Operations Management

Contemporary Concepts and Cases

The McGraw-Hill/Irwin Series
Operations and Decision Sciences

Operations Management

Contemporary Concepts and Cases   Third Edition

Roger G. Schroeder
University of Minnesota
Carlson School of Management

 **McGraw-Hill** **Irwin**

Boston   Burr Ridge, IL   Dubuque, IA   Madison, WI   New York
San Francisco   St. Louis   Bangkok   Bogotá   Caracas   Kuala Lumpur
Lisbon   London   Madrid   Mexico City   Milan   Montreal   New Delhi
Santiago   Seoul   Singapore   Sydney   Taipei   Toronto

OPERATIONS MANAGEMENT: CONTEMPORARY CONCEPTS AND CASES

Published by McGraw-Hill/Irwin, a business unit of The McGraw-Hill Companies, Inc., 1221 Avenue of the Americas, New York, NY, 10020. Copyright © 2007 by The McGraw-Hill Companies, Inc. All rights reserved. No part of this publication may be reproduced or distributed in any form or by any means, or stored in a database or retrieval system, without the prior written consent of The McGraw-Hill Companies, Inc., including, but not limited to, in any network or other electronic storage or transmission, or broadcast for distance learning.

Some ancillaries, including electronic and print components, may not be available to customers outside the United States.

This book is printed on acid-free paper.

1 2 3 4 5 6 7 8 9 0 QPD/QPD 0 9 8 7 6 5

ISBN-13: 978-0-07-313706-3
ISBN-10: 0-07-313706-5

Editorial director: *Stewart Mattson*
Executive editor: *Scott Isenberg*
Development editor II: *Christina A. Sanders*
Senior marketing manager: *Douglas Reiner*
Senior media producer: *Victor Chiu*
Project manager: *Gina F. DiMartino*
Production supervisor: *Debra R. Sylvester*
Coordinator freelance design: *Artemio Ortiz Jr.*
Photo research coordinator: *Kathy Shive*
Photo researcher: *David A. Tietz*
Media project manager: *Brian Nacik*
Cover design: *Graphic Visions*
Typeface: *10/12 Palatino*
Compositor: *GTS – New Delhi, India Campus*
Printer: *Quebecor World Dubuque Inc.*

Library of Congress Cataloging-in-Publication Data
Schroeder, Roger G.
    Operations management : contemporary concepts and cases / Roger G. Schroeder.—3rd ed.
        p. cm.—(McGraw-Hill/Irwin series operations and decision sciences)
    Includes index
    ISBN-13: 978-0-07-313706-3 (alk. paper)
    ISBN-10: 0-07-313706-5 (alk. paper)
    1. Production management. I. Title. II. Series.
TS155.S334 2007
    658.5—dc22
                                                            2005053363

www. mhhe.com

To: My parents, Angela and Martin Schroeder; my wife, Marlene; and my children, Kristen and Bethany

—Roger G. Schroeder

About the Author

Roger G. Schroeder   *University of Minnesota*
holds the Donaldson Chair in Operations Management at the Curtis L. Carlson School of Management, University of Minnesota. He is also the Co-Director of the Joseph M. Juran Center for Leadership in Quality and has earned an appointment as a Distinguished Teaching Professor. He received the B.S. degree in Industrial Engineering with high distinction from the University of Minnesota, the MSIE from the University of Minnesota, and the Ph.D. from Northwestern University. Prior to joining the University of Minnesota, he taught at the U.S. Naval Postgraduate School, Monterey, California, and was an analyst for the office of the Assistant Secretary of Defense. Professor Schroeder has received research grants from the Ford Foundation, American Production and Inventory Control Society, Exxon Education Foundation, and the National Science Foundation. His current research interests include operations strategy, quality improvement, and high-performance manufacturing. He is a recipient of the Morse Award for outstanding teaching at the University of Minnesota. Professor Schroeder has consulted with many public and private organizations and serves on numerous editorial boards. He is a Fellow of the Decision Sciences Institute and received the Lifetime Scholarship Award from the Academy of Management.

Preface

FEATURES

Operations management is an exciting and vital field in today's complex business world. Therefore, students in both MBA and undergraduate courses have an urgent need to understand operations—an essential function in every business.

This textbook on operations management addresses the impact of operations decisions on the firm and emphasizes cross-functional decision making. The text provides materials of interest to general business students and operations management majors. By stressing cross-functional decision making, the text provides a unique and current business perspective for all students. This is the first text to incorporate cross-functional decision making in every chapter.

A unified decision framework organizes the material by grouping decisions into four major categories: process, quality, capacity, and inventory. This framework is intended to make it easy for students to understand the decision role and responsibilities of operations in relation to other functions such as marketing and finance. The text also provides a balanced treatment of both service and manufacturing firms.

The latest content is incorporated, including global operations, supply chain management, virtual operations, e-operations, service blueprinting, competency-based strategy, agile manufacturing, and mass customization. Complete coverage is also provided on traditional topics, including process design, service systems, quality management, JIT, ERP, and inventory control and scheduling.

While covering the concepts of operations management in 17 chapters, the book also provides 20 case studies. The cases are intended to strengthen problem formulation skills and illustrate the concepts presented in the text. Long and short case studies are included. The cases are not just large problems or examples; rather, they are substantial management case studies, including some from the Harvard Business School and Darden School case collections.

This softcover edition with fewer pages than most introductory books is economical for students. It covers all the essentials students need to know about operations, leaving out only superfluous and tangential topics. By limiting the size of the book, I have condensed the material to the basics.

This book is ideal for regular operations management courses and also case courses and modular courses. It is particularly useful for those who desire a cross-functional decision-making perspective. Instructors can easily supplement the text with their own cases, readings, or course materials as desired.

Each copy of the text includes a student CD-ROM containing 21 Excel templates designed to assist in solving problems at the end of chapters and the case studies. The CD-ROM also contains additional technical notes on linear programming, simulation, transportation method, financial analysis, and queuing, which can be assigned by the instructor, if desired. Finally, the CD-ROM contains PowerPoint slides, video clips, and Web links to companies cited in the Student Internet Exercises in the text. A Web site for this textbook (http://www.mhhe.com/schroeder3e) is also linked to the McGraw-Hill operations Web site (http://www.mhhe.com/pom/).

A number of pedagogical features are contained in this book.

- Operations Leader boxes are included in each chapter to illustrate the latest practices being implemented by leading firms.

- Each chapter contains at least three Student Internet Exercises. These exercises generally allow for extended learning about concepts that have already been discussed in the text.
- Points of cross-functional emphasis are noted in each chapter by a special symbol. This highlights the cross-functional nature of this book.
- Solved problems are included at the end of quantitative chapters to provide additional examples for students.
- Excel spreadsheets are keyed to specific problems at the end of chapters. One of these spreadsheets is illustrated in the text for each chapter that contains Excel problems.
- The student CD-ROM can be used to extend students' learning of the basic ideas covered in the text. CD includes technical chapters, video clips, Excel templates, PowerPoint slides, and Web links.

KEY CHANGES TO THE THIRD EDITION

1. *The process view of operations is emphasized in every chapter in addition to the cross-functional approach used in the earlier editions.*
2. *New or expanded sections are added to the various chapters to provide extensive coverage of the following topics:*

- Operations competence as a basis for competitive advantage.
- Service quality measurement including SERVQUAL.
- Illustrations of different types of processes.
- Technology choice by managers.
- Measuring process flows (Little's Law, capacity, flow rate, throughput, inventory, and bottlenecks).
- Six Sigma.
- Supply chain strategies.
- Collaborative Planning, Forecasting, and Replenishment.
- Theory of Constraints.
- Sales and Operations Planning.
- PERT method.
- Lean thinking.

3. *Many new examples are included throughout to illustrate major points:*

- 3M example of process improvement outside operations.
- The process view in General Electric.
- Zara as an example of fast replenishment.
- General Mills example of new cereal design.
- Concurrent engineering at the Centers for Disease Control.
- Modular design at Dell Computer.
- Project management at Boeing.
- TRW legal department's use of Six Sigma.
- Cisco's supply chain management problems.
- Wal-Mart and Whirlpool's use of CPFR.
- Intel investment in Ireland.

- Syngenta's use of S&OP.
- Odessa Texas Police Department uses Theory of Constraints.
- MRP at Coca Cola.
- Health care example of lean thinking.

4. *Service operations coverage is expanded throughout the text:*

- The service chapter has been updated and expanded to provide more complete coverage of the cycle of service at SAS, the profit chain at Harrah, service recovery in car repair, and service design at a ski resort.
- Service examples have been added in every chapter.
- Concepts in the text have been illustrated with both manufacturing and service examples.

5. *Student Internet Exercises:*

- About 60 student Internet assignments with new and updated exercises have been added to the third edition.

6. *Case Studies:*

- 20 case studies have been included. They have been updated and two new cases added:

  The "mi adidas" Mass Customization Initiative
  Southwest Airlines: Singin' the (JET) Blues

- Recent cases have been carried over from the second edition:

  Customer-Driven Learning at Radisson Hotels Worldwide
  Six Sigma at 3M, Inc.
  Ford Motor Company: Supply Chain Strategy

Summary of Chapter by Chapter Revisions

Chapter 1: The Operations Function
Changed focus from "systems" to "process" throughout chapter.
Increased references of service companies:

- GE Capital, Wal-Mart, Nordstrom, Starbucks, Amazon.com., Fed Ex, Citigroup.

Chapter 2: Operations and Supply Chain Strategy
Added new Wal-Mart example of distinctive competence.
Included new Zara (Spanish retailer) example of replenishment.
Moved Section 2.4, "Focused Operations," to Chapter 4.
Added Section 2.4, "Operations Competence," which includes the following:

- Wal-Mart versus Nordstrom order winner example.
- Dell Computer example of distinctive competence.

Chapter 3: Product Design
Revised introduction to product design.
Included new General Mills cereal example for product design.
Added new example of concurrent engineering techniques at the National Center for Disease Control Institute for Occupational Safety and Health.
Added new Dell computer example of modular design.

Chapter 4: Process Selection

Revised Line Flow figure and explanation for Figure 4.1.

Revised Figure 4.2, batch flow, and explanation.

Revised the graphic comparison between MTS, MTO, and ATO.

Included new project examples: Boeing, furniture making, and services, including catering and fund-raising.

Moved Section 4.5, "Focused Operations," from Chapter 2.

Chapter 5: Service Process Design

Revised Table 5.1 on the difference between manufacturing and services for clarity.

Added ski resort service example/exercise.

Provided car repair example regarding service recovery.

Included new service guarantee examples in Table 5.2.

Added SAS business traveler example—moment of truth.

Provided new application of service-profit chain at Harrah's casino.

Chapter 6: Choice of Technology

Deleted old section, "Technology and the Manager."

Revised the introduction on technology choice.

Revised and clarified the section on group technology layout.

Provided new example of Changen auto manufacturing to illustrate ERP.

Heavily revised the "Technology Choice" section.

Chapter 7: Process-Flow Analysis

Added new section 7.3, "Measuring Process Flows," including

- New Little's Law material.
- Pizza parlor example.

Revised figures for clarity.

Condensed section on using process-flow analysis and deleted the material on sociotechnical problems.

Added new solved problems.

Chapter 8: Managing Quality

Added the new section 8.2, "Service Quality," which now includes coverage of SERVQUAL.

Updated Baldrige Award criteria.

Revised TQM costs of quality material.

Chapter 9: Quality Control and Improvement

Revised the explanation of attribute control.

Clarified the discussion of variable measurement use.

Added control chart uses—manufacturing and services explanation.

Added new Six Sigma material:

- TRW Legal Department example.
- Additional discussion of the seven tools of quality.

Chapter 10: Supply Chain Management
Added introduction using Cisco as an example.

Added new discussion of business cycle time and flexibility using Dell as an example.

Provided new time measurement presentation.

Revised the supply chain costs discussion.

Added section 10.5, "Supply Chain Strategies," including new examples: Sport Obermeyer and General Mills.

Chapter 11: Forecasting
Clarified that forecasting should provide a mean and variance.

Added section 11.10, "Collaborative Planning, Forecasting, and Replenishment," with the new Whirlpool example.

Chapter 12: Facilities and Aggregate Planning
Included a definition of nominal capacity.

Updated the Operations Leader box, Intel Irish Operations.

Deleted material comparing cumulative demand and production.

Added Syngenta example of sales and operations planning.

Chapter 13: Scheduling Operations
Included service example (drawn from a hospital) for batch scheduling.

Heavily revised the section on bottleneck and Theory of Constraint.

Revised Priority Dispatching Rules and included new examples on capacity/TOC.

Provided new explanations of Figures 13.4 and 13.5, infinite capacity loading.

Chapter 14: Project Planning and Scheduling
Replaced Figure 14.1 Gantt Chart and provided a new example.

Revised construction of a simple network and network representation.

Heavily revised the section on constant-time networks.

Added a new PERT section.

Deleted PDM from section 14.7.

Added new example, Cadbury Schweppes.

Added new Solved Problems.

Chapter 15: Independent-Demand Inventory
Added new material discussing inventories in the supply chain.

Revised Figure 15.6, the total cost curve.

Added an EOQ example, Hewlett Packard.

Clarified the definition of a periodic review system.

Added a list of service-oriented independent demand inventories.

Chapter 16: Materials Requirements Planning
Explained how the master schedule is driven by the aggregate plan.

Added explanation of MRP as part of ERP.

Added Coca-Cola as an example of MRP.

Chapter 17: Just-in-Time Systems and Lean Thinking
Added material introducing the concept of lean thinking.

Added the new section "Beyond JIT to Lean Thinking."

BOOK SUPPLEMENTS

Book supplements available to instructors include the instructor's Resource CD-ROM with instructor's manual, PowerPoint slides, Web links, Excel templates, additional video clips, technical notes, and a test bank.

- **McGraw-Hill/Irwin video series** is available to book adopters. These videos include 12 volumes containing over 36 segments varying in length from 9 to 25 minutes. The videos provide actual plant and service tours, and students can hear from real operations managers. The topics include concepts such as lean production, quality, manufacturing processes, CIM, inventory management, services, supply chain management, improving operations methods, layout improvements, supplier development, reengineering, value-driven production, scheduling, product and process design, JIT, and international logistics.

McGraw-Hill/Irwin has the following products available for purchase or shrinkwrapped with the text at a discounted price:

- **Interactive Cases for Operations Management and Supply Chain Management** by Byron Finch: This collection of 24 dynamic cases features scenarios utilizing interactive Java applets included on a CD-ROM with the casebook. These innovative case studies require students to utilize the Java-based applets to solve operations and supply chain management problems with an interactive graphical tool, on topics such as production line simulation, variance analysis, overbooking, x-bar and r-charts, waiting lines, forecasting, bullwhip effect, inventory, Kanban, aggregate planning, constraint management, facility layout, and learning curves.

- **HOM Operations Management Software for Windows** by Moses, Seshadri, and Yakir offers powerful Windows-based programs for solving real-world operating problems such as forecasting, process analysis, waiting line design and analysis, project management, MRP and inventory management, and capacity planning. HOM imports and exports files to and from Excel, and each module has a detailed, step-by-step "how-to-solve" dialog box.

- **Mike's Bikes Business Simulation on CD** provides an opportunity to run Mike's Bikes, a bicycle manufacturing company. Through this simulation students apply their knowledge of the functional areas of business, such as marketing, operations, finance, and accounting, to a real business.

ACKNOWLEDGMENTS

The author would like to acknowledge the many individuals who have assisted with this book. Special thanks go to the reviewers for this edition:

Stephen N. Chapman
North Carolina State University

Steven M. D'Ostroph
University of Phoenix

Karen Eboch
Bowling Green State University

Michael Godfrey
University of Wisconsin, Oshkosh

Mark E. Goudreau
Johnson & Wales University

Elias Kirche
Florida Gulf Coast University

Anita Lee-Post
University of Kentucky–Lexington

Samar K. Mukhopadhyay
University of Wisconsin–Milwaukee

Ron Parker
Metropolitan State University

James A. Pope
University of Toledo

Eric Svaan
University of Michigan–Ann Arbor

The author would also like to thank the staff at McGraw-Hill/Irwin who had a direct hand in the editing and production of the text. Brent Gordon, editorial director, encouraged the development of this book from the beginning and supported the concept throughout. Scott Isenberg, executive editor, provided unwavering editorial support for many of the key features and concepts incorporated into the text. My thanks go to Christina Sanders, developmental editor, who ensured that the book faithfully adhered to its concept and coordinated the editing and review process. Gina DiMartino, project manager, was diligent in getting the book through the production process.

I would also like to thank my colleagues at the University of Minnesota who listened to my ideas and provided suggestions for book improvement. Special thanks go to James Pope, University of Toledo, who authored the PowerPoint slides; and Aravind Chandrasekaran, who wrote practice quizzes for the text Web site. I would like to thank Doug Chard, who diligently and carefully prepared the index. Finally, I thank my family for their patience and perseverance during the many months of writing and editing. Without their support and encouragement this textbook would not have been possible.

Roger G. Schroeder

Brief Table of Contents

Contents

Part **One**

Introduction

1. The Operations Function

2. Operations and Supply Chain Strategy

3. Product Design

The introductory part of this book provides an overview of the operations management field and some of the prerequisites for decision making in operations: operations strategy and product design. After reading this part, the student should have an appreciation for the importance of operations to the firm, the major decisions made in operations, the linkages of operations decisions to other functions, and the need for strategy to guide all operations decision making. New-product design is treated as a cross-functional decision responsibility that precedes production of goods or services.

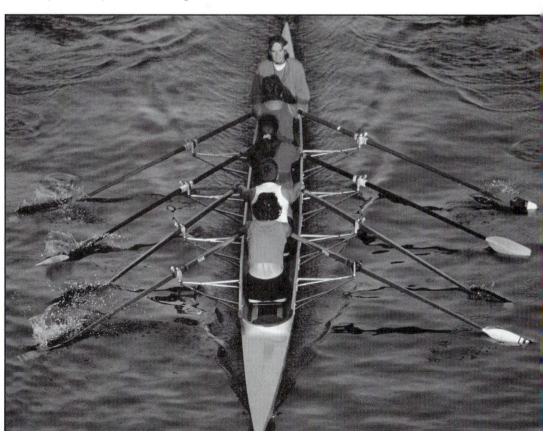

The Operations Function

Chapter outline

Operations management, as a field, deals with the production of goods and services. Every day we come in contact with an abundant array of goods or services, all of which are produced under the supervision of operations managers. Without effective management of operations, a modern industrialized society cannot exist. Operations is the engine that creates wealth for the enterprise and underpins the global economy.

Operations managers have important positions in every company. One example is the plant manager who is in charge of a factory. All other managers who work in the factory—including production and inventory control managers, quality managers, and line supervisors—are also operations managers. Collectively, this group of factory managers is responsible for producing the supply of products in a manufacturing business. Carrying this example one step further, we should also include in the group of operations managers all manufacturing managers at the corporate or divisional level. These managers might include a corporate vice president of operations (or manufacturing) and a group of corporate staff operations managers concerned with quality, production and inventory control, facilities, and equipment.

Operations managers, however, have important responsibilities in **service industries** as well as in **manufacturing** companies. In the private sector, operations managers take leadership roles in hotels, restaurants, airlines, banks, and retail stores. In each of these organizations, operations managers are responsible for providing the supply of services much like their counterparts in manufacturing produce the supply of goods. In the government, there are operations managers in the post office, police department, and housing department, to name only a few.

At first glance, it may appear that service operations don't have much in common with manufacturing operations. However, a unifying feature of these operations is that both can be viewed as **transformation processes.** In manufacturing, inputs of raw materials, energy, labor, and capital are transformed into finished goods. In service operations, these same types of inputs are transformed into service outputs. Managing the transformation process in an efficient and effective manner is the task of the operations manager in any type of organization.

Our economy has dramatically shifted from the production of goods to the production of services. It may come as a surprise that today more than 80 percent of the American workforce is employed in service industries.[1] Even though the predominance of employment is in the service sector, manufacturing remains important to provide the basic goods needed for export and internal consumption. Because of the importance of both service and manufacturing operations, they are treated on an equal basis in this text.

In the past when the field was related primarily to manufacturing, operations management was called **production management.** Later the name was expanded to "production and operations management," or more simply, "operations management," to include the service industries as well. The term "operations management" as used in this text refers to both manufacturing and service industries.

Wealth is created in the global economy through excellent operations management. Wealth creation occurs when the value of outputs in goods and services exceeds the cost of the inputs used. It is reflected in the standard of living of the people and is a function of constantly increasing productivity.

Wealth can only be created by manufacturing and service operations that add more value than the costs of the inputs they use. Raising productivity of operations, the ratio of output to input, is therefore the primary basis for creating wealth. In the global economy, a company and a country cannot prosper in the long run unless they have higher productivity than their domestic and foreign competitors.

The task of the operations manager is one of the **wealth creator.** Operations should lead the way in enhancing our ability to create wealth, improve productivity, and raise the standard of living for all people. This is the challenge for the next decade. An example of an operations leader in creating wealth is Dell Computer Corporation (see the Operations Leader box).

1.1 DEFINITION OF OPERATIONS MANAGEMENT

The essence of operations management can be summarized by the following definition:

> Operations is responsible for supplying the product or service of the organization. Operations managers make decisions regarding the operations function and its connection with other functions. The operations managers plan and control the production process and its interfaces within the organization and with the external environment.

[1] U.S. Bureau of the Census, *Statistical Abstract of the United States,* Washington, DC, 2004–2005 ed.

Three points in this definition deserve emphasis:

1. **Decisions.** The above definition refers to **decision making** as an important element of operations management. Since all managers make decisions, it is natural to focus on decision making as a central theme in operations. This decision focus provides a basis for dividing operations into parts according to major decision types. In this text, we identify the **four major decision responsibilities** of operations management as process, quality, capacity, and inventory. These decisions provide the framework for organizing the text and describing what operations managers do. A hallmark of this book is not only treating decision making within operations but the connection with other functions in the organization.

2. **Function.** Operations is a major function in any organization, along with marketing and finance. The operations function is responsible for supplying or producing products and services for the business. In a manufacturing company, the **operations function** is typically called the manufacturing or production department. In service organizations, the operations function might be called the operations department or some name peculiar to the particular industry (e.g., the policy service department in insurance companies). In general, the generic term "operations" refers to the function that produces goods or services. While separating operations out in this manner is useful for analyzing decision making and assigning responsibilities, we must also integrate the business by considering the cross-functional nature of decision making in the firm.[2]

3. **Process.** As noted above, operations managers plan and control the production process and its interfaces. This **process view** not only provides a common ground for defining service and manufacturing operations as transformation processes but is also a powerful basis for design and analysis of operations.

[2] The "crossed-oars" symbol in the margin identifies a point of cross-functional emphasis and is designed to illustrate that everyone must pull their oars together for a successful company.

Using the process view, we consider operations managers as managers of the conversion process in the firm.

But the process view also provides important insights for the management of productive processes in functional areas outside the operations function. For example, a sales office may be viewed as a production process with inputs, transformation, and outputs. The same is true for an accounts payable office and for a loan office in a bank. In terms of the process view, operations management concepts have applicability beyond the functional area of operations. The 3M Company, for example, uses Six Sigma (described in Chapter 9) to improve processes throughout the firm, including processes in human resources, accounting, finance, information systems, and even the legal department. Process improvement is not restricted to operations.

Since the operations management field can be defined by decisions, function, and processes we will expand on these three elements in detail in this chapter. But first we provide an example of the decisions that would be made by operations in a typical company that makes and markets pizzas in the United States.

1.2 DECISIONS AT PIZZA U.S.A.

Pizza U.S.A. satisfies its customers by carefully managing the four key decision areas in operations. © Steve MASON/Getty Images

Pizza U.S.A., Inc., produces and markets pizzas on a national basis. The firm consists of 85 company-owned and franchised outlets (each called a store) in the United States. The operations function in this company exists at two levels: the corporate level and the level of the individual store.

The major operations decisions made by Pizza U.S.A. can be described as follows:

Process

Corporate staff makes some of the process decisions, since uniformity across different stores is desirable. They have developed a standard facility that is simply sized to fit a particular location. The standard facility incorporates a limited menu with high-volume equipment. As pizzas are made, customers can watch the process through a glass window; this provides entertainment for both children and adults as they wait for their orders to be filled. Because this is a service facility, special care is taken to make the layout attractive and convenient for the customers. The location of facilities is based on a mathematical model that is used to project revenues and costs for particular sites. Each potential site must have an adequate projected return on investment before construction can begin.

Within the design parameters established by the corporate operations staff, the store managers seek to continually improve the process over time. This is done both by additional investment in the process and by the use of better methods and procedures, which are often developed by the employees themselves.

Managers of the pizza stores are responsible for hiring, training, supervising, and, if necessary, firing workers. They must decide on exact job responsibilities and on the number of people needed to operate the store. They also advertise job openings, screen applications, interview candidates, and make the hiring decisions. They must measure the amount of work required in relation to production and also evaluate the performance of each individual. Management of the workforce is one of the most important daily responsibilities of the store manager. Note, we consider the workforce as an integral part of the process.

Quality

Certain standards for quality that all stores must follow have been set by the corporate staff. The standards include procedures to maintain service quality and to ensure the quality of the pizzas served. While service quality is difficult to measure, the quality of the pizzas can be more easily specified by using criteria such as temperature at serving time, the amount of raw materials used in relation to standards, and so on. Service-quality measures include courtesy, cleanliness, speed of service, and a friendly atmosphere. Each Pizza U.S.A. store manager must carefully monitor quality to make sure that it meets company standards. All employees are responsible for quality in their jobs to ensure that service and food quality is "produced at the source" by the employees themselves.

Capacity

Decisions about capacity determine the maximum level of output of pizzas. First, when the initial location and process decisions are made, the corporate staff fixes the physical capacity of each facility. Individual store managers then plan for annual, monthly, and daily fluctuations in service capacity within the available physical facility. During peak periods, they employ part-time help, and advertising is used in an attempt to raise demand during slack periods. In the short run, individual personnel must be scheduled in shifts to meet demand during store hours.

Inventory

Each store manager buys the ingredients required to make the recipes provided by corporate staff. They select their own suppliers and decide how much flour, tomato paste, sausage, and other ingredients to order and when to place orders. Store operators must carefully integrate purchasing and inventory decisions to control the flow of materials in relation to capacity. They do not want to run out of food during peak periods or waste food when demand is low.

The four decision categories provide a framework to describe the important operations decisions made by Pizza U.S.A. It should be recognized, however, that these four types of decisions cannot be made separately; they must be carefully integrated with one another and with decisions made in marketing, finance, and other parts of the business. For example, if marketing wishes to change the prices of pizza, this is likely to affect sales and the capacity needs of operations and the amount of ingredients (materials) used. Also, if finance cannot raise the necessary capital, operations might have to redesign the process to require less capital or manage inventories more efficiently. This in turn may affect the response time to serve customers, costs, and so on. Decision making is highly interactive and systemic in nature.

Because Pizza U.S.A. is only one example of an operation, students often ask: What do operations managers do in more general terms? The Monster.com Operations Leader box provides examples of four typical operations management positions and describes the associated decision-making responsibilities. The descriptions have been greatly simplified, perhaps oversimplified, for illustration purposes.

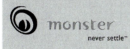

As the box indicates, there are a great variety of management positions in operations. These range from first-level supervisory positions to middle- and top-management positions of considerable responsibility. These positions also cut across all the aspects of operations and apply to both manufacturing and service operations.

There are many opportunities for international employment in operations management since operations are located around the world. Many operations in other countries are seeking to implement world-class best practices, so what is learned in this course can be applied anywhere in the world.

1.3 OPERATIONS DECISIONS—A FRAMEWORK

To generalize from Pizza U.S.A., we introduce a framework that categorizes and defines decisions in operations. Although many different frameworks are possible, the primary one used here is a conceptual scheme for grouping decisions according to decision responsibilities. In this framework, similar decision responsibilities concerning facilities or inventories, for example, are grouped together. This is a novel and useful decision framework.

In the proposed framework, operations has responsibility for four major decision areas: process, quality, capacity, and inventory.

1. **Process.** Decisions in this category determine the physical process or facility used to produce the product or service and the associated workforce practices. The decisions include the type of equipment and technology, process flows, layout of the facility, job design, and workforce policies. Many of these process decisions are long range in nature and cannot be easily reversed, particularly when heavy capital investment is needed. It is therefore important that the physical process be designed in relation to the long-term strategic posture of the business and the capabilities of the workforce. Processes must also be continually improved once they are designed. This requires the cooperation of the workforce and the ideas of all employees.

   Since many process decisions require large capital investments, financial managers are concerned with the investments required by operations processes. Human resource managers are concerned with the recruiting, hiring, staffing, and evaluation decisions concerning the people employed in operations. Operations typically manages more employees than any other function in the firm.

2. **Quality.** The operations function is responsible for the quality of goods and services produced. Quality is an important operations responsibility and it requires total organizational support. Quality decisions must ensure that quality is designed and built into the product in all stages of operations: standards must be set, people trained, and the product or service inspected, preferably by those who produce it, for quality to result.

   Managers from all functions are concerned with management of quality. Operations has a particular responsibility for producing products and services that meet the defined specifications and standards. But operations must also participate with other functions in setting the specifications for all new products and in defining the levels of customer service required. Continuous quality improvement is now a key responsibility of all managers.

3. **Capacity.** Capacity decisions are aimed at providing the right amount of capacity at the right place at the right time. Long-range capacity is determined by the size of the physical facilities built by the firm and its suppliers or by outsourcing the product to a reliable supplier. In the short run, capacity can sometimes be augmented by subcontracting, extra shifts, or rental of space. Capacity planning, however, determines not only the size of facilities but also the proper number of people in operations. Staffing levels are set to meet the needs of market demand and the desire to maintain a stable workforce. In the short run, available capacity must be allocated to specific tasks and jobs in operations by scheduling people, equipment, and facilities.

4. **Inventory.** Inventory management decisions in operations determine what to order, how much to order, and when to order. Inventory control systems are used to manage materials from purchasing through raw materials, work in process, and finished goods inventories. Inventory managers decide how much inventory is needed, where to locate the inventory, and a host of related decisions. They manage the flow of materials within the firm and within the supply chain.

Careful attention to the four decision areas is the key to management of successful operations. Indeed, the well-managed operations function can be defined in terms of the decision framework. If each of the four decision areas is functioning properly and well integrated with the other areas and functions of the firm, the operations function can be considered well managed.

In the past, some students felt that operations management was a hodgepodge of techniques and methods—that there was no central theme. The decision framework was specifically designed to overcome this problem. Each major section of this text is devoted to one of the four decision categories.[3] The framework thus provides an integrating mechanism for the text.

1.4   CROSS-FUNCTIONAL DECISION MAKING

As we have indicated, the operations function is a critical element in every business. No business can survive without it. The operations function is one of the **three primary functions** along with marketing and finance. In addition, the **supporting functions** include human resources, information systems, and accounting.

Functional areas are concerned with a particular focus of responsibility or decision making in an organization. The marketing function is typically responsible for creating demand and generating sales revenue; the operations function is responsible for the production of goods or services (generating supply); and finance is responsible for the acquisition and allocation of capital. Functional areas tend to be closely associated with organizational departments because businesses typically are organized on a functional basis.

Supporting functions are essential to provide staff support to the three primary functions. For example, the human resources function interviews prospective employees, examines compensation rates, engages in negotiations with labor unions, and manages performance appraisal systems. While human resources provides information and advice, operations makes the hiring decisions, determines the pay and salary levels, and conducts the performance appraisals of the employees assigned to operations with the assistance of the human resources staff.

Every function must be concerned not only with its own decision responsibilities but with integrating decisions with other functions. **Functional silos** have developed in many businesses and impede cross-functional decision making. As a result, the overall business suffers due to an emphasis on functional prerogatives.

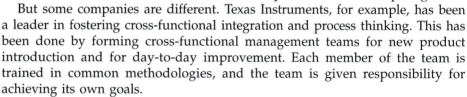

But some companies are different. Texas Instruments, for example, has been a leader in fostering cross-functional integration and process thinking. This has been done by forming cross-functional management teams for new product introduction and for day-to-day improvement. Each member of the team is trained in common methodologies, and the team is given responsibility for achieving its own goals.

Some of the key **cross-functional decision making** relationships are shown in Table 1.1. We discuss these one at a time to examine in detail the relationship between operations decisions and the functional areas of marketing, finance/accounting, human resources, and information systems.

Marketing is concerned with identification of the customer for the business and the associated customer needs. Customer needs impact heavily on the level of quality designed into the product, usually a cross-functional decision, and conformance to quality standards managed by operations. Marketing also has a key role in determining the volume of product that the firm will sell, through selection of the product, and pricing and promotion decisions. Volume in turn heavily affects operations decisions such as selection of process type (line, batch, and project) and capacity required.

---

[3] Students have called these four categories QPIC, pronounced "Q Pick" as a memory aid.

TABLE 1.1
Examples of Cross-Functional Decision Making

Key Decision Area	Interface with Operations Decisions
Marketing	
Who is the customer and what does the customer need?	Quality design and quality management
Market size (volume)	Type of process selected (line, batch, or project) and capacity required
Distribution channels	How much inventory and where to stock it?
Pricing	Quality, capacity, and inventory
New product introduction	Cross-functional teams
Finance and Accounting	
Availability of capital	Inventory levels, degree of automation, process type selected, and capacity
Efficiency of conversion process	Process type selection, process flows, and value-added determination
Net present value and cash flow	Automation, inventory, and capacity
Process costing or job costing	Type of process selected
Measurement of operations	Costing systems used
Human Resources	
Skill level of employees	Process type selected and automation
Number of employees and part-time or full-time employment	Capacity and scheduling decisions
Training of employees	Quality improvement
Job design	Process and technology choice
Teamwork	All decisions in operations
Information Systems	
Determination of user needs	Systems should support all users in operations
Design of information systems	Systems should help streamline operations and support all decisions in operations
Software development	Software is needed for capacity, quality, inventory, and scheduling decisions
Hardware acquisition	Hardware is needed to support automation decisions in operations and to operate software

Another marketing decision is the distribution channel used to deliver the product to the customer. This decision in turn affects how much inventory is carried by operations and where the inventory is stocked. Pricing decisions made by marketing affect not only quality but capacity and inventory levels as well. Decisions made in marketing affect all four of the types of operations decisions; therefore, a high level of integration is needed between decisions made by marketing and operations.

Finance and Accounting decides on the availability of capital, return on capital, risk taken by the firm, cash flows, and measurement of operations. The availability of capital will affect inventory levels, capacity, and the degree of automation that can be financed. Every decision in operations should be viewed in light of its potential return on capital and cash flow as these decisions affect returns to the stockholders. Efficiency of the conversion process is a concern of finance and accounting and is reflected in operations through decisions concerning selection of process type, arrangement of process flows, and elimination of non-value-adding steps in processes. Through selection of the process type (flow or batch), operations also determines the type of costing system used (process costing or job costing). Accountants are trained to ask questions regarding internal control of operations and measurement of operations productivity and output. Thus accounting and finance functions interact with all four decision categories in operations, particularly when capital or measurement of operations is required.

The human resources function affects the type of people recruited, hiring, training and development, teamwork, and compensation systems. The type of people recruited and training in turn affect skill levels of employees and automation decisions in operations. The number of employees recruited and whether they are full-time or part-time affects capacity and scheduling decisions. Also, training of employees is one of the critical elements in quality management. Teamwork affects all decisions made in operations as employees must be able to work toward common goals.

The information systems function plays an important role in supporting decisions in operations and the entire business. One of the decisions made by information systems managers is a determination of user needs and the associated design of the information systems. Because operations is a major internal customer of the information systems function, it is critical that information systems designers accurately understand operations needs and design systems that help operations meet its objectives. The resulting software and hardware from systems design should support specific operations decisions such as capacity determination, forecasting, quality management, inventory control, and scheduling.

It should be clear that no matter what part of business you might select as a major, you will have an important interface with operations. An understanding of operations decisions is critical for all business careers since everyone will be involved with operations decisions in a direct or cross-functional relationship. The decisions of operations are improved when the ideas from all functions have been considered.

Nonmajors will find many valuable ideas in studying operations. Principles of quality management, process improvement, and JIT/lean can be applied in all business functions. Also, techniques learned in this course such as forecasting, project management, Six Sigma, and scheduling can be widely applied. The operations way of process thinking can be applied to all business functions and is widely used in business today.

1.5 OPERATIONS AS A PROCESS

Operations has been defined as a transformation system (or process) that converts **inputs** into **outputs.** Inputs to the system include energy, materials, labor, capital, and information (see Figure 1.1). Process technology is then used to convert inputs into outputs. The process technology is the methods, procedures, and equipment used to transform materials or inputs into products or services.

The process view of operations is very useful in unifying seemingly different operations from different industries. For example, the transformation process in manufacturing is one of material conversion from raw materials into finished products. When an automobile is produced, steel, plastics, aluminum, cloth, and many other materials are transformed into parts that are then assembled into the finished automobile. Labor is required to operate and maintain the equipment, and energy and information are also required to produce the finished automobile.

In service industries a transformation process is also used to transform inputs into service outputs. For example, airlines use capital inputs of aircraft and equipment and human inputs of pilots, flight attendants, and support people to

FIGURE 1.1 An operation as a productive system.

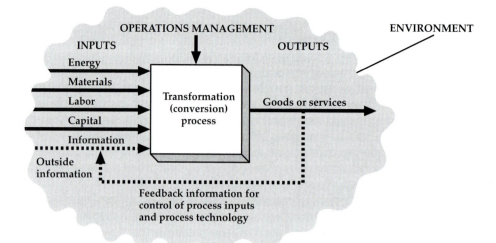

produce safe, reliable, fast, and efficient transportation. Transformations of many types also occur in other industries, as indicated in Table 1.2. By studying these different types of transformation process, you can learn a great deal about how to analyze and identify any operation as a system.

The process view provides a basis for seeing an entire business as a system of interconnected processes. All work performed inside or outside of operations can be described as a process. This makes it possible to analyze an organization and improve it from a process point of view. GE Capital, a service provider, uses the process view and techniques such as Six Sigma and lean thinking to improve all its business processes worldwide.

All systems interact with their **internal and external environments.** We have already indicated the nature of internal interaction through cross-functional decision making. Interaction with the external environment occurs through the economic, physical, social, and political environment of operations. As Figure 1.2 indicates, operations is surrounded by its environment and constantly interacts with it. The interactive nature of these relationships makes it necessary to constantly monitor the environment and to make corresponding changes in operations when needed. In the fast-changing world of today's global business,

TABLE 1.2
Examples of Productive Systems

Operation	Inputs	Outputs
Bank	Tellers, staff, computer equipment, facilities, and energy	Financial services (loans, deposits, safekeeping, etc.)
Restaurant	Cooks, waiters, food, equipment, facilities, and energy	Meals, entertainment, and satisfied customers
Hospital	Doctors, nurses, staff, equipment, facilities, and energy	Health services and healthy patients
University	Faculty, staff, equipment, facilities, energy, and knowledge	Educated students, research, and public service
Manufacturing plant	Equipment, facilities, labor, energy, and raw materials	Finished goods
Airline	Planes, facilities, pilots, flight attendants, maintenance people, labor, and energy	Transportation from one location to another

FIGURE 1.2
Relation of
operations to its
environment.

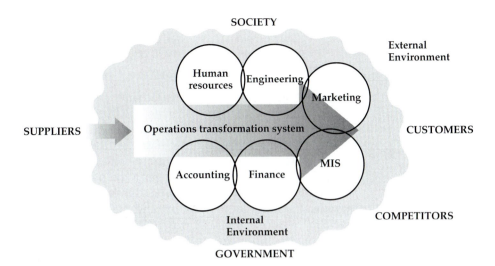

constant change in operations has become essential as a means of survival. The process view helps us understand how operations cannot be insulated from changes in the environment but rather must adapt to them.

1.6 CONTEMPORARY OPERATIONS THEMES

Several contemporary themes are important in operations today and will repeatedly appear throughout the book. These contemporary themes make operations an exciting and interesting place for aspiring managers and those who want the challenge of leadership.

Services and Manufacturing

As we have noted, service and manufacturing are highly interrelated in today's economy. Services such as banking, insurance, consulting, telecommunications, and transportation are critical for support of manufacturing, and likewise, manufactured products support all service industries. While service operations are treated in detail in Chapter 5, services and manufacturing are covered in all chapters through examples and application of concepts. The need to treat both manufacturing and service is a critical theme in operations because of the pervasive and intertwined nature of both manufacturing and service. Leading service businesses that excel in operations are Wal-Mart, Nordstrom, Starbucks, Amazon.com, FedEx, and Citigroup, to name only a few. They excel by applying operations concepts such as service design, process thinking, quality improvement, capacity management, and lean operations.

Customer-Directed Operations

Every operation should be externally directed to meet **customer requirements.** This notion is consistent with the marketing concept taught in marketing courses and is now being integrated into operations courses as well. A key concept is that efficiency need not be sacrificed in the pursuit of meeting customer needs. Rather, the customer can be a powerful driver for reducing waste and improving efficiency of all processes. This idea will be continually developed in the chapters on quality, product design, process design, service operations, scheduling, and inventory control.

For example, the Saturn division of General Motors is a highly directed customer operation in both sales and manufacturing. Saturn operations are responsive to the customer's desire for a high-quality compact automobile at a reasonable price. Extensive benchmarking has been done to ensure that the Saturn processes are the best possible. All Saturn employees, even those in the plant, are trained in customer responsiveness.

Lean Operations

Lean operations are concerned with eliminating waste (non-value-adding) activities in every part of operations and the business. For example, the order entry process may have unnecessary steps that waste time and do not add value for the customer. As a result, order entry can be redesigned to reduce the time it takes to enter an order and to do only what is necessary to meet the customer's needs. Motorola redesigned its pager to be more customer friendly and reduced the time to make a pager from a matter of weeks to two hours. This was done by radical redesign of the product and the production system. Not only was the lead time reduced, but cost was reduced too by eliminating non-value-adding steps from the processes resulting in drastic reduction of inventories. Lean operations employ the concepts of Just-in-Time production and extend those ideas to identifying value provided to the customer along with lean thinking applied to every part of the business and the supply chain. See the Operations Leader box, "Lean Manufacturing: Fat Cash Flow."

Integration of Operations with Other Functions

Integration of operations decisions with other functions in the organization is another contemporary theme. Teaching business functions has been too isolated in the past. Some organizations are still managed as separate departments with little integration between them. The best operations are now seeking increased integration through use of cross-functional teams, information systems, management coordination, rotation of employees, and other methods of integration across functions. Integration is critical as a way of getting everyone pulling in the same direction. Most of the implementation problems with new systems, or new approaches, can be traced to a lack of organizational cooperation and integration. Accordingly, cross-functional decision making is stressed throughout the text and is a hallmark of this book.

Environmental Concerns

Everyone in society must help protect the environment, including those in operations. One company, for example, is measuring the amount of pollution that ends up in landfills, in the water, or in the air. This is being done by weighing all raw materials and supplies that come into the factory and then weighing the finished products that are shipped out the door. The difference between these two weights ends up in the environment. The company has set strong goals to reduce pollution measured in this way. Operations have come a long way in reducing pollution of the environment, but there is still a long way to go. The most progressive companies have found that reduction of pollution often pays. Developing a better process that pollutes less may also reduce the cost of the product through less wasted material.

Supply Chain Management

Another contemporary theme in operations is **supply chain management,** discussed in detail in Chapter 10. It includes the integration of suppliers, producers, and customers. Managing the supply chain requires all managers to consider the entire flow of materials and information along the supply chain, from raw materials through production and distribution to the final customers. Supply chain management is improved by using lean operations to speed up the flow of materials and reduce waste along the supply chain. It is also facilitated by fast and accurate information processing between suppliers and customers that can

Interview with Clifford Ransom II, Vice President, State Street Research, Boston

"Q. Analysts are sometimes blamed for managements taking a short-term quarter-to-quarter view when they should follow a long-term vision. What is your view?

A. Stock analysts frown on companies with no long-term plan or vision. Managements do, sometimes, use analysts or "the market" as an excuse because they are clueless about how to induce better performance from their companies. Short-term grandstanding for the market is a desperate attempt to look good, but it usually is obvious to competent analysts.

However, as stock analysts our ultimate customers are stockholders, so we have a fiduciary responsibility to take an investor's view of a company. If a company's forward plan has no financial promise, we may recommend selling the stock, or most likely just avoid buying it. . . .

Q. Does putting the customer first interfere with returns to stockholders?

A. Long-term it should not. The voice of the customer is critical to success, so analysts want to see a company listen to customers. However, in the long run satisfying customers has to also satisfy investors. Giving products and services away might please customers, but not investors.

Incidentally, the stocks of truly lean manufacturers appear to outperform those that merely have a quality program. Lean ones do better than Baldrige winners. By regularly doing more with less, and doing it well, they have a great formula for financial success, a cash flow machine."

Source: *Target* 17, no. 4 (2001).

be accomplished today via the Internet and other forms of electronic data transfer. These forms of electronic information exchange between suppliers and customers are often called **e-business.** Dell Computer Company is a prime example of a leader in supply chain management and e-business.

Globalization of Operations

Finally, the **globalization of operations** is a pervasive theme in business today. One can hardly pick up a newspaper or a business periodical without reading an article on the accelerating nature of international business. Strategies for operations should be formulated with global effects in mind and not only consider narrow national interests. Facility location should be considered in view of its global implications. Technology can be rapidly transferred across national borders. All aspects of operations are affected by the international nature of business; therefore, international issues will be addressed throughout the book.

Many American companies are powerful global competitors. For example, Coke and Pepsi are sold and manufactured throughout the world. McDonald's has restaurants in 121 different countries. Russian citizens can buy a Big Mac in Moscow, and McDonald's has established restaurants in India and China. Similarly, Asian and European firms have become fierce global competitors with global operations around the world.

The foregoing seven themes are critical to high-performing operations. They need more emphasis in business and can be the basis for rapid and continual improvement of operations. By using these ideas, operations will be not only more efficient but more competitive and more effective in meeting customer needs and in creating wealth for the company and the country.

1.7 KEY POINTS

This book provides a broad overview and introduction to the exciting and dynamic field of operations management. It stresses decision making in operations and the relationship of operations decisions to other functions. The four major decision categories are used as an organizing framework for the text.

Key points emphasized in the chapter are:

- The operations function is essential to every business. Operations create the wealth in a global economy, and thus we cannot survive or prosper without them.
- Operations management is defined as decision making in the operations function and integration of these decisions with other functions. All operations can also be viewed as a transformation system that converts inputs into outputs.
- There are four key types of decisions in operations: process, quality, capacity, and inventory. These decision types are useful for diagnosing existing operations or identifying the types of decisions required in new operations.
- The process view of operations and business is a unifying approach for studying and improving all manufacturing and service companies. Changes in the systems environment, including changes in the global economy, frequently require corresponding changes in operations.
- We identified seven contemporary themes in operations that are emerging and will expand in the future. These themes are services and manufacturing, customer-directed operations, lean operations, integration of operations with other functions, environmental concerns, supply chain management, and globalization of operations.

STUDENT INTERNET EXERCISES

1. Operations Management Center
   http://www.mhhe.com/pom

This site contains many useful references to operations management. Use it to find some information of interest to you on operations and write a short report about what you found.

2. Dell Computer Company
   http://www.dell.com

After reading the Dell Operations Leader box, use the Dell home page to expand your knowledge about the company. Specifically, come to class prepared to discuss one interesting aspect of how Dell conducts its operations.

3. Monster.com
   http://www.monster.com

Check the monster.com Web site for positions and career opportunities in operations management. Come to class prepared to discuss one or two jobs in operations that you found interesting and challenging (not necessarily an entry-level job).

Discussion Questions

1. Why study operations management?
2. What is the difference between the terms "production management" and "operations management"?
3. How does the function of an operations manager differ from the function of a marketing manager or a finance manager? How are these functions similar?
4. How is the operations management field related to the fields of human resources, information systems, or accounting?
5. Describe the nature of operations management in the following organizations. In doing this, first identify the purpose and products of the organization; then use the four decision types to identify important operations decisions and responsibilities.
   a. A college library
   b. A hotel
   c. A small manufacturing firm
6. For the organizations listed in question 5, describe the inputs, transformation process, and outputs of the production system.
7. Describe the decision-making view and the process view of operations management. Why are both these views useful in studying the field of operations management?
8. Write a short paper on some of the challenges facing operations management in the future. Use newspapers and business magazines from the library or the Internet as your primary sources.
9. Review the want ads in *The Wall Street Journal* or use the Internet to look for management positions that are available for operations management graduates.
10. How do changes in the environment, such as demand changes, new pollution control laws, the changing value of the dollar, and price changes, affect operations? Name specific impacts on operations for each change.
11. Find examples of well-run and poorly run operations in recent business periodicals such as *BusinessWeek, Fortune,* and *The Wall Street Journal.* What can you learn from these examples?
12. Identify some of the current trends in operations that you think are of critical importance.

Selected Bibliography

Armstrong, Julie. "Visteon Focuses on Lean Manufacturing at New Plants." *Automotive News* 77 (August 11, 2003), pp. 1–6.

Breen, Bill, and Michael Aneiro. "Living in Dell Time." *Fast Company* 88 (November 2004), pp. 86–93.

Chase, Richard B., Nicholas J. Aquilano, and F. Robert Jacobs. *Operations Management for Competitive Advantage,* 10th ed. New York: McGraw-Hill, 2004.

Flynn, Barbara B., Roger Schroeder, and E. James Flynn. "World Class Manufacturing: An Investigation of Hayes and Wheelwright's Foundation." *Journal of Operations Management* 17, no. 3 (1999), pp. 249–69.

Hall, Robert. "Distribution Excellence and the Dell Model." *Target* 16, no. 2 (2nd quarter 2000), pp. 6–11.

Hazra, Jishnu. "Supply Chain Management in the Internet Era: Discussion." *Management Review* 16, no. 4 (December 2004), pp. 54–75.

Heizer, Jay, and Barry Render. *Operations Management,* 7th ed. Upper Saddle River, NJ: Prentice-Hall, 2004.

Kouvelis, Panagiotis, and Martin A Lariviere. "Decentralizing Cross-Functional Decisions: Coordination through Internal Markets." *Management Science* 46, no. 8 (August 2000), pp. 1049–58.

Krajewski, Lee J., and Larry P. Ritzman. *Operations Management: Strategy and Analysis,* 7th ed. Upper Saddle River, NJ: Prentice-Hall, 2005.

Legare, Thomas L. "How Hewlett-Packard Used Virtual Cross-Functional Teams to Deliver Healthcare Industry Solutions." *Journal of Organizational Excellence* 20, no. 4 (Autumn 2001), pp. 29–38.

Sahay, B. S., K. B. C. Saxena, and Ashish Kumar. "World-Class Manufacturing." *Industrial Management* 43, no. 3 (May–June 2001), pp. 23–28.

Schwab, Klaus, Michael E. Porter, and Jeffrey D. Sachs. *The Global Competitiveness Report 2001–2002: World Economic Forum.* Oxford: Oxford University Press, January 2002.

Stevenson, William J. *Operations Management,* 8th ed. Homewood, IL: Irwin/McGraw-Hill, 2005.

U.S. Bureau of the Census—Statistical Abstract of the United States, Washington, D.C., 2004–2005.

Wren, Daniel A. *The Evolution of Management Thought,* 4th ed. New York: Wiley, 1993.

Operations and Supply Chain Strategy

Chapter outline

There is an increasing awareness that operations should contribute to the global competitive stance of the business and not merely be a place to make the firm's products or services. This can be done by contributing distinctive capability (or competence) to the business and continually improving the products and processes of the business. The Operations Leader box discusses how Corning Inc. competes through a strategy of cycle-time reduction and quality improvement.

Skinner (1969) notes that operations is seldom neutral: "It is either a competitive weapon or a corporate millstone." In his now-classic article, Skinner argues that operations should be fully connected to the business strategy. Operations strategies and decisions should fulfill the needs of the business and should add **competitive advantage** to the firm.

In the previous chapter, we indicated that the operations function is a key wealth creator for the firm. Wealth can be created only by operations that are more productive than competitors' in relation to a known market with the required financing and human resources. In other words, all of the functions of the firm must be well coordinated for wealth to be created and competitive advantage to occur. The cross-functional coordination of decision making is facilitated by an operations strategy that is developed by a team of managers from across the entire business.

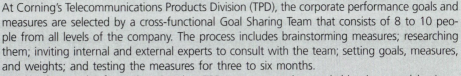

OPERATIONS LEADER
Corning Inc. Competes through Cycle Time and Quality

CORNING
Discovering Beyond Imagination

At Corning's Telecommunications Products Division (TPD), the corporate performance goals and measures are selected by a cross-functional Goal Sharing Team that consists of 8 to 10 people from all levels of the company. The process includes brainstorming measures; researching them; inviting internal and external experts to consult with the team; setting goals, measures, and weights; and testing the measures for three to six months.

The data and information Corning TPD uses to monitor and drive improved business performance are linked to its business strategy, values, and performance analysis. It collects and uses data to support the development of the division strategy, deployment of its strategic initiatives, investment in the company's values, and improvement of results.

Corning TPD also believes that cycle time and quality are much better indicators of business excellence and relative performance than financial indicators. Gerald J. McQuaid, division vice president of Corning TPD, said, "We are unique in that we are willing to put our money on improvement of nonfinancial measures, knowing this improvement will link to financial measures. Most companies tell their employees, 'Meet your financials, and then we will pay you for customer service.' We don't do that. We don't have any thresholds in our system; we pay for customer service if our employees hit it, whether or not they meet their financials. That says we believe in the link."

Source: Laura Struebing, "Measuring for Excellence," *Quality Progress,* December 1996, pp. 25–30; and www.corning.com Web site, 2005.

The following definition of operations strategy is a starting point for our discussion:

> Operations strategy is a strategy for the operations function that is linked to the business strategy and other functional strategies, leading to a competitive advantage for the firm.

This definition will be expanded in the next section as a basis for guiding all decisions that occur in operations and connecting those decisions to other functions. At the end of the chapter we will extend operations strategy to a global context and to the entire supply chain.

2.1 OPERATIONS STRATEGY MODEL

As depicted in Figure 2.1, operations strategy is a **functional strategy** that should be guided by the business strategy and should result in a consistent pattern in decisions [Hayes and Wheelwright (1984)]. The four elements inside the dashed box—mission, distinctive competence, objectives, and policies—are the heart of operations strategy. The other elements in the figure are inputs or outputs from the process of developing operations strategy. The outcomes of the process are operations decisions in the four parts of operations (process, quality, capacity, and inventory), which are well connected with the other functions in the business.

Corporate and Business Strategy

Corporate strategy and business strategy are at the top of Figure 2.1. The **corporate strategy** defines what business the company is pursuing. For example, Walt Disney Productions considers itself in the business of "making people happy." The Disney Corporation includes not only the theme parks but production of cartoons, movie production, merchandizing, and a variety of entertainment-related businesses around the world.

THE MAGIC KINGDOM. Walt Disney is in the business of "making people happy." This business strategy is implemented throughout the company. © Mark Peterson/CORBIS SABA

Business strategy follows from the corporate strategy and defines how a particular business will compete. Most large corporations have several different businesses, each competing in different market segments. Each business must find its own basis for competing in its particular markets. For example, Treacy and Wiersema (1997) define three generic types of business strategies, which can be selected by any particular business: customer intimacy, product leadership, and operational excellence.[1] The operations strategy should then be connected to the particular business strategy selected.

Operations Mission

Every operation should have a mission that is connected to the business strategy and in agreement with the other functional strategies. For example, if the business strategy is product leadership, the operations mission should emphasize new-product introduction and flexibility to adapt products to changing market needs. Other business strategies would lead to other operations missions, such as low cost or fast delivery, as will be illustrated below. The **operations mission** is thus derived from the particular business strategy selected by the business unit. How mission-driven companies can create shareholder value is explained by William George, an operations leader at Medtronic.

Distinctive Competence

All operations should have a **distinctive competence** (or operations capability) that differentiates it from the competitors. The distinctive competence is something that operations does better than anyone else. It may be based on unique resources (human or capital) that are difficult to imitate. Distinctive competence can also be based on proprietary or patented technology or any innovation in operations that cannot be easily copied.

The distinctive competence should match the mission of operations. For example, it does no good to have a distinctive competence of superior inventory management systems when the operations mission is to excel at new-product introduction. Likewise, the distinctive competence must be something that is coordinated with marketing, finance, and the other functions so that it is supported across the entire business as a basis for competitive advantage.

Distinctive competence may be used to define a particular business strategy in an ongoing business. The business strategy does not always emanate from the market; it may be built instead on matching operations' distinctive competence (current or projected) with a market. Both a viable market segment and a unique capability to deliver the product or service offered must be present for the firm to compete. In an insightful article, Clark (1996) argues that distinctive competence is an essential ingredient for a successful business strategy.

[1] They define customer intimacy as catering closely to every customer need, product leadership as having the latest new products, and operational excellence as being the lowest-cost producer.

FIGURE 2.1
Operations strategy
model.

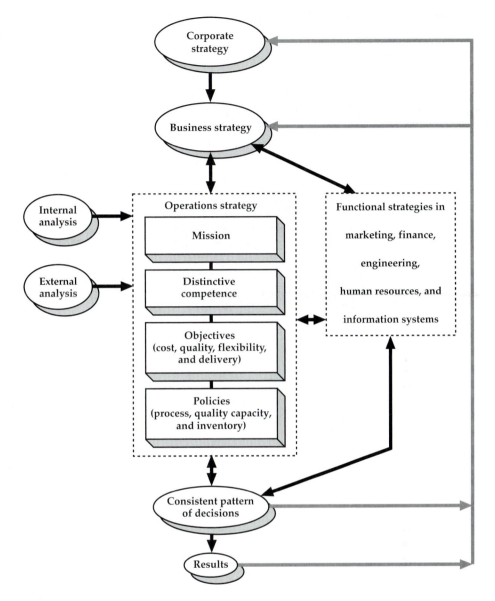

Wal-Mart has a mission to be the low-cost retailer. To achieve this mission they have developed a distinctive competence in cross-docking aimed at lowering costs of shipping. Using cross-docking, goods from suppliers' trucks are transferred across the loading dock to waiting Wal-Mart trucks and delivered to the stores without entering the warehouse. Wal-Mart also has a more sophisticated inventory control system than its competitors and therefore can hold inventories to a minimum. These distinctive competencies help Wal-Mart compete at low cost.

Wal-Mart has distinctive competencies to support its low-cost strategy. Mark Mainz/Getty Images

OPERATIONS LEADER
How Mission-Driven Companies Create Long-Term Shareholder Value: Medtronic's Former CEO Bill George

. . . I have developed a deep conviction that the widely accepted philosophy, that the primary mission of a for-profit corporation is to maximize shareholder value, is flawed at its core. While that philosophy may result in short-term increases in shareholder value, it is simply not sustainable over the long term. Over time, shareholder value will stagnate and eventually decline for companies that drive their strategy simply from financial considerations. . . .

The best path to long-term growth in shareholder value comes from having a well-articulated mission that employees are willing to commit to, a consistently practiced set of values, and a clear business strategy that is adaptable to changing business conditions. Companies that pursue their mission in a consistent and unrelenting manner in the end will create shareholder value far beyond what anyone believes is possible. . . .

The real flaw in the sole mission of maximizing shareholder value is the inability to motivate a large group of employees to exceptional performance. Tying financial incentives of the management team—be they bonuses, incentive compensation, stock grants, or stock options—to immediate results that increase shareholder value will indeed motivate the top people in the organization, at least in the short term. This is well established and documented. Unfortunately, the top people represent only a small fraction of the people doing the work of the organization. . . .

There is a better way to increase long-term shareholder value, but this cannot be the primary objective. It is my belief that corporations are created for a purpose beyond making money. Sustained growth in shareholder value may be the end result, but it cannot be the sole purpose.

The purpose of a company boils down to one thing: serving the customers. This is true across all industries and all types of businesses: stock brokers, banks, aerospace companies, consumer goods, retailing, etc. . . . If it is superior (in serving its customers) to everyone else in the field, and can sustain this advantage over the long term, that company will create ultimate shareholder value. . . .

In the end, motivating employees with a mission and a clear sense of purpose is the only way I know of to deliver innovative products, superior service and unsurpassed quality to customers over an extended period of time. Over time, an innovative idea for a product or a service will be copied by your competitors. Creating an organization of highly motivated people is extremely hard to duplicate.

Source: William George, "Address Given to the Academy of Management," *Academy of Management Executive* 15, no. 4 (November 2001), pp. 39–47.

Operations Objectives

Operations objectives are the third element of operations strategy. The **four common objectives of operations** are cost, quality, delivery, and flexibility.[2] These objectives should be derived from the mission, and they constitute a restatement of the mission in quantitative and measurable terms. The objectives should be long-range oriented (5 to 10 years) to be strategic in nature.

Table 2.1 shows some common measures of objectives that can be used to quantify long-range operations performance. The objectives for 5 years into the future are compared to the current year and also to a current world-class competitor. The comparison to a world-class competitor is for **benchmarking** purposes and may serve to indicate that operations is behind or ahead of the competition. But the objectives should be suited to the particular business, which will not necessarily exceed the competition in every category.

---

[2] In some cases, innovation has been added as a fifth operations objective.

TABLE 2.1
Typical Operations Objectives

	Current Year	Objective: 5 Years in the Future	Current: World-Class Competitor
Cost			
Manufacturing cost as a percentage of sales	55%	52%	50%
Inventory turnover	4.1	5.2	5.0
Quality			
Customer satisfaction (percentage satisfied with products)	85%	99%	95%
Percentage of scrap and rework	3%	1%	1%
Warranty cost as a percentage of sales	1%	0.5%	1%
Delivery			
Percentage of orders filled from stock	90%	95%	95%
Lead time to fill stock	3 wk	1 wk	3 wk
Flexibility			
Number of months to introduce new products	10 mo	6 mo	8 mo
Number of months to change capacity by ±20%	3 mo	3 mo	3 mo

Operations Policies

Operations policies constitute the fourth element of operations strategy. Policies should indicate how the operations objectives will be achieved. Operations policies should be developed for each of the major decision categories (process, quality, capacity, and inventory). These policies should, of course, be well integrated with other functional decisions and policies. This is one of the most difficult things to actually achieve in business and is one of the reasons a truly integrated operations strategy is needed.

Table 2.2 indicates some important policies for operations. Note, these policies may require trade-offs or choices in each case. For example, in the capacity area there is a choice between one large facility or several smaller ones. While

TABLE 2.2
Examples of Important Policies in Operations

Policy Type	Policy Area	Strategic Choice
Process	Span of process	Make or buy
	Automation	Handmade or machine-made
		Flexible or hard automation
	Process flow	Project, batch, line, or continuous
	Job specialization	High or low specialization
	Supervision	Highly decentralized or centralized
Quality	Approach	Prevention or inspection
	Training	Technical or managerial training
	Suppliers	Selected on quality or cost
Capacity	Facility size	One large or several small facilities
	Location	Near markets, low cost, or foreign
	Investment	Permanent or temporary
Inventory	Amount	High levels or low levels of inventory
	Distribution	Centralized or decentralized warehouse
	Control systems	Control in great detail or less detail

the large facility may require less total investment due to economies of scale, the smaller facilities can be located in their markets and provide better customer service. So the choice of policies depends on what objectives are being pursued in operations, availability of capital, marketing objectives, and so forth.

2.2 EMPHASIS ON OPERATIONS OBJECTIVES

It is possible to use the four operations objectives, discussed above, to describe different ways to compete through operations. Suppose we start with the idea of **competing through quality.** For the moment we can think of quality as satisfying customer requirements. This assumes that marketing has identified a particular type of customer for the business or a particular market segment of customers. If we are competing through quality as the first priority, there are many things that we would do in product design and operations. For example, we would work with the selected customers to define their specific requirements; we would also want to be sure that the process that we have is capable of meeting those customers' needs and is under control. We would ensure that workers are trained to provide the product or service needed and so on. The point is that a quality objective leads to certain actions and policies in operations to provide a product or service that the customer wants.

Now, suppose that we had decided to pursue a **low-cost objective** instead of quality. Actually, low cost is compatible with the quality objective in the way that we have defined quality, satisfying a particular set of customers.[3] Perhaps the best way to achieve lower cost is to focus on customer requirements (quality) in both product design and operations, as a way of eliminating rework, scrap, inspection, and other forms of non-value-added steps in operations. It has been found always to be cheaper to prevent errors and mistakes than to correct them after they occur. The cost savings of this approach can be dramatic. But a low-cost objective may require more than just an emphasis on quality. Heavy investment in automation and information systems may also be needed to reduce costs. In this case, some actions required for low cost are the same as those for quality and some are unique.

Had we selected **delivery time** as the key objective, we would also want to use quality improvement as a way of reducing wasted time in operations. When rework, scrap, inspection, and other non-value-added steps are eliminated from operations, the time to order, produce, and deliver the product is also reduced. But focusing on time is different than focusing on quality, although these two are related. Typical products spend most of their time in operations waiting and sitting in line for the next step. The waiting time may be as much as 80 or 90 percent of the total time of production. The best way to reduce time, beyond quality improvement efforts, is to attack time directly. This is done by reducing machine changeover time, by moving processes closer together, by smoothing out flows, by simplifying complex operations, and by redesigning the product or service for fast production. These actions would be taken in addition to those of a quality improvement objective.

Finally, we could choose to emphasize **flexibility** in operations. By reducing time, flexibility will automatically improve. For example, suppose that it originally took 16 weeks to make a product and we have now reduced the production time

---

[3] Later, we will broaden the definition of quality to include superior product attributes or features that may indeed cost more in the short run.

to 2 weeks. This will make it possible to change the schedule within a 2-week time frame rather than a 16-week time frame, thereby making operations more flexible to changes in customer requirements. On the other hand, flexibility can be attacked directly by adding capacity, by buying more flexible equipment, or by redesigning the product for high variety.

What we see from these examples is that operations objectives are connected. If we stress quality improvement, we also get cost reduction, time improvement, and more flexibility. It seems that quality is the place to start, along with time reduction. Then other objectives may be attacked directly by taking unique actions for that objective, as needed. A series of such actions will then result in continuous improvement of all four operations objectives at the same time.[4]

Zara, a giant fashion retailer in Europe, is able to achieve fast replenishment of hot-selling items in its stores within a few weeks rather than the months taken by competitors. By stressing quality processes and supply chain management practices, Zara achieves fast restocking of its stores and lower costs.

2.3 LINKING STRATEGIES

Not only should objectives be linked, but the entire operations strategy should be linked to business strategy and to marketing and financial strategies as well. Table 2.3 illustrates this linkage by showing two diametrically opposite business strategies that can be selected and the resulting functional strategies. First, there is the **product imitator** (or operational excellence) business strategy, which would be typical of a mature, price-sensitive market with a standardized product. In this case, the operations mission would emphasize cost as the dominant objective, and operations should strive to reduce costs through such policies as superior process technology, low personnel costs, low inventory levels, a high degree of vertical integration, and quality assurance aimed at saving cost. Marketing and finance would also pursue and support the product imitator business strategy as shown in Table 2.3.

The second business strategy shown in the table is one of **product innovation** and new-product introduction (or product leadership). This strategy would typically be used in an emerging and possibly growing market where advantage can be gained by bringing out superior-quality products in a short amount of time. Price would not be the dominant form of competition, and higher prices could be charged, thereby putting lower emphasis on costs. In this case, operations would emphasize flexibility to rapidly and effectively introduce superior new products as its mission. Operations policies could include the use of new-product introduction teams, flexible automation that could be adapted to new products, a workforce with flexible skills, and possibly purchase of some of the key services and materials from outside to retain flexibility. Costs would not be emphasized to the same degree as in the first strategy. Once again, finance and marketing also need to support the business strategy to achieve an integrated whole.

What Table 2.3 indicates is that drastically different types of operations are needed to support different business strategies. It also illustrates that flexibility and superior-quality products might cost more for the product innovator strategy. There is no such thing as an all-purpose operation that is best for all circumstances. Thus, when asked to evaluate operations, one must immediately consider the business strategy as well as the mission and objectives of operations.

---

[4] For more details, see the famous "sand-cone model" by Ferdows and De Meyer (1990).

TABLE 2.3
Strategic
Alternatives

Business Strategy	Strategy A Product Imitator	Strategy B Product Innovator
Market Conditions	Price-sensitive Mature market High volume Standardization	Product-features-sensitive Emerging market Low volume Customized products
Operations Mission	Emphasize low cost for mature products	Emphasize flexibility to introduce new products
Distinctive Competence Operations	Low cost through superior process technology and vertical integration	Fast and reliable new-product introduction through product teams and flexible automation
Operations Policies	Superior processes Dedicated automation Slow reaction to changes Economies of scale Workforce involvement	Superior products Flexible automation Fast reaction to changes Economies of scope Use product development teams
Marketing Strategies	Mass distribution Repeat sales Maximizing of sales opportunities National sales force	Selective distribution New-market development Product design Sales made through agents
Finance Strategies	Low risk Low profit margins	Higher risks Higher profit margins

Table 2.3 also suggests that all functions must support the business strategy for the strategy to be effective. For example, in the product imitator strategy marketing should focus on mass distribution, repeat sales, competitive pricing, and maximization of sales opportunities. On the other hand, in the product innovator strategy marketing should focus on selective distribution, new-market development, product design, and perhaps sales through agents. It is not enough for just operations to be integrated with the business strategy; all functions must support the business strategy and each other.

Hill (2000) is an advocate of the above approach that integrates marketing and operations and clearly selects a particular mission for operations. He makes the distinction between **order winners** and **order qualifiers.** An order winner is an objective that will win orders from the customers in a particular segment that marketing has selected as the target market. In the product imitator strategy, the order winner is price for the customer; this implies the need for low cost in operations, marketing, and finance. Other objectives in this case (flexibility, quality, and delivery) can be considered order qualifiers in that the company must have acceptable levels of these three objectives to qualify to get the order. Insufficient levels of performance on order qualifiers can lose the order, but higher performance on order qualifiers cannot by themselves win the order. Only price/cost will win the order in this case.

In the product innovator strategy, the order winner is flexibility to rapidly and effectively introduce superior products; order qualifiers are cost, delivery, and quality. Note how the order winner depends on the particular strategy selected and that all functions must pursue superior levels relative to competition on the order winner, while achieving acceptable levels to the customer on order qualifiers.

What is the order winner at Wal-Mart? It's low cost and everything is geared to keeping costs down. The same cannot be said about Nordstrom's, which competes on upscale merchandise and superior customer service. Since the order winners in these stores are different, so are the operations strategies.

2.4 OPERATIONS COMPETENCE

A recent trend in operations strategy is to stress distinctive competence as the primary basis for a business strategy. The distinctive competence must, of course, have a market and customer. The reverse is also true: a market without a distinctive competence does not provide the basis for a competitive strategy, and at best the operations strategy can be defensive or neutral.

Distinctive competence, as we have defined it above, refers to resources or capabilities that are unique relative to competitors. For the distinctive competence to be sustainable it must be difficult to imitate or copy. Resources or capabilities that are difficult to imitate include the following examples:

- Skills of employees and managers, particularly those that can't be easily learned.
- Proprietary equipment or processes that are patented or otherwise protected.
- An ability to continuously learn and improve operations at a rapid pace.
- Partnerships with customers or with suppliers that are developed and nurtured over the long run.
- An advantageous location for facilities gained by being the first mover (e.g., access to rare natural resources or an attractive retail location).
- Organizational knowledge that has been built up internally over time.
- Proprietary or unique information and control systems.

As can be seen from these examples, a sustainable distinctive competence is not something that can be purchased on the open market. Rather, it is often built up by the organization over time. If it could be purchased from the market, then competitors could easily duplicate it. Competitors cannot easily duplicate internal resources that are developed over time. A sustainable distinctive competence in operations is consistent with the "resource-based view" of the firm that advocates building strategy on resources that are rare, valuable, inimitable, and nonsubstitutable (Schroeder et al., 2002).

The Dell Computer Corporation has a sustainable distinctive competence in both marketing and production. Dell developed its famous direct marketing approach for the sale of computers by Internet and phone orders. This not only leads to a unique marketing channel in the computer business, but also is based on a distinctive competence in operations. When orders for computers are accepted online or by telephone, the customer immediately pays for the computer, usually by credit card. The computer is then assembled directly from the order and shipped to the customer within five days. To accomplish this, Dell has developed proprietary software that allows it to quickly enter orders into its system and to track the order to completion. It has also developed partnerships with suppliers that can immediately supply the assembly lines of the Dell factories with the required parts and components. Dell factory employees have flexible skills so they can assemble a large number of different computers that are built in lot sizes of one. The fast assembly of computers limits Dell's need for inventory, thus providing for rapid turnover of inventory and low costs. Since the product is shipped within five days, the customer payment is received in advance, and suppliers are paid later, Dell has a positive cash-to-cash cycle and can therefore hold working capital to a minimum.

This example gives only one way of building a distinctive competence that is difficult for competitors to copy or find a substitute and also is rare and valuable. While the methods Dell uses are well known to competitors they have not duplicated Dell's efficient and responsive system of production and marketing. Distinctive competencies are sometimes "sticky" and not easily duplicated, even though they could be. This is because the competitors would have to retool their entire production system, write new software, develop long-term supplier relationships, and retrain employees to copy the Dell system.

Distinctive competence provides an advantage for operations and can be the basis for competing. While market positioning is important, it is more powerful when coupled with a distinctive competence in operations. Competitively neutral operations, without a distinctive competence, cannot be expected to provide an advantage in cost, quality, delivery, or flexibility. A sustainable distinctive competence or capability is needed to provide a performance advantage.

2.5 GLOBAL SCOPE OF OPERATIONS

Every day in the popular press we read that markets are becoming global in nature. Due to expanding worldwide communications systems and global travel, consumer demand is more homogenized on an international basis. Many products and services are global in nature, including soft drinks, VCRs, TVs, banking, travel, automobiles, motorcycles, farm equipment, machine tools, and a wide variety of other products. To be sure, there are still market niches that are national in character, but the trend is toward more global markets and products.

As a result of these changes, business and operations are becoming more global. Traditional businesses are operated on a multicountry basis rather than a global basis. In a traditional company, decisions are handled differently in each country around the world. The business sees itself as selling to local markets, there is mostly local competition, and there is limited export and import. Also, each country has its own quality, process technology, and cost structure. Sources of supply are handled locally, or regionally, and export is subject to currency fluctuations. A traditional company is organized with a separate division or subsidiary for each country in which the company operates.

When operating in global markets, a traditional company is at a competitive disadvantage. The scale of operations is wrong, products may be inadequate, and the company is organized the wrong way to produce and market its products. As a result, the **global corporation** has emerged with the following characteristics.

Facilities and plants are located on a worldwide basis, not country by country. Products and services can be shifted back and forth between countries. This is being done in the automobile industry, electronics, and many other industries today. Components, parts, and services are sourced on a global basis. The best worldwide source of supply is found, regardless of its national origin.

Global product design and process technology are used. A basic product or service is designed, whenever possible, to fit global tastes. When a local variation is needed, it is handled as an option rather than as a separate product. Process technology is also standardized globally. For example, Black and Decker has recently designed worldwide hand tools. Even fast food is becoming a global product.

Demand for products is considered on a worldwide, not a local, basis. Therefore, the economies of scale are greatly magnified, and costs can be lower. The VCR came out as a worldwide product and was never marketed locally. Its demand and cost were scaled for a global market right from the start. Local competitors were kept out of the market.

Logistics and inventory control systems are global in nature. This makes it possible to coordinate shipments of products and components on a worldwide basis. For service operations, facilities are interconnected through a worldwide communications system. For example, consulting firms, fast food, banks, and travel services are globally interconnected.

A global corporation is organized into divisions that have global responsibility for the marketing, R&D, and operations functions. These functions are not fragmented into several domestic and international divisions.

Some service have also taken on a global scope of operations. For example, consulting firms, telecommunications, air travel, entertainment, financial services, and software programming have global operations. All parts of the world receive these services, and global consolidation has taken the place of these once fragmented service industries. Certainly, not all service is global. There still remain services that are delivered on a local basis to serve local markets, but the trend toward globalization is undeniable.

The implications for operations management of this change toward global business are profound. Operations strategy must be conceived of as global in nature. A global distinctive competence should be developed for operations, along with a global mission, objectives, and policies. Product design, process design, facility location, workforce policies, and virtually all decisions in operations are affected. To achieve an international perspective, we will provide a global orientation to decisions throughout this text.

2.6 SUPPLY CHAIN STRATEGY

In the same way that operations can be expanded to a global context, operations strategy can also be expanded to supply chain strategy. Today, some firms no longer compete with each other, but entire supply chains compete.

In Chapter 10, we define a supply chain as a sequence of business processes and information that provides a product or service from suppliers through manufacturing and distribution to the ultimate customer. Supply chain strategy thus takes into account not only the business and corporate strategy of the firm but also the strategies of the suppliers and customers in the firm's supply chain.

Supply chain strategy should be aimed at achieving a sustainable competitive advantage for the entire supply chain. This advantage can be achieved by expanding many of the concepts already covered in this chapter. For example, a supply chain should have a distinctive competence that is valuable and difficult to imitate or replace by competitors. This distinctive competence should be based on what the firm does along with actions of its supply chain partners. In a similar way, the supply chain partners and the firm should be working toward the same mission and objectives in order to have a consistent supply chain strategy. Since no single firm controls the entire supply chain, a coherent supply chain strategy can be difficult to achieve. Nevertheless, it is important to realize that sup-ply chain partners that are working at cross purposes will not be competitive with other supply chains that have achieved a high degree of cooperation and consistency.

In this chapter we have contrasted the product innovator and product imitator strategies. By the same token, an entire supply chain can implement these two types of strategies. As a result, not all supply chains have the same strategies but they are configured according to their fundamental purpose and therefore exhibit different missions, objectives, distinctive competencies, and policies.

For example, earlier in this chapter we discussed Wal-Mart's mission to be a low-cost retailer. Because of its enormous size and clear mission, Wal-Mart can impose a low-cost strategy on the entire supply chain. If supply chain partners do not support the low-cost strategy, they will no longer participate in Wal-Mart's supply chain. It is clear from this example how a supply chain strategy can exist beyond the boundaries of a single firm. It will, of course, be more difficult to define and implement such a strategy in smaller and more diffuse supply chains.

In every operations decision it is important to consider the proper context whether it be global or the supply chain of which the firm is only a part. Global operations and the supply chain help to set the context, not only for operations strategy, but also for decision making in all parts of operations.

2.7 KEY POINTS

This chapter has emphasized the idea of achieving a competitive advantage through operations by developing an operations strategy that the market and the customers of the business value. The key points are as follows:

- The strategy for the operations function must be linked to the business strategy and other functional strategies, leading to a consistent pattern of decisions, unique capability, and competitive advantage for the firm.
- Operations strategy consists of mission, distinctive competence, objectives, and policies. These four elements must be tightly integrated with each other and with other functions.
- The operations mission should be aligned with the business strategy. Possible missions for operations include low cost, fast new-product introduction, fast delivery, or best quality.
- The distinctive competence of operations should support the mission and differentiate operations from its competitors. Possible distinctive competencies include proprietary technology, superior human resource practices, best location of facilities, unique organization culture, and ability for rapid change.

- The objectives of operations are cost, quality, delivery, and flexibility. These objectives can work in concert if non-value-adding activities are removed from operations. One of the four objectives should be selected as an order winner; the others are order qualifiers.
- Operations policies indicate how operations objectives will be achieved. Operations policies should be developed for each of the major decision areas (process, quality, capacity, and inventory). Policies require trade-off choices in operations.
- There is no one best strategy for all operations. The mission, distinctive competence, objectives, and policies of operations depend on whether a product imitator, product innovator, or other strategy is being pursued by the business.
- The business strategy can be built on a sustainable distinctive competence that is difficult for competitors to copy or imitate.
- The scope of operations strategy is now expanding to a global basis, particularly for those businesses pursuing a global business strategy.
- In some situations the basis of competition is not the firm, but the entire supply chain. Supply chain strategy is an extension of operations strategy that considers not only the firm but also the strategies of its supply chain partners.

STUDENT INTERNET EXERCISES

\<WWW\>

1. Medtronic
   http://www.medtronic.com

Check the Medtronic Web site for evidence of a mission or vision statement. How can the mission be related to operations strategy and operations decisions?

2. Wal-Mart Company
   http://www.walmartstores.com

Go to "About Wal-Mart" and read about culture and international operations. Come to class prepared to discuss what sets Wal-Mart apart from its competition and how Wal-Mart is approaching global operations.

3. Perpetual Company
   http://www.perpetual.com.au/

What is the Perpetual company mission statement and how is it related to operations?

Discussion Questions

1. What are the reasons for formulating and implementing an operations strategy?
2. Describe a possible mission for operations and some associated strategies that fit the following business situations:
   a. Ambulance service
   b. Production of standard automobile batteries
   c. Production of electronics products that have a short product life cycle

3. An operations manager was heard complaining, "The boss never listens to me—all the boss wants from me is to avoid making waves. I rarely get any capital to improve operations."
   a. Does the business have an operations strategy?
   b. What should be done about the situation?
4. Define the following terms in your own words: mission of operations, order winner, order qualifier, and distinctive competence.

5. How would you determine whether a company has an operations strategy or not? What specific questions would you ask, and what information would you gather?

6. Evaluate your local hospital in terms of its emphasis on the four objectives of operations: cost, quality, delivery, and flexibility. Are all departments focused on the same objectives? What are the order winners and what are the order qualifiers?

7. Define some of the strategic decisions that might be required in grocery store operations depending on whether the mission (order winner) was emphasizing cost or quality.

8. What kinds of external factors might affect the following types of operations?
   a. Airline
   b. Bank
   c. Semiconductor manufacturing

9. Using newspapers, magazines, or the Internet, find examples of operations strategies. Write a few paragraphs describing the situation and the strategies being pursued.

10. Find an example of an operation in your local community that has been successful in simultaneously improving quality, reducing throughput time, improving on-time deliveries, and reducing costs. How has this operation been able to achieve these seemingly conflicting results?

11. Think of an operation where higher quality will cost more money. What is your definition of quality in this case? Why does higher quality cost more? If you use a different definition of quality, will higher quality cost less?

12. What do you consider to be the distinctive competence of the following companies? If you don't know the distinctive competence, see if you can determine it from their Internet site or articles on the company.
    a. Starbucks Coffee Company
    b. Hewlett Packard
    c. Citibank

13. Explain how a distinctive competence in operations can be the basis for competition in the company.

14. Give two examples of a distinctive competence that can be sustained and not easily duplicated. Explain why it is hard to copy these distinctive competencies.

15. Give examples of a global business that you are familiar with. How has globalization of this business affected operations?

16. What are the practical consequences of a lack of strategic linkage between the business and the operations function?

17. Give three examples of supply chains that compete with each other. In each case determine the basis of competition between the supply chains (e.g., quality, low cost, fast delivery, flexibility, etc.).

18. Define the distinctive competence for two different supply chains of your choice. Explain why the distinctive competence is valuable, difficult to imitate, and why it is difficult for competitors to find a substitute.

Selected Bibliography

Ahmad, Sohel, and Roger G. Schroeder. "Dimensions of Competitive Priorities: Are They Clear, Communicated and Consistent?" *Journal of Applied Business Research* 18, no. 1 (2002), pp. 77–86.

Alegre-Vidal, Joaquín, Rafael Lapiedra-Alcamí, and Ricardo Chiva-Gómez. "Linking Operations Strategy and Product Innovation: An Empirical Study of Spanish Ceramic Tile Producers." *Research Policy* 33, no. 5 (July 2004), pp. 829–40.

Barnes, David, Matthew Hinton, and Suzanne Mieczkowska. "The Strategic Management of Operations in e-Business." *Production Planning & Control* 15, no. 5 (July 2004), pp. 484–95.

Boyer, Kenneth K. "Strategic Consensus in Operations Strategy." *Journal of Operations Management* 17, no. 3 (March 1999), pp. 289–305.

Clark, Kim B. "Competing through Manufacturing and the New Manufacturing Paradigm: Is Manufacturing Strategy Passé?" *Production and Operations Management* 5, no. 1 (Spring 1996).

Collin, James, and Jerry Porras. *Built to Last: Successful Habits of Visionary Companies.* New York: HarperCollins, 1997.

Dyer, Davis, and Daniel Gross. *The Generations of Corning: The Life and Times of a Global Corporation.* Oxford: Oxford University Press, 2001.

Edwards, Tim, Giuliana Battisti, and Andy Neely. "Value Creation and the UK Economy: A Review of Strategic Options." *International Journal of Management Reviews* 5/6, no. 3/4 (September 2004), pp. 191–214.

Frohlich, Markham T. "A Taxonomy of Manufacturing Strategies Revisited." *Journal of Operations Management* 19, no. 5 (October 2001), p. 541.

Gunasekaran, A., L. Forker, and B. Kobu. "Improving Operations Performance in a Small Company: A Case Study." *International Journal of Operations & Production Management* 20, no. 3 (2000), p. 316.

Hayes, Robert H., and Kim B. Clark. *Dynamic Manufacturing: Creating the Learning Organization.* New York: Free Press, 1988.

Hayes, Robert H., and David M. Upton. *Strategic Operations: Competing through Capabilities.* New York: Free Press, 1996.

Hayes, Robert H., and Steven C. Wheelwright. *Restoring Our Competitive Edge: Competing through Manufacturing.* New York: Wiley, 1984.

Hill, Terry. *Manufacturing Strategy: Text and Cases,* 3rd ed. New York: McGraw Hill, 2000.

Ketokivi, Mikko, and Roger G. Schroeder. "Manufacturing Practices, Strategic Fit and Performance: A Routine-Based View." *International Journal of Operations & Production Management* 24, no. 2 (2004), pp. 171–190.

McDougall, Paul, and Darrell Dunn. "Fixing HP with Strong Operations Strategy." *Information Week* 1026 (February 14, 2005), pp. 24–26.

Pagell, Mark. "Do Trade-Offs Exist in Operations Strategy? Insights from the Stamping Die Industry." *Business Horizons* 43, no. 3 (May–June 2000), p. 59.

Porter, Michael E. *Competitive Strategy: Techniques for Analyzing Industries and Competitors.* New York: Free Press, 1980.

Safizadeh, Hossein M. "Revisiting Alternative Theoretical Paradigms in Manufacturing Strategy." *Production and Operations Management* 9, no. 2 (Summer 2000), pp. 111–27.

Schroeder, Roger G., John C. Anderson, and Gary Cleveland. "The Content of Manufacturing Strategy: An Empirical Study." *Journal of Operations Management* 6, no. 4 (August 1986), pp. 405–16.

Schroeder, Roger G., Kimberly A. Bates, and Mikko A. Junttila. "A Resource-Based View of Manufacturing Strategy and the Relationship to Manufacturing Performance." *Strategic Management Journal* 23, no. 2 (2002), pp. 105–17.

Skinner, Wickham. "Manufacturing—Missing Link in Corporate Strategy." *Harvard Business Review,* May–June 1969, pp. 136–45.

———. "Manufacturing Strategy on the 'S' Curve." *Production and Operations Management* 5, no. 1 (Spring 1996).

Smith, Thomas M. "The Relationship of Strategy, Fit, Productivity, and Business Performance in a Services Setting." *Journal of Operations Management* 17, no. 2 (1999), pp. 145–61.

Treacy, Michael, and Fred Wiersema. *The Discipline of Market Leaders: Choose Your Customers, Narrow Your Focus, Dominate Your Market.* New York: Perseus Press, 1997.

Ulrich, Dave, and Norm Smallwood. "Capitalizing on Capabilities." *Harvard Business Review,* June 2004, pp. 119–27.

Product Design

Chapter outline

New-product development is a crucial part of business. New products serve to provide growth opportunities and a competitive advantage for the firm. Increasingly there is a challenge to introduce new products more quickly without sacrificing quality. For example, the world's automobile makers can now introduce a new car design in two years, where it used to take four years. Personal computers have a very short product life cycle, sometimes less than a year.

New-product design greatly affects operations by specifying the products that will be made; it is a prerequisite for production to occur. At the same time, existing processes and products can constrain the technology available for new products. Thus, new products must be defined with not only the market in mind but also the production process that will be used to make the product.

Product design refers to either a physical, manufactured product or a service. In this chapter, we emphasize product development for manufactured products. In Chapter 5, we extend this discussion to service products.

Product decisions affect each of the four decision-making areas of operations. Therefore, product decisions should be closely coordinated with operations—to ensure that operations is integrated with product design. Through close cooperation between operations, marketing, and other functions, the product design can be integrated with decisions regarding process, quality, capacity, and inventory. Not coordinating product design and operations can have disastrous results. For example, an analysis by Nissan Motor Company indicated that 6,000 different fasteners were used in the production of its automobiles. Nissan is aiming to cut its number of fasteners in half and then in half again until an economic point is reached.

The product development process is how Ford's vision becomes reality—and how societal needs are arrayed and accommodated through innovative design and engineering.

An automobile is the most complex product that most people are ever likely to own. A typical mid-size family car is made up of more than 20,000 individual parts comprising 600 major subsystems or components. At least 73 different materials are used in a typical vehicle including 24 different types of plastics.

The process of designing and producing a modern vehicle is similarly complex. It begins with information inputs of three major types:

- Ford strategy and goals for performance and leadership
- Market research
- Research and development technical approaches to a variety of environmental, safety, and performance challenges

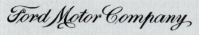

To accomplish its goals Ford spends about $7 billion per year on research and development. The product development process itself is changing in significant ways. E-commerce will revolutionize ordering, sourcing, and manufacturing processes. In early 2000, Ford announced a partnership with General Motors and DaimlerChrysler that created a single electronic marketplace for the three companies—a business-to-business integrated supplier exchange through a single global portal. This venture created the world's largest virtual supplier marketplace.

Source: 2002 Ford Web site: www.ford.com.

Product design is the result of the development of a business strategy. For example, the business strategy might specify a full product line to serve a particular set of customers. As a result, new products would be designed to fill out the product line. These new product designs then become an input into the operations strategy, and operations decisions are adjusted to fit the new-product strategy. See the Operations Leader box on the Ford Motor Company for linkages between strategy and new-product development.

3.1   STRATEGIES FOR NEW-PRODUCT INTRODUCTION

There are three fundamentally different ways to introduce new products. These approaches are called market pull, technology push, and interfunctional.

Market pull. According to this view, the market is the primary basis for determining the products a firm should make, with little regard for existing technology. A firm should make what it can sell. The customer needs are determined, and then the firm organizes the resources and processes needed to supply the customer. The market will "pull" through the products that are made.

Technology push. In this view, technology is the primary determinant of the products that the firm should make, with little regard for the market. The firm should pursue a technology-based advantage by developing superior technologies and products. The products are then pushed into the market, and marketing's job is to create demand for these superior products. Since the products have superior technology, they will have a

FIGURE 3.1 Lack of cooperation in designing a swing.

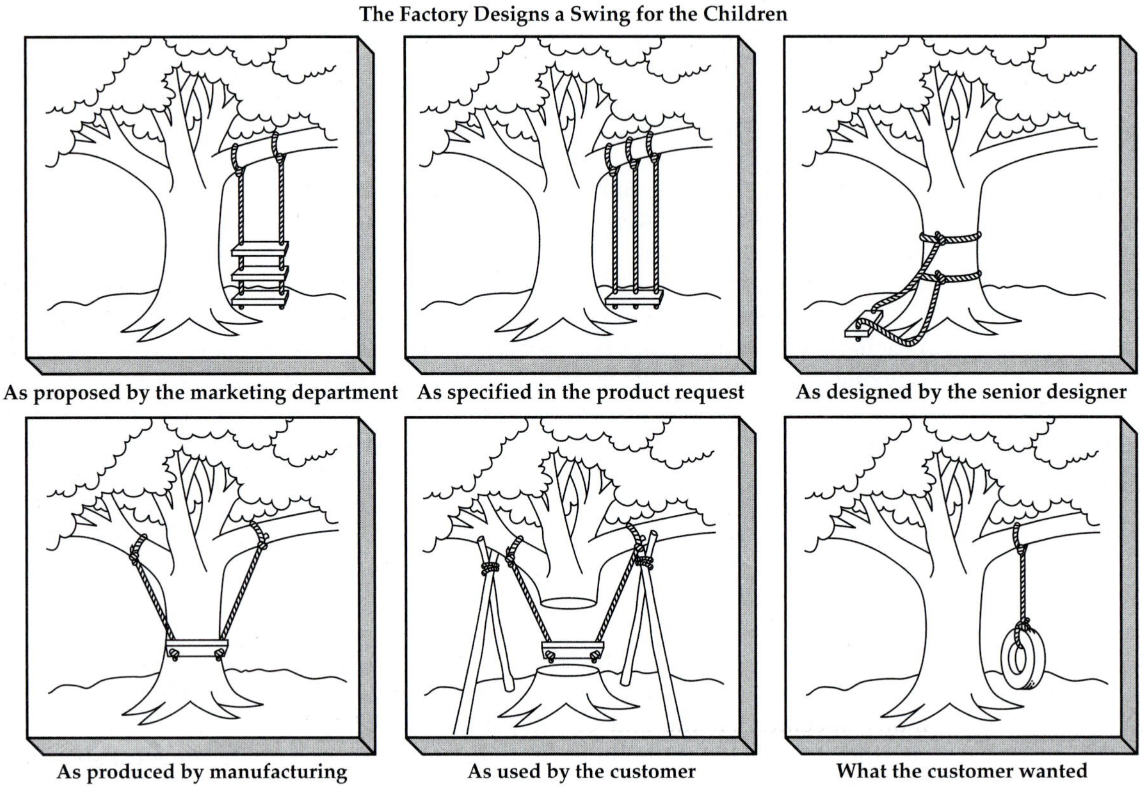

The Factory Designs a Swing for the Children

As proposed by the marketing department	As specified in the product request	As designed by the senior designer
As produced by manufacturing	As used by the customer	What the customer wanted

natural advantage in the market and the customers will want to buy them.

Interfunctional view. This view holds that the product should not only fit the market needs but have a technical advantage as well. To accomplish this, all functions (e.g., marketing, engineering, operations, and finance) should cooperate to design the new products needed by the firm. Often this is done by forming cross-functional teams that are responsible for development of the new product. This is the most appealing of the three views but also the most difficult to implement. Often cross-functional rivalry and friction must be overcome to achieve the degree of cooperation required for interfunctional product development to succeed. If it can be implemented, the interfunctional approach will usually produce the best results, and we emphasize it in the remainder of this chapter. The lack of interfunctional cooperation is depicted in Figure 3.1.

3.2 NEW-PRODUCT DEVELOPMENT PROCESS

Most firms have an organized new-product development (NPD) process that follows specific phases or prescribed steps. These phases may be formally defined in company documents and require sign-offs by senior management between phases. The purpose of such a process is to gain control of product development and to ensure that all important issues are addressed by the NPD team. **ISO 9000** certification requires that a prescribed **NPD process** be defined and followed by the company in development of its products.[1]

The typical phases followed by firms in developing new products are concept development, product design, and pilot production/testing. The names of these phases and the number of phases may vary from one company to the next, but there is a great deal of similarity between the various approaches used.

Concept Development

This phase is concerned with idea generation and evaluation of alternative ideas for the new product. During this phase, several product concepts will usually be generated and evaluated. The physical product is not actually designed during concept development; rather, different approaches to defining and meeting the market need are considered and the best approach is selected by the company. When General Mills designs a new cereal it must start with the concept development. Will the new cereal use wheat, oats, corn, bran, or a combination of these? What shape will appeal to the market (flakes, biscuits, "little Oh's"), and will the new cereal have added sugar and vitamins?

Among the several conceptual designs considered and evaluated, one will be selected for the next phase of product development. The decision to proceed to the product design phase will ordinarily require top management approval. At the time of approval, a **cross-functional team** will be established, if one does not already exist, to actually design the new product.

Product Design

This phase is concerned with designing the physical new product. At the beginning, the firm has a general idea of what the new product will be but not too many specifics. At the end of the product design phase, the firm has a set of product specifications and engineering drawings (or computer images) specified in sufficient detail that production prototypes can be built and tested.

Product design requires consideration of many different trade-offs between product cost, quality (features), and schedule. Engineers will be assigned to work on the various parts of this project. As they work, they will make decisions that will ultimately affect the product cost, its quality (features), and the schedule for product introduction. It is easy to see why marketing, operations, and finance/accounting must also be involved with engineering during this phase so that appropriate trade-offs can be made for the greatest benefit of the entire business.

Engineering will probably use computer software to design the product and simulate its operation before it is made. This will help to ensure that the product works when it is produced. Virtual prototypes, designed and tested inside a computer, are now frequently used to speed up and simplify the engineering design tasks. CAD (computer-aided design) systems, discussed in Chapter 6, are also used to view the product on the computer screen and, in some cases, to eliminate the need for blueprints or drawings. At the end of this phase, the computer images and database are transmitted to production as a basis for pilot production. Continuing the cereal example from above, the product design phase will specify the exact recipe for making the cereal, including the amounts of all the ingredients and the method to make the cereal (mixing method, baking temperature, and so on).

---

[1] ISO stands for the International Organization for Standards. ISO 9000 is a standard that applies to new product development and to production to ensure that quality products are designed and manufactured. The ISO 9000 standard requires that a procedure manual for new-product development be defined and used by the company. For more information on ISO 9000, see Chapter 8.

FIGURE 3.2
New-product design process.

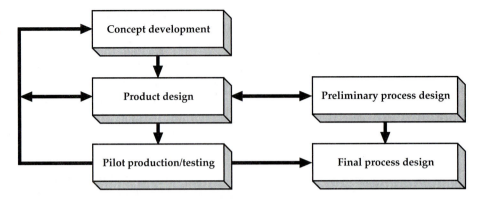

Process design should be taking place simultaneously with product design. Manufacturing should not wait for the final design to be completed before process design begins. As a matter of fact, it is better if process design is done in parallel with product design, so that changes can be made in the product to facilitate the production process before "freezing" the product design. It is also a good idea for the product designers to have some manufacturing experience, so they are aware of the process choices that are available and the pitfalls of designs that can lead to poor production processes. Figure 3.2 shows how process design should proceed in parallel with product design.

Services also require product and process design. For services, however, the product may in fact be the process. For example, a new bank debit card was introduced that provides free long-distance minutes for each use of the card for purchases of $10 or more. This card, introduced by TCF Financial Corporation, required a process change to keep track of the phone credits for the customer and to provide those credits to the customer's phone account. The product was relatively simple to design in this case, but the process change was more complex.

Pilot Production/Testing

Complex products require testing of **production prototypes** before they are actually put into production. For example, in the design of a new laptop computer, several laptops would be built as prototypes and tested for their ability to meet the product specifications. This may include performance tests of hardware and software and lifetime tests of reliability of the laptop. Similar pilot production and testing is done for aircraft, automobiles, new cereals, and many other new products. In some cases, the preliminary product is made in sufficient volume so that it can be test marketed, for example, new consumer products. Pilot testing the cereal design described above requires production of cereal samples and packaging for consumer testing (prototypes). A panel of consumers will be assembled to taste the cereal and determine if they like it. A test market in a city may also be used to test the cereal on a larger scale before full-scale production is launched.

During this phase, the process for production is finalized. Since the product design is nearing completion, the process can be designed in great detail and tested for its capability to make the product that has been designed. Process and product modifications should be considered so that the process is optimized before full-scale production and market introduction begins. To facilitate full-scale production, an **information package** should be finalized that contains not only product specifications but also process design specifications, training procedures for operators, and test results. This will facilitate transition from design to production.

3.3 CROSS-FUNCTIONAL PRODUCT DESIGN

The new-product development process is one of frequent **misalignment.** No matter how excellent the advanced planning or the technology, misalignment between the product design and operations is a common occurrence. Misalignments can occur in technology, infrastructure, and reward systems [Leonard-Barton (1998)].

Technology misalignment occurs when the product designed by engineering cannot be made by operations. This occurs when technologies are new or unproven or not well understood. Operations can also have an infrastructure that is misaligned with the new product in terms of labor skills, control systems, quality assurance, and organization. Finally, reward systems might reinforce the use of current technology rather than the new processes needed.

To overcome these problems in technology development, a concurrent marketing, engineering, and production approach has been suggested. The traditional approach proceeds in stages or steps as shown in part *(a)* of Figure 3.3. It is assumed that technology will be transferred in stages, as a handoff, between marketing, engineering, and operations. This is a **sequential process,** with each function completing its work before the next one starts.

Figure 3.3 *(b)* illustrates a simultaneous development process, also called **concurrent engineering.** All functions are involved from the beginning, frequently by forming a new-product development team, as soon as concept development is started. In the first stage, marketing has the major effort, but other functions also have a role. During the product design phase, marketing reduces its effort, but not to zero, while engineering has the major role. Finally, operations picks up the lead as the new product is tested and launched into the market.

The traditional approach is more like a relay race, while the concurrent approach is like rugby. In a relay race, each runner picks up the baton for one portion of the race. In rugby, the entire team runs down the field together, pushing and shoving in a group, to advance the ball toward the goal.

Concurrent engineering techniques were used at the National Center for Disease Control Institute for Occupational Safety and Health. The concurrent product development team revolutionized the national certification process for industrial respirators used to protect workers in hazardous environments. The team improved procedures to speed up certification and ensure better quality respirators, thereby improving safety for workers.

TEAMWORK IN ACTION, Product design teams are used to involve all functions in the simultaneous design of new products.
© Royalty-Free/CORBIS

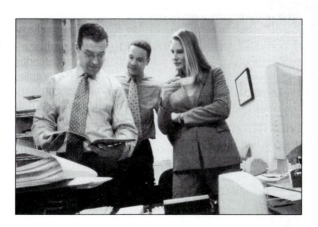

FIGURE 3.3 Sequential and concurrent approaches.

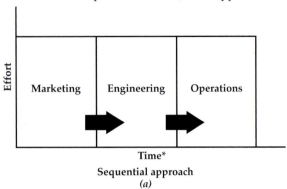

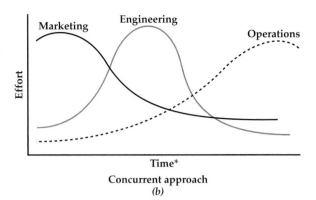

* Elapsed time from the beginning of the development effort.

Concurrent engineering has several benefits. According to a recent survey, design project time has been reduced up to 30 percent and product redesign has been cut in half. A product engineering manager at a midsize producer of air distribution equipment says, "Concurrent engineering has enabled us to do more in less time with limited resources."[2]

3.4 QUALITY FUNCTION DEPLOYMENT

The new-product development process is aided by many different tools and techniques, some of which are covered in the remainder of this chapter. **Quality function deployment** (QFD) is a tool for linking customer requirements as defined by the customer to technical specifications. QFD is very useful in translating the ordinary language obtained from the customers to technical requirements understood by engineers. It also facilitates interfunctional cooperation between marketing, engineering, and manufacturing.

QFD was first used in 1972 at the Mitsubishi shipyard in Japan. It spread from there to Toyota and to American companies. Now, many companies throughout the world are using QFD in industries such as automobiles, electronics, home appliances, and service industries. QFD has been found to be very useful as a communication tool, and it helps ensure that all of the customer requirements are being considered and nothing has been forgotten.

When using QFD, the firm identifies various customer attributes. Each of these attributes can be met by one or more engineering characteristics of the product. By using the matrix shown in Figure 3.4, the customer attributes on the left side of the matrix can be related to the engineering characteristics on the top of the matrix. When the matrix, first popularized by Hauser and Clausing (1988), is completed it is called the **house of quality.**

The house of quality illustrated in Figure 3.4 will be explained in some detail by using a bicycle example. We will work through this example, one step at a time beginning with the customer attributes.

Customer Attributes

The customer attributes (CAs) shown on the left side of the matrix in Figure 3.4 represent the voice of the customer. These attributes are determined through market research in conjunction with potential customers of the bicycle to define

[2] www.scpdnet.org, 2005.

FIGURE 3.4 Relationship matrix.

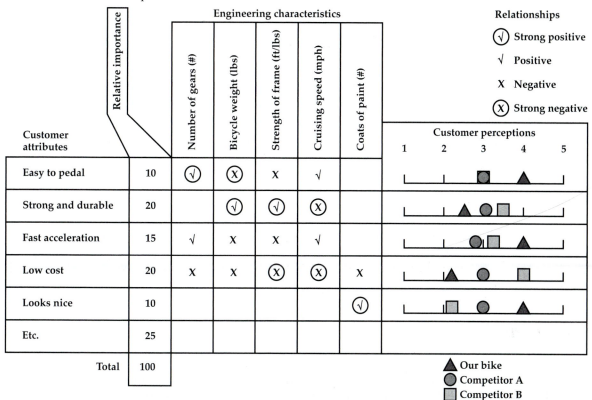

the important attributes of the product. Therefore, a target market must be defined, so that the appropriate type of customers can be contacted. Suppose, in this case, the bicycle is being designed for a very specific market: use by college students on campus. College students would be interviewed or questioned to determine what they consider important features or attributes of a bicycle. Assume students would like a bicycle that is easy to pedal, is strong and durable, has fast acceleration, is low cost, and looks nice. Please note, these CAs are not very specific at this point and need further definition by means of the QFD process.

A few more things are now added to the house of quality. After listing the CAs on the left side of the matrix, they would be rated on their relative importance by customers so as to add to a total of 100 points. This is shown on the "chimney" column of the house of quality in Figure 3.4. On the right side of the matrix is a comparison of how the company's current bicycle compares to the competitor's offerings on each of the CAs.

Engineering Characteristics

The next step in QFD is to translate the customer attributes into engineering characteristics (ECs). This is done by thinking about how each of the customer attributes can be met by the new bicycle design. Engineering characteristics must be measurable and specific and are closely related to the final design specifications for the product.

For the bicycle design, some of the ECs might be the number of gears, weight of the bicycle in pounds, strength of the frame, cruising speed, and number of coats of paint on the frame. These characteristics are put on the top of the matrix in Figure 3.4 and then related to each of the customer attributes. For example,

FIGURE 3.5   House of quality.

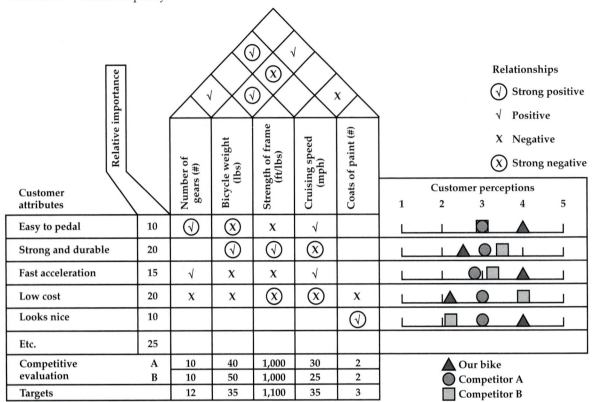

Relationships

- ⓥ **Strong positive**
- √ Positive
- X **Negative**
- ⓧ **Strong negative**

Customer attributes	Relative importance	Number of gears (#)	Bicycle weight (lbs)	Strength of frame (ft/lbs)	Cruising speed (mph)	Coats of paint (#)	Customer perceptions
Easy to pedal	10	ⓥ	ⓧ	X	√		
Strong and durable	20		ⓥ	ⓥ	ⓧ		
Fast acceleration	15	√	X	X	√		
Low cost	20	X	X	ⓧ	ⓧ	X	
Looks nice	10					ⓥ	
Etc.	25						
Competitive evaluation	A	10	40	1,000	30	2	
	B	10	50	1,000	25	2	
Targets		12	35	1,100	35	3	

Customer perceptions: 1   2   3   4   5

▲ Our bike
● Competitor A
■ Competitor B

the CA of "easy to pedal" is strongly related to the number of gears on the bicycle. Generally, the more gears, the easier it is to pedal the bicycle under different conditions and situations. Also "easy to pedal" is inversely related to the weight of the bike. Various symbols are placed in the matrix (see Figure 3.4 for the key) to indicate the nature of the relationship between each particular CA and the ECs. This can be done by conducting engineering tests or by using generally understood relationships.

Next, we switch to Figure 3.5, which adds a roof to the house of quality. The roof shows how each EC is related to the other ECs. This makes it possible to study any of the **trade-offs** that may be required between one EC and another. For example, we see that the weight of the bicycle will negatively affect its cruising speed. Also, the number of coats of paint will have a mild positive effect on bicycle weight.

Finally, on the bottom of the matrix in Figure 3.5 we have indicated the values of each EC achieved by the competitor's bicycles. We have also shown a **target value** that we have set for our new bicycle design. The target value is determined by the importance of various customer attributes, the linkages to ECs, and the desired performance of the new bicycle relative to the competitors. The ultimate result of the house of quality is a translation of the CAs into target values for ECs on the bottom of the matrix.

The house of quality has been found to be very useful in increasing cross-functional communications because it neatly connects the market requirements, which the customer values, with the design characteristics that engineers must consider. Thus, a design can be developed that will meet the needs of the market while still considering all of the design trade-offs required. The house of quality can also

FIGURE 3.6 QFD for Pizza U.S.A. delivery.

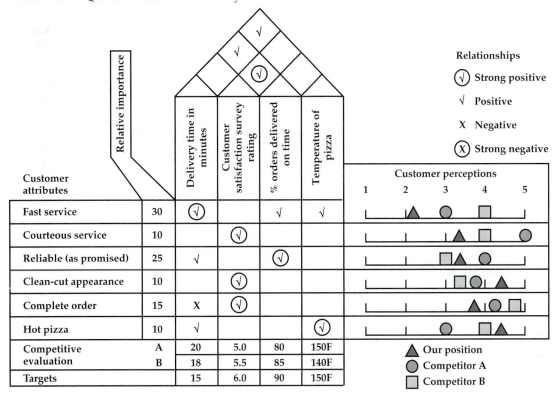

be extended into production by linking the product to various parts and to process design parameters. In this case, the target values for the product design become customer attributes for the part design and process design. Also, the house of quality can be linked to suppliers by considering the target value of the design as customer attributes for the suppliers. In this way, a linked design can be developed between all parties in the supply chain involved in designing and producing the product.

QFD can also be applied to service industries in much the same way as manufacturing. To illustrate, consider an example for Pizza U.S.A., first described in Chapter 1. Pizza U.S.A. is considering adding a take-out delivery service for its pizza and related products.

The CAs for this new service have been determined from customers to be fast, courteous, and reliable service. Also, the delivery agent should have a clean-cut appearance and the order should be delivered complete (no missing items) with hot pizza. The CAs are listed on the left side of the QFD matrix in Figure 3.6.

For services it can be difficult to identify the ECs, which are sometimes hard to define and measure. In this case the ECs are delivery time (minutes), customer satisfaction (from a periodic survey of customers), actual delivery time compared to promised delivery time, and the temperature of the pizza when it is delivered. Please note that the customer survey will measure intangible CAs such as a clean-cut appearance, courtesy, order completeness, and general satisfaction with the service.

The CAs are now related to each of the ECs in the same way as the bicycle example. Also, the roof of the house of quality, customer perceptions, competitive evaluations, and targets are added to complete the analysis as shown in Figure 3.6. While service QFD may be measured somewhat differently than it is for manufacturing, the same general principles apply.

3.5 VALUE ANALYSIS

There is a need not only to meet customer requirements but to ensure that the product is manufacturable. **Design for manufacturing** (DFM) is an approach that consists of two things: (1) simplification of products and (2) manufacture of multiple products using common parts, processes, and modules. In this section, we cover simplification of products based on **value analysis** (or value engineering), preferably conducted before the product is produced.

Value analysis is a method for improving the usefulness of a product without increasing its cost or reducing the cost without reducing the usefulness of the product. It can result in great cost savings or a better product for the customer, or both. A logical step-by-step approach is used in value analysis.

Value is defined as the ratio of usefulness to cost. Cost is an absolute term and measures the amount of resources used to produce the product. Usefulness, on the other hand, is a relative term describing the functionality that the customer ascribes to the product. Usefulness can be described by such terms as product features, performance, or reliability of the product.

In value analysis the following terms are used:

- **Objective:** the primary purpose of the product.
- **Basic function:** a basic function, if eliminated, would render the product useless in terms of its stated objective.
- **Secondary function:** a function that is the result of the way the product is designed and permits accomplishment of the basic function.

For example, to access the contents of a tin can we might have the following:

- **Objective:** remove the contents of the can.
- **Basic function:** open the can.
- **Secondary function:** cut the lid.

It is necessary to open the can to achieve the objective, which is to remove the contents. Therefore, opening the can is a basic function. But it is not necessary to perform the secondary function of cutting the lid. Other methods could be used to open the can, such as a pull tab, flip top, or screw top, as in Figure 3.7.

FIGURE 3.7 Value analysis can be used to determine the best way to open a tin can.

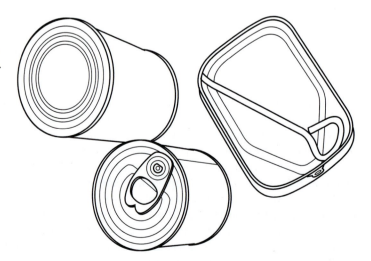

FIGURE 3.8 This example illustrates the progression of a tool box insert from design inception through the evolution of a DFM study that resulted in reducing the design part count from 20 to 2 parts, improving reliability, and lowering product cost.

Source: John Ingalls, "How Design Teams Use DFM/A to Lower Costs and Speed Products to Market," *Target* 12, no. 1 (1996), pp. 13–19.

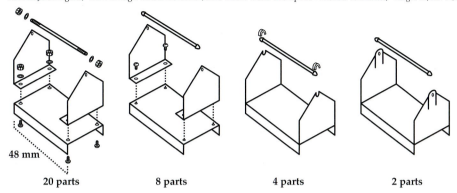

| 20 parts | 8 parts | 4 parts | 2 parts |

Value analysis is the process of examining secondary functions to see if an alternative can be identified that will improve the value ratio. This is done by first identifying the cost of the current secondary function. Then the costs of alternative secondary functions are calculated. If these alternatives have lower cost without sacrificing the usefulness of opening the can to the customer, then value is improved. Also, the usefulness may be improved (e.g., ease of removal of the lid, ability to reseal the can, and so forth) at the same cost, which would also increase the value to the customer.

Value analysis is a way to improve a product in the customer's eyes. After all, the customer is interested in value and purchases products on the basis of value received. Value analysis is frequently related to manufacturability, since a product designed for manufacturability has the lowest cost and most value. Design for manufacturability removes unnecessary parts and makes the product easier to make. This approach will reduce cost or improve the usefulness of the product, or both. See Figure 3.8 for a dramatic example of product simplification that improved manufacturability and value.

3.6 MODULAR DESIGN

Another part of DFM is to simplify the design of multiple products. Usually products are designed one at a time without much regard for commonality of parts or modular properties that can aid production and still meet customer needs.

Modular design makes it possible to have relatively high product variety and low component variety at the same time. The core idea is to develop a series of basic product components, or modules, that can be assembled into a large number of different products. To the customer, it appears there are a great number of different products. To operations, there are only a limited number of basic components and processes. Modular design is a prerequisite to mass customization described in the next chapter.

Controlling the number of different components that go into products is of great importance to operations, since this makes it possible to produce more efficiently for larger volumes while also allowing standardization of processes and equipment. A large number of product variations greatly increases the complexity and cost of operations.

Modular design offers a fundamental way to change product design thinking. Instead of designing each product separately, the company designs products around standard component modules and standard processes. If this is done, the product line must be carefully analyzed and divided into basic modules. Common modules should be developed that can serve more than one product line, and unnecessary product frills should be eliminated. This approach will still allow for a great deal of product variety, but the number of unnecessary product variations will be reduced.

The modular design approach can best be illustrated by an example. A group of students at the University of Minnesota studied the operations of a large manufacturer of beds, a company that produced over 2,000 different combinations of mattresses. The team discovered that 50 percent of those combinations accounted for only 3 percent of sales. Market surveys showed that this much product variety was not advantageous to marketing and at the same time had increased costs.

Using modular design ideas, a mattress product line was designed with four basic sizes: regular, twin, queen, and king. The inside construction of the mattresses was limited to only a few different spring arrangements and foam padding thicknesses. A moderate variety of mattress covers were used to meet consumer preferences for color and type of design. This approach greatly reduced the number of mattress components while providing substantial variety for the customer. For example, with four bed sizes, three types of spring construction, three types of foam, and eight different covers, a total of 288 different mattresses were possible.

$$4 \times 3 \times 3 \times 8 = 288 \text{ combinations}$$

Not all these combinations were produced, since some might be unacceptable to the customer (e.g., the expensive springs with the thin foam pad). Although there are still many product combinations in this example, the number of components has been limited.

The team suggested that marketing, operations, and engineering get together to define the basic components that would be made and the product combinations desired. They also suggested that the company rigorously adhere to those components once the decision had been made, with a periodic revision perhaps once

a year. The team not only dealt with the problem of product proliferation, but by using the concept of modular design, retained the marketing advantages of product variety.

Dell Computer Corporation uses modular design for its computers. Dell notebooks, for example, have many optional choices: 12 processors, four memories, six hard drives, six media devices, five wireless cards, five battery options, five displays, nine graphics cards, and six software choices.[3] This provides a total of 58 different modules (or components) that go into Dell notebooks. The theoretical number of different notebooks that can be produced is:

$$12 \times 4 \times 6 \times 6 \times 5 \times 5 \times 5 \times 9 \times 6 = 11,664,000$$

Of course, not every module is combined with every other module, thereby limiting the total number of choices. Modular design provides the opportunity to streamline production at Dell while offering abundant consumer choices.

3.7 KEY POINTS

New-product design has a great impact on operations, since it determines the specifications for the product. Likewise, operations can constrain the firm's ability to develop new products and make them more costly to produce. As a result, operations should be deeply involved in new-product development.

- There are three ways to develop new products: market pull, technology push, and interfunctional. The interfunctional approach is usually the best since it includes both market and technological considerations in the new-product design.
- The new-product development process is often specified in companies by three phases: concept development, product design, and pilot production/testing.
- Products should be designed from the start for manufacturability. This is done by considering design of the production process as part of product design and utilizing a concurrent engineering approach.
- Concurrent engineering uses overlapping phases for product design rather than a sequential approach. Typically, an NPD team is formed with representation from all major functions (marketing, engineering, operations, and finance/accounting) to ensure cross-functional integration.
- Quality function deployment is used to connect customer attributes to engineering characteristics. This is typically done by a technique called the house of quality that can be used for both manufacturing and services.
- Design for manufacturability can be accomplished by product simplification or modular production.
- Product simplification is done through value analysis, which achieves the maximum usefulness for the customer at the lowest cost.
- Modular design is concerned with minimizing the number of different parts needed to make a product line of related products. This can be done by designing standard modules and considering only the combinations of options that have significant market demand.

---

[3] Dell catalog, Jan 2005.

**STUDENT
INTERNET
EXERCISES**

<WWW>

1. Japan Business Consultants
   http://www.mazur.net/works/jurassic_qfd.pdf
   Read how QFD was used to design animatronic dinosaurs.

2. Society of Concurrent Product Development
   http://www.scpdnet.org/paper.htm
   Read one of the papers on this site and come to class prepared to discuss your findings.

3. 3M Company
   http://www.3m.com
   Describe a new product recently introduced by 3M. How has 3M been able to remain an innovative company?

Discussion Questions

1. Why is interfunctional cooperation important for new-product design? What are the symptoms of a possible lack of interfunctional cooperation?

2. Under what circumstances might a market-pull approach or a technology-push approach to new-product design be the best approach?

3. Describe the steps that might be required in writing and producing a play. Compare these steps to the three steps for new-product development described in Section 3.2. Is there a correspondence?

4. Why has there been an increase in product variety in our economy?

5. How can the modular design concept control production variety and at the same time allow product variety?

6. What is the proper role of the operations function in product design?

7. What form does the product specification take for the following firms: a travel agency, a beer company, and a consulting firm?

8. Perform a value analysis on the following items:
   a. A stapler
   b. A mouse for computer operation
   c. A desk for use by students for studying

9. Find examples of modular design of products in everyday life.

10. Work with one of your classmates as your customer; you are the supplier. Have your customer select a product and specify the customer attributes (CAs) that are desirable. Then, you specify the engineering characteristics (ECs) required to meet the customer's needs. Complete the house of quality matrix by specifying relationships in the matrix. Ask your customer if the resulting ECs will meet their needs.

11. What are the essential benefits of using a QFD approach to product design? Also, identify any negative effects that might apply to the use of QFD.

12. Think of some examples of how QFD can be applied to service design problems.

13. A student would like to design a backpack for student books and supplies. The CAs are for a (1) comfortable backpack that is (2) durable with (3) enough room and (4) not too heavy to carry. Think of some ECs that can be used to measure these customer attributes. Then construct a QFD matrix showing the positive and negative relationships that you expect to see in this case.

14. An entrepreneur is designing a submarine sandwich shop that would be located on campus. Define the CAs that you would like to see for the service (not the product) delivered at this location. Then specify some ECs that can be used for measurement of the service.

15. Suppose a car that you want to buy has five choices for interior colors, three types of radios, three engine choices, two battery types (regular and heavy duty), 10 exterior colors, two transmission choices, and four types of wheel covers. How many possible combinations of the car are possible for the manufacturer? What can be done to limit the number of combinations without limiting customer choice?

Selected Bibliography

Barry, David. "Perfecting the DFM Process." *Printed Circuit Design* 18, no. 7 (July 2001), pp. 14–17.

Boyle, Matthew. "Kraft's Arrested Development." *Fortune* 150, no. 10 (November 15, 2004), pp. 44–47.

Clark, Kim B., and Takahiro Fujimoto. *Product Development Performance.* Boston: Harvard Business School Press, 1991.

Deschamps, Jean-Philippe, and P. Ranganath Nayak. *Product Juggernauts: How Companies Mobilize to Generate a Stream of Market Winners.* Boston: Harvard Business School Press, 1995.

Eldin, Neil. "A Promising Planning Tool: Quality Function Deployment." *Cost Engineering* 44, no. 3 (March 2002), pp. 28–39.

Flynn, Barbara, E. James Flynn, Susan Amundson, and Roger G. Schroeder. "Team Characteristics as Enablers of Fast Product Development Speed." *Advances in Interdisciplinary Studies of Work Teams,* JAI Press, 6 (2000).

Hauser, John R., and Don Clausing. "The House of Quality." *Harvard Business Review,* May–June 1988, pp. 63–73.

Ingalls, John. "How Design Teams Use DFM/A to Lower Costs and Speed Products to Market." *Target* 12, no. 1 (1996).

Lane Davis, Kristin. "Finding Value in the Value Engineering Process." *Cost Engineering* 46, no. 12 (December 2004), pp. 24–28.

Leonard-Barton, Dorothy. *Wellsprings of Knowledge: Building and Sustaining the Sources of Innovation.* Boston: Harvard Business School Press, 1998.

Mallick, Debasish, and Roger G. Schroeder. "An Integrated Framework for Product Development Performance in High Technology." *Production and Operations Management,* to appear.

Maloney. "Modular Designs Carry the Future." *Modern Materials Handling* 54, no. 10 (September 1999), pp. 43–45.

Martins, Alieksiei, and Elaine M. Aspinwall. "Quality Function Deployment: An Empirical Study in the UK." *Total Quality Management* 12, no. 5 (August 2001), pp. 575–88.

McGirt, Ellen. "Harley's Easy Rider." *Money* 32, no. 9 (September 2003), pp. 48–49.

McGrath, Michael E. *Product Strategy for High Technology Companies,* 2nd ed. New York: McGraw-Hill, 2000.

Nonaka, Ikujiro, and Hirotaka Takeuchi. *The Knowledge-Creating Company: How Japanese Companies Create the Dynamics of Innovation.* New York: Oxford Press, 1995.

Olson, Eric M., Orville C. Walker Jr., Robert W. Ruekert, and Joseph M. Bonner. "Patterns of Cooperation during New Product Development among Marketing, Operations and R&D." *Journal of Product Innovation Management* 18, no. 4 (July 2001), pp. 258–71.

Ragatz, Gary L., Robert B. Handfield, and Kenneth J. Petersen. "Benefits Associated with Supplier Integration into New Product Development under Conditions of Technology Uncertainty." *Journal of Business Research* 55, no. 5 (May 2002), pp. 389–400.

Rosenthal, Stephen R. *Effective Product Design and Development: How to Cut Lead Time and Increase Customer Satisfaction.* Homewood, IL: Irwin Business-One, 1992.

Selen, Willem J., and Jos Schepers. "Design of Quality Service Systems in the Public Sector: Use of Quality Function Deployment in Police Services." *Total Quality Management* 12, no. 5 (August 2001), pp. 677–87.

Sturgeon, Timothy J. "Modular Production Networks: A New American Model of Industrial Organization." *Industrial & Corporate Change* 11, no. 3 (June 2002), pp. 451–96.

Zhou, Z. D. "A WWW-Based Integrated Product Development Platform for Sheet Metal Parts Intelligent Concurrent Design and Manufacturing." *International Journal of Production Research* 39, no. 17 (2001), pp. 3829–52.

Part **Two**

Process Design

Among the most important decisions made by operations managers are those involving the design and improvement of the process for producing goods and services. These decisions include choice of process and technology, analysis of flows through operations, and the associated job design in operations. Two themes underlie and unify Part Two: first, the idea of designing and improving a process to enhance the flow of materials, customers, and information; second, the idea of combining social and technical considerations in process design. These principles can be used to design and manage a process that is not only efficient but socially and environmentally acceptable as well.

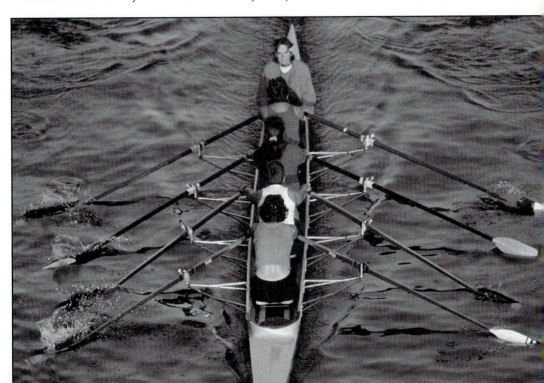

Process Selection

Chapter outline

Process selection decisions determine the type of process used to make the product or service. For example, automobiles are made using an assembly-line type of process, while sailboats are made using a batch production method. The considerations required for process selection include the volume of the product and whether the product is standardized or customized. Generally speaking, high-volume products that are standardized will be made on an assembly line, while low-volume customized products will be made in a batch operation.

Process selection decisions are strategic in nature. They require a long-term perspective and a great deal of cross-functional coordination, since marketing, finance, human resource, and operations issues are all important. Process selection decisions tend to be capital intensive and cannot be easily changed. Therefore, the firm is committed to the process choice and bound by these decisions for years to come.

This chapter describes the various types of processes that can be selected and the corresponding situations where one process or another is preferred. Two main types of process classifications are provided. One classification is by the product flow, including line, batch, and project flows. The second classification is by type of customer order: whether the product is made-to-order or made-to-stock. At the end of this chapter, we consider the dynamic context of the process choice decisions over time and the interaction of operations and other functions in the firm. While this chapter concentrates primarily on manufacturing processes, the next chapter treats service processes in detail.

4.1 PRODUCT-FLOW CHARACTERISTICS

There are three types of product flow: line, batch, and project. In manufacturing, the product flow is the same as the flow of materials, since materials are being converted into the product. In services, there might not be a product flow, but there would be a flow of customers or information. These later flows will be considered the product flow for services.

Line Flow

Line flow is characterized by a linear sequence of operations like an assembly line. The product moves from one step to the next in a sequential manner from beginning to end. Products made by a line flow include automobiles, refrigerators, computers, printers, and a vast array of mass-produced consumer products.

In Figure 4.1 a line process is used to make a metal bracket. The first step in production is to cut a rectangular metal blank in the required shape of the bracket. At the second workstation, two holes are drilled into the metal blank. Then the bracket is bent at a 90-degree angle and finally it is painted. Notice, how the workstations are placed in the proper sequence needed so that the product moves sequentially from one end of the line to the other.

Mass production and continuous flow are other terms used to describe line flows. **Mass production** generally refers to the use of assembly lines to assemble discrete parts into a finished product, for example, a refrigerator. **Continuous production** refers to the so-called process industries such as beer, paper, oil, and electricity. Here, the products are made in a continuous fashion and tend to be highly standardized and automated with very high volumes of production. Often, continuous flow products are liquids or semisolids that can be pumped or flow from one operation to another, while assembly lines make discrete products.

Traditional line operations are very efficient but also very inflexible. The line operation requires high-volume products that are standardized. At the same time, this makes it difficult to make changes in the product itself or the volume of flow leading to inflexibility of operations. For example, it takes several weeks to

FIGURE 4.1 Line flow.

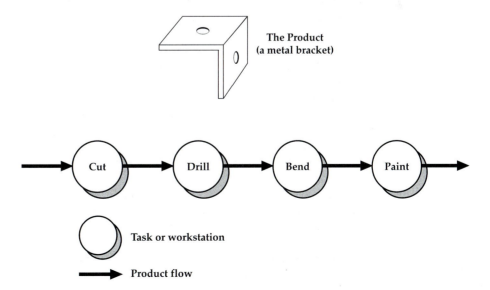

FIGURE 4.2 Batch flow (metal brackets).

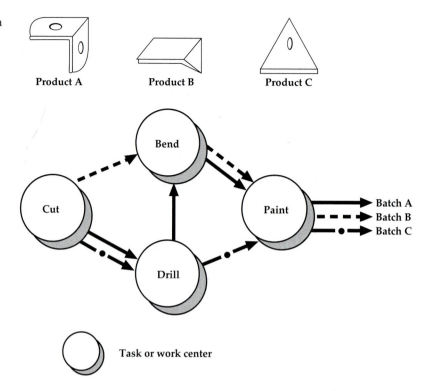

change over an automobile assembly line to the new model year and the line runs at a constant speed. The volume can only be altered by changing the number of hours worked by the plant.

Line operations can only be justified in certain situations. They generally require large amounts of capital investment and must have high volume to justify the investment. For example, a modern plant that makes semiconductor wafers costs over $2 billion in initial investment, and an automobile assembly plant costs about $1 billion. An automobile assembly plant can produce a car every minute off the end of the line or about 350,000 automobiles a year on a two-shift basis. Because of the great amount of capital required, finance is concerned with the choice of a line process along with operations. Also, marketing must be geared toward mass appeal and a high-volume product.

Batch Flow

Batch flow is characterized by production of the product in batches or lots. Each batch of the product flows from one operation or **work center** to another. A work center is a group of similar machines or processes used to make the product.

Figure 4.2 shows various low-volume brackets that are made by a batch process. In this simple example, three different shaped brackets—A, B, and C—flow through the four work centers. Notice how bracket A requires work in all four work centers, but bracket B requires only cutting, bending, and painting, while bracket C requires cutting, drilling, and painting. One characteristic of a batch operation is that it can be used to make many different types of products. Each of these products can have a different flow path and some products actually skip certain work centers. As a result, the flow is jumbled and intermittent in its appearance. Contrast this to the flow of a line process that is regular and sequential.

Batch operations often use **general-purpose equipment** that is not specialized to make just one particular product. This offers equipment flexibility. Labor is also highly skilled and flexible in its ability to make different products. As a result, a batch operation is configured with both equipment and labor to be more flexible than a line process. Lot sizes can be quite small, down to as little as one unit. As a result, batch processes can be configured to handle low-volume orders.

The **jumbled flow** of a batch operation results in considerable production scheduling and inventory problems. When loaded to near full capacity, the batch operation will typically have high inventories, as jobs wait in line to be processed. High capacity utilization results in job interference between the various jobs, as they wait for labor or equipment that is assigned to another job at the time. This results in a loss of efficiency of a batch operation.

One way to measure efficiency of a batch process is by a ratio called the **throughput ratio** (TR)

$$TR = \frac{\text{total processing time for the job}}{\text{total time in operations}} \times 100\%$$

In the numerator of the throughput ratio is total processing time for the job, which includes only the time the job actually spends being processed by machines or labor, excluding any waiting time it spends between operations. The denominator includes the total time the job spends in operations, including both processing and waiting time. Most batch operations have TRs of 10 percent or 20 percent, rarely higher than 40 percent. This means that a typical job spends most of its time waiting to be processed relative to the actual processing time. In contrast, line flow operations have TRs of 90 to 100 percent.

A batch operation uses a so-called **process layout** because the machines and labor are organized by process types into work centers. The line process, however, uses a **product layout** because the machines and labor are organized according to the product flow itself. An example of a process layout is the typical high school where classrooms are organized according to subjects (or processes) such as English, math, and chemistry. The students flow through the facility in batches (classes) going from one process to the next.

Batch operations are sometimes called **job shops,** further confusing the terminology. Job shops typically make products only to customer order in batches using a process layout. A job shop may also design the product for the specific customer. Thus, for purposes of the present discussion, we consider the job shop to be a special case of the batch operation. In a job shop, the product is made in batches even if the product is made to customer order.

Batch operations can be justified when the volume is low or there are many different products. In this case, the batch operation is the most economical and incurs the least risk. Examples of products made in batch operations are furniture, boats, dishware, and other products with large variety and low volumes. Furniture making, for example, requires many different styles and options. Sofas are ordered by customers and also ordered for stock. Each sofa might have a different fabric and may have different features on the arms or back and different lengths. As a result there are a tremendous number of variations that are made in a small batch process or even one at a time.

Project

The project form of operations is used for unique or creative products. Examples of projects are concerts, construction of buildings, and production of large aircraft. Technically speaking, the product doesn't flow in a project since materials and labor are brought to the project site and the project itself is stationary. Projects are characterized by difficult planning and scheduling problems since the product may not have been made before. Also, projects are difficult to automate, but some general-purpose equipment may be used. Labor must be highly skilled because of the unique nature of the product or service being made.

In the project form of operations each unit is made individually and is different from the other units. Projects are used when the customer desires customization and uniqueness. Generally speaking, the cost of production for projects is high and sometimes difficult to control. This is because the project may be difficult to define in all its details, and innovation may be required during production.

Boeing makes large aircraft using a project process. Each airplane is assembled at a fixed site within the factory with materials and labor brought to the site. A complex schedule is made that must balance work across all of the different aircraft being made. The tasks and resources must be sequenced and scheduled to meet the required delivery dates of the individual planes. The construction industry uses projects to construct buildings, roads, dams, and other projects. Service industries also use projects for catering food, fund-raising, political campaigns, concerts, and art fairs.

The characteristics of the three processes we have been discussing—line, batch, and project—are summarized in Table 4.1. This table makes direct comparisons among the three types of processes. Notice that line operations have relatively low-skilled labor and high automation, while project operations are quite the opposite. Also, the objectives and the product characteristics are on opposite extremes for these processes.

TABLE 4.1
Process
Characteristics

Characteristics	Line	Batch	Project
Product			
Order type	Continuous or large batch	Batch	Single unit
Flow of product	Sequenced	Jumbled	None
Product variety	Low	High	Very high
Market type	Mass	Custom	Unique
Volume	High	Medium	Single unit
Labor			
Skills	Low	High	High
Task type	Repetitive	Nonroutine	Nonroutine
Pay	Low	High	High
Capital			
Investment	High	Medium	Medium
Inventory	Low	High	Little
Equipment	Special purpose	General purpose	General purpose
Objectives			
Flexibility	Low	Medium	High
Cost	Low	Medium	High
Quality	Consistent	Consistent	Consistent
Delivery	On time	On time	On time
Control and Planning			
Production control	Easy	Difficult	Difficult
Inventory control	Easy	Difficult	Difficult

At this point, examples from the housing industry may help solidify some of the concepts. At the project end of the continuum is the custom-built house. A unique plan for it may be drawn by an architect, or existing plans may be modified for each house built. Since the construction of the house is customized, planning, sequencing, and control of various construction activities often become major problems. The customer is highly involved in all stages of construction, and sometimes the plans are modified while the house is being built. The process is labor-intensive, time-consuming, and costly, but it is very flexible.

The batch process is characterized by the production of similar houses in batches. In this case, the customer can select one of several standard houses with only minor options on things like colors, fixtures, and carpets. The house is produced with little reference to blueprints, since identical or very similar houses have been built elsewhere. The company may buy materials in large carload lots, and specialized equipment or jigs may be used to speed up construction. A crew that is very familiar with the type of house being built is brought in, and the entire structure—except for final touches—may be put up in only a few weeks. Such a house is usually less expensive per square foot than the custom-built project house, but there is also less flexibility in operations.

The line-flow method of house production is characterized by modular or factory operations. Standard houses are produced in sections, in a factory, by relatively cheap labor. The use of expensive plumbers, carpenters, and electricians is largely avoided by installing complete electrical and plumbing systems at the factory. Special-purpose machines are also used in the factory to cut costs still further. After being built on an assembly line, the house sections are brought to the site and erected in a day or so by a crane. These modular houses are typically the least expensive of all and provide the least flexibility of customer choice.

Obviously, a company faces a major strategic decision in choosing the type of process to use for the construction of houses. All three approaches may be used, but then care must be taken to separate these processes because of their different requirements for labor, management, and capital. If all three types of houses are to be offered, the company might form a separate division for each type of process because they have different labor, equipment, and management requirements.

CUSTOM HOUSE CONSTRUCTION. A custom house is being built using a project type of process. © Royalty-Free/CORBIS

4.2 CLASSIFICATION BY TYPE OF CUSTOMER ORDER

Another critical process choice is whether the product is made-to-order or made-to-stock. There are advantages and disadvantages to each type of process. A **make-to-stock** (MTS) process can provide faster service to customers from available stock and lower costs than a **make-to-order** (MTO) process. But the MTO process has higher flexibility for product customization.

In the MTO process, individual orders can be identified during production. As each order is made to the customer specification, the jobs in process are actually associated with customers. In contrast, the MTS process is building products for inventory, and the jobs in process are not identified for any particular customer. Thus, one can always identify an MTO or MTS process by simply looking at the jobs in production.

In the MTO process, the cycle of production and order fulfillment begins with the customer order. After receiving the order, the design must be completed, if it is not already done, and materials are ordered that are not already on hand or on order. Once the materials begin to arrive, the order can be processed as material and labor are added until the order is completed. Then the order is delivered to the customer. Once the customer pays for the order, the cycle is completed.

The key performance measures of an MTO process are the length of time it takes to design and make the product. This is often referred to as lead time. Another measure of performance in an MTO environment is the percentage of orders completed on time. This percentage can be based on the delivery date the customer originally requested or the date that was subsequently promised to the customer. The date requested by the customer provides, of course, a more strict criterion.

In contrast the MTS process is completely different (see Figure 4.3). The MTS process has a standard product line specified by the producer, not by the customer. The products are carried in inventory to immediately fulfill customer demand. Everything in operations is keyed to producing inventory in advance of actual demand in order to have the proper products in stock when the customer calls. The critical management tasks are forecasting, inventory management, and capacity planning.

The MTS process begins with the producer specifying the product. The customer then requests a product from inventory. If the product is available in inventory, it is delivered to the customer. If it is not available, a back order may be placed or the order can be lost to the firm. Ultimately, the customer pays for the product and the cycle is completed.

As noted above, in an MTS process customer orders cannot be identified during production. The production cycle is being operated to replenish stock. Customer orders follow a completely separate cycle of stock withdrawal. What is being produced at any point in time may bear little resemblance to what is being ordered. Production is geared to future orders and replenishment of inventory.

Performance measures for an MTS process include the percentage of orders filled from inventory. This is called the service level and is typically targeted in the 90 percent to 99 percent range. Other measures are the length of time it takes to replenish inventory, inventory turnover, capacity utilization, and the time it takes to fill a back order. The objective of an MTS process is to meet the desired service level at minimum cost.

In summary, the MTS process is keyed to replenishment of inventory with order fulfillment from inventory, while the MTO process is keyed to customer

FIGURE 4.3   MTS, MTO, and ATO comparison.

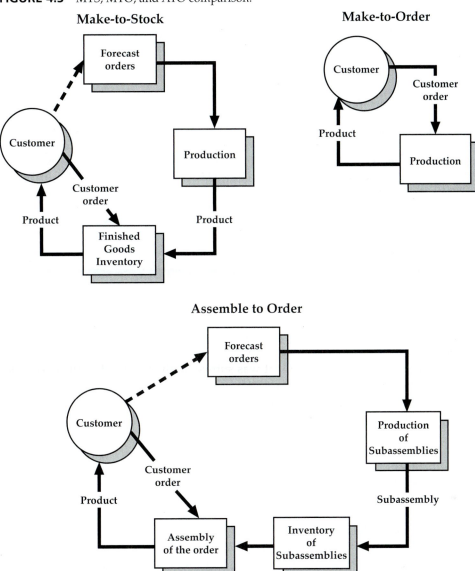

orders. An MTO process can provide higher levels of product variety and has greater flexibility. The performance measures of these two processes are completely different.

While the MTS process is measured by service level and efficiency in replenishing inventory, the MTO process is measured by its response time to customers and the efficiency in meeting its customer orders (see Table 4.2).

Recently, **assemble-to-order** (ATO) processes have come into vogue. The ATO process builds up subassemblies in advance of demand and then puts them together at the last minute to satisfy customer demand. ATO is a hybrid process of make-to-order and make-to-stock. While the subassemblies are made to stock,

OPERATIONS LEADER
FieldWorks, Inc., Configures PCs to Order

Along the broad spectrum of make-to-order manufacturing, there is a growing convergence between strictly assemble-to-order (limited options and features) and completely engineer-to-order (just about anything goes, at a cost) environments. This evolving environment is often referred to as configure-to-order.

Using a rules-based product configuration system, configure-to-order (CTO) manufacturers are able to simplify the order entry process and retain engineer-to-order (ETO) flexibility without maintaining bills of materials for every possible combination of product options.

Minneapolis-based FieldWorks, Inc., designs and builds notebook computers that can withstand environmentally "rugged" conditions for applications such as field testing communications networks or field servicing disabled tractor trailers, where rain, temperature extremes, and other trauma to the computer are common.

FieldWorks needed a system for delivering computers customized with options, features, and degrees of ruggedness. In addition, its products need to be expandable, permitting installation of specific cards or modules, such as those that test for communications cable faults or interface with a vehicle's on-board computer. The company was a perfect candidate for a configure-to-order solution.

Without CTO, engineering had to build a separate bill of material for each customer order. Now the order entry person selects from lists of options available at various levels to configure precisely to customer requirements, and the system automatically builds a bill of material. If incompatible options are chosen, the system informs the order entry person and prompts for a revision in the specifications before proceeding to configure the bill.

FieldWorks controller Steve Manske says the CTO application has already exceeded the company's expectations in the short time they have used it. "I have been involved in many software implementations and I've never seen one go as smoothly," he says. "Configure-to-order is a real advantage for us."

Source: Julie F. Riess, "Go Configure! Planning in a Configure-to-Order Environment," *APICS—The Performance Advantage,* March 1996, pp. 54–59.

the final assembly is made to order. Figure 4.3 shows how the subassemblies are built to a forecast and placed in inventory. When the actual order from the customer arrives, the subassemblies are taken from inventory and assembled together to fill the customer's order. But, of course, the product must be designed in a modular fashion for ATO to be used. There are many other variations on ATO, including configuration to order. The Operations Leader box describes how FieldWorks, Inc., configures PCs to order using a flexible manufacturing process.

Operations are moving toward assemble-to-order and make-to-order processes for standardized products, whenever possible, by reducing production lead times.

TABLE 4.2
Make-to-Stock versus Make-to-Order

Characteristics	Make-to-Stock	Make-to-Order
Product	Producer-specified Low variety Inexpensive	Customer-specified High variety Expensive
Objectives	Balance inventory, capacity, and service	Manage delivery lead times and capacity
Main Operations Problems	Forecasting Planning production Control of inventory	Delivery promises Delivery time

If the standard product can be made quickly, then it need not be placed in finished-goods inventory; rather, it can be made or quickly assembled when ordered by the customer. For example, Allen Bradley can make and ship a motor starter unit in over 300 different configurations in one day from when it is ordered. This product, which had previously been made-to-stock, can now be assembled-to-order with large savings in inventory and improved customer service. Allen Bradley assembles the product with a fast and flexible assembly line.

A classic example of the three types of processes is the production of diamond rings for the jewelry business. A make-to-stock process is used for rings that are carried in finished-goods inventory by the jewelry store. In this case, the customer buys one of the rings from the jeweler's stock. An assemble-to-order process is used when the customer selects the stone first and then makes a separate selection of a stock ring setting. The jeweler will then assemble the stone with the setting selected in an assemble-to-order process. The make-to-order process is illustrated by those jewelers who make custom settings to the customer's design and then order the stone to meet the customer's requirements. The setting and the stone are matched to make a unique ring.

4.3 PROCESS SELECTION DECISIONS

We have been discussing two dimensions that can be used for process classification purposes: product flow and type of customer order. These dimensions are used to construct the six-cell matrix shown in Table 4.3. This matrix contains the six types of processes used in practice. All of these six processes may be used by a single firm, depending on the products and volumes required by the market. However, if more than one process is used in a single facility, then the plant-within-a-plant concept may be used to maintain focus, as described later in this chapter.

All six types of processes are encountered in industry. While it is common for a line operation to be make-to-stock, it can also be make-to-order. For example, an automobile assembly line is used to produce a large variety of different automobile options for particular customers, as well as cars that are being made for dealer stock. Similarly, a project form of process is commonly used to make to order. However, a construction company can build a few speculation houses to stock that are then later sold.

TABLE 4.3
Process Characteristics Matrix

	Make-to-Stock	Make-to-Order/Assemble-to-Order
Line Flow	Automobile assembly line Oil refining Cannery Cafeteria	Automobile assembly line Dell computers Motorola pager
Batch Flow	Machine shop Glassware factory Costume jewelry	Machine shop Restaurant Hospital Custom jewelry
Project	Speculation homes Commercial paintings	Buildings Movies Ships Portraits

Also, note that all six processes apply to service operations. Pure service operations produce only to customer order. But the service may be provided with facilitating goods that are produced to stock. For example, at McDonald's some of the hamburgers are made-to-stock, while the counter service is made-to-order.

The six-cell classification system is used to categorize different processes. Notice that cost, customization, inventory, and scheduling decisions differ greatly by the type of process. Another use for the process classification system is for process selection, which is discussed in the remainder of this chapter.

In discussing the process selection decision, we shall begin with an example and generalize from there. Let us consider the contracting company, mentioned in Section 4.1, which can choose to build houses using either the project, batch, or line-flow process. With any of these processes, the company can also choose to make the houses to stock or to order. What, then, are the factors that should be considered in making this choice?

First of all, the company should consider market conditions. The line approach requires a mass market for inexpensive houses; the batch process requires a lower-volume market for medium-priced houses; and the project process requires a market for expensive houses. Which of these is chosen will require discussions between marketing and operations, which is cross-functional in nature.

But competition in the market should also be considered. Can the company enter the market at the right time and gain an advantageous position? This will depend on competitors' plans and how they react to the company's process choice. In the end, matching the process to the market will be a key strategic decision involving both product and process choices, as discussed at length in Chapter 2.

Second, the company should consider capital. The line-flow process will require a great deal more capital than the project or batch flow. The line flow requires capital to equip the factory assembly line and to finance the partially completed houses. If the houses are built to stock in advance of customer orders, more capital is required to finance finished-goods inventories. By way of contrast, construction of custom project houses would require much less capital since only one or a few houses are being built at any one time and no factory is needed. The finance function will be intimately involved with operations in these capital considerations.

The third factor that should be considered is the availability and cost of labor. The project and batch processes require costly skilled labor such as plumbers, electricians, and carpenters. The factory line approach requires relatively cheap, low-skilled labor. Unionization may affect both the supply and cost of labor. The human resources function will be involved in these considerations along with operations because of the employee selection, training, and compensation issues involved.

Finally, the company should consider the state of technology for both process and product. Are innovations likely to come along that will make a process obsolete before costs are recovered? Assessment of these conditions is part of risk evaluation for the process. Generally speaking, the risk in order of highest to lowest is line, batch, and project.

In summary, four factors appear to influence process selection from among the six processes shown in Table 4.3:

1. Market conditions
2. Capital requirements
3. Labor
4. Technology

FIGURE 4.4 Product-process matrix.

Source: Adapted from Robert H. Hayes and Steven C. Wheelwright, "Link Manufacturing Process and Product Life Cycles," *Harvard Business Review*, January–February 1979, pp. 133–140.

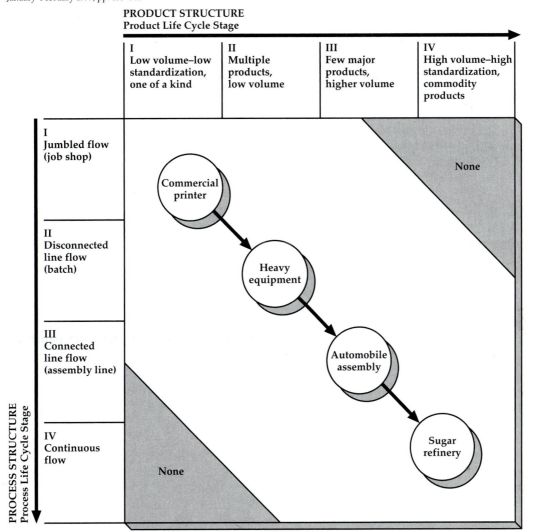

4.4 PRODUCT-PROCESS STRATEGY

To this point, we have been treating process decisions as static. Actually, process decisions are dynamic, since processes evolve from one stage to the next over time. Furthermore, process decisions are closely related to product decisions.

Hayes and Wheelwright (1979) have proposed a product-process matrix that describes the dynamic nature of product and process choices (see Figure 4.4). On the product side (top) of the matrix is the life cycle of a typical product, ranging from a low-volume, one-of-a-kind product to a high-volume, standardized product. A product typically evolves from the left side to the right side of the matrix.

On the process side of the matrix the various processes are represented, ranging from the job shop (jumbled flow) to a continuous process. The process has a similar life cycle to the product life cycle evolving from a very fluid job shop type of production at the top of the matrix to a standardized and high-volume continuous process at the bottom. Many products have followed the product and process life cycle. Automobiles were made in a job shop and batch environment in the early 1900s before Henry Ford invented the moving assembly line. Electronics are also often produced in batches until the volume becomes sufficient to support an assembly-line process.

Most firms should position themselves on the diagonal of the matrix. This means that a low-volume product with high variety would be produced by a job shop, while a highly standardized product with high volume would be produced by a continuous process. The diagonal of the matrix represents a match between the product and process. Any firm operating off the diagonal is likely to have either the wrong product or the wrong process to remain competitive.

The **product-process matrix** represents the strategic choices available to firms in both product and process dimensions. Often, strategy is represented as only consisting of product choice. But the process can provide a unique capability that the firm can exploit in the market. Thus, a patch on the matrix represents a strategic choice of both product and process. This type of strategic position will require cross-functional cooperation between marketing and operations to ensure that both product and process choices have been considered. This is not to say that the firm should use its existing processes when considering new markets and new products. Rather, the product choice should not be made without considering the corresponding process choices that might be required.

Many scholars have studied the nature of product and process choices. They have concluded that changes rarely occur simultaneously. Alternating vertical and horizontal moves are common. For example, the firm may choose to increase the volume and standardization of the product, thus moving horizontally to the right and possibly off the diagonal of the matrix. However, if this product move to the right is not accompanied by a corresponding change in process, the product will probably be too costly, which the competitors may exploit to force the firm to move back to its original position on the diagonal or to change the process and move down the diagonal.

Carrying this example one step further, a firm might be tempted to move down the diagonal ahead of its competitors and thus gain competitive advantage. This would be a good idea provided the customer is ready to accept a more standardized and higher-volume product. If the customer prefers more customization, the firm may be forced to move back up the diagonal to remain competitive.

All firms in the industry, however, do not occupy the same spot on the diagonal of the product-process matrix. Some firms may choose to stay in the upper left-hand corner of the matrix; other firms may move down the diagonal. One example of this behavior is the hand-held calculator business. Hewlett-Packard has chosen to stay with low-volume, high-variety, and high-priced calculators while the rest of the industry has moved down the diagonal toward highly standardized, high-volume, and low-priced calculators. The Hewlett-Packard calculators are suited to various specialized market niches such as accounting, surveying, and electrical engineering, which can command high prices at relatively low volumes.

4.5 FOCUSED OPERATIONS

Often a company will have products with different volumes and different levels of standardization. When a company mixes all these products in the same factory, it can lead to disaster. Skinner (1974), who originated the idea of the focused factory, tells the story of the electronic instrument company that made low-volume custom automatic-pilot instruments and high-volume standardized fuel gauges in the same plant. After years of losing money on the fuel gauges, management decided as a last resort to separate the fuel gauge production from the automatic-pilot production by building a wall down the center of the plant. They also assigned separate quality control and materials management staff to each product as well as separate direct labor, supervision, and equipment. As a result of these changes, the fuel gauges became profitable in four months and the auto-pilots also improved their profitability.

Previously, the auto-pilot production was imposing more stringent requirements in quality, materials, and skills on the fuel gauges. As a result, the fuel gauge costs were inflated and efforts could not be directed to each product separately. When these more stringent requirements were removed, each product could respond to its particular customer and market requirements. The problem essentially resulted from two different missions being mixed in operations, one of low cost for the fuel gauges and one of superior product performance and innovation for the auto-pilot.

Services can also lose their focus by trying to "be all things to all people." A service operation should have a well-defined mission such as low cost or product innovation, not both. For example, Wal-Mart is clearly focused on the low cost of operations to support its "low price always" marketing strategy. Low cost is achieved at Wal-Mart by economies of scale in purchasing, an efficient and well-managed supply chain, and economical store operations. For a time Kmart tried to attack Wal-Mart by offering lower prices, but their costs were too high, subsequently forcing Kmart into bankruptcy. Kmart is an example of loss of focus where operations strategy and capability did not match its marketing strategy.

The lack of focus in manufacturing plants and service operations has resulted from excessive attention to economies of scale. In some cases, product proliferation in the markets served by the company has led to incompatible products being mixed together in the same facility. In the name of efficiency due to economies of scale, different missions are being served by the same operation. The solution is to arrange each product as a **plant-within-a-plant** (PWP), which may sacrifice some economies of scale while doing a better job of meeting market requirements and improving profitability.

Several **types of focus** dimensions need to be considered. These include the following:

1. Product focus.
2. Process type.
3. Technology.
4. Volume of sales.
5. Make-to-stock and make-to-order.
6. New products and mature products.

Several of these dimensions may be combined when focusing operations. For example, a case study of focus in a refrigeration company included separating compressor production for high-volume, standardized, and mature products from compressor production for low-volume and customized products. In this case, one factory was divided into two separate focused factories, with consequent improvements in all measures of operations performance.

Service operations can also be focused by assigning different types of service products to different facilities. For example, in an insurance business mixing the processing of high-priced, service-intensive policies with low-priced, commodity-style policies could cause trouble. The high-priced policies might get too little service, while the low-priced polices receive too much service. The solution to this problem is to segment these policies into two different facilities or two different parts of the same facility with separate workforces and appropriate service levels for each type of policy.

Focus can be thought of as positioning facilities or PWPs along the diagonal of the product-process matrix. For example, a product with low volume, low standardization, and one of a kind should be made in a job shop process while a product with high volume and high standardization should be made on an assembly line process. Since these two types of products occupy different positions on the product-process matrix, they should be produced in different facilities with different processes or at least in different PWPs. Not doing so would result in operating off the diagonal of the matrix and a lack of focus.

4.6   MASS CUSTOMIZATION

To this point we have been discussing traditional forms of production processes. However, with the advent of flexible manufacturing, **mass customization** is now possible. At first blush, mass customization appears to be an oxymoron, two words that are incompatible like jumbo shrimp or a deafening silence. But this dichotomy between mass production and customization can be overcome by modern technologies, including the computer, robotics, modular design, and the Internet.

Traditional mass production is built on **economies of scale** by means of a high-volume standardized product with few options. On the other hand, mass customization depends on **economies of scope,** that is, a high variety of products from a *single process*. So, mass customization comes from a different economic basis, a common process rather than a common product.

Customization refers to making a different product for each customer. But mass customization is customization at approximately the same cost as mass production. This is a stringent requirement and means that some products cannot be mass-customized because the cost would be higher.

One of the early examples of mass customization is the Motorola pager. Faced with stiff offshore competition, Motorola decided to mass customize its pagers by making them in lot sizes of one. That is, each pager would be produced to the specific requirements of the customer. To accomplish this, Motorola put together a cross-functional team that designed a completely computer-integrated assembly line. They reduced the number of parts in the pager and used robots that could be quickly changed over from one pager to the next. This permitted 29 million possible variations, and total manufacturing time was reduced to only two hours from receipt of the order to shipment.

The order-entry process was also streamlined for mass customization. Sales representatives in the field entered customer orders directly into laptop computers that downloaded the order immediately to the factory. Within a few hours, the customer's pager had been ordered, manufactured, and shipped by overnight mail. This example illustrates the potential for mass customization.

There are four forms of mass customization.

1. Mass-customized services.
2. Modular production and assemble-to-order (ATO).
3. Fast changeover (zero setup time between orders).
4. Postponement of options.

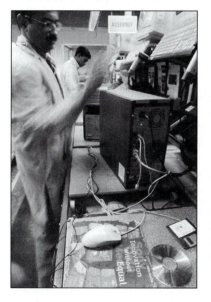

Dell computers are mass customized to meet each customer's order. © INDRANIL MUKHERJEE/AFP/Getty Images

An example of **mass customization of services** is provided by Hertz's Gold Service. For Gold customers, Hertz keeps the customer's preferences in the computer and provides a waiting car for the customer without check-in lines. When the customer returns the car, it is checked in by an attendant using a hand-held computer that reduces waiting time and personalizes service.

Modular production can provide a variety of options using an assemble-to-order process. For example, when Dell receives a computer order by phone or Internet, the company assembles standard modules or components rapidly to meet the customer's order. The order is then shipped by overnight mail so that the customer receives it in five days or less. But, this requires modular design, discussed in Chapter 3.

Fast changeover is the form of mass customization the Motorola pager uses. In this case, it is critical that production is computer controlled and each order uniquely identified by a bar code that specifies the customer's options. It is also essential to have nearly zero changeover time on equipment so that a lot size of one can be economically produced.

Postponement is used to defer a portion of the production until the point of delivery. For example, customized T-shirt shops can put a unique design on the customer's T-shirt at the point of purchase. Hewlett-Packard printers receive their final configuration for various voltages and power supplies at U.S. or overseas warehouses before delivery. Postponement makes it possible to ship standard units anywhere in the world and customize them at the last minute.

From a manufacturing point of view, mass customization has changed the dynamics of the product-process matrix. Some think that mass customization has made obsolete the product-process matrix, but we disagree. Flexible automation makes it possible to make small lot sizes along with large lot sizes without a great cost penalty. Thus, with mass customization a firm can operate over a wider range of product choices without changing its process. This amounts to a wider horizontal operating patch on the matrix. Nevertheless, mass customization does not make it possible to competitively make all volumes with all amounts of customization. There are limits to mass customization, too, but not as many limits as with the traditional forms of production. Operations Leader Lands' End is using mass customization to offer men's and women's "Jeans designed by you."

4.7 CROSS-FUNCTIONAL DECISION MAKING

We have been pointing to many of the cross-functional interactions in process selection decisions. In this section, we will expand on those notions by discussing cross-functional decision making, starting with marketing and operations interactions.

Marketing has a large stake in process selection decisions. Process choices require large capital investments and thus make it difficult to quickly change the process. In many cases, the markets the firm faces may be changing faster than the firm can recover the capital investment from process choices. Thus, marketing should be intimately involved in these decisions to ensure that both current and future market demands can be met.

One way to deal with rapidly changing markets is to move below the diagonal by choosing a batch process when the product is still in a low-volume, high-variety state that would initially warrant a job shop process. As the product moves to the right on the top of the matrix, the firm will already have the correct process. This process selection strategy requires some anticipation of future demand and the willingness to create demand, if necessary. Another way to meet the problem of rapidly changing markets is to choose mass customization, which may be more expensive in the beginning but would allow the firm to meet a wider range of product shifts.

The critical role of marketing in estimating and managing future demand is apparent. While forecasting is always an inexact science, some scenario planning should be done to estimate the appropriate product and process response for different demand scenarios. This will make it possible to manage the risk inherent in making process choices and the associated capital investment. Marketing should also be aware of the process choice implications of managing demand to support the process choices made.

Another role for marketing is in stimulating demand in market segments that marketing and operations have already chosen. If selected segments are cultivated through promotion, advertising, and sales, then sufficient volume can be generated to ensure profitability from the process cost structure already in place. This requires careful selection, development, and maintenance of a target market to fit the process choice.

Finance will also have a key role in process selection decisions because of the capital investment required. Process selection choices should be subjected to standard cash flow and present value analysis. This will ensure that any contemplated process choices will provide the required returns on capital at an acceptable risk. Finance will also be required to raise the capital once the process selection decision is made and to provide capital for future investments as the product and process evolve over time.

The human resources function will have a key role in providing the human capital that is consistent with the process selection choices made. As we have already noted, the skill level of the workforce for job shops and batch processes is much higher than for assembly lines.[1] Also, assembly lines require workers who can accept highly repetitive and routine jobs. The human resource choices must be coordinated with the process choices made by operations.

Information systems and accounting professionals should be aware that different processes have different performance measures and different data requirements. The information and accounting system designed for a make-to-order process will not work in a make-to-stock operation; nor will a job shop information system work in an assembly-line environment, since the methods used for scheduling and inventory control depend on the type of process selected. The information/accounting system will need to evolve with the process chosen. Because large investments are required in hardware and software, information systems and accounting decisions must be closely coordinated with process selection choices.

We have shown that process selection choices affect all parts of the firm. They are strategic decisions and thus involve all functions along with general management. With proper cross-functional coordination, the processes selected can offer competitive advantage to the firm and will be supported by all functions.

[1] With the exception of highly trained maintenance workers in line operations.

4.8 KEY POINTS

This chapter has emphasized two key dimensions for process classification: product flow and customer type. These dimensions can be used to create six different process types. The product-process matrix provides a basis for matching product choices made by marketing with process choices made by operations. The key points made in the chapter are:

- There are three types of processes: line, batch, and project. The line process is suited to high-volume, standardized products that are produced at low cost. But the line process has limited flexibility even if mass customization approaches are used. The batch process is suited to low-volume products that are customized or produced in a high variety. The disadvantage of a batch process is the jumbled flow, which reduces throughput and efficiency. The project process is best for unique or creative products that are made one at a time. It requires intensive planning and scheduling and generally results in costly products or services.

- The second dimension of process is type of customer order: make-to-stock, make-to-order, or the hybrid assemble-to-order. With the MTS process, the replenishment cycle for inventory is separate from the customer order cycle. On the other hand, the MTO process is set in motion by customer orders and geared to delivery performance. The MTS process provides standard products, while the MTO process is suited to custom orders. The ATO process makes subassemblies in advance for inventory, and assembles them into a final product when ordered by the customer.

- The combination of product flow and type of customer order provides six types of processes. Selection from among these six requires consideration of market conditions, capital requirements, labor, and technology. These factors are evaluated by considering economic and market conditions, but the process selection decision is always strategic and cross-functional in nature.

- The product-process matrix provides a dynamic view of the process selection decision by considering the life cycle of both products and processes. Strategy is defined by a patch on the matrix for particular combinations of product and process. The matrix helps provide coordination between marketing decisions about product and operations decisions concerning the process.

- Focused operations are used to separate products and processes that have different volume requirements or different levels of standardization. Each type of process or product family should be assigned to a different factory, PWP, or focused service operation.

- Mass customization is the ability to make a customized product at approximately the same cost as a mass-produced product. This can be done for some products by using flexible automation, robotics, modular design, and computers. There are four types of mass customization: services, modular production/ATO, fast changeover, and postponement.

- Process selection decisions are highly cross-functional in nature because they affect human resources, capital, information systems, and the ability of the firm to deliver products to the market. Therefore, all functions should be knowledgeable about the six choices available for processes and the impact of process selection on their particular functional area.

STUDENT INTERNET EXERCISES

1. Jelly Belly Tour
   http://www.jellybelly.com/Cultures/en-US/Fun/Tours/Virtual+tour.htm
   Take the Jelly Belly plant tour and describe the process used. Is it a line, batch, or project form of process, and how much automation is used?

2. Beachbeat Surfboards
   http://www.beachbeatsurfboards.co.uk/factory/index.html
   Take a tour of Beachbeat surfboard manufacturing. Describe the process used.

3. Endot Company
   http://www.endot.com/home/company_tour.asp
   Take a virtual tour of this plastic pipe maker. Observe the type of process being used.

Discussion Questions

1. Classify the following types of processes as line, batch, or project:
   a. Doctor's office
   b. Automatic car wash
   c. College curriculum
   d. Studying for an exam
   e. Registration for classes
   f. Electric utility

2. Why are line processes usually so much more efficient but less flexible than batch processes? Give three reasons.

3. The rate of productivity improvement in the service industries has been much lower than in manufacturing. Can this be attributed to process selection decisions? What problems would be involved in using more efficient processes in service industries?

4. The project process is typically used for skyscraper construction. Does this lead to higher costs? Could more efficient processes be used? If so, how?

5. Several industries—including those that produce furniture, houses, sailboats, and fashion clothing—have never progressed down the diagonal of the product-process matrix to become highly standardized and efficient. Why do you think this is so? Is this a serious problem?

6. Compare the expensive restaurant, fast-food restaurant, and cafeteria in terms of process characteristics such as capital, product type, labor, planning, control systems, and so forth.

7. An entrepreneur is planning to go into the food business. How would he or she decide whether to open a cafeteria, fast-food restaurant, or fine restaurant? What factors should be considered in this decision?

8. A company is in the business of making souvenir spoons to customer order. The customers select the size of the spoons and may specify the design to be embossed on them. One or more spoons may be ordered. The company is considering going into the make-to-stock spoon business for souvenir spoons and everyday tableware as well. What will it have to do differently? How is the business likely to change?

9. What are the possible consequences of defining a marketing strategy independently of the process strategy?

10. What are the strategies of the following organizations? Is the strategy defined in terms of product or process or both?
    a. McDonald's
    b. AT&T Telephone Co.
    c. General Motors
    d. Harvard Business School

11. Suppose that a firm is considering moving from a batch process to a line process to better meet evolving market needs. What concerns might the following functions have about this proposed process change: marketing, finance, human resources, accounting, and information systems?

Service Process Design

Chapter outline

The service economy today represents more than 80 percent of the jobs in America, and yet service production receives far too little emphasis in operations management courses and business courses in general. In other industrialized economies, including Europe and Asia, service has a similar impact on employment. Service process design clearly needs more emphasis to reflect the importance that service provides to modern economies.

When was the last time you enjoyed really superior service? Unfortunately, the service horror stories far outweigh the stories of world-class service. For example, were you happy with your last service encounter at the automobile garage? Did you enjoy waiting in the doctor's office? And, what do you think of most airline service? The stories of poor service are far too familiar.

What can be done about this? We argue that service process design is an essential ingredient of better service delivery. As a starting point, we take the ideas of process selection from the last chapter and extend them to services. We also expand the discussion here into the domain of service product offering, customer satisfaction, service guarantees, and service system design. For an example of how to deliver world-class service, see AT&T Universal Master Card Services in the Operations Leader box.

5.1 DEFINING SERVICE

Most definitions of service stress the **intangibility of the product.** Services are indeed intangible and cannot be easily quantified or defined, but we think this definition is incomplete. A better definition is that service is produced and consumed simultaneously. Therefore, a service never exists, only the results of the service can be observed. If you get a haircut, the effect is obvious, but the service itself was produced and consumed at the same time.

Simultaneous production and consumption is a critical aspect of service because it implies that the customer must be in the production system while production takes place. The customer can introduce uncertainty into the process by placing demands on the producer at the time of production. Also, the simultaneity of production and consumption indicates that most services cannot be stored or transported; they must be produced at the point of consumption. Exceptions are communications and electricity services that can be provided over long distances. They can be transported, but not stored.

Many services can be defined as acts and interactions that are social contacts. The interaction itself between the producer and customer, at the time of production, is a critical attribute of service. Indeed, production being a social interaction with the customer is quite foreign to the notion of manufacturing. In service companies, this interaction is critical not only to service but to service process design considerations.

Many think that service industries pay less. While there are certainly low-paying jobs in services, particularly unskilled jobs, there are also high-paying jobs in the

TABLE 5.1
Differences
between
Manufacturing
and Service

Manufacturing	Service
The product is tangible	The service is intangible
Ownership is transferred at the time of purchase	Ownership is generally not transferred
The product can be resold	No resale is possible
The product can be demonstrated before purchase	The service does not exist before purchase
The product can be stored in inventory	The service cannot be stored
Production precedes consumption	Production and consumption are simultaneous
The product can be transported	The service cannot be transported (though producers can be)
The seller produces	The buyer takes part directly in the production process and can indeed perform part of the production
Indirect contact is possible between the company and the customer	In most cases direct contact is needed

professional services arena, for example, doctors, lawyers, and consultants. Because pay, and other characteristics of service, vary over a wide range, it is difficult to generalize about services. Therefore, a classification system is needed to distinguish between the different types of services and associated management tasks. Such a classification system, the service matrix, is provided later in the chapter.

Service has been defined as manufacturing with a "few odd characteristics." While there are certainly many similarities between service and manufacturing, there are also many differences. The differences are more than incidental, and service cannot be merely classified as a different type of manufacturing. Some of the important similarities and differences are shown in Table 5.1.

5.2 THE SERVICE-PRODUCT BUNDLE

Before designing the process, the service product must be defined. Most services come bundled with facilitating goods in a service-goods package. For example, when customers go to a fast-food restaurant, they receive not only the food but the service, which they hope is fast, courteous, and pleasant. In this case, the food is the facilitating good for the service. Other services have fixed facilitating goods, such as the dentist's office and equipment that form the basis for dental service.

The **service-product bundle** consists of three elements:

1. The physical goods (**facilitating goods**).
2. The tangible service provided (**explicit service**).
3. The psychological service (**implicit service**).

In the case of a taxi cab ride, the taxi cab is the facilitating good, the tangible service is the sound, sight, smell, and feel of the ride, and the psychological service is the sense of well-being and security with no hassle, which hopefully the cab ride provides. It is important in the design of the service not to overemphasize the facilitating goods or the explicit service to the neglect of the implicit service. New York cab drivers are often accused of making just this mistake.

In Chapter 3, quality function deployment was presented for Pizza U.S.A. delivery service. This example can be used to illustrate the service-product bundle. The facilitating good was the pizza itself that should be delivered hot to the customer.

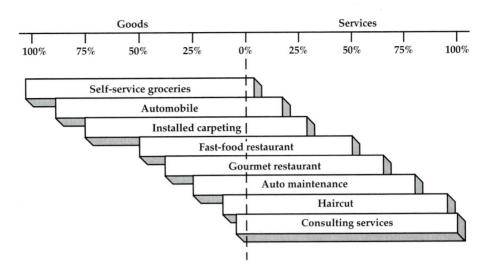

FIGURE 5.1

A comparison of various goods and services packages.

The explicit services were the time it took for delivery and the percentage of orders delivered on time. The implicit services were related to the "clean-cut appearance" and the courtesy provided by the delivery agent. These implicit services contribute to a sense of professionalism and security for the customer.

When customers go out to a restaurant for the evening, restaurant employees may be emphasizing the food when the customers in fact want a good time and atmosphere at the restaurant. So, it is important to properly read the customers' expectations and provide the proper mix of facilitating goods, tangible services, and psychological services. See Figure 5.1 for the mix of facilitating goods and service for typical products.

As an exercise, define the explicit services, implicit services, and facilitating goods for a winter ski resort. The explicit service is the experience that can be gathered by the five senses in the chalet, the shops, and the skiing runs. This includes interactions with the resort employees, the visual experience, the grooming of the slopes, and the challenging nature of the runs. The facilitating goods are the chair lifts, the buildings, and the mountain itself. The psychological service is having fun, feeling secure, and the exhilaration of skiing. The ski resort must ensure that they can appeal to all three aspects of service.

In Chapter 3 we referred to designing the product and processes together. This point is even more important for services. In many cases, the process is the product, so it is impossible to separate product design from process design. Also, the delivery of service is a simultaneous marketing and operations act. Therefore, cross-functional cooperation is the essence of service design and delivery. Service cannot be provided without it.

Service recovery is an important part of the product design. When there is a service failure, service recovery is the ability to quickly compensate for the failure and restore, if possible, the service required by the customer. For example, when there is a power failure, service recovery is the time it takes for the electric company to restore power. In a restaurant, if the waiter spills soup on a customer's lap, service recovery is the time it takes to help dry the clothes with napkins, the depth of the apology provided, and the offer to have the clothes dry cleaned at the restaurant's expense. Often when the service recovery is swift and properly performed, the customer will accept the service failure and can be satisfied with the overall service experience. The important point is that the service recovery must be swift and appropriate in the customer's eyes.

We all have personal examples of service recovery. Recently, the morning newspaper was not delivered to the author's house. After calling the newspaper office, a paper was hand-delivered within 30 minutes together with a verbal and written apology. The author judged this to be excellent service recovery.

What if your car doesn't work after taking it in for repair, an all too common experience? How can service recovery be achieved? In this case, service recovery could be the garage offering to make additional free repairs, providing a free loaner car, and promising the customer that the problem will be promptly and properly fixed. The customer may leave satisfied that the garage did everything possible to make the problem right even though the car was not fixed the first time. But service recovery cannot be instituted too often. If the service failure happens again and again, the customer may look for a different garage.

5.3 SERVICE GUARANTEES

Many companies are now beginning to offer **service guarantees** as a way to define service and ensure its satisfactory delivery to the customer. A service guarantee is like its counterpart the product guarantee, except for one thing: the customer can't return the service if he or she doesn't like it. For example, if you didn't like your haircut, you have to live with it that way until it grows out. The advantage of a service guarantee is that it builds customer loyalty and clarifies exactly what the service process must provide. Such clarification of intent helps immensely in design of the service process and specifies the extent of service recovery required upon service failure.

The service guarantee is not an advertising gimmick or a way for customers to get their money back if they are not satisfied. It is an assurance that the service provider will actually perform as promised. The fewer conditions on the service guarantee the better.

Federal Express has a famous service guarantee for its priority overnight service to many cities in the United States. Your package will be delivered by the time promised (e.g., 10:30 A.M. the next business day), or your money will be refunded—absolutely, positively. FedEx will also seek to trace your package and get it delivered at the next possible opportunity. This service guarantee defines exactly what the operations process must do. Other companies offer somewhat less precise service guarantees. For example, hotels may give you a free room if you are not satisfied. The restaurant server may be authorized to give you a free dessert or a free meal if you don't like the food. These customer satisfaction service guarantees are not as precise in guiding operations as the Federal Express guarantee; nonetheless, they provide assurance of customer satisfaction. The performance of operations can be measured, in part, by how few dollars are spent on service guarantees.

Operations Leader U.S. Bancorp offers "five star service guaranteed." The company does this by carefully defining service and providing more than 80 guarantees in all, delivered by business lines throughout the organization. Motivated employees who are rewarded for providing service deliver this excellent service. Product features and rates may be similar among banks, but guaranteed and outstanding service makes U.S. Bank unique.

Hart (1988) advocates that service guarantees be extended to internal services. Every firm has departments whose sole mission is to provide services to other departments, such as data processing, legal, and human resources. These service

departments can be held to a high standard of service just like delivery of external services. When this is done, the company must first define the customers of the internal service provider, the customer must define the level of service required, and then management must determine a significant cost or penalty if the service is not delivered as required. This approach would probably help provide higher standards for internal services, but it has not been widely adopted to date.

The service guarantee must be "meaty" for it to be effective. If the service guarantee is too small, it will not provide an incentive for better service, nor will it provide customer satisfaction in the face of failure. To accomplish this, Atlantic Fasteners, a distributor of hardware in Massachusetts, provides the following service guarantee for on-time delivery: "We deliver defect free in-stock fasteners on time as promised or we pay you $100."

The importance of a service guarantee to operations is that it provides a concrete definition of the level of service that must be provided. As a result, the service process can be designed to consistently meet this required target, and in the event of service failure, service recovery procedures can be defined. Additional service guarantee examples are provided in Table 5.2.

TABLE 5.2
Service Guarantee Examples

Summit Company (electric product supplier) Southwest United States
We guarantee that when you walk into a Summit counter to order parts, an Associate will serve you in 30 seconds or you get $5.00 toward your next purchase.

Newista (Web service)
Your Web site will be available 99.9% of the time to anyone in the world or we will give you a credit on your monthly service fee as follows: (94% to 99.8% = 20%, 89%–93.9% = 50%, 88.9% or below = 100%).

Pacific Gas and Electric (utility) California
PG&E will meet the agreed-upon appointment time set with our call center or automatically credit your account $30.
PG&E will investigate non-emergency situations (check meter) within seven days of the customer's request or credit your account for $30.

United Community Bank (retail bank) Illinois
If you wait in line for a teller for more than 10 minutes, we pay you $10. If you do not hear a thank you after a teller transaction, we pay you $5. If you call the bank and are placed on hold for more than 4 minutes, we pay you $10.

5.4 CYCLE OF SERVICE

The service provided must be considered not only in light of a single service encounter but in terms of the entire cycle of service delivery. Every service product is delivered in a **cycle of service** beginning with the point of initial customer contact and proceeding through steps or stages until the entire service is completed. For example, when you make an airline reservation, the first contact may be by

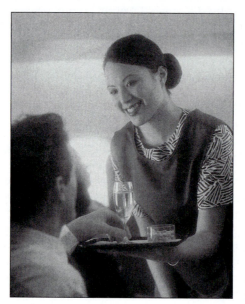

AIRLINE SERVICE. Service provided in flights is one part of the airline service cycle. © DigitalVision/ Getty Images

phone (or Internet) to ask about the schedule of departures. If you find the schedule and price satisfactory, you may then contact the airline for a reservation. After making the reservation, you arrive at the airport, check your baggage, board the plane, make the flight, eat the food, and retrieve your baggage again at your destination. Each of these points of contact is part of the cycle of airline service as shown in Figure 5.2.

Each contact with a service system can be defined as a **moment of truth** [Carlzon (1987)]. It is the cumulative effect of all of the moments of truth that defines the service provided. Therefore, the service process must be designed with the whole extent of the service cycle in mind.

FIGURE 5.2
Cycle of service for an airline.

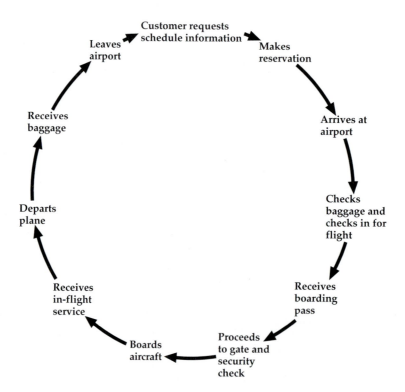

A bad moment of truth can cancel out many positive moments. Even where service recovery is provided, it is better to prevent service failure at each moment of truth than to recover from service failures. As a result, the entire cycle of service should be managed. For example, at SAS airlines there are approximately 50,000 moments of truth each day. Marriott hotel has 6 million moments of truth each day from 140,000 employees. This illustrates the magnitude of the service process design problem and the need to design each service encounter to very high standards to ensure overall service cycle performance.

The above ideas can be summarized by the following formula:

$$\text{Perceived service} = f \text{ (all previous moments of truth)}$$

Managing the moments of truth to achieve a positive experience is the essence of service delivery.

Rudy Peterson was an SAS business traveler who one day happened to leave his airline ticket at the hotel. Upon discovering his problem at the SAS check-in counter, Rudy thought he would not get on his flight. To his surprise, after checking his I.D. and the computer reservation system, the SAS ticket agent gave him a boarding pass and told him not to worry about the ticket. She sent a courier to his hotel to pick up the ticket and cleared his account when the ticket was returned. This moment of truth created a loyal customer due to superior, and unexpected, service. Each year SAS employees have millions of moments of truth lasting an average of 15 seconds each that make a difference in customers' perceptions of service.[1]

The cycle of service illustrates the cross-functional nature of service because different functions often handle different parts of the cycle. For example, a mail-order catalog firm might have the following cycle of service. The service begins with a request for a catalog, which is handled by the catalog service department. Then, if an order is placed, the customer works with the order entry department. The order is then filled by the order-filling department and shipped to the customer by the shipping department. Finally, the customer pays for the order through the accounts receivable department. The handoffs between these departments are critical to ensure that the customer is not lost between departments—a seamless service experience is desired.

5.5   CUSTOMER CONTACT

We now will look at each moment of truth in detail to understand the importance of **customer contact.** Chase and Tansik (1983) relate process design to the extent of customer contact. With a low-contact process, it is possible to buffer the customer from the actual process of production. Separating the customer from the service production system allows for more efficiency and greater standardization of processes. Examples of low-contact systems are catalog order processing and automatic bank teller transactions.

On the other hand, high-contact systems have the customer in the system during the production of the service. Examples are dentistry, hair cutting, and consulting. In these systems, the customer can introduce uncertainty into the process with a resulting loss of efficiency. For example, a customer could require special consideration or more processing time and may impose unique requirements on the service provider.

[1] Jan Carlzon, *Moments of Truth.* Cambridge, MA: Ballinger, 1987.

Chase and Tansik, in their classic article, propose that high-contact systems can lead to a loss of efficiency as follows:

$$\text{Potential inefficiency} = f \text{ (degree of customer contact)}$$

The measure of degree of contact is the amount of time that the customer is in the system while the service is being produced. For example, a highly efficient system is one with no customer contact, where the order can be processed away from the customer. At McDonald's, the degree of customer contact may be about 70 percent. Most of the processing of the customer's order is done at the front counter while the customer is waiting. However, some of the food can be made away from the customer in the back room.

Chase and Tansik advocate separating high-contact and low-contact service systems. This separation is sometimes referred to as the front room (high contact) and the back room (low contact). Front-room operations require intensive customer interaction, while the back room operates more like the traditional factory. The separation of high-contact and low-contact services is an application of the focused operations principle first discussed in Chapter 4.

There are several characteristics of high- and low-contact services:

1. Low-contact services are used when face-to-face interaction is not required. This could be done in bank-by-mail operations or check processing in banks. High-contact operations are used for changing or uncertain customer demand.
2. Low-contact services require employees with technical skills, efficient processing routines, and standardization of the product and process. High-contact services require employees who are flexible, personable, and willing to work with the customer (the smile factor).
3. High-contact service providers must respond immediately as demand occurs in peak situations. Low-contact operations can work to average demand levels and smooth out the peaks and valleys in demand.
4. High-contact services generally require higher prices and more customization due to the variable nature of the service required.

While customer contact is an important ingredient of service, it is not the only consideration. The nature of uncertainty introduced by the customer is also of critical importance. For example, contact can be high, but if the customer interface is standardized, efficiency is still possible. In fast-food restaurants the customer contact is high, but the nature of the contact is highly controlled in contrast to a fine-food restaurant, where there is more uncertainty in the service encounter. Thus, high contact by itself will not introduce inefficiency unless uncertainty introduced by the customer is also present.

5.6 SERVICE MATRIX

There are many ways to think about services, in addition to the degree of customer contact. For example, capital investment varies widely among services. Some service firms are very capital intensive, such as airlines and electric utilities; other services are labor intensive, such as consulting services and professional placement services, where it is said, "All you need is a phone and a desk."

To incorporate both customer contact and capital investment, Schmenner (1995) has suggested the **service matrix** shown in Figure 5.3. On the top of the matrix is the dimension of "degree of interaction and customization." This

FIGURE 5.3

Service matrix.

Source: Roger W. Schmenner, "How Can Service Businesses Survive and Prosper?" *Sloan Management Review,* Spring 1986, p. 25.

Degree of Interaction and Customization

	Low	High
Low	**Service Factory:** —Airlines —Trucking —Hotels —Resorts and recreation	**Service Shop:** —Hospitals —Auto repair —Other repair services
High	**Mass Service:** —Retailing —Wholesaling —Schools —Retail aspects of commercial banking	**Professional Service:** —Doctors —Lawyers —Accountants —Architects

(Degree of Labor Intensity)

dimension incorporates the interaction demanded by the customer and the customization required as a reflection of uncertainty and variation introduced into operations. Operations with low interaction and customization can be highly standardized and routinized, while operations with high interaction and customization must be responsive to high variety and low standardization. The interaction and customization dimension clearly represents the uncertainty and variety introduced into operations by the customer and is thus an extension of the degree of customer contact construct.

The side of the service matrix represents the degree of labor intensity, which is the amount of labor required in relation to the capital utilized. This can be measured by the ratio of the annual cost of labor (all employees) to the book value of buildings and equipment. As Table 5.3 indicates, the ratio varies from .07 for capital-intensive utilities to 6.7 for highly labor-intensive security brokers. Schmenner argues that this ratio will have an effect on efficiency, as well as on the managerial task.

When both dimensions of the matrix are considered, four types of service operations can be identified. The **service factory** is characterized by low labor intensity combined with low interaction and customization. Examples of these services

TABLE 5.3
Labor Intensity of Some Services

Services	Labor-Capital Ratio
Low Labor-Intensive	
Electric utilities, gas, sanitation services	.07
Communications	.19
Amusement and recreation	.40
Hospitals	.61
Auto and other repair	.63
Transportation	.79
Banking	.83
Hotels, etc.	.99
High Labor-Intensive	
Retail trade	1.61
Wholesale trade	1.85
Personal services (laundry, photo, funeral)	1.89
Business services (advertising, consulting, mailing)	2.38
Insurance agents and service	5.55
Securities, commodity brokers	6.66

Adapted from: Roger W. Schmenner, "How Can Service Businesses Survive and Prosper?" *Sloan Management Review,* Spring 1986, p. 22.

include the airlines, trucking, and electric utilities. In this case, each customer is offered a highly standardized service with little customization, and the production of the service is highly automated, much like the goods produced in a factory. If the amount of interaction or customization is increased, the **service shop** occurs as shown in the upper right-hand corner of Figure 5.3. Examples of the service shop are hospitals and automobile repair shops. In this case, the service producer must provide much more customization and interaction with the customer but can still use a high degree of automation. The service shop is somewhat analogous to the job shop described in the last chapter.

Mass services occur in the lower left-hand corner of the service matrix where labor intensity is high but interaction and customization are low. Examples of this type of service occur in retailing, schools, and retail banking. Here, the efficiency of the conversion will be lower than the service factory because of lower automation. In the lower right-hand corner of the service matrix are the **professional services,** which include doctors, lawyers, and accountants. These services have the lowest efficiency of all since the service cannot be standardized, nor can it be automated. For professional service, every case is different and requires a great deal of personal discretion and interaction with the customer.

The service matrix is intended not only to classify the different types of services but to indicate how the operations management task differs between services. For example, the service factory and the service shop will require operations management attention to automation and capital investment. On the other hand, mass service and professional service require more attention to management of human resources and personnel issues.

As Schmenner points out, the highly customized services provide challenges for operations management to hold down costs, maintain quality, control customer interaction, and reduce turnover of highly skilled employees. The highly standardized service requires operations management to present an image of service, to motivate employees doing routine work, and to maintain standard procedures.

The service matrix can also be used for strategic positioning. For example, American Express is moving from mass service to a service factory via the Internet. In 2000, the company launched its own online home page and added a number of new services. Also, the number of cardholders enrolled in "Manage Your Card Account" increased to 3.5 million, up from 1.5 million the year before. American Express also is expanding its capability for online restaurant reservations and voice-enabled customer service. All these moves can be viewed as offering a more automated service than before with perhaps less personalization but greater convenience and speed for Internet users. Product positioning can be used to gain differentiation and provide competitive advantage. When this is done, however, the resulting service will provide different management tasks for the operations manager.

The service matrix indicates the high degree of interaction between marketing and operations. If product positioning is seen as a marketing responsibility, then changes in market position, such as that of American Express, also change the operations task and the process used to produce the service. This illustrates how process design interacts with product design, and the two must be considered simultaneously in any strategic positioning decisions.

Finally, the service matrix illustrates the connection between manufacturing and service. Services in the service factory cell of the matrix are more like manufacturing with high levels of automation and standardization, while professional service has the least similarities with manufacturing. The service matrix is useful in understanding the connections with the last chapter where the product-process matrix, based on manufacturing concepts, was first introduced. The product-process matrix can be used to position different types of manufacturing while the service matrix can be used to position, or classify, different types of services.

5.7 EMPLOYEES AND SERVICE

Recently, the key to service profitability has been linked to focusing on customers and employees as paramount in importance. Often management has focused on setting goals or positioning the service without attention to what really matters. Managers should focus on front-line employees who deliver the service, the technology that supports them, training, and customer satisfaction. By linking these factors, profits will be improved in a **service-profit chain** as described by Heskett and colleagues (1994).

The service-profit chain in Figure 5.4 shows that **customer loyalty** is the key to profitability. Although being number 1 or number 2 in market share has been repeatedly touted as the key to profitability, thinking is now turning toward customer loyalty as an additional factor of equal or greater importance. The lifetime value of a loyal customer can be tremendous. For example, a loyal pizza eater generates a lifetime revenue stream of $8,000, while a loyal Cadillac owner produces $332,000. Even a 5 percent increase in customer loyalty can increase profits in many industries by 25 to 85 percent. Quality of market share with loyal customers is important, as is the quantity of market share.

The service-profit chain shows that customer loyalty is driven by **satisfied customers.** Naturally, if customers are satisfied they will not only provide repeat business but also tell others about their positive experiences. It is important, however, to move beyond barely satisfied customers; customers should feel that service is so exceptional that it is worth telling others.

FIGURE 5.4

The links in the service-profit chain.

Source: James L. Heskett et al., "Putting the Service-Profit Chain to Work," *Harvard Business Review,* March–April 1994, p. 166.

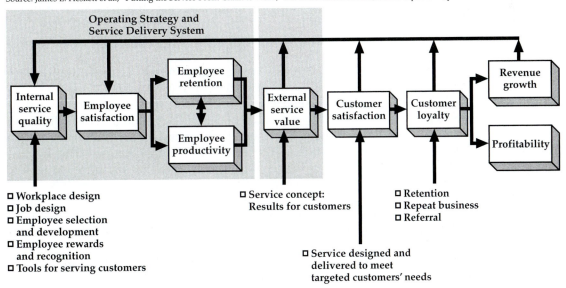

Continuing with the service-profit chain, **external service value** leads to a satisfied customer. External service value is defined here as the benefit the customer receives less the cost incurred in obtaining the service, which is not only the price but the costs of finding the service, traveling to the service location, waiting for the service, and correcting any service problems encountered. For example, the Progressive corporation, an insurance company, has created CAT (catastrophe) teams to fly to the scene of major accidents to provide support services such as transportation, housing, and claims handling quickly. By avoiding legal costs and putting more money quickly into the hands of the insured parties, the CAT team more than makes up for the costs of travel and maintaining the team. The CAT team provides value to the customers, which explains why Progressive has one of the highest margins in the property-and-casualty insurance industry.

Now we come to the employee part of the service-profit chain. **Productive employees** are seen as essential in delivering value to the customer. Productive employees will lower the costs of operations and ensure satisfied customers when supported by management and appropriate technology and systems. For example, Southwest Airlines has the most productive employees and the highest level of customer satisfaction in the airline industry. Southwest accomplishes this by innovative practices such as open seating with simple boarding cards, enabling the boarding of three and four times more passengers per day than competing airlines. Southwest deplanes and reloads two-thirds of its flights in 15 minutes or less. As a result of short routes and fast turnaround, Southwest has 40 percent more aircraft and pilot utilization than its competitors. At Southwest, customer perceptions of value are very high even though the airline does not assign seats, offer meals, or integrate its reservation system with other airlines. The combination of frequent departures, on-time service, friendly employees, and very low fares leads to high value for the customer.

Employee retention and low employee turnover drive productivity and customer value. Traditional studies of cost of employee turnover consider only the cost of recruiting, hiring, and training replacements. In reality, the greatest cost is the lost productivity and decreased customer satisfaction associated with new employees.

According to the service-profit chain, employee retention and productivity can be assured by **satisfied employees.** For example, one study of a property-and-casualty insurance company employees indicated that 30 percent of all dissatisfied employees intended to leave the company, a potential turnover rate three times higher than for satisfied employees. Also, low employee turnover was found to be related to high customer satisfaction. Satisfied employees are the result of what Heskett and his associates call **internal service quality.** This includes employee selection, workplace design, reward systems, and the computer tools used to support service workers. Workers will be satisfied with their jobs when they feel that they can act on behalf of the customer. This will lead to both employee and customer satisfaction. This is achieved, in part, by giving front-line employees latitude to use resources to immediately meet the customer's needs. For example, Xerox front-line employees are authorized to replace up to $250,000 worth of equipment if the customer is not getting results.

The important point for design of service processes is that all the links in the service-profit chain must be strong. Often, studies are done of one or two links, but seldom is the entire chain measured and evaluated. As a result, service and profit can break down at any point in the chain.

The chain also illustrates the central role of employees in delivering service directly to the customer. This can differentiate service from manufacturing, since manufacturing employees rarely have direct contact with the customer.

A manufacturing employee's effect on customer satisfaction is through the product that the customer may receive days, weeks, or months later. On the other hand, the morale, attitude, and satisfaction of service employees is directly, and immediately, related to customer satisfaction and loyalty. There is no buffer zone between service employees and the customer.

Process design should reflect this direct contact between service employees and customers. This can be done by providing customer-friendly computer tools to help service employees do their jobs. It can also be done through so-called smile training, where service workers are trained to be nice to customers and to seek their satisfaction even in pressure situations. Service workers should also be rewarded for both productivity and customer satisfaction. The service-profit chain shows that these two measurements are not in conflict; rather, productivity can actually drive customer satisfaction as illustrated above. Both satisfaction and productivity can often be achieved not by trying harder but by better technology and improved service process flows. These points will be covered in detail in the next two chapters.

A lesson learned by Aquarion, a water utility, is "it takes more than sparkling water to satisfy customers." Aquarion is one of the 10 largest investor-owned (nonmunicipal) water utilities in the United States and the largest operator in New England. Aquarion illustrates the service-profit chain by its excellent levels of customer satisfaction, employee loyalty, and employee satisfaction. Since 1995,

OPERATIONS LEADER

Aquarion Company Mission Statement

AQUARION

Respect means . . .

- Being polite and courteous to one another.
- Appreciating each person's background and opinions—co-worker and customer alike.
- Understanding that differing points of view and open and honest feedback strengthen our work relationships.
- Acknowledging that another's time is as valuable as your own.

Mission and Values

To be the . . .

Employer
Investment
of
Choice

Service Provider
through a *relentless commitment to excellence*

Take Responsibility means . . .

- Being accountable by saying "the buck stops here" and handling the problem.
- Going the extra mile or getting involved, even if it's not in the job description.
- Asking questions to determine the root cause of a problem and finding a solution.
  - Managing your career and educational goals.

Be Responsive means . . .

- Providing information and handling requests promptly.
- Keeping customers and co-workers updated on the status of their requests.
- Anticipating what needs to be done and doing it.
- Replying to messages in a timely manner.

Reach for Excellence means . . .

- Seeking the best way, not always the easiest way, to accomplish our goals.
- Challenging each other on the status quo.
- Pursuing a relentless commitment to higher achievement.
- Incorporating these values into our daily lives.

Source: Company Web site 2002: www.aquarion.com.

this Connecticut utility has received 17 state awards for innovative service or product initiatives that benefit the company or its customers. Aquarion improved customer service ratings for personal service by 19 percentage points in one year. How did this company do it? The approach involved high water quality, reliable service, and motivated employees.

The company's mission is to be the service provider, employer, and investment of choice. Its strategy is to grow the business and differentiate itself not only through quality of the product and process, but also through quality of personal service. Aquarion's achievements are the result of creativity, consistency, and commitment—creativity in finding new ways to meet and exceed customer expectations, consistency in product quality, and the relentless commitment to excellence of every employee at every level.

The Operations Leader box for Aquarion shows how the company's mission statement, "to be the service provider of choice through a relentless commitment to excellence," is translated into actions and values throughout the organization. It illustrates the depth of employee commitment needed to achieve superior customer service and profitability as part of the service-profit chain.

An interesting application of the service-profit chain is being made in Las Vegas, Nevada, at Harrah's. Traditionally the gambling industry has catered to the high rollers. A former professor at the Harvard Business School, Gary Loveman, Harrah's CEO, is revolutionizing the gaming industry by arguing that the key to profitability and growth is not the high rollers but providing exceptional service and treating gamblers like shoppers. "People don't understand that gaming itself is fundamentally entertainment," says Loveman. He is looking for frequent shoppers like teachers, lawyers, and accountants to play the odds again and again and again. This will be done by satisfied employees providing exceptional service to satisfied and loyal customers.[2]

5.8 KEY POINTS

This chapter has emphasized the design of service processes. The key points are as follows:

- A service is defined by simultaneous production and consumption. This makes it impossible to store the service for later use and the service must be located near the customer with the exception of technology-delivered services such as communication and electricity. The customer is part of the service process during production and may introduce inefficiencies. Personal service is a social interaction and requires human interchange.

- Services consist of a bundle of goods and services, including facilitating goods, explicit services, and implicit services. It is important to provide the right mix of these three elements and not to overlook the psychological component of service. When things go wrong, the firm should provide quick and helpful service recovery.

- A service guarantee is offered to ensure that the customer and producer will understand the service being provided. The service guarantee provides a way for operations to know exactly what is required.

- A cycle of service consists of several individual service transactions at different points in time. All elements of the cycle (each moment of truth) must perform for the customer to be satisfied with the service experience.

[2] Julie Schlosser, "Teacher's Bet," *Fortune,* March 8, 2004, pp. 158–63.

- At each point in the service cycle, customer contact can be either high or low, depending on the service. Generally, high-contact services are performed in the front room; low-contact services are performed away from the customer in the back room. It is not only contact that is important but the degree of uncertainty and customization demanded by the customer while in contact with the service system.

- The service matrix is formed by a combination of customer interaction/customization together with the degree of labor intensity. Four types of service combinations are formed by this matrix: service factory, service shop, mass service, and professional service. Each of these four types of services has different requirements for operations managers to meet.

- The service-profit chain indicates how customer satisfaction and loyalty along with employee satisfaction and loyalty are important to profitability. Attention to selection, job design, training, support tools, and rewards for employees are important drivers of the chain. Any weak link in the chain will reduce the level of customer loyalty and profit.

STUDENT INTERNET EXERCISES

<WWW>

1. United Parcel Service (UPS)
   https://www.sonicair.ups.com/ups/cust-support-guarantee.jsp

   Read the UPS service guarantee and come to class prepared to discuss it. Do you think it is simple, understandable, and provides confidence in the service provided?

2. Summit Electric Supply
   http://www.summit.com/services/guarantees/index.asp

   What is the Summit 30 second and 20/20 service guarantee? Compare it to the UPS service guarantee in number 1.

3. Pike Place Fish
   http://pikeplacefish.com

   Visit this site to learn how friendly and "fun" employees can lead to satisfied customers and a "world famous" company. Explain how they do it!

Discussion Questions

1. Classify the following services by their degree of customer contact (high, medium, or low). Also, determine how much uncertainty the customer introduces into the system by the ability to make customized service demands (high, medium, or low).
   a. Check clearing in a bank
   b. Bank teller
   c. Bank loan officer

2. Who is the customer in a school, a jail, and a personnel office in a firm? Identify some moments of truth experienced by these customers.

3. Locate each of the following services on the service matrix:
   a. Vending machine business
   b. Housecleaning service
   c. Appliance repair

4. How do the managerial tasks differ among the services described in question 3?

5. Describe the service-product bundle for each of the following services:
   a. Hospital
   b. Lawyer
   c. Trucking firm

6. Critique the customer contact model. What are its strengths and weaknesses?

7. Identify the front-room and back-room services for the following organizations. Could these services be improved by increasing or decreasing the degree of customer contact? By separating low- and high-contact services?
   a. Hospital
   b. Trucking firm
   c. Grocery store
   d. Appliance repair firm

8. Define the cycle of service for the following services:
   a. Registration for college classes
   b. Going to a movie
   c. Buying a used car

9. Define a possible service guarantee for each of the services listed in question 8.

10. Give an example of the service-profit chain for the movie business. Define each of the points in the chain and how you would measure each point.

11. Why is the service-profit chain important to operations management?

12. Find some service guarantees in everyday life and bring them to class for discussion.

13. What attributes are required of a service guarantee to make it effective?

14. What are the pros and cons of having a service guarantee?

15. How can we use the service matrix to improve service operations?

Selected Bibliography

Bannan, Karen J. "Customer Relationship Management." *PC Magazine* 20, no. 13 (July 3, 2001), pp. 136–38.

Beckett, Antony. "From Branches to Call Centres: New Strategic Realities in Retail Banking." *Service Industries Journal* 24, no. 3 (May 2004), pp. 43–63.

Berry, Leonard L., Valerie A. Zeithaml, and A. Parasuraman. "Five Imperatives for Improving Service Quality." *Sloan Management Review,* Summer 1990, pp. 29–38.

Carlzon, Jan. *Moments of Truth.* Cambridge, MA: Ballinger, 1987.

Chase, Richard B., and David A. Tansik. "The Customer Contact Model for Organization Design." *Management Science* 29, no. 9 (September 1983), pp. 1037–50.

Donnelly, Robert A. Jr. "Managing the Moment of Truth for a Service Organization." *Supervision* 65, no. 12 (December 2004), pp. 3–7.

Fitzsimmons, James A., and Mona J. Fitzsimmons. *Service Management: Operations, Strategy and Information Technology,* 3rd ed. Burr Ridge, IL: Irwin/McGraw-Hill, 2001.

Fox, Justin. "Hang-Ups in India." *Fortune (Europe)* 148, no. 13 (December 22, 2003), pp. 16–19.

Hart, Christopher W. L. "The Power of Unconditional Service Guarantees." *Harvard Business Review,* July–August 1988, pp. 54–62.

Henderson, Liza. "A Juicy Service Guarantee." *Telephony* 233, no. 4 (1997).

———. "The Power of Internal Guarantees." *Harvard Business Review,* January–February 1995.

Heskett, James L. *Managing in the Service Economy.* Boston: Harvard Business School Press, 1986.

Heskett, James L., Earl W. Sasser, and Leonard A. Schlesinger. *The Service Profit Chain: How Leading Companies Link Profit and Growth to Loyalty, Satisfaction, and Value.* New York: Free Press, 1997.

Heskett, James L., Thomas O. Jones, Gary W. Loveman, W. Earl Sasser, Jr., and Leonard Schlesinger. "Putting the Service-Profit Chain to Work." *Harvard Business Review,* March–April 1994.

Lee, John. "Service Guarantee." *Wireless Review* 18, no. 6 (March 15, 2001), pp. 94–96.

O'Brien, Jeanne. "U.S. Bancorp Builds Up B-to-B Service." *Bank Systems & Technology* 37, no. 2 (February 2000), p. 30.

Parasuraman, A., Leonard L. Berry, and Valerie A. Zeithaml. "Understanding Customer Expectations of Service." *Sloan Management Review,* Spring 1991, pp. 39–48.

Schlosser, Julie. "Teacher's Bet." *Fortune*, March 8, 2004, pp. 158–63.

Schmenner, R. "How Can Service Businesses Survive and Prosper?" Sloan Management Review. Spring 1986, p. 22.

Sergeant, Andrew, and Stephen Frenkel. "When Do Customer Contact Employees Satisfy Customers?" *Journal of Service Research* 3, no. 1 (August 2000), pp. 18–34.

Silvestro, Rhian, and Stuart Cross. "Applying the Service Profit Chain in a Retail Environment." *International Journal of Service Industry Management* 11, no. 3 (2000), pp. 244–68.

Swank, Cynthia Karen. "The Lean Service Machine." *Harvard Business Review* 81, no. 10 (October 2003), pp. 123–30.

Wirtz, Jochen, Doreen Kum, and Khai Sheang Lee. "Should a Firm with a Reputation for Outstanding Service Quality Offer a Service Guarantee?" *Journal of Services Marketing* 14, no. 6/7 (2000), pp. 502–12.

Zemke, R. *Service Wisdom: Creating and Maintaining the Customer Service Edge.* Minneapolis, MN: Lakewood, 1989.

Choice of Technology

Chapter outline

As they say, "Technology marches on." But does it? Isn't technology a matter of choice on the part of managers, and don't they have the will to pick and choose appropriate technologies? Technology choice is not merely a matter of implementing the latest innovation. Rather, managers have the ability and responsibility to choose technology that not only is efficient but protects the environment and meets the needs of society.

We must become managers of technology, as Peter Drucker argues, not only users of technology. For example, the United States has halted the construction of new nuclear power plants because of the potentially dangerous environmental impact. A business, too, must choose the technology it uses and not merely be driven by market and competitive forces. Also, government has a role in ensuring that technologies used by business ultimately meet the needs of society at large.

There are two **definitions of technology.** A very broad definition is that technology is the application of knowledge to solve human problems. A narrower definition, and the one used in the remainder of this chapter, is that technology is a set of processes, tools, methods, and equipment used to produce goods and services. This is clearly a definition of process technology rather than product technology.

In the last two chapters, we have discussed process selection. Within the context of the process selected it is still possible to choose a level of technology. For example, a line process need not be highly automated; it could be labor intensive. Likewise, a job shop could be highly automated with general-purpose equipment. So, technology choice is mostly independent of process selection.

Technology choice is an extremely important decision and one of interest to managers in all functions. These decisions are not only technical in nature; they affect capital, human resources, and information systems. Thus, all managers are interested in the choice of technology and how it affects the business as a whole.

It is important to understand the technologies available before discussing the choice of technology. The first part of the chapter discusses newly emerging technologies in manufacturing, automated offices, and services. The chapter ends with a discussion of the factors that managers should consider when choosing technology.

6.1 COMPUTER-INTEGRATED MANUFACTURING

Most business students are not going to work in factories. But, it is nevertheless important to understand factory technology and its capabilities. Investment in factory technology is a concern for finance and accounting students. Marketing students need to know how the products are made that are being marketed. Human resource students need to know how technology affects jobs and people. The focus here is on the capabilities of technology and not its details.

Stop to think of the **factory of the future.** What can you expect to see? One popular conception is that the factory of the future will be populated by robots, not people. However, the essence of the factory of the future is not fewer people but a factory centered on computer integration. The factory of the future will use computers for new-product introduction, process design, forecasting, and production and inventory control. The key concept is integration of all manufacturing and business functions through a **common database.** It is the integration of decision making and data that is at the heart of **computer-integrated manufacturing** (CIM).

IBM has a CIM factory that produces laptop computers. Actually, any electronic product can be made in this factory provided it fits into a 2-foot by 2-foot by 14-inch cube. Considerable flexibility is provided in this CIM factory by robots, product/process design, and computerized routing and scheduling of the product. But CIM factories are still more the exception than the rule. While many factories make extensive use of computers, they are not fully integrated.

CIM has the following elements, all integrated through a common database: computer-aided design, computer-aided manufacturing, robotics, and a manufacturing planning and control system (see Figure 6.1). When the CIM system is extended to include accounting, order entry, and sales information, it becomes an **enterprise resource planning system** (ERP), which encompasses the entire business and is discussed later in this chapter.

Computer-Aided Design

Computer-aided design (CAD) is a term used to describe computer support of the engineering design function. In the mid-1960s, General Motors and IBM set out to put engineering drawings (blueprints) into computer storage so that they could be easily updated and changed. The input of the initial drawings is done through a computer terminal or by use of a special drawing table that permits the engineer to draw the product design on a computer screen. The geometry of the part being designed is stored in the computer database. If desired, a drawing can be printed out or the electronic design information can be accessed directly by manufacturing. Some CAD facilities today, however, still do not have this link through the database directly to manufacturing. Rather, they are stand-alone facilities used for automated drafting. Even so, CAD has greatly simplified engineering changes and allowed designers to update products rapidly.

FIGURE 6.1
Computer-
integrated
manufacturing.

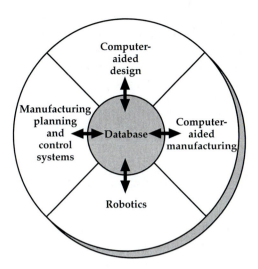

But CAD goes further than mere automated drafting. Three additional features are needed for a full CAD system: design calculations, parts classification, and a link to manufacturing. Once the part geometry is stored in the computer, **engineering design calculations** can be made, including stress analysis, strength of materials, thermal calculations, and so on. As a result, engineering is simplified, and design problems can be uncovered without building expensive prototypes for testing.

Parts classification is used to code and classify existing parts so that they can be easily identified by shape and function. When designing a new part, the designer may find a similar part already in production or one that can be easily modified to perform the new function. Analysis has shown that in many companies only 20 percent of the parts initially thought to require new designs actually need them; of the remaining parts 40 percent could be built from an existing design and the other 40 percent could be created by modifying an existing design.

The final element of CAD is a **link to manufacturing.** The choice of manufacturing process should be closely integrated with product design choices. This requires choosing the proper type of machines and designing the tooling used to facilitate production of the product. These design steps are simplified if the product geometry and specifications are already in the computer database. The efficiency of different machine processes can be simulated, and tools can be matched to the product shape. As a matter of fact, it is advisable that various manufacturing steps be simulated before the design is completed as a coordinated effort between the engineering design department and manufacturing. In a CIM factory, this will be done by use of a common database linking design and manufacturing.

CAD is already being heavily used in several industries, including aircraft, autos, shipbuilding, construction, and electronics. The application of CAD frequently reduces labor in design and manufacturing, and it has brought striking benefits to manufacturers. For example, at General Motors, the redesign of a single automobile model was reduced from 24 months to 14 months. Another company reduced the time needed to design custom valves from 6 months to 1 month. Many companies have installed CAD to get these benefits and to remain competitive. One example is described in the Ford Motor Company Operations Leader box.

Computer-Aided Manufacturing

Computer-aided manufacturing (CAM) may well provide batch manufacturing companies with the efficiencies long enjoyed in the process and line-flow industries. Line production implies manufacturing at high volume in a predetermined sequence with resulting low costs. Batch production, on the other hand, implies small volumes, high product variety, and a jumbled flow of materials. Through use of CAM it is now possible to streamline batch manufacturing, which constitutes about 35 percent of all U.S. manufacturing.

CAM utilizes the computer to design production processes, to control machine tools, and to control the flow of materials in batch manufacturing. By use of the computer it is possible to change over machines rapidly when producing small lot sizes. It is also possible to operate machines automatically following a prescribed set of instructions and to move materials from one machine to the next under computer control. To do so, however, it is necessary to organize the products to be produced by similar families or groups using an approach called **group technology** (GT). The process of classifying parts by families and subsequently dedicating production equipment to a specific family or families of parts is called group technology, or cellular manufacturing.

The typical batch (process) layout is shown in Figure 6.2*a*. In this layout, also described in Chapter 4, machines are grouped by similar type, and the product follows a jumbled flow pattern as it moves through the factory. In Figure 6.2*b*, this facility has been reorganized by group technology cells. In this case, all machines needed to produce a given part family are grouped together, and a line flow is achieved.

When a similar parts family is produced in a cell, some machines may be duplicated from one cell to the next and capacity utilization may be reduced over the jumbled flow alternative. Nevertheless, the overall benefits of GT are significant, provided that a large enough number of parts can be included in each cell.

The principal benefits of GT or **cellular manufacturing** are to speed up the manufacturing process and to reduce in-process inventories. This is done by moving parts more quickly through the manufacturing process. In a typical batch

FIGURE 6.2 Batch layout versus group technology layout.

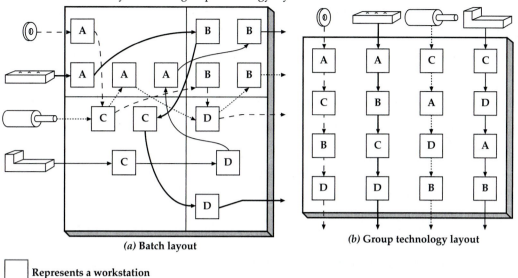

(a) **Batch layout**   *(b)* **Group technology layout**

☐ **Represents a workstation**

facility, parts may spend as much as 95 percent of the time waiting in line for machines to become available. Given a GT layout, it is possible to speed up the flow of materials between machines.

Once the products have been grouped into product families by GT, it is possible to lay out the physical configuration of the manufacturing cells. From practice, the concept of the U-shaped cell has been developed as shown in Figure 6.3. Here

FIGURE 6.3
U-shaped cell
layout.

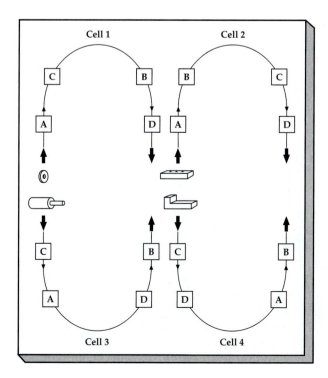

the products from Figure 6.2 have been configured into four U-shaped cells. This U-shaped configuration allows visual control of the work. For teamwork and scheduling purposes it is important to have visual control during manufacturing.

Strategos, a consulting company, provides the following example of cellular manufacturing used for an assembly line.

> A firm that assembles air-handling products faced high inventories and erratic delivery. They originally assembled units on a traditional line. Long setups and logistics required long production runs. Often, they pulled products from finished goods and rebuilt them for custom orders. We built twelve small (1–3 person) assembly workcells that were always set up and ready. People worked in different cells each day and assembled to customer order. Finished goods inventory dropped by 96%. Lead-time was 24 hours. Productivity improved by 20–30%.

CAM also utilizes **computer-aided process planning** (CAPP) as one component of the CAM system. With CAPP each process in manufacturing is planned with assistance from the computer. After the parts design is downloaded from the CAD system, CAPP is then used to decide on routings, equipment, and tools for producing the part.

Computer-aided manufacturing thus involves designing the manufacturing process and tooling through the database. This can be accomplished by organizing batch manufacturing, and even some assembly lines, by cellular manufacturing. This speeds up the flow of the product and increases machine utilization in manufacturing environments.

Robotics

Robots have captured the minds of the public, science fiction writers, moviemakers, and the press. An industrial robot, however, is nothing more than a computer-controlled machine programmed to perform various production tasks. The distinctive part of the robot is its "hand," or gripper, and the arm, which can make humanlike movements. The first applications of robots involved hot, dirty, or heavy work for which humans were not well suited. Use of robots has subsequently been expanded into a variety of production jobs, including welding, painting, fixed assembly work, and materials handling.

Robots are still limited in their ability to perform many production jobs. The most serious limitation is the ability to pick up a randomly positioned part. To do so, a robot would need to "see" and to position its hand accordingly. Most current applications are limited to parts that have a fixed and known location, but the technology is rapidly developing to provide more visual ability.

ROBOTS. Automobile frame assembly makes use of robots for welding.
© Royalty-Free/CORBIS

A related form of automation is the **numerically controlled** (NC) machine tool. While NC tools are not normally thought of as robots, they are controlled by a computer and can be programmed for a variety of different tasks. The NC machine, however, does not have the distinctive robotic arm or hand and is not, perhaps, as flexible as a robot. Nevertheless, the factory of the future is likely to consist of a mixture of NC machines, conventional machines, and robots.[1]

While robots can sometimes be justified by reduction of direct labor, they provide many more benefits, including flexibility to redesign parts, 24-hour operation, performance of hazardous tasks, and more uniform quality. The traditional return-on-investment justification tends to ignore these benefits and emphasizes only cost reduction. As a result, the use of robots in the United States is not as extensive as some have predicted.

It seldom pays to introduce one robot into a production process because of the maintenance and software support needed. These costs should be spread over several robots. Also, a single robot operating 24 hours a day will simply pile up inventory waiting for other machines. A coordinated flow of material is needed to achieve true economies. This requires a long-range plan of automation and not simply replacement of humans by robots in an incremental fashion.

Some have noted that robots should not be substituted for people on a one-for-one basis in existing processes. Actually, the production process, and possibly the product, should be redesigned to take maximum advantage of robots and other automation. After this redesign, certain steps may be eliminated or combined, thereby eliminating the need for a robot at that step. Processes should always be simplified before being automated. This can hardly be overemphasized. Robots are not mechanical people; they are part of an integrated production process.

Implementation of CIM

If a strategy for computer-integrated manufacturing is adopted, many steps must be taken to transform the factory. It is likely that **islands of automation** will be built up as certain machines are computerized and parts of the information system are put on the computer. If the ultimate goal is CIM, all the computerization should be linked through a common database so that separate islands of automation can eventually be tied together. As this occurs, the benefits of CIM will become more apparent.[2]

Since CIM is not just another type of automation effort where one machine type is replaced by another, this level of automation is more difficult to achieve and more expensive than past efforts. But CIM promises benefits beyond mere cost reduction. Those companies that can effectively implement CIM can reap the benefits of a competitive advantage through better delivery, better quality, or more flexibility. This is the promise and the hope of CIM implementation.

Generally speaking, the greater the integration achieved in CIM implementation, the greater the benefits. But integration is difficult to achieve because of the high degree of cross-functional participation required. Nevertheless, it is important to recognize this problem and to address it directly when planning for CIM implementation through such mechanisms as **cross-functional implementation teams** and high-level management direction.

---

[1] NC machines are also called CNC (computer numerically controlled) machines. DNC (direct numerical control) refers to several NC or CNC machines controlled through a network.

[2] See *Manufacturing Engineering* (1997) for an example of linking islands of automation at Toyo Tanso, U.S.A.

The CIM factory, particularly in batch manufacturing, should be justified on the basis of **economies of scope** rather than economies of scale. Economies of scope are defined as the ability to efficiently produce a wide variety of products rather than a large volume of standardized products. CIM technology reduces changeover costs and product modification costs. As a result, small batches of similar products can be economically produced. It is not necessary to standardize the product and to develop associated mass markets using an economies-of-scale rationale. Thus, companies can compete on the basis of economies of scope by offering more customized products, faster delivery, and smaller lots. This opens up a whole new realm of competition through what is essentially mass customization, agile manufacturing, and cellular manufacturing.

CIM presents an opportunity for manufacturing companies to compete in new ways. But CIM systems can fail to provide the promised benefits when the organization is not ready, training is insufficient, or top management leadership is lacking. The biggest problems in CIM implementation have not been the hardware; rather, they involve the organization and the software. These problems, however, can be overcome by sensible implementation.

CIM should be implemented in stages under the guidance of a master plan. The master plan is needed to identify the future software modules planned, the interfaces between modules, and the common database elements. Then one module (e.g., CAD or CAM) at a time can be implemented. Once a particular module is up and running, more modules are added and driven off the common database. The database serves to integrate the various CIM modules.

Is CIM for everyone? Probably not. Effective use of CIM depends on doing a thorough analysis of the costs and benefits. The benefits will include more flexibility in changing both products and volumes. The cycle time will be reduced both for new-product introduction and production throughput time of existing products. Costs may or may not be higher, depending on inventory reduction achieved and labor saved in relation to the cost of the CIM system. In most cases, revenue should be higher as a result of quicker response or more flexible response to customer needs. After a careful analysis of the benefits and costs of CIM, it should be possible to determine its effect on discounted cash flow and the bottom line.

6.2 AUTOMATED OFFICES AND SERVICES

As indicated in the last section, factory technologies are rapidly changing. However, office and service technologies are changing just as fast.

Office Technology

Until the 1980s, office technology had not advanced much since the invention of the typewriter. To be sure, offices used electric typewriters, electronic copiers, and Dictaphones; but most office work was still labor-intensive and largely fragmented. With the development of the personal computer and interconnected networks, an office revolution was under way.

In offices, the transformation process consists of the following activities:

1. Handling messages.
2. Typing or keyboarding files.
3. Copying printed or electronic materials.
4. Filing.
5. Keeping a calendar.

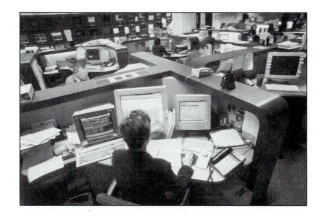

INTEGRATED WORKSTATIONS. Information flow in this office is entirely automated.
© Amy Etra/PhotoEdit

How have these activities been changed by the automated office?

The **automated office** has a computer terminal or PC for each secretary and each manager, connecting them together in a network fashion. The office is also connected to the outside world through e-mail, the Internet, or other electronic networks. By using e-mail, communication is faster and more efficient.

In the fully automated office, all the activities identified above are performed through electronic media. Paperwork can be drastically reduced or eliminated; however, it may actually increase if everything is printed out. The expansion of paperwork happens when the office is only partially automated and not fully integrated. Repetitive tasks are simplified by electronic filing, online correction of errors, and the use of standard responses. This drastically reduces the cost of office functions and increases productivity when fully implemented.

The automated office can also have other impacts on society. For example, offices can be dispersed to outlying sites or even to homes. There is no need to have all office functions centralized in skyscrapers with the associated high transportation and energy costs.

For certain types of businesses, such as life insurance companies, the automated office provides a reprieve from an avalanche of paperwork. In this type of office, each person performs his or her task on a computer terminal and then passes the work electronically on to the next workstation. With automated offices, managers can easily track the flow of transaction processing to manage and improve the process-flow characteristics. Such an application is very similar to the concept of control of work flow used in factories. The Operations Leader box describes how IBM is trying to implement this idea in the insurance industry.

The largest impact of the automated office will be on professional and managerial jobs, the so-called **knowledge workers,** and not on secretarial jobs. Today, about 80 percent of office compensation is paid to knowledge workers and only 20 percent to clerical workers. Therefore, improved productivity will need to focus on the knowledge workers. Fortunately, automated office systems can save a great deal of knowledge-worker time and improve the effectiveness of managers and professionals. However, proposed office automation projects must be directed toward knowledge workers and not merely toward clerical cost reduction.

The key concept in office automation is the same as it is in the factory, namely, integration of the functions. Previously separate departments and functions are linked together by means of the computer. As islands of automation become linked, the benefits of the integrated office become apparent: not only a reduction

in costs, but faster throughput, better coordination, greater utilization of knowledge, and lower error rates. Office automation affects all functions in the firm, not just operations.

Service Industries

Technology has had a profound effect on services of various types. Table 6.1 shows how technology has impacted services ranging from medical care to education to telecommunications. But how much should service be automated? Should all services be automated, or does automation change the very nature of service itself?

In a classic article, Levitt (1972) describes what he calls the **production-line approach to service.** With this approach, services are standardized and delivered in an efficient and cheerful manner. The service facility itself is designed so that mistakes are minimized. Various stages of service delivery are automated so that costs are reduced and standardization is achieved.

Levitt uses the McDonald's chain to demonstrate these concepts. He points to the special widemouth scoop that has been developed to fill French fry bags to the correct levels more efficiently. All the food inputs at McDonald's are carefully

TABLE 6.1
Impact of
Technology on
Service Operations

Service	Technology
Medicine	Intensive care units, MRI scanners, medical records, automated diagnostic testing, pacemakers
Telecommunications	Cellular phones, TV, video conferencing, satellite communications, e-mail, Internet
Retail	Point-of-sale scanners, bar-code readers, inventory control computers
Education	Computerized libraries, Internet, interactive learning
Legal	Computerized searches, databases for evidence, word processing
Hotels	TV checkout, keycard security, reservations systems, heating/ventilation controls, guest computers, Internet access
Airlines	Air traffic control system, electronic cockpits, reservation systems

FIGURE 6.4
Production-line approach to service.

specified to ensure consistency. Procedures for cleaning the restaurants are prescribed. All this is done to standardize the service and to deliver it in a controlled and efficient manner (see Figure 6.4).

Levitt indicates that service people tend to think their problems are different from those of manufacturing. Service is often thought of as something that is delivered "out there in the field" under highly variable conditions, whereas manufacturing is done in a factory under highly controlled and automated conditions. He argues that until the delivery of services is thought of as a transformation process similar to that of manufacturing, little improvement in efficiency or quality will be possible.

In contrast, manufacturing problems are often seen in technocratic terms. If there is poor quality or high cost, an analysis is made of the tasks performed, the work flow, and the equipment used. A solution is sought in the technology of the process.

But automating services is not the solution to all service problems. As we have seen in the last chapter, there are four types of services in the service matrix. Automation simply moves a service into the "service factory" or "service shop" category. While the resulting service may be more efficient, automation can change the very nature of the service itself toward a more standardized service. The market will ultimately determine how much automation customers want, how standardized service should be, and what service will cost. At the present time, all four types of service seem to have market appeal.

Schlesinger and Heskett (1991) argue that in designing technological solutions for services, managers should view employees, not equipment, as the center of the service delivery system. They suggest that a new model of industrialization is emerging in which service companies:

- Use technology to support the employees on the front line, not to just monitor or replace them.
- Make recruitment and training just as important for service workers as for managers and staff employees.
- Value investments in employees as much as investments in machines, sometimes more.
- Link compensation to performance for employees at every level, not just for those at the top.

This approach offers an alternative to the production-line approach to service by emphasizing both technology and people in the service delivery system. It promises to break the cycle of poor service by training, motivating, and rewarding the people who deliver the service within the context of a well-designed system.

6.3 ENTERPRISE RESOURCE PLANNING SYSTEMS

So far, we have been discussing the use of computer-integrated technology in manufacturing, offices, and service operations. While integrated technology is the base for operations, it can also be extended into all other business functions through the use of an enterprise resource planning (ERP) system. For example, when operations transactions are computerized they can be fed directly to the accounting and finance system. Accounting transactions can be seen as putting operations transactions into dollars-and-cents terms. Accounting control in dollars is closely related to control of the physical units and the physical flow of operations in number of units produced.

Likewise, the integrated information system in operations can be extended into marketing. Marketing and sales transactions should be closely integrated as inputs to the operations system through order entry. Not only is the number of units sold the input, but units forecast for future sales are input to form the basis for operations planning. Often, marketing and sales systems are developed and designed as separate systems that are not fully integrated with operations. As a result, the functions of marketing and operations are isolated from an information systems point of view.

Finally, operations transactions from a CIM system in manufacturing or a service delivery system should be integrated with the human resource systems in the company. This takes place not only through payroll transactions but through recruiting and selection functions as well. For example, when operations make a decision to expand capacity by hiring more people, this decision should be fed directly to the HR system and the hiring process tracked through to completion. The payroll system should pick up the new people hired by operations, and these employees should be followed through their lifetime of employment.

When operations, finance/accounting, marketing/sales, and HR systems are integrated through a common database, the ERP system is completed. The ERP system will track transactions from their origin at the customer, to order entry, through operations and accounting until the transaction is completed. Also, all decisions made in one function will be apparent to other functions and reflected in their information systems. No longer will the various functional information systems be isolated; rather, they will be integrated through the common company database.

For example, the type of ERP system we have been discussing has been developed by SAP, a German company. SAP has an ERP system that has been adopted by 15,000 firms in 120 different countries.[3] One advantage of the SAP system is that it can be tailored to different companies and industries. Standard processes, including order entry, payroll, inventory management, accounts payable, and accounts receivable, have been designed into the SAP system. A company can select those processes that fit its needs and customize them to its particular business (see Table 6.2).

Changan Automobile makes faster management decisions with ERP. Changan is one of China's major automobile manufacturers with a market share of 30 percent and over one million vehicles produced annually. The company implemented the Oracle ERP system using the following modules: financials, manufacturing, order management, general ledger, payables, and assets. The Oracle database was

---

[3] See the SAP Internet site at www.sap.com for more details.

TABLE 6.2
ERP: Cross-
Functional
Integration through
Data Sharing

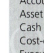

An ERP system integrates data across functions in the firm. This list shows some of the many functions supported by SAP's R/3 package.	
Financial Systems	**Operations and Logistics**
Accounts receivable and payable	Inventory management
Asset accounting	Material requirements planning
Cash management and forecasting	Materials management
Cost-element and cost-centered accounting	Plant management
Executive information system	Production planning
Financial consolidation	Project management
General ledger	Purchasing
Product-cost accounting	Quality management
Profitability analysis	Routing management
Profit-center accounting	Shipping
Standard and period-related costing	Vendor evaluation
Human Resources	**Sales and Marketing**
Human-resources accounting	Order management
Payroll	Pricing
Personnel planning	Sales management
Travel expenses	Sales planning

the key to integration of these modules and to the use of common data. Before implementing ERP many of the diverse functions had developed information islands and data within isolated applications.

ERP systems are becoming very popular in business and are the basis for cross-functional integration. When all functions share information through the common database of the company, the functional silos are minimized and functions can effectively communicate with each other. While integration is a worthwhile and interesting concept, ERP systems are expensive and time-consuming to implement. Nevertheless, many companies have determined that their existing information systems, which have grown up separately, can no longer meet the needs of the business and must be integrated through an ERP approach.

6.4   THE INTERNET AND E-BUSINESS[4]

The Internet is rapidly spreading in connecting businesses to each other and to the end consumer. These interconnections are providing integration between companies, just like ERP has integrated functions within a company. Generally speaking, a company must have attained internal integration via ERP or other systems before attempting external integration since internal integration facilitates information exchange with other companies and end customers.

While the trials and tribulations of the start-up dot-com companies are well known, e-business as a larger concept is thriving and growing. For example, **BtoB** (business-to-business) connections have been growing at a rapid rate as businesses are seeking Internet connections with each other. These connections take the form of electronic purchasing, order entry, Internet auctions, and the like. In the **BtoC** (business-to-consumer) arena, the so-called "bricks and mortar" companies are establishing Web sites and offering merchandise and services over the Internet at increasing rates.

[4] Information for the specific examples and illustrations in this section comes from company Web sites.

TABLE 6.3
Types of E-Business Companies

	E-Marketplace Companies	E-Service	E-Retailers and Wholesalers	E-Producers
Purpose	Manage complex marketplace exchanges	Provide service via the Internet	Sales of products by linking customers and producers	Procure, manufacture, and sell by the Internet
Activities	Dynamic pricing, information, and transactions	Value added services and information	Selling, distributing, and delivery of goods	Manage partnerships online
Operations Role	Maintain and improve the databases and Web sites	Fast, convenient, and efficient service	Back-end fulfillment and front-end service	Online purchasing, ordering, and information sharing
Operations Performance	Accuracy and access to information at low cost	Customer satisfaction, fast service, and low costs	Inventory turnover, stockouts, and accuracy of shipments	Fast, efficient transactions and decisions
Examples	eBay.com priceline.com newview.com covisint.com	ING.com e-trade.com Visa.com FedEx.com UPS.com	Amazon.com Barnesandnoble.com Target.com	Dell.com Cisco.com Ford.com

For purposes of discussion, we have classified **e-business** into the following four categories:

- E-marketplace companies
- E-service providers
- E-retailers and wholesalers
- E-producers

Companies in each of these categories play a unique role and require a specific type of operations support as explained in Table 6.3.

Examples of **e-marketplace** companies are eBay, priceline.com, newview.com, and covisint.com. These companies provide a complex exchange that matches buyers and sellers. Dynamic pricing is used as goods and services are either offered or requested for sale. Buyers and sellers can access these sites to conduct market transactions electronically. Founded in 1995, eBay is today the world's largest online marketplace. In 2005, eBay had 100 million registered users and was the most popular trading site on the Internet. The company's mission is "to provide a global trading platform where practically anyone can trade practically anything on earth."

The operations role in the e-marketplace companies is to maintain and improve the database and the Web sites used. This is an information-intensive role that cannot be separated from marketing, information systems, and other functions. The primary operations measures of performance for this type of business are accuracy of information, speed of access to information, satisfaction with support services, and low-cost operations. These measures can be equated to the customary quality, cost, flexibility, and delivery dimensions of operations performance.

In Table 6.3 the e-service providers have the primary purpose of providing fast and convenient service over the Internet. Examples of leaders in this category are ING (financial services), Visa, Federal Express, UPS, SAP, Blue Cross–Blue Shield, and many others. Most of the e-service providers are traditional companies that are now providing service over the Internet, but there are also examples of new service providers such as Expedia.com (travel) and e-trade (financial). A leader in providing e-service is ING, a traditional financial services company that is investing heavily in Web enhancement of its 150 different businesses.

The role of operations in **e-service** is to provide fast, efficient, and convenient service over the Internet through a combination of technology and human service providers. Technology alone cannot provide all of the service required, but it can augment or replace some of the traditional human service providers. For example, at Travelocity.com you can make a travel reservation on the Internet, but when you run into trouble or have questions, you can also talk with a person for help.

The third type of e-business is the familiar **e-retailer** or **e-wholesaler.** Examples in this category are Amazon.com, Barnesandnoble.com, Target.com, and Baxter International (a medical supply wholesaler). Amazon.com is the world's leading shopping site, with millions of customers in more than 200 countries. While their customer base and product offerings have grown considerably since opening in 1995, they maintain their founding commitment to the delivery of a convenient, inspiring, and educational shopping experience. By way of contrast, Baxter International is a traditional worldwide distributor of health-care products. It has saved over $30 million a year through strategic sourcing via the Internet while improving customer service. The Internet is a tremendous productivity improvement engine for Baxter.

In e-retail and e-wholesale, company operations serve the more traditional role of "back-end fulfillment" of orders while also providing services on the front end. Fulfillment is concerned with order entry, inventory control, and distribution of products. It can become a bottleneck, since orders may need to be consolidated for efficient shipping and warehouse location. Fulfillment operations for these businesses can be measured by traditional measures such as inventory turnover, stockouts, and accuracy of order shipment.

The fourth category of e-business is the **e-producers** that engage in procurement, manufacturing, distribution, and sales of products via the Internet. A few examples are Dell, Cisco, and Ford Motor Company. Cisco is a leader in this category by taking 90 percent of its orders online and resolving over 80 percent of its service calls over the Internet. According to Operations Leader Cisco, it has realized over $2.1 billion in annual financial benefits from this strategy, and customer satisfaction has improved. Many traditional producers are turning to the Internet to accomplish electronic purchasing, order entry, and after sales services.

The operations role in e-producers is to utilize electronic methods for transaction processing and decision making. For example, purchasing transactions can be handled online and supply decisions improved by immediate access to information. For e-producers, tremendous efficiency can be gained by electronically connecting customers and suppliers. They can share not only purchasing information and orders online but also planned orders and forecasts to help improve overall supply chain performance.

OPERATIONS LEADER
The Cisco Story

CISCO SYSTEMS

Cisco Systems, Inc., is the worldwide leader in networking for the Internet. Cisco's Internet Protocol–based (IP) networking solutions are the foundation of the Internet and most corporate, education, and government networks around the world. . . . Cisco employs 34,000 people worldwide.

Cisco has set the standard for business transformation by using Internet technology to integrate its core processes and culture. The results have been phenomenal:

- 90 percent of orders taken online.
- Monthly online sales exceed $1 billion.
- 82 percent of support calls now resolved over the Internet.
- Customer satisfaction has increased significantly.

Cisco's CEO John Chambers says, "Cisco's success and our increased productivity gains are due largely to the implementation of Internet applications to run our business. The ability to harness the power of the Internet to create a New World business model is driving survival and competition in today's fast-paced economy."

Source: Cisco Web site 2002 and 2005: www.cisco.com.

As can be seen, many different types of companies fall under the e-business umbrella, and the operations role varies by the type of company. In the future we expect these companies and their operations to continue to expand. Use of technology to connect companies, suppliers, and customers in this way can improve operations and business performance.

6.5 TECHNOLOGY CHOICE

Choice of technology should be based on a sound technology strategy. A technology strategy is aimed at obtaining the right amount and type of technological investment. A technology strategy begins with a business strategy and operations strategy that describe the vision and mission of the firm. For example, if the mission is to be a low-cost producer, the technology strategy should be aimed at developing technologies that enable low cost, and new technologies should be evaluated on their ability to lower costs. On the other hand, if the mission is to produce differentiated products, the technology strategy, the technologies developed, and the evaluation criteria should be oriented toward product differentiation.

A technology strategy sets an overall framework for development of new technology to support the mission. It ensures that technologies are not merely developed and justified one at a time, or for the wrong reasons, but implemented as part of a coherent strategy over time. As a result, the technology is integrated and provides a competitive advantage not easily imitated. Many firms justify their technology one proposal at a time and do not have a comprehensive technology development strategy.

A second aspect of evaluation of technology is the financial return on investment. Various methods are available such as net present value and internal rate of return to determine whether the investment provides an acceptable return on the investment. Very careful analysis is needed to ensure that the firm remains competitive and is not depleted of capital. Aversion to capital investment is a problem

FIGURE 6.5
Sociotechnical systems design.

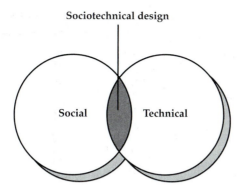

in some industries where management seems more aware of the dangers of too much investment rather than too little. Acceptable financial returns can be seen as a constraint on technology strategies. The technology strategy must provide at least the minimum acceptable return on investment.

In addition to considering the technology strategy and return on investment, technology choice should consider the effect on human resources. For example, job choice need not be determined by the technology. The concept of a **sociotechnical system** posits that both jobs and technology should be simultaneously chosen, as shown in Figure 6.5, to achieve joint optimization. In the past, it was often assumed that jobs were merely a fallout from the choice of technology, so-called **technological determinism.** In other words, the choice of technology determined the jobs and the social system. Now we understand that technology choice must consider not only technology but social and human consequences as well.

An example of this problem occurred in a small manufacturing company that installed an ERP system and encountered unforeseen problems.[5] It installed bar code readers and workstations on the shop floor so parts could be easily tracked during production. After 18 months the system was still not being used. A new IS manager was brought in and found that workers were not technically proficient in computers. They also found significant resistance from other employees. This example indicates a lack of attention to social factors when implementing a new system or technology.

[5] Ryan and Harrison (2000).

Technology investments should support a comprehensive technology strategy, meet financial objectives, and provide a sociotechnical system. Managers in all functions should work to develop a technology choice that considers operations, financial, human resources, marketing, and information systems perspectives. Choosing technology on a cross-functional basis will ensure that all these factors are properly considered.

6.6 KEY POINTS

This chapter has considered the issue of technology choice on a cross-functional basis. The key points are as follows:

- Technology is defined as a set of processes, tools, methods, and equipment used to produce goods or services. The definition is broader than merely equipment selection; it includes the choice of processes, methods, and tools.

- Computer-integrated manufacturing is achieved through a common database that supports applications in computer-aided design, computer-aided manufacturing, robotics, and manufacturing planning and control systems. The key is integration of these systems within manufacturing and with the accounting, financial, and marketing systems as well.

- Office automation is achieved through computerization and integration of information processing and communications between offices. The focus should be on improving the work of knowledge workers and not merely automation of clerical work.

- The automation of services also offers great potential. As services are viewed in technical rather than humanistic terms, automation and standardization become possible. This can result not only in lower costs but also in more uniform quality and faster service. Nevertheless, service should be automated only if it meets a true customer need.

- Enterprise resource planning systems integrate not only operations information but information from marketing, finance/accounting, and human resources through a common database. ERP systems can form the basis for cross-functional integration through shared information.

- E-business is rapidly changing the economy by connecting suppliers, companies, and customers via the Internet. There are four types of e-businesses: e-marketplace companies, e-service providers, e-retailers and wholesalers, and e-producers. Each of these types of companies has different business activities and different roles for operations.

- Technology choice should be based on a technology strategy that seeks to help obtain a competitive advantage through minimizing cost or product differentiation. The required return on investment sets a minimum acceptable level that the technology strategy should meet or exceed.

- The choice of technology automatically determines the jobs and thus has a social and human impact. As a result, a sociotechnical approach should be used to jointly choose the jobs and technology at the same time. Then technology will be selected that not only is efficient but considers the impact on human resources as well.

- The choice of technology should consider the effects on customers, employees, finance, and the environment. A cross-functional strategy is needed to ensure that technological choices are integrated over time and help the firm achieve a competitive advantage.

STUDENT INTERNET EXERCISES

<WWW>

1. SAP
http://www.sap.com

Write a short essay on the SAP approach to enterprise resource planning. Describe how their ERP systems are used by customers.

2. IBM
http://www.ibm.com

Come to class prepared to discuss the CAD/CAM product available from IBM called CATIA (computer-aided three-dimensional interactive application). Search the IBM Web site for information on CATIA.

3. Cisco Systems
http://www.cisco.com

Go to this Web site and find information about the history, strategy, and technology of the company. Come prepared to discuss the development of technology by Cisco.

Discussion Questions

1. How is the problem of technology choice related to process selection and product design?

2. How much detailed technical knowledge on the part of managers is required to make a decision regarding the selection of computer hardware?

3. Suppose you need to select a personal computer to use in your office. What performance characteristics of the technology would you assess? How would you get the necessary information to make the selection?

4. What are the pertinent sociotechnical considerations for selection of a personal computer workstation for the office?

5. Suppose your boss has asked you to evaluate the possibilities of further office automation through linkage to the Internet. How would you approach this problem? What information would you gather?

6. What is meant by a manufacturing or technocratic approach to the delivery of services?

7. Is the success of McDonald's chain attributable to a marketing concept or an operations concept? Discuss.

8. What is the main obstacle to using a manufacturing approach to the delivery of services?

9. It has been proposed that robots replace several people who do painting on an automobile assembly line. Explain why robots should not replace people on a one-for-one basis.

10. What are the common pitfalls encountered when justifying a CIM project or an ERP project?

11. What are the major benefits one can expect from implementing CIM and ERP? How can these benefits be incorporated into financial calculations?

12. Explain what is meant by the terms CAD, CAM, CAPP, CIM, GT, and ERP.

13. Under what circumstances can the use of a group technology cell be expected to be economically justified over traditional batch manufacturing?

14. Explain the differences between economies of scale and economies of scope.

15. Use the Internet or find some newspaper or magazine articles that deal with technology choice issues or examples of automated factories, offices, or services. Summarize the key points in each article.

16. What is the difference between a BtoB business and a BtoC business?

17. Take a supply chain view of operations and discuss the impact of e-business on the relationships among suppliers, companies, and their customers.

18. Suppose you work for a bank, and a major customer has come to you and said that all suppliers, including you, are going to be integrated with the customer by the Internet. What possible impact might this have on your bank and its operations?

19. How would the answer to question 18 change if you were a manufacturer of parts and components instead of a bank?

Selected Bibliography

Ahmad, Sohel, and Roger Schroeder. "The Impact of Electronic Data Interchange on Delivery Performance." *Production and Operations Management* 10, no. 1 (2001), pp. 16–30.

Akturk, Selim M., and Serkan Ozkan. "Integrated Scheduling and Tool Management in Flexible Manufacturing Systems." *International Journal of Production Research* 39, no. 12 (2001).

Blodgett, Mindy. "Hotels Seek to Answer Needs of Business Traveler." *Computerworld* 31, no. 18 (May 5, 1997), pp. 67–68.

Boström, Gert-Olof, Peter Zackariasson, and Timothy Wilson. "CAD and Consequences in the Swedish Architectural Industry." *Services Marketing Quarterly* 25, no. 2 (2003), pp. 25–42.

Bruno, Giorgio, and Rakesh Agarwal. "Modeling the Enterprise Engineering Environment." *IEEE Transactions on Engineering Management* 44, no. 1 (February 1997), pp. 20–30.

Burger, Katherine. "IBM Is Force for Change in Insurance." *Insurance and Technology* 22, no. 7 (July 1997), p. 6.

Byrne, John A., and Ben Elgin. "CISCO behind the Hype." *BusinessWeek,* January 21, 2002, pp. 54–61.

Chang, Hsin Hsin. "The Implementation and Integration of Information Systems for Production Management in Manufacturing: An Empirical Study." *International Journal of Computer Integrated Manufacturing* 13, no. 5 (September 2000), pp. 369–87.

Christen, Alan. "CAD/CAM, eBusiness and the Internet." *Modern Machine Shop* 72, no. 11 (April 2000), pp. 184–85.

Co, Henry C. "Managing Flexible Manufacturing Technology: Must Parts in an FMS Always Move in a Job-Shop Manner?" *International Journal of Production Research* 39, no. 13 (2001).

Davenport, Thomas H. "Putting the Enterprise into the Enterprise System." *Harvard Business Review,* July–August 1998.

Goldhar, J. D., and Mariann Jelinek. "Plan for Economies of Scope." *Harvard Business Review,* November–December 1983, pp. 141–48.

Gunasekaran, A. "Next Generation Computer-Integrated Manufacturing Strategies and Techniques." *International Journal of Computer Integrated Manufacturing* 14, no. 2 (March–April 2000).

Gupta, Mahesh. "Operations Effectiveness for a Successful Implementation of CIM." *Technovation* 16, no. 10 (October 1996), pp. 589–94.

Karwowski, W., and G. Salvendy, eds. *Organization and Management of Advanced Manufacturing.* New York: Wiley, 1994.

Kickul, Jill, and Lisa K. Gundry. "Breaking through Boundaries for Organizational Innovation: New Managerial Roles and Practices in E-Commerce Firms." *Journal of Management* 27, no. 3 (2001), pp. 347–61.

Leondes, C. T., ed. *Computer-Aided Manufacturing/Computer Integrated Manufacturing.* San Diego, CA: Academic Press, 1994.

Levitt, Theodore. "Production-Line Approach to Service." *Harvard Business Review,* September–October 1972, pp. 41–52.

Mathews, Joseph R. "Riding the ERP Wave." *Siliconindia* 9, no. 1 (February 2005), pp. 44–46.

McGaughey, Ronald E., and David W. Roach. "CIM Planning: An Exploratory Study of Factors Practitioners Perceive Important to CIM Planning Success." *International Journal of Computer Integrated Manufacturing* 14, no. 4 (August 2001), pp. 353–66.

Ming-Chyuan, Lin, and Yan Ing-Horng. "Development of a Computer-Assisted Procedure for Car Style Design." *International Journal of Vehicle Design* 35, no. 4 (2004), pp. 289–307.

Motwani, Jaideep, Dinesh Mirchandani, Manu Madan, and A. Gunasekaran. "Successful Implementation of ERP Projects: Evidence from Two Case Studies." *International Journal of Production Economics* 75, no. 1/2 (2002), pp. 83–96.

Prasad, Biren. "Converting Computer-Integrated Manufacturing into an Intelligent Information System by Combining CIM with Concurrent Engineering and Knowledge Management." *Industrial Management & Data Systems* 100, no. 7 (2000), pp. 301–16.

Rehg, James A. *Introduction to Robotics and CIM,* 5th ed. Englewood Cliffs, NJ: Prentice Hall, 2002.

Ryan, Sherry, and David Harrison, "Considering Social Subsystem Costs and Benefits in Information Technology Investment Decisions: A View from the Field on Anticipated Payoffs." *Journal of Management Information Systems* 16, no. 4 (Spring 2000), pp. 11–40.

Schlesinger, Leonard A., and James L. Heskett. "The Service-Driven Service Company." *Harvard Business Review,* September–October 1991, pp. 71–81.

Vizard, Michael, and Tom Sullivan. "SAP Embraces Web Services." *InfoWorld* 24, no. 13 (April 1, 2002), p. 14.

Waltner, Charles. "B-to-B Integration: Cost Savings, Improved Efficiencies." *Information Week,* May 7, 2001, pp. 106–8.

Wetmore, Pete. "Misfiring in the Midlands." *Seybold Report: Analyzing Publishing Technologies* 4, no. 12 (September 22, 2004), pp. 13–16.

Process-Flow Analysis

Chapter outline

In the previous three chapters, we have been dealing with macro questions concerning process selection, service system design, and technology choice. Now, we turn to micro questions regarding **process-flow analysis.** The transformation process can be viewed as a series of process flows connecting inputs to outputs. In process-flow analysis we will be analyzing how the product or service is made. When the sequence of steps connecting inputs to outputs is analyzed, better methods or procedures can usually be found.

Measuring process flows is essential to improving them. We describe several process measures including throughput time, flow rate, inventory, and capacity. We also define bottlenecks and provide methods for calculating these measures.

The flowchart is essential to process-flow analysis. Flowcharts should consider not only process flows but customers, suppliers, and employee inputs in designing better processes.

In this chapter we discuss process-flow decisions, beginning with process thinking. This is one of the most powerful ideas and neglected concepts in business education and in practice. We then describe various types of measurement and flowcharting for materials, information, and services. We complete the chapter with a discussion of business process reengineering.

7.1 PROCESS THINKING

A prerequisite to process-flow analysis is defining the operations transformation process as a system. System boundaries, inputs, outputs, suppliers, customers, and systems flows must all be defined. General **process thinking** is needed before detailed measurement and flowcharting can begin.

A system is often defined as a collection of interrelated elements whose whole is greater than the sum of its parts. The human body, for example, is a system. The heart, lungs, brain, and muscles cannot function without each other. They are interrelated, and the function of one part affects the others. The whole of the body is greater than any of its individual parts or components.

A business organization can also be viewed as a system. Its parts are the functions of marketing, operations, finance, accounting, human resources, and information systems. Each of these functions accomplishes nothing by itself. A business cannot sell what it can't produce, and it does no good to produce a product that can't be sold. The functions in an organization are highly interactive and can accomplish more by working together than separately.

Every operation can be viewed as a system by identifying the transformation or conversion system as described in Chapter 1. The transformation system must be isolated from its environment by specifying the **system boundary.** The boundary should encompass all the important interacting elements for purposes of the analysis or decision being made. Identification of the system boundary is always difficult and somewhat arbitrary, but it must be done to separate the system under study from the larger system or organization.

To illustrate these concepts, consider the case of a bank that is installing a new computer system. The new system will replace the current one, with larger capacity, new hardware, and some new software. The accounting systems will not be affected by this conversion because the same accounting transactions will be produced by the new computer in the same way, so accounting can safely be assumed to be outside the system boundary. Training will be required to operate the new system, so human resources can be considered part of the system. Operations will be affected by the new software and must also be included within the system boundary since some new operational software is being added. Each part of the organization that is affected by the new computer installation should be included within the system boundary, and functions not affected can be excluded as outside the system boundary. In this way, the appropriate system boundary can be identified for purposes of analysis.

A **cross-functional team** should be formed consisting of those functions that are affected by the computer conversion. This team should be responsible for converting to the new system and should deal with all of the interactions between functions. By doing so, a systems view will be taken of the project by considering all of the interacting parts within the system boundary when making the conversion.

7.2 THE PROCESS VIEW OF BUSINESS

One of the most important contributions of process thinking is that a business can be viewed as a collection of interconnected processes. Some of these processes include strategic planning, order entry, supplying the product, receiving payment from the customer, customer satisfaction, and human resources management. Note that each of these processes cuts across the usual functional

FIGURE 7.1 The process view of business.

Source: V. Grover and M. K. Malhorta, "Business Process Reengineering: A Tutorial on Concept, Evolution, Method, Technology and Application," *Journal of Operations Management* 15 (1997), p. 200.

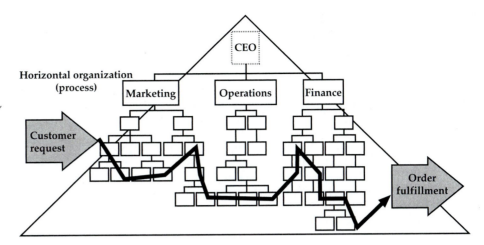

departments of marketing, operations, finance, and so forth. The **process view of a business** is horizontal in nature; the functional view is vertical. This is shown graphically in Figure 7.1.

Viewing a business as a collection of processes emphasizes the cross-functional nature of decision making. It illustrates that functions must make a handoff from one to another in executing a process. As a result, time and information can be lost between processes. In some cases, the number of steps in a process is so large that the system cannot function in an efficient and effective manner.

One example of this problem occurred in the Banca di America e di Italia (BAI).[1] Prior to application of process thinking, the bank operated in a traditional manner with many bureaucratic structures and departments. For example, a check deposited by a customer required 64 activities, nine forms, and 14 accounts. The BAI design team systematically diagnosed the present check-processing system and then redesigned it without considering the constraints of the existing organization. They traced out in detail the information flow for a check deposit and designed a new streamlined check-processing system. For example, the new system required only 25 activities, two forms, and two accounts. This greatly simplified system required adjustments in work assignments and organization responsibility. It also resulted in changed incentive systems and other organizational changes to accommodate the new technical system.

But checking deposits was just one process that needed redesign at BAI. In the complete redesign of the organization, a total of 10 families of retail banking processes were redesigned, including payments, deposits, withdrawals, money orders, bills, consumer credit, foreign exchange, credit cards, sourcing, and end-of-the-day branch closing processes. As a result of the radical redesign using the systems view, the bank was able to support growth and made impressive gains in profitability.

This example illustrates how operations is only a part of a larger organization that includes many other functions. No decisions can be confined entirely to operations. All operations decisions are related to at least one other part of the organization. The process view of business through systems thinking provides a vehicle

[1] For details see Gene Hall, Jim Rosenthal, and Judy Wade, "How to Make Reengineering Really Work," *Harvard Business Review*, November–December 1993, pp.119–33; and Web site www.globalff.org (2002).

for understanding the interactions between various organizational functions and decisions that typically cross functional lines. These interactions can be streamlined and improved by applying process thinking and measurements described next.

7.3 MEASURING PROCESS FLOWS

Before discussing flowcharts aimed at process improvement some basic process measurements must be described. Let's assume we study the airport security process during check-in at a major airport. We notice that there is a line of passengers waiting to clear security, sometimes a long line. There are also a number of security x-ray stations for examining carry-on luggage and we note the total time it takes from entering the security line until passengers are cleared to catch their flights. It turns out that these three observations are related: the average rate at which security can process passengers, the average time it takes to get through the line, and the average length of the line. This relationship is called **Little's Law,** named after the operations researcher who discovered it. Little's Law basically says that the average number of items in a system is the product of the average arrival rate to the system and the average length of time that any item stays in the system. In mathematical terms Little's Law is:

$$I = T \times R$$

where I = average number of things in the system (or "inventory").

T = average throughput time (or flow time).

R = average flow rate into the process.

In the case of airport security, if the security screeners can process an average of five passengers a minute ($R = 5$), and it takes an average of 20 minutes to get through the security check line ($T = 20$), then the average number of passengers in line will be 100 ($R \times T = 100$). An assumption is that the process is in steady state where the average output rate equals the average input rate to the process.

Little's Law is very powerful and widely used in practice. It applies to manufacturing and service processes. For example, suppose that a factory can produce an average of 100 units of product per day ($R = 100$). Also, suppose the throughput time including all processing and waiting time of the product equals an average of 10 days ($T = 10$). Throughput time is the time from when the product first starts being processed in the factory until it is finished and shipped. Then the average inventory of work in process (partly finished product) in the factory will be 1,000 units ($I = 10 \times 100$). So, Little's Law applies to any process in steady state including manufacturing, people waiting in lines, invoice processing, transactions in a legal office, and even accounts receivable processing.

For example, the amount of money in accounts receivable can be considered as inventory or the stock of money. Using Little's Law, if there are $2 million in accounts receivable (I), and $20,000 per day enters (and flows through) accounts receivable (R), then the throughput time is 100 days ($T = I/R = 2,000,000/20,000$). We would say accounts receivable has 100 days of outstanding receivables.

Little's Law is useful when any two of the three variables in the formula are known and the third can be calculated. In the above example, we know the average level of accounts receivable and the average input/output rate from the accounting books, thus permitting a calculation of the average time an account spends in accounts receivable before it is collected.

Next, we extend process measurements to include capacity, supply, and demand. **Capacity** is the maximum rate of output of a process or the maximum flow rate that can be sustained over a period of time. In the airport security example, the average flow rate was five passengers per minute, but the *capacity* of the security checkpoint may have been, say, eight passengers per minute. With random arrivals it is actually necessary to have capacity that exceeds the average arrival rate or the line will build up to an infinite length. This occurs because there are periods of time when the arrivals are less than the average and the full capacity can't be used during those times. Queuing (or waiting line) theory covered in a technical chapter on the CD-ROM explains this phenomena in detail.

Most processes are composed of several resources that must process the transactions. In the airport screening example there are workers who check each passenger's identification and boarding pass and operators who run the X-ray equipment. This system has two resources that must process each passenger. In general if there are n resources that process each transaction then

Process capacity = minimum (capacity of resource$_1$, ..., capacity of resource$_n$)

Note the capacity of the entire process can't be larger than the capacity of the most constraining (the smallest capacity) resource, also called the **bottleneck.**

The amount a process actually produces will depend not only on its capacity, but also on the supply and demand of the process. The flow rate is:

Flow rate = minimum (supply, demand, capacity)

In the factory example above, assume that capacity was 200 units per day, demand was 75 units per day, and supply was 100 units per day. The flow rate would be 75 units per day (the minimum of the three variables) assuming you can only produce what you can sell, and the factory utilization would be $75/200 = 37.5$ percent. If we were able to increase demand to 150 units per day, the flow rate would only be 100 units per day unless supply could also be increased.

We illustrate the concepts of process measurement with an example from Pizza U.S.A. first described in Chapter 1. Suppose that one of the pizza stores produces fresh pizza with seven different topping choices including the most popular "everything dump" pizza. The store is staffed by two employees, a pizza chef and an assistant. It has an oven that can bake up to four pizzas at a time. The process (sequence of steps) followed at the store is:

	Minutes	**Who**
Take the order	1	Assistant
Make the crust	3	Chef
Prepare and add ingredients	2	Chef
Bake the pizza	24	Oven
Cut pizza and box the order	1	Assistant
Take payment	1	Assistant

1. *What is the capacity of this process?*

   Looking at the three resources we have:

   The assistant takes 3 minutes per order (1 + 1 + 1) and thus can process 20 orders per hour.

   The chef takes 5 minutes per order (3 + 2) and can process 12 orders per hour.

   The oven takes 6 minutes per order up to its capacity (24 ÷ 4) or 10 orders per hour.

For simplicity, we have assumed that each order is for one pizza and that pizzas can be added to the oven any time during the cooking cycle. The minimum of the three resource capacities is 10 orders per hour, so the system can produce 10 orders per hour.

The bottleneck in this case is the oven. The assistant is busy only half of the time and the chef has one minute of idle capacity out of every 6 minutes. Reallocating the jobs between the chef and the assistant to balance the workload will make the chef happy, but won't increase the flow rate of the process. Something must be done to accelerate the flow of pizzas through the oven or add another oven. The lesson here is that the process can't produce more than the bottleneck can process. This is covered more completely in Chapter 13 when we discuss scheduling and the Theory of Constraints.

2. *What is the throughput time?*

We simply add the times of all the steps to fill an order.

$$1 + 3 + 2 + 24 + 1 + 1 = 32 \text{ minutes}$$

It takes 32 minutes to complete all the steps and make one pizza. Note that adding an oven would improve the capacity and move the bottleneck to the chef, but it would not improve the throughput time. Changes would have to be made in the actual process of cooking, preparation, or other flow times to reduce throughput time.

3. *What is the flow rate?*

Assuming demand and supply exceed capacity, the flow rate is determined by the capacity of 10 orders per hour. However, this is the maximum flow rate; the actual flow rate could be much less.

4. *What does it cost to make a pizza if the average demand is 60 percent of capacity?*

Assume the chef gets paid $10 per hour, the assistant gets paid $8 per hour, and overhead cost is 50 percent added to direct labor cost.

At 60 percent of capacity, the average flow rate is six pizzas per hour.
The cost per hour of operations is $10 + $8 = $18 for labor plus 50 percent added for overhead = $27 per hour or $27/6 = $4.50 per pizza.
Assume the cost of ingredients is $2.00 per pizza.
The total cost is $4.50 + $2.00 = $6.50 per pizza.

5. *How can the unit cost of pizzas be reduced?*

Three possibilities are:

- Increase demand through pricing, advertising, and the like.
- Increase the flow rate of the process by automation or process improvements.
- Reduce the unit cost of labor, materials, or overhead.

As you can see, these three approaches are interconnected because increasing demand will also require an increase in capacity at some point, and increasing the flow rate does no good unless demand is increased to sell the additional product.

We have covered several ways to measure a process that are useful not only in operations but in any process in a business. Next we turn to flowcharts that are useful tools to make process improvements.

7.4 FLOWCHART ANALYSIS

Flowcharts are used to describe and improve the transformation process in business. In improving the effectiveness or efficiency of productive processes, some or all of the following process elements might be changed:

1. Raw materials
2. Product (output) design
3. Job design
4. Processing steps used
5. Management control information
6. Equipment or tools
7. Suppliers

Process analysis can, therefore, have a wide effect on all parts of the organization.

As noted above, process-flow analysis is heavily dependent on process thinking. To analyze process flows, a relevant system is selected, and the customers, outputs, inputs, suppliers, boundaries, and transformations are described. In effect, the process-flow problem is described as a system.

Using the systems approach, the following steps are then taken in a process flowchart analysis:

1. Select a relevant productive process (or system) for study, for example, the whole business or some part of it.
2. Form a team, or designate an individual, to analyze and improve the system. Usually a cross-functional team is formed if the system cuts across organizational boundaries.
3. Decide on the objectives of the analysis, for example, to improve efficiency, throughput time, effectiveness, capacity, or worker morale.
4. Define the customers and suppliers for the system. In some cases, the next process is the customer and the previous processes are the suppliers. Customers and suppliers can be internal or external to the organization.
5. Describe the existing transformation process by means of flowcharts and efficiency measurements.

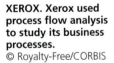

XEROX. Xerox used process flow analysis to study its business processes.
© Royalty-Free/CORBIS

6. Develop an improved process design by revising the process flows or inputs used. Usually the revised process is also described by a flowchart.
7. Gain management approval for the revised process design.
8. Implement the new process design.

Notice that this method assumes an existing process. If there is no existing process, steps 5 and 6 are combined to describe the desired process, but the rest of the method is still used. This general method of flowchart analysis will be illustrated below for specific situations.

In Section 7.5, materials flows will be treated in detail. This will be followed by analysis of information flows in Section 7.6 and service flows in Section 7.7. One of our objectives is to show how these three types of process flows can be analyzed by the same procedure even though they are often thought of as being quite different.

7.5 MATERIALS-FLOW ANALYSIS

The analysis of **materials flows** in factories was one of the first applications of process-flow analysis ideas. These ideas were developed in the early 1900s by industrial engineers applying the principles of Taylor's scientific management. First they broke down the manufacturing process into detailed elements, and then they carefully studied each element and the interrelationship between elements to improve overall process efficiency.

Today, materials-flow analysis has come back into vogue through emphasis on reducing **manufacturing throughput time** (cycle time), the total time to order, manufacture, and distribute a product from beginning to end. This is being done by seeking to reduce **waste** in the process. Waste is defined as any operation that does not add value during the production process, including the time the product sits in storage, the time the product is being moved from one location to another, inspection time, and so forth. Only actual processing time of the material by machine or by labor adds value. The tools for eliminating waste through analyzing materials flows are described next.

As part of the materials-flow analysis, it is necessary to describe the flow of materials in great detail. This is done in manufacturing through flow-process charts. For analysis purposes, a flow-process chart (or, more simply, a process chart) is usually constructed; it breaks the process down in terms of the symbols shown in Figure 7.2.

We take an example from the grocery industry to illustrate the **flow-process chart.** In this example, groceries are selected, assembled, and delivered in response to customer telephone orders. As the first step in the process, customer orders are received by phone and entered directly into a computer. The computer then generates picking lists for each of the various aisles (dry groceries, produce, meat, dairy, and so on) in the grocery warehouse. The items are picked by employees in each aisle and then assembled into a complete order for delivery to the customers.

Figure 7.3 is a flow-process chart for a portion of this operation, which includes the groceries that are picked from the produce, dairy, and meat aisles. Notice the use of the special symbols for operations, transportation, inspection, delays, and storage. Only the operations activity adds value to the product. The other activities (transportation, inspection, delays, and storage) are considered as

FIGURE 7.2

Symbols used in a flow-process chart.

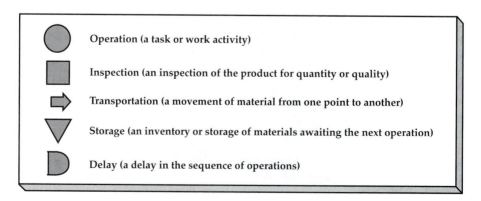

Operation (a task or work activity)

Inspection (an inspection of the product for quantity or quality)

Transportation (a movement of material from one point to another)

Storage (an inventory or storage of materials awaiting the next operation)

Delay (a delay in the sequence of operations)

FIGURE 7.3 Flow-processing chart.

Subject Charted	Produce,Dairy,Meat Depts.		

FLOW PROCESS CHART

Summary	Pres.	Prop.	Save
Operations	7		
Transports	5		
Inspections	1		
Delays	5		
Storages	0		
Time			
Distance	215		

Operation	Picking
Chartered by	RGS
Chart No.	01 Sheet 1 of 1
Date	1/8/02

Can I Eliminate?
Can I Combine?
Can I Change Sequence?
Can I Simplify?

Present ☒ Proposed ☐

	Dist. in Feet	Time in Min.	Oper.	Tran.	Insp.	Delays	Store	Descriptions	Notes
1		5						Computer prints order sheets	
2	90	60						To the warehouse	
3		120						On distribution desk	
4		3						Separated according to work areas	
5	30	10						Taken to start points	
6		80						Wait for order picker	
7		4						Picker separates them order by order	
8		20						(Produce) picker fills order	
9	20	15						To Dairy aisle	
10		25						On conveyor waiting for picker	
11		10						(Dairy) picker fills order	
12	30	30						To Meat aisle	
13		60						On conveyor waiting for picker	
14		5						(Meat) picker fills order	
15	45	15						To inspection	
16		4						Inspected	
17		10						Loaded onto carts route-by-route	
18		50						Waits to be taken to the warehouse	
19		=							
20		526						Total Time	
21									

waste, or non-value-adding activities, and should be reduced or eliminated. In Figure 7.3, the time and the distance are noted on the chart to identify and assess possible improvements. It is evident that groceries spend most of the time waiting for the next operation (symbol D) or in transit (symbol T) and very little time in value-adding operations (symbol O). As a matter of fact, the total throughput time is 526 minutes (add all times in Figure 7.3) and only 57 minutes are value-adding operations (10.8 percent). The remainder of the time is a candidate for reduction or elimination.

The flow-process chart is a key tool for improving the flow of materials. After examining it, the analyst or team may be able to combine certain operations, eliminate others, or simplify operations to improve overall efficiency and reduce throughput time. This may, in turn, require changes in layout, equipment, and work methods and possibly even changes in product design.

But it is not enough simply to draw flow-process charts. A key to analyzing these charts is to ask the following types of questions:

1. **What.** What does the customer need? What operations are really necessary? Can some operations be eliminated, combined, or simplified? Should the product be redesigned to facilitate production?

2. **Who.** Who is performing each operation? Can the operation be redesigned to use less skill or fewer labor hours? Can operations be combined to enrich jobs and thereby improve productivity or working conditions? Who are the suppliers? Should different suppliers be used or can the present suppliers be used more effectively? Should some, or all, of the operations be outsourced to suppliers?

3. **Where.** Where is each operation conducted? Can the layout be improved to reduce distance traveled or to make the operations more accessible?

4. **When.** When is each operation performed? Is there excessive delay or storage? Are some operations creating bottlenecks? How can the waiting time be reduced?

5. **How.** How is the operation done? Can better methods, procedures, or equipment be used? Should the operation be revised to make it easier or less time-consuming?

The application of these questions can be illustrated by using the grocery warehouse example. After the questions were asked, the following types of changes were made:

1. **Layout.** The layout of the facility was revised to be more efficient and compact. Some aisles were moved from one part of the warehouse to another.

2. **Methods and jobs.** Methods of picking groceries were revised to reduce bottlenecks and labor.

3. **Equipment.** Special carts were designed to make loading of the delivery vans easier and faster. An overhead conveyor was also installed to consolidate orders and speed up the flow of materials.

These changes contributed significantly to better materials flow and improved efficiency. More value was added to the service produced by reducing wasted time and effort.

It should be noted that analysis of materials flow extends far beyond manufacturing. The grocery warehouse example is a service operation. Other examples of service operations with a substantial flow of materials are restaurants, laundries, the U.S. Postal Service, warehousing, and retail trade.

7.6 INFORMATION-FLOW ANALYSIS

Information flows can be analyzed in a manner analogous to that used for the flow of materials. Although information flows are sometimes recorded on a flow-process chart using the standard symbols, different forms of flowcharting are also used for information flows. However, the purpose of information-flow analysis is the same as for the analysis of materials flow: to improve the efficiency and effectiveness of the process.

There are two types of information flows. In the first, information is the product of the operation. This is typical, for example, of clerical processing in offices, where the office can be thought of as an "information-processing factory" converting the inputs from "raw material" to "finished goods." In Chapter 5, we briefly described information-flow analysis for service operations. The emphasis was on designing the flows with an awareness of customer contact points and moments of truth. Since information is the product for many service operations, information-flow analysis becomes a key tool, much like analyzing materials flow for factories.

In the second case, the information flow is used for management or control purposes. Examples of this are order entry, purchasing documents, electronic documents, and paperwork used in manufacturing. In this case, the information is used to control the flow of materials. Although the methods of analysis are the same, the purposes of these two types of information flows are quite different.

It is usually insufficient to analyze a materials-flow process without also analyzing the flow of information. This is because the materials flow may be improved but management control of the process may still be lacking. To illustrate this concept, we have shown in Figure 7.4 the information flow from the

FIGURE 7.4 Information flows in a grocery warehouse.

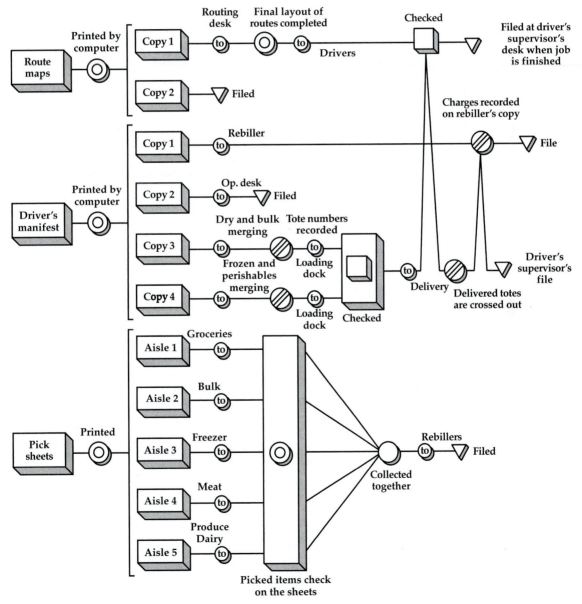

FIGURE 7.5

Symbols used in an information-processing flowchart.

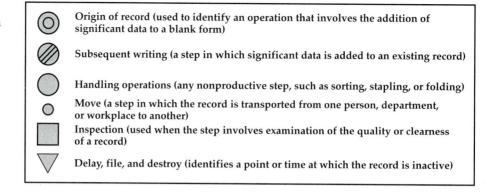

◎	Origin of record (used to identify an operation that involves the addition of significant data to a blank form)
◐	Subsequent writing (a step in which significant data is added to an existing record)
◯	Handling operations (any nonproductive step, such as sorting, stapling, or folding)
∘	Move (a step in which the record is transported from one person, department, or workplace to another)
▢	Inspection (used when the step involves examination of the quality or clearness of a record)
▽	Delay, file, and destroy (identifies a point or time at which the record is inactive)

grocery warehouse example. (See Figure 7.5 for an explanation of the symbols used. Although these are not the only symbols used in flowcharting, they illustrate the concepts involved.)

As Figure 7.4 indicates, three key types of information are used to control the flow of groceries: (1) route maps, (2) drivers' manifests, and (3) pick sheets. A route map tells the driver which route to follow in delivering the groceries for a particular run. The computer constructs the routes for each delivery on the basis of the locations of the customers' homes. The driver's manifest is simply a listing of the groceries to be delivered to each customer. Finally, the pick sheets are used to list the groceries by warehouse aisle so as to facilitate picking. In this case, all these types of information are used to control the delivery of grocery services. The information flow itself is not the "product."

After the information flowchart is completed, the analysis proceeds in much the same way as the analysis of materials flow. The analysis should include the five key questions of what, who, where, when, and how. It might also include some recording of times and information-flow volumes.

As a result of the analysis, it should be possible to consolidate or simplify information flows. This may result in changes in equipment (perhaps involving the computer), in jobs, and in procedures. In the case of the grocery example, some of the copies and paperwork might be eliminated through the use of a common database that all employees can access by remote electronic terminals or displays.

The analysis of information flows is sometimes seen as different from the analysis of materials flows. This may be because industrial engineers deal with materials flows while computer systems analysts deal with information flows. As we have seen, however, systems analysts might be considered "industrial engineers of the office."

7.7 SERVICE BLUEPRINTING

For service operations flowcharting is called **service blueprinting.** A service blueprint shows how the customer and service providers interact at each step of the service delivery process. Each horizontal row on the blueprint is for a specific person, the customer or one of the service providers.

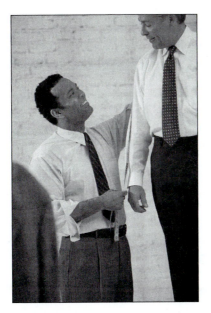

The tailor checks the suit for alterations as part of the service blueprint. © Comstock Images/AGE Fotostock

Figure 7.6 shows a service blueprint for the purchase of a man's ready-made suit from a retail store. The top left side of the figure shows the customer arrival at the store. The customer is greeted by a sales representative and asked what he is generally looking to purchase in terms of style, size, and price range. The sales representative then takes the customer to the appropriate racks to look at the suits available. After searching the available suits, the customer decides if there is a suit that he would like to try on for size. If there is, he tries the suit and looks in the mirror. Otherwise, the customer exits the store. If the customer likes the suit, he will move to the tailor, as shown on the lower part of the service blueprint. The tailor and customer determine the alterations needed, and the suit is then sent to the tailor shop (below the line of visibility). It is customary to draw a line of visibility on the service blueprint to separate those parts that come in direct contact with the customer from those that don't. The customer then pays for the suit or makes a deposit and then returns later to pick up the altered suit.

Service blueprinting is a very good way to show all points of interaction between the customer and one or more service providers. Referring back to Chapter 5, each point on the flowchart is a "moment of truth" where the customer can receive either excellent or poor service. In total, the service blueprint shows the "cycle of service" from beginning to end. Managing the cycle of service and all of the moments of truth is essential to providing excellent service.

After drawing the service blueprint, an analysis can be conducted just like we did for materials and information flowcharts. The analysis proceeds by asking the previously indicated questions: *what, who, where, when,* and *how.*

Returning to Figure 7.6 when buying a suit, *what* does the customer need? For example, if sales representatives are trained to be better listeners to customer requests, will operations improve? Also, could a customer call ahead to the sales representative and ask for some suits to be waiting for his examination, thereby cutting out several steps in the service blueprint?

The analysis of *who* can be accomplished by asking if the sales representative can be trained to do the alteration fitting. In this case, a step in the process and possible waiting for the tailor can be eliminated. While this might improve the efficiency of the process, will it be perceived by the customer to reduce the level of expertise provided?

Similarly, the *where* question might result in rearranging some of the store layout to make it more convenient for the customer. Answering the question *when* might result in taking some of the steps in the service blueprint "off-line" so they can be performed earlier or later in the process. Finally, the question of *how* can be related to equipment or methods used. One men's store, for example, has a laser measurement device that can immediately measure the suit alterations needed more accurately and quickly than the traditional tailor can.

FIGURE 7.6 Service blueprint for men's suit purchase.

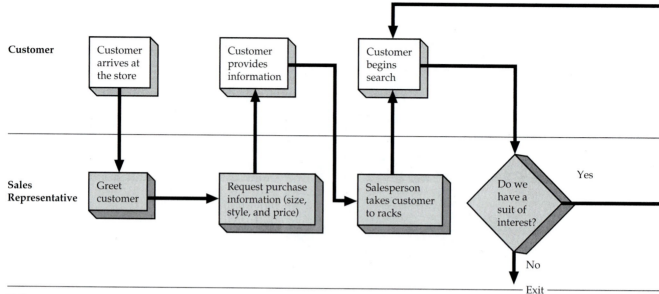

Cross-functional teams of store employees could do the analysis of the service blueprint, perhaps with outside assistance. The analysis might even include focus groups of customers to get their ideas about improvements that are desirable. It is always advisable to get customer and employee input into process improvement.

As can be seen, service blueprinting is very similar to analysis of manufacturing and information flow for manufacturing firms. One important difference, however, is that the customer is in the system and interacts with the service provider during production of the service. Rather than interfering with efficiency, the interaction with the customer can provide many opportunities for the improvement of the service process itself.

In summary, process-flow analysis describes the transformation process used to convert inputs into outputs. The analysis may be used to describe materials flows, information flows, or service flows. First, an appropriate process or system is isolated, customers and suppliers are identified, and a flowchart is constructed of the process. After the flowchart is prepared, questions of what, who, where, when, and how are asked to improve the process. From the answers to these questions, improvements might be made in procedures, tasks, equipment, raw materials, layout, suppliers, or management control information. Basically, the objective is to add more value to the product or service by eliminating waste or unnecessary activities at all stages. As we have shown in the examples, a variety of processes can be improved by following this relatively simple form of analysis.

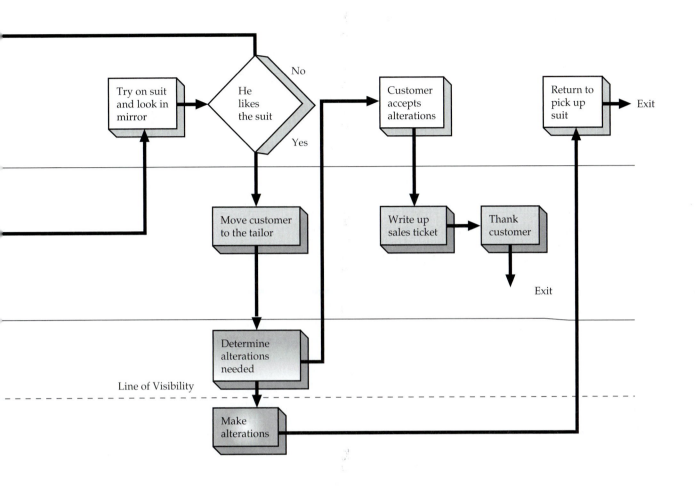

7.8 BUSINESS PROCESS REENGINEERING

At present, the principles of process-flow analysis are being applied as **business process reengineering** (BPR). This usually starts with the entire business and identifies critical processes required to meet the customers' needs. Then, these critical processes, many of which cut across organization boundaries, are analyzed in detail using the methods described in this chapter. As a result, major business processes are redesigned and integrated to better serve the customer.

BPR is a term coined by Hammer and Champy in their famous book *Reengineering the Corporation* (2001). They argue that most business processes are antiquated and need to be completely redesigned. Many existing processes have been designed within the confines of individual functions such as marketing, operations, and finance and furthermore do not make use of modern computer systems for information processing. As a result, these processes take far too long to provide customer service and are very inefficient and wasteful.

Consider a typical major insurance company that had just this problem. When the customer called the home office about an insurance problem, the call was taken by the incoming calls department. The problem was entered into the computer and passed electronically to one of several departments: underwriting, policy service, accounting, or another. The problem then waited in line, often for several days, until a clerk had time to check it out. In some cases, the customer's problem had been routed to the wrong department and had to be routed to another department again taking several days in the queue. If the problem required more than one department to answer the question, the process of waiting was repeated. Finally, someone in customer service would get back to the customer after several weeks. In many cases, the original question was not completely answered or answered in the wrong way.

This process was reengineered by completely reorganizing the entire insurance operation around customer service representatives who would attempt to handle the customer's request on the phone, if possible, using detailed computer protocols and standard scripts. If more detailed work was required, the customer service representative checked with other specialists and got back to the customer in one week or less with an answer. The customer service representatives had been cross-trained in all the various disciplines required and were supported by the other departments. Although this required more training of customer service representatives, it greatly improved the speed and accuracy of the service while saving many millions of dollars. It also provided a single point of contact, and less hassle, for the customer.

BPR assumes radical redesign of business processes. Many processes simply cannot be further improved in small steps and require a complete redesign to improve them in a major way, like the insurance office described above. Hammer and Champy advocate radical redesign as compared to the more incremental approach associated with total quality management, a subject discussed in detail in the next chapter.

The famous BPR project at Ford Motor Company is another example of radical process redesign.[2] The accounts payable department at Ford employed 500 people before reengineering and represented an opportunity for major improvement. Ford had formed a joint venture with Mazda and decided to benchmark their accounts payable department only to learn that Mazda had only five accounts payable employees. Even after accounting for the difference in sizes of the two companies this could only be attributed to a much different process.

The process that Ford was using before reengineering started with the purchasing department issuing a purchase order to the supplier with a copy to accounts payable. When the merchandise was received from the supplier, a receiving document was sent to accounts payable. Later, the supplier sent an invoice to Ford accounts payable for the merchandise. If accounts payable could match the three documents, they would authorize payment to the supplier. Most of the time in accounts payable, however, was spent on mismatches among documents. A clerk would hold up payment until the source of the mismatch could be identified and the problem resolved.

Under the reengineered system, the purchasing department entered the purchase order into a database and did not send a copy to anyone. When the merchandise arrived, the receiving clerk would enter the database and determine if the shipment agreed with the electronic purchase order. If it did, payment was authorized to be made at the appropriate time. If it didn't match, the merchandise would be returned or the Ford purchasing department would be notified

[2] Adapted from Michael Hammer, "Reengineering Work: Don't Automate, Obliterate," *Harvard Business Review,* July–August 1990, pp.104–12.

to give the okay to receive the material. Ford also instituted "invoiceless purchasing" where the supplier did not need to send an invoice to be paid. This greatly simplified the process for all concerned. As a result, Ford was able to reduce the work of its accounts payable department and the headcount by 75 percent.

There are four principles of BPR, as follows:

1. **Organize around outcomes, not tasks.** The insurance company described above was organized according to tasks using the classic division of labor. One department handled customer phone calls, others handled policy service, underwriting, and accounting. By reorganizing around the outcome, which is customer service, dramatic improvements were made. A customer service representative handles all activities associated with the desired outcome. Although it is not always possible to have one person do everything, jobs can be broadened and handoffs between departments minimized when using BPR.

2. **Have the people who do the work process their own information.** In the Ford example, the accounts payable department was responsible for reconciling information that was received from other departments and from the customer. In the redesigned system, everyone processed their own information. Purchasing put information directly into the database, and receiving reconciled the material received with the purchase order. There was no need for accounts payable to match the purchase order, the receiving document, and the invoice. This principle can be applied in many situations where information is passed from one department to another and unnecessary information is generated.

3. **Put the decision point where the work is performed, and build control into the process.** It is always better to push decision making to the lowest possible level. This will eliminate layers of bureaucracy and speed up the decision-making process. After reengineering in the Ford Motor case, the receiving department made the decisions as to whether the material received was equal to the material ordered. In the insurance example, the case worker received greater latitude to make decisions directly for the customer rather than referring decisions to other departments. To accomplish this, however, information and controls must be built into the process itself.

4. **Eliminate unnecessary steps in the process.** Simplifying the processes frequently means that unnecessary steps and paperwork are eliminated. Every step is examined using the flowcharting techniques discussed earlier, and only those that add value for the customer are retained. As a result, greatly streamlined and simplified processes are designed.

While BPR has achieved outstanding results, it has also resulted in failures. Hammer and Champy (2001) suggest that 70 percent of reengineering projects have been less than successful. Why does such a promising approach often lead to disappointment and problems? These results have been ascribed to both the approach itself and the way it is implemented. Proponents of BPR often point to the lack of top management support, a narrow implementation effort, the assignment of the wrong people to the project, or lack of changes in incentive systems as reasons for failure. At the same time, BPR itself may lead to some of these problems. The early insistence of **radical redesign** has now been somewhat softened to allow less radical change and continuous improvement. The essential

OPERATIONS LEADER

Reengineering in Health Care: Continental Rehabilitation Hospital

Reengineering can radically improve health care. Looking at the basic patient–provider interaction, however, one might ask: What is the essential nature of work, and what is reengineered? At its core, health care delivery is a chain of hand-offs. Three aspects of hand-off processes that are open to redesign are the overall chain length, the amount of variation within each link, and the degree of coordination between links.

Continental Rehabilitation Hospital of San Diego, CA, provides health care services to people with complex and catastrophic injuries or illnesses. One of its services to insurers is to provide comprehensive medical and/or legal evaluations of such individuals. These services are low volume, complex, and provider intensive. Each patient is different and requires a unique and extensive evaluation process. A typical process includes physical capacity assessments and radiological tests, such as computerized tomography, magnetic resonance imaging, and bone scanning. Evaluations are conducted by four to eight physicians from different specialties, and two or three specialty therapy evaluations are made. In addition, the process requires the work of 10 to 25 other staff members, including those from nursing, technical support, and administrative support. Activities must be coordinated among as many as 10 organizations, as most of the providers of radiological testing and physical evaluations are separate business entities.

A process action team was formed to study and improve the evaluation process. The team started by mapping out who was supposed to do what, by when, and with whom. Based on its observations the team redesigned the process.

The team's redesign required only six hours of meeting time over a six-week period and 10 to 12 additional hours of support work. Immediately, after implementing the newly redesigned process, the time from arrival of the patient to submittal of the final evaluation report was reduced from a mean of 50 days to 18 days.

Source: Edward Chaplin, "Reengineering in Health Care: Chain Hand-Offs and the Four-Phase Work Cycle," *Quality Progress,* October 1996, pp.105–9; and www.aitriz.org (2002).

idea of BPR may be the process view of the organization, not the need for radical redesign in every instance. See, for example, how reengineering was done, with fairly minor disruptions, at Operations Leader Continental Rehabilitation Hospital.

BPR has come under attack due to its association with downsizing of American corporations. While this association might be true, the fault probably does not lie with BPR itself. Rather, some corporations have failed to grow their businesses and are so inefficient that they can no longer compete. BPR is simply a way to catch up with problems that have been created over the years. A more enlightened use of BPR would be to use it, along with continuous improvement, so that inefficiencies do not build up to a disastrous extent coupled with a strategic growth plan to protect and enhance employment.

BPR is just one of many tools that can be used to improve operations. It provides a process view of the organization and a way of improving processes. As a result of process reengineering, processes will be simplified, process flows improved, and non-value-added work eliminated. Other tools for improving processes will be covered in the next two chapters on quality.

7.9 KEY POINTS

This chapter has emphasized process-flow analysis by building upon the ideas of systems, measurement, flowcharting, and business process reengineering. The key points are as follows:

- A prerequisite to process-flow analysis is definition of the system to be analyzed. Systems definition requires isolation of the system of interest from its environment by defining a boundary, customers, outputs, inputs, suppliers, and process flows.

- The process view leads to the idea that a business is a set of horizontal processes that are interconnected with the objective of meeting customer needs.

- Measurement is essential to process improvement. Some key measurements of a process are throughput time, flow rate, inventory, and capacity. The bottleneck resource determines the capacity of the entire process.

- Materials, information, and service flows can be analyzed by flowcharts and answering the questions: What is done? Who does it and where? When and how is it done? The result of the analysis may lead to changes in output, raw materials, tools, equipment, jobs, methods, and information.

- Information flows can be analyzed either as the product itself or as management information used to plan and control production of the product or service. In the same way as materials flows, information flows and service flows are depicted in flowcharts, which are then analyzed to find ways to improve the process.

- A service blueprint is used to describe and analyze the service delivery system. Each point of contact between the service providers and the customer is shown. The questions of what, who, when, where, and how assist in analyzing the service blueprint for improvements.

- Business process reengineering is used for radical redesign of processes. BPR is cross-functional in nature and requires a complete overhaul of work methods, flows, and information systems.

STUDENT INTERNET EXERCISES

1. BPR Online Learning Center
   http://www.prosci.com

   Read one or more tutorials about BPR on this site and come to class prepared to discuss your findings.

2. Q-Skills
   http://www.q-skills.com/flowchrt.html

   Read the summary of flowcharting and write a short report on some of the problems and pitfalls in using flowcharts.

3. Little's Law (Section 7.4 of Programming Pearls)
   http://www.cs.bell-labs.com/cm/cs/pearls/sec074.html

   Read this short article on Little's Law for more background information.

SOLVED PROBLEMS

Problem

1. A ticket line for the Minnesota Vikings football team has an average of 100 fans in line to buy tickets and an average flow rate of 5 fans a minute. What is the average time that a ticket buyer can expect to wait in line?

Solution

Using Little's Law $I = T \times R$, solve for T

$$T = I/R = 100/5 = 20$$

A ticket buyer can expect to spend an average of 20 minutes in line.

Problem

2. Joe's commercial laundry has contracts to wash bed sheets for hotels. Joe intakes each batch of sheets, which takes 1 minute, then the sheets are washed taking 20 minutes and dried taking 30 minutes. The batch of sheets is ironed taking 10 minutes for each batch and there are two employees ironing sheets. Finally, Joe packages the sheets and bills the customer, taking 2 minutes. Joe has five wash machines and seven dryers that can each process one batch of sheets.

   a. What is the capacity of the laundry system and what is the bottleneck?
   b. What is the average throughput time of a batch of sheets?
   c. If the flow rate is 10 batches per hour, what is the average number of batches of sheets in the system (inventory)?

Solution

a. The capacity of each resource is as follows:

   Joe takes 3 minutes for each batch and can thus handle 20 batches per hour.

   Ironing takes 10 minutes so each employee can handle 6 batches per hour and the total capacity for two employees is 12 batches per hour.

   Washing machines take 20 minutes per batch or three loads per hour for each machine and there are five machines for a total capacity of 15 batches per hour.

   Dryers take 30 minutes per batch or two loads per hour from each machine times seven machines for a capacity of 14 batches per hour.

   The most constraining (minimum capacity) resource is the ironing so the system capacity is 12 batches per hour and ironing is the bottleneck.

b. The average throughput time of the system for each batch of sheets is:

$$T = 1 + 20 + 30 + 10 + 2 = 63 \text{ minutes}$$

c. $I = T \times R = 63/60 \times 10 = 10.5$ batches (note, the 63 minutes must be converted to hours using 60 minutes in an hour).

Problem

3. A small restaurant has 30 tables. When the guests arrive the manager seats them, servers serve them, and they pay their bill. The process is shown with

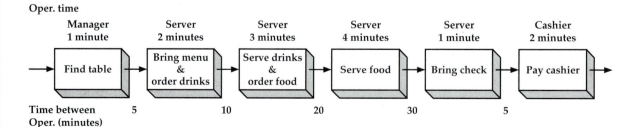

Oper. time					
Manager 1 minute	Server 2 minutes	Server 3 minutes	Server 4 minutes	Server 1 minute	Cashier 2 minutes
Find table	Bring menu & order drinks	Serve drinks & order food	Serve food	Bring check	Pay cashier

Time between Oper. (minutes) 5   10   20   30   5

operations times on the top of the figure and times between operations on the bottom. There is one manager, one cashier, and four servers available.

a. What is the capacity of the system and the bottleneck resource?

b. What is the throughput time for each customer?

c. If there are 20 arrivals per hour, what is the number of tables filled?

Solution

a. The capacity of each resource is as follows:

The manager takes 1 minute each and can handle 60 customers (or tables) per hour.

The cashier takes 2 minutes each and can handle 30 customers per hour.

Each server takes 10 minutes per table and can handle 6 tables per hour. There are four servers, so the total capacity for servers is 24 tables per hour.

There are 30 tables available.

The resource with the minimum capacity is the servers so the system capacity is 24 tables per hour and the bottleneck is the servers.

b. The throughput time of the system for each customer is:

$$1 + 2 + 3 + 4 + 1 + 2 + 5 + 10 + 20 + 30 + 5 = 83 \text{ minutes}$$

c. If there are 20 arrivals per hour, there will be

$$I = T \times R = 83/60 \times 20 = 27.7 \text{ tables being used}$$

Discussion Questions

1. In the following operations, isolate a system for analysis and define customers, services produced, suppliers, and the primary process flows.
   a. A college
   b. A fast-food restaurant
   c. A library

2. Explain how the process view of an organization is likely to uncover the need for greater interfunctional cooperation and greater decentralization of the organization.

3. Explain Little's Law in your own words. How can it be used and what are the limitations of this law?

4. Provide a definition of a bottleneck. Why is it important to find the bottleneck?

5. Explain the differences between capacity, flow rate, and demand.

6. How is the analysis of material similar to and different from the analysis of information?

7. Give three reasons why the flow of materials and the flow of control information should be analyzed together, at the same time.

8. What kinds of problems are presented by the redesign of existing processes that are not encountered in the design of a new process?

9. What is the best approach, radical improvement or continuous improvement of processes? Under what circumstances might either approach be preferred?

10. Why is it important to define the system of interest before embarking on improvement? Give three reasons.

11. Find an article in the library or on the Internet that describes business process reengineering. Write a short report on how the BPR approach was used.

12. Visit the data-processing department of a company and ask them to show you a sample of systems flowcharts that they have developed. Also ask them how flowcharts are used to make improvements in information systems.

13. Describe service blueprinting in your own words to a fellow classmate.

14. How does service blueprinting differ from flowcharting for manufacturing or information systems?

Problems

1. In a company that processes insurance claims, the average flow rate is 10 claims per hour and the average throughput time is 6 hours.

   a. How many claims are in the system on average?

   b. If the demand for claims to be processed is seven per hour and the capacity is eight per hour what is the flow rate?

   c. What assumptions have you made in your answers?

2. Suppose a bank clears checks drawn upon customers' checking accounts using the following process

   a. If the capacity for receiving checks is 1,000 checks per hour, sorting checks is 800 checks per hour, and shipping checks is 1,200 per hour, what is the capacity of the system to process checks?

   b. If the flow rate is an average of 600 checks per hour and there are an average of 200 checks in the system, what is the average throughput time of checks?

   c. What could be done to decrease the throughput time?

3. The Stylish Hair Salon has three stylists that provide services to women. After checking in with the receptionist, which takes an average of one minute, the customer's hair is washed, dried, and styled taking an average of 25 minutes. The payment takes 3 minutes and is also performed by the receptionist.

   a. What is the capacity of the process and what is the bottleneck?

   b. What is the average throughput time, and if the average flow rate is five customers per hour, what is the average number of customers in the system?

   c. If the input to the system is random, what will happen as the flow rate approaches the capacity of the system?

4. Judy's Cake Shop makes fresh cakes to customer orders. After receiving the order by Judy's assistant, which takes 2 minutes, Judy then takes 8 minutes to mix the ingredients for the cake and loads a cake pan for baking. Then the cake is put into the oven for 30 minutes. The oven can hold

three cakes at one time. When the cake is taken out of the oven it is cooled for 1 hour. The assistant then takes 2 minutes to pack the cake for pickup and bills the customer, taking 3 minutes.

   a. What is the capacity of the process and what is the bottleneck?

   b. What is the throughput time for a typical cake?

   c. If on average five orders are taken per hour, how many cakes are there in the process (work in process inventory)?

5. The Swanky Hotel provides room service for its guests. The process for room service consists of a room service manager who takes orders by phone in an average of 2 minutes per order. The manager then sends the order to the kitchen where it takes an average of 16 minutes to prepare the food for each order. There are four chefs in the kitchen. If the customer requires a beverage (alcoholic or nonalcoholic), the room service manager sends the order to the bar at the same time the order is sent to the kitchen. It takes 3 minutes to fill the order by one bartender and 80 percent of the orders require a beverage. When the kitchen and bar orders are both ready, a waiter will take them to the room and bill the guest. There are six waiters to provide the service and each order takes 20 minutes for the waiter to complete.

   a. What is the capacity of the process and what is the bottleneck?

   b. What is the throughput time of a typical order?

   c. Assume that on Friday evenings an average of 10 room-service orders per hour are placed. How many orders are in the system on average on Friday nights?

   d. Assume the following pay rates for employees. Waiters are paid $6 per hour (not including tips), cooks are paid $10 per hour, the bartender is paid $7 per hour, and the room service manager is paid $12 per hour. Also assume that 60 percent overhead is added to direct labor and that the cost of food and beverages averages $6 per order.

What is the average cost of an order when operating at 10 orders per hour?

What is the minimum cost per order that the system can achieve?

e. What assumptions have you made in these calculations that may not be reasonable?

6. A furniture factory makes two types of wooden tables, large and small. Each table flows through the following process.

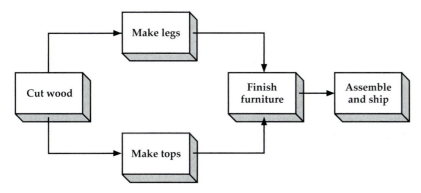

Small tables are made in batches of 100 and large tables are made in batches of 50 at a time. A batch includes a fixed setup time for the entire batch at each process and a run time for each piece in the batch. Both large and small tables have the same processing times and capacities shown below.

	Setup time minutes	Run time per piece minutes	Capacity pieces per hour
Wood Cutting	30	5	15
Make Four Legs	60	10	10
Make Tops	60	12	8
Finish the Wood	20	8	12
Assemble and Ship	20	17	14

a. What is the capacity of the system and what is the bottleneck?

b. What is the throughput time for large and small batches?

c. When producing at a rate of six large tables per hour on average, how many tables will be in the system?

7. Draw a flowchart of the following processes:

a. The procedure used to keep your checkbook

b. College registration

c. Obtaining a book from the library

8. Using the special symbols, draw a flow-process chart of the processes listed in problem 7.

9. Use the key questions of what, who, where, when, and how on problem 7 or 8 to suggest improvements in the process.

10. Using the special operations symbols, draw a flow-process chart of the following processes:

a. Preparing yourself for a job interview

b. Going to the library to study and returning to your room

11. Use the what, who, when, where, and how questions to make improvements in problems 10a and 10b.

12. Draw a service blueprint for the following services:

a. Pizza delivery

b. Automobile repair

13. Analyze the service blueprints in problem 12 for possible improvements. Use the what, who, when, where, and how questions.

Selected Bibliography

Ahadi, Hamid Reza. "An Examination of the Role of Organizational Enablers in Business Process Reengineering and the Impact of Information Technology." *Information Resources Management Journal* 17, no. 4 (2004), pp. 1–19.

Bliemel, Michael, and Hassanein, Khaled. "E-Health: Applying Business Process Reengineering Principles to Healthcare in Canada." *International Journal of Electronic Business* 2, no. 6 (2004), pp. 1–2.

Bryne, J. A. "The Horizontal Corporation: It's about Managing Across, Not Up and Down." *BusinessWeek,* October 20, 1993, pp. 76–81.

Champy, J. A. *Reengineering Management: The Mandate for New Leadership.* London: HarperCollins, 1996.

Chaneski, Wayne S. "Process Flow Chart: A Tool for Streamlining Operation." *Modern Machine Shop* 72, no. 10 (March 2000), pp. 52–54.

Chaplin, Edward. "Reengineering in Health Care: Chain Hand-Offs and the Four-Phase Work Cycle." *Quality Progress,* October 1996.

Godfrey, Michael, and D. Brent Bandy. "Applying Little's Law and the Theory of Constraints." *Six Sigma Forum Magazine* 4, no. 2 (February 2005), pp. 37–41.

Grant, Delvin. "A Wider View of Business Process Reengineering." *Communications of the ACM* 45, no. 2 (February 2002), pp. 85–90.

Hall, Gene, Jim Rosenthal, and Judy Wade. "How to Make Reengineering Really Work." *Harvard Business Review,* November–December 1993.

Hammer, Michael. *Beyond Reengineering: How the Process Centered Organization Is Changing Our Work and Lives.* New York: HarperCollins, 1996.

———. "Reengineering Work: Don't Automate, Obliterate." *Harvard Business Review,* July–August 1990.

Hammer, Michael, and James A. Champy. *Reengineering the Corporation: A Manifesto for Business Revolution.* New York: Harper Business, 2001.

Marshall, Simon. "Systems Thinking." *Communications International,* November 2001, p. 53.

Rohleder, Thomas, and Edward Silver. "A Tutorial on Business Process Improvement." *Journal of Operations Management* 15 (1997), pp. 139–54.

Rubenstein-Montano, B., J. Liebowitz, J. Buchwalter, D. McCaw, B. Newman, and K. Rebeck. "A Systems Thinking Framework for Knowledge Management." *Decision Support Systems* 31, no. 1 (May 2001), pp. 5–16.

Senge, Peter M. *The Fifth Discipline: The Art and Practice of the Learning Organization.* New York: Doubleday, 1990.

Smetzer, Judy. "Systems Thinking: Tap into Staff Creativity for Innovation." *AHA News* 37, no. 40 (October 8, 2001), p. 5.

Taylor, Frederick W. *Scientific Management.* New York: Harper Bros., 1911.

Zemke, Ron. "Systems Thinking." *Training* 38, no. 2 (February 2001), pp. 40–43.

Part **Three**

Quality

8. Managing Quality

9. Quality Control and Improvement

Quality is one of the objectives of operations and one of the four decision-making responsibilities. To meet the quality objective, it is important to manage and control all aspects of quality. Chapter 8 begins this part with a discussion of managing quality, and Chapter 9 addresses quality control and improvement.

The main contribution of Part Three is a broad treatment of quality, which includes management, planning, and policy concerns in addition to the more traditional statistical topics. In practice, quality is primarily a management problem, and statistical methods are used to achieve continuous improvement of a stable system.

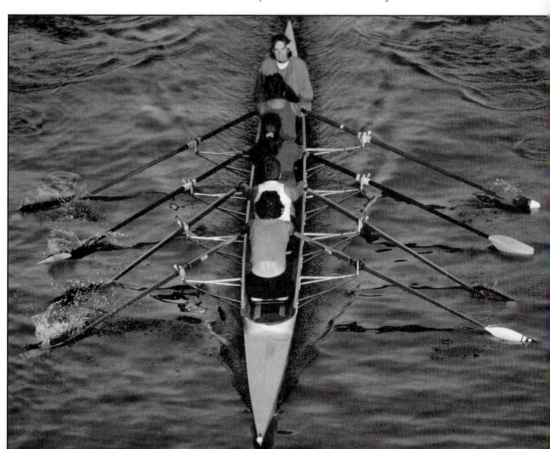

Chapter **Eight**

Managing Quality

Chapter outline

Quality is one of the four key objectives of operations, along with cost, flexibility, and delivery. While quality management is cross-functional in nature and involves the entire organization, operations has a special responsibility to produce a quality product for the customer. This requires the cooperation of the entire organization and careful attention to management and control of quality. This chapter discusses the management of quality, and the next chapter deals with quality control.

There has been tremendous interest in managing quality in recent years. One can hardly pick up a newspaper without reading about the Baldrige Award, ISO 9000, Six Sigma, or the approach used by a particular company to improve its quality. These subjects are treated here along with other aspects of managing for quality.[1]

Quality management has had many different meanings over the years. In the early 1900s, quality meant inspection, which was the primary method used to ensure quality products. In the 1940s, quality took on a statistical connotation as statistical methods were first used to control quality within the natural variation of the process. Statistics pioneers such as Shewhart, Dodge, Romig, and Nelson developed statistical control charts and other methods to maintain a process within a state of statistical control and thus reduce the amount of inspection required. In the 1960s, the meaning of the term "quality management" was

---

[1] For a comprehensive searchable bibliography on quality go to the Web site www.carlsonschool.umn.edu/jurancenter/bodyofknowledge.

The Ritz-Carlton Hotel Company, L.L.C., is a premier hotel management company that develops and operates 57 luxury hotels and resorts worldwide. The company targets primarily industry executives, meeting planners, and prestigious travelers. It employs 28,000 people who are highly trained and motivated to provide quality service. The Ritz-Carlton Hotel Company, now owned by Marriott, has won numerous quality awards and is the only company to win two Malcolm Baldrige Awards.

Ritz-Carlton translates customer requirements into employee requirements through its Gold Standards and its strategic planning process. They have taken the things their customers want most and come up with the simplest ways to provide them. Ritz-Carlton's data show that its employees' understanding of the Gold Standards is directly correlated with guest satisfaction.

Employees respond to a customer's requirements at both the team and individual levels. They provide highly personal, individual service. Customer likes and dislikes are captured and entered into a computerized guest history that provides information on the personal preferences of hundreds of thousands of repeat Ritz-Carlton guests. When a customer returns, the information is provided to the employees serving that customer. Service is then delivered at the lowest possible levels in the organization.

If an employee detects a dislike or problem, the employee is empowered to spend up to $2,000 on the spot to make the customer happy, or the employee can call on any other employee to assist. This is called lateral service. Such a system depends on well-trained, perceptive, and motivated employees along with a well-defined service delivery system. With more than a million customer contacts on a busy day, Ritz-Carlton understands that its customer and quality requirements must be driven by each individual employee at the lowest level of the organization.

Based on results, the Ritz-Carlton hotels are doing an exceptional job of translating customer requirements into employee behavior and excellent systems. Ninety-seven percent of Ritz-Carlton's customers report having a "memorable experience" while staying in one of their hotels.

Source: Adapted from Stephen George and Arnold Weimerskirch (1998); and www.ritzcarlton.com (2005). Logo reprinted with permission. All rights reserved.

expanded to include the entire organization as all functions helped in designing and producing quality. Quality was not seen as just an act of production; rather, it was something the entire organization should strive to provide for the customer. Now, quality is taking on a broader meaning, including continuous improvement, competitive advantage, and customer focus. The Operations Leader box shows how Ritz-Carlton Hotel, twice a winner of the Malcolm Baldrige National Quality Award, is implementing modern quality principles.

8.1 QUALITY DEFINITIONS

Quality is defined here as "meeting, or exceeding, customer requirements now and in the future." This means that the product or service is fit for the customer's use.

Fitness for use is related to benefits received by the customer and to customer satisfaction. Only the customer, not the producer, can determine it.

Customer satisfaction is a relative concept that varies from one customer to another. Also, a customer may be satisfied with today's products but not satisfied in the future. For example, while one customer may consider a Ford automobile

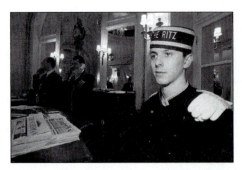

RITZ-CARLTON. Any of the "Ladies and Gentlemen of the Ritz-Carlton" can spend up to $2,000 to immediately correct a guest's problem or handle a complaint. Its employees are the key factor in Ritz-Carlton's receipt of two Malcolm Baldrige National Quality Awards and the highest guest satisfaction level in the luxury hotel industry. © Doug Scott/AGE Fotostock

perfectly satisfactory, another may not. But if the Ford customer wins the lottery, the Ford may no longer be satisfactory; now the customer may prefer a Mercedes or a Jaguar. Each person defines quality in relation to his or her own expectations at a particular point in time.

From the producer's viewpoint, variation from specifications cannot be tolerated. The producer must specify quality attributes of the product or service as carefully as possible and then strive to meet those specifications while improving the process over time. Whether the resulting product meets the customer's requirements or not will then be judged by the customer.

Producers should continuously strive to improve quality, that is, doing a better job of meeting customer needs by reducing variability in all processes and by introducing new products when needed. **Continuous improvement** is a never-ending process and is driven by knowledge and problem solving. As producers gain a better understanding of customer expectations, and as better technology becomes available, quality can be continuously improved.

Whether the product is a service or a good, the following dimensions of quality may be defined:

- Quality of design
- Quality of conformance
- The "abilities"
- Field service

Quality of design is determined before the product is produced. This determination is usually the primary responsibility of a cross-functional product design team, including members from marketing, engineering, operations, and other functions.

Quality of design is determined by market research, design concept, and specifications. Market research is ordinarily aimed at assessing customer needs. Since there are different ways to meet these needs, a particular design concept must be developed. For example, the customer may need inexpensive and energy-efficient transportation—a need that can be met by a large number of different automobiles, each representing a different design concept. The design concept then results in a set of specifications for the product, for example, a blueprint, bill of materials, or service specification.

Quality of conformance means producing a product to meet the specifications. When the product conforms to specifications, operations considers it a quality product regardless of the quality of the design specifications. For example, an inexpensive pair of shoes will have high quality if they are made according to specifications, and they will have low quality if they do not meet specifications. Quality of design and quality of conformance thus represent two different uses of the term "quality."

Another aspect of quality involves the so-called abilities: availability, reliability, and maintainability. Each of these terms has a time dimension and thus extends the meaning of quality beyond the beginning or starting quality level. The addition of time to the definition of quality is, of course, necessary to reflect continued satisfaction by the customer.

Availability defines the continuity of service to the customer. A product is available if it is in an operational state and not down for repairs or maintenance. In the military, availability is equated with operational readiness. Availability can be measured quantitatively as follows:

$$\text{Availability} = \frac{\text{uptime}}{\text{uptime} + \text{downtime}}$$

Reliability refers to the length of time that a product can be used before it fails. Formally speaking, reliability is the probability that a product will function for a specified period of time without failure. The reliability of a light bulb for 1,000 hours might, for example, be 80 percent. In this case, if many light bulbs are tested for 1,000 hours, 80 percent of them will remain lighted the entire time and 20 percent will fail within the 1,000 hours. The reliability of a product is also related to mean time between failure (MTBF), which is just the average time that the product functions from one failure to the next. The longer the MTBF, the more reliable the product.

Maintainability refers to the restoration of a product or service once it has failed. All customers consider maintenance or repairs a nuisance. Thus, a high degree of maintainability is desired so that a product can be restored to use quickly. For example, the Caterpillar Company supports excellent maintainability by supplying spare parts anywhere in the world within 48 hours. Maintainability can be measured by the mean time to repair (MTTR) the product.

Availability, then, is a combination of reliability and maintainability. If a product is high in both reliability and maintainability, it will also be high in availability. The above relationship for availability can be restated in terms of MTBF and MTTR:

$$\text{Availability} = \frac{\text{MTBF}}{\text{MTBF} + \text{MTTR}}$$

For example, if a product has an MTBF of eight hours and an MTTR of two hours each time it fails, then its availability will be 80 percent.

Field service, the last dimension of quality, represents warranty and repair or replacement of the product after it has been sold. Field service is also called customer service, sales service, or just service. Field service is intangible, since it is related to such variables as promptness, competence, and integrity. The customer expects that any problems will be corrected quickly, in a satisfactory manner, and with a high degree of honesty and courtesy.

The four different dimensions of quality are summarized in Figure 8.1.[2] As can be seen, quality is more than just good product design; it extends to quality control of production, quality over the life of the product, and quality of field service after the sale.

8.2 SERVICE QUALITY

The definition and measurement of **service quality** is quite different from manufacturing quality. As defined in Chapter 5, service quality has dimensions of the facilitating good, tangible (explicit) service, and psychological (implicit) service. While the facilitating good quality can be measured using the dimensions of manufacturing, the tangible and psychological dimensions of service quality require different measurements.

---

[2] These dimensions are closely related to Garvin's (1987) well-known dimensions of quality.

FIGURE 8.1
Different types of
quality.

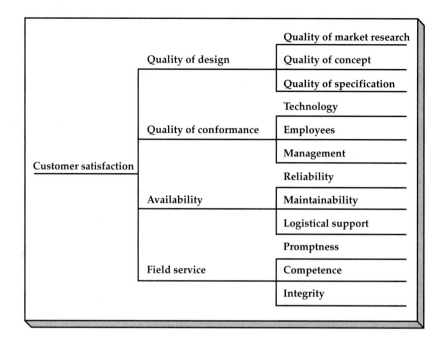

Manufacturing measurements can be largely objective while many service measures are perceptual or subjective. For example, manufacturing design quality can be measured by the product features offered such as the speed of acceleration of an automobile and its normal braking distance. The conformance quality can be measured by the cost of scrap and rework in the factory. While not everything is measured objectively in manufacturing, service quality is the opposite where most measures are subjective.

The most popular measure of service quality is called **SERVQUAL**.[3] It is measured by a customer questionnaire based on five perceptual measures of service:

1. **Tangibles.** The appearance of the company's physical facilities, equipment, and personnel. If a restaurant, for example, is dirty, not presentable and the employees are disheveled looking the tangible quality will be low.

2. **Reliability.** The ability of the company to perform the promised service dependably and accurately without errors. For example, if a restaurant takes a reservation for 7:00 P.M. and you are not seated promptly or they bring the wrong meal, the reliability will be low. Note that reliability for service (which is more accurately called conformance) is defined differently than reliability for manufacturing.

3. **Responsiveness.** The willingness of the company to provide service that is prompt and helpful to the customer. In the restaurant, for example, the meal should be provided in a timely fashion and with help when needed to understand the menu.

4. **Assurance.** The knowledge and courtesy of the company's employees and their ability to convey trust and confidence. In the restaurant example, does the server know the menu and is the server courteous in providing the service?

5. **Empathy.** The caring, individualized attention the company provides to its customers. Does the server in the restaurant help each customer and show concern for the customer?

[3] Parasuraman et al. (1991, 1988).

As can be seen, these dimensions of service are very different from manufacturing and reflect the close interaction that the employees have with the customer in service delivery.

SERVQUAL uses a questionnaire consisting of 22 items (or questions) that in aggregate measure the above five dimensions. Service quality is based on the gap (or mathematical difference) between what the customer expects on each dimension and what is provided. For example, if the customer doesn't expect much empathy, then the quality can be high even though not much empathy is provided. The use of gaps as a measure of service quality has been vigorously debated. While some argue the perceived level of service provided should simply measure service quality, others claim the gap between what is provided and what is expected is a better measure of quality. Although the five dimensions of SERVQUAL have a high level of acceptance for overall quality measurement, the specifics of SERVQUAL measurement have been hotly debated in the literature.[4] Nevertheless SERVQUAL is widely used in practice to measure retail services such as banking, telephone service, and repair services.

8.3 QUALITY PLANNING, CONTROL, AND IMPROVEMENT

In this section we will explain how the dimensions of manufacturing or service quality can be part of a process to manage quality. The process of quality planning, control, and improvement requires a continuous interaction between the customer, operations, and other parts of the organization. Figure 8.2 illustrates

[4] L. J. Morrison Coulthard, 2004.

FIGURE 8.2 The quality cycle.

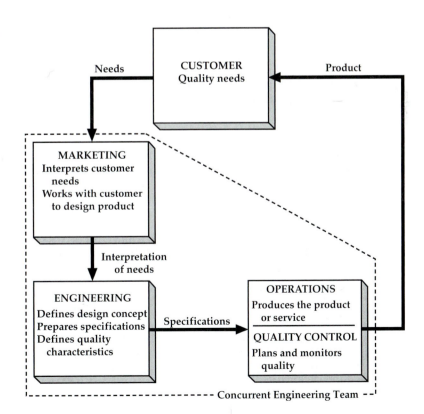

how these interactions occur through a **quality cycle.** The customer needs are determined, usually through the marketing function. These needs are either expressed directly by the customer or discovered through a process of market research. Engineering, in conjunction with other departments, designs a product to meet those needs or works with the customer on design specifications that fit within current or future production capabilities. Quality function deployment covered in Chapter 3 is a useful technique for aligning the voice of the customer (customer needs) with the engineering specifications.

Once the design concept and specifications have been completed, the quality of design has been established. Operations, as part of the quality team, then produces the product as specified. Operations must continually ensure that the product is produced as specified by insisting on quality of conformance. This is ordinarily done through proper training, supervision, machine maintenance, and operator inspections. In addition to meeting specifications, operations should strive to reduce the variance of its processes and products over time. In this way continuous improvement occurs.

Figure 8.3 is a description of the quality cycle for a mass transit system. In this case, a planning agency, in place of marketing, interprets customer needs. Another planner, working in greater detail, then determines the design concept and the specifications for service. The operations function delivers the service, and the public then restates its needs or confirms that the present service is satisfactory. The quality cycle should exist in every organization to ensure that all aspects of quality are planned, controlled, and continually improved. Feedback from the customer is essential to produce quality products and services.

The implementation of planning, control, and improvement of quality through the quality cycle requires this sequence of steps:

1. Define quality attributes on the basis of customer needs.
2. Decide how to measure each attribute.
3. Set quality standards.
4. Establish appropriate tests for each standard.
5. Find and correct causes of poor quality.
6. Continue to make improvements.

FIGURE 8.3 The quality cycle in a mass transit system.

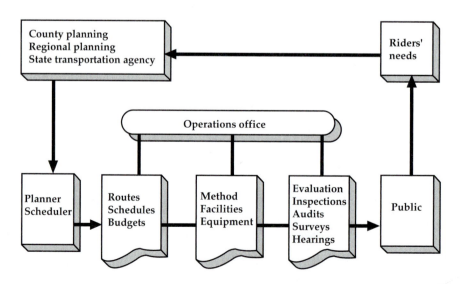

The Operations Leader box describes how this six-step approach is used in practice at Motorola, a Baldrige Award winner.

Planning for quality must always start with the **product attributes.** The quality planner determines which attributes are important to customer satisfaction and which are not. For example, the manufacturer of L'eggs panty hose has determined three important quality attributes for its product: (1) a comfortable fit, (2) an attractive appearance, and (3) a wear life that is considered reasonable by the customer. It has also decided that the correct amount of material in various parts of the panty hose will provide a comfortable fit; that fabric dyed in popular colors and free from defects will provide an attractive appearance; and that choice yarns and selected stitch formations will provide acceptable wear life.

OPERATIONS LEADER

Motorola's Quality Improvement Process

Motorola is a leading manufacturer of semiconductors and related electronics applications, including paging systems, cellular telephones, and two-way communications radios. It employs more than 145,000 employees around the world who are committed to continuous quality improvement. Motorola was the first winner of the Malcolm Baldrige National Quality Award and has been named as the country's top quality management practitioner by the Business Roundtable.

Motorola's fundamental objective is total customer satisfaction. To reach this objective it has five initiatives in place:

- Produce products and services to a Six Sigma standard (no more than 3.4 defects per million actions).
- Reduce total cycle time in all activities.
- Lead in the area of products, manufacturing, and the environment.
- Improve profitability.
- Provide a creative, cooperative workplace in which employees are empowered.

These initiatives for customer satisfaction are led by all levels of management from the bottom to the top.

Motorola is a strong believer in the value of education for all employees. To empower employees, they have found the need for continuous education. Employees continually renew their skills and knowledge in quality, design, manufacturing, and their own specializations.

Motorola believes that it has been successful because of its management process. Simply put, the process is (1) have a set of metrics, (2) determine results, (3) pick a problem, (4) address the problem, (5) analyze the solution, and (6) move on. This process is far from earthshaking; it's just an application of continuous improvement and the quality planning and control cycle.

Motorola's stretch goals are 10 times improvement in two years in whatever is being measured. If cycle time for an activity is 100 days, it would be cut to 10 days. If defects were 100 parts per million (ppm), they would be cut to 10 ppm.

At Motorola all employees take responsibility for quality. Quality is not an assignable task. It must be rooted and institutionalized in every process. Motorola believes that it is everyone's responsibility to improve the system for total customer satisfaction.

Source: Adapted from Karen Bemowski, "Motorola's Fountain of Youth," *Quality Progress,* October 1995, pp. 29–31; Stephen George and Arnold Weimerskirch, *Total Quality Management,* New York: John Wiley and Sons, 1998; and Motorola Web site: www.Motorola.com (2005). MOTOROLA and the stylized M logo are registered in the U.S. Patent and Trademark office. © Motorola Inc. 2001. The Motorola logo is used with the permission of Motorola, Inc.

A method must then be devised to test and **measure quality** for each of the product attributes. For example, the manufacturer of L'eggs has developed a special cross-stretcher that can be used to test the strength of its product, and this is used on a certain percentage of all its panty hose. L'eggs are also inspected visually for fabric defects, seaming defects, and shade variations.

After deciding on the measurement techniques to use, the quality planner should set **standards** that describe the amount of quality required on each attribute. Usually these standards are stated as tolerances (± quantities), or minimum and maximum acceptable limits. Standards can also be set as desired targets. For example, a standard on L'eggs panty hose is the amount of pressure that the garment must withstand on the cross-stretcher.

After standards have been set, a **testing program** should be established. In the case of L'eggs, this program is based on sampling procedures since it would be far too costly to test and inspect each of the millions of pairs of panty hose produced each year. How such testing and inspection plans can be set up will be treated in the next chapter.

It is not enough simply to inspect the products for defects. As the saying goes, "You cannot inspect quality into a product, you must build it in." Upon discovering defects, quality personnel and workers should find the **underlying causes** and correct them. Causes of poor quality could include improper raw materials, lack of training, unclear procedures, a faulty machine, and so on. When the causes of poor quality are regularly found and corrected, the production system will be under constant control and improvement will be possible.

An even better approach is to prevent errors from occurring in the first place. This requires designing products and internal procedures that are **foolproof,** working with suppliers to prevent errors, training employees before problems occur, and performing preventive machine maintenance. Nevertheless, when errors do occur, they need to be quickly corrected and the system itself changed to prevent errors of the same type from recurring.

The concept of foolproofing was first developed in the 1960s by Shigeo Shingo, who worked for Toyota Motors in Japan. It was called *Poka-yoke* (pronounced poh-kah-yoh-kay), which means "mistake proofing" in Japanese. The idea of Poka-yoke is to design the product and process so it is impossible to make mistakes or they are easily detected when mistakes do occur. For example, your microwave won't start if the door is open, and your car doors won't lock when the key is in the ignition. Parts should be designed so they cannot be put on backward or left off the product by mistake. Service should be designed so that the customer gets exactly what he or she ordered. If the error cannot be prevented from occurring, it should be made easy to detect. This is the Poka-yoke approach.

8.4   THE QUALITY GURUS

Now that we have defined quality and the general theory of planning, control, and improvement as it applies to quality, we turn to different approaches for managing quality. This discussion begins with a brief historical review of the approaches advocated by the so-called **quality gurus:** Deming, Juran, and Crosby. We will then describe ISO 9000 and the Baldrige approach to quality management, which are in wide use in industry today.

W. Edwards Deming

W. Edwards **Deming** emphasized the role that management should take in quality improvement. Deming defined quality as continuous improvement of a stable system. This definition emphasizes two things. First, all systems (administrative, design, production, and sales) must be stable in a statistical sense. This requires that measurements be taken of quality attributes throughout the company and monitored over time. If these measurements have a constant variance around a constant average, the system is stable. The second aspect of Deming's definition is continuous improvement of the various systems to reduce variation and better meet customer needs.

Deming expressed his philosophy toward quality in his famous **14 points,** shown in Table 8.1. He stressed that top executives should manage for the long run and not sacrifice quality for short-run profits. Deming argued that excessive attention to quarterly profit reports and short-run objectives distracts top management from focusing on customer service and long-run quality improvement. He also argued, as others do, that management should cease dependence on mass inspection to achieve quality and stress prevention of defects instead. Deming suggested that this should be accomplished by training all employees, good supervision, and use of statistical procedures.

Deming went on to exhort management to break down barriers between departments and to encourage people to work together to produce quality products and services. He thought that many of the work standards, individual performance pay systems, and quotas companies use get in the way of cooperation among individuals and departments and thus impede quality improvement.

TABLE 8.1
Deming's 14 Management Principles

Requirements for a business whose management plans to remain competitive in providing goods and services that will have a market.	
1. Create constancy of purpose toward improvement of products and services with the aim of being competitive and staying in business for long-run, rather than short-run, profits.	7. Focus management and supervisors on leadership of their employees to help them do a better job.
2. Adopt the new philosophy by refusing to allow commonly accepted levels of mistakes, defects, delays, and errors. Accept the need for change.	8. Drive out fear. Don't blame employees for "systems problem." Encourage effective two-way communications. Eliminate management by control.
3. Cease dependence on mass inspection. Rely instead on building quality into the product in the first place and on statistical means for controlling and improving quality.	9. Break down barriers between departments. Encourage teamwork among different areas such as research, design, manufacturing, and sales.
4. End the practice of awarding business on the basis of price tag alone. Instead minimize total cost. Reduce the number of suppliers by eliminating those who cannot provide evidence of statistical control of processes.	10. Eliminate programs, enhortations, and slogans that ask for new levels of productivity without providing better methods.
5. Improve constantly, and forever, systems of production to improve quality and productivity and thus constantly reduce costs.	11. Eliminate arbitrary quotas, work standards, and objectives that interfere with quality. Instead, substitute leadership and continuous improvement of work processes.
6. Institute training on the job for all employees.	12. Remove barriers (poor systems and poor management) that rob people of pride in their work.
	13. Encourage life-long education and self-improvement of all employees.
	14. Put everyone to work on implementing these 14 points.

Adapted from W. Edwards Deming, *Out of the Crisis,* Cambridge, MA: MIT Center for Advanced Engineering Study, 1986.

Deming was a strong advocate of statistical process control ideas that are covered in the next chapter. Quality cannot be improved by trying harder. Workers and managers must have the proper tools to identify causes of variation, to control variation, and to reduce variation in the product.

Deming and the other gurus are advocates of the idea that most quality problems are caused by poor systems, not by the workers. They argue that quality problems should not be blamed on the workers; rather, management must change the system to improve quality. Quality responsibility must be accepted by all levels of management.

Deming successfully taught his ideas to the Japanese and is credited, along with Juran, with helping to improve quality in Japanese industry. The Japanese attribute much of their success to American ideas, which they have thoroughly implemented. Lately, American industry is also rediscovering many of these basic ideas and is once again implementing quality ideas as a key to survival and success.

Joseph Juran

The textbook author (left) learns from Joseph Juran at a conference.
Courtesy of Roger Schroeder

Juran originated the idea of the **quality trilogy:** planning, control, and improvement of quality. In the planning area he suggested that companies should identify the major business goals, customers, and products required. New products should

be introduced only after they are carefully tested and when they meet a verified customer need. He also suggested that much of quality improvement requires careful planning to ensure that the most important quality problems are attacked first—"the vital few."

Juran stressed control of quality through use of statistical methods covered in the next chapter. He argued that management should institute the procedures and methods needed to ensure quality and then work to continuously keep the system in control. Like Deming, Juran believed strongly in the statistical approach to quality as a way of achieving process control.

The third leg of the quality trilogy is improvement. Juran suggested both breakthrough improvement and continuous improvement of processes. He argued that this could be done once the system was brought under statistical control. Juran also believed that training and involvement of all employees was necessary to ensure continuous quality improvement.

Phillip Crosby

Phillip **Crosby** advocated that organizations should seek to produce **zero defects** or to "make it right the first time." He argued that we are conditioned to believe it is all right to make errors. Crosby pointed to such common sayings as "To err is human," "Everybody makes mistakes," and "Nobody's perfect," all of which serve to justify the lack of conformance in the work place. The problem is further compounded by inspectors whose job it is to catch the errors made by workers.

We are conditioned to expect errors in the work place but not in other forms of human activity. For example, when we attend a concert we do not expect the soloists to play a certain percentage of bad notes. Why should we settle for poor quality in the work place? The usual reply is that high quality costs too much. But in fact high quality may cost less. Crosby argued that it is cheaper to make the product right the first time than to correct errors or to pay for scrap, rework, or failures in the field. Table 8.2 gives many examples of when 99.9 percent quality is not good enough.

TABLE 8.2
When 99.9 Percent Quality Is Not Enough

If 99.9 percent quality standards were in effect, the following would happen:

- Two million documents would be lost by the IRS each year.
- 22,000 checks would be deducted from the wrong bank account.
- 1,314 phone calls would be misrouted each day.
- 12 babies would be given to the wrong parents each day.
- Two plane landings daily at O'Hare would be unsafe.

Source: Natalie Gabel, "Is 99.9% Good Enough?" *Training Magazine,* March 1991, pp. 40–41.

Of course, it may be unrealistic to expect that the delivered product will literally have zero defects; but according to the zero-defects approach, everyone should strive toward this goal. Even when they do, however, a few defective items may be produced and shipped to the customer because of unknown (random) causes of process variation. However, the defects may be measured in parts per million (ppm) or parts per billion, which is nearly zero defects for all practical purposes. When the zero-defects approach is being used, the workforce should strive to make the product exactly to specifications or get the specifications changed. No worker should knowingly produce defects on the grounds that it is too expensive to do it right the first time.

Crosby defined a zero-defects program in terms of 14 implementation steps that require cross-functional participation. These steps provide a basis for quality improvement regardless of the particular quality philosophy used, since they stress management commitment, training, worker involvement, measurement of quality, and prevention of defects in all parts of the business.

Crosby's 14-step program is very extensive and time-consuming. It is not simply a motivational effort, but rather an educational program aimed at improving quality. This requires not only a change in employee and management attitudes but a system to identify and remove causes of errors. The Crosby approach is organizationwide and improves quality while simultaneously reducing costs.

While the specific details of quality improvement might vary among the three gurus, they have much in common. Some of their common ideas and those of other major contributors to the quality field are shown in Table 8.3.

TABLE 8.3
Changing Quality Assumptions

From	To
Reactive	Proactive
Inspection	Prevention
Meet the specifications	Continuous improvement
Product-oriented	Process-oriented
Blame placing	Problem solving
Quality versus schedule	Quality *and* schedule
Cost *or* quality	Cost *and* quality
Operations only	Marketing, engineering, and operations
Predominantly blue-collar caused	Predominantly white-collar caused
Defects should be hidden	Defects should be highlighted
Quality department has quality problems	Purchasing, R&D, marketing, and operations have quality problems
Subordinated to management team	Part of management team
General managers not evaluated on quality	Quality performance part of general manager review
Quality costs more	Quality costs less
Quality is technical	Quality is managerial
Schedule first	Quality first

As can be seen from the table, there is a common thread running through modern quality thinking.

8.5 ISO 9000 STANDARDS

ISO 9000 is one of the major approaches that companies are using to ensure quality today. When it was first established in 1987, ISO 9000 was oriented toward compliance, or what we have termed conformance quality. Customer needs were not included in the original ISO 9000 standard—you could make any product you liked, even if it did not sell—as long as the company had a quality system to ensure that it could make what it said it could. In 2000 the ISO 9000 standard was revised to include customer requirements, continuous improvement, and management leadership to ensure that quality meets customer needs and not just conformance to specifications.

ISO (International Organization for Standardization) is an international body consisting of members from 155 countries. The ISO 9000 standards are meant to describe how a company should go about ensuring quality whether the company is large or small and whether the product is complex or simple. ISO 9000 standards also apply to services and to software development.

The ISO 9000 standards specify that a company must have a quality system in place, including procedures, policies, and training to provide quality that consistently meets customer requirements. A quality manual and careful record keeping is usually required as part of the documentation. ISO 9000 requires that the company have process flowcharts, operator instructions, inspection and testing methods, job descriptions, organization charts, measures of customer satisfaction, and continuous improvement processes. It is also expected that employees will be trained in the procedures and actually follow them in practice. To ensure compliance, certified ISO 9000 registrars audit the organization and determine whether the company has a well-documented quality system, whether training is completed, and whether the actual system in use conforms to the formal system description. If no discrepancies are found, the registrar, who is external to the company, will then certify the company's plant or facility. The product itself is not certified as having high quality; only the process for making the product is certified. The ISO 9000 certification must be periodically renewed via return audits by a registrar.

ISO 9000 has had a major impact on worldwide quality practice. Many companies are requiring ISO 9000 certification as a condition for doing business. The European Community has adopted ISO 9000 as a standard for selling in their markets, and compliance with ISO 9000 is required by some European customers. ISO 9000 certification is catching on not only in Europe; companies in many other countries, including the U.S.A., are also requiring ISO 9000 certification of their suppliers.

ISO 9000 does not provide a complete quality system because it does not address competitive strategy, information systems, and business results. A company can be making a product that satisfies the customer for a shrinking market and going out of business and still be ISO 9000 certified. Nevertheless, ISO 9000 is a good first step that addresses the fundamental processes needed to ensure a quality product and high levels of customer satisfaction. The Baldrige system has similar requirements to ISO 9000, but strategy, information systems, and business results are also required.

8.6 MALCOLM BALDRIGE AWARD

MALCOLM BALDRIGE NATIONAL QUALITY AWARD. Courtesy of the United States Department of Commerce, The National Institute of Standards and Technology

The U.S. Congress established the Malcolm Baldrige National Quality Award in 1987 to promote better quality management practices and improved quality results by American industry. The criteria for the award have gained wide acceptance and have become a de facto standard for "best quality practice" in America. We will summarize the Baldrige criteria as a framework for evaluating and implementing quality principles and concepts.

Each year, the **Baldrige Award** is given to at most two companies in each of three categories: manufacturing, service, and small business. In 2000 the award was also made available for education and health care organizations. A few of the past winners are Motorola, Milliken & Co., Federal Express, Sunny Fresh Foods, Ritz-Carlton, 3M, IBM, University of Wisconsin at Stout, and Pearl River School District. To win this award these organizations, or the subsidiary that won the award, exhibited high levels of quality management practice and performance results as indicated by the Baldrige criteria.

The **Baldrige criteria** recognize quality efforts that have senior management leadership, business results, employee involvement, control of internal processes, strong customer satisfaction, and so on. The specific categories of quality evaluated by the Baldrige examiners are listed in Table 8.4. These seven Baldrige categories are judged by a self-evaluation report prepared by each applicant for the award and a site visit by Baldrige examiners for those applicants who pass an initial screening of their self-evaluation report.

The Baldrige criteria are based on 1,000 points total, which are allocated among the seven categories shown in Table 8.4. The first category, leadership (120 points), is scored based on senior management commitment, active involvement by all managers in the process, and the extent to which quality values have permeated the entire organization. It also includes societal responsibilities and community involvement, which ensure a "quality company."

The second category, strategic planning (85 points), is the glue that holds the quality effort together. Successful applicants have established high-level goals and plans for quality that are specific and implemented. Often, the strategic plans for quality management will be indistinguishable from the company's strategic plan.

Category three is customer and market focus (85 points). Winning companies collect objective customer data from a variety of sources, including focus groups, market research surveys, and one-on-one contacts. The information should be acted upon and used to direct the company toward customer needs and satisfied customers. Baldrige winners strive to delight their customers, not just minimally satisfy them. They often exceed customer expectations and anticipate customer needs.

Category four is measurement, analysis, and knowledge management (90 points). This category includes decision making based on hard data, sometimes called "management by fact." The company's database should be accessible to

TABLE 8.4
Malcolm Baldrige
National Quality
Award: Criteria for
Performance
Excellence, 2005

2005 Categories and Items	Point Values
1 Leadership	**120**
1.1 Senior Leadership	70
1.2 Governance and Social Responsibilities	50
2 Strategic Planning	**85**
2.1 Strategy Development	40
2.2 Strategy Deployment	45
3 Customer and Market Focus	**85**
3.1 Customer and Market Knowledge	40
3.2 Customer Relationships and Satisfaction	45
4 Measurement, Analysis, and Knowledge Management	**90**
4.1 Measurement, Analysis, and Review of Organizational Performance	45
4.2 Information and Knowledge Management	45
5 Human Resource Focus	**85**
5.1 Work Systems	35
5.2 Employee Learning and Motivation	25
5.3 Employee Well-Being and Satisfaction	25
6 Process Management	**85**
6.1 Value Creation Processes	45
6.2 Support Processes and Operational Planning	40
7 Business Results	**450**
7.1 Product and Service Outcomes	100
7.2 Customer-Focused Results	70
7.3 Financial and Market Results	70
7.4 Human Resource Results	70
7.5 Organizational Effectiveness Results	70
7.6 Leadership and Social Responsibility Results	70
TOTAL POINTS	**1000**

Source: U.S. Department of Commerce, 2005.

employees and should have comprehensive information on suppliers, internal processes, and customers. The information system must also be integrated and used for decision making in the company.

The fifth category is human resource focus (85 points), a very broad and extensive area. Human resource focus includes employee involvement, continuous education and training, teamwork, and decision making by the workers. Past Baldrige winners have been strong advocates of human resources as the basis for all quality improvement efforts.

Process management (85 points), the sixth category, includes process definition, documentation, statistical process control, and the tools of quality improvement. The poorest performing companies have little understanding of their processes, have not integrated them, and have not defined and controlled them.

The seventh, and last, Baldrige criterion, business results, receives 450 points. This category includes customer-focused results, product and service outcomes, financial and market results, human resource results, organization effectiveness results, and leadership and social responsibility results. Standard quality measures such as percent defective product, customer returns, and on-time deliveries are considered, along with profitability, return on investment, and market share. Successful companies can demonstrate improvement trends over time, not stellar results in one year only.

These seven categories represent a comprehensive framework for quality management and performance improvement in general. No standard approach is required to win the Baldrige Award. Each organization is free to choose its own specific techniques and approaches within the overall goals and criteria described above, and there is enormous variety among the past winners. This is a strength of the Baldrige Award—that it does not require a particular dogma but allows flexibility in defining "good quality management" by individual companies [George and Weimerskirch (1998)].

Many companies are now using the Baldrige criteria as a vehicle for internal assessment of their quality and performance improvement systems. They train their own managers to make Baldrige assessments of other divisions. The objective is not to win an award but to diagnose strengths and weaknesses of their management system in the various divisions of the company.

As noted by the breadth of the criteria, the Baldrige Award represents more than mere quality assurance and amounts to a comprehensive system for management of the company. Actually, quality cannot be isolated from management, and progressive management is needed to consistently produce a product or service that meets true customer needs now and in the future.

8.7 QUALITY AND FINANCIAL PERFORMANCE

Quality and financial performance are intimately related. First, we consider the relationship between quality and cost. A powerful idea in the area of quality is to calculate the **cost of quality,** which includes prevention, appraisal, internal failure, and external failure categories. All these, except prevention, are costs of not doing things right the first time. By assigning a cost to poor quality, it can be managed and controlled like any other cost. Since managers speak the language of money, putting quality in cost terms offers a powerful means of communication and control.

Most companies have no idea how much they spend to manage quality. Those who have measured it find that the cost of quality is about 30 percent of sales, with ranges from 20 to 40 percent. Since these figures are two or three times greater than profit margins in many companies, a reduction in the cost of quality can lead to a significant improvement in profit. The best-managed companies have been able to reduce their costs of quality from 30 percent of sales to as little as 3 percent over a period of several years. This has been done while improving the quality of the product. The potential for doing this in most companies is untapped.

The cost of quality may be divided into two components: **control costs** and **failure costs.** The control costs are related to activities that remove defects from the production stream. This can be done in two ways: by prevention and by appraisal. Prevention costs include activities such as quality planning, new-product reviews, training, and engineering analysis. These activities occur prior to production and are aimed at preventing defects before they occur. The other category of control costs comprises appraisal or inspection aimed at eliminating defects after they occur but before the products reach the customer.

TABLE 8.5
Costs of Quality

Prevention Costs

Quality planning: Costs of preparing an overall plan, numerous specialized plans, quality manuals, procedures.

New-product review: Review or prepare quality specifications for new products, evaluation of new designs, preparation of tests and experimental programs, evaluation of vendors, marketing studies to determine customers' quality requirements.

Training: Developing and conducting training programs.

Process planning: Design and develop process control devices.

Quality data: Collecting data, data analysis, reporting.

Improvement projects: Planned failure investigations aimed at chronic quality problems.

Appraisal Costs

Incoming materials inspection: The cost of determining quality of incoming raw materials.

Process inspection: All tests, sampling procedures, and inspections done while the product is being made.

Final goods inspection: All inspections or tests conducted on the finished product in the plant or the field.

Quality laboratories: The cost of operating laboratories to inspect materials at all stages of production.

Internal Failure Costs

Scrap: The cost of labor and material for product which cannot be used or sold.

Rework: The cost of redoing product which can be made to conform.

Downgrading: Product which must be sold at less than full value due to quality problems.

Retest: Cost of inspection and tests after rework.

Downtime: Idle facilities and people due to quality failures.

External Failure Costs

Warranty: The cost of refunds, repairing, or replacing products on warranty.

Returned merchandise: Merchandise which is returned to the seller.

Complaints: The cost of settling customer complaints due to poor quality.

Allowances: Cost of concessions made to customers due to substandard quality.

Adapted from J. M. Juran and A. B. Godfrey, eds., *Juran's Quality Handbook*, 5th ed. (New York: McGraw-Hill, 1999).

Failure costs are incurred either during the production process (internal) or after the product is shipped (external). Internal failure costs include such items as scrap, rework, quality downgrading, and machine downtime. External failure costs include warranty charges, returned goods, allowances, and the like. A more complete listing of all these costs is given in Table 8.5.

The cost of quality can be a confusing term. Three of the four costs in Table 8.5 can be called the cost of nonconformance or the **costs of poor quality** (appraisal, internal failure, or external failure). The three costs of poor quality can be reduced by increasing the fourth cost, prevention. Many companies have found that by investing in prevention activities such as training, process planning, and new product review they can then avoid costs that occur later in production (appraisal, internal failure) or after production (external failure). Prevention is a tremendous leverage factor. Suppose for example that a company is spending 2 percent of its sales on prevention and 18 percent on the cost of poor quality (appraisal, internal failure, and external failure). By doubling the amount spent on prevention to 4 percent, suppose the cost of poor quality can be cut in half to 9 percent. Assume additional investments in prevention to a total of 6 percent can further reduce the cost of poor quality to as little as 2 percent. At this point the total cost of quality is only 8 percent of sales instead of 20 percent. It should be noted that the entire 12 percent of sales saved would flow to the bottom line.

A construction company investigated its cost of poor quality and found a total of 72 instances of nonconformance on one highway construction project.[5] These could be classified into the following types of preventable errors.

- Design problems that caused the reworking of a portion of the highway several times.
- Noncompliance by a cement contractor that required repair of the poured concrete.
- Subcontractor problems that resulted in failure to deliver by some subcontractors.

The company found that it could save considerable costs in future projects by seeking to prevent these errors before they occur.

A health care research study estimated that a combination of administrative inefficiencies and overuse and misuse of medical services wastes 30 cents of every dollar spent on health care.[6] These costs can all be considered the costs of poor quality and are preventable. Applying the principles of quality management and control can reduce them.

The cost of quality can be a powerful tool for quality improvement when it is properly used. It focuses management attention on waste due to excess failures or high control costs. It also provides a quantitative basis for monitoring progress in reducing quality costs. The cost of quality is easily understood; it brings quality out of a "goodness" or "value" area that cannot be measured into a dollars-and-cents basis.

Quality improvement programs can also dramatically increase revenues through either a more consistent product or new products or services that better meet customer needs. Improving customer satisfaction can be a powerful driver of revenue and market share when customers receive a product or service that they really like.

The effect of cost reduction *and* revenue improvement is shown in Figure 8.4, which indicates how quality affects financial results. Both conformance quality and design quality affect reduced waste, greater productivity, and greater value.

FIGURE 8.4 How quality contributes to profitability.

Adapted from: Stephen George, and Arnold Weimerskirch, *Total Quality Management* (New York: John Wiley and Sons, 1998).

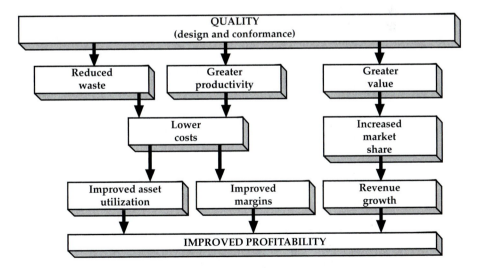

[5] H. Abdul-Rahman, 1995.

[6] C. Gunsauley, 2002.

This creates a chain effect in lowering costs and increased market share, which ultimately results in improved profitability. Both conformance and design quality have significant effects on profit.

8.8 WHY SOME QUALITY IMPROVEMENT EFFORTS FAIL

Quality improvement is a proven strategy that has yielded significant financial benefits for many companies. Yet quality efforts have also failed, or yielded marginal results, in other companies. Some studies have indicated that only one-third of companies had obtained significant results from their quality improvement programs, one-third had achieved moderate results, and one-third were dissatisfied with the results. Why has this happened, and what separates the winners from the losers?

It's not the approach a company uses to improve quality that makes the difference; it's the implementation process. To improve quality, a company must change its values and management philosophy, which is not easy. Brown, Hitchcock, and Willard (1994) describe some of the reasons implementation has failed, as follows.

Managers may continue to focus on short-term financial results to the exclusion of system improvement. Excessive focus on financial results tends to destroy the underlying quality system as layoffs are encountered or training is slashed to improve short-term financial numbers. Quality improvement requires a change in thinking to manage the underlying system and not the immediate financial outcome.

Some managers instinctively blame the employees when there is a quality failure; it doesn't occur to them to look in the mirror. Only managers can change the underlying system that causes the quality problem, not the employees. It is easier for managers to blame someone else than themselves or the system that they control.

There are managers who believe in trade-offs. To them, consistent quality cannot be achieved without sacrificing the schedule or cost. When a decision is required to ship the product or to fix a quality problem, these managers will ship the product and fix it later. They also feel that it is too expensive to have high quality. These managers don't realize they can have it all, if they use consistent quality and prevention as a driver of better results in schedule, flexibility, and cost.

Managers sometimes interfere with true teamwork. Either they don't really delegate decision making to the team or they continue to reward individual performance over team performance. Actually, they should reward teams for what teams do and individuals for what individuals do. The reward system is ingrained in the organization and is one of the most difficult things to change.

Some firms have very sloppy procedures and processes and yet fail to realize how this hurts quality. One example is universities and colleges that have the most intelligent employees in the world and the worst systems for delivery of the educational service. But intelligent employees or good management can't compensate for a bad system.

So, producing quality requires a systems approach to management, which must be driven by customer needs. This approach conflicts with the philosophies and values that some companies have. Quality improvement therefore requires deep cultural change. Executives have to lead by example to make the transformation. A quality improvement program introduced as the "flavor of the month" or a fad program will fail.

The only way to institute true quality improvement is through extensive education of all employees and constant leadership at all levels of management. With this approach, a quality system can be introduced into any service or manufacturing organization, and the financial, human, and market results will be impressive.

8.9 KEY POINTS

The chapter's key points include the following:

- Quality can be defined as meeting, or exceeding, customer requirements now and in the future. There are four dimensions of quality that contribute to customer satisfaction: quality of design, quality of conformance, the "abilities," and field service.

- Five dimensions can define service quality: tangible, reliability, responsiveness, assurance, and empathy. These measures can be obtained by surveying customers.

- There is a cycle of product quality—from customer needs through quality of design, production, quality of conformance, and use by the customer. This cycle is controlled by specifying quality attributes, determining how to measure each attribute, setting quality standards, establishing a testing program, and finding and correcting causes of poor quality. Continuous improvement of the system through prevention of defects is the preferred approach.

- The three quality gurus, Deming, Crosby, and Juran, have taken somewhat different approaches to quality but also have much in common. Deming argued that management needs to change in order for quality to improve. He also advocated the aggressive use of statistical quality control techniques. Juran advocated the quality trilogy: planning, control, and improvement. Crosby emphasized a zero-defects approach or making it right the first time.

- ISO 9000 process certification is a quality approach based on compliance and meeting customer requirements. It requires well-defined and documented procedures along with trained operators who implement them in order to ensure a quality process and a consistent quality product.

- The Baldrige Award recognizes companies that achieve a total quality system as defined and measured by the Baldrige criteria. Criteria specified for the award have become the de facto definition for excellence in management practice.
- Quality can both improve revenues and reduce costs. The cost of quality measures the lack of conformance to customer requirements. Quality costs can be conveniently divided into control costs and failure costs. Control costs are due to prevention or appraisal. Failure costs may be due to internal or external failures.
- Quality improvement efforts fail when management does not lead by example and does not take a systems approach driven by customer needs.

STUDENT INTERNET EXERCISES

1. **The Ritz-Carlton Hotels**
   http://www.ritzcarlton.com

   Access the Ritz-Carlton Web site and find the information on the "Gold Standard." Come to class prepared to discuss the Gold Standard and its relationship to Quality.

2. **Malcolm Baldrige National Quality Award**
   http://www.quality.nist.gov

   Find the latest award winners on this site and write a short report on the approach used by one of the recent winners.

3. **American Society for Quality (ASQ)**
   http://www.asq.org

   Click on the "Books & Publications" heading and find publications of interest to you on quality management. Some suggested topics might be ISO 9000, Baldrige Award, Quality Tools, Basic Concepts, and organizationwide approaches. Write a short report on your findings using the abstracts and articles provided by the search.

Discussion Questions

1. How can quality be measured for the following products?
   a. Telephone service
   b. Automobile repair
   c. Manufacture of ballpoint pens

2. Describe the differences between the quality of design and the quality of conformance.

3. Product A has an MTBF of 30 hours and an MTTR of 5 hours. Product B has an MTBF of 40 hours and an MTTR of 2 hours.
   a. Which product has the higher reliability?
   b. Which product has greater maintainability?
   c. Which product has greater availability?

4. Check the Internet or your library for articles on SERVQUAL. Briefly summarize one of the items that you found in a paragraph or two.

5. Describe service problems that you encountered in a recent service experience. Then categorize the service failures that occurred as tangible, reliability, responsiveness, assurance, or empathy.

6. Suppose you manufacture 10,000 wooden pencils per day. Describe a quality planning and control system for this product, including possible attributes, measures of quality, tests, and so forth.

7. Name some products or services that in your opinion have relatively poor quality.

8. Name some products that have a high degree of quality. Are these products generally associated with successful companies?

9. The following costs have been recorded:

Incoming materials inspection	$20,000
Training of personnel	40,000
Warranty	45,000
Process planning	15,000
Scrap	13,000
Quality laboratory	30,000
Rework	25,000
Allowances	10,000
Complaints	14,000

What are the costs of prevention, appraisal, external failure, and internal failure?

10. How could a zero-defects policy be applied to student term papers?

11. Which of Deming's 14 points do you agree with and which ones do you disagree with?

12. Contrast and compare the Deming, Crosby, and Juran approaches to quality improvement.

13. Critique the seven categories used by the Baldrige Award. Are there some items that you think are missing, or do some categories receive too much weight?

14. How could the Baldrige Award categories be used by a company to improve quality? Explain.

15. Compare the Baldrige-based approach to the use of ISO 9000.

16. Why is ISO 9000 considered a first step, or basic, approach to quality?

17. Which of the four manufacturing quality dimensions are most likely to improve revenue? Which ones are related more to cost reduction or to both revenue and cost?

18. Find an example of a quality failure and determine the reasons for the failure. Use the references at the end of this chapter or recent newspaper or magazine articles to help find an example.

19. Define what is meant by a successful quality improvement implementation effort. How have you defined success?

Selected Bibliography

Aaker, David A. *Baldrige Award Winning Quality: How to Interpret the Baldrige Criteria for Performance Excellence.* Milwaukee, WI: ASQ Quality Press, 2001.

Abdul-Rahman, H. "The Cost of Non-conformance during a Highway Project: A Case Study." *Construction Management and Economics* 13 (1995), pp. 23–32.

Anderson, John C., Manus Rungtusanatham, and Roger G. Schroeder. "A Theory of Quality Management Underlying the Deming Management Method." *Academy of Management Review* 19, no. 3 (1994), pp. 472–509.

Bemowski, Karen. "Motorola's Fountain of Youth." *Quality Progress,* October 1995, pp. 29–31.

Brown, Mark G., Darcy E. Hitchcock, and Marsha L. Willard. *Why TQM Fails and What to Do about It.* Burr Ridge, IL: Irwin, 1994.

Crosby, Philip B. *Quality Is Free.* New York: McGraw-Hill, 1979.

———. *Completeness: Quality for the 21st Century.* New York: Penguin, 1992.

Deming, W. Edwards. *Out of the Crisis.* Cambridge, MA: MIT Press, 1986.

Dimitriades, Zoe S. "Total Involvement in Quality Management." *Team Performance Management* 6, no. 7/8 (2000), pp. 117–21.

Evans, James R., and William M. Lindsay. *The Management and Control of Quality,* 6th ed. Cincinnati: South-Western Publishing, 2004.

Feigenbaum, A. V. *Total Quality Control,* 3rd ed. New York: McGraw-Hill Professional Publishing, 1991.

Flynn, Barbara B., Roger G. Schroeder, and Sadao Sakakibara. "The Impact of Quality Management Practices on Performance and Competitive Advantage." *Decision Sciences,* September–October 1995, pp. 659–91.

Flynn, B. B., and Brooke Saladin. "Further Evidence on the Validity of the Theoretical Models Underlying the Baldrige Criteria." *Journal of Operations Management* 19, no. 6 (November 2001), pp. 617–52.

Gabel, Natalie. "Is 99.9% Good Enough?" *Training Magazine,* March 1991, pp. 40–41.

Garvin, David A. "Competing on the Eight Dimensions of Quality." *Harvard Business Review,* November–December 1987, pp. 101–9.

George, Stephen, and Arnold Weimerskirch. *Total Quality Management: Strategies and Techniques Proven at Today's Most Successful Companies (Portable MBA Series),* 2nd ed. New York: John Wiley and Sons, 1998.

Gunsauley, C. "Estimate: 30% of Health Spending Is Wasted." *Employee Benefit News* 16, no. 10 (August 2002), pp. 1–4.

Hendricks, K. B., and V. R. Singhal. "Firm Characteristics, Total Quality Management, and Financial Performance." *Journal of Operations Management* 19, no. 3 (May 2001), pp. 269–85.

Juran, J. M. *Juran on Quality by Design: The New Steps for Planning Quality into Goods and Services,* rev. ed. New York: Free Press, 1992.

Juran, J. M., and A. B. Godfrey, eds. *Juran's Quality Handbook,* 5th ed. New York: McGraw-Hill, 1999.

Linderman, K., R. G. Schroeder, S. Zaheer, C. Liedtke, and A. S. Choo. "Integrating Quality Management Practices with Knowledge Creation Processes." *Journal of Operations Management* 22, no. 6 (December 2004), pp. 589–607.

Morrison Coulthard, L. J. "Measuring Service Quality: A Review and Critique of Research Using SERVQUAL." *International Journal of Market Research* 46, no. 4, 2004.

Parasuraman A., L. Berry, and V. Zeithmal. "Refinement and Reassessment of the SERVQUAL Scale." *Journal of Retailing,* 67, no. 4, 1991.

Parasuraman, A., V. Zeithmal, and L. Berry. "SERVQUAL: A Multiple Item Scale for Measuring Consumer Perceptions of Service Quality." *Journal of Retailing* 64, no. 1, 1988, pp. 14–40.

Ritchie, L., and B. G. Dale. "Self-Assessment Using the Business Excellence Model: A Study of Practice and Process." *International Journal of Production Economics* 66, no. 3 (July 20, 2000), pp. 241–54.

Salegna, Gary, and Farzaneh Fazel. "Obstacles to Implementing Quality." *Quality Progress* 33, no. 7 (July 2000), pp. 53–57.

Schultz, Louis E. *Profiles in Quality: Learning from the Masters.* White Plains, NY: Quality Resources, 1994.

Shingo, Shigeo. *Zero Quality Control: Source Inspection and the Poka-Yoke System,* trans. A. P. Dillon. Portland, OR: Productivity Press, 1986.

Tennant, Charles, and Paul Roberts. "Using Hoshin Kanri for Strategy Deployment." *International Journal of Manufacturing Technology and Management* 2, no. 1–7 (2000), pp. 517–31.

United States Department of Commerce. *2005 Award Criteria: Malcolm Baldrige National Quality Award.* Washington, DC: National Institute of Standards and Technology, 2005.

Wilson, Darryl, and David A. Collier. "An Empirical Investigation of the Malcolm Baldrige National Quality Award Causal Model." *Decision Sciences* 31, no. 2 (Spring 2000), pp. 361–91.

Zeitmal, V. A., A. Parasuraman, and L. Berry. *Delivering Quality Service.* New York: Free Press, 1990.

Quality Control and Improvement

Chapter outline

In the last chapter, we reviewed the long history of quality management. In the early 1900s, inspection shifted from the workers to a formal quality control department. This created tension between the workers and the inspectors, which is still evident in some companies today. But those who use the modern ideas of quality control are able to avoid these tensions and create a positive environment for quality improvement.

In 1924, **Walter A. Shewhart** of the Bell Telephone Labs developed a statistical quality control chart. Two others from the Bell Labs, H. F. Dodge and H. G. Romig, further developed the theory of statistical quality control in the 1930s. But little was done in industry until World War II in the early 1940s. The war created the demand for huge quantities of military goods from industry. The military required that industry adopt the new methods of statistical quality control to help ensure that the goods they ordered would meet government standards. As a result, statistical methods for control of quality were widely adopted by industry during the early 1940s. In later years, however, these methods were abandoned, only to be rediscovered in the 1980s as a valid way to ensure quality products and services.

The service industries have been reluctant to adopt the methods of statistical quality control. While some service companies have made impressive gains in use of these methods, many others have lagged behind. As a result, there is a tremendous opportunity to use the methods of statistical quality control and improvement in service companies.

After World War II, in 1946, the American Society for Quality (ASQ)[1] was formed. While the initial emphasis was on statistical quality control methods, the focus has now broadened to include customer needs, total quality management, and continuous improvement. The ASQ has also been focusing on spreading the ideas of quality management to service industries.

Our emphasis in this chapter will be on **process definition, statistical quality control,** and **continuous improvement.** We adopt the point of view that quality control is the continuous improvement of a stable process. We also advance the idea that organizations consist of many interrelated processes that need to be controlled in order to produce quality goods and services. It follows that quality control is highly cross-functional in nature and requires the participation and support of the entire organization. The Operations Leader box about implementing **statistical process control** (SPC) at Milliken & Co. explains how these ideas are being applied in industry.

9.1 DESIGN OF QUALITY CONTROL SYSTEMS

All quality control must start with the process itself. Actually, a process of production is composed of many subprocesses, each having its own intermediate product or service. A process can be an individual machine, a group of machines, or any of the many clerical and administrative processes that exist in the organization. Each of these processes has its own **internal customers** and its own products or services that are produced. The customer is the next process (or processes) that receives the work output. For example, the customer of the design department is the machine shop that makes the parts. The customer of the machine shop is the assembly department that uses the parts. By breaking down a large production system into many smaller systems or processes, quality can be defined and controlled at each point along the way.

After identifying each of the processes that need to be controlled, **critical control points** can be identified where inspection or measurement should take place. The types of measurement or tests required and the amount of inspection required at each of these points should be determined. Finally, management should decide who will do the inspection, the workforce itself or separate inspectors. Usually **operator inspection** is preferred because it places responsibility on those who make the product or service. Once these decisions are made, it is possible to design a complete system of quality control, which ensures continuous improvement of a stable system.

1. The first step in designing a quality control system is to identify the critical points in each of the processes where inspection and testing are needed. The guidelines for doing this are as follows:

   • Ensure that incoming raw materials or purchased services will meet specifications. Ideally, incoming inspection can be eliminated by certifying the supplier. **Supplier certification** is normally granted to those suppliers that

[1] This society was called the American Society for Quality Control (ASQC) until 1997 when its name was changed to more accurately reflect its scope and mission, beyond mere control of quality.

OPERATIONS LEADER

Implementing SPC at Milliken & Co.

Milliken & Company is one of the world's largest privately held textile and chemical companies, with headquarters in Spartanburg, South Carolina. The company's more than 14,000 associates work at over 65 manufacturing facilities worldwide to produce high-quality textiles and specialty chemicals. The company is the winner of the Malcolm Baldrige National Quality Award and the European Quality Award.

Implementing SPC at Milliken & Co. was not treated as a staff program or an edict by top management. This is a sure way to kill SPC before it starts. Also, training workers in SPC before they have a need to use it can produce poor results. The best way to implement SPC is to start with a real problem concerning control of an important process. With this approach, employees responsible for the process will see not only the need for SPC but the results from process improvement. It's best to start with the problem rather than the solution.

Christopher Wozniak, process improvement specialist at Milliken & Company, writes, "When I was working on my first SPC program, a plant superintendent told me, 'Don't get too excited about this SPC stuff. I've been around for 15 years, and I give SPC a year before the next program comes along.' He was right. The program started to fizzle out. Soon after, however, a companywide commitment was made to SPC, and the proper system developed. The SPC program has since flourished."

In one example at Milliken, SPC was used after an out-of-control process was found. To solve this problem, several people from different departments spontaneously joined together. The informal team leader rallied everyone around the out-of-control process by explaining the importance of the process, showing them examples of defects, and defining how team members could help. Feedback on how the process was being improved was given to everyone as the improvement proceeded. As a result, within six months the process capability improved from a C_{pk} of 0.15 to a C_{pk} of 0.95.*

* C_{pk} is explained later in this chapter.

Source: Christopher Wozniak, "Proactive vs Reactive SPC," *Quality Progress,* February 1994; and the company Web site in 2002: www.milliken.com.

have demonstrated they use statistical process control and other methods to achieve consistent quality performance. In this case, the products or services of the supplier can be used directly by the customer without incoming inspection.

- Test work in process or the service while it is being delivered. As a general rule, the product or service should be inspected by operators before irreversible operations take place or before a great deal of value is added to the product. In these cases, the cost of inspection is less than the cost of adding more value to the product. A precise determination of where the product should be inspected should be made from the process flowchart.

- The third critical inspection point is the finished product or service. In manufacturing, final products are frequently inspected or tested prior to shipping or prior to placing the product in inventory. At one automobile assembly plant, for example, a sample of cars is taken directly off the assembly line and thoroughly inspected for appearance and function. The defects are noted and fed back to assembly-line personnel so that they can correct the underlying causes. The defects are also used to compute a quality score for comparison among assembly plants.

It is usually far better to **prevent defects** from occurring than to inspect and correct defects after production. Nevertheless, some measurement via sampling inspection is necessary to maintain processes in a continuous state of control and to facilitate improvement. So inspection (or measurement) cannot be eliminated, but it can be reduced by a vigorous process of prevention.

2. The second step in designing a quality control system is to decide on the type of measurement to be used at each inspection point. There are generally two options: measurement based either on variables or on attributes. **Variables measurement** utilizes a continuous scale for such factors as length, height, and weight. Examples of variables measurement are the dimensions of parts, the viscosity of liquids, and the time that it takes to wait on tables in a restaurant.

   Attribute measurement uses a discrete scale by counting the number of defective items or the number of defects per unit. When the quality specifications are complex, it will usually be necessary to use attribute measurements. In this case, a complicated set of criteria can be used to define a defective unit or a defect. For example, a color TV set may be classified as defective if any of a number of functional tests fail or if the appearance of the cabinet is not satisfactory. In inspecting cloth, a defect can be defined as a flaw in the material and the number of defects per 100 yards can be counted during inspection. Determining the type of measurement to use also involves the specification of measuring equipment. A wide variety of devices are available for measurement. However, the selection of these devices is beyond the scope of this text.

3. The third step in defining the quality control system is to decide on the amount of inspection to use. Generally, statistical process control is preferred to minimize the amount of inspection needed. Exceptions to this might be when process variables are difficult to define or when the consequences of failure are very high. For example, when human lives are at stake both process control and 100 percent testing of output might be used.

4. The final step in designing a quality control system is deciding who should do the inspection. Usually it is best to have the workers inspect their own output and be responsible for the quality of their work (sometimes called quality at the source). If a philosophy of zero defects or "make it right the first time" is used, workers will be given much of the responsibility for inspection and only a minimum of outside inspection will be used. There is much evidence to suggest that a prevention program along with worker responsibility for quality will be less expensive than an extensive outside inspection program.

   In some cases, the customer will be involved in inspecting the product. Service customers always take this role as they receive the service. Some customers station inspectors at the vendor's plants to examine and accept or reject shipments before they are sent on to the customer. The government has inspectors in a variety of industries to ensure quality in the interest of public health and safety. Thus, many people may be involved in the inspection process.

   A well-designed quality control system requires a series of management judgments and the participation of all functions. The control principles themselves are elementary, requiring performance standards, measurement, and feedback of results to correct the process. The application of these principles in any given situation is complex. The guiding principle is to first control the system and then aim for continuous improvement of the resulting stable system.

9.2   PROCESS QUALITY CONTROL

Process quality control utilizes inspection (or testing) of the product or service while it is being produced. Periodic samples of the output of a production process are taken. When, after inspection of the sample, there is reason to believe that the process quality characteristics have changed, the process is stopped and a search is made for an **assignable cause.** This cause could be a change in the operator, the machine, or the material. When the cause has been found and corrected, the process is started again.

Process control is based on two key assumptions, one of which is that random variability is basic to any production process. No matter how perfectly a process is designed, there will be some random variability, also called common causes, in quality characteristics from one unit to the next. For example, a machine filling cereal boxes will not deposit exactly the same weight in each box; the amount filled will vary around some average figure. The aim of process control is to find the range of natural random variation of the process and to ensure that production stays within this range.

The second principle of process control is that production processes are not usually found in a state of control. Due to lax procedures, untrained operators, improper machine maintenance, and so on, the variation being produced is usually much larger than necessary. The first job of process control managers is to seek out these sources of unnecessary variation, also called special causes, and bring the process under statistical control where the remaining variation is due to random causes.

Administrative processes in accounting, human resources, sales, marketing, and finance in most organizations are also not usually under statistical control. These processes can be controlled just like the production processes themselves. The same principles used to control production are also used to control administrative processes.

A process can be brought to a **state of control** and can be maintained in this state through the use of quality control charts (also called process charts or control charts). In the control chart shown in Figure 9.1, the *y* axis represents the

FIGURE 9.1
Quality control chart.

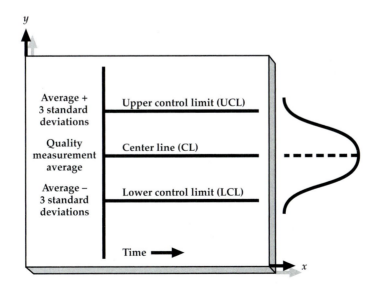

FIGURE 9.2
Quality control
chart example.

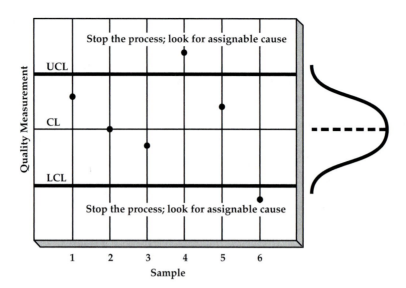

quality characteristic that is being controlled, while the *x* axis represents time or a particular sample taken from the process. The **center line** of the chart is the average quality characteristic being measured. The **upper control limit** represents the maximum acceptable random variation, and the **lower control limit** indicates the minimum acceptable random variation when a state of control exists. Generally speaking, the upper and lower control limits are set at ± three standard deviations from the mean. If a normal probability distribution is assumed, these control limits will include 99.74 percent of the random variations observed.

On the side of Figure 9.1 a normal probability distribution is shown. It indicates that the distribution mean (average) is located on the center line of the control chart and the tails of the distribution are outside the control limits by just a small amount. Thus 99.74 percent of the sample observations that are taken and plotted on the graph in Figure 9.1 will fall inside the control limits provided the process is still in control. When the process mean shifts up or down, it is more likely that sample points will fall outside the control limits and thus indicate an assignable cause that needs correction.

After a process has been brought to steady-state operation, periodic samples are taken and plotted on the control chart (see Figure 9.2). When the measurement falls within the control limits, the process is continued. If the measurement falls outside the control limits, the process is stopped and a search is made for an assignable cause.[2] Assignable causes have also been termed "special causes," those that cause points to fall outside the control limits and can be corrected to bring the process back under control. In contrast, common causes of variation are those that randomly occur when the process is under statistical control and cannot be changed unless the process is redesigned. Through use

---

[2] Another indication of a possible process shift, but outside the scope of this discussion, is a trend in the points plotted on the control chart indicating a possible downward or upward drift in the process average.

of control charts, the process is maintained in a constant state of statistical control and there is only natural random variation (common causes) in the process's output.

Quality can be measured for control charts by attributes or by variables. We will cover each of these cases in turn below.

9.3 ATTRIBUTE CONTROL

Attribute control occurs when the quality characteristic is measured on a discrete scale (e.g., an item is either good or defective) rather than a continuous scale. In this section we consider the percentage of defectives occurring in a sample as the attribute measured. Examples of attribute measurements are the percentage of phone calls not answered within three rings, the percentage of customers who are dissatisfied, or the percentage of parts from a supplier that are defective. The percentage defective is estimated by taking a sample of n units at random from a process at specified time intervals. For each sample, the observed percent defective (p) in the sample is computed. These observed values of p are plotted on the p control chart, one for each sample.

To get the center line and control limits of the p control chart, we take a large number of samples of n units each. The p value is computed for each sample and then averaged over all samples to yield a value $\bar{p}$. This value of $\bar{p}$ is used as the center line since it represents the best available estimate of the true average percent defective of the process. We also use the value of $\bar{p}$ to compute upper and lower control limits as follows:

$$\text{UCL} = \bar{p} + 3\sqrt{\frac{\bar{p}(1 - \bar{p})}{n}}$$

$$\text{LCL} = \bar{p} - 3\sqrt{\frac{\bar{p}(1 - \bar{p})}{n}}$$

In this case, the process's standard deviation is the quantity under the square root sign. We are adding and subtracting three standard deviations from the mean to get the control limits. An example of this computation is given on the next page for controlling computer data entry operations.

After the p control chart is constructed with its center line and upper and lower control limits, samples of the process being controlled are taken and plotted on the chart. If the sample percentage falls within the control limits, no action is taken. If the sample percentage falls outside the control limits, the process is stopped and a search for an assignable cause (material, operator, or machine) is made. After the assignable cause is found and corrected—or, in very rare cases, no assignable cause is found—the process is restored to operating condition and production or service is resumed.

9.4 VARIABLES CONTROL

Control charts are also used for measurements of variables. In this case, a measurement of a continuous variable is made when each item is inspected. As a result, two values are computed from the sample: a measure of central tendency (usually the average) and a measure of variability (the range or standard

ATTRIBUTE CONTROL CHART EXAMPLE

Example of Control Chart

Suppose samples of 200 records are taken from a data entry operation at 2-hour intervals to control the data entry process. The percentage of records in error for the past 11 samples is found to be .5, 1.0, 1.5, 2.0, 1.5, 1.0, 1.5, .5, 1.0, 1.5 and 2.0 percent. The average of these 11 sample percentages yields a $\bar{p}$ = 1.27 percent, which is the center line of the control chart. The upper and lower control limits are

$$UCL = .0127 + 3\sqrt{\frac{.0127(.9873)}{200}} = .0364$$

$$LCL = .0127 - 3\sqrt{\frac{.0127(.9873)}{200}} = -.0110$$

When the LCL is negative, it is rounded up to 0 because a negative percentage is impossible. Thus, we have the following chart:

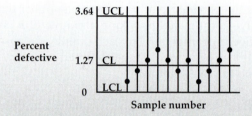

Since all sample points are found to be in control, these 11 samples can be used to establish the center line and control limits.

deviation). With these values, two control charts are developed: one for the central tendency and the second for variability of the process. When the process is found to be out of control on either of these charts, it is stopped and a search for an assignable cause is made.

When variable measurement is used, two control charts are needed because the normal distribution is assumed and it has two parameters (mean and variance). Either the mean of the distribution can change or the variance (as measured by range) can change. As a result, we monitor both the average of a process and the range for control purposes.

Suppose that the average $\bar{x}$ and range R are computed each time a sample is taken. Then a control chart for average and a chart for range will be used. The control limits for the average chart are computed as follows:

$$CL = \bar{\bar{x}}$$
$$UCL = \bar{\bar{x}} + A_2\bar{R}$$
$$LCL = \bar{\bar{x}} - A_2\bar{R}$$

where $\bar{\bar{x}}$ is the grand average of several past $\bar{x}$ averages and $\bar{R}$ is the average of several past R values. Recall that the range (R) is simply the largest value minus the smallest value in a sample. In the above formulas, A_2 is a constant that includes three standard deviations in terms of the range. Table 9.1 provides values of A_2 for various sample sizes for the normal distribution.

TABLE 9.1
Control Chart
Constants

Sample Size n	A_2	D_3	D_4
2	1.880		3.267
3	1.023	0	2.575
4	0.729	0	2.282
5	.577	0	2.115
6	.483	0	2.004
7	.419	.076	1.924
8	.373	.136	1.864
9	.337	.184	1.816
10	.308	.223	1.777
12	.266	.284	1.716
14	.235	.329	1.671
16	.212	.364	1.636
18	.194	.392	1.608
20	.180	.414	1.586
22	.167	.434	1.566
24	.157	.452	1.548

Source: Factors reproduced from 1950 *ASTM Manual on Quality Control of Materials* by permission of the American Society for Testing and Materials, Philadelphia.

The control limits for the range chart are computed as follows:

$$\text{CL} = \bar{R}$$
$$\text{UCL} = D_4\bar{R}$$
$$\text{LCL} = D_3\bar{R}$$

The constants D_3 and D_4 provide three standard deviation limits for the range. Values for these constants are also given in Table 9.1. The purpose of these constants is to help calculate the upper and lower control limits as a function of

**VARIABLES
CONTROL
CHART
EXAMPLE**
*Example of
Control by
Variables*

The Midwest Bolt would like to control the quality of the bolts produced by its automatic screw machines. Each machine produces 100 bolts per hour and is controlled by a separate control chart. Every hour, a random sample of six bolts is selected from the output of each machine and the diameter of each sample bolt is measured. From each six diameters, an average and range are computed. For example, one sample produced the following six measurements: .536, .507, .530, .525, .530, and .520. The average of these measurements is $\bar{x} = .525$ and the range is $\bar{R} = .029$. We also know that the grand average of all past samples has been running $\bar{\bar{x}} = .513$ and the grand average range is $\bar{R} = .020$. From these grand averages, the control chart parameters are computed as follows (see Table 9.1 for control chart constants with $n = 6$).

$\bar{X}$ Chart	R Chart
CL = .513	CL = .020
UCL = .513 + .483(.020) = .523	UCL = 2.004(.020) = .040
LCL = .513 − .483(.020) = .503	LCL = 0(.020) = 0

On the basis of these control limits, the sample of six bolts is found to be out of control on average measurement and in control on range. (*Note*: $\bar{x} = .525$ is outside the upper control limit on the $\bar{x}$ chart.) We should therefore stop the process and look for an assignable cause that would tend to produce bolts that are too large in diameter.

sample size. A given sample size can be used in Table 9.1 to look up the appropriate values of A_2, D_3, and D_4 for average and range charts. The example below the table illustrates how to compute control limits and how to determine whether or not a sample is in control.

9.5 USING CONTROL CHARTS

There are several issues of concern in using control charts. First, the problem of sample size must be faced. For an attribute control chart, samples should be fairly large, frequently in the range of 50 to 300 observations. As a general rule, the sample must be at least large enough to allow for the detection of one defective unit. For example, if the process being controlled produces 1 percent defective units, a sample size of at least 100 should be used to detect one defective unit on average. Control charts for variables require much smaller sample sizes, usually in the range of 3 to 10 items, because each variable measurement provides much more information.

The second issue is how frequently to sample. This issue is often decided on the basis of the rate of production and the cost of producing defects in relation to the cost of inspection. A high-volume production process should be sampled frequently since a large number of defective units could be produced between samples. When the cost of producing defective units is high in relation to the cost of inspection, the process should also be sampled frequently. An example of a costly situation is one where the entire production output must be screened when the process is found to be out of control. In these cases, samples should be taken frequently, provided that the cost of sampling is not too high. What is the cost of sampling from an accounting process, personnel records, or a process that receives sales orders? These costs can be rather high and may warrant statistical control through infrequent sampling.

Another issue in the use of control charts is the relationship of product specifications to control limits. If the process is in control and yet too many units are outside the specifications, as judged by management, then the process is not capable of meeting product specifications. In this case, the specifications should be relaxed, a better process used, or 100 percent inspection instituted temporarily to screen out the bad items until the process or specifications can be changed. Control charts illustrate very clearly the need to match product specifications to the characteristics of the process. In practice, a product can be overspecified, and it will then have apparently poor quality of conformance when the process itself is inadequate.

Control charts are widely used in industry for both manufacturing and service. In manufacturing companies control charts are frequently located on each machine to control the quality output of that machine. Quality measurements are taken periodically and plotted on the chart to ensure that the machine is still producing at its required tolerances and the average and range haven't changed.

In service industries control charts are used to control the time or the percentage of defects from various processes—for example, the time it takes to answer a phone, the time it takes to serve a customer, or the time it takes to collect accounts receivable. Service industries also use control charts to monitor and control the percentage of dissatisfied customers or the percentage of late payments, for example.

9.6 CONTINUOUS IMPROVEMENT

We have defined quality control as continuous improvement of a stable process. As we have seen, a stable process can be maintained by the methods of process control. Next, we will turn to approaches that are useful for achieving continuous improvement over time.

The aim of continuous improvement is to reduce variability of the product or process. This generally requires problem solving or changes in the design of the product or process itself. Such changes make it possible to make a more consistent product or service with less variation from one unit to the next. In the language of control charts, we are seeking to reduce the common causes of variation, which have been assumed to be random until now. In effect, continuous improvement techniques will narrow the control limits themselves.

Three techniques for continuous improvement will be reviewed in this section: Pareto analysis, cause-and-effect diagrams, and process capability charts. Each of these methods relies on data collection and analysis in order to improve product or process quality.

Using **Pareto analysis,** data can be collected on the various modes of failure of the product or service produced. Vilfredo Pareto in 1906 observed that a few items in any population constitute a significant percentage of the entire group—the vital few. Data are tabulated to identify the most frequent modes of failure. As a result, the most important problems can be attacked first.

Table 9.2 provides a count of possible reasons for hydraulic leaks found in assembling front-end tractor loaders in a factory. As noted in the table, the most frequent reason for a leak (defect) is loose connections, followed by cracked connectors, and so on. These data are transferred to the Pareto diagram in Figure 9.3. By graphing the reasons for leaks in decreasing order of occurrence, the Pareto diagram readily shows the importance of the various types of defects that have been found. According to Pareto's law, a few of the failure modes account for most of the defects.

The Pareto diagram shows which defects we should try to eliminate first. By reference to Figure 9.3, we should investigate loose connections first because they occur most frequently. Of course, cracked connectors is a close second and should be investigated too, especially if cracked connectors are easier or less costly to correct than loose connections. Pareto analysis is very helpful when first studying a quality problem because it helps break the problem down into smaller pieces. Leaking hydraulics has been defined as due primarily to loose connections or cracked connectors (78.6 percent combined failures).

TABLE 9.2
Defectives in
Front-End Loader
Hydraulics

Number Inspected (*N*) = 2347		
Defective Items	**Number of Defectives**	**Percent Defective**
O-rings missing	16	3.9%
Improper torque	25	6.1
Loose connections	193	46.8
Fitting burrs	47	11.4
Cracked connectors	131	31.8
Total	412	100.0%

FIGURE 9.3
Pareto diagram.

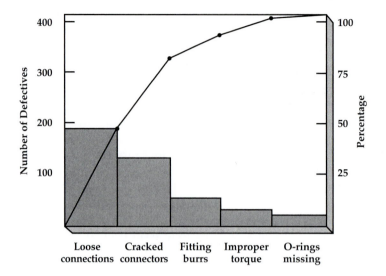

The next step in the analysis is to take one of these failure modes, say, loose connections, and to analyze the causes of failure. This is done by use of the cause-and-effect diagram, also called an Ishikawa diagram, after Dr. Ishikawa (1986) who first used these diagrams in Japan.

A **cause-and-effect** (CE) **diagram** is shown in Figure 9.4 for the loose connections. The problem itself, or the effect, is shown on the right side of the diagram. The various potential causes of this problem are shown along the spine of the diagram as materials, workers, inspection, and tools. The appearance of this diagram suggests a fishbone analogy. The bones of the fish are probable causes

FIGURE 9.4
Cause-and-effect diagram for loose connections.

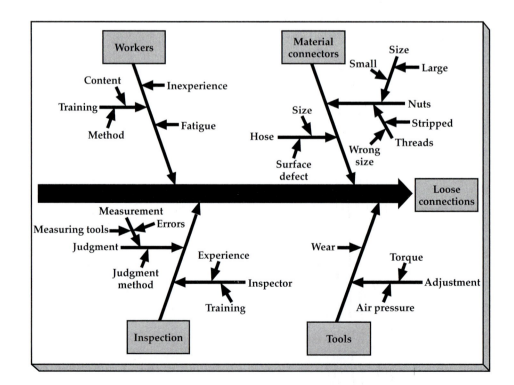

of quality problems, but any cause can be listed. Each of the major causes is then broken down into more detailed causes, giving rise to more bones on the fish. For example, the worker cause is split into three possibilities: inexperience, fatigue, or training. Training is in turn divided into content and method.

By constructing a CE diagram, the potential causes of a problem become readily apparent. Each of these can then be evaluated one by one in order to find the true causes of the problem.

CE diagrams are frequently constructed by using quality improvement teams or problem-solving teams. By use of brainstorming, the team will develop a wide variety of possible causes for a problem. Then the team, or an individual, can collect data to narrow down the potential causes before taking corrective action.

By using Pareto and CE diagrams, it is possible to reduce defects and thus improve quality. For example, in the case of hydraulic leaks, the loose connections may be found to be caused by the torque adjustment of the tools and the improper training of operators. After these causes are corrected, the number of defects will be reduced. It is then possible to move to the second problem, which is cracked connectors. In this way, continuous improvement is achieved.

Once a process is under control, another aspect of continuous improvement is the ability of the process to meet, or exceed, its specifications. This ability can be determined by the **process capability index** C_p—the ratio of the specification (spec) width to the process width:

$$C_p = \frac{\text{spec width}}{\text{process width}}$$

If the process is centered within the specification range, as shown in Figure 9.5, $C_p \geq 1$ will be a good indicator of the capability of the process to meet its specifications, since the process width will be within the specification width.

FIGURE 9.5   Process capability index examples.

$$C_p = \frac{\text{spec width}}{\text{process width}} = \frac{\text{USL} - \text{LSL}}{6\sigma}$$

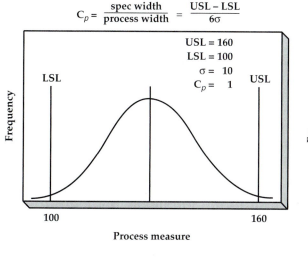

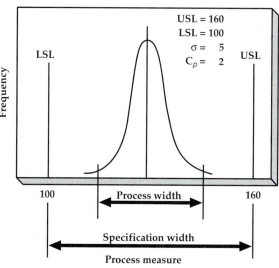

In practical use, the specification width is computed as the difference between the upper specification limit (USL) and the lower specification limit (LSL). The process width is computed by using six standard deviations of the process measurement being monitored (6σ). The logic for 6σ is that most of the variation of a process measurement is included within ±3 standard deviations of the mean, or a total of 6 standard deviations. Thus we have

$$C_p = \frac{\text{USL} - \text{LSL}}{6\sigma}$$

If the process is centered in the specification range and $C_p = 1$, the process is considered to be minimally capable of meeting the specifications. A process with $C_p < 1$ must be improved by reducing the standard deviation or increasing the specification width if possible, to become capable.

For the normal distribution, if $C_p = 1$ and the process is centered within the specifications and under statistical control, then 99.74 percent of the product produced will lie within the specifications, corresponding to 2,600 parts per million (ppm) defective.[3] The figure of 99.74 percent can be obtained by using the normal probability distribution tables from Appendix A. If $C_p = 1.33$, then 99.994 percent of the product will lie within the specifications, corresponding to 60 ppm defective. Thus a slight increase in C_p causes a dramatic drop in the defective rate of the process. Customers often specify C_p values from 1 to 1.5, or even as high as 2.0, depending on their particular quality requirements.

One problem with the C_p measure is that it requires the process to be centered in the specification range for an accurate measure of process capability. Because of this problem, another more widely used measure (C_{pk}) has been devised:

$$C_{pk} = \min\left(\frac{\text{USL} - \mu}{3\sigma}, \frac{\mu - \text{LSL}}{3\sigma}\right)$$

where μ = the process mean value and σ = the process standard deviation.

This more complicated measure of process capability overcomes the centering problem by calculating the process capability for each half of the normal distribution and then taking the minimum of the two calculations. The result is shown in Figure 9.6a, where the value of $C_{pk} = 0$, while $C_p = 1$. This figure illustrates

[3] Note that 99.74 percent good product corresponds to $(100 - 99.74) = .26$ percent bad. The .26 percent can be converted to 2,600 ppm by multiplying .0026 by 1,000,000.

FIGURE 9.6 Computation of C_{pk}.

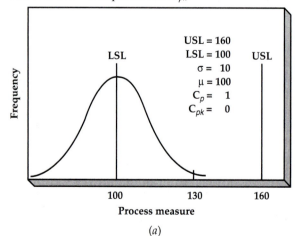

(a)

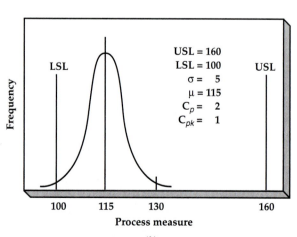

(b)

that the use of the C_p index when the process is not centered gives the wrong answer, since the process is not fully capable of meeting the specifications, whereas C_{pk} gives the correct answer with $C_{pk} = 0$. A further example is given in Figure 9.6b, where $C_{pk} = 1$, even though the distribution is not centered. In this case, the process is capable of meeting the specifications but could be improved by shifting the mean closer to the center of the specification range. Because C_{pk} more accurately reflects the actual process capability, it is the measure commonly used by industry.

9.7 SIX SIGMA

The tools of quality control and improvement should be used in an organized fashion by firms. Tools by themselves will not lead to improvement; they need to be incorporated into an improvement approach such as **Six Sigma.** See the Operations Leader box "Six-Sigma Quality" for background information on this approach.

Six Sigma is a systematic method for process improvement that often uses the five steps defined by the acronym: **DMAIC.**

1. **Define:** The process is selected for improvement and the project charter is specified.
2. **Measure:** Quality variables valued by the customer are measured and goals are set for improvement.
3. **Analyze:** The root causes of the current defect levels are identified and alternatives are considered for process changes.
4. **Improve:** The process is changed and checked for improvement.
5. **Control:** This step ensures that the process improvement is not lost over time.

The Six Sigma approach can be applied to processes in manufacturing, service, or administrative areas.

Before improving a specific process, however, a strategic choice of process should be made. Senior management should choose critical processes that are needed to implement the strategy of the firm. For example, top management might determine that the sales processes, the processes for hiring new employees, or a particular manufacturing process should be selected for improvement.

Motorola originally developed the Six Sigma methodology.
© Colin Young-Wolf/Photo Edit

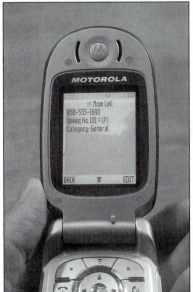

Once a process is selected for improvement a cross-functional team is formed since most processes cut across functional lines. A full-time trained process improvement specialist, usually called a **"Black-Belt,"** is chosen to lead the improvement team. The team then sets out to make improvements by using the DMAIC approach.

The team begins improvement by defining process defects using measures that are critical to the customer. Data is collected on these measures to establish a current process baseline and goals for improvement. For example, if the process is currently producing 1 defect in 100 opportunities (1 percent defective), a goal might be to improve the process to 1 defect in 1,000 opportunities, a 10 times (10X) improvement factor. This kind of aggressive improvement approach is taken by Six Sigma

OPERATIONS LEADER
Six-Sigma Quality

Motorola invented the term "six-sigma quality" in the mid-80s to reflect a desire for very high levels of consistent quality in all its processes. A level of six sigma equates to a defect level of 3.4 parts per million (ppm), which is much better than most processes in companies can achieve.

Six-sigma quality is related to the normal probability distribution with sigma (σ) denoting the standard deviation of the process. Motorola assumed that the process mean would experience a 1.5σ shift before a ±6σ change. Thus six sigma corresponds to a 4.5σ deviation on one side of the mean and a 7.5σ deviation on the other side of the mean resulting in 3.4 ppm defects. This can be verified by referring to the normal probability tables tails at +4.5 and −7.5 standard deviations.

The six-sigma criterion is equivalent to a process capability of $C_{pk} = 1.5$. This can be seen by referring to the formula for C_{pk} with USL − μ = 4.5σ. As a result, the six-sigma criterion will ensure processes that are not just barely capable of producing the specifications but will provide somewhat better process capability.

Six-sigma quality can be applied to not only manufacturing processes but administrative and service processes as well. For example, Motorola has applied six sigma in the finance department. It measures the cycle time to close the books at the end of the month. It used to take a couple of weeks to close the books; now they are closed in about three days. The department also measures how many errors were made in closing, tracking the sigma level each month.

In another application, Texas Instruments uses the six-sigma criterion to improve levels of customer satisfaction. A defect is defined as a level of customer service rated by the customer as less than satisfactory. The percentage of defects from a large survey of customers is then equated to the corresponding sigma level and tracked on a periodic basis for improvement.

Source: Adapted from Pandu R. Tadikamalla, "The Confusion over Six-Sigma Quality," *Quality Progress,* November 1994, pp. 83–85; and Karen Bemowski, "Motorola's Fountain of Youth," *Quality Progress,* October 1995, pp. 29–31.

teams to ensure that significant change is achieved. Of course, the improvement goal must not be set arbitrarily; rather, it is set based on the economic benefit of improvement and the time available for the team to accomplish its goal, with six months being the typical project length.

Once the goal has been set, the team seeks the **root causes** of the current defect levels. The team must be careful to go beyond symptoms and find the real causes. This is often done by brainstorming and careful collection of data to analyze the situation. A variety of tools such as CE diagrams and Pareto charts are used at this stage.

After finding root causes, alternatives for improvement are considered and improvements made. Then, further data is collected to ensure that improvements have occurred, savings have been generated, and a control plan is put in place to ensure the changes are permanent. Quality control charts can be used at this point to maintain the new process in a state of statistical control.

While the use of Six Sigma is well established in manufacturing, an example of improvement in a transaction process might be informative. The TRW legal department improved its processes for worldwide trademark renewal and saved $1.8 million.[4] Prior to Six Sigma improvement the legal department and associated

[4] R. Das, S. Colello, and H. Davidson (2004).

business units reviewed 2,500 trademark registrations each year at a cost of $1,200 per registration. It was thought that many of these registrations might no longer be needed or were not critical to the businesses. But, how could this be determined?

The Six Sigma process started by defining a defect as either an unnecessary registration that was renewed or a necessary registration that was not renewed because response for verification from the business unit was not received before expiration of coverage. The baseline defect rate was 25 percent—that is, one in four registrations was a defect.

The first step in the analysis was to draw a flowchart of all the steps required for renewal of a trademark. This resulted in 41 steps, of which only 11 added value. As a result of this analysis, the process of renewal was greatly streamlined.

The next step was to determine the causes of the defects. It was hypothesized that potential causes were too much time waiting for approval from the business unit, too much time waiting for evidence of use, or a foreign country renewal. Data were collected to test the relationship of these potential causes to the number of defects. An analysis of the data was conducted by use of statistical regression analysis to establish the root causes. As a result the number of renewals that needed processing was drastically reduced.

After designing a new process to reduce defects and shorten the time for review, employees were trained and a control plan was implemented to keep the defects from reappearing. The resulting defect rate from the revised process was 1 defect in 300 renewals or .33 percent.

This example illustrates how Six Sigma methods can be applied to any process, even those in the legal department. The application may be different for each type of process, but the steps followed (DMAIC) and the underlying principles are the same.

Six Sigma has produced dramatic results in companies such as Motorola, General Electric, Citigroup, American Express, and Honeywell. These results are only possible through aggressive senior management leadership, widespread training in Six Sigma, use of full-time improvement specialists, and careful tracking of financial results.[5] Six Sigma is not merely a quality improvement approach, but also a way to improve the net income of the company. GE, for example, reports adding more than $2 billion to the bottom line from Six Sigma.[6]

9.8 QUALITY CONTROL IN INDUSTRY

Industry has made widespread use of the quality control methods described in this chapter as indicated by several surveys of industry practice. These surveys indicate that about three-fourths of all firms use process control charts. There is greater use of $\bar{x}$ and R charts than p charts due to the small samples that are possible with variables control. Other more sophisticated charts are not as widely used as $\bar{x}$, R, and p charts.

Pareto charts, CE diagrams, and C_{pk} calculations have also achieved significant use in industry. Recently, employees and managers at all levels, and in all functions, have received intensive training in these techniques through quality

---

[5] In a few cases companies have used part-time improvement specialists rather than full-time employees.
[6] GE Annual Report (1999).

teams and quality improvement programs. As a result, awareness of quality control ideas has increased greatly in the last 10 years in American business. The popular quality control tools used by industry have been termed the "seven tools of quality control," as shown in Figure 9.7.[7]

We have studied three of the seven tools in this chapter and flowcharting in Chapter 7. The remaining three tools are as follows. The histogram is simply a chart of the frequency of occurrence versus a quality measurement. It provides a convenient way to show how the data are distributed. The run chart is a plot of the quality measurement over time. It indicates the trend in the data. The scatter diagram shows the relationship between two variables. It can be used to demonstrate the strength of the relationship and the correlation of the variables. All these techniques are helpful in analyzing data to improve quality.

Six Sigma is rapidly gaining acceptance in manufacturing and service industries as a proven approach for using the seven tools of quality control. Although there is no reliable survey of adoption of Six Sigma, the list of companies reporting Six Sigma implementation continues to grow.

While use of quality methods has now spread beyond operations, there is much room for further use in administrative and office functions in manufacturing firms and in service firms. Quality control education must be concentrated on all functions in the firm and on the firm's suppliers as well. Some firms have still not internalized the concept of total quality management. As a result, quality control efforts are focused primarily on production operations.

Quality control in the service industries has lagged behind that in manufacturing for several reasons. First, services are more difficult to measure because they are intangible, whereas the characteristics of a manufactured product can be measured and specified. For example, steel can be measured by its strength, hardness, ductility, and other properties. The quality of a service is related to intangibles such as atmosphere in a restaurant, the waiter's smile, and the customer's sense of well-being. Nevertheless, quality cannot be controlled unless it is measured. Therefore, it is imperative that the service industries measure what they can and develop new, innovative measurement techniques for what is now considered intangible.

One way to measure service is to quantify the transactions that take place. Transactions might include the number of tables served in a restaurant per employee, the percentage of customers who are satisfied or very satisfied with the service, and the number of power outages at an electric utility company. Once the important dimensions of service delivery are determined, then a way can be found to measure these dimensions by either objective or perceptual data.

Another way to measure service is to use the dimensions of SERVQUAL described in the last chapter. These perceptual measures can help management understand and improve the quality of service offered.

A characteristic of managing quality of services is the perishability of the product, which requires that quality be controlled while the service is being delivered. As a result, a great burden for service quality is placed on the workforce; when bad quality is delivered, the customer is immediately aware of it. Thus, service organizations should emphasize selection of the proper employees, workforce training, and process control. Of course, these are also good practices for manufacturing firms to prevent errors from occurring.

---

[7] There are also seven new tools of quality described in Mizuno (1988). These additional seven tools are more suited to problem identification than problem solving.

FIGURE 9.7 The seven tools of quality control.

Source: Gitlow et al., *Tools and Methods for Quality Improvement*, 2d ed. (Burr Ridge, IL: Irwin, 1994).

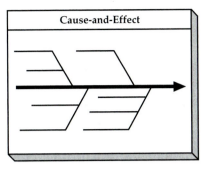

Cause-and-Effect

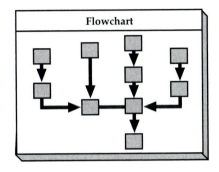

Flowchart

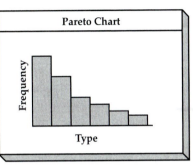

Pareto Chart

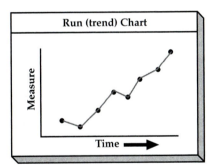

Run (trend) Chart

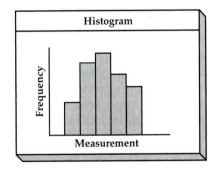

Histogram

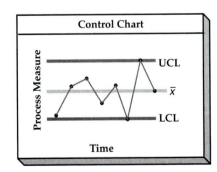

Control Chart

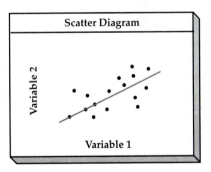

Scatter Diagram

Why should accounting, human resources, marketing, and finance people be interested in the ideas expressed in this chapter? First, accounting is interested in accurate costs and financial information. When all production processes are in statistical control, the special causes of variation in the processes and thus in costs have been eliminated. Accounting can also benefit directly by applying these ideas to the control of quality in the input transactions received by the accounting system and the accounting outputs produced. In other words, they can bring the accounting system of the company under statistical control. Outside auditors can audit whether the processes producing accounting transactions are under control, rather than just auditing the transactions themselves.

From a human resources perspective, the ideas in this chapter offer many possibilities. Implementation of statistical quality control requires in-depth training of the workforce. The workers are no longer blamed for errors that are in fact due to the underlying system. Workers take more pride in their work when they are responsible for inspecting their own output and controlling their own processes. A greater sense of satisfaction and productivity occurs when people are contributing to reducing errors and satisfying their customers (the next process).

Needless to say, marketing does not like to see dissatisfied customers who have received a defective product. Implementing the ideas of statistical quality control reduces the number of defects produced in a never-ending cycle of improvement. As a result, there are fewer customer complaints and revenues can be increased by marketing the consistent quality of the company. Marketing and sales are made easier by aggressive implementation of the ideas in this chapter.

Finally, finance can see the results of a progressive quality control and improvement approach on the bottom line. Financial processes can also be controlled, and a company that implements these ideas will save money and improve its financial results.

9.9 KEY POINTS

This chapter's key points include the following:

- Quality control is defined as the continuous improvement of a stable process. The process is actually a sequence of interconnected subprocesses, each with its own internal customers. Critical points must be defined for inspection and measurement in order to control and improve these processes.

- Process control charts should be considered for the inputs (by the suppliers), as part of the process, and for the outputs. The critical control points are best described by a flowchart of the process.

- Using process quality control, periodic samples are taken from a continuous production or service process. As long as the sample measurements fall within the control limits, production is continued. When the sample measurements fall outside the control limits, the process is stopped and a search is made for an assignable cause—operator, machine, or material. With this procedure, a production or service process is maintained in a continual state of statistical control.

- It is preferable to use statistical process control instead of inspection whenever possible, because SPC is prevention-oriented. SPC can be used as a basis for internal quality control and achieving a certified supplier status, which requires a stable production process.

- Six Sigma is an organized and systematic approach for process improvement. It often utilizes the five DMAIC steps: define, measure, analyze, improve, and control. Careful analysis using statistical tools is needed to identify root causes of defects perceived by customers, to analyze changes, and to control the improved process.

- There are seven tools of quality control and improvement. These methods can be used to bring a process under control or to improve it.

- A high percentage of manufacturing companies use the seven tools of quality control. However, the use of these methods has less acceptance in service industries and in administrative functions.
- Every function in the company can benefit from the application of the ideas in this chapter. All functions should bring the administrative processes they manage under statistical quality control and improvement. Other functions outside operations, and the company, will also benefit directly when quality control principles are used.

STUDENT INTERNET EXERCISES	

STUDENT INTERNET EXERCISES

1. Society of Manufacturing Engineers (SME)
  http://www.sme.org

From the home page of SME search the site for "six sigma" and click on a recent article of interest to you. Come to class prepared to discuss your findings.

2. Milliken & Company
  http://www.milliken.com

Find out what quality awards Milliken & Company has won. Why is Milliken considered a leading company in America?

3. Statistical Quality Software (SAS)
  http://www.sas.com

Use an internal search of the SAS site to find information on statistical process control software. Write a short report on your findings.

4. iSixSigma
  http://www.isixsigma.com

After finding the home page, click on "New to Six Sigma?" and read more about Six Sigma history, DMAIC, certification, and the like.

SOLVED PROBLEMS

Problem

1. *P* Control Chart A company that makes golf tees controls its production process by periodically taking a sample of 100 tees from the production line. Each tee is inspected for defective features. Control limits are developed using three standard deviations from the mean as the limit. During the last 16 samples taken, the proportion of defective items per sample was recorded as follows:

.01	.02	.01	.03	.02	.01	.00	.02
.00	.01	.03	.02	.03	.02	.01	.00

a. Determine the mean proportion defective, the UCL, and the LCL.
b. Draw a control chart and plot each of the measurements on it.
c. Does it appear that the process for making tees is in control?

Solution

a. The mean proportion defective (center line) is

$$CL = \frac{\begin{pmatrix} .01 + .02 + .01 + .03 + .02 + .01 + .00 + .02 + \\ .00 + .01 + .03 + .02 + .03 + .02 + .01 + .00 \end{pmatrix}}{16}$$

$$= .015$$

$$UCL = .015 + 3\sqrt{\frac{.015(.985)}{100}}$$

$$= .015 + .0365$$

$$= .0515$$

$$LCL = .015 - 3\sqrt{\frac{.015(.985)}{100}}$$

$$= .015 - .0365$$

$$= -.0215 \text{ which is negative}$$

Therefore, the LCL = 0

b.

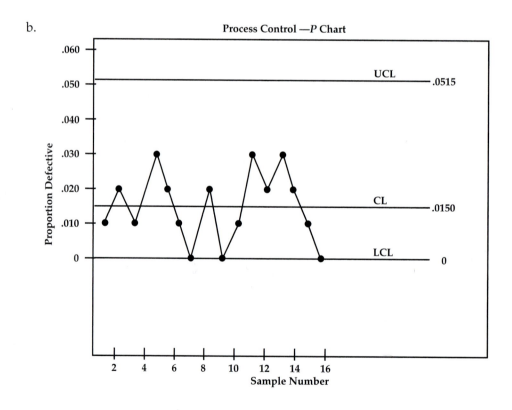

Process Control —*P* Chart

c. All the points are within the control limits. We can conclude that the process is in control.

Problem

2. **$\bar{x}$ and R Control Charts**   A cereal manufacturer fills cereal boxes to an average weight of 20 ounces, and has an average range of 2 ounces when the filling process is in control. A sample size of 10 boxes is used in sampling the process.

a. What are the CL, UCL, and LCL for the $\bar{x}$ and R charts?

b. A sample with the following 10 measurements was just taken: 20, 21, 19, 18, 19, 21, 22, 20, 20, 19. Is the process still in control?

Solution

a.

$\bar{x}$ Chart	R Chart
CL = 20	CL = 2
UCL = 20 + .308(2)	UCL = 1.777(2)
= 20.616	= 3.554
LCL = 20 − .308(2)	LCL = 0.223(2)
= 19.384	= 0.446

Note: Table 9.1 is used to get the control chart constants.

b. Process control charts need to be checked for both mean and range. The sample mean is 199/10 = 19.9 and the sample range is 22 − 18 = 4. The range is out of control, above the upper control limit, but the mean is still in control. They should stop the process and look for an assignable cause.

Problem

3. **Process Capability (C_{pk} and C_p)**   The operations manager of an insurance claims-processing department wants to determine the claims-processing capability of the department. Claims usually take a minimum of four days to handle. The company has a commitment to handle all claims within 10 days. On the average, claims are processed in eight days and processing has a standard deviation of one day.

a. Compute C_p and C_{pk} for the claims-processing department. Based on these computations, should the claims department improve its process?

b. Using the same data, recompute C_{pk}, but use an average claims-processing time of seven days instead of eight days.

c. Using the original data, recompute C_{pk}, but use a standard deviation of 2/3 of a day. Which change made the most improvement—the change in mean in part *(b)* or the change in standard deviation? Can you explain the results?

Solution

a. $C_p = \dfrac{10 - 4}{6(1)} = 1.000$

$$C_{pk} = \min\left\{\frac{10 - 8}{3(1)}, \frac{8 - 4}{3(1)}\right\}$$

$$= \min\{0.667, 1.333\} = 0.667$$

The C_p calculation seems to indicate that the process is capable of performing within specification; however, since C_{pk} is less than 1.0, the process needs improvement if it is to become even minimally capable of meeting the customer service specifications.

b. Using reduced mean claim-processing time of seven days per claim,

$$C_{pk} = \min\left\{\frac{10 - 7}{3(1)}, \frac{7 - 4}{3(1)}\right\}$$

$$= \min\{1.0, 1.0\} = 1.0$$

c. Using reduced standard deviation of claim-processing time of .667 day per claim,

$$C_{pk} = \min\left\{\frac{10 - 8}{3(.667)}, \frac{8 - 4}{3(.667)}\right\}$$
$$= \min\{1.0, 2.0\} = 1.0$$

Either change would result in the process being capable of meeting specifications. Since the mean processing time was not centered within the specification limits to begin with, shifting the mean processing time toward the center of the specification limits has exactly the same effect as decreasing the variation in claims-processing time. Ideally, the manager should strive for a reduction in both the mean and variation of claims-processing time to enhance process capability.

Discussion Questions

1. Why did statistical quality control ideas catch on in the 1940s?

2. Suppose you make electronic calculators that contain a chip purchased from a local vendor. How would you decide how much inspection to perform on the chips supplied to you?

3. For the following situations, comment on whether inspection by variables or by attributes might be more appropriate:
   a. Filling packaged food containers to the proper weight.
   b. Inspecting for defects in yard goods.
   c. Inspecting appliances for surface imperfections.
   d. Determining the sugar content of candy bars.

4. It has been said that workers should be given more control over the inspection of their own work. Discuss the pros and cons of this proposition.

5. Why is it that most processes are not in statistical control when they are first sampled for control chart purposes?

6. It has been suggested that a sample of six items be taken four times a day to control a particular process. How would you go about evaluating this suggestion?

7. Define the purpose of continuous improvement of quality.

8. How can a Pareto chart be used to improve quality?

9. Which technique would be useful for each of the following situations?
   a. To rank-order the causes of a quality problem.
   b. To brainstorm the various reasons why a product might have failed.
   c. To find an assignable cause.
   d. To determine if a process is under control in range.
   e. To reduce the variability of failures found in the field under actual use of the product.
   f. To achieve the smallest possible variance in the time that it takes to wait on tables in a restaurant.

10. A cause-and-effect diagram is used to identify the possible causes of defects. Draw a CE diagram for the following situations.
    a. Your car doesn't start in the morning.
    b. You received a low grade on your last exam.
    c. A student fails to graduate from college.

11. It has been said that Six Sigma is a metric, a process for improvement, and a philosophy for managing a business. Explain these different perspectives.

12. Use the DMAIC steps to describe and improve the process of ordering a book from an Internet provider. From the perspective of the company, what would be done in each of the steps?

13. What are the pros and cons of using the Six Sigma approach?

Problems

1. Golden Gopher Airline issues thousands of aircraft boarding passes to passengers each day. In some cases a boarding pass is spoiled for various reasons and discarded by the airline agent before issuing the final boarding pass to a customer. To control the process for issuing boarding passes, the airline has sampled the process for 100 days and determined the average proportion of defective

passes is .005 (5 in every 1,000 passes are spoiled and discarded). In the future, the airline plans to take a sample of 500 passes that are issued each day and calculate the proportion of spoiled passes in that sample for control chart purposes.

a. What is the sample size (n) for this problem? Is it 100, 500, or 1,000? Explain the significance of the 100 days used to determine the average proportion defective.

b. Calculate the CL, UCL, and LCL using three standard deviations for control purposes.

2. We have taken 12 samples of 200 letters each from a typing pool and found the following proportions of defective letters: .01, .02, .02, .00, .01, .03, .02, .01, .00, .04, .03, and .02. A letter is considered defective when one or more errors are detected.

a. Calculate the control limits for a p control chart.

b. A sample of 200 letters has just been taken, and 6 letters were found to be defective. Is the process still in control?

eXcel 3. Each day 400 inventory control records are cycle-counted for errors. These counts have been made over a period of 20 days and have resulted in the following proportion of records found in error each day:

.0025 .0075 .0050 .0150 .0125 .0075 .0050 .0025 .0175 .0200 .0150 .0050 .0150 .0125 .0075 .0150 .0200 .0125 .0075 .0100

a. Calculate the center line, upper control limit, and lower control limit for a p control chart.

b. Plot the 20 points on the chart and determine which ones are in control.

c. Is the process stable enough to begin using these data for quality control purposes?

4. A process for producing electronic circuits has achieved very high yield levels. An average of only 10 defective parts per million is currently produced.

a. What are the upper and lower control limits for a sample size of 100?

b. Recompute the upper and lower control limits for a sample size of 10,000.

c. Which of these two sample sizes would you recommend? Explain.

5. Widgets are made in a two-shift operation. Management is wondering if there is any difference in the proportion of defectives produced by these two shifts. They suspect that the second shift has a higher rate of defectives, since the workforce is not as highly trained and supervision may be lacking.

a. How would you use the p control chart to determine if there is a difference between the two shifts? Explain.

b. On the first shift, samples of size 200 have been used and $\bar{p} = .04$. Calculate CL, UCL, LCL for the first shift.

c. On the second shift, six samples of size 200 have been taken with the proportion of defectives .04, .06, .10, .02, .05, and .03. Using the samples from the second shift, has the process mean shifted upward or downward? Explain.

6. In a control chart application, we have found that the grand average over all past samples of size 7 is $\bar{\bar{x}} = 30$ and $\bar{R} = 5$.

a. Set up a control chart for this application.

b. The following measurements are taken: 38, 35, 27, 30, 33, 28, and 32. Is the process still in control?

7. The producer of electronic circuits in problem 4 has reconsidered the method of quality control and has decided to use process control by variables instead of attributes. For variables control a circuit voltage will be measured based on a sample of only five circuits. The past average voltage for samples of size 5 has been 3.1 volts, and the range has been 1.2 volts.

a. What would the upper and lower control limits be for the resulting control charts (average and range)?

b. Five samples of voltage are taken with the following results:

Sample	1	2	3	4	5
$\bar{x}$	3.6	3.3	2.6	3.9	3.4
R	2.0	2.6	0.7	2.1	2.3

What action should be taken, if any?

c. Discuss the pros and cons of using this variables control chart versus the control chart described in problem 4. Which do you prefer?

8. A machining operation requires close tolerances on a certain part for automobile engines. The current tolerance for this measurement is 3.0 cm ±.001. The quality control procedure is to take a sample of size 4 and measure each of the parts. On the basis of past samples of size 4, $\bar{\bar{x}} = 3.0$ and $\bar{R} = .0015$.

a. Construct an average and range chart for this part.

b. On the basis of the following data, is the process in control?

Sample	1	2	3	4	5
$\bar{x}$	3.0005	2.9904	3.0010	3.0015	3.0008
R	0.0024	0.0031	0.0010	0.0040	0.0010

c. Is the process running outside of its tolerances?

(continues page 185)

Excel Spreadsheet Tips

Two Excel spreadsheets are provided on the student CD-ROM for assistance in solving problems 3 and 11 in this chapter. The spreadsheet for problem 3, with different data than problem 3, is shown below. Inputs to this spreadsheet are the proportion of defects from 20 samples of 400 items each. Outputs are the center line and the upper and lower control limits for an attribute control chart. The sample data are plotted on the *p* control chart below, which indicates that all the sample points are in control.

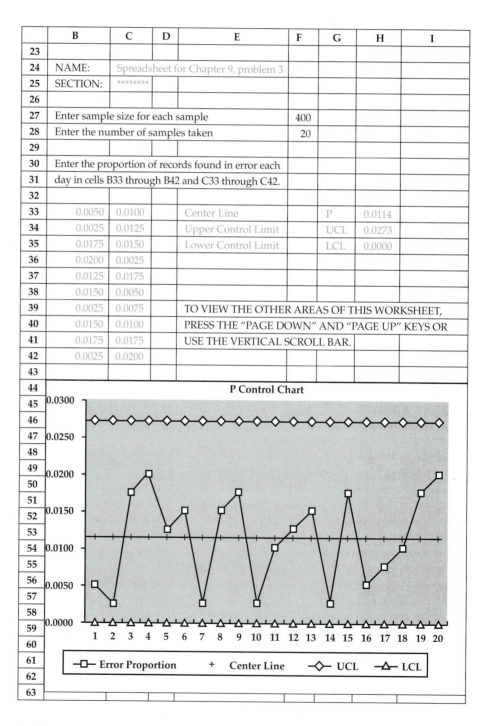

	B	C	D	E	F	G	H	I
23								
24	NAME:	Spreadsheet for Chapter 9, problem 3						
25	SECTION:	********						
26								
27	Enter sample size for each sample				400			
28	Enter the number of samples taken				20			
29								
30	Enter the proportion of records found in error each							
31	day in cells B33 through B42 and C33 through C42.							
32								
33	0.0050	0.0100		Center Line		P	0.0114	
34	0.0025	0.0125		Upper Control Limit		UCL	0.0273	
35	0.0175	0.0150		Lower Control Limit		LCL	0.0000	
36	0.0200	0.0025						
37	0.0125	0.0175						
38	0.0150	0.0050						
39	0.0025	0.0075		TO VIEW THE OTHER AREAS OF THIS WORKSHEET,				
40	0.0150	0.0100		PRESS THE "PAGE DOWN" AND "PAGE UP" KEYS OR				
41	0.0175	0.0175		USE THE VERTICAL SCROLL BAR.				
42	0.0025	0.0200						
43								

9. The Robin Hood Bank has noticed an apparent recent decline in the daily demand deposits. The average daily demand deposit balance has been running at $106 million with an average range of $10 million over the past year. The demand deposits for the past six days have been 110, 102, 96, 87, 115, and 106.

   a. What are the CL, UCL, and LCL for the $\bar{X}$ and R charts based on a sample size of 6?

   b. Compute an average and range for the past six days. Do the figures for the past six days suggest a change in the average or range from the past year?

10. A grocery store purchases fresh fish every day from its supplier. It has ordered 100 pounds of fish each day, but the weight actually received varies from day to day with an average range of 4 pounds. Over the past five days it received the following weights of fish: 106, 94, 102, 100, and 97 pounds.

   a. Using this five-day sample is the process of the fish supplier in control in average and range?

   b. How can the supplier more carefully control the process to provide nearly 100 pounds of fish each day?

eXcel 11. As cereal boxes are filled in a factory, they are weighed for their contents by an automatic scale. The target value is to put 10 ounces of cereal in each box. Twenty samples of three boxes each have been weighed for quality control purposes. The fill weight for each box is shown below.

Observation

Sample	1	2	3
1	10.01	9.90	10.03
2	9.87	10.20	10.15
3	10.04	9.89	9.76
4	10.17	9.94	9.83
5	10.21	10.13	10.04
6	10.16	10.02	9.85
7	10.14	9.89	9.80
8	9.86	9.91	9.99
9	10.18	10.04	9.93
10	9.91	9.87	10.06
11	10.08	10.14	10.03
12	9.82	9.87	9.92
13	10.14	10.06	9.84
14	10.16	10.17	10.19
15	10.13	9.84	9.92
16	10.16	9.81	9.83
17	10.20	10.10	10.03
18	9.87	9.93	10.06
19	9.84	9.91	9.99
20	10.06	10.19	10.01

a. Calculate the center line and control limits for the $\bar{x}$ and R charts from these data.

b. Plot each of the 20 samples on the $\bar{x}$ and R control charts and determine which samples are out of control.

c. Do you think the process is stable enough to begin to use these data as a basis for calculating $\bar{\bar{x}}$ and $\bar{R}$ and to begin to take periodic samples of 3 for quality control purposes?

12. A certain process has an upper specification limit of 200 and a lower specification limit of 160. The process standard deviation is 6 and the mean is 170.

   a. Calculate C_p and C_{pk} for this process.

   b. What could be done to improve the process capability C_{pk} to 1.0?

13. A certain process is under statistical control and has a mean value of $\mu = 130$ and a standard deviation of $\sigma = 10$. The specifications for this process are USL = 150, LSL = 100.

   a. Calculate C_p and C_{pk}.

   b. Which of these indices is a better measure of process capability? Why?

   c. Assuming a normal distribution, what percent of the product can be expected to fall outside the specifications?

14. A customer has specified that they require a process capability of $C_p = 1.5$ for a certain product. Assume that USL = 1000, LSL = 800, and the process is centered within the spec range.

   a. What standard deviation should the process have?

   b. What is the process mean value?

   c. What can the company do if it is not capable of meeting these requirements?

Selected Bibliography

Abbot, James C. *SPC: Practical Understanding of Capability by Implementing Statistical Process Control*, 3rd ed. Greenville, SC: R. Houston Smith, 1999.

Bemowski, Karen. "Motorola's Fountain of Youth." *Quality Progress*, October 1995, pp. 29–31.

Besterfield, Dale H. *Quality Control*, 6th ed. Englewood Cliffs, NJ: Prentice Hall, 2000.

Byrne, John A. *Jack: Straight from the Gut*. New York: Warner, 2001.

Crossley, Mark L. *The Desk Reference of Statistical Quality Methods*. Milwaukee, WI: ASQ Quality Press, 2000.

Das, R., S. Colello, and H. Davidson. "Six Sigma in Corporate Law." *Six Sigma Forum* 4, no. 1 (November 2004), pp. 30–36.

Deming, W. Edwards. *Out of the Crisis*. Cambridge, MA: MIT Center for Advanced Engineering Study, 1986.

Eckes, George. *The Six Sigma Revolution: How General Electric and Others Turned Process into Profits*. Somerset, NJ: John Wiley, 2000.

Evans, James R., and William M. Lindsay. *The Management and Control of Quality*, 5th CD-ROM ed. Cincinnati: South-Western Publishing, 2001.

Gitlow, H. *Planning for Quality, Productivity and Competitive Position*. Homewood, Ill.: Irwin, 1990.

Gitlow, H., S. Gitlow, A. Oppenheim, and R. Oppenheim. *Tools and Methods for Quality Improvement*, 2nd ed. Homewood, Ill.: Dow Jones-Irwin, 1994.

Hahn, Gerald J., N. Doganaksoy, and R. Horel. "The Evolution of Six Sigma." *Quality Engineering* 2, no. 3 (2000), pp. 317–26.

Harry, Mikel, and Richard Schroeder. *Six Sigma: The Breakthrough Management Strategy Revolutionizing the World's Top Corporations*. Westminster, MD: Doubleday, 2000.

Ishikawa, Kaoru. *Guide to Quality Control*, 2d ed. Tokyo: Asian Productivity Organization, 1986.

Juran, J. M. *Juran on Quality by Design: The New Steps for Planning Quality into Goods and Services*, rev. ed. New York: Free Press, 1992.

Juran, J. M., and A. B. Godfrey, eds. *Juran's Quality Handbook*, 5th ed. New York: McGraw-Hill, 1999.

Linderman, K., R. G. Schroeder, A. Choo, and S. Zaheer, "Six Sigma: A Goal Theoretic Perspective." *Journal of Operations Management* 21, no. 2 (March 2003), pp. 193–203.

Meadows, Becki, and Forest W. Breyfogle III. "Frontiers of Quality: Bottom-Line Success with Six Sigma." *Quality Progress* 34, no. 5 (May 2001), pp. 101–4.

Mitra, Amitava. *Fundamentals of Quality Control and Improvement*. New York: Macmillian, 1993.

Mizuno, S., ed. *Management for Quality Improvement: The 7 New Tools*. Cambridge, MA: Productivity Press, 1988.

Montgomery, D. *Introduction to Statistical Quality Control*, 4th ed. New York: John Wiley & Son, 2000.

Pande, Peter S., Robert P. Neuman, and Roland R. Cavanagh. *The Six Sigma Way: How GE, Motorola and Other Top Companies Are Honing Their Performance*. New York: McGraw-Hill, 2000.

Riebling, N. B., S. Condon, and D. Gopen. "Toward Error Free Lab Work." *Six Sigma Forum* 4, no. 1 (November 2004), pp. 23–29.

Smith, Gerald M. *Statistical Process Control and Quality Improvement*, 4th ed. Old Tappan, NJ: Prentice Hall, 2001.

Tadikamalla, Pandu. "The Confusion over Six Sigma Quality." *Quality Progress* 27, no. 1 (November 1994), pp. 83–85.

Wheeler, Donald J. *Understanding Variation: The Key to Managing Chaos*, 2nd ed. Knoxville, TN: SPC Press, 1999.

Wozniak, Christopher. "Proactive vs. Reactive SPC." *Quality Progress* 27, no. 2 (February 1994), pp. 49–50.

Part **Four**

Capacity and Scheduling

Operations managers are responsible for providing sufficient capacity to meet their firms' needs. Capacity decisions should be made by forecasting demand and by developing plans to provide capacity for the long, medium, and short time ranges within the context of the supply chain being served. After discussing supply chain management and forecasting, the remaining chapters are devoted to the long-, medium-, and short-range capacity and scheduling decisions.

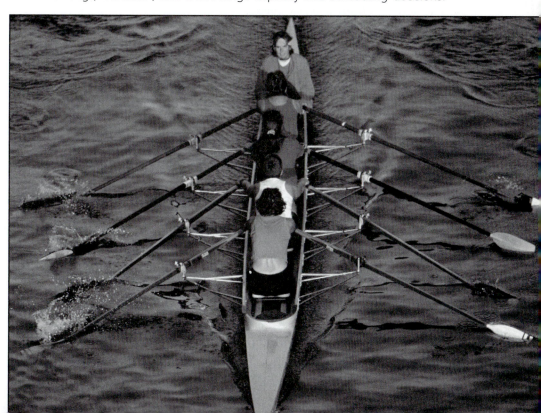

Supply Chain Management

On April 16, 2001, Cisco's supply chain broke. The world's largest network equipment maker shocked the stock market by announcing that it would write off $2.5 billion in inventories, and its stock price subsequently dropped by 6 percent. What happened that this paragon of U.S. industry misread demand by $2.5 billion? Although the market was headed for recession, there was more to the story.

Cisco does not manufacture its own product, but relies on outside suppliers for parts, components, and assembly. The incentives provided to these suppliers had encouraged them to overproduce and the resulting product ended up in Cisco's warehouses. This chapter shows how a strategic approach to supply chain design and operation can help avoid such mistakes.

Supply chain management is an essential aspect of business today. It is discussed here to provide an overview of the capacity and inventory sections of the text. We are taking a strategic approach by describing the big picture before getting into more detailed scheduling and inventory topics.

A company can identify its supply chains by first selecting a particular product group or product family. Then it should trace the flow of materials and information from the final customer (end-user) backward through the distribution system, to the manufacturer, and then to the suppliers and the sources of raw materials. This entire chain of activities and processes is known as the supply chain for that product group.

A large company will have several supply chains. In a multidivisional company with many product groups there could be many different supply chains. For example, large companies such as Procter & Gamble or General Electric may use 50 to 100 different supply chains to bring their products to market. Some of these supply chains utilize distribution through company-owned warehouses, some use direct distribution, some use outside manufacturing, and some use in-house manufacturing sites. The elements in a supply chain can be arranged in many different ways.

The subject of supply chain management has generated a great deal of interest recently in industry and academia. There are several reasons for this sudden interest. First, the total time for materials to travel through the entire supply chain can be six months to a year or more. Since the materials spend so much time waiting in inventory, there is a great opportunity to reduce the total supply chain cycle time, leading to a corresponding reduction in inventory, increased flexibility, reduced costs, and better deliveries. Also, many companies have drastically improved their internal operations and now find it necessary to consider relations with external customers and suppliers in the supply chain to gain further improvements in operations. Finally, supply chain thinking is an application of systems thinking and provides a basis for understanding processes that cut across a company's internal departments and processes that extend outside the company as well.

In this chapter, we will discuss supply chain management from several perspectives. We begin with some formal definitions and concepts, then move to measuring the performance of supply chains and ways to improve their performance. The chapter ends with a discussion of virtual supply chains. The Operations Leader box shows the supply chain for the front-end of the Ford Explorer vehicle.

10.1 DEFINITIONS AND TERMINOLOGY

The definitions presented in this section will help clarify terminology used throughout the chapter.

Supply chain. The sequence of business processes and information that provides a product or service from suppliers through manufacturing and distribution to the ultimate consumer.

Supply chain management. Planning, design, and control of the flow of information and materials along the supply chain in order to meet customer requirements in an efficient manner, now and in the future.

Distribution channel. The route from the producer forward through the distributors to the customer.

Note that the distribution channel, a term frequently used in marketing, is only a part of the supply chain. It is the forward (or downstream) part of the supply chain from the producer out to the customer.

Also, supply chain management is defined here as something different from the supply chain itself. It is important to note that supply chain management requires attention to both information and materials flow. The information feedback loop

OPERATIONS LEADER
Front-End of the Ford Explorer

The supply chain for the front-end of the Ford Explorer is shown below:

Manufacturing example: Supplier web superimposed on product BOM

Shows clearly who delivers what and how long the chains of delivery are

Part count: 9
Part sources: 7
Tool count: 5
Tool sources: 4
Check fixture count: 2
Check fixture sources: 2
Dispersal index: 81%

Closure panel check fixture: Fixture Vendor G

Assembly fixture for hood: Fixture Vendor A

Hood (Ford-Chicago)

Contact chain

Organizational boundary

Customer feature: Hood fit to fender

Assembly fixture for fender: Fixture Vendor A

Structural check fixture: Fixture Vendor E

Fender (Patt: Budd-Shelbyville Check Fixture Vendor D)

Fixture Vendor C

D-pillar assembly station: Fixture Vendor B

Assembly tooling

Reinforcements

Fender skin (Budd-Shelbyville)

Radiator support

Inner fenders (Budd-Philadelphia)

Cowl top Part Vendor A

Parts Vendor B Fixture Vendor F

Part Vendor C

Body frame (Ford LAP)

Illustrated in the figure is the web of nine suppliers of parts and tooling. The fit of the hood to the fender is determined by the quality of supplier interfaces.

Source: Paul Hermes, "Design Partners: Faster and Smarter," *Target* 12, no. 3 (1996), p. 46.

is critical to effective management of the supply chain, as we shall see in the next section. Delays in information can lead to fluctuations in orders and in ineffective movement of materials.

Two other terms need some clarification:

Demand management. Managing the demand for goods or services along the supply chain. Demand can be managed through such mechanisms as products, pricing, promotion, and distribution—tasks that are generally assigned to marketing.

Demand management is an important but often overlooked consideration in managing supply chains. It is really the flip side of supply chain management and is essential in controlling the levels of demand on the system. We consider demand management as equally important to supply chain management in managing the flow of materials and services.

Logistics management: When logistics management is broadly defined, it is identical to supply chain management. Some managers, however, define logistics narrowly as only concerned with inbound transportation and outbound distribution, in which case logistics is a subset of supply chain management.

Logistics has experienced a surge of interest with the renewed attention to supply chain management. Modern logistics thinking in terms of the systems approach can be traced back to the 1960s, along with such topics as industrial dynamics. These approaches highlight the interactions between various parts of the supply chain and how they could affect decisions in other parts of the chain. Systems thinking is an essential idea and is covered in the next section.

The surge of interest in supply chains can be traced to companies such as Hewlett-Packard, which realized that many of its assets were tied up in inventories and that total supply times were hindering improved performance. Many other companies have adopted programs for supply chain excellence, including 3M, Procter & Gamble, Motorola, Supervalu, and Federal Express. Supply chain thinking has permeated all industries, including retail, consumer goods, autos, and manufacturing.

Most analysis and discussion of supply chain management begins with a picture of a typical supply chain, as shown in Figure 10.1. For analysis purposes, it is important to identify the various parts and elements of the supply chain that will be considered. Note that in Figure 10.1 we have shown several suppliers, manufacturing plants, warehouses, and retail sites. These facilities may be under the control of a single firm, but more likely they will be controlled by several firms. Figure 10.1 is intended to show a typical example of those elements of a supply chain that might be considered for purposes of analysis and improvement.

FIGURE 10.1
A typical supply chain.

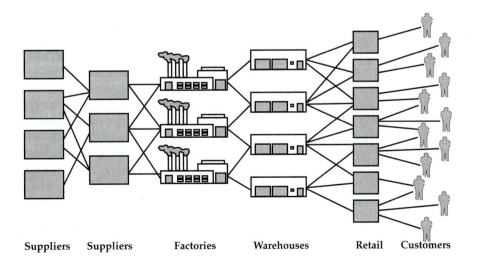

Suppliers Suppliers Factories Warehouses Retail Customers

10.2   SYSTEM INTERACTIONS

To illustrate the system dynamics inherent in supply chains, we will take a small example and introduce a sudden change in retail demand. We then observe the effect on the rest of the system.[1]

In this example, there are three levels in the supply chain: retail, wholesale, and factory. The retail level consists of 500 stores; the wholesale level has five warehouses; and there is one factory, which makes a widely known product, widgets. For simplicity, assume that the demand at each retail store is five cases of widgets a week and it has been steady at this level for some time. The stores each carry 10 cases of widgets in inventory (a two-week supply) to handle the usual fluctuations in demand. Each store orders five cases a week to replenish its stock, and it takes two weeks to process the order and ship it from a warehouse to the store.

In week two, all of the stores unexpectedly receive a demand increase from 5 to 10 cases of widgets per week. The stores immediately increase their weekly orders of widgets to 10 cases per week to cover the increased demand, even though they are not sure that the higher demand level will continue.

At the wholesale level, the warehouses have been receiving a total demand of 2,500 cases per week (5 cases per store × 500 stores). When the sudden increase in orders to 5,000 cases per week occurs, the warehouses can fill the additional demand from inventory, at least for a while. To be on the safe side, the warehouses also increase their orders to the factory to 5,000 cases per week, just in case the increased demand continues. It takes four weeks for the factory to replenish the warehouses. Assume that each of the five warehouses faces the same demand, 500 cases a week before the increase and 1,000 cases per week after the increase.

Meantime at the factory, the production scheduler notes the increase in orders from all the warehouses from the usual of 2,500 cases per week to 5,000 cases per week. The scheduler immediately plans to add a second shift to handle this doubling of demand. The second shift will be ready to produce more widgets in four weeks, the time it takes to hire and train more workers and to give advanced notice to suppliers of the increased requirements. Actually, to everyone's surprise the increased demand at the retail level continues to flow in week after week, so the quick actions at the retail, wholesale, and factory levels are justified after all.

What is the effect on the supply chain of this rather large, and sudden, increase in demand at the retail level? As we shall see, the effect is quite dramatic and in fact magnified by the replenishment lead times involved. The total replenishment lead time, also called total supply chain cycle time, is 10 weeks (2 weeks at retail + 4 weeks at wholesale + 4 weeks at the factory). It takes 10 weeks from the time a decision is made to increase production at the factory until the widgets will reach the retail level and be available to be sold to customers.

As Figure 10.2 shows, the retail level has just enough inventory to cover the demand increase without running out of stock. Although the retail inventory level is reduced to zero for several weeks, the customers get their widgets as the replenishment shipments arrive from the warehouses just in time to meet the demand. When the demand increase occurs in week two (from 5 to 10 cases),

---

[1] This example is similar to the well-known "Beer Game," which has been used at MIT since the 1960s [Senge (1990)].

FIGURE 10.2
Widget example.

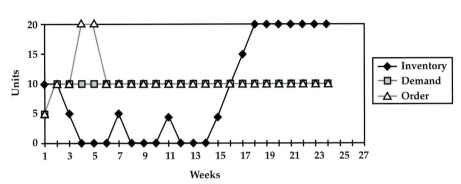

Retail Status (each store)

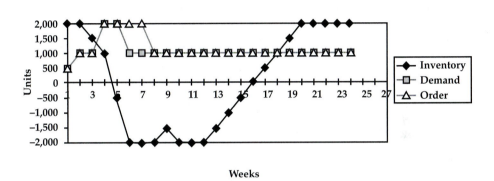

Wholesale Status (each warehouse)

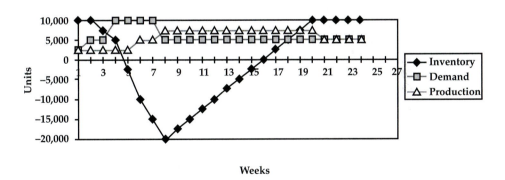

Factory Status

each retail store increases its order to 10 cases, which arrive two weeks later. In week four, the retail stores notice their stocks have been depleted and increase their orders to 20 cases per week, not only to meet the new demand but to rebuild their own inventories. This is the prudent thing to do. In week four, the wholesale level starts to run out of inventory and can only supply 15 cases of the 20 cases ordered. In week five it's worse; the wholesale level can only supply 5 of the 20 cases ordered. Nevertheless, the cases not supplied are back ordered for later delivery. The retail level then intelligently cuts its orders back in week six to the demand level of 10 units per week in order to not ultimately overshoot demand. In reality, retailers often continue to make large orders and then cancel the back orders when the stock actually arrives. This will further distort demand levels back (upstream) in the supply chain.

In the meantime, things are getting worse at the wholesale level. First, even though true demand has only doubled at the retail level, each of the five wholesale sites sees a fourfold increase in orders, from 500 per week to 2,000 per week. This occurs because the retailers not only need to meet the new demand, but also must rebuild their inventories used to meet the sudden surge in demand. Economists call this the **accelerator effect,** also commonly called the **bullwhip effect,** as the demand change is magnified the further back you go in the supply chain. The wholesale level tries to keep up with the increased demand by placing more orders on the factory, but it finally runs out of inventory in week five and is unable to recover from the back-order condition for several weeks until the factory is able to provide more widgets.

Meanwhile at the factory, quick action in adding the second shift turns out to be prudent. The second shift starts producing more widgets in week six, but this additional production is just barely enough to meet the increased demand. The factory itself goes into a back-order situation and must add a third shift to recover. Actually, this third shift is only rebuilding inventories and filling back orders in the supply chain; it will not be needed in the long run. If the third shift is kept on too long, there will eventually be too much inventory in the system—overshooting the true demand is another consequence of the accelerator effect.

Could managers have acted more prudently and prevented this situation? The answer is no. We tend to blame individuals when the root cause of the problem is the system itself, a condition that commonly occurs in supply chains. The root cause of the problem was the 10-week total replenishment lead time and the lack of a forecast of increased demand at the retail level.

The wholesale level could have avoided back orders if it had more inventory at the beginning. But the retail level was never actually out of stock, so the extra inventory would only have served to rebuild the retail inventories faster. The accelerator effect would still have been there.

The best thing management could have done was shorten the total replenishment time of 10 weeks. This would have permitted the supply chain to react faster to the sudden demand changes and would also have decreased the total inventories required to handle any given demand shift. The time lags experienced here in ordering, shipping, and adding capacity were at the core of the problem.

Of course, better forecasting also could have helped at the retail level. This would have permitted the system to build up inventories in anticipation of the demand shift rather than afterward. It might have been unnecessary to add the third shift at the factory if an accurate forecast led to the addition of the second shift before the demand increase occurred. However, it is extremely difficult to predict demand changes, so shorter replenishment cycle times are often the best solution in this situation.

In actual practice, things are often worse than shown here. Typically, the retail and wholesale levels will delay their orders to see if the demand is actually going to continue. However, waiting to order only accentuates the problem. In this example, the flow of information and orders to the wholesale and factory level is immediate—the factory decided to add the second shift in the same week that the demand increase occurred at the retail level so there was no information time lag. If there were both information and replenishment time lags, back orders would have been worse. The discussion questions at the end of the chapter address this point.

This example illustrates three key points about **supply chain dynamics:**

1. The supply chain is a highly interactive system. Decisions in each part of the supply chain affect the other parts.

2. There is an accelerator effect of demand changes. Upstream elements (warehouses and the factory) must be careful to not overreact to inflated orders from downstream elements rather than real demand changes at the end-user level. Even with perfect information at all levels, there will be an accelerator effect in the supply chain due to replenishment lead times.

3. The best way to improve the supply chain is to reduce the total replenishment time and to feed back actual demand information to all levels. The time lags in the supply chain only serve to create fluctuations in orders and inventories. Forecasting of demand changes can also serve to dampen the effect of the actual change, and demand management can smooth changes in the demand profile.

One of the best ways to achieve the changes needed for effective supply chain management is to increase coordination within and between organizations. This is the subject of the next section.

10.3   COORDINATION IN THE SUPPLY CHAIN

Although the example we have been discussing may be fictitious, these problems occur in everyday life. For example, the grocery business has a very stable consumer demand for most grocery items. At the retail level, the demand only varies by about ±5 percent from week to week, yet the demand at the wholesale and supplier levels varies by factors of 2 to 4 times this amount due to the accelerator effect and the failure to use demand management principles. For instance, it is common to have grocery price specials that greatly increase the demand in one week and depress it the following week. The grocery industry has now realized that this problem can only be solved by cooperation and coordination among everyone in the industry. The industry has, therefore, formed a partnership of retailers, wholesalers, and manufacturers to implement what is called **efficient consumer response (ECR).** The basic elements of this program are aimed at managing both demand and the supply chain.

To make improvements, it is important to increase **coordination** both across firms and within firms. The typical firm is organized into **functional silos.** These separate departments manage different aspects of the supply chain. For example, purchasing takes care of the suppliers and raw materials inventory; operations takes care of manufacturing and work-in-process inventory; and marketing manages demand and finished-goods inventory. When these departments lack coordination, as they often do, there are dramatic effects on the supply chain within the firm as well as outside the firm.

Coordination can be increased in several ways, including **cross-functional teams,** partnerships with customers and suppliers, better information systems, a flatter organizational structure, and so on. Each of these mechanisms serves to get people to work together toward overall system goals rather than narrowly defined individual or departmental goals. When this occurs, major improvements in the supply chain will result.

Many firms still view supply chain management as an area of cost control. They assign supply chain responsibility to various executives each with their own cost control objectives. This strategy is sure to fail. What is needed is overall coordination by general managers of the supply chain across organizational boundaries and a revision of the way supply chains are structured and managed.

Part of the renewed interest in industry in supply chain management is that the time for replenishment is too long, as much as one year in some cases. Companies are also starting to think in terms of total delivered cost to the consumer. This includes not only the initial cost of the product but transportation costs; warranty, repair, and return costs; inventory carrying charges for the time the product spends in the supply chain; and the carrying cost for accounts receivable until the company is actually paid. When the awareness of the magnitude of these measures becomes clear, executives then understand that the only solution is to increase coordination among the various parties involved to manage the supply chain as an integrated system. Read the next Operations Leader box to learn how a multicompany strategy is being used for quick response in industry.

There is a close parallel between supply chains and quality improvement. Quality improvement requires coordination across organizational boundaries and recognition of systems interactions. Organizations can combine quality

---

OPERATIONS LEADER
Multicompany Strategy for Quick Response

The need was for multicompany planning. Milliken and Company, a large, privately held textile and chemical producer, led an effort that was successful in forging planning linkages forward through its customer chains.

A Milliken team, headed by CEO Roger Milliken, invited several leading apparel houses plus four of the largest U.S. department store chains to a meeting in Chicago. The Kurt Salmon consulting firm had done a thorough study showing that the industry was losing the most profitable sales of all: resales of the most popular garments in the same season. Many-week lead times from fabric to retail had made same-season resupply of sold-out stocks impossible.

The Chicago textile-apparel-department store cabal hammered out an audacious plan. They would synchronize the entire supply chain (or from Milliken's position, customer chain) to recent sales at the four big department stores. Point-of-sale bar-code technology made the plan feasible, although a crude version of the plan could have been carried out using telephones and fax machines. What was most important was the agreement among the diverse players in the chain to use sales to final customers as the basis for synchronizing their activities. They called the creation the quick response (QR) program. When implemented, QR had the effect of linking production and distribution companies at several echelons in the chain all at once. A response time of three weeks from fabric ordering to receipt in the department store—down from eighteen weeks—had been achieved through a few of Milliken's customers' chains.

Within a few years, many other sectors besides textiles and apparel had forged similar chain-of-customer linkages. An annual QR international convention and exhibition emerged to tout the concept and the technology. At a Quick Response conference, special sessions were devoted to housewares, apparel, health and beauty aids, footwear, menswear, consumer electronics, textiles, toys, tools, hardware, and jewelry. Attendees came from dozens of other business sectors as well.

Source: Adapted from Richard Schonberger, "Strategic Collaboration: Breaching the Castle Walls," *Business Horizons,* March–April 1996, pp. 20–26.

improvement across the supply chain along with their cost and time improvement efforts. This leads us into the question of measurement of supply chain performance and various improvement approaches.

10.4 MEASURING SUPPLY CHAIN PERFORMANCE

Measuring supply chain performance is the first step toward improvement. A baseline of performance needs to be established and goals set for improvement. There are generally five measures of supply chain performance, which compare closely to the cost, quality, flexibility, time, and delivery measures for operations discussed in Chapter 2.

The specific measures for supply chain performance are as follows:

Delivery

This actually refers to **on-time delivery:** the percentage of orders delivered complete and on the date requested by the customer. Note that orders are not counted as delivered on time when only part of the order is filled or when the customer does not get the delivery on the requested date. This is a stringent definition, but it measures performance in getting the entire order to the customer when he or she wanted it.

Quality

A direct measure of quality is **customer satisfaction,** which can be measured in several ways. First, it can be measured relative to what the customer expected. For example, one company asks its customers, How well did we do in meeting your expectations? Responses are given on a five-point scale: (5) greatly exceeded expectations, (4) exceeded expectations, (3) met expectations, (2) didn't meet expectations, (1) greatly disappointed. The company wants a high percentage of responses of 4 or 5, indicating that it is exceeding customer expectations. This is, of course, a tough standard.

Another way to measure customer satisfaction is to ask the customers one or more of the following types of questions: (1) How satisfied are you with the overall product experience? (2) How strongly would you recommend our product to a friend for purchase? (3) How likely is it that you would purchase our product again in the future when needed? These questions can be rated on a five- or seven-point scale, and an average or percentage score of customer responses can be computed.

A measure closely related to quality is **customer loyalty.** This can be measured by the percentage of customers who are still purchasing the product after having purchased it at least once. Customer loyalty is something that companies are very interested in achieving since it is much more expensive to find a new customer than to keep an existing one. Companies should compare both loyalty and customer satisfaction to that of their competitors; they should also monitor improvement made over time.

Time

The **total replenishment time** can be computed directly from inventory levels. If we assume there is a constant usage rate from the inventory, then the time in inventory is just the level of inventory divided by the usage rate. This is an application of Little's Law discussed in Chapter 7. For example, if the inventory level is $10 million and we sell (or withdraw) $100,000 per day out of inventory, we have 100 days of inventory. In other words, a product spends 100 days on average from the time it enters inventory until it is withdrawn. The time spent in inventory should be computed for each part of the supply chain (supplier, manufacturer, wholesaler, and retailer) and added to get the total replenishment lead time.

But it is important to also consider the time it takes to get paid for the product once it is sold. It is not enough to reduce inventories; the company must also get the cash from sales so that it can use the money to make and sell more products. A measure of this time is the number of days in accounts receivable. Accounts receivable in days can also be added along the entire supply chain as a measure of payment time.

The number of days in accounts payable is a benefit to the firm since the firm is using materials from suppliers that have not yet been paid. So, the number of days in accounts payable can be subtracted from the days in accounts receivable and days in inventory.

The number of days in inventory plus the number of days in accounts receivable minus the number of days in accounts payable is called the **business cycle** needed to make the product and get the money:

$$\text{Business cycle} = \text{days in inventory} + \text{days in accounts receivable} - \text{days in accounts payable}$$

Sometimes, the business cycle is called the "cash to cash" cycle. At Dell Computer the cash to cash cycle is −37 days (days in inventory = 4, days in accounts receivable = 32, days in accounts payable = 73). This is one of the fastest business cycles in industry due to low inventories and accounts receivable, coupled with relatively high accounts payable. It is made possible by Dell's very effective management of its supply chain.

Flexibility

Flexibility is the time it takes to change volume or product mix by a certain percentage or amount. For example, suppose it takes six weeks to add 20 percent to the volume of production. If instead, we could add 20 percent to volume in a shorter length of time, then the supply chain would be more flexible. Also, flexibility can be measured by the maximum percentage of change in volume or product mix possible in a fixed period of time, say one month. For example, suppose we can make at most a 10 percent change in product mix in one month. This means if 20 different products are planned for production in the month, we could add 2 more products (a 10 percent change) in the mix in that month. Supply chain flexibility is an extremely important measure, but is not often quantified by firms.

Cost

There are two ways to measure cost. First, a company can measure **total delivered cost,** including manufacturing, distribution, inventory carrying costs, and accounts receivable carrying costs. Often these separate costs are the responsibility of different managers and are therefore not minimized from a total cost standpoint.

The second way to measure cost along the supply chain is to measure efficiency in **value added** or **productivity.** One measure of efficiency is as follows:

$$\text{Efficiency} = \frac{\text{sales} - \text{cost of materials}}{\text{labor} + \text{overhead}}$$

This measure has value added in the numerator and the total cost of adding the value in the denominator.

TABLE 10.1
Supply Chain Example

Measures	Supplier	Factory	Wholesaler	Retailer
Inventory in days	20	60	30	20
Accounts receivable in days	20	40	30	50
Purchase cost	$10	$20	$60	$ 80
Added cost	$ 5	$20	$ 5	$ 30
Sales	$20	$60	$80	$120
On-time delivery (%)	85	90	95	95
Customer satisfaction (%)	50	80	70	80
Accounts payable in days	30	40	60	30
% vol. change in a month	20	10	30	20

It is important for management to set goals for these five separate areas of measurement. By doing so, the supply chain can be improved by considerable amounts in most organizations. Table 10.1 gives an example of these measurements in a typical supply chain for illustration purposes. The set of numbers in Table 10.1 is for a supplier, factory, wholesaler, and retailer. We assume that there is just one of each in this example.

Delivery in the supply chain can be represented by the average on-time delivery of all participants.[2]

$$\text{Average on-time delivery} = (85 + 90 + 95 + 95)/4 = 91.25\%$$

Likewise, customer satisfaction can be represented by the average customer satisfaction of all participants in the supply chain.[3]

$$\text{Average customer satisfaction} = (50 + 80 + 70 + 80)/4 = 70\%$$

Time can be measured in three ways, by total replenishment time (inventory), by total days to pay (accounts receivable), and by total time to pay suppliers (accounts payable).

Total replenishment time $= 20 + 60 + 30 + 20 = 130$ days

Total accounts receivable $= 20 + 40 + 30 + 50 = 140$ days

Total accounts payable $= 30 + 40 + 60 + 30 = 160$ days

Then the total business cycle (cash to cash) is $130 + 140 - 160 = 110$ days.

The volume flexibility of the supply chain is the minimum volume flexibility of all participants since that will be the most constraining part of the supply chain, the bottleneck. From Table 10.1 the volume flexibility of the supply chain as a whole is therefore

Volume flexibility $=$ minimum $(20, 10, 30, 20) = 10\%$ change in one month

Cost can be measured by total delivered cost as a percentage of sales and by value-added efficiency. These numbers are shown in Table 10.2 for each part of the supply chain and for the supply chain as a whole. Costs are computed sequentially through the supply chain. Starting with the supplier, the cost is $10 in purchased cost plus $5 in added cost for a total of $15 at the supplier level.

[2] Alternatively it can be argued that only the delivery time to the final customer matters. The intermediate delivery times are already reflected in the delivery time at retail. In this case the measure of the supply chain is the retail on-time delivery of 95 percent.

[3] Likewise it can be argued that the only customer satisfaction that matters is the final customer satisfaction at retail. In this case the measure of the supply chain is 80 percent customer satisfaction.

TABLE 10.2
Cost Calculations

	Cost % of Sales	Efficiency Value-Added
Supplier	$\dfrac{15}{20} = 75\%$	$\dfrac{20 - 10}{5} = 2$
Factory	$\dfrac{40}{60} = 67\%$	$\dfrac{60 - 20}{20} = 2$
Wholesaler	$\dfrac{65}{80} = 81\%$	$\dfrac{80 - 60}{5} = 4$
Retailer	$\dfrac{110}{120} = 92\%$	$\dfrac{120 - 80}{30} = 1.33$
	$\dfrac{10 + 5 + 20 + 5 + 30}{120}$	$\dfrac{120 - 10}{5 + 20 + 5 + 30} = \dfrac{110}{60}$
Total	$= \dfrac{70}{120} = 58.3\%$	$= 1.833$

The supplier sells its product to the factory for $20, so the supplier's cost to sales ratio is $15/20 = 75$ percent. The factory adds $20 in cost to the $20 purchase price from the supplier for a total cost of $40 and sells the product to the wholesaler for $60. This yields a cost-to-sales ratio at the factory of $40/60 = 67$ percent. Similarly the cost-to-sales ratio can be computed for the wholesale and retail levels. The total cost-to-sales ratio for the supply chain as a whole is the supplier purchase cost plus the costs added at each level divided by the sales at retail. Efficiency and value added are computed at each level using a similar sequential approach.

After constructing these measures, the company must then set goals for those it can control. For example, it might decide to cut inventories in half, to cut accounts receivable days by one-third, to improve efficiency by 20 percent, to increase on-time deliveries to 95 percent, and to improve customer satisfaction to a level better than any of its competitors. The goals set should be consistent with the business strategy and overall business needs.

A company should also meet with its customers and suppliers and set supply chain goals as a group. It is important that the overall chain be improved, not just one portion. Also, improvement in the company's part of the supply chain could work to the detriment of others and needs to be coordinated for overall system benefit. For example, if a company unilaterally cuts its finished-goods inventory, it could reduce its costs but increase stockouts, thereby affecting its ability to supply its customers.

Any goals for improvement should be converted into financial terms. This can be done by taking the set of operational goals described above and converting them into changes in the income statement and balance sheet. As a result, it will be possible to determine the effect on net income, on assets, and on such financial measures as return on assets, return on equity, cash flow, and economic value added. Needless to say, the operational improvements must be in the financial interest of each party in the supply chain.

10.5 SUPPLY CHAIN STRATEGIES

Sport Obermeyer is in the fashion skiwear business. Each year up to 95 percent of its ski clothes is new or redesigned. The company must plan production and forecast demand well in advance of sales (more than a year), and as a result it often has stockouts or overstock situations that result in markdowns at the end of the season. The problem facing Sport Obermeyer is that its supply chain doesn't match the nature of its product. The supply chain is oriented to efficiency and low cost, whereas Sport Obermeyer needs a shorter, more flexible supply chain with better forecasting that responds to uncertain demand. There are two types of supply chains, and this company appears to have the wrong one.

To identify the proper supply chain, companies should first sort their products into two categories: functional and innovative. Functional products are like commodities—they have predictable demand and low profit margins. As a result, functional products should have a very efficient low-cost supply chain. Examples are toothpaste, standard automobiles (not the new hybrid cars), and most food. On the other hand, innovative products have unpredictable demand and high profit margins. They need a flexible and fast supply chain to deal with uncertainty in demand. Examples are fashion clothing, hybrid cars, new electronic products, and DVDs. The characteristics of these two types of products are shown on the top of Table 10.3. Note, that the product life cycle, contribution margin, average forecasting error, stockout rate, and forced end of the year markdowns are all dramatically different for functional and innovative products.

Firms often make the mistake of using one type of supply chain strategy for both types of products. For example General Mills, a food company, might use an efficient supply chain with high inventory turnover and high utilization of its factories since most of its products are functional in nature. But, General Mills also needs a different supply chain that is highly flexible and responsive to meet the uncertain demand of its new and innovative products. When firms face this dilemma, they should not make the mistake of choosing only one supply chain strategy for all products.

The two types of supply chain strategies are summarized in the bottom half of Table 10.3. The objectives of these two strategies are different. While functional supply chains should aim at predictable supply at low cost, the innovative supply chains should aim for quick response to unpredictable demand to minimize stockouts, lost sales, and markdowns. While better forecasting is helpful for unpredictable demand, it can't be relied on to achieve low inventories and full

TABLE 10.3
Supply Chain Strategies

Source: Adapted from Fisher (1997).

Product Differences	Functional Products	Innovative Products
Product life cycle	Greater than 2 years	3 months to 1 year
Contribution margin	5% to 20%	20% to 60%
Average forecast error when production is planned	10%	40% to 100%
Average stockout rate	1% to 2%	10% to 40%
Average forced end of the year markdown	0%	10% to 25%
Supply Chain Strategy		
Objective	Predictable supply at low cost	Respond quickly to unpredictable demand to minimize stockouts, lost sales, and markdowns.
Manufacturing	High utilization and low-cost production	Excess buffer capacity and short throughput time. May have low utilization of capacity.
Inventory	High turnover	Deploy significant buffers of parts or finished goods. May have low turnover.
Suppliers	Selected for cost and quality	Selected for speed, flexibility, and quality.

capacity utilization for innovative products. In innovative supply chains the high margins can absorb the higher costs of buffer capacity and buffer inventories needed to deal with uncertainty.

By better forecasting, additional capacity, and lead-time reductions for their innovative products, Sport Obermeyer was able to cut the cost of both overproduction and underproduction in half—enough to increase profits by 60 percent. Retailers were very happy that product availability exceeded 99 percent, making Sport Obermeyer the best in the industry for service.

Before making improvements to supply chains, a company should sort its products into two categories (functional and innovative) and then apply supply chain strategies that fit the nature of these products. In the next two sections we discuss approaches that can be used to improve supply chain structure and infrastructure. The choice of specific improvement decisions, however, should fit the product type and the supply chain strategy.

10.6 STRUCTURAL IMPROVEMENT

There are two basic ways to improve supply chains: by changing structure or infrastructure. Changes in **structure** are related to bricks and mortar, while infrastructure changes are related to people and systems [Hayes and Wheelwright (1984)]. Structural changes include capacity, facilities, process technology, and vertical integration. These changes are frequently long-range in nature and require considerable capital. Changes in structure rearrange the elements of the supply chain usually in a major and dramatic way.

Infrastructure includes people, information systems, organization, production and inventory control, and quality control systems. These changes are in the "soft" side of the supply chain. They involve changing the way the supply chain operates within the given structural arrangements.

Whether the improvement is in structure or infrastructure, it should reduce either uncertainty or replenishment time. Uncertainty can be reduced in demand or in supply times along the chain. This in turn reduces the need for inventory. For example, in the extreme case where demand uncertainty is zero and resupply is completely reliable, no inventory is needed except that in transit. The material can be scheduled to arrive just as it is needed by the customer.

Reducing replenishment time is a major approach to supply chain improvement, as seen in the widget example. This allows the supply chain to react rapidly to real demand changes and reduces the inventory needed. Replenishment time can be reduced by changing either the structure or the infrastructure along the supply chain.

Below, we will discuss improvements by structural change and then address infrastructure approaches in the next section. Each of these approaches addresses some combination of reduction in uncertainty along with replenishment time reduction.

There are five forms of structural change of the supply chain:

1. Forward and backward integration.
2. Major process simplification.
3. Changing the configuration of factories, warehouses, or retail locations.

4. Major product redesign.

5. Outsourcing logistics to a third party.

Forward and backward integration refers to ownership within the supply chain. If a manufacturer, for example, decides to buy a wholesale firm and distribute its products only through that wholesaler, then the integration is forward toward the market. On the other hand, if the manufacturer buys a supplier company, the integration is backward in the supply chain. If one firm owns the entire supply chain, there is total vertical integration.

Benetton is an international designer, manufacturer, and distributor of fashion merchandise. The company is highly vertically integrated because it owns its own factories and warehouses and has franchised retail outlets and captive suppliers. The high degree of vertical integration allows Benetton to make 75 percent of the requirements for a particular garment in advance and keep 25 percent in "gray" goods, which can be dyed at the last minute to meet shifting demand patterns.

In the Benetton case, one of the benefits of vertical integration is control of the supply chain. Another benefit is to reap the profits of suppliers or distributors provided there is an attractive return on investment. Vertical integration also has its drawbacks, such as loss of flexibility to changing technology or loss of economies of scale. Nevertheless, forward and backward integration decisions can be evaluated like any other investment choice of the firm and may be the key to improving supply chain performance.

Major **process simplification** is used to improve supply chains when the processes are so complex, or hopelessly out of date, that a major change is required. In this case, a clean slate approach is used, where the processes are designed from scratch without regard for the existing processes.[4] This could include major conceptual changes in how business is conducted and major information systems changes. For example, consider the changes 3M made in its Post-It notes supply chain. The plant implemented a pull system driven by customer demand, which utilized quick changeovers, daily replenishment of branch stock, and responsive production scheduling based on daily customer demand.[5] This resulted in a 99 percent fill rate, work-in-process inventory of less than one day, machine changeovers reduced from two hours to 13 minutes, and new-product introductions reduced from 80 days to less than 30 days.

The third way to restructure supply chains is to change the number and **configuration** of suppliers, factories, warehouses, or retail sites. Sometimes the distribution system is just no longer configured in the right way. For example, many companies have determined that they have too many suppliers and are reducing the number of suppliers by one-half or more. This is being done to partner with the best suppliers to ensure JIT deliveries and certified sources of material. Another structural change of this type is occurring in Europe as it becomes a more unified market. As a result, companies are finding they need fewer plants and warehouses in different locations. A complete reconfiguration of the production and distribution facilities is under way at many companies.

---

[4] Also see the discussion on business process reengineering in Chapter 7.

[5] Actually, this involved changes in both structure (process) and infrastructure.

Major product design is often needed to make improvements in the supply chain. Some companies have found that they have too many different product variations and types, some with extremely low sales. As a result, product lines are trimmed and redesigned to be more modular in nature. For example, Hewlett-Packard found that it had to make many different models of laser printers because of the different power requirements in different countries. To get around this problem, the company decided to have a common laser printer design with a power supply module that could be inserted at the last minute to configure the printer for the particular country where it would be used. This **postponement strategy** saved the company millions of dollars.

Some companies have simply thrown up their hands and decided that the best approach is to **outsource** all inventory management, distribution, and logistics to a third party. For example, National Semiconductor concentrates on making semiconductors. When the product is produced it is given to Federal Express for inventory or distribution. FedEx then warehouses the product, takes incoming orders, and ships the product to the customer.

Now that we have described some of the structural changes that can be made in supply chains, we turn to infrastructure improvements. The distinction is that infrastructure change is made within a given structure or configuration of the supply chain. Decisions concerning such issues as vertical integration, the number and type of factories and warehouses, and major process designs have been made. This is not to say that infrastructure change cannot have a major impact; it can be just as dramatic and important as structural change.

10.7 IMPROVEMENT IN INFRASTRUCTURE

The objective of infrastructure change is the same as structural change: to remove sources of uncertainty or time from the supply chain. This can be done in five ways:

1. Cross-functional teams
2. Partnerships
3. Setup time reduction
4. Information systems
5. Cross-docking

The use of **cross-functional teams** is pervasive in many businesses today. Their purpose is to provide coordination that is lacking across the various departments and functions of a business. For example, a cross-functional team is often used to plan and control the master schedule for manufacturing. The team consists of representatives from marketing/sales, production, human resources, and accounting/finance. The team develops a forecast of future expected orders, plans the capacity of manufacturing, and schedules customer orders. Everyone then agrees to work toward executing this plan. Without a cross-functional team of this type, marketing makes a forecast, production uses a different forecast to plan production, and the capital is not made available to provide the capacity needed. Without a cross-functional team, the functional silos are very effective in destroying any semblance of a master schedule that everyone can implement.

SUPPLIER AND CUSTOMER RELATIONSHIPS. A key to supply chain management is strong customer and supplier relationships along the entire supply chain. © Roy Morsch/CORBIS

Partnerships with suppliers and customers provide coordination across businesses just like cross-functional teams provide coordination within the business. Partnerships start with a commitment by both firms to establish a long-term business relationship that will be mutually beneficial. The partners must develop trust for each other to make this work. Also, the partners will probably establish teams of employees from the two different firms to work together on important improvement projects. For example, a new product was developed over several months by a team of engineers from an appliance company and its key customer's site. This team worked very effectively together and made a final presentation to the senior executives from both firms. One executive turned to the other and said, "Which employees are yours and which ones are ours?" The team had become so integrated that it was difficult to tell the members apart.

In supply chain improvement it is often necessary to dramatically reduce the **setup time** of equipment so that smaller lots of the product can be economically produced. Once the lot size is reduced, inventory will also be reduced; the inventory will turn over more quickly, thereby more closely meeting the market need. Reducing setup time requires imagination and can be done for any piece of production equipment by simply getting ready for changeover before the machine is stopped and then making changes quickly once the machine is no longer running so that it can be put back into production as soon as possible. Watching the pit crews work during a road race gives a good idea of how quickly tires can be changed and cars refueled and put back on the track. A similar type of thinking can drastically reduce setup times in manufacturing and service from hours to a matter of minutes. Reducing setup time is one of the changes that can take many days out of the supply chain.

Changes to **information systems** are important in supply chains. One of the changes occurring in industry is obtaining sales data from the final customer and feeding this information back through the supply chain. Suppliers no longer just get orders from their customers; they also know the sales and inventory positions of the customers as well. This gives the supplier a basis for forecasting future orders and planning capacity. Sharing this kind of information is easy once partnerships have been established. However, using the downstream demand information will require improved information systems and new decision rules for capacity planning. These can be integrated into a revised information system.

Cross-docking is an innovation in transportation attributed to Wal-Mart. The basic idea is that a supplier's shipments are taken from various docks at the warehouse when they arrive and transferred directly to a Wal-Mart truck at another dock. The items do not spend time in the warehouse inventory; they are simply moved from one dock to another. This provides the economy of full truckload shipments while also drastically reducing warehouse inventory. Cross-docking is now being widely used wherever there is sufficient volume to make it possible.

As we can see, both structural and infrastructure improvements can make major changes in the supply chain that help reduce uncertainty or time. These changes have a dramatic effect, as we have shown, but require immense coordination both within the firm and across firms. The opportunity for supply chain improvement is substantial in most companies.

10.8 THE INTERNET AND SUPPLY CHAINS

Electronic commerce is enabling supply chain management in many ways. The Internet and World Wide Web make it possible to process information more rapidly and provide information not previously available. This has enabled companies to speed up their supply chains and reduce costs.

There are two fundamental processes in all supply chains:

1. Order placement
2. Order fulfillment

The process of **order placement** includes not only the actual entry of an order from the customer but information supplied before the order is entered. For example, a customer might like to know before ordering a particular item whether it is in stock, where it is located, and how long it will take to be delivered. When this information is available on the supplier's Web site, the customer can access it quickly.

The Internet can facilitate faster order taking and increased accuracy of the order. As the order is taken online, it can be checked for missing information, and selection menus can be provided to ensure that the customer makes only correct choices. When the customer makes a special order, the specifications can be provided to the supplier and then checked for consistency when the order is filled. After the order is entered, the Internet can provide the customer with manufacturing and shipment status. With the Internet, the order placement process can be streamlined and made more efficient and less error prone.

In the same way, the Internet can also enhance **order fulfillment.** Once the order has been taken the producer can enter the information directly into its ERP system as described in Chapter 6. The ERP system is used to schedule production of the order or replenishment of inventory, and it is also used to plan the internal manufacturing of parts and external procurement of materials as needed. Orders to suppliers are provided directly to the suppliers' computer system to provide visibility of current and future planned orders. In this way the entire supply chain is linked electronically.

E-procurement plays an important role in both the order placement and fulfillment process. It allows a company to interact electronically with its suppliers through BtoB (business-to-business) connections. Several processes are included in e-procurement, as shown in Figure 10.3. Each of these processes can be done electronically by the Internet.

FIGURE 10.3

Processes for e-procurement.

Source: Adapted from E. A. Ageshin, "E-Procurement at Work: A Case Study," *Production and Inventory Management Journal*, 1st Quarter, 2001.

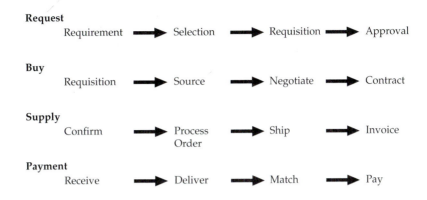

There are generally three types of e-procurement services:

1. Online catalogs listing products, prices, specifications, sales, and delivery terms.
2. Third-party auctions for buyers and sellers.
3. Private exchanges conducted by major corporations.

Many large and small suppliers have put their catalogs online so customers can easily purchase standard parts and components. This has greatly simplified order placement. However, order fulfillment must still be done physically by making and shipping the product with electronic assistance for order confirmation, billing, and payment.

An example of **third-party auctions** in the auto industry is Covisint, sponsored by GM, Ford, DaimlerChrysler, and others. This reverse auction site provides easy access to suppliers who wish to bid on parts and component contracts. In 2001 DaimlerChrysler conducted the world's largest auction event, exceeding $3 billion.

Numerous companies have now formed their own **private exchanges** for e-procurement, including Dell Computer, Siemens, GE, Herman-Miller, IBM, and Procter & Gamble. For example, IBM has 15,000 suppliers connected via the Internet and all procurement transactions at IBM are Web-based. See the IBM Operations Leader box.

E-procurement and BtoB marketplaces have been growing rapidly. In 2004 e-procurement transactions reached $1.5 trillion, with over 10,000 BtoB marketplaces. This huge growth, however, has created significant problems including:

• Too much focus has been placed on technology without adequate attention to process redesign and process coordination issues.
• Joint value propositions have not been carefully developed so that both partners benefit from the BtoB exchange.
• There have been too many fragmented efforts across divisions within the same company and also fragmented approaches across companies.
• Multitudes of record accuracy and data issues have plagued the process.

Despite these problems, the progress in integrating supply chains and the promise for the future is bright. E-procurement is rapidly becoming a standard practice in industry.

OPERATIONS LEADER
IBM and E-Procurement

This is a portion of an interview with IBM Vice President and Chief Procurement Officer M. Paterson about how the Web has changed the way IBM does business.

Q. A manufacturer of IBM's size must have a complex supply chain. About how many outside suppliers does IBM use?

A. We probably have a total of a couple of hundred thousand suppliers across all our manufacturing lines. Of those, a few hundred are key suppliers. We may place hundreds of millions of dollars in orders with a key supplier in a year.

Q. Supply chain management has become an industry buzzword and concern in manufacturing in the last year. How important is improving external supply chain management for manufacturers today?

A. For IBM, its life or death. Fifteen years ago we were the primary designers of the technologies in all our products. Today, the speed of technological change has forced us to become integrators of other people's technology for many products.

It is not unusual in the PC line to bring out new products every four to six months using the latest and greatest technologies. The only way we can do that is to buy subsystems from multiple suppliers and assemble them into our products. We depend on those suppliers to keep us current with fast-changing technologies. So having tight integration with our suppliers determines whether we succeed or fail.

Q. A number of web-based tools and services have appeared in the last year in the supply chain arena. What types of web services are valuable for manufacturers, and which should they be cautious of using?

A. Too many web services have a heavy bias toward the buy side of the supply chain. Web services only work when they benefit both the buy side and the sell side. When a service promises buyers they will save 15 percent, and that is coming out of suppliers' margins, you can imagine how suppliers feel.

The real value of web services is in the integration of the supply chain rather than in being able to plug suppliers in and out based on price. Web-based services that tout spot buying and options are of little value to large manufacturers. We want to develop continuity, quality, assured levels of supply from our OEMs [original equipment manufacturers]. . . .

Q. To what extent has the web replaced personal contact with your suppliers?

A. It hasn't. If anything, we have more personal contact. Our relationships with core suppliers occupy a lot of our time. Those relationships are crucial to success, and personal contact by senior management is vital to building and maintaining that level of trust. We want to select suppliers whom we can work with for a large period of time, and we work hard to build and maintain those relationships. . . .

Source: G. B. Latamore, "Get Personal," *APICS—The Performance Advantage*, October 2000.

10.9 VIRTUAL SUPPLY CHAINS

A **virtual corporation** produces a product or a service without employees or buildings. It exists to coordinate other companies that do the design, production, and distribution work. The virtual company can quickly form partnerships and then dissolve them when the need no longer exists. It is a very flexible form of organization that responds quickly to changing conditions.

Suppose that you wish to form a virtual corporation. The first thing you would do is to rent space for your offices, not buy the space. Then you would rent computers and phones to communicate with other companies, and you may hire a few contract employees from an employment firm to assist you. To design the product that you plan to produce, you would contract with a design engineering firm, which would suggest alternative product designs and carry the product design through to specifications. You would also hire a contract market research firm to assess the market and make marketing and distribution plans for you. Once the design was finished, you would contract out the manufacturing to one or more of the many firms that do this type of work. Then you would line up manufacturers' representatives to sell your product along with other products that they already handle. Finally, you would contract for the transportation, distribution, and warehousing through third-party distribution firms. Now you have a virtual company. It produces a product or service without facilities or people; it has no fixed assets on the balance sheet. If the company is successful, the return on net assets (RONA), a common measure of financial performance, will be phenomenal.

But is this a good idea? When markets are rapidly changing and the company must adapt quickly, the virtual firm works well. On the other extreme, in a stable market the virtual firm may be too expensive to operate and unable to compete with traditional companies. We have described the extreme case; however, many firms only contract out a portion of their businesses and use traditional employees and assets for their core competencies. Using this approach, they protect their intellectual property and their knowledge of technology only in those areas where they plan to create a competitive advantage—core competency areas.

The virtual corporation is being made feasible by use of computers and the Internet. Rapid communications and access to well-organized information about suppliers and contractors make it possible to quickly put together groups of people who are not in the same physical location. Conferences can be held by two-way video links. Routine communications can be handled by e-mail. It seems that this technology will lead to more virtual companies in the future.

Notice, however, that even with the virtual corporation there are still companies with people and assets. These are firms that specialize in certain functions and then contract their services out to the virtual corporations. These contract companies have the traditional forms of organization. Not every firm can be a virtual company.

The virtual corporation is not a panacea; it can actually be the wrong thing in many cases. It leads to the so-called hollow corporations that do not make anything or provide a service. In the past, these companies were thought of as

shell companies; but now the time might be right for companies seeking a high degree of flexibility to be at least partly hollow and virtual in their approach to organization.

The **virtual supply chain** then consists of at least one virtual company that coordinates all the activities of the supply chain. No company owns the entire supply chain, but it can control the design of products and the movement of material through the supply chain by use of contracts and partnerships with other companies. The Benetton company mentioned earlier is probably the best example of a virtual supply chain. They own very little of the supply chain but are able to control all aspects of supply, production, and distribution through contracts and franchise arrangements.

10.10 KEY POINTS

Every firm must manage one or more supply chains. An understanding of supply chain management is essential to improving performance in all parts of the supply chain. This chapter's key points include the following:

- A supply chain is the sequence of business processes and information that provides a product or service from suppliers through manufacturing and distribution to the ultimate customer.

- According to systems thinking, all elements of the supply chain are interconnected and dependent on each other. The elements should be coordinated to achieve overall systems goals.

- Demand changes by the end-user create an accelerator effect in the supply chain, which magnifies the size of demand changes on upstream supply chain elements. Information time lags and replenishment time lags account for the dynamics observed.

- Coordination within the firm and between firms is the key to supply chain improvement.

- Measurement of supply chain performance should be made in five areas: on-time delivery, quality, flexibility, cost, and time.

- There are two types of supply chain strategies: (1) flexible supply chains for innovative products with uncertain demand, and (2) efficient supply chains for low-margin functional products with predictable demand. The proper supply chain strategy must be matched to the product type.

- Structural improvement in supply chains can be achieved by vertical integration; major process simplification; changing warehouse, factory, and retail configurations; major product redesign; and outsourcing logistics to a third party.

- Infrastructure improvement in supply chains can be accomplished by cross-functional teams, setup time reduction, partnerships, information systems, and cross-docking.

- The Internet is cutting costs and accelerating order placement and order fulfillment in supply chains. There are three types of e-procurement services: online catalogs, third-party auctions, and private exchanges.

- The virtual company contracts for most of its major functions except those related to its core competency. The virtual firm can react quickly to changes in its environment, but it can have greater costs when contracting in a stable environment.

1. Federal Express
   http://www.fedex.com/us/supplychain/services/?link=1

From this Web site, find what supply chain management services FedEx offers. Under what circumstances might a company want to use these services?

2. Supply Chain Council
   http://www.supply-chain.org/slides/SCOR5.0OverviewBooklet.pdf

Access this site to find an overview of the SCOR (Supply Chain Operations Reference) model. Come to class prepared to discuss how the model works and how it can be used.

3. PriceWaterhouseCoopers
   http://www.pwcglobal.com/

Do a quick search of the PriceWaterhouseCoopers home page using the words "supply chain" to find some of the latest ideas that this consulting firm is using.

4. Covisint
   http://www.covisint.com/res/studies/

Read about Covisint solutions offered to suppliers and customers in the auto industry. Come to class prepared to discuss your findings.

Discussion Questions

1. What is the difference between supply chain management and demand management?
2. Define the supply chains for the following products from the first source of raw material to the final customer.
   a. Big Mac
   b. Gasoline
   c. Automobile repair
   d. A textbook
3. Why is supply chain management an important area to study?
4. Suppose the widgets example described in Section 10.2 has a second demand change in week 10 back to 5 units a week. Assume this shift in demand is not known to the factory for 10 additional weeks at week 20. Draw graphs like Figure 10.2 for these new assumptions, and compare the new graphs to the original graphs.
5. Add an information time lag to the example in Section 10.2. Assume the retail level has a three-week lag before it orders additional units. Also assume the wholesale and factory levels also have three-week time lags until they order additional materials. Draw the graphs like Figure 10.2 for these new assumptions and compare them to the original graphs.

6. Why is increased coordination needed to manage supply chains? Give three examples.
7. How can coordination be increased both internally to the firm and with customers and suppliers?
8. A supply chain has the following information.

	Supplier	Factory	Wholesale	Retailer
Inventory in days	30	90	40	20
Accounts receivable in days	20	45	30	40
Accounts payable in days	30	45	60	37
Purchasing cost	$5	$20	$55	$70
Added cost	$10	$25	$10	$30
Sales	$20	$55	$70	$110
On-time delivery (%)	85	95	75	95
Customer satisfaction (%)	80	95	70	85

   a. Compute measures of total replenishment lead time, total accounts receivable, total accounts payable, and total business cycle time for the supply chain.

b. Compute average customer satisfaction and average on-time delivery.

c. Compute the total delivered cost as a percentage of sales and the total value-added efficiency of the supply chain.

9. Considering the data and calculations from question 8:

a. Where should improvements be made to benefit the supply chain as a whole?

b. Explain how improvements are related to operations strategy for each member of the supply chain.

10. Describe the supply chain strategy that should be used for an innovative product. How does it differ from the strategy that should be used for a functional product?

11. How is structural improvement in supply chain management related to business process reengineering described in Chapter 7? Where are they the same and where are they different?

12. How would you decide whether a supply chain needs improvement in structure, infrastructure, or both?

13. Suppose that management has decided to use structural supply chain improvement. How would you decide which of the five approaches to structural improvement to use?

14. Under what circumstances would a firm decide to outsource all of its inventory, distribution, and logistics to a third party?

15. Explain how setup time reduction can have a powerful effect on the entire supply chain.

16. Why are cross-functional teams so widely used for supply chain improvement?

17. Explain what is meant by cross-docking, and describe the associated benefits.

18. Describe a specific company that has e-procurement using an online catalog, third-party auction, or private exchange. If you are not familiar with any company, find one on the Internet that is using one of these approaches.

19. What problems with fulfillment can a company expect to encounter using online order placement to order from its suppliers?

20. How can the entire supply chain benefit from the use of e-procurement?

21. What is a virtual firm?

22. How does management of the supply chain for a virtual firm differ from traditional supply chain management?

Selected Bibliography

Ageshin, E. A. "E-Procurement at Work: A Case Study." *Production and Inventory Management Journal*, 1st Quarter, 2001.

Badoc, Jean Luc. "The Context of E-Supply Chain Management." *Industrial Management*, September–October 2001, pp. 20–23.

Baliga, John. "Supply Chain Collaboration." *Semiconductor International*, January 2001, pp. 81–85.

Blaser, Jim, and Bruce Westbrook. "The Supply Chain Revolution." *APICS—The Performance Advantage*, January 1995, pp. 43–48.

Chopra, Sunil, and Peter Meindl. *Supply Chain Management: Strategy, Planning and Operations*, Englewood Cliffs, NJ: Prentice Hall, 2000.

Davis, Tom. "Effective Supply Chain Management." *Sloan Management Review*, Summer 1993, pp. 35–46.

Fahey, L., R. Srivastava, J. S. Sharon, and D. S. Smith. "Linking E-Business and Operating Processes: The Role of Knowledge Management." *IBM Systems Journal* 40, no. 4 (2001), pp. 889–908.

Fisher, M. "What Is the Right Supply Chain for Your Product?" *Harvard Business Review*, March–April 1997.

Gray, Paul, and Magid Igbaria. "The Virtual Society." *OR/MS Today*, December 1996, pp. 44–48.

Hayes, Robert, and Steven Wheelwright. *Restoring Our Competitive Edge: Competing through Manufacturing*. New York: Wiley, 1984.

Hermes, Paul. "Design Partners: Faster and Smarter." *Target* 12, no. 3 (1996), pp. 46–49.

Knolmayer, Gerhard, Peter Mertens, and Aleaxander Zeierrt. *Supply Chain Management Based on SAP Systems*. New York: Springer-Verlag, 2001.

Krizner, Ken. "Covisint Strikes Integration Platform Deal." *Frontline Solutions* 2, no. 11 (October 2001), pp. 66–68.

Kurt Salmon Associates, Inc. "Efficient Consumer Response: Enhancing Consumer Value in the Grocery Industry." Monograph, 1993.

Latamore, G. B. "Get Personal." *APICS—The Performance Advantage*, October 2000.

Lee, Hau L. "The Evolution of Supply-Chain Management Models and Practice at Hewlett-Packard." *Interfaces* 25, no. 5 (September–October 1995), pp. 42–63.

Lee, H. L. "The Triple-A Supply Chain." *Harvard Business Review*, October 2004, pp. 102–113.

Narayanan, V. G., and Ananth Raman. "Aligning Incentives in Supply Chains." *Harvard Business Review*, November 2004, pp. 94–103.

Schonberger, Richard, J. "Strategic Collaboration: Breaching the Castle Walls." *Business Horizons*, March–April 1996, pp. 20–26.

Senge, Peter M. *The Fifth Discipline: The Art & Practice of the Learning Organization.* New York: Currency Doubleday, 1990.

Senge, Peter M., Art Kleiner, Charlotte Roberts, Rick Ross, and Bryan Smith. *The Fifth Discipline Fieldbook: Strategies and Tools for Building a Learning Organization.* New York: Currency Doubleday, 1994.

Shah, Jennifer Balko. "FedEx's Hub of Supply Chain." *Electronic Component News*, April 2001.

Sohal, Amrik S., Damien J. Power, and Mile Terziovski. "Integrated Supply Chain Management from the Wholesaler's Perspective." *International Journal of Physical Distribution & Logistics Management* 32, no. 1/2 (2002), pp. 96–110.

Stadtler, Hartmut, and Christopher Kilger. *Supply Chain Management and Advanced Planning,* 2nd ed. New York: Springer-Verlag, 2002.

Tobin, Walter. "Globalizing the Supply Chain." *Electronic Component News* 46, no. 5 (May 2002), pp. 27–32.

Chapter **Eleven**

Forecasting

Chapter outline

Forecasting is the art and science of predicting future events. Until the last decade, forecasting was largely an art, but it has now become a science as well. While managerial judgment is still required for forecasting, managers today are aided by sophisticated mathematical tools and methods. Forecasting has indeed come a long way from the black art of fortune-telling by use of the stars, tea leaves, or crystal balls.

Many different methods of forecasting and their uses are described here. One of the main points in the chapter is that a forecasting method must be carefully selected for the particular use it is intended to serve. There is no universal forecasting method for all situations.

Forecasts will almost always be wrong. It is rare for sales to equal the exact amount forecast. A little variation from the forecast can often be absorbed by extra capacity, inventory, or rescheduling of orders. But large variations can wreak havoc in the business. For example, suppose 100,000 cases of a product are forecast to be sold in a particular year, and only 80,000 cases are actually sold.

The extra 20,000 cases can end up in inventory, or perhaps employment might be cut to reduce production levels. It is also equally painful if the forecast is too low. Then capacity is strained, extra people may be added in a rush, or sales may be lost owing to stockouts. From these examples it is clear that forecasting has a strong impact on operations and, indeed, all functions in the business.

There are three ways to accommodate forecasting errors. One is to try to reduce the error through better forecasting. The second is to build more flexibility into the operations and the supply chain. The third is to reduce the lead time over which forecasts are required. Even good forecasts will have some error, but the lowest possible error is the goal consistent with reasonable forecasting costs.

In recognition of inherent forecasting error, all forecasts should have at least two numbers: one for the best estimate of demand (e.g., mean, median, or mode) and the other for forecasting error (standard deviation, absolute deviation, or range). To produce forecasts with only one number is to ignore error, but this is a common occurrence in practice.

Forecasting problems are often very complex and difficult. One example is forecasting the 50,000 different items carried by a typical grocery store. Stockout of a particular brand or size package can cause a loss of sale for both the retailer and the producer. Thus, forecasting occupies a central role in the firm, and all along the supply chain, because of its complexity and its impact on the business. How Wal-Mart handles complex forecasting in its supply chain is described in the Operations Leader box.

The first part of this chapter presents a descriptive framework for forecasting. Several methods and their potential applications are then discussed at length. Following this, the uses of forecasting in organizations are described.

OPERATIONS LEADER

Wal-Mart's Supply Chain Forecasting

WAL★MART

In 1962 Sam Walton opened his first Wal-Mart store. Today, Wal-Mart has over 5,300 stores worldwide that sold over $280 billion in merchandise in 2004. To help manage this complex business, Wal-Mart has developed a data warehouse for Collaborative Planning, Forecasting and Replenishment (CPFR) with its suppliers.

The data warehouse contains data for each item carried in each store for each day for the past 65 weeks. Today, this system has eight terabytes (one trillion bytes) of data on inventories, sales, forecasts, demographics, prices, markdowns, returns, and market baskets. Wal-Mart's buyers, merchandisers, logistics, and forecasting associates, along with its 3,500 merchandise suppliers, have access to this data. More than 30 computer applications are available so that the users can ask practically any question they want.

Wal-Mart provides each of its suppliers with a monthly profit and loss statement for each item supplied, along with a past history of demand and a forecast of future sales. This information appears on the supplier's server and the supplier can interact with Wal-Mart planners to arrive at an agreed forecast for planning and replenishment purposes. Suppliers can also do their own analysis using Wal-Mart's vast data warehouse. Using this state-of-the-art system, both Wal-Mart and its suppliers engage in collaborative planning, forecasting, and replenishment decisions.

Source: Adapted from Paul Foote and M. Krishnamurthi, "Forecasting Using Data Warehousing Model: Wal-Mart's Experience," *Journal of Business Forecasting Methods & Systems,* Fall 2001; and Wal-Mart Web site, 2005.

11.1 A FORECASTING FRAMEWORK

Although there are many types of forecasting, this chapter will focus on forecasting demand for output from the operations function. Demand and sales, however, are not always the same thing. Whenever the demand is not constrained by capacity or other management policies, the forecasting of demand will be the same as the forecasting of sales. Otherwise, sales may be somewhat below real customer demand.

We should also clarify at the outset the difference between forecasting and planning. Forecasting deals with what we think *will* happen in the future. Planning deals with what we think *should* happen in the future. Thus, through planning, we consciously attempt to alter future events, while we use forecasting only to predict them. Good planning utilizes a forecast as an input. If the forecast is not acceptable, a plan can sometimes be devised to change the course of events.

Forecasting is one input to all types of business planning and control, both inside and outside the operations function. Marketing uses forecasts for planning products, promotion, and pricing. Finance uses forecasting as an input to financial planning. Forecasting is an input for operations decisions on process design, capacity planning, and inventory.

For process design purposes, forecasting is needed to decide on the type of process and the degree of automation to be used. For example, a low forecast of future sales might indicate that little automation is needed and the process should be kept as simple as possible. If greater volume is forecast, more automation and a more elaborate process, including line flow, might be justified. Since process decisions are long range in nature, they can require forecasts for many years into the future.

Capacity decisions utilize forecasts at several different levels of aggregation and precision. For planning the total capacity of facilities, a long-range forecast several years into the future is needed. For medium-range-capacity decisions extending through the next year or so, a more detailed forecast by product line will be needed to determine hiring plans, subcontracting, and equipment decisions. Besides being more detailed, the medium-range forecast should be more accurate, if possible, than the long-range forecast. Short-range-capacity decisions, including assignment of available people and machines to jobs or activities in the near future, should be detailed in terms of individual products, and they should be highly accurate.

Inventory decisions resulting in purchasing actions tend to be short range in nature and deal with specific products. The forecasts that lead to these decisions must meet the same requirements as short-range scheduling forecasts: They must have a high degree of accuracy and individual product specificity. For inventory and scheduling decisions, because of the many items usually involved, it will also be necessary to produce a large number of forecasts. Thus, a computerized forecasting system will often be used for these decisions.

Forecasting is used for many purposes in marketing, including sales planning, new-product introduction, design of marketing programs, pricing decisions, advertising, and distribution planning. Forecasting isn't limited to one aspect of marketing; rather, it affects all marketing decisions. In fact, forecasting responsibility may sometimes be assigned to marketing or to a cross-functional team consisting of marketing, operations, and finance personnel.

TABLE 11.1
Forecasting Uses and Methods

	Time Horizon	Accuracy Required	Number of Forecasts	Management Level	Forecasting Method
Uses of Forecasting for Operations Decisions					
Process design	Long	Medium	Single or few	Top	Qualitative or causal
Capacity planning facilities	Long	Medium	Single or few	Top	Qualitative and causal
Aggregate planning	Medium	High	Few	Middle	Causal and time series
Scheduling	Short	Highest	Many	Lower	Time series
Inventory management	Short	Highest	Many	Lower	Time series
Uses of Forecasting in Marketing, Finance, and Human Resources					
Long-range marketing programs	Long	Medium	Single or few	Top	Qualitative
Pricing decisions	Short	High	Many	Middle	Time series
New-product introduction	Medium	Medium	Single	Top	Qualitative and causal
Cost estimating	Short	High	Many	Lower	Time series
Capital budgeting	Medium	High	Few	Top	Causal and time series

The finance, accounting, and human resources functions are also keenly interested in forecasting. Even the routine task of making a budget or estimating costs requires a volume forecast and financial plans grounded on forecasts of sales. Human resources requires a forecast to anticipate hiring decisions and personnel budgets.

In summary, there are different types of decisions in operations and different forecasting requirements, as shown in Table 11.1. The table also shows some of the decisions in marketing, finance/accounting, and human resources that require a forecast. And it indicates the three types of forecasting methods associated with these decisions: qualitative, time series, and causal.

In general terms, **qualitative forecasting methods** rely on managerial judgment; they do not use specific models. Thus, different individuals can use the same qualitative method and arrive at widely different forecasts. Qualitative methods are useful, however, when there is a lack of data or when past data are not reliable predictors of the future. In this case, the human decision maker can utilize the best available data and a qualitative approach to arrive at a forecast.

There are two types of **quantitative forecasting methods:** time-series and causal forecasting. In general, quantitative methods utilize an underlying model to arrive at a forecast. The basic assumption for all quantitative forecasting methods is that past data and data patterns are reliable predictors of the future. Past data are then processed by a time-series or causal model to arrive at a forecast.

In the remainder of this chapter, we will be referring to long, medium, and short time ranges. "Long range" will mean two years or more into the future, a common horizon for the planning of facilities and processes. "Medium range" is defined as from six months to two years, the normal time frame for aggregate planning decisions, budgeting, and other resource acquisition and allocation decisions. "Short range" will refer to less than six months, where the decisions involve procurement of materials and scheduling of particular jobs and activities. For short-range decisions, forecasts that extend through procurement or production lead times are sufficient.

TABLE 11.2
Qualitative Forecasting Methods

Qualitative Methods	Description of Method	Uses	Accuracy				Relative Cost
			Short Term	Medium Term	Long Term	Identification of Turning Point	
1. Delphi	Forecast developed by a panel of experts answering a series of questions on successive rounds. Anonymous responses of the panel are fed back on each round to all participants. Three to six rounds may be used to obtain convergence of the forecast.	Long-range sales forecasts for capacity or facility planning. Technological forecasting to assess when technological changes might occur.	Fair to very good	Fair to very good	Fair to very good	Fair to good	Medium to high
2. Market surveys	Panels, questionnaires, test markets, or surveys used to gather data on market conditions.	Forecasts of total company sales, major product groups, or individual products.	Very good	Good	Fair	Fair to good	High
3. Life-cycles analogy	Prediction based on the introduction, growth, and saturation phases of similar products. Uses the S-shaped sales growth curve.	Forecasts of long-range sales for capacity or facility planning.	Poor	Fair to good	Fair to good	Poor to fair	Medium
4. Informed judgment	Forecast may be made by a group or an individual on the basis of experience, hunches, or facts about the situation. No rigorous method is used.	Forecasts for total sales and individual products.	Poor to fair	Poor to fair	Poor to fair	Poor to fair	Low

Source: Reprinted by permission of the *Harvard Business Review*. Exhibit adapted from David M. Georgoff and Robert Murdick, "Manager's Guide to Forecasting," *Harvard Business Review*, January–February 1986, pp. 110–20.

11.2 QUALITATIVE FORECASTING METHODS

As we have indicated, qualitative forecasting methods utilize managerial judgment, experience, relevant data, and an *implicit* mathematical model. Because the model is implicit, two different managers both using qualitative methods often arrive at widely different forecasts.

Some people think that qualitative forecasts should be used only as a last resort. This is not strictly true. Qualitative forecasts should be used when past data are not reliable indicators of future conditions. When this happens, past data must be tempered by judgment before a forecast can be developed. Qualitative forecasting must also be used for new-product introductions, where a historical database is not available. In this case, qualitative methods can be used to develop a forecast by analogy or by the selective use of market research data. Note, a systematic approach to qualitative forecasting is possible even though an explicit mathematical model is not formulated.

Table 11.2 describes four of the best-known qualitative methods and some of the characteristics of each. As can be seen, qualitative methods are typically used for medium- and long-range forecasting involving process design or capacity of facilities. For these decisions, past data are not usually available or, if they are, may show an unstable pattern.

Although we are not describing qualitative methods in detail in this chapter, we note their usefulness for certain situations. We also note that the qualitative methods are costly, especially when multiple forecasts are required. Next, we turn to the other extreme: time-series methods, which are well suited to multiple forecasts of a short-range nature.

11.3 TIME-SERIES FORECASTING

Time-series methods are used to make detailed analyses of past demand patterns over time and to project these patterns forward into the future. One of the basic assumptions of all time-series methods is that demand can be divided into components such as average level, trend, seasonality, cycle, and error. A sample of these components for a representative time series is shown in Figure 11.1. When the components are added together (or in some cases multiplied), they will equal the original time series.

SEASONALITY. Snow skiing is an industry that exhibits several different patterns of behavior. It is primarily a seasonal (i.e., winter) industry and over a long period of time the snow skiing industry has exhibited a generally increasing growth trend. Random factors can cause variations, or abrupt peaks and valleys, in demand.
© Masterfile Royalty Free

FIGURE 11.1
Decomposition of
time-series data.

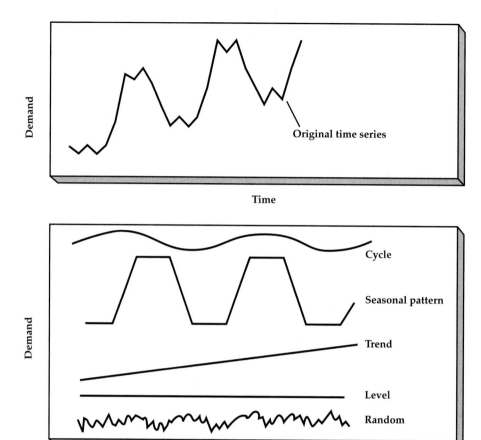

The basic strategy used in time-series forecasting is to identify the magnitude and form of each component on the basis of available past data. These components, except the random component, are then projected forward into the future. If only a small random component is left over and the pattern persists into the future, a reliable forecast will be obtained.

One example of the **decomposition** of a time series is as follows:

$$y(t) = (a + bt)[f(t)] + e \qquad\qquad \textbf{(11.1)}$$

where $y(t)$ = demand during period t

a = level

b = trend

$f(t)$ = seasonal factor (multiplicative)

e = random error

As can be seen, this time-series model has a **level, trend, seasonal factor,** and **random-error** term. Each of these terms would be estimated from past data to develop an equation that is then used to forecast future demand. See the chapter Supplement for an example of this method.

In discussing time-series forecasting, the following symbols and terminology are used:

Data										
	D_1	D_2		D_{t-2}	D_{t-1}	D_t	F_{t+1}	F_{t+2}	F_{t+3}	
Period	1	2	. . .	$t-2$	$t-1$	t	$t+1$	$t+2$	$t+3$	. . .

Observed Demands   **Forecasts at Time t**

↑
Present Time

D_t = demand during period t

F_{t+1} = forecast demand for period $t + 1$

$e_t = D_t - F_t$ = forecast error in period t

A_t = average computed through period t

The general picture is that we are at the end of period t, just having observed the value of D_t, and are making a forecast for periods $t + 1$, $t + 2$, $t + 3$, and so on.

11.4 MOVING AVERAGE

The simplest method of time-series forecasting is the **moving-average method.** For this method, it is assumed that the time series has only a level component plus a random component. No seasonal pattern, trend, or cycle components are assumed to be present in the demand data. More advanced versions of the moving average can, however, include all the various components.

When the moving average is used, a given number of periods (N) is selected for the computations. Then the average demand A_t for the past N periods at time t is computed as follows:

$$A_t = \frac{D_t + D_{t-1} + \cdots + D_{t-N+1}}{N} \tag{11.2}$$

Since we are assuming that the time series is flat (or horizontal), the best forecast for period $t + 1$ is simply a continuation of the average demand observed through period t. Thus, we have

$$F_{t+1} = A_t$$

Each time F_{t+1} is computed, the most recent demand is included in the average and the oldest demand observation is dropped. This procedure maintains N periods of demand in the forecast and lets the average *move* along as new demand data are observed.

In Table 11.3, a three-period moving average is used for forecasting purposes. Notice how the moving *average* is offset by one period to obtain the moving *forecast*. The forecast error is also shown in the table as the difference between actual and forecast demand. Always use the forecast for period t (F_t) in computing forecast errors, not the average for period t (A_t).

Let's calculate some of the numbers in Table 11.3 for illustrative purposes starting with period 3. Since we are using a three-period moving average, A_3 is just the sum of demands from periods 3, 2, and 1 averaged over these three periods.

$$A_3 = (29 + 18 + 10)/3 = 19$$

TABLE 11.3
Moving-Average
Forecasts

Period	D_t (Demand)	A_t (Three-Period Moving Average)	F_t (Three-Period Forecast)	$D_t - F_t$ (Error)
1	10			
2	18			
3	29	19.0		
4	15	20.7	19.0	−4.0
5	30	24.7	20.7	+9.3
6	12	19.0	24.7	−12.7
7	16	19.3	19.0	−3.0
8	8	12.0	19.3	−11.3
9	22	15.3	12.0	10.0
10	14	14.7	15.3	−1.3
11	15	17.0	14.7	0.3
12	27	18.7	17.0	10.0
13	30	24.0	18.7	11.3
14	23	26.7	24.0	−1.0
15	15	22.7	26.7	−11.7

The forecast for period 4 is equal to the moving average through period 3, therefore $F_4 = 19$. After seeing the actual demand in period 4, which turns out to be $D_4 = 15$, the forecast error in period 4 is calculated as $(D_4 - F_4) = 15 - 19 = -4$. Check some of the numbers in this table for yourself to make sure you understand the concepts.

The graph in Figure 11.2 shows the demand data from the example, the three-period moving average, and a six-period moving average. It is a good idea to always plot the data and forecasts before making comparisons. Notice how the six-period moving average responds more slowly to demand changes than the three-period moving average. As a general rule, the longer the averaging period, the slower the response to demand changes. A longer period thus has the advantage of providing stability in the forecast but the disadvantage of responding more slowly to real changes in the demand level. The forecasting analyst must select the appropriate trade-off between stability and response time by selecting the averaging length N.

One way to make the moving average respond more rapidly to changes in demand is to place relatively more weight on recent demands than on earlier ones. This is called a **weighted moving average,** which is computed as follows:

$$F_{t+1} = A_t = W_1 D_t + W_2 D_{t-1} + \ldots + W_N D_{t-N+1} \qquad \textbf{(11.3)}$$

FIGURE 11.2
Time-series data.

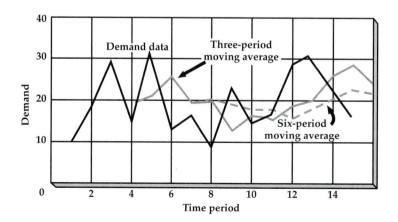

With the condition

$$\sum_{i=1}^{N} W_i = 1$$

In the weighted moving average, any desired weights can be specified so long as they add up to 1. For example, if we have the three demands $D_1 = 10$, $D_2 = 18$, and $D_3 = 29$, the ordinary three-period moving average is 19.0. With weights of .5, .3, and .2, the three-period weighted moving average is 21.9. In this case, the weight of .5 was applied to the third period, .3 to the second period, and .2 to the first period. Notice, for this example, how the weighted moving average has responded more rapidly than the ordinary moving average to the increased demand of 29 in the third period. Notice also that the simple moving average is just a special case of the weighted moving average with all weights equal, $W_i = 1/N$.

One of the disadvantages of a weighted moving average is that the entire demand history for N periods must be carried along with the computation. Furthermore, the response of a weighted moving average cannot be easily changed without changing each of the weights. To overcome these difficulties, the method of exponential smoothing has been developed.

11.5   EXPONENTIAL SMOOTHING

Exponential smoothing is based on the very simple idea that a new average can be computed from an old average and the most recent observed demand. Suppose, for example, we have an old average of 20 and we have just observed a demand of 24. It stands to reason that the new average will lie between 20 and 24, depending on how much weight we want to put on the demand just observed versus the weight on the old average.

To formalize the above logic, we can write

$$A_t = \alpha D_t + (1 - \alpha)A_{t-1} \tag{11.4}$$

In this case, A_{t-1} is the old average (20), D_t the demand just observed (24), and α the proportion of weight placed on the new demand versus the old average ($0 \leq \alpha \leq 1$).

To illustrate, suppose we use the values $\alpha = .1$, $D_t = 24$, and $A_{t-1} = 20$. Then, from Equation (11.4), we have $A_t = 20.4$. If $\alpha = .5$, we have $A_t = 22$, and if $\alpha = .9$, we have $A_t = 23.6$. Thus A_t can vary between the old average of 20 and the demand of 24, depending on the value of α used.

If we want A_t to be very responsive to recent demand, we should choose a large value of α. If we want A_t to respond more slowly, then α should be smaller. In most forecasting work, α is given a value between .1 and .3 to maintain reasonable stability.

In **simple exponential smoothing,** just as in the case of moving averages, we assume that the time series is flat with no cycles and that there are no seasonal or trend components. Then the exponentially smoothed forecast for the next period is simply the average obtained through the current period. That is,

$$F_{t+1} = A_t$$

In this case the forecast is also offset one period from the smoothed average.

We can substitute the preceding relationship into Equation (11.4) to obtain the following equation:

$$F_{t+1} = \alpha D_t + (1 - \alpha)F_t \tag{11.5}$$

Sometimes this alternative form of simple, or first-order, exponential smoothing is more convenient to use than Equation (11.4) because it uses forecasts instead of averages.

Another way to view exponential smoothing is to rearrange the terms on the right-hand side of Equation (11.5) to yield

$$F_{t+1} = F_t + \alpha(D_t - F_t)$$

This form indicates that the new forecast is the old forecast plus a proportion of the error between the observed demand and the old forecast. The proportion of error used can be controlled by the choice of α.

For example, suppose that we had forecasted for period 5, $F_5 = 100$, and have just observed the demand for period 5, $D_5 = 120$. In this case we have an error of $D_5 - F_5 = 20$. If $\alpha = .1$, then we add only 10 percent of this error to the old forecast to make the adjustment for the fact that demand has exceeded the forecast. Therefore, in this case the forecast for period 6 is $F_6 = 100 + .1 (20) = 102$. Note that in using a smoothing constant of .1 we are not overreacting to the fact we have just observed a demand that exceeded our forecast. However, if we want to react more quickly to demand increases such as this, we could just raise the value of α. For example, what would be the forecast for period 6 if $\alpha = .5$ or $\alpha = .7$? (Answer: $F_6 = 110$ for $\alpha = .5$ and $F_6 = 114$ for $\alpha = .7$.)

Students often wonder why the name "exponential smoothing" has been given to this method. It can be mathematically shown that the weights on each preceding demand data point decrease exponentially, by a factor of $(1 - \alpha)$, until the demand from the first period and the initial forecast F_1 is reached. Since the weights on the previous demands decrease exponentially over time and all the weights add up to 1, exponential smoothing is just a special form of the weighted moving average.

In Table 11.4, two exponentially smoothed forecasts are computed for $\alpha = .1$ and $\alpha = .3$ using the same demand data as in Table 11.3. As can be seen, the $\alpha = .3$ forecast responds more rapidly to demand changes but is less stable than $\alpha = .1$. Which of these forecasts is then the best?

Before answering this question let's look at a few rows in Table 11.4. In row 1 the initial forecast for period 1, $F_1 = 15$, is given as a starting value. The demand for period 1 is only 10 units, so the forecast for period 2 will be decreased. For $\alpha = .1$, the new forecast F_2 will be 14.5 and for $\alpha = .3$, the new forecast will be 13.5. (Check these numbers yourself.) That is why we say that the forecast reacts more quickly to demand changes for higher values of α but is less stable, since we don't know if the underlying long-term average has changed or whether we are just seeing random fluctuation in the first period.

To answer the question of which is the best forecast, we need to look at data and forecast errors over a relatively long period of time. Two measures of forecast error are computed in Table 11.4 for 15 periods. One measure is simply the arithmetic sum of all errors, which reflects the bias in the forecasting method. Ideally this sum should be zero, since the positive and negative errors should cancel out over time. In Table 11.4, both methods have a positive bias, with $\alpha = .1$ producing more bias than $\alpha = .3$. The reason for this positive bias in both methods is that the starting point chosen for the forecast at $F_1 = 15$ was, perhaps, a bit low. A better starting point, from hindsight, would have been $F_1 = 20$.

The second measure of forecast error is the absolute deviation. In this case the absolute value of the errors is added, so that negative errors do not cancel positive errors. The result is a measure of variance in the forecasting method. The total absolute deviation for $\alpha = .1$ is less than for $\alpha = .3$.

TABLE 11.4
Exponential
Smoothing*

Period	D_t (demand)	$\alpha = .1$ F_t (forecast)	$D_t - F_t$ (error)	$\alpha = .3$ F_t (forecast)	$D_t - F_t$ (error)	MAD_t ($\alpha = .3$)	TS (tracking signal)
1	10	15	−5.0	15	−5.0	6.4	−.8
2	18	14.5	3.5	13.5	4.5	5.8	−.1
3	29	14.85	14.15	14.85	14.15	8.3	1.6
4	15	16.26	−1.26	19.09	−4.09	7.1	1.3
5	30	16.14	13.86	17.86	12.14	8.6	2.5
6	12	17.52	−5.52	21.50	−9.50	8.8	1.4
7	16	16.97	−.97	18.65	−2.65	7.0	1.4
8	8	16.87	−8.87	17.85	−9.85	7.9	−.1
9	22	15.98	6.02	14.90	7.10	7.6	.9
10	14	16.58	−2.58	17.03	−3.03	6.2	.6
11	15	16.33	−1.33	16.12	−1.12	4.7	.6
12	27	16.19	10.81	15.78	11.22	6.7	2.1
13	30	17.27	12.73	19.15	10.85	7.9	3.1
14	23	18.54	4.46	22.40	0.60	5.7	4.4
15	15	18.99	−3.99	22.58	−7.58	6.4	2.8
$\Sigma(D_t - F_t)$ Bias			36.01		17.74		
$\Sigma|D_t - F_t|$ Absolute Deviation			95.05		103.38		

*Assume $F_1 = 15$, as an arbitrary starting point. Also assume $MAD_0 = 7$. See the text for definitions of MAD and tracking signal.

Thus, we have the interesting result that the $\alpha = .1$ forecast has more **bias** but less **absolute deviation** than the $\alpha = .3$ forecast. In this case, there is no clear choice between the two methods; it just depends on one's preference between bias and deviation. However, if a forecast has both lower deviation and lower bias, then it is clearly preferred.

The procedure for choosing a value of α is now clear. A forecast should be computed for several values of α. If one value of α produces a forecast with less bias and less deviation than the others, then this value is preferred. If no clear choice exists, trade-offs between bias and deviation must be considered in choosing the preferred value of α.

Unfortunately, simple exponential smoothing cannot always be used in practice because of trends or seasonal effects in the data. When these effects are present, second-order smoothing, third-order smoothing, trend-corrected smoothing, or seasonal smoothing might be used. Some of these more advanced methods are presented in the chapter Supplement.

11.6 FORECAST ERRORS

When exponential smoothing is used, whether it is simple smoothing or more advanced smoothing, an estimate of forecast error should be computed along with the smoothed average. This error estimate might be used for several purposes:

1. To monitor erratic demand observations or outliers, which should be carefully evaluated and perhaps rejected from the data.
2. To determine when the forecasting method is no longer tracking actual demand and needs to be reset.
3. To determine the parameter values (e.g., N and α) that provide the forecast with the least error.

4. To set safety stocks or safety capacity and thereby ensure a desired level of protection against stockout.

The first three uses will be covered next; the fourth use is covered later in Chapter 15.

In forecasting work, there are four different ways to measure the long-run cumulative forecast error over several periods of time. (Recall that $e_t = D_t - F_t$ is the forecast error for period t, as defined above.)

Cumulative sum of forecast errors	$CFE = \sum_{t=1}^{n} e_t$	
Mean square error	$MSE = \dfrac{\sum_{t=1}^{n} e_t^2}{n}$	
Mean absolute deviation of forecast errors	$MAD = \dfrac{\sum_{t=1}^{n} |e_t|}{n}$	
Mean absolute percentage errors	$MAPE = \dfrac{\sum_{t=1}^{n} \left|\dfrac{e_t}{D_t}\right| 100}{n}$	(expressed as a percentage)

Note that n is the number of past periods used to compute the cumulative error measurements.

We have already referred to the value of CFE as the bias in the forecast. Ideally, the bias will be zero, if positive errors are offset by negative errors. However, if the forecast is always low, for example, the error will be positive in each period and the CFE will be a large positive number, indicating a biased forecast. In this case the chosen starting point is too low and the forecasting method should be reset with a higher starting point.

The second and third formulas measure the variance in the forecast. The square root of MSE is the well-known standard deviation (σ). MSE uses the square of each error term so that positive and negative errors do not cancel each other out. The other measure of variance, MAD, is computed from the absolute values of the error in each period instead of the squared errors. MAD is just the average error over n periods without regard to the sign of the error in each period. In practice, MAD has been widely used in forecasting work because it is easy to understand and easy to use.

The last measure of cumulative forecast error (MAPE) normalizes the error calculations by computing a percentage error. This will make it possible to compare forecast errors for different time-series data. For example, if one time series has low demand values and another has much higher demand values, MAPE will be an accurate way of comparing the errors for these two time series.

When exponential smoothing is used, it is common to calculate the smoothed mean absolute deviation, which is defined as follows:

$$MAD_t = \alpha|D_t - F_t| + (1 - \alpha)MAD_{t-1}$$

In this case, the new MAD, or MAD_t, is simply a fraction α of the current absolute deviation plus $(1 - \alpha)$ times the old MAD. This is analogous to Equation (11.4), since the MAD is being smoothed in the same way as the average. MAD_t is just an exponentially weighted average of absolute error terms.

The current MAD_t should be computed for each period along with the forecast average. The MAD_t can then be used to detect an outlier in demand by comparing the observed deviation with the MAD_t. If the observed deviation is greater than 3.75 MAD_t, we have reason to suspect that the demand may be an extreme value. This is comparable to determining whether an observed demand value lies outside three standard deviations (σ) for the normal distribution. This is true because $\sigma = 1.25\ MAD_t$ for the normal distribution. In Table 11.4, MAD_t was computed for $\alpha = .3$. As can be seen, none of the demand errors fall outside 3.75 MAD_t, so no outliers are suspected in the data.

The second use of MAD_t is to determine whether the forecast is tracking with the actual time-series values. To determine this, a tracking signal is computed, as follows:

$$\text{Tracking signal} = \text{TS} = \frac{\text{CFE}}{\text{MAD}_t}$$

The tracking signal is thus a computation of bias (cumulative forecast error) in the numerator divided by the most recent estimate of MAD_t. If demand variations are assumed to be random, then control limits of ±6 on the tracking signal should ensure only a 3 percent probability that the limits will be exceeded by chance.[1] Thus, when the tracking signal exceeds ±6, the forecasting method should be stopped and reset to more nearly equal observed demand. In Table 11.4, the tracking signal does not exceed ±6 in any period. Therefore, the forecast is considered to be tracking sufficiently close to actual demand.

In computerized forecasting systems, it is extremely important to incorporate error controls of the type discussed above. This will ensure that the system does not run out of control. Instead, the user is notified when outliers in demand are detected or when the tracking signal becomes too large.

As an example of these computations, refer to the first few rows of Table 11.4. In the last two columns of the table we have computed smoothed MAD and tracking signal. Starting with the arbitrary assumption that $MAD_0 = 7$, we can compute MAD_1 from the previously given formula as follows using $\alpha = .3$

$$MAD_1 = .3|10 - 15| + .7(7) = 6.4$$

In a similar way, the tracking signal for period 1 is the cumulative error divided by MAD_1:

$$\text{TS} = -5/6.4 = -.8$$

As an exercise, compute MAD_2 and the tracking signal for period 2 and compare your results to Table 11.4.

As we said earlier, forecasting should produce two numbers, not only one. The forecast of average demand should be produced along with an estimate of forecasting error. This provides management with more than a point estimate

---

[1] These numerical limits and probabilities are based on the normal probability distribution and a value of $\alpha = .1$ [see Thomopoulos (1980), p. 306].

for decision making based on the forecast average alone. The forecast error is also provided and forms the basis for understanding the inherent risk in the forecast.

11.7 ADVANCED TIME-SERIES FORECASTING

A variation of exponential smoothing that has received considerable attention is **adaptive exponential smoothing.** In one form of this approach, first-order smoothing is used but the smoothing coefficient is varied at each forecast by ±5 to determine which of the three forecasts has the lowest forecast error. The resulting value of α is used for the next-period forecast. The smoothing coefficient is allowed to increase to a maximum of .95 and to decrease to a minimum of .05.

Another type of adaptive smoothing is to continually adjust α on the basis of current forecast error. For example, α could be adjusted for the value of the smoothed forecasting error. If there is a large forecasting error, α will be large until the forecast comes back on track. When the error is smaller, α will also be small and a stable forecast will result. This method appears to work quite well for inventory forecasting situations.

Table 11.5 summarizes four time-series forecasting methods. We have already discussed two of them, moving average and exponential smoothing, at some length. The remaining two are described briefly below.

Any desired mathematical model can be fitted to a time series such as the one shown in Equation (11.1), with level, trend, and seasonal components. For example, a model can be fitted by the methods of linear regression or the use of nonlinear methods. In some cases, the resulting model may provide a more accurate forecast than exponential smoothing. However, a custom-fitted model is more expensive, so the trade-off between accuracy and model cost must be made.

To aid analysts in forecasting work, the sophisticated **Box-Jenkins method** has been developed for time-series forecasting. This technique has a special phase for model identification, and it permits more precise analysis of proposed models than is possible with the other methods. The Box-Jenkins method, however, requires about 60 periods of past data and is too expensive to use for routine forecasting of many items. For a special forecast of sales involving a costly decision, however, the use of Box-Jenkins may be warranted.

In summary, time-series methods are useful for short- or medium-range forecasts when the demand pattern is expected to remain stable. Time-series forecasts are often inputs to decisions concerning aggregate output planning, budgeting, resource allocation, inventory, and scheduling. Time-series forecasts are not typically useful for decisions on facility planning or process selection because of the long time spans involved.

11.8 CAUSAL FORECASTING METHODS

In general, **causal forecasting methods** develop a cause-and-effect model between demand and other variables. For example, the demand for ice cream may be related to population, the average summer temperature, and time. Data can be collected on these variables and an analysis conducted to determine the

TABLE 11.5
Time-Series Forecasting Methods

Time-Series Methods	Description of Method	Uses	Accuracy				Identification of Turning Point	Relative Cost
			Short Term	Medium Term	Long Term			
1. Moving averages	Forecast is based on arithmetic average or weighted average of a given number of past data points.	Short- to medium-range planning for inventories, production levels, and scheduling. Good for many products.	Poor to good	Poor	Very poor		Poor	Low
2. Exponential smoothing	Similar to moving average, with exponentially more weight placed on recent data. Well adapted to computer use and large number of items to be forecast.	Same as moving average.	Fair to very good	Poor to good	Very poor		Poor	Low
3. Mathematical models	A linear or nonlinear model fitted to time-series data, usually by regression methods. Includes trend lines, polynomials, log-linear, Fourier series, etc.	Same as moving average but limited, due to expense, to a few products.	Very good	Fair to good	Very poor		Poor	Low to medium
4. Box-Jenkins	Autocorrelation methods are used to identify underlying time series and to fit the "best" model. Requires about 60 past data points.	Limited, due to expense, to products requiring very accurate short-range forecasts.	Very good to excellent	Fair to good	Very poor		Poor	Medium to high

Source: Reprinted by permission of the *Harvard Business Review*. Exhibit adapted from David M. Georgoff and Robert Murdick, "Manager's Guide to Forecasting," *Harvard Business Review*, January–February 1986, pp. 110–20.

validity of the proposed model. One of the best-known causal methods is regression, which is usually taught in statistics courses.

For regression methods, a model must be specified before the data are collected and the analysis is conducted. The simplest case is the following single-variable linear model:

$$\hat{y} = a + bx$$

where $\hat{y}$ = estimated demand

x = independent variable (hypothesized to cause $\hat{y}$)

a = y intercept

b = slope

Data are collected for this model and the parameters a and b are estimated. Then estimates of demand can be made from the above equation. Of course, more complicated multiple regression models can also be developed.

We will illustrate linear regression forecasting with a simple example. Suppose we are interested in estimating the demand for newspapers on the basis of local population. The demand for newspapers over the past eight years (y_i) and the corresponding population in a small town (x_i) are shown in Table 11.6. Using the available data, the first step is to compute the values of a and b for the line. This is done by using one of many statistics packages, such as Excel, Minitab, SPSS, or SAS. The result in this case is $a = -1.34$ and $b = 2.01$. The best (least squares) equation for predicting demand for newspapers is thus $y = -1.34 + 2.01x$. From this equation we can see that the rate of increase in newspapers is 2.01 (thousands of copies) for each 10,000 person increase in population. This rate of increase, or trend, would allow us to project newspaper demand in future years from population estimates, assuming that a linear equation continues to be a good fit with population as a predictor variable.

Other forms of causal forecasting—econometric models, input-output models, and simulation models—are described in Table 11.7. In general, these models are more complex and more costly to develop than regression models. However, in situations where it is necessary to model a segment of the economy in detail, the econometric or input-output models may be appropriate.

Simulation models are especially useful when a supply chain or logistics system is modeled for forecasting purposes. For example, suppose that you want to estimate the demand for TV picture tubes. In this case, a simulation model can be built representing the distribution pipeline from the glass tube manufacturer to the TV tube manufacturer to the TV set manufacturer and finally to wholesale and retail distribution chains; all imports, inventories, and exports from the supply chain would be included. Through the use of this model, a reasonable forecast for glass TV tubes several years into the future is obtained.

One of the most important features of causal models is that they are used to predict turning points in the demand function. In contrast, time-series models can be used only to predict the future

TABLE 11.6
Regression
Example*

i	y_i	x_i
1	3.0	2.0
2	3.5	2.4
3	4.1	2.8
4	4.4	3.0
5	5.0	3.2
6	5.7	3.6
7	6.4	3.8
8	7.0	4.0
	39.1	24.8

*The demand for newspapers y_i is expressed in thousands of copies. The population x_i is expressed in ten thousands of people.

TABLE 11.7
Causal Forecasting Methods

| Causal Methods | Description of Method | Uses | Accuracy | | | Identification of Turning Point | Relative Cost |
			Short Term	Medium Term	Long Term		
1. Regression	This method relates demand to other external or internal variables that tend to cause demand changes. The method of regression uses least squares to obtain a best fit between the variables.	Short- to medium-range planning for aggregate production or inventory involving a few products. Useful where strong causal relationships exist.	Good to very good	Good to very good	Poor	Very good	Medium
2. Econometric model	A system of interdependent regression equations that describes some sector of economic sales or profit activity.	Forecast of sales by product classes for short- to medium-range planning.	Very good to excellent	Very good	Good	Excellent	High
3. Input-output model	A method of forecasting that describes the flows from one sector of the economy to another. Predicts the inputs required to produce required outputs in another sector.	Forecasts of company- or countrywide sales by industrial sectors.	Not available	Good to very good	Good to very good	Fair	Very high
4. Simulation model	Simulation of the distribution system describing the changes in sales and flows of product over time. Reflects effects of the distribution pipeline.	Forecasts of companywide sales by major product groups.	Very good	Good to very good	Good	Good	High

Source: Reprinted by permission of the *Harvard Business Review*. Exhibit adapted from David M. Georgoff and Robert Murdick, "Manager's Guide to Forecasting," *Harvard Business Review*, January–February 1986, pp. 110–20.

FAMOUS QUOTATIONS ABOUT FORECASTING	"I have seen the future and it is very much like the present, only longer." 　—Kehlog Albran, *The Profit* "Prediction is very difficult, especially if it's about the future." 　—Nils Bohr, Nobel laureate in physics "An economist is an expert who will know tomorrow why the things he predicted yesterday didn't happen today." 　—Evan Esar "I always avoid prophesying beforehand because it is much better to prophesy after the event has already taken place." 　—Winston Churchill "Wall Street indices predicted nine out of the last five recessions." 　—Paul Samuelson, 1966 "The herd instinct among forecasters makes sheep look like independent thinkers." 　—Edgar R. Fiedler, 1977

demand pattern on the basis of the past; they cannot predict upturns and downturns in the demand level.

Because of this ability to predict turning points, causal models are usually more accurate than time-series models for medium- to long-range forecasts. Causal models are, therefore, more widely useful for facility and process planning in operations.

Nevertheless, forecasting remains an inexact science. This is demonstrated by some famous quotations about forecasting shown in the boxed insert. They warn about the dangers of forecasting, including the instability of time series, the uncertainties of the future, difficulties in predicting turning points, and "20-20 hindsight."

11.9 SELECTING A FORECASTING METHOD

In this section, we will present a framework for selecting from among qualitative, time-series, and causal methods. The most important factors in selecting a model are as follows:

1. User and system sophistication. How sophisticated are the managers, inside and outside of operations, who are expected to use the forecasting results? It has been found that the forecasting method must be matched to the knowledge and sophistication of the user. Generally speaking, managers are reluctant to use results from techniques they do not understand.

Another related factor is the status of forecasting systems currently in use. Forecasting systems tend to evolve toward more mathematically sophisticated methods; they do not change in one grand step. So the method chosen must not be too advanced or sophisticated for its users or too far advanced beyond the current forecasting system. Furthermore, simpler models can sometimes perform better, so sophistication is not the ultimate goal.

2. Time and resources available. The selection of a forecasting method will depend on the time available in which to collect the data and prepare the forecast. This may involve the time of users, forecasters, and data collectors. The preparation of a complicated forecast for which most of the data must be collected may take several months and cost thousands of dollars. For routine forecasts made by computerized systems, both the cost and the amount of time required may be very modest.

3. Use or decision characteristics. As was pointed out in the beginning of the chapter, the forecasting method must be related to the use or decisions required. The use, in turn, is closely related to such characteristics as accuracy required, time horizon of the forecast, and number of items to be forecast. For example, inventory, scheduling, and pricing decisions require highly accurate short-range forecasts for a large number of items. Time-series methods are ideally suited to these requirements. On the other hand, decisions involving process, facility planning, and marketing programs are long range in nature and require less accuracy for, perhaps, a single estimate of total demand. Qualitative or causal methods tend to be more appropriate for those decisions. In the middle time range are aggregate planning, capital-budgeting, and new-product introduction decisions, which often utilize time-series or causal methods.

4. Data availability. The choice of forecasting method is often constrained by available data. An econometric model might require data that are simply not available in the short run; therefore, another method must be selected. The Box-Jenkins time-series method requires about 60 data points (five years of monthly data). The quality of the data available is also a concern. Poor data lead to poor forecasts. Data should be checked for extraneous factors or unusual points.

5. Data pattern. The pattern in the data will affect the type of forecasting method selected. If the time series is flat, as we have assumed in most of this chapter, a first-order method can be used. However, if the data show trends or seasonal patterns, more advanced methods will be needed. The pattern in the data will also determine whether a time-series method will suffice or whether causal models are needed. If the data pattern is unstable over time, a qualitative method may be selected. Thus, the data pattern is one of the most important factors affecting the selection of a forecasting method. One way to detect the pattern is to plot the data on a graph. This should always be done as the first step in forecasting.

Another issue concerning the selection of forecasting methods is the difference between **fit** and **prediction**. When different models are tested, it is often thought that the model with the best fit to historical data (least error) is also the best predictive model. This is not true. For example, suppose demand observations are obtained over the last eight time periods and we want to fit the best time-series model to these data. A polynomial model of degree seven can be made to fit exactly through each of the past eight data points.[2] But this model is not necessarily the best predictor of the future.

The best predictive model is one that describes the underlying time series but is not force fitted to the data. The correct way to fit models based on past data is to separate model fit and model prediction. First, the data set is divided into two parts. Several models based on reasonable assumptions about seasonality,

---

[2] The model would be $Y = a_1 + a_2 t + a_3 t^2 + \ldots + a_8 t^7$, where t = time.

trend, and cycle are then fitted to the first data set. These models are used to predict values for the second data set, and the one with the lowest error on the second set is the best model. This approach utilizes fit on the first data set and prediction on the second as a basis for model selection.

11.10 COLLABORATIVE PLANNING, FORECASTING, AND REPLENISHMENT

Collaborative planning, forecasting, and replenishment (CPFR) is a relatively new approach aimed at achieving more accurate forecasts. The basic idea is to share information between customers and suppliers in the supply chain during the planning and forecasting process. For example, a customer may have information on future planned sales promotions or inventory adjustments that are not known to the supplier. In this case a forecast based on time-series data alone by the supplier would be inaccurate, but it could be adjusted if the customer information were made available.

Using CPFR the customer and supplier exchange information on their respective forecasted demands. When there is a discrepancy in the forecasts, a discussion ensues to discover the basis for the difference. After discussion, an agreed forecast is developed that becomes the basis for replenishment planning. Note, this is a forecast and not an actual order from the customer that would typically be placed at a later time. The collaborative forecast gives visibility into the replenishment planning processes beyond the usual ordering cycle.

CPFR is only useful in certain situations. It works best in BtoB relationships where there are only a few customers that reflect the bulk of demand. Wal-Mart, for example, would not use CPFR with its large numbers of retail customers, but Wal-Mart does supply forecasted orders to its suppliers. Wal-Mart does this by item and by store for all of its major suppliers as explained in the Operations Leader Box. As a result the suppliers gain visibility into expected demand shifts, special sales promotions, or inventory adjustments that Wal-Mart is planning. CPFR helps coordinate the Wal-Mart supply chain.

Whirlpool uses CPFR to forecast sales of appliances by its key trading partners (e.g., Sears). Traditionally, Whirlpool and its trading partners each had independently created a sales forecast for each market. Using CPFR they share their forecasts on a Web site and then work to reduce differences. Before CPFR, the average

Whirlpool uses CPFR to reduce forecast errors for its appliances.
©Tim Boyle/Getty Images

forecast error was 100 percent of demand due to the small quantity of appliances sold in the typical store. After using CPFR, the forecast error was reduced to 45 percent of demand. Just to understand the impact of this change, each percentage point reduction in forecast error across the system reduced Whirlpool's inventory by several million dollars.[3]

11.11 KEY POINTS

Demand forecasts are crucial inputs to planning decisions within operations and other parts of business. In this chapter, we have highlighted several important uses and methods of forecasting. Some of the chapter's main points are the following:

- Different decisions require different forecasting methods, including the following decisions in operations: process design, capacity planning, aggregate planning, scheduling, and inventory management. Some of the decisions outside of operations that require forecasts are long-range marketing programs, pricing, new-product introduction, cost estimating, and capital budgeting. The available methods may be classified as qualitative, time-series, and causal methods.

- Four of the most important qualitative methods are Delphi, market surveys, life-cycle analogy, and informed judgment. These methods are most useful when historical data are not available or are not reliable in predicting the future. Qualitative methods are used primarily for long- or medium-range forecasting involving process design, facilities planning, and marketing programs.

- Time-series forecasting is used to decompose demand data into its principal components and thereby to project the historical pattern forward in time. The primary uses are short- to medium-term forecasting for inventory, scheduling, pricing, and costing decisions. Some of the best-known time-series techniques are the moving average, exponential smoothing, mathematical models, and the Box-Jenkins method.

- Causal forecasting methods include regression, econometric models, input-output models, and simulation models. These methods attempt to establish a cause-and-effect relationship between demand and other variables. Causal methods can help in predicting turning points in time-series data and are therefore most useful for medium- to long-range forecasting.

- Two types of errors in forecasting are bias and deviation. Both these errors should be monitored routinely to control the accuracy of the forecasts obtained.

- A forecasting method should be selected on the basis of five factors: user and system sophistication, time and resources available, use or decision characteristics, data availability, and data pattern.

[3] R. E. Sloan, 2004.

- There is a distinction between forecasting and planning. Forecasting is predicting what will happen, and planning is determining what should happen.
- CPFR is a method used to share and improve forecasts between customers and suppliers along the supply chain and thereby reduce forecasting errors.

STUDENT INTERNET EXERCISES

1. ForecastPro Software
   http://www.forecastpro.com/

   This site contains a description of the ForecastPro software. Read the description and download the demo file. Write a short summary report on the features of the software.

2. Institute for Business Forecasting
   http://www.ibf.org

   This site provides a listing of jobs in the forecasting field. Examine the listing and gain an appreciation for the types of degrees desired, experience required, and companies who are looking for forecasting professionals.

3. Journal of Business Forecasting
   http://www.ibf.org

   Read a sample article from this site and come to class prepared to discuss your findings.

4. Delphus
   http://www.delphus.com

   Examine the types of software available from this company. Prepare a short report on the various features available in their forecasting systems.

SOLVED PROBLEMS

Problem

1. **Moving Average, Weighted Moving Average, and Exponential Smoothing**
   The weekly demand for chicken wings at a local restaurant during the past six weeks has been

Week	1	2	3	4	5	6
Demand	650	521	563	735	514	596

   a. Forecast the demand for week 7 using a five-period moving average.

   b. Forecast the demand for week 7 using a three-period weighted moving average. Use the following weights to obtain your forecast: $W_1 = .5$, $W_2 = .3$, $W_3 = .2$.

   c. Forecast the demand for week 7 using exponential smoothing. Use an α value of .1 and assume that the forecast for week 6 was 600 units.

   d. What assumptions are made in each of the above forecasts?

Solution

a. $F_7 = A_6 = \dfrac{D_2 + D_3 + D_4 + D_5 + D_6}{n}$

$= \dfrac{521 + 563 = 735 + 514 + 596}{5}$

$= 585.8$

b. $F_7 = A_6 = (W_1 \times D_6) + (W_2 \times D_5) + (W_3 \times D_4)$
$= (.5 \times 596) + (.3 \times 514) + (.2 + 735)$
$= 599.2$

c. $F_7 = A_6 = [(\alpha) \times D_6] + [(1 - \alpha) \times F_6]$
$= [(.1) \times 596] + [(1 - .1) \times 600]$
$= 599.6$

d. We assumed the following: Future demand will be like past demand in terms of quantity demanded. No trend, seasonality, or cyclical effects are present. In the weighted moving average model, the more recent demand is considered more important than older demand in predicting future demand. In the exponential smoothing model, an α value of .1 puts very little weight on current demand (10 percent), while most of the weight is put on past demand (90 percent).

Problem

2. **Exponential Smoothing, Exponentially Smoothed MAD, and Tracking Signal**
The XYZ Company was flooded by a thunderstorm and lost part of their forecasting data. Positions in the table that are marked [a], [b], [c], [d], [e], and [f] must be recalculated from the remaining data.

Period	D_t (demand)	$F_t(\alpha = .3)$ (forecast)	$e_t = D_t - F_t$ (error)	$\alpha = .3$ (MAD$_t$)	Tracking Signal
0				10.0	
1	120	100.0	20.0	[a]	1.5
2	140	106.0	34.0	19.3	[b]
3	160	[c]	[d]	[e]	[f]

Solution

a. $\text{MAD}_t = (\alpha \times |D_t - F_t|) + [(1 - \alpha) \times \text{MAD}_{t-1}]$
$\text{MAD}_1 = (\alpha \times |D_1 - F_1|) + [(1 - \alpha)\text{MAD}_0]$
$= (.3 \times |120 - 100|) + [(1 - .3) \times 10.0]$
$= 13.0$

b. $\text{TS}_t = \dfrac{\text{CFE}}{\text{MAD}_t}$

$\text{TS}_2 = \dfrac{(D_1 - F_1) + (D_2 - F_2)}{\text{MAD}_2}$

$= \dfrac{20.0 + 34.0}{19.3}$

$= 2.8$

c. $F_{t+1} = (\alpha \times D_t) + [(1 - \alpha) \times F_t]$
$F_3 = (\alpha \times D_2) + [(1 - \alpha) \times F_2]$
$= (.3 \times 140) + [(1 - .3) \times 106.0]$
$= 116.2$

d. $e_t = D_t - F_t$

$\quad e_3 = D_3 - F_3$

$\qquad = 160 - 116.2$

$\qquad = 43.8$

e. $\text{MAD}_t = (\alpha \times |D_t - F_t|) + [(1 - \alpha) \times \text{MAD}_{t-1}]$

$\quad \text{MAD}_3 = (\alpha \times |D_3 - F_3|) + [(1 - \alpha) \times \text{MAD}_2]$

$\qquad = (.3 \times |160 - 116.2|) + [(1 - .3) \times 19.3]$

$\qquad = 26.7$

f. $\text{TS}_t = \dfrac{\text{CFE}}{\text{MAD}_t}$

$\quad \text{TS}_3 = \dfrac{(D_1 - F_1) + (D_2 - F_2) + (D_3 - F_3)}{\text{MAD}_3}$

$\qquad = \dfrac{20.0 + 34.0 + 43.8}{26.7}$

$\quad = 3.7$

Discussion Questions

1. Is there a difference between forecasting demand and forecasting sales? Can demand be forecast from historical sales data?

2. What is the distinction between forecasting and planning? How can organizations become confused over forecasting when this distinction is not clear?

3. Define the terms "qualitative method," "time-series method," and "causal forecast."

4. It has been said that qualitative forecasting methods should be used only as a last resort. Comment.

5. Describe the uses of qualitative, time-series, and causal forecasts.

6. It has been said that qualitative forecasts and causal forecasts are not particularly useful as inputs to inventory and scheduling decisions. Why is this statement true?

7. What type of time-series components would you expect for the following items?
   a. Monthly sales of a retail florist.
   b. Monthly sales of milk in a supermarket.
   c. Daily demand for telephone calls.
   d. Monthly demand for newspapers.

8. What are the advantages of exponential smoothing over the moving average and weighted moving average?

9. How should the choice of α be made for exponential smoothing?

10. Describe the difference between "fit" and "prediction" for forecasting models.

11. A request has gone out to all salespeople in a company to make forecasts for their sales territories for next year. These forecasts will be aggregated by product lines, districts, regions, and—finally—at the national level. Describe the problems in using this forecast for planning aggregate levels of operations for the next year and for specific inventory and scheduling decisions.

12. In the Stokely Company, marketing makes a sales forecast each year by developing a salesforce composite. Meanwhile, operations makes a forecast of sales based on past data, trends, and seasonal components. The operations forecast usually turns out to be an increase over last year but still 20 percent less than the forecast of the marketing department. How should forecasting in this company be done?

13. Explain the CPFR approach and how it is used to reduce forecasting error.

14. Under what circumstances might CPFR be useful and when is it not useful?

Excel Spreadsheet Tips

Four Excel spreadsheets are provided on the student CD-ROM for assistance in solving problems in this chapter and the chapter supplement. The spreadsheet for problem 8 is illustrated below, but with different data than problem 8. Inputs to the spreadsheet are the value of alpha, demand for periods 1 to 14, and the forecast for period 1. This spreadsheet calculates the first-order exponentially smoothed forecast, error, the MAD, tracking signal, absolute error, and cumulative sum error for each period.

H	A I	B J		C		D	E	F	G
21									
22									
23		NAME:	Example			Chapter 11, Problem 8			
24		SEC:	**********						
25									
26				ALPHA	0.2				
27									
28						Tracking	Absolute	Cum Sum	
29		Day	Demand	Forecast	Error	MAD	Signal	Error	Error
30		------------	------------	------------	------------	------------	------------	------------	------------
31		1	107	110.0	–3.0	0.6	–5.0	3.0	–3.0
32		2	121	109.4	11.6	2.8	3.1	11.6	8.6
33		3	117	111.7	5.3	3.3	4.2	5.3	13.9
34		4	111	112.8	–1.8	3.0	4.0	1.8	12.1
35		5	94	112.4	–18.4	6.1	–1.0	18.4	–6.3
36		6	99	108.7	–9.7	6.8	–2.4	9.7	–16.1
37		7	104	106.8	–2.8	6.0	–3.1	2.8	–18.8
38		8	116	106.2	9.8	6.8	–1.3	9.8	–9.1
39		9	123	108.2	14.8	8.4	0.7	14.8	5.7
40		10	129	111.1	17.9	10.3	2.3	17.9	23.6
41		11	92	114.7	–22.7	12.8	0.1	22.7	0.9
42		12	95	110.2	–15.2	13.2	–1.1	15.2	–14.3
43		13	104	107.1	–3.1	11.2	–1.6	3.1	–17.4
44		14	102	106.5	–4.5	9.9	–2.2	4.5	–22.0
45				---------	---------	-------	------	------	-------

Problems

1. Daily demand for marigold flowers at a large garden store is shown below. Compute:
   a. A three-period moving-average.
   b. A five-period moving-average.

Period	Demand
1	80
2	95
3	71
4	100
5	97
6	78
7	89

2. In the Atlanta area, the number of daily calls for repair of Speedy copy machines has been recorded as follows:

October	Calls
1	92
2	127
3	103
4	165
5	132
6	111
7	174
8	97

a. Prepare a three-period moving-average forecast for the data. What is the error on each day?

b. Prepare a three-period weighted-moving-average forecast using weights of $w_1 = .5, w_2 = .3, w_3 = .2$.

c. Which of the two forecasts is better?

3. The ABC Floral Shop sold the following number of geraniums during the last two weeks:

Day	Demand	Day	Demand
1	200	8	150
2	134	9	182
3	157	10	197
4	165	11	136
5	177	12	163
6	125	13	157
7	146	14	169

Develop a spreadsheet to answer the following questions.

a. Calculate a forecast of the above demand using a three- and five-period moving average.

b. Graph these forecasts and the original data using Excel. What does the graph show?

c. Which of the above forecasts is the best? Why?

4. The Handy-Dandy Department Store had forecast sales of $110,000 for the last week. The actual sales turned out to be $125,000.

a. What is the forecast for this week, using exponential smoothing and $\alpha = .1$?

b. If sales this week turn out to be $120,000, what is the forecast for next week?

5. The Yummy Ice Cream Company projects the demand for ice cream using first-order exponential smoothing. Last week the forecast was 100,000 gallons of ice cream, and 80,000 gallons were actually sold.

a. Using $\alpha = .1$, prepare a forecast for next week.

b. Calculate the forecast using $\alpha = .2$ and $\alpha = .3$ for this problem. Which value of α gives the best forecast, assuming actual demand is 95,000 gallons?

6. Using the data in problem 2, prepare exponentially smoothed forecasts for the following cases:

a. $\alpha = .1$ and $F_1 = 90$

b. $\alpha = .3$ and $F_1 = 90$

7. Compute the errors of bias and absolute deviation for the forecasts in problem 6. Which of the forecasting models is the best?

 8. At the ABC Floral Shop, an argument developed between two of the owners, Bob and Henry, over the accuracy of forecasting methods. Bob argued that first-order smoothing

with $\alpha = .1$ would be the best method. Henry argued that the shop would get a better forecast with $\alpha = .3$.

a. Using $F_1 = 100$ and the data from problem 3, which of the two managers is right?

b. Graph the two forecasts and the original data using Excel. What does the graph reveal?

c. Maybe the forecast accuracy could be improved even more. Try additional values of $\alpha = .2, .4,$ and .5 to see if better accuracy is achieved.

9. Only a portion of the following table for exponential smoothing has been completed. Complete the missing entries using $\alpha = .2$.

Period	D_t	F_t	e_t	MAD_t	Tracking Signal
0				20	
1	300	290			
2	280				
3	309				

10. A candy store has sold the following number of pounds of candy for the past three days. Assuming $\alpha = .4$, $A_0 = 18$, and $MAD_0 = 1$, complete the following table.

Period	D_t	A_t	F_t	e_t	MAD_t	Tracking Signal
0		18			1	
1	20					
2	26					
3	14					

eXcel 11. A grocery store sells the following number of frozen turkeys over the one week period prior to Thanksgiving:

Turkeys Sold	
Monday	80
Tuesday	55
Wednesday	65
Thursday	40
Friday	85
Saturday	105

a. Prepare a forecast of sales for each day, starting with $F_1 = 85$ and $\alpha = .2$.

b. Compute the MAD and the tracking signal for the data given above in each period. Use $MAD_0 = 0$.

c. On the basis of the criteria given in the text, are the MAD and tracking signal within tolerances?

d. Recompute parts *a* and *b* using $\alpha = .1, .3,$ and .4. Which value of α provides the best forecast?

12. The famous Widget Company uses simple exponential smoothing to forecast the demand for its best-selling widgets. The company is considering whether it should use $\alpha = .1$ or $\alpha = .4$ for forecasting purposes. Use the following data for daily sales to arrive at a recommendation:

Day	Demand	Day	Demand
1	35	8	39
2	47	9	24
3	46	10	26
4	39	11	36
5	26	12	43
6	33	13	46
7	24	14	29

Develop an Excel spreadsheet to answer the following questions.

a. For the first seven days of data compare the absolute deviation for forecasts using $\alpha = .1$ and $\alpha = .4$. Start with $A_0 = 33$. Which method is best?

b. Use the second week of seven days of data (days 8 to 14) to make the same comparison. Use $A_7 = 32$ for both methods. Which method is best now?

c. What does this example illustrate?

13. The Easyfit tire store had demand for tires shown below. Split the data into two equal parts of seven days each. Assume $F_1 = 198$.

a. Develop a spreadsheet using the first seven days of demand to determine the best exponential smoothing model for values of $\alpha = .2$, $\alpha = .3$, and $\alpha = .4$. Select the model with the smallest absolute deviation for seven periods.

b. Develop another spreadsheet using the hold-out sample for the second seven days to compare the best exponential smoothing model found in part *a* with a three-period moving average model. Compare the predictions on the basis of the total absolute deviation for the second seven periods.

c. What principles does this problem illustrate?

Day	Demand	Day	Demand
1	200	8	208
2	209	9	186
3	215	10	193
4	180	11	197
5	190	12	188
6	195	13	191
7	200	14	196

14. The ABC Floral Shop from problem 3 is considering fitting various forecasting models on the first seven days of demand and using the second seven days as a hold-out sample for comparing prediction accuracy of the models. They have decided to use $\alpha = .3$, but aren't sure what starting value of forecast, F_1, to use.

a. Try values of $F_1 = 160$, $F_2 = 170$, and $F_3 = 180$ to determine the best exponential model for the first seven days using the minimum total absolute deviation as the criterion. You may modify the spreadsheet from problem 8 for the calculations.

b. Compare the best model from part *a* to a three-period moving average model on the second set of data. Which one has the smallest sum of absolute errors?

c. What principles does this problem illustrate?

Selected Bibliography

Armstrong, J. Scott. *Principles of Forecasting.* New York: Kluwer, 2001.

Basu, Shankar, and Roger G. Schroeder. "Incorporating Judgments in Sales Forecasts: Application of the Delphi Method at American Hoist & Derrick." *Interfaces* 7, no. 3 (May 1977), pp. 18–27.

Bowerman, Bruce, and Richard O'Connell. *Forecasting and Time Series: An Applied Approach.* New York: Wadsworth, 1993.

Box, G. E. P., G. M. Jenkins, G. C. Reinsel, and G. Jenkins. *Time Series Analysis, Forecasting, and Control,* 3rd ed. Upper Saddle River, NJ: Prentice Hall, 1994.

Brander, A. "One Total Forecast." *APICS—The Performance Advantage,* May 2003, pp. 54–57.

Brockwell, Peter J., and Richard Davis. *Introduction to Time Series and Forecasting,* 2nd ed. New York: Springer Verlag, 2002.

Chow, W. M. "Adaptive Control of the Exponential Smoothing Constant." *Journal of Industrial Engineering,* September–October 1965.

Delurgio, Stephen, and Amir Aczel. *Forecasting Theory and Applications.* Homewood, IL: Irwin, 1996.

Deutsch, Claudia H. "A Giant Awakens to Yawns." *The New York Times,* December 22, 1996.

Dorsey, Thomas J. *The Essential Application for Forecasting and Tracking Market Prices,* 2nd ed. New York: John Wiley, 2001.

Foote, Paul, and M. Krishnamurthi. "Forecasting Using Data Warehousing Model: Wal-Mart's Experience." *Journal of Business Forecasting Methods & Systems,* Fall 2001.

Georgoff, David M., and Robert Murdick. "Manager's Guide to Forecasting." *Harvard Business Review,* January–February 1986, pp. 110–20.

Hanke, John, Arthur Reitsch, and Dean Wichern. *Business Forecasting,* 7th ed. Upper Saddle River, NJ: Prentice Hall, 2001.

Kakouros, S., D. Kuettner, and B. Cargille, "Measure, Then Manage." *APICS—The Performance Advantage,* October 2002, pp. 25–29.

Kress, George, and John Snyder. *Forecasting and Market Analysis Techniques: A Practical Approach.* Westport, CT: Quorum, 1994.

Lapide, Larry. "New Developments in Business Forecasting." *Journal of Business Forecasting Methods & Systems* 19, no. 4 (Winter 2000–2001), pp. 17–19.

Loudin, Amanda. "Forecasting the Future." *Warehousing Management* 7 no. 4 (May 2000), pp. 34–37.

Makridakis, Spyros. *Forecasting, Planning and Strategy for the 21st Century.* New York: Free Press, 1990.

Makridakis, Spyros, Steven Wheelwright, and Rob Hyndman. *Forecasting Methods and Applications,* 3rd ed. New York: Wiley, 1998.

Nelson, Charles L. *Applied Time Series Analysis.* San Francisco: Holden-Day, 1973.

Slone, R. E. "Leading a Supply Chain Turnaround." *Harvard Business Review,* October 2004, pp. 114–21.

Thomopoulos, Nick T. *Applied Forecasting Methods.* Englewood Cliffs, NJ: Prentice Hall, 1980.

Wallace, Thomas F., and Robert A. Stahl. *Sales Forecasting: A New Approach.* Alexandria, VA: APICS, 2002.

Wilson, J. Holton, Barry Keating, and John Galt Solutions, Inc. *Business Forecasting with Accompanying Excel-Based Forecast X™ Software.* New York: McGraw-Hill, 2002.

Winters, Peter R. "Forecasting Sales by Exponentially Weighted Moving Averages." *Management Sciences,* April 1960, pp. 324–42.

Supplement

Advanced Methods

This supplement describes three additional methods for time-series forecasting that have trend and seasonal components. These methods are extensions of the techniques described in the chapter.

When the time-series model has a trend component, an exponential smoothing model can be developed that is based on updating two variables in each time period: an average level and a trend. The average level is computed as an expanded version of the first-order equation to include trend, as follows:

$$A_t = \alpha D_t + (1 - \alpha)(A_{t-1} + T_{t-1})$$

This average is then, in turn, used to update the estimate of trend by taking the difference in averages and smoothing this difference with the old trend. The updated trend is thus

$$T_t = \beta(A_t - A_{t-1}) + (1 - \beta)T_{t-1}$$

In this case, the smoothing constant β, which can be the same as or different from the constant α used for level, is used for trend. The model requires initial estimates of A_0 and T_0 to get started. These estimates can be based either on judgment or on past data.

Using the above values, we can compute forecasts for the future. The procedure is now slightly different from the first-order case, because a constant trend is assumed in the time series. The forecast for period $t + K$ in the future is therefore

$$F_{t+K} = A_t + KT_t \quad K = 1, 2, 3, \ldots$$

One unit of trend is added for each period into the future. An example using these formulas is shown in Table S11.1.

Time series having both trend and seasonal components can be forecast by a method developed by Winters (1960). In this case, three variables—average, trend, and a seasonal factor—are updated for each time period.

The average is computed for period t as follows:

$$A_t = \alpha\left(\frac{D_t}{R_{t-L}}\right) + (1 - \alpha)(A_{t-1} + T_{t-1})$$

In this case, the demand is adjusted by the seasonal ratio and smoothed with the old average and old trend. The trend for period t is

$$T_t = \beta(A_t - A_{t-1}) + (1 - \beta)T_{t-1}$$

TABLE S11.1
Trend-Adjusted
Exponential
Smoothing*

t	D_t (demand)	A_t (average)	T_t (trend)	F_t (forecast)	$D_t - F_t$ (error)
1	85	85	15	85	0
2	105	100.5	15.05	100	5.00
3	112	115.2	15.01	115.55	−3.55
4	132	130.4	15.03	130.21	1.79
5	145	145.4	15.03	145.43	−.43

*Assume $A_0 = 70$, $T_0 = 15$, $\alpha = .1$, $\beta = .1$.

TABLE S11.2
The Winters's
Seasonal
Exponential
Smoothing
Method*

t	D_t (demand)	A_t (average)	T_t (trend)	R_t (seasonal ratio)	F_t (forecast)	$D_t - F_t$ (error)
1	66	80.5	10.1	.804	64	2.0
2	106	90.1	10.0	1.195	108.7	−2.7
3	78	99.5	9.9	.799	80.4	−2.4
4	135	110.1	10.0	1.201	130.7	4.3

*Assume $A_0 = 70$, $T_0 = 10$, $L = 2$, $R_{-1} = .8$, $R_0 = 1.2$, $\alpha = .2$, $\beta = .2$, $\gamma = .2$.

The seasonal ratio for period t is

$$R_t = \gamma\left(\frac{D_t}{A_t}\right) + (1 - \gamma)R_{t-L}$$

In this case, we are assuming that the seasonal cycle is L periods. There are L seasonal ratios, one for each period. If the demand is monthly and the seasonal cycle repeats on an annual basis, then $L = 12$. Each month, one of the seasonal ratios will be updated to a new value, along with the trend and average.

The model requires initial estimates of A_0, T_0 and R_0, R_{-1}, . . . , R_{-L+1}. These initial estimates can be based on judgment or data, if available.

Using the updated values, the forecast for future periods in period t is

$$F_{t+K} = (A_t + KT_t)(R_{t-L+K})$$

An example of this method is shown in Table S11.2.

If there is no trend, Winters's method can also be used with seasonal factors alone. In this case, the above trend equation and T_t values are simply dropped from the method.

One of the techniques used frequently in time-series forecasting is **classical decomposition.** This involves decomposing a time series into level, trend, seasonal, and possibly cyclic components. Decomposition will be illustrated by means of an example with three years of quarterly data from a store that sells children's toys. It is assumed that the seasonal pattern is quarterly in nature, and there may be trend and level components in the data as well. Since only three years of data are available, no cyclic component will be estimated.

The quarterly data on the sales of toys are shown in Table S11.3. The biggest sales of toys, by far, are in the fourth quarter, at Christmas time. Visual inspection of the data indicates an upward trend—but how can this trend be disentangled from the seasonality of the data? This is done by first computing a four-quarter moving average. Decomposition requires the same number of periods in the moving average as the seasonality of the data (i.e., 4 periods for quarterly seasonality, 12 periods for monthly seasonality). This is done to average out the high periods and the low periods of demand over the seasonal cycle. The four-period moving average is shown in the third column of Table S11.3. These moving averages are centered between periods because a four-period average should represent a point with two periods on each side. From column 3, the upward trend is clear, because the seasonality has been removed from the data.

To calculate seasonal ratios, we need an average for each period. This is done in column 4 of Table S11.3 by constructing a two-period moving average of column 3. These new averages are then once again centered on the periods of data instead of in between periods. Column 4 then represents the best average of the data for estimating the trend. It is also used to calculate seasonal ratios directly by dividing sales by column 4 to produce the seasonal ratios in column 5. Interpretation of these

TABLE S11.3
Classical Decomposition Method

Quarter	Sales*	Four-Period Moving Average	Two-Period Moving Average	Seasonal Ratio
1	30			
2	42			
3	55	56.75	57.4	.958
4	100	58	58.5	1.709
5	35	59	59.5	.588
6	46	60	62.5	.736
7	59	65	66.0	.894
8	120	67	68.4	1.754
9	43	69.75	71.3	.603
10	57	72.75	75.5	.755
11	71	78.25		
12	142			

	Seasonal Ratios Quarter			
	1	2	3	4
			.958	1.709
	.588	.736	.894	1.754
	.603	.755		
Average	.596	.746	.926	1.732

*Sales are in thousands of dollars.

ratios is as follows: Demand in the third quarter is 95.8 percent of the annual average, demand in the fourth quarter is 170.9 percent of the yearly average, and so on. To obtain a best estimate of the seasonal ratios, we simply average the ratios for corresponding quarters. This calculation is shown on the bottom of Table S11.3. Note that the seasonal ratios are quite stable in this example, but we have a minimal amount of data to work with. Ordinarily, at least four years of data should be used to establish seasonal ratios.

The original sales data and the deseasonalized moving average, from column 4, are plotted in Figure S11.1. The moving average indicates an upward trend line. Actually, the trend might be slightly nonlinear, but let us assume for this

FIGURE S11.1
Seasonal toy sales.

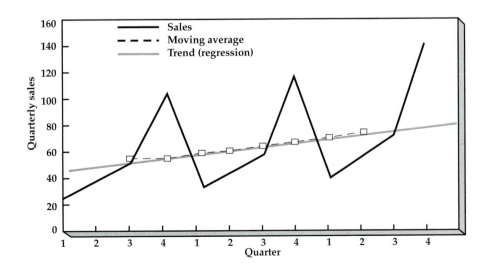

example a linear trend line. Then a regression line can be fitted through the eight moving-average points shown on the graph. The result is

$$Y(t) = 47.8 + 2.63t$$

where $Y(t)$ = sales and t = time.

A trend line could also be fitted to the original sales data, but it is customary in classical decomposition to use moving averages before fitting the trend line. This seems to give a slightly more stable forecast.

To forecast sales for the coming year, the following method is used. First, use the trend-line equation to predict the average for quarters 13, 14, 15, and 16 by plugging these values of time into the above regression equation. This yields column 2 in Table S11.4. Then multiply the seasonal ratio for each quarter by the predicted average. The result is a forecast for each quarter of the next year, as shown in Table S11.4.

TABLE S11.4
Seasonal Forecast Calculations

Quarter	Predicted Average	×	Seasonal Factor	=	Forecast
13	82.0		.596		48.8
14	84.6		.746		63.1
15	87.2		.926		80.7
16	89.9		1.732		155.7

Supplement Problems

1. Ace Hardware handles spare parts for lawn mowers. The following data were collected for one week in May when replacement lawn-mower blades were in high demand:

Day	Demand
1	10
2	12
3	13
4	15
5	17
6	20
7	21

a. Simulate a forecast for the week, starting with $F_1 = 10$, $T_0 = 2$, $\alpha = .2$, and $\beta = .4$. Use the trend model given in the chapter supplement.

b. Compute the MAD and tracking signal for the data. Use $MAD_0 = 0$.

c. Are the MAD and tracking signal within tolerances?

d. Simulate a forecast using simple smoothing for the week, starting with $F_1 = 10$ and $\alpha = .2$. Plot the forecast and the data on graph paper. Note how the forecast lags behind the data.

 2. The daily demand for chocolate donuts from the Donut-Hole Shop has been recorded for a two-week period.

Day	Demand	Day	Demand
1	80	8	85
2	95	9	99
3	120	10	110
4	110	11	90
5	75	12	80
6	60	13	65
7	50	14	50

a. Simulate a forecast of the demand using trend-adjusted exponential smoothing. Use values of $A_0 = 90$, $T_0 = 25$, and $\alpha = \beta = .2$.

b. Plot the data and the forecast on a graph.

c. Does this appear to be a good model for the data?

3. The SureGrip Tire Company produces tires of various sizes and shapes. The demand for tires tends to follow a quarterly seasonal pattern with a trend. For a particular type of tire the company's current estimates are as follows: $A_0 = 10,000$, $T_0 = 1000$, $R_0 = .8$, $R_{-1} = 1.2$, $R_{-2} = 1.5$, and $R_{-3} = .75$.

a. The company has just observed the first quarter of demand $D_1 = 6000$ and would like to update its forecast for each of the next four quarters using $\alpha = \beta = \gamma = .4$.

b. When demand is observed for the second quarter, $D_2 = 15,000$. How much error was there in the forecast?

c. Update the forecasts again for the coming year, using the second-quarter demand data.

eXcel 4. Management feels there is a seasonal pattern in the above data for the Donut-Hole Shop (see problem 2), with the first two days of a week representing one level; the third and fourth days representing a second level; and the fifth, sixth, and seventh days a third level. Thus, three seasonal factors have been suggested: $R_0 = .9$, $R_{-1} = 1.3$, and $R_{-2} = .8$.

a. Simulate a forecast of demand for days 1 to 7 using $A_0 = 85$, $T_0 = 0$, and $\alpha = \beta = \gamma = .1$. Use Winters's method from the supplement to this chapter.

b. Comment on the appropriateness of the forecasts developed.

5. Management of the ABC Floral Shop feels that its sales are seasonal in nature with a monthly seasonal pattern and no trend. The demand data and seasonal ratios for the past three years are given below.

Month	Year 1 Demand	Year 2 Demand	Year 3 Demand	Seasonal Ratio
Jan.	$12,400	$11,800	$13,600	0.8
Feb.	23,000	24,111	21,800	1.8
Mar.	15,800	16,500	14,900	0.9
Apr.	20,500	21,000	19,400	1.6
May	25,100	24,300	26,000	2.0
June	16,200	15,800	16,500	1.0
July	12,000	11,500	12,400	0.7
Aug.	10,300	10,100	10,800	0.6
Sept.	11,800	11,000	12,500	0.7
Oct.	14,000	14,300	13,800	1.2
Nov.	10,700	10,900	10,600	0.9
Dec.	7,600	7,200	8,100	0.6

a. Calculate a forecast for the past year using $A_0 = 15,000$, $\alpha = \gamma = .3$, and the seasonal ratios shown above. For each period, calculate the forecast and the updated seasonal ratio.

b. Plot the original data and the forecast on graph paper.

c. Calculate the tracking signals for the past year using $MAD_0 = 0$. Are they within tolerances?

d. Using the classical decomposition method described in the chapter supplement, calculate the seasonal ratios from the data, and determine the trend and average levels. Use these ratios and estimates of trend and level to make a forecast for the next year.

Chapter Twelve

Facilities and Aggregate Planning

Chapter outline

In Chapters 12 to 14 we discuss long-, medium-, and short-range capacity decisions. These follow naturally from supply chain decisions already made and forecasting as an input.

As discussed in the last chapter, long-range decisions are concerned with facilities and process selection, which typically extend more than two years into the future.[1] The first part of this chapter describes facilities decisions and a strategic approach to making them. We also deal with medium-range aggregate planning in this chapter, extending from six months to two years into the future. The next chapter discusses short-range capacity decisions of less than six months regarding the scheduling of available resources for ongoing operations.

---

[1] In some cases, facilities that follow a standard design, such as fast-food or other service facilities, can be built in one year or less.

FIGURE 12.1
Hierarchy of
capacity decisions.

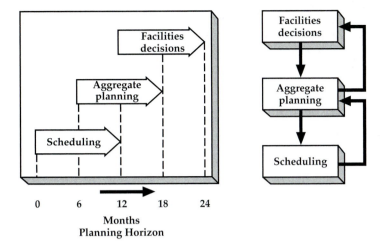

Facilities, aggregate planning, and scheduling form a **hierarchy of decisions** concerning the capacity of operations extending from long to medium to short range in nature. Facility planning establishes physical capacity that cannot be exceeded by aggregate planning. Then, aggregate planning determines the workforce level and production output level for the medium term within the physical capacity available. Finally, scheduling is constrained by aggregate planning and allocates the available capacity by assigning it to specific tasks, activities, or jobs.

This hierarchy of capacity decisions is shown in Figure 12.1. Notice that the decisions proceed from the top down and that there is also a feedback loop from the bottom up. Thus, scheduling decisions often indicate a need for revised aggregate planning, and aggregate planning may also uncover facility needs.

Before proceeding we define **capacity** as the maximum output that can be produced over a given period of time such as a day, week, or year. In some cases not only physical assets may limit capacity but also labor availability. For example, capacity depends on the assumptions made concerning facilities, equipment, and workforce availability for one, two, or three shifts and the possibility of operating 7 days a week and up to 365 days a year. If we assume two eight-hour shifts are available for five days a week, then the capacity of a facility is $16 \times 5 = 80$ hours per week, and $80 \times 52 = 4,160$ hours per year. Capacity can be measured in terms of not only hours of output but also output measures such as number of units produced, tons produced, or number of customers served over a specified period of time.

We have just defined the theoretical capacity, but there is also a **nominal capacity** or effective capacity that is obtained by subtracting downtime for maintenance, shift breaks, and equipment utilization that decreases the theoretical capacity available. The nominal capacity is then the maximum amount that can be used when planning for actual facility output over some period of time.

12.1   FACILITIES DECISIONS

Facilities decisions are of great importance to the business and to the operations function. These decisions place physical constraints on the amount that can be produced, and they require investment of scarce capital. Therefore, facilities decisions involve all organizational functions and are often made at the highest corporate level, including top management and the board of directors.

Because of the construction required, the lead time for many facilities decisions can range from one to five years. The one-year time frame generally involves buildings and equipment that can quickly be constructed or leased. The five-year time frame involves large and complex facilities such as oil refineries, paper mills, steel mills, and electricity generating plants.

In facilities decisions, there are four crucial questions:

1. How much total capacity is needed?
2. How large should each unit of capacity be?
3. When is the capacity needed?
4. What type of facilities/capacity are needed?

The questions of how much, how large, when, and what type can be separated conceptually, but they are often intertwined. As a result, facilities decisions are exceedingly complex and difficult to analyze.

In the next section, the above four types of facilities decisions will be considered in detail. We stress the notion of a facilities strategy, cross-functional decision making, and the relationship of facilities strategy to business strategy.

12.2 FACILITIES STRATEGY

Chapter 2 noted that a facilities strategy (or policy) is one of the major parts of an operations strategy. Since major facilities decisions affect competitive success, they need to be considered as part of the total operations strategy and not simply as a series of incremental capital-budgeting decisions. This point of view also applies to other major strategic decisions in operations, as we have already noted, for certain process design, supply chain, and quality management decisions.

As indicated above, a **facilities strategy** typically considers the amount of capacity, size of units, the timing of capacity changes, and the types of facilities needed for the long run. These elements of a facilities strategy need to be considered in an integrated fashion and are affected by the following factors:

1. **Predicted demand.** Formulating a facility strategy requires a forecast of demand, even if the variance is quite large. Techniques for making these forecasts were considered in the last chapter. Marketing will often be involved in forecasting future demand.
2. **Cost of facilities.** Cost will enter into the facility strategy in considering whether large or small facilities should be built. Cost also affects the amount of capacity added at any one time, the timing, and the location of capacity. Accounting and finance will be involved in estimating future costs and cash flows from facility strategies.
3. **Likely behavior of competitors.** An expected slow competitive response may lead the firm to add capacity to grab the market before competitors become strong. On the other hand, an expected fast competitive response may cause the firm to be more cautious in expanding capacity.
4. **Business strategy.** The business strategy may dictate that a company put more emphasis on cost, service, or flexibility in facilities choices. For example, a business strategy to provide the best service can lead to facilities with some excess capacity or several market locations for fast service. Other business strategies can lead to cost minimization or other types of facilities choices.

5. **International considerations.** As markets become more global in nature, facilities must be located globally. This involves not merely chasing cheap labor but locating facilities globally for the best strategic advantage. The Operations Leader box explains why Intel decided to locate a modern semiconductor plant in Ireland.

Amount of Capacity

One part of a facilities strategy is the amount of capacity provided in relation to expected demand. This can best be described by the notion of a **capacity cushion,** defined as follows:

$$\text{Capacity cushion} = \text{capacity} - \text{average demand}$$

Since the capacity cushion is expressed relative to the average demand level, a positive cushion provides excess capacity over the average demand and a negative cushion means that average demand will exceed capacity. Of course, the ideal is to provide no capacity cushion, but this is impossible in the face of uncertain demand.

Three strategies can be adopted with respect to the amount of capacity cushion.

1. **Try not to run out.** In this case a positive capacity cushion is used. The firm would be going beyond the average demand forecast to provide some additional capacity. Such a strategy is appropriate when there is an expanding market, or when the cost of building and operating capacity is inexpensive relative to the cost of running out of capacity. Electric utilities adopt this approach, since blackouts or brownouts are generally not acceptable. Companies in growing markets may also adopt a positive capacity cushion, since it allows them to capture market share ahead of their competitors. Also, in growth markets there is less risk of having idle capacity for long since the market is expanding.

2. **Build to average forecast.** In this case, the firm is more conservative with respect to capacity provided. Building to average forecast will provide a 50 percent probability of running out of capacity and a 50 percent probability of having excess capacity.[2] This strategy would be used when the cost (or consequences) of running out is approximately in balance with the cost of excess capacity.

[2] This, of course, assumes a symmetrical probability distribution of demand.

3. **Maximize utilization.** In this case, a small or negative capacity cushion is planned to maximize utilization. This strategy is appropriate when capacity is very expensive, relative to stockouts, as in the case of oil refineries, paper mills, and other capital-intensive industries. These facilities operate profitably only at very high capacity rates approaching 90 to 100 percent. While this strategy tends to maximize short-run earnings it could damage the long-run market share, especially if competitors adopt larger capacity cushions and demand develops in excess of capacity.

In the Solved Problems section at the end of the chapter, we provide an example of how to compute the capacity cushion required using probabilities of demand and costs of capacity. This method provides a quantitative basis to estimate the amount of capacity cushion that may be required.

Size of Units/Facilities

After deciding on the level of capacity to be provided, a facility strategy must also address the question of how large each unit of capacity should be. This is, of course, a question involving **economies of scale.** Scale economies are based on the notion that large units are more economical because fixed costs can be spread over more units of production. These economies occur for two reasons. First, the cost of building and operating large production equipment does not increase linearly with volume. A machine with twice the output rate generally costs less than twice as much to buy and operate. Also, in larger facilities the overhead due to managers and staff can be spread over more units of production. As a result, the unit cost of production falls as facility size increases, when scale economies are present as shown in the left part of Figure 12.2.

This is a good news–bad news story, for along with economies of scale come **diseconomies of scale.** Diseconomies occur as the facility gets larger for several reasons. First, there are transportation diseconomies present. For example, a large facility incurs more transportation costs than two smaller facilities that are closer to their markets. Diseconomies of scale also occur because communications, coordination, and control costs increase in large bureaucratic organizations. As more layers of staff and management are added to manage the organization, the cost ultimately increases faster than the output level. Furthermore, costs of complexity and confusion arise as more products are added and a facility becomes larger. For these reasons, the curve in Figure 12.2 rises on the right-hand side due to the diseconomies of scale.

As Figure 12.2 indicates, there is a minimum unit cost for a certain facility size. This particular optimum size will depend on how high the fixed costs are and how rapidly diseconomies of scale occur. As an example, Hewlett-Packard

FIGURE 12.2
Optimum unit size.

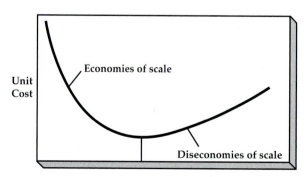

Facility Size (units produced per year)

FACILITIES STRATEGY.
This Bacardi Rum
factory supplies the
entire North American
market from a single
modern automated
distillery in Puerto
Rico. Courtesy of
Roger Schroeder

tends to operate small plants of less than about 300 people. This plant size is used because Hewlett-Packard wants to encourage innovation and it has many small product lines with relatively low fixed costs. On the other hand, IBM operates very large plants in the range of 5,000 to 10,000 people for producing large computers. IBM plants tend to be highly automated, and they use a decentralized management approach to minimize diseconomies of scale. Every company seems to have an optimum facility size, depending on its cost structure, product structure, and particular operations strategy, which may emphasize cost, delivery flexibility, or service. Cost is, after all, not the only factor that affects facility size.

Timing of Facility Additions

Another element of facility strategy is the timing of additions to capacity. There are basically two opposite strategies here.

1. **Preempt the competition.** In this case, the firm will lead the market by building capacity in advance of the need. This strategy tends to provide a positive capacity cushion; it may actually stimulate the market and could prevent competition from coming in for a while. An example of this strategy was followed by Apple Computer in the early days of the personal computer market. Apple built a factory in advance of demand and had a lion's share of the market before competitors moved in. McDonald's also followed this strategy in the early days of the fast-food industry.

2. **Wait and see.** In this case, the firm will wait to add capacity until demand develops and the need is clear. As a result, the company will be following the leader and taking a lower-risk strategy. A small or negative capacity cushion could develop, and a loss of potential market share may result. However, this strategy can also be very effective since superior marketing channels or technology can allow the follower to capture market share. For example, IBM followed the leader (Apple) in the personal computer market but was able to take away market share because of its superior brand image, size, and market presence. On the other hand, U.S. automobile companies followed the wait-and-see strategy, to their chagrin, for small compact autos. While U.S. automakers waited to see how demand for small cars would develop, the Japanese grabbed a dominant position in the U.S. small-car market.

Types of Facilities

The final element in facility strategy considers the question of multiple facilities. There are four different types of facility choices:

1. Product-focused (55 percent)
2. Market-focused (30 percent)

3. Process-focused (10 percent)

4. General-purpose (5 percent)

The figures in parentheses indicate the approximate percentages of companies in the *Fortune* 500 using each type of facility.

Product-focused facilities produce one family or type of product, usually for a large market. An example is the Anderson Window plant, which produces various types of windows for the entire United States from a single product-focused plant. Product-focused plants are often used when transportation costs are low or scale economies are high. This tends to centralize facilities into one location or a few. Other examples of product-focused facilities are large bank credit card processing operations and auto leasing companies that process leases for cars throughout the United States from a single site.

Market-focused facilities are located in the markets they serve. Many service operations fall into this category since services cannot be transported. Plants that require quick customer response or customized products or that have high transportation charges tend to be market focused. Consider, for example, plants that produce mattresses. Due to the bulky nature of the product and high shipping charges, it makes sense to locate small mattress plants in regional markets. International facilities also tend to be market focused because of tariffs, trade barriers, and potential currency fluctuations.

Process-focused facilities have one technology, or at most two. These facilities frequently produce components or parts that are shipped to other facilities for further processing or assembly. This is common in the auto industry, where engine plants and transmission plants feed the final assembly plants. Process plants can also supply plants outside the company, and they can make a wide variety of products within the given process technology. Process-focused facilities are not widely used compared with product or market facilities, but they are nonetheless important in certain cases.

General-purpose facilities may produce several types of products and use several different processes. They tend to be used by thousands of small companies that do not have sufficient volume to justify more than one facility. For example, general-purpose facilities are used by small companies to print books, to make sailboats, and to produce specialty office products. Larger companies usually specialize their facilities according to product, market, or process. The disadvantage of a general-purpose facility, of course, is that it can be unfocused, as described in Chapter 4, unless a plant-within-a-plant strategy can be used.

We have shown how a facility strategy can be constructed by considering questions of capacity, size of units, timing, and types of units. Of course, a facility strategy needs to be supported by medium-term capacity decisions covered in the remainder of this chapter.

12.3 AGGREGATE PLANNING DEFINITION

Aggregate planning is concerned with matching supply and demand of output over the medium time range, up to approximately 12 months into the future. The term "aggregate" implies that the planning is done for a single overall measure of output or, at the most, a few aggregated product categories. The aim of aggregate planning is to set overall output levels in the near to medium future in the face of fluctuating or uncertain demand.

As a result of aggregate planning, decisions and policies should be made concerning overtime, hiring, layoff, subcontracting, and inventory levels. Aggregate planning determines not only the output levels planned but also the appropriate resource input mix to be used. For aggregate planning purposes, facilities are assumed to be fixed and cannot be expanded or contracted.

Aggregate planning might seek to influence demand as well as supply. If this is the case, variables such as price, advertising, and product mix might be used. If changes in demand are considered, then marketing, along with operations, will be intimately involved in aggregate planning.

We will be using a broad definition of the term "aggregate planning," which has the following characteristics:

1. A time horizon of about 12 months, with updating of the plan on a periodic basis, perhaps monthly.
2. An aggregate level of demand for one or a few categories of product. The demand is assumed to be fluctuating, uncertain, or seasonal.
3. The possibility of changing both supply and demand variables.
4. A variety of management objectives, which might include low inventories, good labor relations, low costs, flexibility to increase future output levels, and good customer service.
5. Facilities that are considered fixed and cannot be expanded or reduced.

Aggregate planning is closely related to other business decisions involving, for example, budgeting, personnel, and marketing. The relationship to budgeting is particularly strong. Most budgets are based on assumptions about aggregate output, personnel levels, inventory levels, purchasing levels, and so forth. An aggregate plan should thus be the basis for initial budget development and for budget revisions as conditions warrant.

Personnel, or human resource planning, is also greatly affected by aggregate planning because aggregate planning results in hiring, layoff, and overtime decisions. In the service industries, where inventory is not a factor, aggregate planning is practically synonymous with budgeting and personnel planning.

Marketing must always be closely related to aggregate planning because the future supply of output, and thus customer service, is being determined. Furthermore, cooperation between marketing and operations is required when both supply and demand variables are being used to determine the best business approach to aggregate planning. Aggregate planning is the primary responsibility of the operations function, but it requires cross-functional coordination and cooperation with all parts of the firm, including accounting, finance, human resources, and marketing. An aggregate planning and scheduling application at Libby-Owens-Ford is illustrated in the Operations Leader box.

The next section contains a detailed discussion of the options available to modify demand and supply for aggregate planning. This will be followed by the development of specific strategies that can be used to plan aggregate output for both manufacturing and service industries. The chapter is completed with an example of aggregate planning cost calculations.

12.4 PLANNING OPTIONS

The aggregate planning problem can be clarified by a discussion of the various decision options available. These will be divided into two types of decisions: (1) those modifying demand and (2) those modifying supply.

OPERATIONS LEADER

Savings from Aggregate Planning/ Scheduling at Libby- Owens-Ford

Libby-Owens-Ford is a supplier of glass component parts, windows, and windshields to the automobile industry. When the company decided to replace its manual scheduling and planning system, it had two objectives: reduce costs and react more quickly to changes. Before the new system was installed, the Sherman, Texas, plant had a manual system for calculating materials and developing schedules. Carolyn Labanara, the project manager for the new system, said, "Having a longer scheduling horizon is essential to the company. We deal with automotive systems which give us 12-week forecasts, which are updated weekly to reflect any changes in demand."

The new computerized system produced two schedules. One was a medium-term schedule for the next eight weeks, which used weekly time periods and was updated weekly. The second short-range schedule was for the next two weeks and was updated daily. Where the manual schedules took four hours to update, the new computerized scheduling system took 20 minutes. The new scheduling system also made it possible to evaluate the costs of proposed schedules. These costs included the inventory-carrying costs and the changeover costs of proposed changes. Labanara commented, "The schedule puts focus on costs under the scheduler's control. It helps them develop the most cost-efficient schedule. The system gets our schedulers to think in dollars and cents terms."

The new system has saved Libby-Owens-Ford $600,000 in inventory costs by making it possible to cut the raw glass inventory by 33 percent. The system also made it possible to quickly evaluate the effect of proposed changes and saved schedulers time, so they can devote their efforts to more productive work.

Source: Abstracted from *Production and Inventory Review,* August 1989, pp. 36–37; and "HR Is Solving Shift-Work Problems," *Personnel Journal* 72, no. 8 (August 1993), pp. 36–48.

Demand can be modified or influenced in several ways:

1. **Pricing.** Differential pricing is often used to reduce peak demand or to build up demand in off-peak periods. Some examples are matinee movie prices, off-season hotel rates, factory discounts for early- or late-season purchases, weekend telephone rates, and two-for-one prices at restaurants. The purpose of these pricing schemes is to level demand through the day, week, month, or year.

2. **Advertising and promotion.** This is another method used to stimulate or in some cases smooth out demand. Advertising is generally timed so as to promote demand during slack periods and to shift demand from the peak periods to the slack times. For example, ski resorts advertise to lengthen their season, and turkey growers advertise to stimulate demand outside the Thanksgiving and Christmas seasons.

3. **Backlog or reservations.** In some cases, demand is influenced by asking customers to wait for their orders (backlog) or by reserving capacity in advance (reservations). Generally, this has the effect of shifting demand from peak periods to periods with slack capacity. However, the waiting time may result in a loss of business. This loss can sometimes be tolerated when the aim is to maximize profit, although most operations are extremely reluctant to turn away customers.

4. **Development of complementary products.** Firms with highly seasonal demands may try to develop products that have countercyclic seasonal trends. The classic example of this approach is a lawn-mower company that begins

building snow-blowers. In the service industry, an example is provided by fast-food restaurants that begin to offer breakfast so as to smooth out demand and utilize capacity more fully.

The service industries, using all the mechanisms cited above, have gone much further than their manufacturing counterparts in influencing demand. This can probably be attributed to one crucial difference: the inability of service operations to inventory their product.

There are also a large number of variables that can be used to modify supply through aggregate planning. These include:

1. **Hiring and layoff of employees.** The use of this variable differs a great deal between companies and industries. Some companies will do almost anything before reducing the size of the workforce through layoffs. Other companies routinely increase and decrease their workforce as demand changes. These practices affect not only costs but also labor relations, productivity, and worker morale. As a result, company hiring and layoff practices may be restricted by union contracts or company policies. One of the purposes of aggregate planning, however, is to examine the effect of these policies on costs or profits.

2. **Using overtime and undertime.** Overtime is sometimes used for short- or medium-range labor adjustments in lieu of hiring and layoffs, especially if the change in demand is considered temporary. Overtime labor usually costs 150 percent of regular time, with double time on weekends or Sundays. Because of its high cost, managers are sometimes reluctant to use overtime. Furthermore, workers are reluctant to work more than 20 percent weekly overtime for a duration of several weeks. "Undertime" refers to planned underutilization of the workforce rather than layoffs or perhaps a shortened workweek. Undertime can be thought of as the opposite of overtime. Another term for undertime is "idle time."

3. **Using part-time or temporary labor.** In some cases, it is possible to hire part-time or temporary employees to meet peak or seasonal demand. This option may be particularly attractive because part-time employees are often paid significantly less in wages and benefits. Unions, of course, frown on the use of part-time employees because the latter often do not pay union dues and may weaken union influence. Part-time employees are, however, essential to many service operations, such as restaurants, hospitals, supermarkets, and department stores. These operations are highly dependent on their ability to attract and utilize part-time and temporary workers for periods of peak demand.

4. **Carrying inventory.** In manufacturing companies, inventory can be used as a buffer between supply and demand. Inventories for later use can be built up during periods of slack demand. Inventory thus uncouples supply from demand in manufacturing operations, thereby allowing for smoother operations. Inventory can be viewed as a way to store labor for future consumption. This option is, of course, not available for service operations (excluding facilitating goods) and leads to a somewhat different and more difficult aggregate planning problem for them.

5. **Subcontracting.** This option, which involves the use of other firms, is sometimes an effective way to increase or decrease supply. The subcontractor may supply the entire product or only some of the components. For example, a manufacturer of toys may utilize subcontractors to make plastic parts during

certain times of the year. The manufacturer may furnish the molds and specify the materials and methods to be used. Service operations may subcontract for secretarial help, catering services, or facilities during peak periods.

6. **Making cooperative arrangements.** These arrangements are very similar to subcontracting in that other sources of supply are used. Examples include electric utilities that are hooked together through power-sharing networks, hospitals that send their patients to other hospitals for certain specialized services, and hotels or airlines that shift customers among one another when they are fully booked.

In considering all these options, it is clear that the aggregate planning problem is extremely broad and affects all parts of the firm. The decisions that are made must, therefore, be strategic and cross-functional, reflecting all the firm's objectives. If aggregate planning is considered narrowly, suboptimization may occur and inappropriate decisions result. Some of the multiple trade-offs that should be considered are customer service level (through back orders or lost demand), inventory levels, stability of the labor force, and costs. All these conflicting objectives and trade-offs are sometimes combined into a single cost function. A method for evaluating cost will be described later.

12.5 BASIC STRATEGIES

Two basic operations strategies can be used, along with many combinations in between, to meet fluctuating demand over time. One basic strategy is to level the workforce; the other is to chase demand with the workforce. With a perfectly **level strategy,** the rate of regular-time output will be constant. Any variations in demand must then be absorbed by using inventories, overtime, temporary workers, subcontracting, cooperative arrangements, or any of the demand-influencing options. What has essentially been done with the level strategy is to fix the regular workforce by using one of the above 10 variables available for aggregate planning.

With the **chase strategy,** the workforce level is changed to meet, or chase, demand. In this case, it is not necessary to carry inventory or to use any of the other variables available for aggregate planning; the workforce absorbs all the changes in demand.

LEVEL STRATEGY. A level strategy can result in a large amount of inventory at certain times of the year. © Andersen-Ross/Brand X Pictures/Age Fotostock

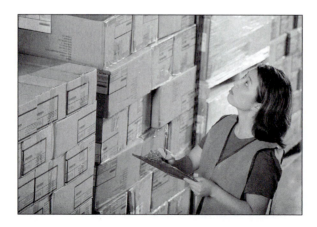

TABLE 12.1
Comparison of
Chase versus Level
Strategy

	Chase Demand	Level Capacity
Level of labor skill required	Low	High
Job discretion	Low	High
Compensation rate	Low	High
Working conditions	Sweatshop	Pleasant
Training required per employee	Low	High
Labor turnover	High	Low
Hire-layoff costs	Low	High
Amount of supervision required	High	Low
Type of budgeting and forecasting required	Short-run	Long-run

Of course, these two strategies are extremes; one strategy makes no change in the workforce and the other varies the workforce directly with demand changes. In practice, many combinations are also possible, but the basic strategies help focus on the issues.

Consider, for example, the case of a brokerage firm that utilized both strategies. The data processing department maintained a capacity to process 17,000 transactions per day, far in excess of the average load of 12,000. This capacity allowed the department to keep a level workforce of programmers, systems analysts, and computer operators even though capacity exceeded demand on many days. Because of the skilled workforce, the high capital investment, and the difficulty in hiring replacements, it made sense for the data processing department to follow this strategy.

Meanwhile, in the cashiering department, a chase strategy was being followed. As the transaction level varied, part-time workers, hiring, and layoffs were used. This department was very labor-intensive, with a high personnel turnover and a low skill level. The manager of the department commented that the high turnover level was an advantage, since it helped facilitate the reduction of workforce in periods of low demand.

In can be seen from this situation that the characteristics of the operation seem to influence the type of strategy followed. This observation can be generalized to the factors shown in Table 12.1. While the chase strategy may be more appropriate for low-skilled labor and routine jobs, the level strategy seems more appropriate for highly skilled labor and complex jobs.

These strategies, however, cannot be properly evaluated unless specific decision criteria are stated. One way to do this is to reduce all the most important criteria to cost, as described in the next section.

12.6 AGGREGATE PLANNING COSTS

Most aggregate planning methods determine a plan that minimizes costs. These methods assume that demand is fixed; therefore, strategies for modifying demand are not considered. If both demand and supply were simultaneously modified, it would be more appropriate to maximize profit since demand changes affect revenues along with costs.

When demand is considered given, the following costs should be included:

1. **Hiring and layoff costs.** The hiring cost consists of the recruiting, screening, and training costs required to bring a new employee up to full productive skill. For some jobs, this cost might be only a few hundred dollars; for more

highly skilled jobs, it might range up to several thousand. The layoff cost includes employee benefits, severance pay, and other costs associated with layoff. The layoff cost may also range from a few hundred dollars to several thousand dollars per person. In some cases, where an entire shift is hired or laid off at one time, a shift cost can be included.

2. **Overtime and undertime costs.** The overtime costs often consist of regular wages plus a 50 to 100 percent premium. The cost of undertime is often reflected by the use of employees at less than full productivity.

3. **Inventory-carrying costs.** Inventory-carrying costs are associated with maintaining the product in inventory; they include the cost of capital, variable cost of storage, obsolescence, and deterioration. These costs are often expressed as a percentage of the dollar value of inventory, ranging from 15 to 35 percent per year. This cost can be thought of as an interest charge assessed against the dollar value of inventory held in stock. Thus, if the carrying cost is 20 percent and each unit costs $10 to produce, it will cost $2 to carry one unit in inventory for a year.

4. **Subcontracting costs.** The cost of subcontracting is the price that is paid to a subcontractor to produce the units. Subcontracting costs can be either more or less than the cost of producing units in-house.

5. **Part-time labor costs.** Because of differences in benefits and hourly rates, the cost of part-time or temporary labor will probably be less than that of regular labor. Although part-time workers often get no benefits, a maximum percentage of part-time labor may be specified by operational considerations or by union contract. Otherwise, there might be a tendency to use all part-time or temporary labor. However, the regular labor force is essential for task continuity and training to effectively utilize part-time and temporary personnel.

6. **Cost of stockout or back order.** The cost of taking a back order or the cost of a stockout should reflect the effect of reduced customer service. This cost is extremely difficult to estimate, but it can be related to the loss of customer goodwill and the possible loss of future sales. Thus, we may think of stockout or back-order costs in terms of forgone future profits.

Some or all of these costs may be present in any particular aggregate planning problem. The applicable costs will be used to "price out" alternative strategies. In the example below, only a few strategies will be priced out. When using mathematical models, a very large number of strategies can be considered (see the chapter supplement for details).

12.7 EXAMPLE OF COSTING

The Hefty Beer Company is constructing an aggregate plan for the next 12 months. Although several types of beers are brewed at the Hefty plant and several container sizes are bottled, management has decided to use gallons of beer as the aggregate measure of capacity.

The demand for beer over the next 12 months is forecast to follow the pattern shown in Figure 12.3. Notice how the demand usually peaks in the summer months and is decidedly lower in the winter.

The management of the Hefty brewery would like to consider three aggregate plans:

FIGURE 12.3

Hefty Beer
Company—forecast
of demand for beer.

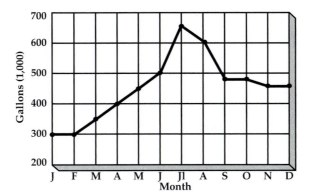

1. **Level workforce.** Use inventory to meet peak demands.
2. **Level workforce plus overtime.** Use 20 percent overtime along with inventory in June, July, and August to meet peak demands.
3. **Chase strategy.** Hire and lay off workers each month as necessary to meet demand.

To evaluate these strategies, management has collected the following cost and resource data:

- Each worker can produce 10,000 gallons of beer per month on regular time. On overtime, the same production rate is assumed, but overtime can be used for only three summer months during the year. Assume the starting workforce is 40 workers.
- Each worker is paid $2,000 per month on regular time. Overtime is paid at 150 percent of regular time. A maximum of 20 percent overtime can be used in any of the three months.
- It costs $1,000 to hire a worker, including screening costs, paperwork, and training costs. It costs $2,000 to lay off a worker, including all severance and benefit costs.
- For inventory valuation purposes, beer costs $2 a gallon to produce. The cost of carrying inventory is assumed to be 3 percent a month (or 6 cents per gallon of beer per month).
- Assume that the starting inventory is 50,000 gallons. The desired ending inventory a year from now is also 50,000 gallons. All forecast demand must be met; no stockouts are allowed.

The next task is to evaluate each of the three strategies in terms of the costs given. The first step in this process is to construct spreadsheet charts like those shown in Tables 12.2 through 12.4, which show all the relevant costs: regular workforce, hiring/layoff, overtime, and inventory. Notice that subcontracting, part-time labor, and back orders/stockouts have not been allowed as variables in this case.

In evaluating the first option, we must calculate the size of the workforce required to meet the demand and inventory goals. Since ending and beginning inventories are assumed to be equal, the workforce must be just large enough to meet total demand during the year. When the monthly demands from Figure 12.3 are added, the annual demand is 5,400,000 gallons. Since each worker can produce 10,000(12) = 120,000 gallons in a year, a level workforce of

TABLE 12.2

Aggregate Planning Costs—Strategy 1, Level Workforce*

	Jan.	Feb.	Mar.	Apr.	May	June	July	Aug.	Sept.	Oct.	Nov.	Dec.	Total
Resources													
Regular workers	45	45	45	45	45	45	45	45	45	45	45	45	
Overtime (%)	0	0	0	0	0	0	0	0	0	0	0	0	
Units produced	450	450	450	450	450	450	450	450	450	450	450	450	5,400
Sales forecast	300	300	350	400	450	500	650	600	475	475	450	450	5,400
Inventory (end of month)	200	350	450	500	500	450	250	100	75	50	50	50	
Costs													
Regular time	$90.0	$90.0	$90.0	$90.0	$90.0	$90.0	$90.0	$90.0	$90.0	$90.0	$90.0	$90.0	$1,080.0
Overtime	0.0	0.0	0.0	0.0	0.0	0.0	0.0	0.0	0.0	0.0	0.0	0.0	0.0
Hire/layoff	5.0	0.0	0.0	0.0	0.0	0.0	0.0	0.0	0.0	0.0	0.0	0.0	5.0
Inventory carrying	12.0	21.0	27.0	30.0	30.0	27.0	15.0	6.0	4.5	3.0	3.0	3.0	181.5
Total cost	$107.0	$111.0	$117.0	$120.0	$120.0	$117.0	$105.0	$96.0	$94.5	$93.0	$93.0	$93.0	$1,266.5

*All costs are expressed in thousands of dollars. All production and inventory figures are in thousands of gallons. Starting inventory is 50,000 gallons.

5,400,000 ÷ 120,000 = 45 workers is needed to meet the total demand. On the basis of this workforce figure, the inventories for each month and the resulting costs have been calculated in Table 12.2.

Consider the calculations for the first month, January, in Table 12.2. With 45 workers entered at the top of the table, 450,000 gallons of beer can be produced, since each worker produces 10,000 gallons in a month. The production exceeds the sales forecast by 150,000 (450,000–300,000) gallons, which is added to the beginning inventory of 50,000 gallons to yield an inventory at the end of the month of January of 200,000 gallons.

Next the costs in Table 12.2 are calculated as follows. Regular time costs are $90,000 in January (45 workers × $2,000 each). There is no overtime cost, but 5 workers have been hired, since the starting workforce level was given above at 40 workers. The cost of hiring these five workers is $5,000. Finally, it cost 6 cents to carry a gallon of beer in inventory for a month, and Hefty is carrying 200,000 gallons at the end of the month, which costs $12,000.[3] These costs are totaled to yield $107,000 for the month of January. The calculations are continued for each month and then added for the year to yield the total cost of $1,266,500 for the first strategy.

The second strategy is a bit more complicated since some overtime can be used. If X is the workforce size for option 2, we must have

$$9(10,000X) + 3[(1.2)(10,000X)] = 5,400,000 \text{ gallons}$$

For nine months we will produce at 10,000X gallons per month, and for three months we will produce at 120 percent of 10,000X, including overtime. When the above equation is solved for X, we have $X = 43$ workers on regular time. In Table 12.3 we have once again calculated the inventories and resulting costs for this option.

The third option requires that the workforce be varied in each month to meet the demand by hiring and laying off workers. Straightforward calculations produce the number of workers and associated costs for each month. In this case, as shown in Table 12.4, a constant level of 50,000 gallons in inventory is maintained as the minimum inventory level.

The annual costs of each strategy are collected and summarized in Table 12.5. On the basis of the assumptions used, strategy 3 is the least-cost strategy. However, cost is not the only consideration. For example, strategy 3 requires building from a minimum workforce of 30 to a peak of 65 workers, and then layoffs are made back down to 45 workers. Will the labor climate permit this amount of hiring and layoff each year, or will this lead to unionization and ultimately to higher costs of labor? Maybe a two-shift policy should be considered for part of the year and one shift for the remainder of the year. These ideas, and others, should be considered in attempting to evaluate and possibly improve on the chase strategy, as we have done in the chapter supplement.

We have shown how to compare costs in a very simple case of aggregate planning for a few strategies. Advanced methods have been developed to consider many more strategies and more complex aggregate planning problems. These methods, which are too complex to discuss here, include linear programming, simulation, and decision rules of various types. See the chapter supplement for advanced techniques.

[3] For convenience we use the end of month inventory to calculate inventory carrying costs rather than the average monthly inventory.

TABLE 12.3

Aggregate Planning Costs—Strategy 2, Use of Overtime*

	Jan.	Feb.	Mar.	Apr.	May	June	July	Aug.	Sept.	Oct.	Nov.	Dec.	Total
Resources													
Regular workers	43	43	43	43	43	43	43	43	43	43	43	43	
Overtime (%)	0	0	0	0	0	20	20	20	0	0	0	0	
Units produced	430	430	430	430	430	516	516	516	430	430	430	430	5,418
Sales forecast	300	300	350	400	450	500	650	600	475	475	450	450	5,400
Inventory (end of month)	180	310	390	420	400	416	282	198	153	108	88	68	
Costs													
Regular time	$86.0	$86.0	$86.0	$86.0	$86.0	$86.0	$86.0	$86.0	$86.0	$86.0	$86.0	$86.0	$1,032.0
Overtime	0.0	0.0	0.0	0.0	0.0	25.8	25.8	25.8	0.0	0.0	0.0	0.0	77.4
Hire/layoff	3.0	0.0	0.0	0.0	0.0	0.0	0.0	0.0	0.0	0.0	0.0	0.0	3.0
Inventory carrying	10.8	18.6	23.4	25.2	24.0	25.0	16.9	11.9	9.2	6.5	5.3	4.1	180.8
Total cost	$99.8	$104.6	$109.4	$111.2	$110.0	$136.8	$128.7	$123.7	$95.2	$92.5	$91.3	$90.1	$1,293.2

*All costs are expressed in thousands of dollars. All production and inventory figures are in thousands of gallons. Starting inventory is 50,000 gallons.

264

TABLE 12.4
Aggregate Planning Costs—Strategy 3, Chase Demand*

	Jan.	Feb.	Mar.	Apr.	May	June	July	Aug.	Sept.	Oct.	Nov.	Dec.	Total
Resources													
Regular workers	30	30	35	40	45	50	65	60	48	47	45	45	
Overtime (%)	0	0	0	0	0	0	0	0	0	0	0	0	
Units produced	300	300	350	400	450	500	650	600	480	470	450	450	5,400
Sales forecast	300	300	350	400	450	500	650	600	475	475	450	450	5,400
Inventory (end of month)	50	50	50	50	50	50	50	50	55	50	50	50	
Costs													
Regular time	$60.0	$60.0	$70.0	$80.0	$90.0	$100.0	$130.0	$120.0	$96.0	$94.0	$90.0	$90.0	$1,080.0
Overtime	0.0	0.0	0.0	0.0	0.0	0.0	0.0	0.0	0.0	0.0	0.0	0.0	0.0
Hire/layoff	20.0	0.0	5.0	5.0	5.0	5.0	15.0	10.0	24.0	2.0	4.0	0.0	95.0
Inventory carrying	3.0	3.0	3.0	3.0	3.0	3.0	3.0	3.0	3.3	3.0	3.0	3.0	36.3
Total cost	$83.0	$63.0	$78.0	$88.0	$198.0	$108.0	$148.0	$133.0	$123.3	$99.0	$97.0	$93.0	$1,211.3

*All costs are expressed in thousands of dollars. All production and inventory figures are in thousands of gallons. Starting inventory is 50,000 gallons.

TABLE 12.5
Cost Summary

Strategy 1	
Regular-time payroll	$1,080,000
Hire/layoff	5,000
Inventory carrying	181,500
Total	$1,266,500
Strategy 2	
Regular-time payroll	$1,032,000
Hire/layoff	3,000
Overtime	77,400
Inventory carrying	180,800
Total	$1,293,200
Strategy 3	
Regular-time payroll	$1,080,000
Hire/layoff	95,000
Inventory carrying	36,300
Total	$1,211,300

12.8 SALES AND OPERATIONS PLANNING

Sales and Operations Planning (S&OP) is a current term manufacturing companies use to describe a form of aggregate planning. S&OP matches supply and demand using a cross-functional team approach. The cross-functional team consisting of marketing, sales, engineering, human resources (HR), operations, and finance meets with the general manager to agree on the sales forecast, the supply plan, and any steps needed to modify supply or demand. The resulting Sales and Operations Plan is updated monthly using a 12-month or longer rolling planning horizon.

S&OP is done by product family and can be more detailed than aggregate planning. Usually no more than 10 product families are used for S&OP to limit the complexity of the planning process. Inconsistencies between supply and demand are resolved on a monthly basis by revising the plan as conditions change.

Demand is decoupled from supply. For each product family the cross-functional team must decide whether to produce inventory, manage customer lead-time (backlog), provide additional capacity (internal or external), or restrict demand. Once demand and supply are in balance, however, the current S&OP may not agree with previous financial plans or HR plans or budgets that also need to be modified.

S&OP can replace a flawed annual business planning process that only provides a plan once a year. In essence S&OP provides flexible budgeting as conditions change. It reduces misalignment among functions by insisting on a common plan that will be implemented by all parties. Strong general manager leadership is required to resolve conflicts that arise.

Syngenta is a world leader in agribusiness products with 19,000 employees in 90 countries. The highly seasonal agricultural market is difficult to forecast and experiences large demand shifts. Syngenta uses S&OP to create collaboration across functions and with its supply chain partners. Managers across several countries are using the S&OP process and software to gain better agreement on forecasts, sales promotions, inventory levels, sales plans, and aggregate production plans. Real-time Web collaboration allows each business unit to manage the S&OP process to achieve targeted business goals.[4]

S&OP is not a stand-alone system. It provides a key input into the Enterprise Resource Planning (ERP) system discussed in Chapter 6. ERP tracks all detailed transactions from orders to shipments to payments, but requires a high-level aggregate plan for future sales and operations as an input. Using the S&OP process, various scenarios and assumptions can be tested via simulation to arrive at an agreed-upon plan that all functions will implement. The ERP system then accepts, as input, the S&OP plan and projects the detailed transactions (shop orders, purchase orders, inventories, and payments) that are required to support the agreed plan. This is covered in greater depth in Chapter 16.

Since S&OP is a form of aggregate planning, it precedes detailed scheduling, which is covered in the next chapter. Scheduling uses the resources provided by aggregate planning or S&OP to deal with individual orders and jobs that must be scheduled on a daily or hourly basis. Scheduling serves to allocate the capacity made available by aggregate planning to specific jobs, activities, or orders, after adjustments have been made for inventories by the ERP system. In the case of services, S&OP or aggregate plans can be translated directly into schedules since there are no inventory adjustments to be made.

12.9 KEY POINTS

The following key points are discussed in the chapter:

- Facilities decisions consider the amount of capacity, size of units, timing of capacity changes, and types of facilities needed. These decisions are on the long-range end of a hierarchy of capacity decisions that successively constrain the capacity available to operations. Facilities decisions are crucial because they determine future availability of output and require the organization's scarce capital.

- A facility strategy should be implemented rather than a series of incremental facility decisions. A facilities strategy answers the questions of how much, how large, when, and what type.

- The amount of capacity planned should be based on the desired risk of meeting forecast demand. A capacity cushion will be the result of the level of risk taken. The firm can choose to either preempt the competition or wait and see how much capacity is needed.

- Both economies and diseconomies of scale should be considered when setting an optimum facility size. The type of facility selected will be focused on product, market, process, or general-purpose needs.

- Facilities decisions are often made by the chief executive and the board of directors. Because these decisions are strategic in nature, they require the input not only of operations but of all other functional areas as well.

- Aggregate planning serves as a link between facilities decisions and scheduling. The aggregate planning decision sets overall output levels for the medium time range. As a result, decisions regarding aggregate inventory levels, workforce size, subcontracting, and back-order levels are also made. These decisions must fit within the level of facilities available, and they constrain the resources that will be available for scheduling.

---

[4] R. Herrin, 2004.

- Aggregate planning is concerned with matching supply and demand over the medium time range. In the aggregate planning problem, the overall output level is planned so as to use the best possible mix of resource inputs. Because human resources, capital, and demand are affected, all functions in the firm should be involved in aggregate planning decisions.

- Supply variables that may be changed by aggregate planning are hiring, lay-off, overtime, idle time, inventory, subcontracting, part-time labor, and cooperative arrangements. Variables that are available to influence demand are pricing, promotion, backlog or reservations, and complementary products.

- When demand is given, two basic strategies are available for adjusting supply: the chase strategy and the level strategy. There are also many other strategies between these two extremes. A choice of strategy can be made by determining the total cost of each of the strategies available.

- Sales and Operations Planning (S&OP) is a form of aggregate planning that seeks to balance supply and demand. S&OP is updated on a monthly basis for product families using a cross-functional team with at least a 12-month rolling planning horizon.

STUDENT INTERNET EXERCISES

1. Course site:
   http://www.uoguelph.ca/~dsparlin/aggregat.htm
   Read this synopsis of aggregate planning from Professor Dave Sparling's course in Canada.

2. Spreadsheet example from Georgia Southern University
   http://et.nmsu.edu/~etti/winter97/computers/spreadsheet.html
   Work through the details of this example to gain a deeper understanding of aggregate planning.

3. Sales and Operations Planning (S&OP) overview
   http://www.sopoverview.com
   Read about S&OP from this site and come to class prepared for discussion.

SOLVED PROBLEMS

Problem

1. **Probabilistic Capacity Planning** The XYZ Chemical Company has estimated the annual demand for a certain product as follows:

Thousands of Gallons	100	110	120	130	140
Probability	.10	.20	.30	.30	.10

a. If capacity is set at 130,000 gallons, how much capacity cushion is there?

b. What is the probability of idle capacity?

c. What is the average utilization of the plant at 130,000 gallons of capacity?

    d. If lost business costs \$100,000 per thousand gallons and it costs \$5000 to build 1000 gallons of capacity, how much capacity should be built to minimize total costs?

Solution

a. Capacity cushion = capacity − average demand

$$= 130 - [(.1 \times 100) + (.2 \times 110) + (.3 \times 120) + (.3 \times 130) + (.1 \times 140)]$$

$$= 9 \text{ thousand gallons}$$

b. Probability of idle capacity = probability of demand < 130

$$= .10 + .20 + .30$$

$$= .60$$

c. Average Utilization = $(.1 \times 100/130) + (.2 \times 110/130) + (.3 \times 120/130) + (.4 \times 130/130)$

$$= 92.31\%$$

d. To determine the amount of capacity that minimizes total costs, we must determine the cost of capacity and then add on the penalty cost for not supplying the quantity demanded. This is done for each amount of possible capacity.

    To build 100,000 gallons of capacity, the

Total cost = capacity cost + penalty cost

$$= (100 \times \$5000) + \{\$100,000 \times [(0 \times .1) + (10 \times .2) + (20 \times .3) + (30 \times .3) + (40 \times .1)]\}$$

$$= \$2,600,000$$

    To build 110,000 gallons of capacity, the

Total cost = capacity cost + penalty cost

$$= (110 \times \$5000) + \{\$100,000 \times [(0 \times .1) + (0 \times .2) + (10 \times .3) + (20 \times .3) + (30 \times .1)]\}$$

$$= \$1,750,000$$

    To build 120,000 gallons of capacity, the

Total cost = capacity cost + penalty cost

$$= (120 \times \$5000) + \{\$100,000 \times [(0 \times .1) + (0 \times .2) + (0 \times .3) + (10 \times .3) + (20 \times .1)]\}$$

$$= \$1,100,000$$

    To build 130,000 gallons of capacity, the

Total cost = capacity cost + penalty cost

$$= (130 \times \$5000) + \{\$100,000 \times [(0 \times .1) + (0 \times .2) + (0 \times .3) + (0 \times .3) + (10 \times .1)]\}$$

$$= \$750,000$$

    To build 140,000 gallons of capacity, the

Total cost = capacity cost + penalty cost

$$= (140 \times \$5000) + \{\$100,000 \times [(0 \times .1) + (0 \times .2) + (0 \times .3) + (0 \times .3) + (0 \times .1)]\}$$

$$= \$700,000$$

    The choice which minimizes total costs is to build 140,000 gallons of capacity which has an estimated total cost of \$700,000.

Problem

2. **Services Aggregate Planning** Ace Accounting Associates (AAA) provides annual income tax filing services for individuals. Customers pay for the service according to the type of form they file. Customers with complex returns (i.e., 1040) are charged $200. Customers with simpler forms are charged $50. Five permanent accountants work for AAA at a rate of $600 per week. During the busy season—the five weeks prior to the due date for tax filing—temporary accountants can be hired for $600 per week. A one-time fee of $200 is paid to an employment service each time the company hires a temporary accountant. All accountants (permanent and temporary) access a computerized system, which costs the company $175 per accountant per week. On the average, any accountant (permanent or temporary) can process 4 complex forms per week or 20 simple forms per week. Demand for simple and complex forms for the upcoming tax season is given in the table below. All demand must be filled by the end of the fifth week.

Week	1	2	3	4	5
Demand (simple)	40	60	80	100	100
Demand (complex)	10	17	21	30	20

a. Determine the total profit that would result from having enough accountants to meet demand each week.

b. Find a more profitable arrangement that will complete all forms by the end of the fifth week, but that is not required to complete all filings in the same week in which they were demanded.

c. If one or more permanent accountants will work up to an additional 40 hours overtime per week at 1.5 times the regular pay rate for the overtime hours worked, how would that change your solution to part *b*?

d. Are there any limitations or assumptions in your answers to parts *a*, *b*, and *c* above that might affect the decisions regarding whom and when to hire or lay off?

Solution

The revenue and permanent employee costs are the same for all the solutions, so they are shown here once:

Revenue					
Simple returns	2000	3000	4000	5000	5000
Complex returns	2000	3400	4200	6000	4000
Total revenues	4000	6400	8200	11,000	9000
Costs of permanent employees					
Accountants	3000	3000	3000	3000	3000
Computer system	875	875	875	875	875
Permanent costs	3875	3875	3875	3875	3875

a. First, the number of total accountants needed is computed as follows:

Number of accountants:					
Simple forms	2.00	3.00	4.00	5.00	5.00
Complex forms	2.50	4.25	5.25	7.50	5.00
	4.50	7.25	9.25	12.50	10.00
Round-up total	5	8	10	13	10

Number of temporary accountants (subtract five permanent accountants from the total).

Costs of Temporary Accountants

Number of Temp. Accts.	0	3	5	8	5
Hiring fees	0	600	400	600	0
Accountants (pay)	0	1800	3000	4,800	3000
Computer system	0	525	875	1,400	875
Temporary costs	0	2925	4275	6,800	3875
Total costs	3875	6800	8150	10,675	7750
Profit (loss)	125	(400)	50	325	1250

Five-week profit (loss) = $1350

b. In this case we do not need to round up the number of accountants to meet demand in each period.

Costs of Temporary Accountants

Number of Temp. Accts.	0	2	4	8	5
Hiring fees	0	400	400	800	0
Accountants	0	1200	2400	4,800	3000
Computer system	0	350	700	1,400	875
Temporary costs	0	1950	3500	7,000	3875
Total costs	3875	5825	7375	10,875	7750
Profit (loss)	125	575	825	125	1250

Five-week profit (loss) = $2900

c. Suppose we use only the five temporary accountants in week 4 and meet total demand in that week by overtime.

Costs of Temporary Accountants

Number of Temp. Accts.	0	2	4	5	5
Hiring fees	0	400	400	200	0
Temp. accountants	0	1200	2400	3,000	3000
Overtime (perm. accts.)	0	0	0	2,700	0
Computer system	0	350	700	875	875
Temporary costs	0	1950	3500	6,775	3875
Total costs	3875	5825	7375	10,650	7750
Profit (loss)	125	575	825	350	1250

Five-week profit (loss) = $3125

d. Aggregate planning is rarely as simple as this sample problem. For example, in this problem, costs of termination are not considered. It is doubtful that the customers of this imaginary tax filing firm would want to allow their filings to be put off until it was convenient for the firm to file them—if they were expecting a refund.

Problem

3. **Manufacturing Aggregate Planning** Manufacturers Inc. (MI) currently has a labor force of 10, which can produce 500 units per period. The cost of labor is now $2,400 per period per employee. The company has a long-standing rule that does not allow overtime. In addition, the product cannot be subcontracted due to the specialized machinery that MI uses to produce it. As a result, MI can only increase/decrease production by hiring or laying off employees. The cost is $5,000 to hire an employee and $5,000 to lay off an employee. Inventory-carrying costs are $100 per unit remaining at the end of each period. The inventory level at the beginning of period 1 is 300 units. The forecast demand in each of six periods is given in the table below.

	Period 1	Period 2	Period 3	Period 4	Period 5	Period 6
Aggregate demand	630	520	410	270	410	520

a. Compute the costs of the chase strategy.
b. Also, compute the costs for a level strategy.
c. Compare the two strategies.

Solution

a. First, decide on the workforce level to be used for the chase strategy so that production meets demand in each period. For example, in period 1, demand is 630 units, which requires 12.6 workers (each worker can make 50 units). The answer is rounded up to 13 workers. The tables for number of units produced and for cost calculations are as follows:

	Period 1	Period 2	Period 3	Period 4	Period 5	Period 6
Units						
Aggregate demand	630	520	410	270	410	520
Number of workers	13	10	8	5	8	10
Units produced	650	500	400	250	400	500
Ending inventory	320	300	290	270	260	240
Costs						
Cost of labor	$31,200	$24,000	$19,200	$12,000	$19,200	$24,000
Hiring/layoff cost	15,000	15,000	10,000	15,000	15,000	10,000
Inventory-carrying cost	32,000	30,000	29,000	27,000	26,000	24,000
Cost per period	$78,200	$69,000	$58,200	$54,000	$60,200	$58,000
Total costs						$377,600

b. For the level strategy, also decide first on the workforce level. To be comparable with part *a*, we must set the workforce level to produce the same number of total units over six periods. The total units produced in part *a* are

$$650 + 500 + 400 + 250 + 400 + 500 = 2{,}700$$

A level strategy produces an equal number of units each period or 2,700/6 = 450 units per period. This requires exactly nine workers each period. The resulting number of units and costs calculations are

	Period 1	Period 2	Period 3	Period 4	Period 5	Period 6
Units						
Aggregate demand	630	520	410	270	410	520
Number of workers	9	9	9	9	9	9
Units produced	450	450	450	450	450	450
Ending inventory	120	50	90	270	310	240
Costs						
Cost of labor	$21,600	$21,600	$21,600	$21,600	$21,600	$21,600
Hiring/layoff cost	5,000	0	0	0	0	0
Inventory-carrying cost	12,000	5,000	9,000	27,000	31,000	24,000
Cost per period	$38,600	$26,600	$30,600	$48,600	$52,600	$45,600
Total costs						$242,600

c. The level strategy is much less costly. This is because it is relatively expensive to hire and lay off workers. Also, the chase strategy is penalized by the relatively high starting inventory of 300 units, which is not needed by the chase alternative but is needed by the level strategy to avoid stockouts.

Discussion Questions

1. Approximately how long would one need to plan ahead for the following types of facilities?
   a. Restaurant
   b. Hospital
   c. Oil refinery
   d. Toy factory
   e. Electric power plant
   f. Public school
   g. Private school

2. What problems are created by mixing the capacity questions of how much, how large, when, and what type?

3. A school district has forecast student enrollment for several years into the future and predicts excess capacity for 2,000 students. The school board has said that the only alternative is to close a school. Evaluate.

4. Why are facilities decisions often made by top management? What is the role in these decisions of operations, marketing, finance, and personnel?

5. In what ways does corporate strategy affect capacity decisions?

6. Aggregate planning is sometimes confused with scheduling. What is the difference?

7. The XYZ Company manufactures a seasonal product. At the present time, the company uses a level labor force as a matter of company policy. The company is afraid that if it lays off workers, it will not be able to rehire them or to find qualified replacements. Does this company have an aggregate planning problem? Discuss.

8. It has been said that aggregate planning is related to personnel planning, budgeting, and market planning. Describe the nature of the relationship between these types of planning.

9. Every company has multiple objectives such as good labor relations, low operation costs, high inventory turnover, and good customer service. What are the pros and cons of treating these objectives separately in an aggregate planning problem versus combining them all into a single measure of cost?

10. How is the choice between a level strategy and a chase strategy influenced by the skill level of the workforce and the degree of automation? After all, isn't the choice between these strategies just a matter of the lowest cost?

11. What factors are important in choosing the length of the planning horizon for aggregate planning?

12. What cost factors should be included in calculating the total cost of an aggregate strategy?

13. A barbershop has been using a level workforce of barbers five days a week, Tuesday through Saturday. The barbers have considerable idle time on Tuesday through Friday, with certain

peak periods during the noon hours and after 4 P.M. each day. On Friday afternoon and all day Saturday, all the barbers are very busy, with customers waiting a substantial amount of time and some customers being turned away. What options should this barbershop consider for aggregate planning? How would you analyze these options? What data would be collected and how would the options be compared?

14. Compare S&OP to aggregate planning. Describe the similarities and differences.
   a. How many units of capacity should be built to minimize the total cost of providing capacity plus lost sales?
   b. State a general rule regarding the amount of capacity to build.
   c. What principle does the problem illustrate?

Problems

1. Suppose we are considering the question of how much capacity to build in the face of uncertain demand. Assume that the cost is $18 per unit of lost sales due to insufficient capacity. Also assume that there is a cost of $5 for each unit of capacity built. The probability of various demand levels is as follows:

Demand—X Units	Probability of X
0	.05
1	.10
2	.15
3	.20
4	.20
5	.15
6	.10
7	.05

2. The Ace Steel Mill estimates the demand for steel in millions of tons per year as follows:

Millions of Tons	Probability
10	.10
12	.25
14	.30
16	.20
18	.15

   a. If capacity is set at 16 million tons, how much capacity cushion is there?
   b. What is the probability of idle capacity, and what is the average utilization of the plant at 16 million tons of capacity?
   c. If it costs $10 million per million tons of lost business and $100 million to build a million tons of capacity, how much capacity should be built to minimize total costs?

3. A barbershop has the following demand for haircuts on Saturdays, which is its busiest day of the week.

Number of Haircuts	Probability
10	.1
15	.3
20	.4
25	.1
30	.1

   a. What is the average demand for haircuts on Saturday?
   b. If the capacity is 30 haircuts, what is the average utilization of the shop?
   c. If capacity is 30 haircuts, how much capacity cushion does it have?
   d. If it costs $50 per lost haircut due to customer dissatisfaction and $100 for each unit of capacity provided, how much capacity should be built to minimize costs?

4. Assume a fast-food restaurant operates from 7 A.M. to 11 P.M. seven days a week.
   a. How much capacity does the restaurant have on a weekly and annual basis in hours?
   b. If the restaurant can serve a maximum of 50 customers per hour, how much capacity does the restaurant have in a week?
   c. What implicit assumptions are made in your calculation for part *b?*

5. The Speedy Mail Service processes millions of pieces of junk mail advertising each year. The company prints, addresses, and mails literature for its customers. The costs of operating the plant are given by the following equation:

$$C(x) = x^2 - 600x + 90{,}200$$

where $C(x)$ is the unit cost, and x is the volume of the plant.
   a. Plot a graph of cost versus volume.
   b. What is the minimum-cost point?
   c. At $x = 500$, what is the dollar magnitude of the diseconomies of scale?

Excel Spreadsheet Tips

Three Excel spreadsheets are provided for this chapter on the student CD-ROM to assist in solving the chapter problems. The spreadsheet for problem 10 is shown below with different data than problem 10. Inputs are shown in the input section of the spreadsheet and the outputs are an aggregate plan with costs for the next six months.

	A	B	C	D	E	F	G	H
19	NAME:	Example				CHAPTER 12, PROBLEM 10		
20	SECT:	* * * * * * * * * * * * * * *				DATE:		
21								
22								
23	INPUT SECTION:							
24	PRESENT LABOR FORCE (employees)					80		
25	TOYS PER WORKER PER MONTH IN $000					$20		
26	REGULAR WAGE RATE PER MONTH					$3,000		
27	OVERTIME RATE (% of regular time)					150%		
28	INVENTORY CARRYING CHARGE (% per year)					30%		
29	HIRING COSTS ($ per worker)					$2,000		
30	LAYOFF COSTS ($ per worker)					$4,000		
31	BEG INVENTORY IN $000					$80		
32								
33								
34			DEMAND IN THOUSANDS OF DOLLARS					
35								
36		JULY	$1,500		OCT	$2,000		
37		AUG	$2,000		NOV	$1,800		
38		SEPT	$2,500		DEC	$1,600		
39								
40			TOTAL $11,400					
41								
42								
43								
44			STRATEGY:		level			
45								
46				MONTH				
47			JULY	AUG	SEPT	OCT	NOV	DEC	TOTAL
48	RESOURCES:	{PRODUCTION, SALES, AND INVENTORIES IN $000}						
49	REG WORKER:	90	90	90	90	90	90	
50	O.T.%	0%	0%	0%	0%	0%	0%	
51	PRODUCTION	1,800	1,800	1,800	1,800	1,800	1,800	10,800
52	SALES:	1,500	2,000	2,500	2,000	1,800	1,600	11,400
53	INVENTORY	380	180	(520)	(720)	(720)	(520)	
54		---------------	---------------	---------------	---------------	---------------	---------------	---------------
55	COSTS: {IN DOLLARS}							
56	REG. TIME:	270,000	270,000	270,000	270,000	270,000	270,000	1,620,000
57	OVERTIME:	0	0	0	0	0	0	0
58	HIRE/FIRE:	20,000	0	0	0	0	0	20,000
59	INVENTORY:	9,500	4,500	(13,000)	(18,000)	(18,000)	(13,000)	(48,000)
60		=========	=========	=========	=========	=========	=========	=========
61	TOTAL:	299,500	274,500	257,000	252,000	252,000	257,000	1,592,000
62								

eXcel 6. The Chewy Candy Company would like to determine an aggregate production plan for the next six months. The company makes many different types of candy but feels it can plan its total production in pounds provided the mix of candy sold does not change too drastically. At the present time, the Chewy Company has 70 workers and 9,000 pounds of candy in inventory. Each worker can produce 100 pounds of candy a month and is paid $5 an hour (use 160 hours regular time per month). Overtime, at a pay rate of 150 percent of regular time, can be used up to a maximum of 20 percent in addition to regular time in any given month. It costs 80 cents to store a pound of candy for a year, $200 to hire a worker, and $500 to lay off a worker. The forecast sales for the next six months are 8,000, 10,000, 12,000, 8,000, 6,000, and 5,000 pounds of candy.

   a. Determine the costs of a level production strategy for the next six months, with an ending inventory of 8,000 pounds.

   b. Determine the costs of a chase strategy for the next six months.

   c. Calculate the costs of using the maximum overtime for the two months of highest demand.

   d. Draw a cumulative graph of demand and of the three production strategies considered above.

7. A company produces to a seasonal demand, with the forecast for the next 12 months as given below. The present labor force can produce 500 units per month. Each employee added can produce an additional 20 units per month and is paid $1,000 per month. The cost of materials is $30 per unit. Overtime can be used at the usual premium of time and a half for labor up to a maximum of 10 percent per month. Inventory-carrying cost is $50 per unit per year. Changes in production level cost $100 per unit due to hiring, line changeover costs, and so forth. Assume 200 units of initial inventory. Extra capacity may be obtained by subcontracting at an additional cost of $15 per unit over and above the company's producing them itself on regular time. What plan do you recommend? What is the incremental cost of this plan?

Month	J	F	M	A	M	J	J	A	S	O	N	D
Demand	600	700	800	700	600	500	600	700	800	900	700	600

8. Approximately 40 percent of a medical clinic's weekly incoming calls for doctors' appointments occur on Monday. Due to this large workload, 30 percent of the callers receive a busy signal and have to call back later. The clinic now has one clerk for each two doctors to handle incoming calls. Each clerk handles calls for the same doctors all week long and thus is familiar with the doctors' hours, scheduling practices, and idiosyncrasies. Consider the following alternatives to solve this problem:

   • Continue the present system, which results in some customer inconvenience, loss of business, and perceived poor service. About 1,000 patients attempt to call the clinic on Mondays. The clinic has 50,000 patients in all.

   • Expand the phone lines and add more people to handle the peak load. Estimated cost for adding two more lines and two clerks is $50,000 per year.

   • Install a computer to speed up appointments. In this case, the peak load could be handled with present personnel. Estimated cost to lease and maintain the equipment and programs is $25,000 per year.

   • Expand the phone lines and ask people to call back later in the week for an appointment. Add two lines and two phone-answering clerks part time at $30,000 per year.

   a. Analyze these options from the standpoint of an aggregate planning problem. What are the pros and cons of each option?

   b. Which option do you recommend? Why?

   c. How does this problem differ from the other aggregate planning problems given above?

9. The Restwell Motel in Orlando, Florida, would like to prepare an aggregate plan for the next year. The motel has a maximum of 200 rooms, which are fully utilized in the winter months but largely vacant in the summer, as shown by the schedule below. The motel requires one employee, paid $800 per month, for each 20 rooms rented on regular time. It can utilize up to 20 percent overtime at time and a half and can also hire part-time workers at $700 per month. The regular-time workers are hired at a cost of $500 and laid off at a cost of $200 per worker. There is no hiring and layoff cost for the part-time workers.

Month	J	F	M	A	M	J	J	A	S	O	N	D
Demand (rooms)	185	190	170	160	110	100	100	80	100	120	140	160

   a. With a regular workforce of six employees and 20 percent overtime when needed, how many part-time workers are required in each month and how much does this strategy cost per year?

b. What is the best strategy to follow if a level workforce of six regular workers is used? You may use various amounts of overtime and part-time workers.

eXcel 10. The Bango Toy Company produces several types of toys to seasonal demand. The forecast for the next six months in thousands of dollars is given below:

	July	Aug.	Sept.	Oct.	Nov.	Dec.
Forecast	$1000	$1500	$2000	$1800	$1500	$1000

A regular employee can produce $10,000 worth of toys per month, and the company has 80 regular employees at the end of June. Regular-time employees are paid $1,500 per month, including benefits. An employee on overtime produces at the same rate as regular time but is paid at 150 percent of the regular pay. Up to 20 percent overtime can be used in any one month. A worker can be hired for $1,000, and it costs $2,000 to lay off an employee. Inventory-carrying costs are 30 percent per year. The company wishes to end the year with 80 employees. Beginning inventory of toys is $900,000.

a. Calculate the cost of a chase strategy.

b. What is the cost of a level strategy?

c. Using the Excel template, simulate several other strategies.

d. Determine the effect on the chase strategy, in part *a*, of changing the hiring cost to $1,500, $2,000, and $2,500. What do these changes suggest the relationship is between hiring cost and total cost?

e. Use the Excel software to study the effect of demand changes on the total cost of the chase strategy. Assume various percentage increases and decreases in demand (e.g., +10%, +20%, −10%, −20%, etc.).

11. A small textile company makes various types of sweaters. Of course, demand is very seasonal, as shown by the following quarterly demand estimates. Demand is estimated in terms of standard hours of production required.

	Fall	Winter	Spring	Summer
Forecast	10,000	15,000	8,000	5,000

An hour of regular time costs the company $8. Employees are paid $12 per hour on overtime, and labor can be subcontracted from the outside at $10 per hour. A maximum of 1,000 overtime hours is available in any given month. A change in the regular level of production (either increase

or decrease) incurs a one-time cost of $5 per hour for adding or subtracting an hour of labor. It costs 2 percent per month to carry an hour of labor in inventory. Materials and overhead costs in inventory are equal to the direct labor costs. At the beginning of fall quarter, there are 5,000 standard hours in inventory and the workforce level is equivalent to 10,000 standard hours.

a. Suppose management sets the level of regular workers for the year equal to the average demand and subcontracts out the rest. What is the cost of this strategy?

b. What is the cost of a chase strategy?

eXcel 12. Beth's Broasted Chicken shop offers a variety of fast-food items. Beth uses regular and part-time workers to meet demand. The demand for the next 12 months has been forecast in thousands of dollars as follows:

	J	F	M	A	M	J	J	A	S	O	N	D
Demand	25	33	40	55	50	58	50	44	37	33	28	32

Assume that each employee can produce $5,000 worth of demand in a month. The company pays regular workers $7 per hour, including benefits, and part-time workers $5 per hour. Of course, management would like to use as many part-time workers as possible, but must limit the ratio to one regular worker to one part-time worker in order to provide adequate supervision and continuity of the workforce. Demand cannot be inventoried and must be met on a month-by-month basis. It costs $500 to hire and $200 to lay off a regular worker. No costs are associated with hiring and laying off part-time workers. A maximum of 20 percent slack is allowed in months when the company would prefer to not lay off people and rehire them in the following months. In other words, the regular and part-time workforce cannot exceed 120 percent of demand in any given month.

a. Develop a strategy for this problem by using the maximum amount of part-time workers and by not laying off people when they would be needed the following month. What is the cost of this strategy?

b. Simulate several other strategies using the Excel template.

13. Valley View Hospital faces a somewhat seasonal demand. Patients defer elective surgery in the summer and in the holiday season at the end of the year. As a result, the forecast of patient days of demand is as follows (a patient day is one patient staying for one day in the hospital):

	Fall	Winter	Spring	Summer
Forecast	90,000	70,000	8,5000	65,000

The hospital uses regular nurses, part-time nurses (when the hospital can get them), and contract nurses (who are not employees). Contract nurses work a number of hours, which varies depending on their contract established with the hospital. Regular nurses are paid a sum of $5,000 per quarter for 60 days of work; part-time nurses are paid $2,000 per quarter for 30 days of work. Contract nurses get an average of $6,000 per quarter for 60 days of work. It costs $1,000 to hire or lay off any of these three types of nurses.

a. Suppose that regular nurses are set at a level of 800 nurses for the year. Each regular nurse works the equivalent of 60 days per quarter. The remainder of the demand is made up by 50 percent part-time and 50 percent contract nurses on a quarter-by-quarter basis. What is the cost of this plan starting at the beginning of spring with a level of 800 regular nurses, 200 part-time nurses, and 200 contract nurses? Assume it takes 0.8 nurse days to provide around-the-clock care for each patient day.

Selected Bibliography

Bradley, Perry. "The Operations Planning Guide." *Business & Commercial Aviation* 87, no. 2 (August 2000), p. 9.

Buxey, Geoff. "A Managerial Perspective on Aggregate Planning." *International Journal of Production Economics* 41, no. 1 (October 1995), pp. 127–33.

Copacino, William C., and Peter Bradley. "Beyond Demand Planning." *Logistics Management & Distribution Report* 37, no. 5 (May 1995), p. 38.

Erkut, Erhan, and Umit Ozen. "Aggregate Planning for Distribution of Durable Household Products: A Case Study." *Journal of Business Logistics* 17, no. 2 (1996), pp. 217–34.

Goddard, Walter E. "Don't Let Internal Communication Links Be Bad Connections!" *Modern Materials Handling* 49, no. 2 (February 1994), p. 41.

Haussmann, R., and S. W. Hess. "A Linear Programming Approach to Production and Employment Scheduling." *Management Technology* 1 (January 1960), pp. 46–52.

Hayes, Robert H., and Steven Wheelwright. *Restoring Our Competitive Edge: Competing through Manufacturing.* New York: Wiley, 1984.

Herrin, Richard. "John Galt Atlas Planning Suite: Syngenta Improves S&OP Process." *DM Review* 14, no. 6 (June 2004), p. 89.

Holt, C., F. Modigliani, and H. Simon. "A Linear Decision Rule for Production and Employment Scheduling." *Management Science* 2, no. 1 (October 1955), pp. 1–30.

Johnston, Robert. "Operations: From Factory to Service Management." *International Journal of Service Industry Management* 5, no. 1 (1994), pp. 49–63.

Lapide, Larry. "Sales and Operations Planning Part 1: The Process." *Journal of Business Forecasting* 23, no. 3 (Fall 2004), pp. 17–19.

Lee, S. M., and L. J. Moore. "A Practical Approach to Production Scheduling." *Production and Inventory Management* (1st quarter 1974), pp. 79–92.

Mellichamp, Joseph, and Robert Love. "Production Heuristics for the Aggregate Planning Problem." *Management Science* 24, no. 12 (August 1978), pp. 1242–51.

Schmenner, Roger W. "Multiplan Manufacturing Strategies among the Fortune 500." *Journal of Operations Management* 2, no. 2 (February 1982), pp. 77–86.

Schroeder, Roger G., and Paul Larson. "A Reformulation of the Aggregate Planning Problem." *Journal of Operations Management* 6, no. 3 (May 1986), pp. 245–56.

Smith, Barry C., Dirk P. Gunther, Richard M. Ratlife, and Venkateshwara B. Rao. "E-Commerce and Operations Research in Airline Planning, Marketing, and Distribution." *Interfaces* 31, no. 2 (March–April 2001), pp. 38–56.

Vergin, R. C. "Production Scheduling under Seasonal Demand." *Journal of Industrial Engineering* 17 (May 1966).

Wallace, Thomas F. *Sales & Operations Planning—The How-To Handbook.* Alexandria, VA: APICS, 1999.

Supplement

Mathematical Models

A wide variety of aggregate planning models have been developed over the years. In this supplement, we will formulate the general mathematical model for aggregate planning and then discuss three alternative solution approaches: decision rules, simulation, and linear programming.

GENERAL MODEL

The aggregate planning problem has three general variables: P_t = the amount produced during period t, I_t = the inventory level at the end of period t, and F_t = the forecasted demand for period t. We can define the inventory at the end of period I_t in terms of these variables.

$$I_t = I_{t-1} + P_t - F_t \quad \text{for} \quad t = 1, 2, \ldots N \qquad \text{(S12.1)}$$

The inventory at the end of any period I_t is just the inventory at the end of the preceding period, plus the production during the period, minus the demand during the period. We have, of course, calculated the inventory in precisely this fashion in the Hefty Beer Company example.

We also want to specify that the inventory and the production levels will not be chosen as negative values:

$$I_t, P_t \geq 0 \qquad \text{(S12.2)}$$

We need a cost function to evaluate the various production strategies used. A cost function for the aggregate planning problem is as follows:

$$\text{Cost} = \sum_{t=1}^{t=N} (a_t I_t + b_t P_t + c_t F_t) \qquad \text{(S12.3)}$$

The cost is a function of the inventory carried, the production rate, and the forecasted demand over all periods.

Now we can state the mathematical problem as finding that set of variables P_t and I_t, given F_t, which will minimize the cost given by Equation (S12.3), subject to the constraints given by Equations (S12.1) and (S12.2).

The chase strategy and the level strategy, which we have described in the chapter, will be two particular (feasible) solutions to this problem. For the chase strategy, we set $P_t = F_t$ for all values of t; the production level is just equal to the forecast. And for the level strategy, we set P_t = a constant value for all periods; the production level does not vary. The mathematical model will allow us to evaluate the cost of these strategies and any other strategies that we may choose. It will also allow us to find, under certain conditions, an optimal strategy that minimizes the total cost equation.

DECISION RULES

One approach to solving the above problem is to construct a decision rule that specifies the value of production for each period as a function of the forecast, inventory levels, and other parameters of interest. A manager can use such a decision rule to determine production levels dynamically at any time *t*. For example, we can specify the following decision rule:

$$P_t = P_{t-1} + \alpha(F_t - P_{t-1}) \text{ for } t = 1, 2, \ldots N$$

where α is the smoothing constant $0 \leq \alpha \leq 1$.

For this rule, if we set $\alpha = 0$, we will get the level strategy ($P_t = P_{t-1}$), and if we set $\alpha = 1$, we will get the chase strategy ($P_t = F_t$). Values of α in between 0 and 1 will produce various other decision rules. Note the similarity of this rule to the exponential smoothing approach used for forecasting. This particular decision rule will simply smooth out production over time to respond to changes in the forecast.

As an example of this decision rule, we set $\alpha = .7$ for the Hefty Beer example and compute the corresponding costs. We construct a cost table similar to Table 12.2 once we know the production level in each period. We are given the starting level of $P_0 = 40$ workers, so we calculate:

$$P_1 = P_0 + .7\ (F_1 - P_0) = 40 + .7(30 - 40) = 33 \text{ workers}[1]$$

Similarly we calculate:

$$P_2 = P_1 + .7\ (F_2 - P_1) = 33 + .7\ (30 - 33) = 30.9 \text{ workers}$$

This process is continued for 12 months, and the resulting production profile is costed out using the same method as in Table 12.2. The total cost for the year of this decision rule is $1,200,100, a savings over the lowest-cost strategy previously found.

Many other decision rules have been proposed in the literature. The first study of aggregate planning, done in a paint factory in 1955, used the so-called linear decision rule [Holt, Modigliani, and Simon (1955)]. In this case, the cost function was quadratic in nature, and the resulting optimal decision rules were linear in terms of forecasted demand, inventory, and previous production levels. Later studies, such as those by Mellichamp and Love (1978), considered more general cost functions and other types of decision rules.

Mellichamp and Love observed that managers seem to favor one large change in the workforce (and production level) rather than a series of smaller continuous changes. As a result, Mellichamp and Love formulated a three-level decision rule for production, with levels of high, medium, and low. This production switching rule determines when to jump from one production level to the next. As a result, production increases and decreases in a series of steps.

SIMULATION

Another technique that can be used to evaluate the models described above is simulation. This technique can be used to rapidly evaluate a large number of different decision rules or production choices. The first application of simulation to aggregate planning was in 1966 by Vergin. He showed how complex cost structures could be used and how simulation could be controlled to systematically search for a "good" solution.

In 1986, Schroeder and Larson reformulated the aggregate production planning problem in terms of random demands. This was done since most practical problems have unpredictable future demands. In addition, management seems

---

[1] If desired, the production level could also be computed in terms of thousands of gallons.

to be primarily concerned with evaluating the probabilities of stockouts and associated inventory levels for a few feasible strategies. Management needs to know how any given strategy will affect probable inventory levels and the ability to meet demand estimates. This problem was solved through the use of simulation.

Today, the availability of commercial spreadsheets, such as Excel, has made simulation easy to use for aggregate planning problems. Spreadsheet models can be easily built, and many alternatives can be evaluated. Excel spreadsheets have been provided for some of the problems at the end of this chapter in the software that accompanies this text.

LINEAR PROGRAMMING

In 1960, Haussmann and Hess proposed the use of linear programming to solve aggregate planning problems. This method offers powerful solutions provided that costs can be expressed in a linear or piecewise linear form. In the linear programming formulation, the constraints represent inventory balances from period to period, the use of overtime, and the hiring and layoff levels. The simplex method and other methods can be used to find the minimum-cost solution to the linear programming formulation.

Linear programming makes it possible to evaluate an infinite number of production strategies and find the minimum-cost alternative. It provides a powerful methodology for not only solving the problem but evaluating other solutions that might be suggested, relative to the best one.

For example, we can calculate the lowest-cost strategy for the Hefty Beer example by formulating it as a linear programming problem. We have done this using Excel and the Solver option for linear optimization. The minimum cost solution is $1,197,500, which is the lowest-cost plan for any conceivable pattern of production.[2] The production strategy in this case is something like the chase strategy in that it follows the forecasted demand each period but is less dynamic than the chase strategy.

Linear programming has also been extended to more complex situations. Lee and Moore (1974) have suggested that a goal programming formulation be used. They used an example with multiple goals specified in the following priority order:

P_1 = operate within the limits of productive capacity
P_2 = meet the contracted delivery schedule
P_3 = operate at a minimum level of 80 percent of regular-time capacity
P_4 = keep inventory less than a maximum number of units
P_5 = minimize total production and inventory costs
P_6 = hold overtime production to a minimum

The solution procedure seeks satisfaction of these goals, starting with P_1 and proceeding to P_2, P_3, and so on. Through the use of this approach, trade-offs can be made between the goals of capacity, delivery schedule, stable workforce, production, inventory, and overtime cost. This makes it possible to consider a richer goal structure than cost alone.

---

[2] Assumes an integer number of workers during each period.

Supplement Problems

1. The Zoro Company manufactures fast-cutting lawn mowers. The company has devised the following decision rule.

$$P_t = P_{t-1} + \alpha(F_t - P_{t-1})$$

   a. If at the present time Zoro has a production level of 1,000 units, a forecast for next period of 1,500 units, and a smoothing constant of .5, what should the production level be for the next period?

   b. If the forecast for period 2 is 1,200 units, what will be the production level for period 2?

   c. Suggest a procedure for bringing inventory into the above equation.

2. Solve the Chewy Candy Company (problem 6 in the chapter) aggregate planning problem using linear programming. The Excel Solver or other linear programming package can be used.

   a. How does the minimum-cost linear programming solution compare to the costs of the chase and level strategies from the chapter?

   b. If a decision rule from problem 1 is used, what is the cost and the resulting strategy obtained?

3. Solve Beth's Broasted Chicken problem (problem 12 in the chapter) using linear programming.

   a. How does the minimum-cost linear programming strategy compare to the strategies from problem 10?

   b. What practical problems might be encountered in implementing the minimum-cost strategy?

4. Solve Valley View Hospital (problem 13) in the chapter using linear programming. You can use Excel Solver for this problem.

   a. How does the minimum cost solution compare to your computation from problem 13 part *a*?

   b. Do you foresee any practical problems that might be encountered in implementing the optimal solution?

Scheduling Operations

Chapter outline

Scheduling decisions allocate available capacity or resources (equipment, labor, and space) to jobs, activities, tasks, or customers over time. Since scheduling is an allocation decision, it uses the resources made available by facilities decisions and aggregate planning. Therefore, scheduling is the last and most constrained decision in the hierarchy of capacity planning decisions.

In practice, scheduling results in a **time-phased plan,** or schedule, of activities. The schedule indicates what is to be done, when, by whom, and with what equipment. Scheduling should be clearly differentiated from aggregate planning. Aggregate planning seeks to determine the resources needed, while scheduling allocates the resources made available through aggregate planning in the best manner to meet operations objectives. Aggregate planning is done on a time frame of about one year; scheduling is done on a time frame of a few months, weeks, or hours.

Scheduling seeks to achieve several conflicting objectives: high efficiency, low inventories, and good customer service. Efficiency is achieved by a schedule that maintains high utilization of labor, equipment, and space. Of course, the schedule should also seek to maintain low inventories, which unfortunately may lead to low efficiency due to lack of available material or high setup times. Thus, a **trade-off decision** in scheduling between efficiency and inventory levels is required in the short run. In the long run, however, efficiency can be increased, customer service improved, and inventory simultaneously reduced by changing the production process itself through cycle time reduction and quality improvement efforts. Scheduling, then, is primarily a short-run activity that involves trade-offs among conflicting objectives.

Because of the conflicting objectives, everyone in the business is interested in scheduling. Marketing wants to make sure the most important customers are scheduled first. If salespeople are rewarded on the basis of dollars sold, they want the big orders shipped on time. Finance and accounting want to be sure that the schedule is cost-efficient and makes the best use of available resources. Operations is often at the intersection of a cross-functional scheduling problem that requires coordination across all of the business functions.

It is not possible to treat scheduling for all types of operations as a single subject. To highlight the differences, scheduling can be classified by the type of process: line, batch, and project. This chapter addresses the scheduling of batch operations for both manufacturing and service operations. The next chapter deals with scheduling for projects.

13.1 BATCH SCHEDULING

For scheduling batch operations, much of the terminology ("shop," "job," "work center") comes from traditional manufacturing job shops. The concepts, however, apply equally to batch operations of all types, including factories, hospitals, offices, and schools. For service operations, the term "job" can be replaced by "customer," "patient," "client," "paperwork," or whatever flows through the process instead of materials or jobs. Furthermore, the term "work center" can be replaced by "room," "office," "facility," "skill specialty," or whatever the processing centers are. In this way, the concepts can be generalized to all types of operations.

Batch scheduling is a very complex management problem. First, each unit flowing through a batch process typically moves along with many starts and stops, not smoothly. This irregular flow is due to the layout of the batch process by machine group or skills into work centers. As a result, jobs or customers wait in line as each unit is transferred from one work center to the next. Work-in-process (WIP) inventory builds up, or people wait in lines, and scheduling becomes complex and difficult.

The batch scheduling problem can be thought of as a **network of queues.** A queue of WIP inventory is formed at each work center as jobs wait for the facilities to become available. These queues are interconnected through a network of material or customer flows. The problem of scheduling batch processes is how to manage these queues.

As we have noted in Chapter 4, one of the characteristics of a batch operation is that jobs or customers spend most of their time waiting in line. The amount of time spent waiting will, of course, vary with the load on the process. If the process is highly loaded, a job may spend as much as 95 percent of its total production time waiting in queues. Under these circumstances, if it takes one week to actually process an order, it will take 20 weeks on average to deliver it to the customer. On the other hand, if the process is lightly loaded, the waiting time will be reduced since all the jobs flow through the process more rapidly. Regardless of the load on the process, however, the challenge is to develop scheduling procedures that will effectively manage the flow of jobs, customers, and work.

The scheduling of batch processes in manufacturing is closely related to materials requirements planning (MRP) systems, which are discussed in Chapter 16. Since MRP deals with a variety of topics—inventory, scheduling, and manufacturing control—the discussion of MRP is deferred until later. Much of the material discussed in this chapter, however, can be considered a component of an MRP system, in addition to the broader scheduling and service-industry applications.

We begin this chapter with a discussion of Gantt charting, a very simple form of scheduling. We then extend this to more complex and realistic settings with discussions of finite and infinite capacity scheduling and dispatching rules. The chapter is completed with some examples of scheduling systems used in actual practice.

13.2 GANTT CHARTING

One of the oldest scheduling methods, the **Gantt chart,** was proposed by Henry L. Gantt in 1917. Although there are many variations of the Gantt chart, we shall restrict its use in this chapter to the batch facility scheduling problem.

The Gantt chart is a table with time across the top and a scarce resource, such as machines, people, or machine hours, along the side. In the example below, we shall assume that machines are the scarce resource to be scheduled.

Gantt charting is best illustrated by example.

Example

Suppose we have a very simple shop with three work centers (A, B, C) consisting of one machine each and five jobs (1, 2, 3, 4, 5) to be scheduled. The processing time of each job in each work center is shown in Figure 13.1 along with sequencing of the jobs through the work centers. For example, job 2 is processed in work center C for six hours followed by four hours in work center A. This is denoted by C/6, A/4 in Figure 13.1.

The jobs are scheduled forward in time within the finite capacity of one machine of each type (A, B, and C). We also assume, arbitrarily, that the jobs should be scheduled in the sequence 1, 4, 5, 2, 3.

The Gantt chart resulting from these assumptions is shown in Figure 13.2. This chart is constructed by first scheduling job 1 on all three machines. Job 1 starts on machine A for two hours; then it is placed on machine B for three hours (time 2 to time 5); and finally it is processed on machine C for four hours (time 5 to time 9). There is no waiting time for the first job scheduled, since there can be no job interference or waiting. Next, according to the assumed sequence, job 4 is scheduled on the Gantt chart for machines C, B, and then A. Job 4 can begin immediately on machine C, since the machine is open until time 5 and only four hours are needed. After a waiting time of one hour, job 4 can start on machine B. Job 4 can finally be scheduled on machine A from time 8 to 11. Next, job 5 is scheduled on the Gantt chart. Job 5 is processed on machine A first; but machine A is already scheduled until time 2. So job 5 starts at time 2 and is completed by time 7. After completion

FIGURE 13.1 Job data for scheduling.

Job	Work center/ Machine hours	Due date
1	A/2, B/3, C/4	3
2	C/6, A/4	2
3	B/3, C/2, A/1	4
4	C/4, B/3, A/3	4
5	A/5, B/3	2

FIGURE 13.2
Gantt chart. Jobs are sequenced in order 1, 4, 5, 2, 3.

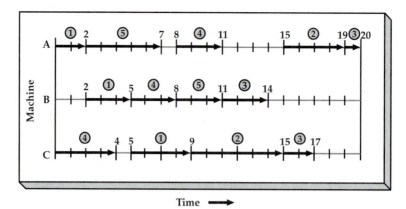

	Machine idle (hr)
A	5
B	8
C	4
	17

Makespan = 20 hr

Job	Job waiting time (hr)	Delivery time (hr)
1	0	9
2	9	19
3	14	20
4	1	11
5	3	11

on machine A, job 5 is moved to machine B, which is busy until time 8. Job 5 is then scheduled from time 8 to 11 on machine B. This process of scheduling is continued until all jobs have been placed in the Gantt chart.

After a Gantt chart has been constructed, it should be evaluated with respect to both job and machine performance. One way to evaluate machine performance is on the basis of the time it takes to complete all work, the **makespan.** In Figure 13.2, the makespan is 20 hours, since it takes 20 hours to complete all five jobs.

Another measure of the Gantt chart performance is **machine utilization.** Utilization may be measured in Figure 13.2 by adding up the idle time for each machine (5 + 8 + 4 = 17) and computing a utilization or idle percentage. The idle-time percentage is 17/60 = 28.3 percent, and the utilization percentage is 43/60 = 71.7 percent. Notice that utilization is closely related to makespan. In the five jobs, a total of 43 hours of processing time is required (simply add machine times for all jobs from Figure 13.1). The 43 hours of processing time is a constant regardless of the schedule used. Notice also that idle time = 3(makespan) − 43. Therefore, minimizing makespan will also minimize machine idle time.

A measure of job performance is the sum of the delivery times for each job. Minimizing this measure would also be equivalent to minimizing total job waiting time, since the two times are complementary. In Figure 13.2, the delivery times and job-waiting times are listed for each job. These figures are obtained directly from the Gantt chart. The delivery time and waiting times will, of course, depend greatly on the job sequence used. Since job 1 was scheduled first, it has no waiting time and is completed as soon as possible, ahead of the due date. Jobs 2 and 3, which were scheduled last, have considerable waiting time.

In general, the waiting times of jobs and machine utilization are highly dependent on the sequence of the jobs scheduled. In this case, we have five jobs to schedule and 5! (five factorial) = 120 possible sequences of jobs. If we were to construct 120 Gantt charts, one for each possible sequence, we could determine the job

**VISIBLE SCHEDULES.
A good schedule must
be available for all
employees to see.**
© David Young-Wolff/
PhotoEdit

sequence with the minimum makespan, or the one with the minimum total job waiting time. In general, for n jobs there will be $n!$ possible sequences to evaluate to find the optimal sequence by complete enumeration of all possibilities. Complete enumeration is, of course, impossible even with the fastest computer in practical situations where there may be several hundred or more jobs.

A great deal of attention has been given in the literature to optimal job-sequencing algorithms, which attempt to find an optimal solution without enumeration of all possible job sequences. These algorithms typically optimize one or more measures of schedule performance, such as makespan; but they utilize a highly restrictive set of assumptions, such as constant processing times, no passing of jobs, no job splitting, and so forth. One particular problem is called the $m \times n$ **machine-scheduling problem,** where m is the number of machines and n is the number of jobs. To suggest the nature of the research that has been done on this problem we will review a simple case.

The $m \times n$ machine-scheduling problem has been solved for $m = 1, 2, 3$ and arbitrary values of n. Efficient optimal algorithms have not been developed for $m > 3$ because of the extremely large number of possible sequences. However, fairly good heuristics that seem to develop good solutions for any values of m and n are available.[1]

Although these optimal sequencing rules have a great deal of theoretical interest, they have not been applied much in practice. This is because real sequencing problems involve a great deal of variability in processing times, multiple objectives, and other complicating factors. Nevertheless, the rules are useful for gaining insight into scheduling problems and for suggesting approaches that might be of value in practice. Some of these are reviewed in detail below.

In summary, the following conclusions about batch scheduling can be drawn from Gantt chart scheduling:

1. Schedule performance (makespan, job waiting times, job delivery times, machine utilization, and inventory level) is highly sequence dependent (which job is scheduled first, second, third, and so on).
2. The waiting time of a job depends on the job interference encountered in the schedule and the capacity available on machines.
3. Finding the optimal schedule is computationally intensive and cannot be done for practical size applications. However, good heuristic procedures that in most cases closely approximate the optimal schedule are available.

[1] See Campbell, Dudek, and Smith (1970); and Schniederjans and Carpenter (1996).

Batch scheduling methods have many applications in both manufacturing and service industries. A service example is the scheduling of patients in a hospital. Patients flow through the hospital and require the services of multiple resources (human and equipment). At one cancer treatment unit, for example, waiting time for appointments for radiology treatments was reduced from 40 days to 16 days despite a 14 percent increase in workload. The new scheduling system allowed radiology staff to schedule all sequential treatments, pretreatment appointments, and other linked appointments. This also meant that patients can see the full extent of their treatment plan at the outset.[2]

13.3 FINITE CAPACITY SCHEDULING

Finite capacity scheduling (FCS) is just an extension of the Gantt chart reasoning. With the advent of modern computers, FCS has been vastly improved, and sophisticated software is now available to accomplish this type of scheduling. First, we will describe the nature of FCS and then give an example of how a finite capacity schedule is constructed.

FCS assumes that jobs are being scheduled through a number of work centers, each with one or more machines. We also assume that jobs can pass each other, or change their order, as they are processed depending on their priority. Furthermore, the job can be split into two or more parts if this will facilitate scheduling. For example, if the job consists of making 100 parts, the job could be split into two lots of 50 parts each if that would help the schedule. Alternate routings of a job through the work centers may also be available. In FCS, attention is paid to scarce resources in order to facilitate job flow and improve the performance of the shop.

Example

Let's take a simple example for purposes of illustration. Assume the same situation as in Figure 13.1 that was used for Gantt charting, except now there are two machines of each type in each work center. In other words, there will be two machines of type A, two of type B, and two of type C.

We can now construct a Gantt chart with this new information, as shown in Figure 13.3. In this figure, the two machines of type A are labeled A_1 and A_2, and we also show two machines of type B and type C. We use the same sequence of scheduling as before, with jobs scheduled in the order 1, 4, 5, 2, 3. Note that the Gantt chart will not change for job 1, since this job was scheduled before without job interference and no job waiting time. The next job scheduled, job 4, is impacted only slightly by the additional machine added to each work center. But job 5 could not start immediately before, since machine A was already scheduled. Now that we have two machines, job 5 is scheduled on machine A_2. Also, job 5 no longer needs to wait for machine B, since job 4 has been scheduled on the second machine of type B. Next we schedule job 2, which is benefited substantially by the addition of a second machine of type C; it can be scheduled to start immediately. Also job 3 can start earlier than before.

This addition of capacity substantially improves the completion dates of jobs and reduces their waiting times. The makespan is now 11 instead of 20 as before. But we are not only interested in demonstrating reduced waiting time from increased capacity. We wish to show the effect of bottleneck work centers on job scheduling. The formal definition of a **bottleneck** is a work center whose capacity is less than the demand placed on it and less than the capacities of all other resources. A bottleneck resource will constrain the capacity of the entire shop

---

[2] Huber (2004).

FIGURE 13.3
Work center Gantt chart (jobs are sequenced in order 1, 4, 5, 2, 3).

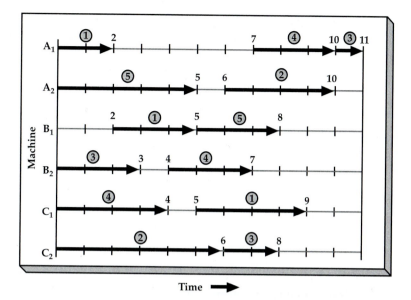

Machine center idle (hr)	
A	7
B	10
C	6
	23

Makespan = 11 hr

Job	Job waiting time (hr)	Delivery time (hr)
1	0	9
2	0	10
3	5	11
4	0	10
5	0	8

and an hour added to a bottleneck will add an hour of capacity to the entire factory. An hour added to a nonbottleneck work center will not help the schedule at all, since excess capacity exists there. This definition of a bottleneck is consistent with the one given in Chapter 7 where we noted that the capacity of the entire system is determined by the minimum of the capacities of all the resources.

In the example in Figure 13.3, work center C is a bottleneck from time 3 to 6 since it is fully utilized then and job 3 is waiting to be processed.[3] Demand exceeds capacity and no other work center provides a constraint at that time. Work center A is a bottleneck from time 8 to 10 for similar reasons. Note, the bottleneck is not constant; it shifts from one work center to another.

The **theory of constraints,** described below, argues that scheduling can be improved by adding capacity at the bottleneck work center. If this were done in the example in Figure 13.3, the makespan could be further reduced from 11 to 10 hours. But, 10 hours is the minimum makespan since job 2 has 10 hours of processing time. Capacity can be added in many ways: by adding machine time, reducing setup time, adding overtime, and subcontracting, to name a few. An important principle in scheduling is to find the bottlenecks and work to remove them by improving flow through the bottleneck resources. FCS can be used to identify the bottlenecks at any point in time.

---

[3] We assume for this example that job 3 cannot be split into two or more lots for processing.

13.4 THEORY OF CONSTRAINTS

In his book *The Goal*, Eliyahu Goldratt argues that the only **goal of operations** in a factory setting is to make money. If the plant does not make money for the company, it will cease to exist. According to Goldratt, other traditional measures of operations such as productivity improvement, cost reduction, direct labor utilization, delivery time, and quality are often misleading and secondary to the goal of making money.

Goldratt goes on to argue that making money can be broken down into three measurable quantities: **throughput, inventory,** and **operating expenses.** He defines these terms in rather nontraditional ways. *Throughput* is defined as the sales of the plant minus the cost of raw materials used to produce those sales. It is not enough just to make a product; it must be sold to the customer in order to make money. So, if operations has excess capacity, then the task of operations is to help the sales department increase sales (and thus throughput) by doing whatever it can to help meet the customer's needs. On the other hand, if the plant is operating at capacity, it must then push orders through the plant faster in order to increase throughput. This is done by identifying the bottleneck operations in the plant and increasing the capacity of these bottlenecks, often without buying more equipment but by more creative scheduling, overtime work hours, better workforce policies, and so forth. Goldratt calls this the **theory of constraints** (TOC) since the most important constraint, either sales or the production bottleneck, is being relieved in order to increase throughput.

In addition to throughput, the plant must reduce inventory to make money. Goldratt defines *inventory* as only the raw material value of any goods being held in inventory, a rather unconventional definition. He puts all labor and overhead costs into the operating expense category, not into inventory. *Operating expense* is then the cost of turning raw materials into throughput. His logic is that true costs are distorted by putting labor and overhead into inventory on the assumption that the inventory will be sold, when in fact no money is made for the company until the inventory is actually sold.

Goldratt's theory of constraints has many implications for scheduling. First, the bottleneck is the critical resource and constraint that should be scheduled to achieve maximum output. As noted above, each hour of capacity gained at the bottleneck is an hour gained for the entire plant. All nonbottleneck resources should be scheduled to be sure that the bottleneck is not starved for materials and can keep busy processing orders needed for sale. Also, a queue should be formed in front of the bottleneck resource to ensure that it stays busy. Nonbottleneck resources do not need to operate at full capacity provided they process enough to keep the bottleneck busy. Thus, some of the nonbottleneck work centers may have idle time in their schedule. Nonbottleneck resources should not produce inventory just to increase resource utilization. They should be idle when their capacity is not needed to supply the bottleneck.

Many steps can be taken at the bottleneck resource to increase capacity. These steps include reduction of setup time so that the work center can be quickly changed from one job to the next. Another step is to be sure that the bottleneck resource is used 24 hours a day and is not shut down for breaks, lunch, or even for maintenance that can be deferred. Resources should be added to the bottleneck work center via additional labor or machines on a temporary basis if possible. When this is done the operation will progress toward its goal of making money.

A few examples might be helpful here. A printing company, constrained by the number of presses available to print jobs, made more efficient use of its presses by routing jobs to different types of presses in a way that maximized the total output of the presses. This increased the capacity of the shop relative to the demand placed on it. A company that made plastic pipe was limited by its ability to saw pipes into required lengths. They put into service an old, inefficient saw that removed the bottleneck and increased capacity and profits considerably. They made more money even though efficiency was reduced in the sawing department.

These examples illustrate the fallacy of traditional cost accounting based on standard costs and cost variances. Although the cost variance of the sawing work center in the above example increased due to the use of the inefficient saw, the company made more money. Traditional cost accounting attempts to maximize the utilization of all resources and work centers even if they build inventory that is not needed and even if the work centers are not bottlenecks. The theory of constraints argues that the capacity of the bottleneck should be improved to reach the goal of making money, and nonbottleneck resources can remain idle some of the time, provided they do not constrain the bottleneck. Maximizing the efficiency of each resource, or reducing their standard cost variances to zero, does not make more money for the company.

It then becomes a matter of analyzing how best to reduce the bottleneck or constraint on the system to increase throughput more than associated increases in inventory or operating expenses.

- Can more capacity be added, even if it is less efficient or uses antiquated equipment, expensive overtime, or is outsourced to a vendor?
- Can you divert the work that doesn't need to go through the bottleneck to another nonbottleneck resource?
- Can you prevent work from reaching the bottleneck that has poor quality and will be scrapped later?
- Can you increase the output rate of the bottleneck by running larger batches or reducing the setup time?

The theory of constraints has had a huge impact on scheduling philosophy, software design, and practice. Modern software using finite capacity scheduling can identify bottlenecks and make it possible to configure schedules that achieve the goal of making more money.

The theory of constraints can also be applied to service operations. The Odessa, Texas, police department used TOC to improve its process for hiring new police officers.[4] The existing process consisted of eight steps including application, written exam, background investigation, oral interview, polygraph exam, medical exam, psychological exam, and drug screening. The entire hiring processes took 117 days from initial application to successful hiring of a candidate. While most of the steps were completed in a few days, the background investigation took 104 days and became the critical constraint or the bottleneck in the process. Of the 60 applicants each year, only 10 were able to complete the entire process and were hired. Because of the long waiting time, many of the applicants became discouraged and found jobs elsewhere. As a result the Odessa Police Department had a shortage of qualified police officers.

---

[4] Taylor et al., 2003.

To relieve the bottleneck, it was decided that the background check should be divided into two parts, a cursory initial background check followed by a complete background check. The cursory initial check could be done in one day and would eliminate some applicants immediately. The complete background check would only be done after an applicant passed most of the other steps, thus saving capacity for those applicants who were nearly qualified. As it turned out it only took 3 days of processing to complete the entire background check and most of the 114 days was queuing time. As a result of reducing the bottleneck, the total process time was reduced from 117 days to 16 days, and the yield of the process improved to provide the badly needed 20 officers per year instead of 10 per year without sacrificing quality of the new recruits.

13.5 PRIORITY DISPATCHING RULES

Dispatching is used to decide on job priority at any particular work center. Typically, a job is not scheduled through the entire shop on the basis of a single priority. In the example in sections 13.2 and 13.3, job 1 was always scheduled first in every work center. The **priority** of a job may change from one work center to the next, depending on the particular dispatch rules chosen. In FCS, the dispatch rule is used to select the particular job to schedule next in a work center when more than one job is waiting in line to be processed.

In practice, schedules are difficult, if not impossible, to maintain because conditions often change: a machine breaks down, a qualified operator becomes ill, materials do not arrive on time, and so on. As a result, the schedule must be adjusted in real time to determine which job to process next. A complete new schedule cannot be made every time there is a change. Rather, real-time adjustments to the schedule are made by use of dispatch rules during execution of the schedule.

A **dispatch rule** specifies which job should be selected for processing next from among a queue of jobs, whether scheduling or during real-time processing. When a machine or worker becomes available, the dispatch rule is applied and the next job selected. A dispatch rule is thus dynamic in nature and continually sets the priority based on changing conditions.

In practice several types of priority rules are used. For services it is common to use the **first come, first served (FCFS)** rule. This has to do with fairness since people are waiting in line. In a manufacturing plant, however, FCFS is not used because it performs poorly in meeting due dates, minimizing makespan, or making money.

For manufacturing, two types of rules are commonly used:

1. **Critical ratio (CR).** The critical ratio is computed as:

$$CR = \frac{\text{remaining time until due date}}{\text{remaining processing time}}$$

The job with the minimum value of CR is scheduled first. The job with the next largest value of CR is scheduled next and so on. This rule calculates the ratio of demand time to supply time. When the ratio exceeds a value of 1, there is sufficient time available to complete the job if the queue times are properly managed. If the ratio is less than 1, the job will be late unless processing times can be compressed. The CR rule has a precise meaning; for example, a ratio of 2 means there is twice as much time remaining as the processing time.

2. **Minimum processing time (MINPRT).** For this rule, the job with the shortest processing time on the machine (or resource) is selected. This rule is based on the idea that when a job is finished quickly due to its short processing time, other machines downstream will receive work resulting in a high flow rate and high utilization.

While the MINPRT rule is very good at achieving efficiency and high throughput, it is poor at meeting due dates, primarily because due dates are not considered in its calculation. On the other hand, due dates are very critical in practice. This is understandable because of the emphasis placed on schedule performance relative to promises made to customers. The CR ratio does a much better job of meeting due dates since it explicitly considers them in its calculation.

The use of priority rules in dispatching or scheduling jobs illustrates a very important principle: "Lead time is what you say it is." If a job is given a very tight due date, perhaps just a little greater than total processing time, a rule such as CR will speed the job through the shop because of the high priority. Of course, too many of these high-priority jobs will ruin the system. Using this rule, if a long lead time is promised, the entire time will be taken since the job will have a relatively low priority. With dispatching rules, lead time can be expanded or contracted by a large factor.

It comes as a surprise to some people that lead times can be managed. The common view is that lead time is a relatively fixed or a statistical phenomenon. There is little realization that lead time is a function of both priority and capacity. If an operation is producing at near capacity, average lead times will be extended. Even though the average lead time is long, an individual job can still have a short delivery if its priority is high enough. Thus, lead time is a function of both capacity and priority decisions.

In summary, dispatching rules are used to determine the priority of a job during scheduling and in real time during processing. The priority of a job can be changed dynamically as it is processed through the shop. Lead time is a function of both priority and capacity.

13.6 INFINITE CAPACITY LOADING

Infinite loading is used for a different purpose than the scheduling approaches we have discussed so far. The purpose of infinite loading is to determine the capacity required for processing and the approximate start dates, assuming that capacity is available and that average lead times are experienced.

Infinite capacity loading typically works in conjunction with materials requirements planning (MRP) systems. These systems schedule backward in time, starting with the due date of a job and working backward to determine the start date of each operation at each work center. MRP systems also calculate the materials required by offsetting for available inventories and parts available, as will be described in Chapter 16. Here we are concentrating on the scheduling aspects of these systems.

Example

Suppose that we take the previous example from Figure 13.1 and do an infinite capacity load. First, the due dates must be converted to hours, so assume that the shop works eight hours per day and multiply the due dates given in Figure 13.1 by eight hours each. This means that job 1 will be due in $3 \times 8 = 24$ hours of shop time, job 2 will be due in $2 \times 8 = 16$ hours of shop time, and so on. These due date times are used to establish the

FIGURE 13.4
Time lines for
infinite capacity
loading.

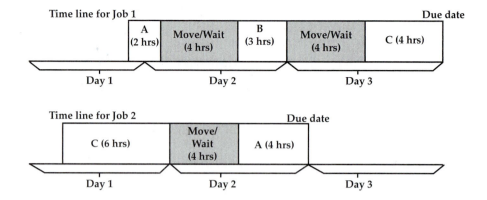

end point for backward scheduling. Also assume that each job spends an average of four hours in the queue for each work center, just for simplicity. The average queuing time could vary by job and work center, if desired.

Next, for illustration we backward load only jobs 1 and 2 starting with job 1. The first step in creating a backward load is to develop a time line for each job as shown in Figure 13.4. For job 1, start at the due date of day 3 and load four hours into the time line for work center C, then load four hours of move/wait time between work centers. This will require a total of eight hours, or one day of elapsed shop time. Then in day 2, load three hours for work center B and another four hours of move/wait time. Finally, load two hours for work center A, one hour in day 2, and one hour in day 1. A similar pattern is created for job 2, starting with the due date of job 2 and working backward in time.

These time lines can be used to define the load on each work center shown in Figure 13.5. The number of hours required in each work center is put into the appropriate day for each work center and job. This process is continued until all the jobs have been loaded. For example, from the time line in Figure 13.4, job 1 requires four hours of time in work center C in day 3. The four hours of time is placed on the graph in Figure 13.5 in day 3 on work center C. Job 1 also requires three hours of time in day 2, except this time in work center B, and this is also placed on the graph in Figure 13.5. Finally job 1 requires one hour in day 2 and one hour in day 1 in work center A, which is placed in Figure 13.5. The process is continued moving the data from the time lines in Figure 13.4 to the loading charts in Figure 13.5.

Once the load is completed, a determination can be made on capacity required to meet the due dates. The bottleneck work centers can easily be spotted. Capacity should be added to these work centers, if possible, by splitting lots, adding overtime, using alternative routings, and other methods available.

FIGURE 13.5 Infinite capacity load.

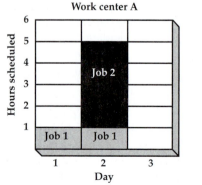
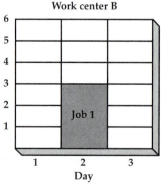
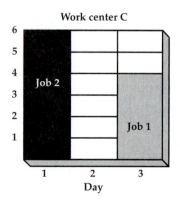

Let us compare finite capacity scheduling to infinite capacity loading. FCS is the best approach to use if the complexity of scheduling can be managed. It calculates the actual waiting times of jobs based on their assigned priority and the capacity available at each work center. Job priorities can be assigned by dispatching rules or other algorithms that determine the sequence of processing at each work center. A true schedule is created by FCS.

On the other hand, backward loading to infinite capacity is used to obtain a rough-cut estimate of the capacity required to produce the jobs just in time to meet their due dates, assuming that jobs at each work center experience average wait times. In infinite loading, we do not assume a fixed capacity but rather calculate the capacity required.

There are many other possible scheduling approaches. For example, we could forward schedule to infinite capacity. This would also allow us to calculate the capacity required at each work center to get the jobs completed in the smallest amount of time. In this case, there would be no queuing time of jobs, only move time between work centers.

We could also backward schedule to finite capacity. This would allow us to compute the latest start time to meet the due dates within available capacity. The actual waiting times, not the averages, would be computed at each work center. This approach would put more emphasis on due dates than FCS since it starts with the due date and works backward in time. Which of these various approaches is used just depends on the objective of the scheduling or loading exercise.

13.7 PLANNING AND CONTROL SYSTEMS

As a popular TV advertisement said, "The system is the solution." This principle applies to scheduling operations, where a planning and control system is needed. This system should not only facilitate the development of good schedules (planning) but also ensure that schedules are implemented and corrected as needed (control). These scheduling systems will usually incorporate some of the methods described above. But without the system, the methods are useless.

Every scheduling system should answer several questions:

1. **What delivery date do I promise?** The promised delivery date should be based on both marketing and operations considerations. These considerations include available capacity, the customer's work requirements, and efficiency of operations. We have seen how the promised date can be derived for batch-process operations through Gantt chart scheduling or finite capacity scheduling. But marketing needs to input appropriate customer priorities and realistic due dates into the scheduling process. Finance needs to make the capital available in time or unduly constrained schedules will result. All functions need to work together for the best interests of the customers and the bottom line of the business.

2. **How much capacity do I need?** A scheduling system can answer this question by forecasting and developing workloads for individual activities. This question is answered by infinite loading of the available or projected future jobs. Infinite loading provides a quantitative forecast of capacity required by finance in order to provide the capital and human resources needed in time.

3. **When should I start on each particular activity or task?** This question is answered by using dispatching rules or a Gantt chart/FCS schedule.

4. **How do I make sure that the job is completed on time?** Dispatching helps to answer this question partially, but the answer also requires feedback on job status and constant activity monitoring. If progress is continually or periodically evaluated, corrective action can be taken as needed to make sure that deliveries are made on time. In manufacturing, this question is answered by a shop-floor control system.

Currently, the term **Advanced Planning and Scheduling** (APS) has been applied to what we refer to as a planning and control system. APS includes various scheduling methods such as finite capacity scheduling, constraint-based bottleneck scheduling, loading, and dispatching at the plant-floor level. APS systems consider materials requirements and plant capacity to generate new plans, and some of these systems sequence production optimally to achieve the factory goals such as maximum throughput with minimum inventory while meeting customer due dates. An APS system applies the methods and approaches we have described in this chapter.

To illustrate the principles of scheduling and control, two examples of scheduling systems will be discussed.

Courtroom Scheduling

Courtroom scheduling urgently requires more systematic scheduling and control systems. Sometimes court calendars are overloaded, with the result that police officers, witnesses, lawyers, and defendants spend long times waiting. After a day in court without being heard, some witnesses will not return.

On the other hand, the same court may also suffer from case underload, with judges kept waiting and inefficient use of courtrooms. This condition occurs when cases finish early or cases scheduled to appear are delayed.

In an attempt to correct these problems, a court-scheduling system was developed for the New York City Criminal Court. The system was designed to achieve the following five objectives: (1) there should be a high probability that judges will be kept busy, (2) there should be a high probability that cases will be heard when scheduled, (3) several cases should be batched together for a police officer on the same day, (4) high-priority cases should be scheduled as soon as possible, and (5) a maximum waiting-time limit should be set for all cases.

The heart of the system was a priority-dispatching rule. The rule determined priorities for cases based on such factors as seriousness of the charge, whether the defendant was in or out of jail, and elapsed time since arraignment. When the priority of a case reached a certain threshold, it was inserted into the court calendar; otherwise it was returned to the unscheduled pool.

When a case was scheduled, the time required was predicted by a multiple regression equation that utilized causal variables such as plea of the defendant, seriousness of the offense, number of witnesses, and presiding judge. The predicted time was then scheduled for the first available spot on the calendar. Some slots, however, were kept open for emergencies and future rescheduling.

Each day the priorities were revised on the basis of the current conditions. Any new cases with a high enough priority were placed on the schedule with the required amount of predicted time.

This example illustrates how a service operation can use a dispatching rule as part of a logical scheduling and control system. The methods used were embedded in an information system, which provided overall planning and control of the schedule. The system helped answer the crucial questions required to develop and implement the schedule.

Finite Capacity Scheduling System[5]

Dixie Iron Works in Alice, Texas, makes special parts for gas compressors and engine components used in the oil fields. This $8 million business must respond quickly to customers who bring in broken parts from the oil fields to be repaired. In the past, shop performance was poor due to use of a manual and obsolete scheduling system. They were scheduling a 24-hour-a-day business with a system that was updated every two weeks. As a result, only 20 percent of the orders were delivered on time, business was lost, and profitability was poor.

Dixie Iron installed new software for an FCS system that incorporates the theory of constraints. This system scheduled new jobs as they arrived at the shop based on real-time information. Each new job was scheduled forward in time using FCS logic and a promised delivery time was given to the customer. If this delivery time was unsatisfactory, other jobs might be rescheduled, capacity added through overtime, or other measures taken to meet the customer's requirements.

The new system was also used to identify bottleneck work centers in the shop. In one case, Dixie Iron had ordered an expensive new machine to increase the capacity at a bottleneck work center, only to learn that it wasn't a bottleneck after all. The expensive machine order was canceled, and a less expensive machine was ordered for another work center that was the actual bottleneck.

After only four months of running the new FCS system, Dixie Iron had doubled its due date performance, increased inventory turns from 4 to 12 turns per year, and increased operating profits by three times. The FCS system had given the company a better way to use the resources available to the shop while improving customer service and profits.

13.8 KEY POINTS

In this chapter, we have treated scheduling decisions for batch operations. The chapter's theme is that all scheduling decisions deal with the allocation of scarce resources to jobs, activities, tasks, or customers. We assume, for scheduling purposes, that resources are fixed as a result of aggregate planning and facilities decisions.

The following are among this chapter's key points:

- Within the available resources, scheduling seeks to satisfy the conflicting objectives of low inventories, high efficiency, and good customer service. Thus, trade-offs are always implicitly or explicitly made whenever a schedule is developed. Because of the conflicting objectives, cross-functional coordination is required for effective scheduling.

- Gantt charting is the simplest form of scheduling. It is used to schedule jobs one at a time according to priorities on the resources available. Gantt charting will determine the waiting time of each job, the job completion dates, resource (machine) utilization, and the makespan of all jobs.

- Finite capacity scheduling is used to schedule multiple jobs through a number of different work centers. The jobs are scheduled in a manner similar to Gantt charting except that each work center may have multiple machines (or resources). In finite scheduling, the bottleneck work centers are detected. Efforts are made to improve job flow through the bottlenecks by splitting jobs, using alternative routings, use of overtime, and other methods.

[5]Abstracted from Gerard Danos, "Dixie Reengineers Scheduling and Increases Profit 300 Percent," *APICS—The Performance Advantage,* March 1996, pp. 28–32.

- The theory of constraints (TOC) is a logical extension of finite capacity scheduling that maximizes operations throughput by identifying and scheduling bottleneck resources. Bottlenecks are scheduled to maximize flow and non-bottlenecks are scheduled to keep the bottleneck busy.
- Dispatching is used to decide on the priority of jobs as they pass through the factory or service facility. Various dispatching rules can be used to decide which job or activity to process next at each work center.
- Infinite capacity loading works from job due dates backward to determine the capacity required at each work center to meet the due dates for each job. Average waiting times are used at each work center, and job load profiles are obtained for each work center.
- To be useful, scheduling methods must be embedded in an information system. Scheduling systems, in general, should answer the following questions: (1) What delivery date do I promise? (2) How much capacity do I need? (3) When should I start each particular activity or task? (4) How do I make sure that the job is completed on time? To handle constantly changing situations, these systems are usually computerized, and they require constant feedback on job status.
- Lead time for completion of a job is not a statistical phenomenon. Lead time is a function of both capacity and priority decisions.

STUDENT INTERNET EXERCISES

1. AGI: Goldratt Institute
   http://www.goldratt.com/

Explore this site for information on the theory of constraints.

2. APS Insight
   http://www.apsinsight.com/Contents.html

Read any of the many articles here concerning APS and come to class prepared to discuss your findings.

3. Waterloo Manufacturing Software
   http://www.waterloo-software.com/

Read one of the papers on this site concerning APS. Look under Technology on the sidebar for technology papers that refer to APS.

SOLVED PROBLEMS

Problem

1. **Gantt Charting** The table below includes information about four jobs and three work centers. Assume that six hours are required to transfer a job from one work center to another (move time not including waiting time for busy machines). Sequence the jobs with a Gantt chart. Use the following priority order: 1, 2, 3, 4. Can you tell if any jobs will be late? Which ones? Can a simple reordering of job priorities alleviate the problem?

Job	Work Center/Machine Hours	Due Date (days)
1	A/2, B/1, C/4	3
2	C/4, A/2	2
3	B/4, A/2	2
4	B/4, A/2, C/3	3

Solution

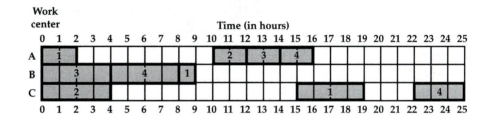

Job 4 will be one day late, since it is due at the end of day 3 and it will still need one hour of processing on day 4 to be completed. But moving job 4 in front of job 3 in the schedule priority would allow job 4 to be completed one hour before it is due. Job 3 would still be done on time.

Problem

2. **Priority Dispatching Rules** The five jobs listed below are waiting for their final operation at a work center. Determine the order of processing for the jobs using the following rules: MINPRT, FCFS, and CR.

Job	Processing Time	Due Date	Order of Arrival
A	5	10	3
B	7	18	1
C	6	29	2
D	2	12	5
E	10	19	4

Solution

The order of processing for each rule is given below. The MINPRT rule assigns jobs with the smallest amount of processing time first. The job with the next least amount of processing time is assigned to be produced next, and so on. Using this rule, the following assignments would be made:

D–A–C–B–E

The CR rule assigns the jobs based on the minimum ratio of total time remaining to total processing time remaining. In this case we take the ratio of due date to processing times in the table and arrange the jobs in sequence from the minimum to the maximum CR ratio resulting in the sequence:

$$E\text{–}A\text{–}B\text{–}C\text{–}D$$

The FCFS rule assigns the job that arrived before all others to be processed first, and so on. Using this rule, the following assignments would be made:

$$B\text{–}C\text{–}A\text{–}E\text{–}D$$

Problem

3. **Work-Center Loading** The table below includes information about four jobs and three work centers. Assume that an average of six hours is required to transfer a job from one work center to another, including move and wait time.

   a. Prepare a backward time load to infinite capacity and load all jobs on the work centers.

   b. Assuming eight hours of production per day on any one workstation, are any workstations overloaded? Which workstations and when?

Job	Work Center/Machine Hours	Due Date (days)
1	A/2, B/1, C/4	3
2	C/4, A/2	2
3	B/4, A/2	2
4	B/5, A/2, C/3	3

Solution

a. Time lines and workloads for backward-loaded jobs are shown below:

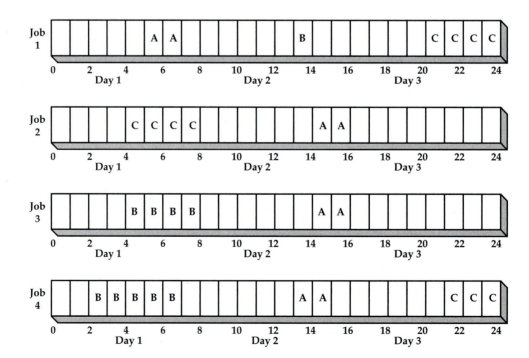

b. Work center B is over capacity by one hour in day 1.

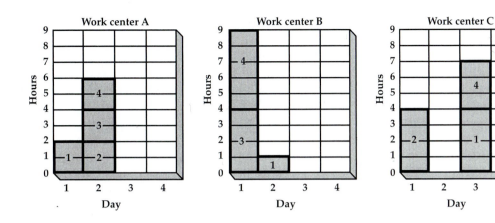

Discussion Questions

1. What types of scheduling decisions is management likely to encounter in the following operations? Describe the scheduling decisions in terms of types of resources to be scheduled and the associated customers or jobs scheduled.
   a. Hospital
   b. University
   c. Movie making
   d. Make-to-order factory

2. Specify the kinds of objectives that might be appropriate for each of the situations listed in question 1.

3. Why is it important to view a batch-process operation as a network of interconnected queues?

4. How is the scheduling of patients in a doctor's clinic similar to or different from the scheduling of jobs in a factory?

5. Describe the differences between Gantt charting, FCS, and infinite capacity loading.

6. What is the purpose of backward loading to infinite capacity?

7. How can production lead time be managed in operations? Why isn't lead time a constant value?

8. Why do you suppose that $m \times n$ machine-scheduling algorithms are not widely used in practice? Should optimal rules be more widely used?

9. What is the purpose of a shop-floor control system? Can effective scheduling be done without shop-floor control?

10. What is the goal as stated by the theory of constraints (TOC) and how is that goal achieved?

11. What is the definition of a bottleneck according to TOC?

12. What scheduling rule should be applied to bottleneck work centers, and what scheduling rule should be applied to nonbottleneck work centers?

13. What measures can be taken to provide more capacity at a bottleneck work center?

Problems

1. Students must complete two activities in order to register for class: registration and payment of fees. Because of individual differences, the processing time (in minutes) for each of these two activities for five students varies as shown at the right:

Student	Minutes	
	Registration	Pay Fees
A	12	5
B	7	2
C	5	9
D	3	8
E	4	6

a. Construct a Gantt chart to determine the total time required to process all five students. Use the following sequence of students: E, D, C, B, A.

b. Can you construct a better sequence to reduce the total time required?

c. What problems might be encountered in using this approach for registration in colleges?

2. Six jobs must be processed through machine A and then B as shown below. The processing time for each job is also shown.

Machine (minutes)

Job	A	B
1	10	6
2	6	12
3	7	7
4	8	4
5	3	9
6	6	8

a. Develop a Gantt chart to determine the total time required to process all six jobs. Use the following sequence of jobs: 1, 2, 3, 4, 5, 6.

b. Can you develop a better sequence to reduce the total time required for processing?

3. The following information is given for four jobs and three work centers:

Job	Work Center/Machine Hours	Due Date (days)
1	A/3, B/2, C/2	3
2	C/2, A/4	2
3	B/6, A/1, C/3	4
4	C/4, A/1, B/2	3

Assume there are six hours of move and queue time between work centers for each job. Perform a backward load to infinite capacity of all jobs.

4. Sequence the jobs given in problem 3 using a Gantt chart. Assume that the move time between machines is one hour. Sequence the jobs in priority order 1, 2, 3, 4.

a. What is the makespan?

b. How much machine idle time is there?

c. When is each job delivered compared with its due date?

d. How much idle time (waiting time) is there for each job?

e. Devise a better job sequence for processing.

5. In problem 4, assume there are two machines of type A, two of type B, and two of type C.

a. Prepare a finite capacity schedule.

b. Compare the FCS to the Gantt chart of problem 4.

6. In problem 2, assume there are two machines of Type A and two of Type B.

a. Prepare a finite capacity schedule.

b. How does your FCS compare to the performance of the Gantt chart from problem 2?

7. The Security Life Insurance Company processes all new life insurance policies through three departments: incoming mail (I), underwriting (U), and policy control (P). The incoming mail department receives applications and customer payments and then routes the files to the underwriting department. After checking on the applicants' qualifications for life insurance, the underwriting department forwards the file to policy control for the issue of the policy. At the present time, the company has five new policy applications waiting to be processed. The time required for processing in each department is shown below.

Policy	Department/Hours
1	I/3, U/6, P/8
2	I/2, P/10
3	I/1, U/3, P/4
4	I/2, U/8, P/6
5	I/1, P/6

a. Perform a backward load to infinite capacity for each policy. Assume there are eight hours of move/wait time between departments. Assume that the due dates for all jobs are 40 hours in the future.

b. Prepare a Gantt chart schedule for these policies. Compare the Gantt chart with the backward load. Which is best? Why?

8. At the University Hospital, five blood samples must be scheduled through a blood testing laboratory. Each sample goes through up to four different testing stations. The times for each test and the due dates for each sample are as follows:

Sample	Test Station/Hours	Due Date (hours)
1	A/1, B/2, C/3, D/1	10
2	B/2, C/3, A/1, D/4	6
3	C/2, A/3, D/1, C/2	8
4	A/2, D/2, C/3, B/1	12
5	D/2, C/1, A/2, B/4	14

a. Using a Gantt chart, schedule these five samples; schedule them in priority order of earliest due date first.

b. Prepare a backward load of these samples. Use a move/wait time of one hour between test stations.

c. Assume that the capacity of each test station (A, B, C, and D) is doubled. Prepare an FCS for this situation.

d. What are the bottleneck work centers with reference to part *a* of the problem? Suggest capacity additions that might be needed.

9. A secretary is considering three dispatching rules for typing term papers. The following information is given on jobs that are waiting to be typed:

Paper	Hours until Due Date	Total Remaining Processing Time* (hours)	Processing Time (typing hours)	Order of Arrival
A	20	14	10	4th
B	19	15	15	3d
C	16	9	6	2d
D	10	5	5	1st
E	18	11	7	5th

*Includes typing, corrections, and copying.

Use the following dispatching rules to determine the order of processing by the typing activity.

a. MINPRT

b. FCFS

c. CR

10. Suppose you are in charge of dispatching for the University Hospital laboratory described in problem 8. Use the following dispatching rules for the first station (A) at the beginning of processing to determine which job should be processed first through station A. *Hint:* Decide between jobs 1 and 4.

a. MINPRT

b. CR

11. Using the Gantt charts developed in the following problems, which is the bottleneck work center?

a. Problem 2.

b. Problem 4.

c. Problem 7.

12. How would the theory of constraints be used to improve output for the operations in the following problems?

a. Problem 2.

b. Problem 4.

c. Problem 7.

Selected Bibliography

Breen, Anne M., Tracy Burton-Houle, and David C. Aron. "Applying the Theory of Constraints in Health Care: Part 1—The Philosophy." *Quality Management in Health Care* 10, no. 3 (Spring 2002), pp. 40–47.

Campbell, H. G., R. A. Dudek, and M. L. Smith. "A Heuristic Algorithm for the *n* Job *m* Machine Sequencing Problem." *Management Science* 16, no. 10 (June 1970), pp. B630–37.

Danos, Gerard. "Dixie Reengineers Scheduling and Increases Profit 300 Percent." *APICS—The Performance Advantage*, March 1996, pp. 28–32.

Goldratt, Eliyahu M. *The Theory of Constraints.* Croton-on-Hudson, NY: North River Press, 1999.

Goldratt, Eliyahu M., and Jeff Cox. *The Goal*, 3rd ed. Croton-on-Hudson, NY: North River Press, 2004.

Green, Jason, and Ali Kiran. "Manufacturers Meet Global Market Demands with FCS Software." *IIE Solutions* 28, no. 8 (August 1996), pp. 26–30.

Holmes, L. E., and A. B. Hendricks. "Is TOC for You?" *Business Management*, April 2005.

Huber, N. "Scheduling System Slashes Radiotherapy Waiting Times by 60% at Wirral Cancer Unit." *Computer Weekly*, May 4, 2004, pp. 39–40.

Kirchmier, Bill, and Johannes Gerhard. *Finite Capacity Scheduling: Management, Selection, and Implementation.* New York: Wiley, 2000.

Odwazny, M. C. "The Theory of Constraints and Medical Error: A Conversation with Robert A. McNutt." *Quality Management in Health Care* 13, no. 3 (July–September 2004), pp. 183–87.

Rudberg, Martin, and Jan Olhager. "Linking Manufacturing Strategy Decisions on Process Choice with Manufacturing Planning and Control Systems." *International Journal of Production Research* 40, no. 10 (July 2002), pp. 2335–52.

Schniederjans, Marc J., and Donald A. Carpenter. "A Heuristic Job Scheduling Decisions Support System—A Case Study." *Decision Support Systems* 18, no. 2 (October 1996), pp. 159–66.

Shapiro, Samuel: "An Automated Court Scheduling System." Paper presented at the 12th American Meeting of the Institute of Management Sciences, Detroit, MI, September 1971.

Sheu, Chwen, and J. G Wacker. "Effectiveness of Planning and Control Systems: An Empirical Study of U.S. and Japanese Firms." *International Journal of Production Research* 39, no. 5 (March 2001), pp. 887–905.

Shih, Michael S. H., and Yong Lee-Chien. "Relationship of Planning and Control Systems with Strategic Choices: A Closer Look." *Asia Pacific Journal of Management* 18, no. 4 (December 2001), pp. 481–504.

Studebaker, David. "Improving Customer Satisfaction through Advanced Scheduling." *IIE Solutions* 29, no. 3 (March 1997), pp. 14–17.

Taylor, L. J. III, B. J. Moersch, G. M. Franklin. "Applying the Theory of Constraints to a Public Safety Hiring Process." *Public Personnel Management* 32, no. 3 (Fall 2003), pp. 367–82.

Taylor, Sam G., "Finite Capacity Scheduling Alternatives." *Production & Inventory Management Journal* 42, no. 3/4 (2001), pp. 70–75.

Woeppel, Mark J. *Manufacturer's Guide to Implementing the Theory of Constraints.* Boca Raton: Lewis Publishers, 2000.

Young, Hae Lee, Chan Seok Jeong, and Chiung Moon. "Advanced Planning and Scheduling with Outsourcing in Manufacturing Supply Chain." *Computers & Industrial Engineering* 43, no. 1/2 (2002), pp. 351–75.

Project Planning and Scheduling

Chapter outline

In the previous chapter's discussion of scheduling we did not include one important type of operation—the project. As originally defined in Chapter 4, the project form of operations is used to produce the unique product, a single unit. Projects are also frequently used for new-product development, construction, and other unique activities. Because of this, the management of a project is quite different from that of an ongoing operation.

Although many decisions in projects differ from those in ongoing operations, our main concern in this chapter will be with project planning and scheduling decisions. In the first part of the chapter, a broad framework for project planning will be established; this will include the objectives of projects and the planning and control activities they require. In the last part of the chapter, specific scheduling methods will be described in detail.

Projects include a wide range of manufacturing and service activities. Large objects such as ships, passenger airplanes, and missile launchers are manufactured on a project basis. Each unit is made as a unique item, and the manufacturing process is often stationary, so that materials and labor must be brought to the project. The construction of buildings is typically organized on a project basis.

TABLE 14.1
Examples of Projects

Building construction	Movie making
New-product introduction	Teaching a course
Research and development	Designing an advertising campaign
Computer system design	Startup or shutdown of a plant
Installation of equipment	Manufacture of aircraft, ships, and large machines
Space shots	Auditing accounts
Fund-raising	Planning a military invasion

Services such as movies, R&D, and fund-raising are also delivered on a project basis. Table 14.1 lists a wide range of manufacturing and service activities which are managed as projects.

14.1 OBJECTIVES AND TRADE-OFFS

In projects, there are usually three distinct objectives: cost, schedule, and performance. The **project cost** is the sum of direct and allocated costs assigned to the project. The project manager and project team's job is to control those costs that are directly controllable by the project organization. These costs typically cover labor, material, and some support services. Ordinarily, the project will have a project budget, which includes the costs assigned to the project.

The second objective in managing projects is **schedule.** Frequently, a project completion date and intermediate milestones are established at the outset. Just as the project team/manager must control the project costs within budget, they must also control the schedule to meet established dates. Frequently, the budget and schedule conflict. For example, if the project is behind schedule, overtime may be needed to bring it back on. But there may be insufficient funds in the budget to support the overtime costs. Therefore, a trade-off decision between time and cost must be made. Management must determine whether the schedule objective is of sufficient importance to justify an increased cost.

The third objective in project management is **performance,** that is, the performance characteristics of the product or service being produced by the project. If the project is research and development on a new type of machine, "performance" refers to the performance specifications of the new machine. If the project is a movie, "performance" refers to the quality of the movie produced and its subsequent box-office receipts. In this case, performance may be specified by a variety of movie standards regarding casting, sound, filming, and editing. Performance for a service project, such as a movie, is ordinarily much more difficult to specify than for a manufactured product.

Performance may also require **trade-offs** with both schedule and cost. In a movie, for example, if the picture is not meeting performance expectations, additional shots or script revisions may be required. These performance requirements may, in turn, cause cost and schedule changes. Since it is rarely possible to predict performance, schedule, and cost requirements accurately before a project begins, numerous trade-offs may be required while the project is under way.

14.2 PLANNING AND CONTROL IN PROJECTS

A general sequence of management decisions required in all projects is planning, scheduling, and control decisions. **Planning** refers to those decisions, required in the beginning of a project, that establish its general character and direction. Generally speaking, project planning establishes the major project objectives, the

TABLE 14.2
Project
Management
Activities and
Decisions

A. Planning
Identify the project customer
Establish the end product or service
Set project objectives
Estimate total resources and time required
Decide on the form of project organization
Make key personnel appointments (project
    manager, etc.)
Define major tasks required
Establish a budget

B. Scheduling
Develop a detailed work-breakdown structure
Estimate time required for each task

Sequence the tasks in the proper order
Develop a start/stop time for each task
Develop a detailed budget for each task
Assign people to tasks

C. Control
Monitor actual time, cost, and performance
Compare planned to actual figures
Determine whether corrective action is needed
Evaluate alternative corrective actions
Take appropriate corrective action

resources required, the type of organization used, and the key people who will manage and implement the project. Project planning is usually a function of top and middle managers with a cross-functional team often making all major decisions. When completed, project planning should be documented by a project authorization form or letter, which is used to initiate further project activities. The project authorization form should specify all the planning decisions listed in part A of Table 14.2.

In the **scheduling** phase of project management, the cross-functional team specifies the project plan in more detail. This phase begins with the construction of a detailed list of project activities, called a **work-breakdown structure.** A detailed time schedule for each activity in the work-breakdown structure is then established, using the methods described later in this chapter. When the time schedule is completed, a time-phased budget, which is keyed to the start and completion times of each of the project activities, can be developed. Finally, the project personnel can be assigned to individual project activities.

Project control is maintained by the cross-functional team, which monitors each activity as the work is performed on the project. Activities should be monitored for time, cost, and performance in accordance with the project plan. When a significant discrepancy exists between actual results and the plan, corrective action should be taken. These corrective actions might include revision of the plan, reallocation of funds, personnel changes, or other changes in resources. Such corrective actions should make the plan feasible and realistic once again.

BOEING PRODUCTION.
Large aircraft are
produced using
project management
methods. © Matthew
McVay/Stock Boston

The study of project management should ideally treat all aspects of planning, scheduling, and control, including behavioral and quantitative issues. Owing to space limitations, however, the remainder of this chapter will be restricted primarily to quantitative scheduling methods.

14.3 SCHEDULING METHODS

Several types of scheduling methods are in use. These may be generally classified as **Gantt chart** or **network** methods. The Gantt chart methods utilize a bar chart as shown in Figure 14.1. The network methods use a graph or network to show precedence relations.

The Gantt chart method of scheduling has a great deal in common with Gantt chart scheduling for batch processes, described in the last chapter. In each case, the activity durations are shown on the chart by a bar or line. These charts also show when each activity is scheduled to begin and when it will be completed.

Example

Figure 14.1 is a simplified Gantt chart for establishing a new office location for a business. Time is shown across the top and activities are shown down the side. Each activity in the project is depicted as a bar on the chart over the period of time for which the particular activity is scheduled. The first activity in the chart is to decide the location and to lease the office space. After this is decided, the company can begin to hire workers, to arrange for furnishings and arrange for phones. Thus activities 2, 3, and 5 occur in sequence after activity 1. The chart also shows that arranging for furnishings, hiring, and installing phones occur in parallel during the same time frame. The Gantt chart, therefore, shows not only how much time is required for each activity, but also when each activity takes place.

Gantt charts are very commonly used in project scheduling because they are easy to use and quite widely understood. In complex projects, however, a Gantt chart becomes inadequate because it does not show the interdependencies and relationships between activities. For complex projects, it is difficult to schedule the project initially and even more difficult to reschedule it when changes occur. The network method of project scheduling overcomes these difficulties.

The advantage of the network method over the Gantt chart is that the precedence relationships in network scheduling are explicitly shown on the network. This permits development of scheduling algorithms that account for all precedence relations when the schedule is developed. With Gantt charts, the precedence relations must be kept in the scheduler's head. On complex projects, this cannot

FIGURE 14.1
Gantt chart project example.

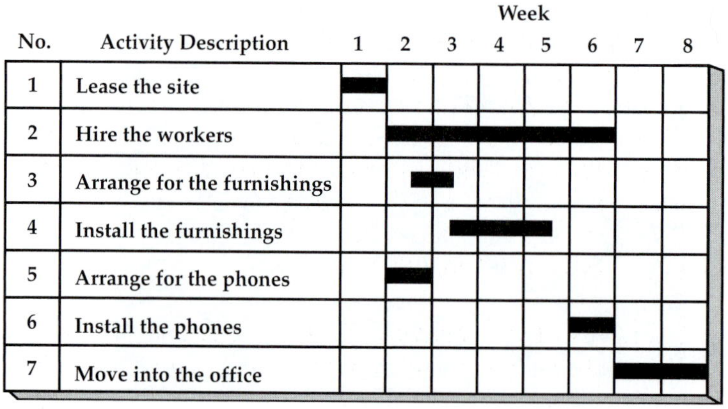

The Kuala Lumpur City Centre in Malaysia was scheduled with the aid of Primavera software. This project will transform a 100-acre tract of land into more than 18 million square feet of commercial, retail, hotel, recreational, and entertainment facilities in a park-like setting that will be developed in phases over 10 to 15 years.

The centermark of this development effort is the twin 88-story Petronas towers, linked by a unique sky bridge at the 41st and 42nd floors. Each tower reaches a height of 1,482 feet above the street level; it was, at least for a short period of time, the world's tallest building.

For projectwide planning and scheduling, project managers used the Primavera Project Planner, a standard project management software utilized by all general contractors and subcontractors on this project. To facilitate coordination and integration of the various programs and schedules, the project manager established a master schedule for the whole development with a series of subprojects for each building or major contract within the development.

PRIMAVERA®

"We manage the schedule for the design and procurement aspects," says Les Brown, senior planning manager, "while the contractors develop and maintain the individual subprojects. As part of the process, the contractors are required to prepare and submit regular standard written and graphical reports along with a Primavera data diskette for their project."

Networks for the twin towers contained nearly 7,000 activities each, and they dealt with a total of nearly 25,000 activities and 40,000 relationships in 29 subprojects. To help them manage this volume of data, they operated the project management software on a local area network, so that individual proj-

© Macduff Everton/CORBIS

ect management teams could directly track their own specific information but also access project-related information from other contracts. Project planning and scheduling software helped bring the project in on schedule with the twin towers opening on time.

Source: Adapted from the Primavera Internet site, www.primavera.com, September 1998.

easily be done, and Gantt charts become unwieldy. Furthermore, when a single activity time changes on the Gantt chart, the entire chart must be rescheduled by hand. Rescheduling can be done automatically by a network algorithm. On the other hand, networks are more complex, more difficult to understand, and more costly to use than Gantt charts. Thus, networks should be used in complex projects, such as construction of one of the world's tallest buildings, as described in the Operations Leader box.

Network scheduling methods involve the use of some important scheduling concepts, such as critical path and slack. These network scheduling concepts will be described next by means of the constant-time network. More complicated networks, using random times and time–cost trade-offs, will be discussed later in the chapter.

14.4   CONSTANT-TIME NETWORKS

In **constant-time networks,** the time for each activity is assumed to be a constant. This is the simplest case from the standpoint of scheduling. Other, more complicated methods are then derived from these constant-time network methods.

TABLE 14.3
Write a Business Report

Activity	Description	Immediate Predecessors	Duration in Days
A	Decide on the topic	None	1
B	Collect data	A	2
C	Search the Internet	A	3
D	Write the report	B and C	5

Next we illustrate the construction of a simple network. Table 14.3 shows the activities required to write a typical business report. The first activity A is to decide on the topic and scope of the report. Then two activities B (collect data) and C (search the Internet) proceed in parallel. Once B and C are completed, then the report can be written (activity D). Table 14.3 indicates the immediate predecessors of the activities that we have just described. Activity A has no immediate predecessor, since it is the first thing that must be done. Activities B and C each have activity A as the immediate predecessor, as noted above. Activity D has B and C as immediate predecessors, because the final report can't be written until the data is collected and the Internet searched. The times for completion of each activity are also shown in Table 14.3.

The above information can be put into a network representation. The **activity-on-node** (AON) network representation is shown in Figure 14.2.[1] Here each of the four activities is shown as a node (circle) in the diagram and the arrows indicate the precedence relationships between the activities. In Figure 14.2 activities B and C cannot start until activity A is completed and activity D cannot start until both activities B and C are completed. The convention is that all preceding activities must be completed before a successor activity can start.

We use the business report example from Table 14.3 and Figure 14.2 to illustrate constant-time network scheduling. Once the network has been defined, the scheduling calculations can be made. To calculate activity start and finish times the following notation is needed.

$ES(a)$ = early start of activity a

$EF(a)$ = early finish of activity a

$LS(a)$ = late start of activity a

$LF(a)$ = late finish of activity a

Each activity has four scheduled times, as defined above. For convenience we sometimes abbreviate them as ES, EF, LS, and LF. These times may be calculated by a forward and backward pass through the network.

First, a forward pass is made to calculate the **early start** (*ES*) and **early finish** (*EF*) times directly from the network diagram. This is done by starting at the beginning of the network and proceeding through to the end of the network in precedence order. We will illustrate this calculation by using the previous example from Figure 14.2. A convention is that we place the ES and EF times on top of the nodes as shown in Figure 14.3. Starting at node A we assign an early start time of zero since it is the first activity (ES = 0 on node A). The EF of activity A is the ES plus the activity duration (from Table 14.3) which is 0 + 1 = 1. The

---

[1] There is also an activity-on-arrow convention for drawing networks. We use the AON convention here because it is easier to understand and is the basis for most scheduling software (e.g., Microsoft Project).

FIGURE 14.2
Network for writing
a business report.

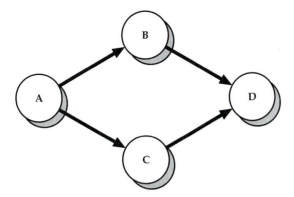

ES of activities B and C, the successors of activity A, is the early finish (EF) of activity A because B and C cannot start until A is finished. It follows that the EF of activities B is its ES time (1) plus the activity duration of B, which is 2 days, EF(B) = 3. Likewise the EF(C) is its ES time (1) plus the activity duration of C, which is 3 days, EF(C) = 4. Now we can schedule the early start of activity D that cannot begin until both activities B and C are completed. Therefore, the earliest start time of activity D is determined by the maximum of the EF of both B and C. In this case ES(D) = max (3,4) = 4. The earliest finish of activity D is now its ES plus the activity D duration time (EF(D) = 4 + 5 = 9). We have now completed the forward pass for this network. The project completion time is 9, which is the EF of the last activity.

The logic we have been using in these calculations can be expressed by the following formulas:

ES(a) = 0 for starting activities

EF(a) = ES(a) + t(a)

ES(a) = max [EF (all predecessors of a)]

Project completion time = max [EF (all ending activities)]

where t(a) denotes the duration of activity a.

FIGURE 14.3
Forward pass for
writing a business
report.

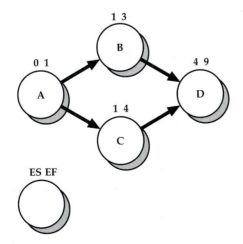

FIGURE 14.4
Forward and
backward pass
writing a business
report.

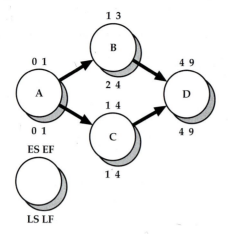

A backward pass is also needed to calculate the **late start** (LS) and **late finish** (LF) times. The backward pass is based on the following calculations:

LF(a) = min [LS (all successors of a)]

LS(a) = LF(a) − t(a)

These late times are computed starting with the last activity in the network and proceeding backward through the entire network. The LF time for activity D in Figure 14.4 is the same as the EF since this is the last activity. Also, the LS for activity D is the same as the ES. The LF for activities B and C is equal to the LS of activity D since it is the only successor. The LS for activities B and C is obtained by subtracting their activity times. For activity A there are two successors, B and C, so the LF for activity A should be the minimum of the LS for the successors, Min (1, 2) = 1. The reason we use the minimum is that activity A must finish in time for both B and C to achieve their late start times if necessary, or the project completion will be delayed. The LS for activity A is its LF minus the activity time, 1 − 1 = 0.

As a check on your computations, determine whether the ES = LS and EF = LF for activity A, the first one in the network. After going backwards, you should always end up with the same numbers that you started with when going forward.

Also, we can now identify the **critical path** as the longest path in the network from start to finish. It consists of all those activities where ES = LS and EF = LF. In this case the critical path of activities is A–C–D. For these activities the earliest they can start is also the latest they can start. As they say, there is no slack in the activities on the critical path. The critical path constrains the completion time of the project since it is the longest path of activity times from the start to the end of the project. In the example in Figure 14.4 there are only two paths through the network: A–B–D and A–C–D. The length of these paths is 8 and 9, respectively. These lengths are obtained by adding the times of activities along each path. It is apparent from these calculations that path A–C–D is the longer of the two and is therefore the critical path. Notice that the length of the critical path is the project completion time we have just computed.

In large examples it is not possible to evaluate all paths, as we have just done to find the longest path, because there are simply too many. Therefore, the forward and backward passes are used to find the critical path by noting those activities where ES = LS or equivalently EF = LF. In other words, the critical activities comprise the longest chain because the earliest they can start is also the latest they can start and the earliest they can finish is also the latest they can finish.

TABLE 14.4
Precedence and
Times for Opening
a New Office

Activity	Description	Immediate Predecessors	Activity Time	Computed Slack
1	Lease the site	None	1	0
2	Hire the workers	1	5	0
3	Arrange for the furnishings	1	1	1
4	Install the furnishings	3	2	1
5	Arrange for the phones	1	1	3
6	Install the phones	4,5	1	1
7	Move into the office	2,6,4	2	0

Slack is defined as the mathematical difference between LS and ES or equivalently LF–EF. In Figure 14.4 there is only one activity with slack—activity B with one unit of slack. This means the duration of activity B can slip by one day and still not affect the project completion date. In this case it is easy to see that once activity B has slipped by one day then it also is on a critical path and the project has two critical paths at that point.

In managing a project, all activities on the critical path must be carefully monitored. If any of the critical activities slips (takes more time than planned), the completion date of the project will slip by a like amount. In a typical project, with a few hundred activities, only 5 to 10 percent of all activities are on the critical path. Therefore, the monitoring of critical activities provides a significant reduction in managerial effort.

It is now apparent that network calculations have several advantages over the Gantt chart. Networks allow precise determination of the critical path and slack, and they allow the rapid evaluation of proposed schedule changes. In addition, the ideas of critical path and slack are important in their own right.

Example

We take the example of opening a new office used in the Gantt chart (Figure 14.1) and schedule it using a network representation. First, we need to specify the precedence relationships and the activity times. These are shown in Table 14.4. It's logical that we can't install the furnishings before we arrange for them, and we can't install the phones before we make the phone arrangements. We have also specified that the furnishings be installed before the phones are installed in order to know where to place the phone jacks, and, of course, everything must be completed before we can move into the office. These precedence relationships are shown in the network in Figure 14.5.

A forward and backward pass was made on Figure 14.5 to determine the ES, EF and LS, LF for each activity. When making the forward pass, activity 6 cannot start until both activity 5 and 4 are finished. Activity 7 cannot start until activities 2, 6, and 4 are finished, therefore ES(7) = max[EF(2), EF(6) and EF(4)] = max[6,5,4] = 6. When making the backward pass we start with the LF of activity 7 and work backwards. Take a close look at the LF for activity 4. It is the min[LS(6), LS(7)] = min (5,6) = 5. The remaining backward calculations are straightforward. As a check on our math, we note for activity 1 that ES = LS and the EF = LF.

The critical path consists of those activities where ES = LS and EF = LF, that is, path 1–2–7. Just to check our logic, there are four paths in this network with the following lengths obtained by adding the times along each path.

Activities	Total time
1–2–7	8
1–5–6–7	5
1–3–4–6–7	7
1–3–4–7	6

FIGURE 14.5
Network for opening a new office.

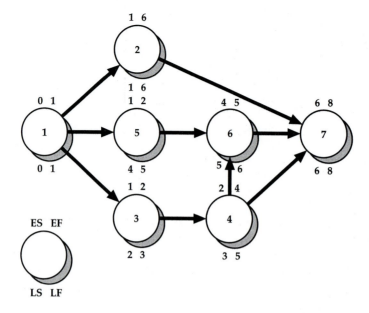

FIGURE 14.6
Gantt chart project example.

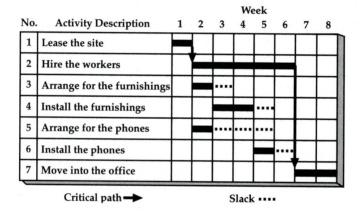

No.	Activity Description	1	2	3	4	5	6	7	8
1	Lease the site								
2	Hire the workers								
3	Arrange for the furnishings								
4	Install the furnishings								
5	Arrange for the phones								
6	Install the phones								
7	Move into the office								

Critical path ➡   Slack ••••

As we can see, path 1–2–7 is the longest path through the network and thus the critical path. Those activities not on the critical path have some slack, as shown in Table 14.4. These figures are obtained by simply subtracting LS − ES or LF − EF for each activity. Slack is the amount of time an activity can slip before affecting the project completion date.

It is possible to put the results from the critical path calculations into a Gantt chart format. In this case we start each activity at its early start time and follow it with a dashed line to show the slack in each activity. This provides a useful display of the critical path along with the slack; see Figure 14.6. Next, we expand on the constant time network to consider PERT and CPM.

14.5 PERT METHOD

The **Program Evaluation Review Technique (PERT)** is a network method for project scheduling that was first developed in the mid-1950s for the Polaris nuclear submarine project. The technique was used to schedule over 3,000 contractors, suppliers, and agencies and is credited with bringing the first nuclear powered submarine into service up to two years ahead of schedule.

FIGURE 14.7
PERT activity times.

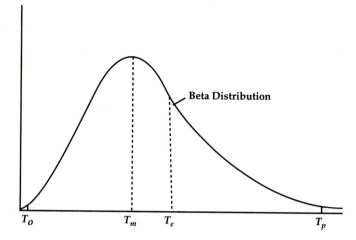

PERT, as originally defined, requires three time estimates for each activity: an optimistic time estimate T_o, a most likely time estimate T_m, and a pessimistic time estimate T_p. These three estimates recognize the uncertainty in activity time that is typical of R&D projects and many other projects where activity times are difficult to predict. The PERT technique also assumes that the actual activity times are distributed according to the beta probability distribution. The beta distribution is skewed to the right with time estimates that are more likely to exceed the average than to be less than the average (see Figure 14.7 for the typical shape of the beta distribution).

Based on experience, time estimates often exceed the most likely time or best estimate in project activities because people tend to be overly optimistic in their time estimating. This leads to a distribution that is skewed to the right, as shown in Figure 14.7. Actual times exceed the most likely time more frequently than they come before it.

From the beta distribution, it is possible to convert the PERT network into a constant-time network. This is done by using the expected times T_e for each activity. According to the beta distribution, the average or expected time can be computed as follows:

$$T_e = \frac{T_o + 4T_m + T_p}{6}$$

In this formula, the most likely time is weighted four times more heavily than the optimistic or pessimistic times. The value of T_e is then used as the single constant-time estimate for each activity. Using these expected times, the constant-time method of the last section can be used to compute ES, EF, LS, and LF times.

But, the problem of uncertainty in activity times cannot be eliminated so easily. When the individual activity times are uncertain, the total project completion time will also be uncertain. To deal with this problem, PERT calculations assume that the statistical variance in total project completion times can be computed by adding the variances along the critical path. This is a reasonable assumption when there are no near-critical paths in the network. In this case, the variance (var_i) for each activity i on the critical path is estimated as follows:

$$\text{var}_i = \left(\frac{T_p - T_o}{6}\right)^2$$

This formula is based on the assumption that the pessimistic and optimistic times will cover six standard deviations on the beta distribution.[2] The variance is then the square of the standard deviation.

If we let T be the total completion time of the project, we can then compute:

$$E(T) = \sum_{\text{critical path}} T_e$$

$$\text{var}(T) = \sum_{\text{critical path}} \text{var}_i$$

Where $E(T)$ denotes the expected value of T and $\text{var}(T)$ denotes the variance of T.

We also assume that the distribution of project completion times is normal. This assumption is based on the central limit theorem, which assures us that the sum of random times will tend to a normal distribution under rather general conditions. Since we know the mean and variance of the normal distribution of project completion times, it is possible to compute the probability of completing the project by any given date. This is done by standardizing the normal variable and using a table of normal probabilities. An example of these calculations is given next.

Example

The PERT network and three time estimates for each activity are given below. Compute the probability that the project will be completed by time 12.

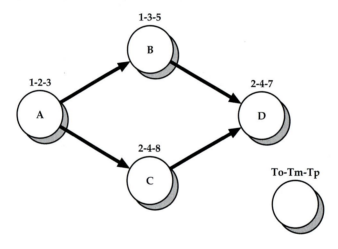

Using the formulas given in the text, the expected time and variance for each activity are computed as follows:

Activity	T_e	Activity Variance
A	2.00	.111
B	3.00	.444
C	4.33	1.000
D	4.17	.694

Using the values of T_e, a forward pass is made to calculate the expected project completion time of 10.5 as follows.

[2] This assumption, in turn, implies that T_o should be set at about the first percentile, while T_p is set at the 99th percentile.

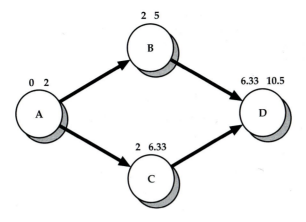

The variance of project completion time (1.80) is the sum of the variances along the critical path (A–C–D).

$$Var(T) = .111 + 1.000 + .694 = 1.80$$

The project completion time is assumed to have a normal distribution with mean 10.5 and standard deviation $= \sqrt{1.80} = 1.342$. The probability that the project completion time will be 12 days or less is obtained by calculating the standard normal variate which is

$$Z = \frac{12 - 10.5}{1.342} = 1.12$$

From the table of normal probabilities (Appendix A), the probability of completion by time 12 (for $Z = 1.12$) is .8686. The diagram below shows the probability area under the normal curve.

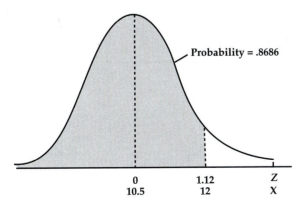

Dealing with uncertainty or randomness of individual time estimates is the essence of the PERT network. When the individual activity times are random, the project completion time will also be random. It is therefore not appropriate, in this case, to set concrete project completion dates. Each completion date will have a certain probability of being met, which is a function of the uncertainties in the individual activities and the precedence relationships. From a management standpoint, it is much better to recognize the uncertainty in completion dates than to force the problem into a constant-time framework.

Another concept that emerges from the PERT network is the idea of a probabilistic critical path. Following PERT logic, there is no certain critical path. Rather each activity has a probability of being on the critical path, some activities having probabilities near zero and others near one. The critical path itself is random when activity times are uncertain.

PERT calculations have been extended to reduce the assumptions inherent in PERT methodology. One way to do this is to simulate the network by sampling random times for each activity. As a result, an exact distribution of project completion time and a probability that each activity is on the critical path can be computed.

14.6 CPM METHOD

The **critical path method** (CPM) was developed by E.I. du Pont de Nemours & Co. as a way to schedule the start-up and shutdown of major plants. Since these plant activities were repeated frequently, the times were fairly well known. However, the time of any activity could be compressed by expending more money. Thus CPM assumes a time–cost trade-off rather than the probabilistic times used in PERT.

The CPM method of project scheduling uses a time–cost function of the type shown in Figure 14.8 for each activity. The activity can be completed in proportionally less time if more money is spent. To express this assumed linear time–cost relationship, four figures are given for each activity: normal time, normal cost, crash time, and crash cost.

The project network is solved initially by using normal times and normal costs for all activities. If the resulting project completion time and cost are satisfactory, all activities will be scheduled at their normal times. If the project completion time is too long, the project can be completed in less time at greater cost.

FIGURE 14.8
Time–cost
relationship in CPM.

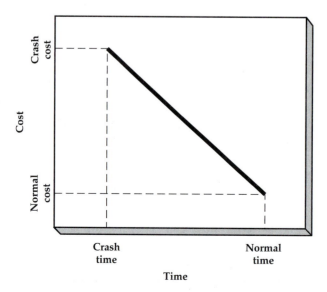

For any given project completion time that is less than the normal time, a great number of network possibilities exist, each at a different total cost. This occurs because a variety of different activity times can be decreased to meet any specified project completion time. All these possibilities can be evaluated by means of a linear programming (LP) problem. The LP problem is used to find the solution representing the minimum total project cost for any given project completion time. [For details on this formulation, see Antill and Woodhead (1990).]

To illustrate the principles involved, an example is given below. The example shows how to calculate normal times and normal costs and how to determine the best way to reduce project completion by one day. Although this simple example is easily evaluated, it will, as the network becomes more complex, be necessary to use linear programming to evaluate all the combinations.

Example

A project network—along with activity times and costs—is given below. Calculate the normal project time and normal cost. Also, calculate the least-cost way to reduce the normal project completion time by one day.

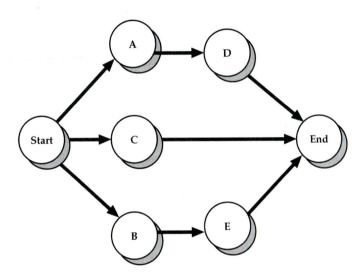

Note that when there is more than one beginning node (in this case A, B, and C), a start node is added to the network. Also, when there is more than one ending node (in this case D, C, and E), an end node is added to the network.

Activity	Normal Time	Normal Cost	Crash Time	Crash Cost
A	3	40	1	80
B	2	50	1	120
C	6	100	4	140
D	4	80	2	130
E	3	60	1	140

Solution

The normal project completion time is computed by setting all activities at their normal times and making a forward pass. The resulting normal project completion time = 7. See the ES, EF time calculations below.

```
        0 3              3 7
        ┌───┐            ┌───┐
        │ A │──────────▶│ D │
        └───┘            └───┘
       ╱                      ╲
  0 0 ╱      0 6                ╲  7 7
 ┌─────┐    ┌───┐              ┌─────┐
 │Start│───▶│ C │─────────────▶│ End │
 └─────┘    └───┘              └─────┘
       ╲                      ╱
        ╲  0 2            2 5╱
        ┌───┐            ┌───┐
        │ B │──────────▶│ E │
        └───┘            └───┘
```

The normal project cost is the sum of normal costs for all activities, which equals $330.

The project completion time can be reduced to 6 days by crashing either activity A or D by one day. It costs $20 per day, (80 − 40)/2, to crash activity A and $25 per day, (130 − 80)/2, to crash activity D. Therefore it is less costly to crash activity A by one day in order to achieve an overall project completion time of 6 days and a cost of $350.

Note from this example that the project completion time can be decreased one unit at a time by incurring more cost. This can be continued until all activities on the critical path are "crashed" to their minimum times or until other paths become critical. Remaining activities can have some slack in them. Management can determine how much it will cost to obtain any given project completion time between the normal time and minimum full-crash time by simply decreasing project completion time one unit at a time until full crash times are reached.

14.7 USE OF PROJECT MANAGEMENT CONCEPTS

Project management requires a great deal more than scheduling. Planning for the project is required before the scheduling begins, and control is required after the schedule is developed. Project management requires a blend of behavioral and quantitative skills often involving the use of cross-functional teams. Thus, scheduling methods should be seen as only one part of a complete approach to project management.

In selecting project scheduling methods, a conscious trade-off should be made between sophisticated methods and cost. Gantt chart methods should not be seen as outdated or naive. Rather, Gantt charts are justified for projects where the activities are not highly interconnected or for small projects. In these cases where the Gantt chart is warranted, a network method may not provide enough additional benefits in relation to its costs.

If a network method is justified, a choice must be made between constant-time, PERT, CPM, or more advanced methods. The constant-time method is adequate for cases where activity times are constant or nearly so. If activity

OPERATIONS LEADER *The U.S. Government Rates Project Software Packages*	Four packages were examined to determine their suitability for project management. The government raters chose Microsoft Project as the most advanced package, followed closely in second place by Primavera Systems, Inc., Sure Trak 2.0. Not as highly rated were Scitor Corp's Project Scheduler 7 and Kidasa Sofware, Inc., Milestones, Etc. 5.0. All of these packages were found to be reasonably priced in the $400 to $600 range at retail. They all performed the basic functions required of project management, but the more highly rated packages contained more features that were judged to be easier to use by the raters. **Source:** *Government Best Buys,* October 6, 1997.

times are random, a PERT network should be chosen to reflect the uncertainty directly. PERT may therefore be applied to situations such as R&D, computer system design, and military invasions, where activity times are expected to vary.

CPM methods, on the other hand, should be used where activity times are fairly constant but can be reduced by spending more money. CPM might apply in cases such as construction projects, installation of equipment, and plant start-up and shutdown. More advanced network methods include generalized networks, resource-constrained networks, and project management based on the theory of constraints. These methods are still in development and have not yet been widely used in practice.

Computerized network scheduling methods are used in practice. A large number of different standard software packages are available to cover the entire range of scheduling methods. The Operations Leader box describes how the U.S. government rates the various project software packages. These packages not only support scheduling but also assist in project accounting and in controlling progress.

Cadbury Schweppes, an international confectionery and beverage company, implemented a new portfolio and process computer system aimed at supporting worldwide growth and innovation. This project management system will assist 2,400 managers in product development, marketing, and commercial strategy in 45 countries. It will be a central repository for new product development information, support product portfolio planning, and facilitate new product development projects.[3]

14.8 KEY POINTS

The planning and scheduling of projects is concerned with the unique, one-time production activity. Because projects are unique, the scheduling problem is quite different from that of ongoing operations.

The key points covered in this chapter include the following:

- The three objectives in projects are time, cost, and performance. Because these objectives are conflicting, trade-offs among them must constantly be made in the course of managing projects.

---

[3] Vignette Corporation (2005).

- All projects go through three phases: planning, scheduling, and control. The planning phase establishes the objectives, organization, and resources for the project. The scheduling phase establishes the time schedule, cost, and personnel assignments. The control phase monitors the progress of the project in cost, time, and performance; it also corrects the plan as necessary to achieve project objectives.
- The Gantt chart is a scheduling method for displaying project activities in a bar-chart form. The Gantt chart is useful for small projects or projects where activities are not highly interrelated.
- There are three network scheduling methods: constant-time, PERT, and CPM. All these methods rely on a network or graph to represent the precedence relationship between activities.
- A network allows one to identify the critical path, slack, and activities that need to be rescheduled. The critical path is the longest time path of activities from the beginning to the end of the network. Activities on the critical path have zero slack—they must be completed on time to prevent slippage of the project completion date. Slack is the amount of time that an activity can be extended while still allowing the project to be completed on time.
- The early start, late start, early finish, and late finish times for each activity can be computed by means of a forward and backward pass through the network.
- PERT is a network-based project scheduling method that requires three time estimates for each activity: optimistic, most likely, and pessimistic. Using these three time estimates, a probability of project completion by any specified date can be computed, along with the standard start and finish times for each activity or event.
- CPM is a network-based method that uses a linear time–cost trade-off. Each activity can be completed in less than its normal time by crashing the activity for a given cost. Thus, if the normal project completion time is not satisfactory, certain activities can be crashed to complete the project in less time at greater cost.

STUDENT INTERNET EXERCISES

1. Primavera, Inc.
   http://www.primavera.com/

Gather information about this project planning and scheduling software. Come to class prepared to discuss your findings.

2. Microsoft Project
   http://www.microsoft.com/office/project

Select the latest project management software (Project 2003 when this book went to press) and write a short report on its main features and capabilities for planning, scheduling, and controlling projects. You can run the demo version of Project 2003 to learn about the package.

3. Job Listings
   http://www.pmi.org/careerhq/

This site contains job listings for project management talent. Study the listings and come to class prepared to comment on the type and number of jobs available in the project management field.

SOLVED PROBLEMS

Problem

1. **Activity-on-Node Method**   A list of activities, precedence relations, and activity times for a project is given below:

Activity Name	Predecessor	Activities
A	—	5
B	A	4
C	B	2
D	A,C	6
E	D	8
F	E	5
G	C	4
H	D,E,G,I	13
I	C	2
J	G,H	1
K	F,H,J	6

a. Draw an activity-on-node network diagram.

b. Compute the early start (ES), late start (LS), early finish (EF), and late finish (LF) times for each activity in the network.

c. What is the critical path? What is the expected completion time for the project?

Solution

a.

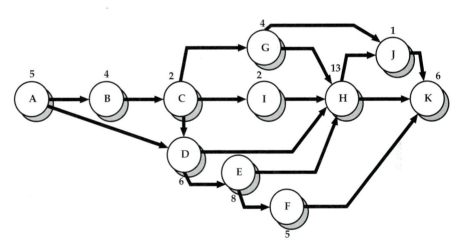

b.

Activity Name	ES	LS	EF	LF	Slack
A	0	0	5	5	0
B	5	5	9	9	0
C	9	9	11	11	0
D	11	11	17	17	0
E	17	17	25	25	0
F	25	34	30	39	9
G	11	21	15	25	10
H	25	25	38	38	0
I	11	23	13	25	12
J	38	38	39	39	0
K	39	39	45	45	0

c. The critical path is those activities that have no slack:

A–B–C–D–E–H–J–K

Problem

2. A PERT network drawing and optimistic, most likely, and pessimistic activity times, listed under each node, are given below for a secret military project.

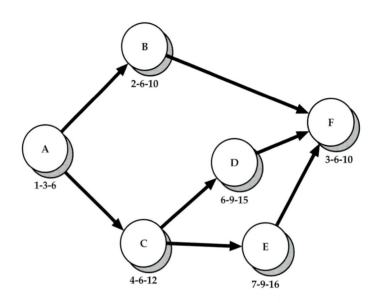

a. What is the expected time for each activity in the project?
b. What is the variance associated with each activity time in the project?
c. What is the critical path for the project?
d. What is the expected completion time of the project?
e. What is the variance of the completion time of the project?
f. What is the probability that the project will be completed in 24 days and in 26 days?

Solution

a. and b.

Activity	T_o	T_m	T_p	Expected Time $(T_o + 4T_m + T_p)/6$	Variance $[(T_p - T_o)/6]^2$
A	1	3	6	3.167	0.694
B	2	6	10	6.000	1.778
C	4	6	12	6.667	1.778
D	6	9	15	9.500	2.250
E	7	9	16	9.833	2.250
F	3	6	10	6.167	1.361

c. The critical path for the project is determined by making a forward pass below. The critical path is A–C–E–F.

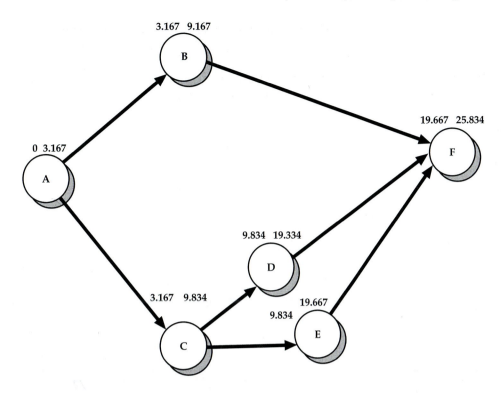

d. The expected project completion time is the sum of expected times along the critical path which is also the EF time for node F: E(T) = 25.834.

e. Variance of completion time is the sum of variances along the critical path: var(*T*) = .694 + 1.778 + 2.250 + 1.361 = 6.083.

f. The probability that the project can be completed in a specified time limit (TL) can be written as

P[Z ≤ [TL − E(T)]/SD(T)]
Where SD(T) = $\sqrt{var(T)}$ = $\sqrt{6.083}$ = 2.466
P[TL ≤ 24] = P[Z ≤ (24 − 25.834)/2.466)] = P[Z ≤ −0.744] = .5 − .2703 = .2297
P[TL ≤ 26] = P[Z ≤ (26 − 25.834)/2.466)] = P[Z ≤ 0.067] = .5 + .0279 = .5279

Use the table in Appendix A to look up the above values with round-off. There is a 23 percent chance the project can be completed in 24 days and a 53 percent probability the project can be completed in 26 days.

Problem

3. The following information is given for a CPM network.

Activity	Predecessor	Successor	Normal Time	Normal Cost	Crash Time	Crash Cost
A	—	B,C	4	$50	2	$100
B	A	D,C	3	60	2	80
C	A,B	D	5	70	3	140
D	B,C	—	2	30	1	60

a. Draw the network showing the normal times.
b. Make a forward and backward pass to calculate ES, LS, EF, LF for each activity.
c. What is the normal project completion time and the normal cost?
d. What should be done to crash the network by one day? By two days?

Solution

a.

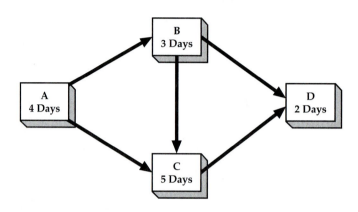

b.

Activity	ES	EF	LS	LF
A	0	4	0	4
B	4	7	4	7
C	7	12	7	12
D	12	14	12	14

c. Normal project completion time = 14, normal cost = $210.

d. To crash by one day, any of the activities on the critical path (A, B, C, or D) can be crashed. The cost of crashing per day is (A = $25, B = $20, C = $35, D = $30). The lowest cost of crashing one day is therefore activity B. In this case project cost is $210 + $20 = $230 for 13-day project completion. To crash two days, also consider the critical path, since no other path is longer than 11 days. Activity B cannot be crashed for another day, so the next lowest cost is to crash activity A by one day. The total cost for 12-day project completion is $210 + $20 + $25 = $255.

Discussion Questions

1. How, precisely, does project scheduling differ from the scheduling of ongoing operations?
2. How would you, after the fact, audit a project to determine whether it was successful or not?
3. Give three examples of projects not given in the text. Are these projects unique, or are they repeated in some way?
4. Contrast and compare CPM and PERT as project scheduling techniques.
5. Define the terms *critical path, ES,* and *LF.*
6. What is the management significance of finding the critical path through a network?
7. How is the Gantt chart used as a scheduling tool? When should the Gantt chart be used in preference to network-based methods?
8. What is meant by the need to make trade-offs between cost, performance, and schedule? Give examples.

9. Why are a forward pass and a backward pass needed to produce a project schedule?

10. What is the definition of the earliest and latest start time of an activity and the earliest and latest finish time of an activity?

11. What statistical assumptions are made in PERT? Under what conditions are those assumptions realistic?

12. An R&D manager told you that the statistical part of PERT seems complicated and perhaps too complex for scheduling R&D. What would your response be?

13. Suppose that a particular activity has a very high variance in a PERT chart. How would this affect the result?

Problems

1. A public accounting firm requires the following activities for an audit:

Activity	Immediate Predecessor	Activity Time
a	—	3
b	a	2
c	—	4
d	b, c	2
e	a	5
f	b, c	6
g	e, d	5

   a. Draw a network for this project.
   b. Make a forward and backward pass to determine ES, LS, EF, and LF.
   c. What is the critical path and the project completion time?
   d. If the project completion must be reduced by two days, which activities might be affected?

2. The following activities are required in starting up a new plant:

Activity	Immediate Predecessor	Activity Time
a	—	3
b	—	2
c	a	1
d	b	4
e	b	4
f	c, d	2
g	e, c, d	3

   a. Draw a network for this project.
   b. Make a forward and backward pass to determine ES, LS, EF, and LF.
   c. Calculate slack.
   d. Prepare a Gantt chart for this project.

3. A construction project has the following network and activity times:

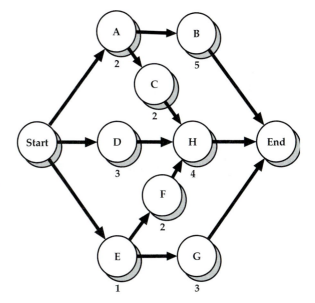

(activity times are given below the nodes)

   a. Make a forward and backward pass on the activity times.
   b. Find the slack for each activity.
   c. Prepare a Gantt chart for this project.
   d. Activity D will be delayed by one day. What effect will this have on the project?

4. A plant start-up is based on the following network:

Activity	Immediate Predecessor	Activity Time
a	—	4
b	—	8
c	—	2
d	a	3
e	a	5
f	c	5
g	b, d	6

a. Draw a network for this project.

b. What is the project completion time?

c. Identify the critical path.

5. An entrepreneur is starting a new business. The activities and times required are given below:

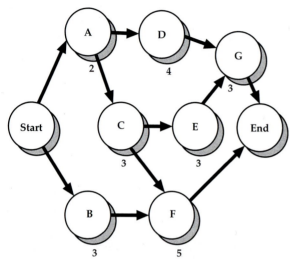

(activity times are given below the nodes)

a. Find the critical path and the project completion time.

b. What is the ES, LS, EF, and LF for each activity?

c. How much slack is there in activity D?

6. In preparing to teach a new course, the professor has estimated the following activity times.

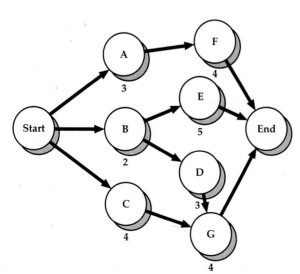

(activity times are given below the nodes)

a. Find the completion time of the project.

b. What is the critical path?

7. A PERT chart includes the following information:

Activity	Immediate Predecessor	T_o	T_m	T_p
A	None	3	6	10
B	A	4	8	14
C	B and A	1	3	8
D	B and C	5	7	10
E	C	2	4	8
F	D and E	2	5	9

a. Draw a network and label each activity with its expected time and variance.

b. Calculate the expected completion time of the project.

c. What is the probability that the project is completed in 30 days?

d. Are the PERT assumptions used to calculate the probability in part (c) realistic in this case? Why or why not?

e. What is the effect of the large variance in activity B?

8. The Widget company is planning to manage a small R&D project with PERT. The following information has been estimated.

Activity	Immediate Predecessor	T_o	T_m	T_p
A	None	6	8	11
B	A	2	3	5
C	A	4	7	12
D	A and C	1	3	6
E	B and D	2	4	7
F	E and C	1	2	4
G	F and E	4	5	7

a. Draw the network diagram.

b. Calculate the expected time and variance for each activity.

c. What is the expected completion time and variance for the entire project?

d. What is the probability that the project completion time will be less than 25?

9. Construction of a building is based on the following CPM network:

Activity	Predecessor	Successor	Normal Time	Normal Cost	Crash Time	Crash Cost
A	—	B,C,D	4	$100	2	$150
B	A	E	8	80	2	140
C	B,A	F	2	40	1	60
D	A	F,G	3	80	2	120
E	B	G	5	80	3	140
F	C,D	G	5	60	1	100
G	E,F,D	—	6	120	2	160

a. Draw the network for this project and label the events.

b. What is the normal project completion time and normal cost?

c. Identify the critical path.

d. How much will it cost to crash the project completion by one day? by two days?

e. What is the minimum time for project completion?

10. The professor from problem 6 is considering reducing the time for completion of the project. He can hire a teaching assistant (TA) to help with the new course, but this will cost additional money. The TA can only help reduce the times for activities A, D, and C. In each case the TA can reduce the time required by one day for $150 and 2 days for $300.

a. Which activity should the TA perform to reduce the project completion time by one day?

b. Which activities should the TA perform to reduce the project completion time by two days?

c. Can the network be crashed by three days in total? Explain why or why not?

Selected Bibliography

Antill, J. M., and R. W. Woodhead. *Critical Path Methods in Construction Practice*, 4th ed. New York: Wiley, 1990.

Burke, Rory. *Project Management: Planning and Control*, 4th ed. New York: Wiley, 2003.

Gelbard, Roy, Nava Pliskin, and Israel Spiegler. "Integrating System Analysis and Project Management Tools." *International Journal of Project Management* 20, no. 6 (August 2002), pp. 461–69.

Kerzner, Harold. *Project Management: A Systems Approach to Planning, Scheduling and Controlling*, 8th ed. New York: Wiley, 2003.

Lewis, James. *Fundamentals of Project Management: Developing Core Competencies to Help Outperform the Competition*, 2nd ed. New York: American Management Association, 2002.

Lientz, Bennet. *Project Management for the 21st Century*, 3rd ed. San Deigo, CA: Academic Press, 2001.

Lock, Dennis. *Project Management*, 7th ed. Aldershot, U.K.: Gower, 2000.

Meredith, Jack, and Sam Mantel, Jr. *Project Management: A Managerial Approach*, 5th ed. New York: Wiley, 2002.

Newbold, Robert C. *Project Management in the Fast Lane: Applying the Theory of Constraints*. Boca Raton, FL: St. Lucie Press, 1998.

Nikander, Ilmari O., and Eero Eloranta. "Project Management by Early Warnings." *International Journal of Project Management* 19, no. 7 (October 2001), pp. 385–400.

Slevin, Dennis P., and Jeffrey K. Pinto. *The Frontiers of Project Management Research*. Newtown Squre, PA: Project Management Institute Publications, February 2002.

Steyn, H. "Project Management Applications of the Theory of Constraints beyond Critical Chain Scheduling." *International Journal of Project Management* 20, no. 1 (January 2002), pp. 75–81.

Thiry, Michel. "Combining Value and Project Management into an Effective Programme Management Model." *International Journal of Project Management* 20, no. 3 (April 2002), pp. 221–28.

Verwey, Anton, and Dennis Comninos. "Business Focused Project Management." *Management Services* 46, no. 1 (January 2002), pp. 14–22.

Vignette Corporation. "A Sweet Solution from Sopheon." *KM World* 14, no. 5 (May 2005), p. 6.

White, Diana, and Joyce Fortune. "Current Practice in Project Management—an Empirical Study." *International Journal of Project Management* 20, no. 1 (January 2002), pp. 1–12.

Whittaker, Roy. *Project Management in the Process Industries*. New York: Wiley, 1996.

Wysocki, Robert, and Rudd McGary. *Effective Project Management: Traditional, Adaptive, Extreme*, 3rd ed. New York: Wiley, 2003.

Part **Five**

Inventory

The basis for organizing Part Five is the distinction between independent-demand and dependent-demand inventories. Chapter 15 treats independent demand, which is subject to market forces and thus independent of operations (e.g., finished goods and spare parts). Chapters 16 and 17 treat dependent demand, which is derived from the demand for another part or component (e.g., work-in-process inventory and raw-materials inventories). MRP and JIT systems are used to manage dependent-demand inventories.

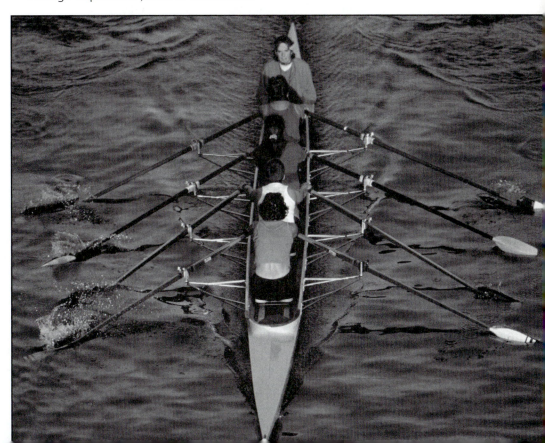

Independent-Demand Inventory

Chapter outline

Inventory management is among the most important operations management responsibilities because inventory requires a great deal of capital and affects the delivery of goods to customers. Inventory management has an impact on all business functions, particularly operations, marketing, accounting, and finance. Inventories can be managed in a logical and consistent manner, which is the main subject of this chapter.

It is, perhaps, best to begin our discussion with a definition of inventory. An **inventory** is a stock of materials used to facilitate production or to satisfy customer demands. Inventories typically include raw materials, work in process, and finished goods. This definition fits nicely with the view of operations as a transformation process. In Figure 15.1, an operation is shown as a materials-flow process with raw-materials inventories waiting to enter the productive process, work-in-process inventories in some intermediate stage of transformation, and finished-goods inventories already completely transformed by the production system.

FIGURE 15.1 A materials-flow process.

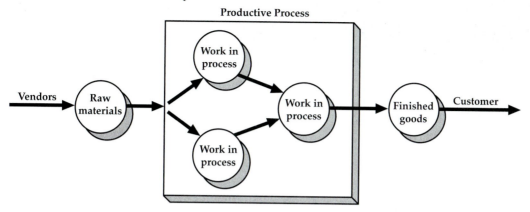

Our definition of inventory as a stock of materials is narrower than that given by others. Some authors define inventory as an idle resource of any kind that has potential economic value. This definition allows one to consider equipment or idle workers as inventory, but we consider all idle resources other than materials as capacity. From a management and accounting perspective, it is important to distinguish between inventory and capacity. Capacity provides the potential to produce, while inventory, as defined here, is the product at some point in the conversion and distribution process.

Inventory stocks are located at various points in the production process, with flows connecting one stock point to another. The rate at which a stock can be replenished is the supply capacity, and the rate of stock depletion is demand. Inventory acts as a buffer between the different demand and supply rates.

The water tank shown in Figure 15.2 is a good analogy for these concepts of flows and stocks. In this figure, the level of water in the tank corresponds to inventory. The rate of flow into the tank is analogous to supply capacity, and the rate of flow out corresponds to demand. The water level (inventory) is thus a buffer between supply and demand. If demand exceeds supply, the water level will drop until the demand and supply rates come back into balance or until the water is depleted. Likewise, if supply exceeds demand, the water level will rise.

Imagine a number of these tanks connected together, each with varying inputs and outputs. This situation, illustrated in Figure 15.3, is a good analogy to the inventory management problem. Here, one tank represents raw materials; there

FIGURE 15.2
A water tank
analogy for
inventory.

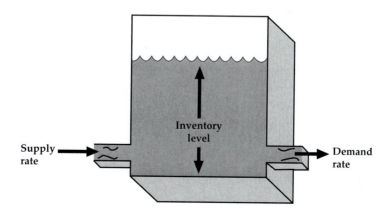

FIGURE 15.3 A water tank system analogy.

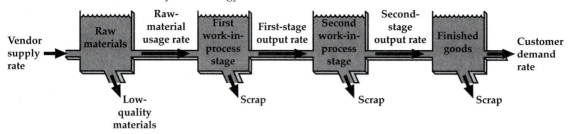

are two tanks for work in process and one for finished goods. The tanks serve as buffers to absorb variations in flow rates within the system. In Chapter 17, we will show how the size of the buffers (inventory levels) can be drastically reduced by smoothing out flow rates and reducing variations in the production system through a just-in-time approach.

Inventories in the supply chain serve the same purpose as inventories in a factory—to buffer the difference in flows between supply and demand. In a supply chain, however, one firm typically does not control all inventories; rather, inventory must be coordinated across the supply chain partners. Many of the concepts covered in this chapter apply to the broader context of a supply chain, although coordination between parties with different interests and objectives must also be considered.

15.1 PURPOSE OF INVENTORIES

The primary purpose of inventories is to uncouple the various phases of operations and the supply chain. Raw-materials inventory uncouples a manufacturer from its suppliers; work-in-process inventory uncouples the various stages of manufacturing from each other; and finished-goods inventory uncouples a manufacturer from its customers.

Within the overall uncoupling purpose, there are four reasons to carry inventory:

1. **To protect against uncertainties.** In inventory systems, there are uncertainties in supply, demand, and lead time. Safety stocks are maintained in inventory to protect against those uncertainties. If customer demand were known, it would be feasible—although not necessarily economical—to produce at the same rate as consumption. In this case, no finished-goods inventory would be needed; however, every change in demand would be immediately transmitted to the production system in order to maintain customer service. Instead of such tight coupling, safety stocks of finished goods are maintained to absorb changes in demand without immediately changing production. In a similar way, safety stocks of raw materials are maintained to absorb uncertainties in delivery by suppliers, and safety stocks of in-process inventories are maintained to allow for poor maintenance, unreliable workers, or fast schedule changes. These safety stocks, however, can often be reduced by better coordination of suppliers and customers in the supply chain.

2. **To allow economic production and purchase.** It is often economical to produce materials in lots. In this case, a lot may be produced over a short period of time, and then no further production is done until the lot is nearly depleted. This makes it possible to spread the setup cost of the production machines over a large number of items. It also permits the use of the same production equipment for different products. A similar situation holds for the purchase of raw materials. Owing to ordering costs, quantity discounts, and transportation costs, it is sometimes economical to purchase in large lots, even though part of the lot is then held in inventory for later use. The inventory resulting from the purchase or production of material in lots is called cycle inventory since the lots are produced or purchased on a cyclic basis. There is a trend under way in industry today, however, to reduce setup times and costs drastically by altering the product or process. This will result in smaller lot sizes and much lower inventories. In some cases, the setup time can be reduced so that the economical lot size is one unit. This possibility will be discussed further in Chapter 17 on just-in-time systems.

3. **To cover anticipated changes in demand or supply.** There are several types of situations where changes in demand or supply may be anticipated. One case is where the price or availability of raw materials is expected to change. Companies often stockpile steel prior to an expected steel industry strike. Another source of anticipation is a planned market promotion where a large amount of finished goods may be stocked prior to a sale. Finally, companies in seasonal businesses often anticipate demand in order to smooth employment, as discussed in Chapter 12. For example, a producer of air conditioners may select a nearly uniform rate of production, although a great deal of the product is sold in the summer.

4. **To provide for transit.** Transit inventories consist of materials that are on their way from one point to another in the supply chain. These inventories are affected by plant location decisions and by the choice of carrier. Sometimes the inventory in transit is called pipeline inventory because it is in the "distribution pipeline."

The first two categories of inventory will be treated extensively in this chapter; the remaining two categories are treated in other parts of the book.

15.2 INVENTORY COST STRUCTURES

Many inventory decision problems can be solved by using economic criteria. One of the most important prerequisites, however, is an understanding of the cost structure. Inventory cost structures incorporate the following four types of costs:

1. **Item cost.** This is the cost of buying or producing the individual inventory items. The item cost is usually expressed as a cost per unit multiplied by the quantity procured or produced. Sometimes item cost is discounted if enough units are purchased at one time.

2. **Ordering (or setup) cost.** The ordering cost is associated with ordering a batch or lot of items. Ordering cost does not depend on the number of items ordered; it is assigned to the entire batch. This cost includes typing the purchase order, expediting the order, transportation costs, receiving costs, and so on. When the item is produced within the firm, there are also costs associated with placing

an order that are independent of the number of items produced. These so-called setup costs include paperwork costs plus the costs required to set up the production equipment for a run. In some cases, setup costs can amount to thousands of dollars, leading to significant economies for large runs. Later, we will discuss how setup times can be reduced by changes in the production system or the product. Setup cost is often considered fixed when, in fact, it can be reduced by changing the way operations are designed and managed.

3. **Carrying (or holding) cost.** The carrying, or holding, cost is associated with keeping items in inventory for a period of time. The holding cost is typically charged as a percentage of dollar value per unit time. For example, a 15 percent annual holding cost means that it will cost 15 cents to hold $1 of inventory for a year. In practice, holding costs typically range from 15 to 30 percent per year. The carrying cost usually consists of three components:

- **Cost of capital.** When items are carried in inventory, the capital invested is not available for other purposes. This represents a cost of forgone opportunities for other investments, which is assigned to inventory as an opportunity cost.

- **Cost of storage.** This cost includes variable space cost, insurance, and taxes. In some cases, a part of the storage cost is fixed, for example, when a warehouse is owned and cannot be used for other purposes. Such fixed costs should not be included in the cost of inventory storage. Likewise, taxes and insurance should be included only if they vary with the inventory level.

- **Costs of obsolescence, deterioration, and loss.** Obsolescence costs should be assigned to items that have a high risk of becoming obsolete; the higher the risk, the higher the costs. Perishable products should be charged with deterioration costs when the item deteriorates over time, for example, food and blood. Many products have an expiration date printed on them and become obsolete at that time. The costs of loss include pilferage and breakage costs associated with holding items in inventory.

4. **Stockout cost.** Stockout cost reflects the economic consequences of running out of stock. There are two cases here. First, suppose items are back-ordered or backlogged for the customer and the customer waits until the material arrives. In this case, there may be some loss of future business associated with each back order because the customer had to wait. This opportunity loss is counted as a stockout cost. The second case is where the sale is lost if material is not on hand. The profit is lost from the sale, and future profits may also be lost.

Given the above costs, it is easy to see why inventory management is a cross-functional problem. Marketing may be particularly interested in minimizing the stockout costs associated with lost sales. Accounting and finance may be interested in minimizing the amount of inventory that needs to be financed. Operations may want a sufficient level of inventory to ensure smooth scheduling and production control. Since these objectives may be at odds, it is important that the total cost minimization approach described in this chapter be taken. This approach is inherently cross-functional in nature and does what is best for the entire firm.

A similar situation exists in a supply chain when all parties do not have the same objectives. As mentioned above, coordination among parties with different interests must be considered. The minimum cost principle still applies where the supply chain partners attempt to minimize the total cost across the entire supply chain. In this case, however, it may be difficult to achieve a minimum when higher costs to one party incur lower costs for another. Nevertheless, market forces, financial incentives, or negotiations among parties can be used to seek the minimum cost across the supply chain.

15.3   INDEPENDENT VERSUS DEPENDENT DEMAND

A crucial distinction in inventory management is whether demand is independent or dependent. **Independent demand** is influenced by market conditions outside the control of operations; it is therefore independent of operations. Finished-goods inventories and spare parts for replacement usually have independent demand. **Dependent demand** is related to the demand for another item and is not independently determined by the market. When products are built up from parts and assemblies, the demand for these components is dependent on the demand for the final product.

A toy wagon can be used to illustrate the difference between independent and dependent demand. The demand for wagons is independent because it is influenced by the market. The demand for wagon wheels is dependent because it is mathematically related to the demand for wagons; it takes four wheels to complete each wagon produced. Likewise, the demand for wagon handles is dependent on the demand for finished wagons.

Independent and dependent demands exhibit very different usage or demand patterns. Since independent demand is subject to market forces, it often exhibits some fixed pattern while also responding to random influences, which usually stem from a great many different customer preferences. On the other hand, dependent demand exhibits a lumpy, on-again, off-again pattern when production is scheduled in lots. A quantity of parts is required when a lot is made; then no parts are required until the next lot is made. These demand patterns are shown in Figure 15.4.

Different demand patterns call for different approaches to inventory management. For independent demand, a **replenishment philosophy** is appropriate. As the stock is used, it is replenished in order to have materials on hand for customers. Thus, as inventory begins to run out, an order is triggered for more material and the inventory is replenished.

FIGURE 15.4
Demand patterns.

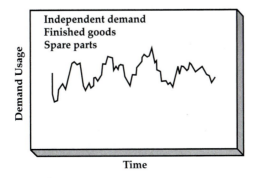

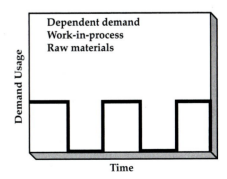

For dependent-demand items, a **requirements philosophy** is used. The amount of stock ordered is based on requirements for higher-level items. As one begins to run out, additional raw material or work-in-process inventory is *not* ordered. More material is ordered only as required by the need for other higher-level or end items.

The nature of demand, therefore, leads to two different philosophies of inventory management. These philosophies, in turn, generate different sets of methods and computer software systems. In this chapter, the independent-demand case will be covered, including the following types of inventories:

1. Finished-goods inventories and spare parts in manufacturing companies.
2. Maintenance, repair, and operating supplies (MRO) inventories.
3. Retail and wholesale finished goods.
4. Service-industry (e.g., hospitals, schools, etc.) inventory.

In Chapters 16 and 17, we will study the management of dependent-demand inventories specifically for work-in-process and raw material inventories.

15.4 ECONOMIC ORDER QUANTITY

In 1915, F. W. Harris developed the famous **economic order quantity** (EOQ) formula. Later, this formula gained wide use in industry through the efforts of a consultant named Wilson. Thus, the formula is often called the Wilson EOQ even though it was developed by Harris. The EOQ and its variations are still widely used in industry for independent-demand inventory management.

The derivation of the EOQ model is based on the following assumptions:

1. The demand rate is constant, recurring, and known. For example, demand (or usage) is 100 units a day with no random variation, and demand is assumed to continue into the indefinite future.
2. The lead time is constant and known. The lead time, from order placement to order delivery, is therefore always a fixed number of days.
3. No stockouts are allowed. Since demand and lead time are constant, one can determine exactly when to order material to avoid stockouts.
4. Material is ordered or produced in a lot or batch, and the lot is placed into inventory all at one time.
5. A specific cost structure is used as follows: The unit item cost is constant, and no discounts are given for large purchases. The carrying cost depends linearly on the average inventory level. There is a fixed ordering or setup cost for each lot, which is independent of the number of items in the lot.
6. The item is a single product; there is no interaction with other products.

Under these assumptions, the inventory level over time is shown in Figure 15.5. Notice that the figure shows a perfect sawtooth pattern, because demand has a constant rate and items are ordered in fixed lot sizes.

In choosing the lot size, there is a **trade-off** between ordering frequency and inventory level. Small lots will lead to frequent reorders but a low average inventory level. If larger lots are ordered, the ordering frequency will decrease but more inventory will be carried. This trade-off between ordering frequency and inventory level can be represented by a mathematical equation using the following symbols:

FIGURE 15.5
EOQ inventory levels.

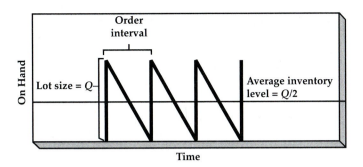

D = demand rate, units per year

S = cost per order placed, or setup cost, dollars per order

C = unit cost, dollars per unit

i = carrying rate, percent of dollar value per year

Q = lot size, units

TC = total of ordering cost plus carrying cost, dollars per year

The annual ordering cost is

$$\text{Ordering cost per year} = (\text{cost per order}) \times (\text{orders per year}) = SD/Q$$

In the above equation, D is the total demand for a year, and the product is ordered Q units at a time; thus D/Q orders are placed in a year. This is multiplied by S, the cost per order placed.

The annual carrying cost is:

$$\text{Carrying cost per year} = (\text{annual carrying rate}) \times (\text{unit cost}) \times (\text{average inventory}) = iCQ/2$$

In this equation, the average inventory is $Q/2$. A maximum of Q units is carried just as a batch arrives in inventory; the minimum amount carried is zero units. Since the stock is depleted at a constant rate, the average inventory is $Q/2$. The carrying rate per year (i) times the unit cost (C) gives the cost of holding *one* unit in inventory for a year. This unit charge multiplied by the average inventory level gives the total carrying cost on an annual basis.

The total annual cost of inventory is then:[1]

$$\text{Total cost per year} = \text{ordering cost per year} + \text{carrying cost per year}$$
$$TC = SD/Q + iCQ/2 \qquad \textbf{(15.1)}$$

Figure 15.6 is a plot of TC versus Q, with each component of TC shown separately along with the total. As Q increases, the ordering-cost component decreases because fewer orders are placed per year; at the same time, however, the carrying-cost component increases because more average inventory is held. Thus, ordering and carrying costs are offsetting: one decreases while the other increases. This is precisely the trade-off between ordering and carrying costs that we mentioned earlier. Because of this trade-off, the function TC has a minimum.

---

[1] Notice that the item cost of procurement is the constant CD, which is independent of Q and can therefore be removed from further consideration. It will not affect the minimum of TC.

FIGURE 15.6
Total cost of
inventory.

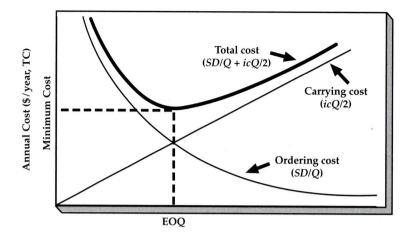

Finding the value of Q that minimizes TC is a classic problem in calculus.[2] We take the derivative of TC, set it equal to zero, and then solve for the resulting value of Q.

$$TC' = -\frac{SD}{Q^2} + \frac{iC}{2} = 0$$

$$\frac{SD}{Q^2} = \frac{iC}{2}$$

$$Q^2 = \frac{2SD}{iC}$$

$$Q = \sqrt{\frac{2SD}{iC}} \qquad \textbf{(15.2)}$$

Equation (15.2) is the classic Wilson economic order quantity, which minimizes the cost of operating the inventory. Although we have minimized cost on an annual basis, any unit of time can be used provided the demand rate and carrying rate are compatible. For example, if demand is expressed on a monthly basis, the carrying rate must also be expressed on a monthly basis.

Example

To illustrate the use of the EOQ formula, suppose we are managing a carpet store and want to determine how many yards of a certain type of carpet to buy. The carpet has the following characteristics:

$$D = 360 \text{ yards per year}$$
$$S = \$10 \text{ per order}$$
$$i = 25\% \text{ per year}$$
$$C = \$8 \text{ per yard}$$

Thus,

$$Q = \sqrt{\frac{2(10)(360)}{.25(8)}} = \sqrt{3,600} = 60$$

The manager should order 60 yards of carpet at a time. This will result in $360/60 = 6$ orders per year, or one order every two months.

[2] Without the use of calculus, the EOQ formula can be rationalized as follows: Observe from Figure 15.6 that the minimum of TC occurs where the two curves intersect. Determine this intersection by setting $SD/Q = iCQ/2$ and solve for the resulting value of Q. This approach is not generalizable but works in this case due to the special nature of the functions involved.

The minimum cost of operating this inventory will be $120 per year as follows:

$$TC = 10(360/60) + .25(8)(60/2) = 60 + 60 = 120$$

Notice that the minimum cost occurs when the ordering-cost component equals the carrying-cost component.

The total-cost curve for inventory is very flat in the neighborhood of the minimum. For example, if 50 or 70 units of carpet instead of 60 units are ordered, the cost change is very slight, about a 1 percent increase. Even if 80 units are ordered instead of 60, the cost increase is about 4 percent. Thus, the manager can adjust the order quantity by a fair amount if necessary, with little effect on the total cost of the inventory.

Even though the EOQ formula is derived from rather restrictive assumptions, it is a useful approximation in practice. The formula at least provides a "ballpark" figure, provided the assumptions are reasonably accurate. Furthermore, the total-cost curve is rather flat in the region of the minimum; thus, the EOQ can be adjusted somewhat to conform to reality without greatly affecting the costs.

Markdowns occur when inventories are poorly managed.
© Amy Etra/Photo Edit, Inc

The most important idea in this section is not the EOQ at all but rather the concept of **total cost.** Regardless of the situation, if one can identify the relevant total-cost equation, then an economic lot size can be found. The idea of minimizing a total-cost equation is basic to all lot-sizing formulas and situations. For example, the supplement to this chapter shows the total cost equation and associated minimization procedure when price discounts are given for large orders.

Hewlett Packard has extended the total cost concept to its entire supply chain.[3] In producing personal computers (PCs) they identified four costs associated with supplying the PC market:

- Component devaluation costs.
- Price protection costs (lowest price guarantees given to retailers).
- Product return costs.
- Obsolescence costs (end of life write-off).

All of these costs are associated with the declining value of a PC once it is placed in inventory due to the risk of not selling the product before a new model is introduced to the market. These costs often exceed the profit margin on a product and must be aggressively managed by limiting the amount of inventory, as part of the total cost of supplying the market.

15.5 CONTINUOUS REVIEW SYSTEM

In practice, one of the most serious limitations of the EOQ model is the assumption of constant demand. In this section, we will relax this assumption and allow random demand. The result will be a model that is sufficiently flexible to use in practice for independent-demand inventory management. All other EOQ

[3] Callioni et al. (2005).

assumptions except constant demand and no stockouts will remain in effect. In this section, we will be assuming that the stock level is reviewed continuously; in Section 15.6, a periodic review model will be developed.

In inventory work, decisions to reorder stock are based on the total on-hand plus on-order quantity. On-order material is counted the same as on-hand for reorder decisions because the on-order material is scheduled to arrive, even if nothing more is done. The total of on-hand and on-order material is called **stock position,** or available stock. One should be careful on this point. A common mistake in inventory problems is failure to consider amounts already on order.

In a **continuous review system,** the stock position is monitored after each transaction, or continuously. When the stock position drops to a predetermined order point, or reorder point, a fixed quantity is placed on order. Since the order quantity is fixed, the time between orders will vary depending on the random nature of demand. The continuous review system is sometimes called the fixed-order quantity system and we call it the Q system, for convenience, here.

A formal definition of the Q-system decision rule follows:

> Continually review the stock position (on-hand plus on-order). When the stock position drops to the reorder point R, a fixed quantity Q is ordered.

A graph of the operation of this system is shown in Figure 15.7. The stock position drops on an irregular basis until it reaches the **reorder point** R, where an order for Q units is placed. The order arrives later, after a lead time L, and the cycle of usage, reorder, and stock receipt is then repeated.

The Q system is completely determined by the two parameters, Q and R. In practice, these parameters are set by using certain simplifying assumptions. First, Q is set equal to the EOQ value from Equation (15.2) by using the average demand for D. In more complicated models, Q and R must be determined simultaneously. Using the EOQ formula for Q is, however, a reasonable approximation provided that demand is not highly uncertain.

The value of R can be based on either stockout cost or stockout probability. Formulations that utilize stockout cost, however, become quite complicated mathematically, and the stockout cost is difficult to estimate anyway. Therefore, **stockout probability** is commonly used as a basis to determine R.

A widely used term in inventory management is **service level,** which is the percentage of customer demands satisfied from inventory. Service level is also called the fill rate. A 100 percent service level represents meeting all customer demands from inventory. The stockout percentage is equal to 100 minus service level.

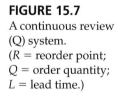

FIGURE 15.7
A continuous review (Q) system.
(R = reorder point; Q = order quantity; L = lead time.)

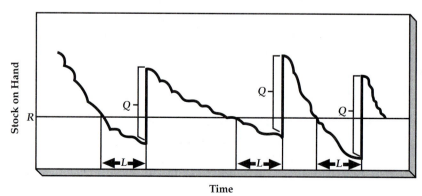

FIGURE 15.8
Probability
distribution of
demand over lead
time. (*m* = mean
demand; *R* = reorder
point; *s* = safety
stock.)

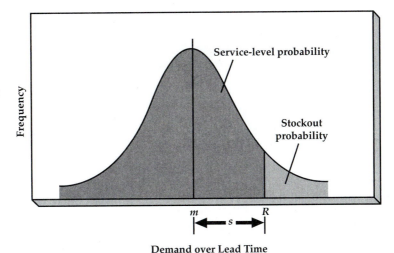

There are several different ways to express service level:

1. Service level is the probability that all orders will be filled from stock during the replenishment lead time of one reorder cycle.
2. Service level is the percentage of demand filled from stock during a given period of time (e.g., a year).
3. Service level is the percentage of time the system has stock on hand.

Each of these definitions of service level will lead to different reorder points. Furthermore, one must determine whether to count customers, units, or orders when applying any of these definitions. In this text, for the sake of simplicity, only the first definition of service level will be used.[4]

The reorder point is based on the notion of a probability distribution of demand over the lead time. When an order has been placed, the inventory system is exposed to stockout until the order arrives. Since the reorder point is usually greater than zero, it is reasonable to assume that the system does not run out of stock unless an order has been placed; the only risk of stockout is during replenishment lead time.

Figure 15.8 shows a typical probability distribution of independent demand over lead time. The reorder point in the figure can be set sufficiently high to reduce the stockout probability to any desired level. However, in calculating this probability, it will be necessary to know the statistical distribution of demand over the lead time. In the remainder of this discussion, we will assume a normal distribution of demand. This assumption is quite realistic for many independent-demand inventory problems.

The reorder point is defined as follows:

$$R = m + s \qquad\qquad (15.3)$$

where R = reorder point

m = mean (average) demand over the lead time

s = safety stock (or buffer stock)

---

[4] In this case, the percentage of orders filled from stock during a given period of time will be a function of the reorder frequency.

TABLE 15.1
Normal Demand
Percentages

z	Service Level (%)	Stockout (%)
0	50.0	50.0
.5	69.1	30.9
1.0	84.1	15.9
1.1	86.4	13.6
1.2	88.5	11.5
1.3	90.3	9.7
1.4	91.9	8.1
1.5	93.3	6.7
1.6	94.5	5.5
1.7	95.5	4.5
1.8	96.4	3.6
1.9	97.1	2.9
2.0	97.7	2.3
2.1	98.2	1.8
2.2	98.6	1.4
2.3	98.9	1.1
2.4	99.2	.8
2.5	99.4	.6
2.6	99.5	.5
2.7	99.6	.4
2.8	99.7	.3
2.9	99.8	.2
3.0	99.9	.1

We can express safety stock as

$$s = z\sigma$$

where z = safety factor

σ = standard deviation of demand over the lead time

Then we have

$$R = m + z\sigma$$

Thus, the reorder point is set equal to the average demand over lead time m plus a specified number of standard deviations σ to protect against stockout. By controlling z, the number of standard deviations used, one can control not only the reorder point but also the service level. A high value of z will result in a high reorder point and a high service level.

The percentages in Table 15.1 are from the normal distribution. These percentages represent the probability that the demand will fall within the specified number of standard deviations from the mean. Given a particular service level desired, it will be possible to determine z from Table 15.1 and then the reorder point.

Example

An example might help cement some of these ideas. Suppose we are managing a warehouse that distributes a certain type of breakfast food to retailers. The breakfast food has the following characteristics:

Average demand = 200 cases per day
Lead time = 4 days for resupply from the vendor
Standard deviation of daily demand = 150 cases
Desired service level = 95%
S = $20 per order
i = 20% per year
C = $10 per case

Assume that a continuous review system will be used and that the warehouse is open five days a week, 50 weeks a year, or 250 days a year. Then average annual demand = 250(200) = 50,000 cases per year.

The economic order quantity is

$$Q = \sqrt{\frac{2(20)(250)(200)}{10(.20)}} = \sqrt{10^6} = 1,000 \text{ cases}$$

The average demand over the lead time is 200 cases a day for four days; therefore, $m = 4(200) = 800$ cases. The standard deviation of demand over the lead time is $\sqrt{4}(150) = 300$ units.[5]

The 95 percent level requires a safety factor of $z = 1.65$ (see Table 15.1). Thus, we have

$$R = m + z\sigma = 800 + 1.65(300) = 1,295$$

The Q-system decision rule is to place an order for 1,000 cases whenever the stock position drops to 1,295 cases. On average, 50 orders will be placed per year, and there will be an average of five working days between orders. The actual time between orders will vary, however, depending on demand.

To complete this example, Table 15.2 simulates the operation of the Q-system decision rule. Here a series of random demands were generated on the basis of an average of 200 cases per day and a standard deviation of 150 cases per day. It is assumed that 1,100 units are on hand at the beginning of the simulation and none are on order. An order for 1,000 cases is placed whenever the stock position reaches 1,295 units. The stock position is reviewed each day, as demands occur, for a possible order. The result is that orders are placed in periods 1, 7, 10, and 15. The lowest inventory level is 285 units at the beginning of day 10. It will be good practice to verify the numbers in part of the box.

---

[5] The standard deviation of demand over the four-day lead time can be computed from the daily standard deviation by assuming that the daily demands are independent. In this case, the variance is additive and the variance for four days is four times the daily variance. This equates to $\sigma^2 = 4(150)^2$ or $\sigma = \sqrt{4}(150)$.

TABLE 15.2
A Q-System Example*

Day	Demand	Beginning Period on Hand	Beginning Period on Order	Beginning Period Stock Position	Amount Ordered	Amount Received
1	111	1,100	—	1,100	1,000	
2	217	989	1,000	1,989		
3	334	772	1,000	1,772		
4	124	438	1,000	1,438		
5	0	1,314	—	1,314	—	1,000
6	371	1,314	—	1,314		
7	135	943	—	943	1,000	
8	208	808	1,000	1,808		
9	315	600	1,000	1,600		
10	0	285	1,000	1,285	1,000	
11	440	1,285	1,000	2,285	—	1,000
12	127	845	1,000	1,845		
13	315	718	1,000	1,718		
14	114	1,403	—	1,403	—	1,000
15	241	1,289	—	1,289	1,000	
16	140	1,048	1,000	2,048		

*For this table, we have used $Q = 1,000$ and $R = 1,295$.

15.6 PERIODIC REVIEW SYSTEM

In some cases, the finished-goods stock position is reviewed periodically rather than continuously. Suppose a supplier will only take orders and make deliveries at periodic intervals, for example, every two weeks, as his truck makes the rounds to your store. In this case, the stock position is reviewed every two weeks and an order is placed if material is needed.

In this section, we are assuming that the stock position is reviewed periodically and the demand is random. All EOQ assumptions in Section 15.4 except constant demand and no stockouts will remain in effect.

In a **periodic review system,** the stock position is reviewed at fixed intervals. When the review is made, the stock position is "ordered up" to a target inventory level. The **target level** is set to cover demand until the next periodic review plus the delivery lead time. A variable quantity is ordered depending on how much is needed to bring the stock position up to target. The periodic review system is often called the fixed-order-interval system or the fixed-order-period system. We call it the P system, for convenience, here.

A formal definition of the P-system rule follows:

> Review the stock position (on-hand plus on-order) at fixed periodic intervals P. An amount equal to target inventory T minus the stock position is ordered at each review.

A graph of the operation of this system is shown in Figure 15.9. The stock position drops on an irregular basis until the fixed review time is reached. At that time, a quantity is ordered to bring the stock position up to the target level. The order arrives later, after a lead time L, then the cycle of usage, reorder, and stock receipt repeats.

The P system functions in a completely different manner than the Q system because (1) it does not have a reorder point but rather a target inventory; (2) it does not have an economic order quantity since the quantity varies according to demand; and (3) in the P system, the order interval is fixed, not the order quantity.

The P system is completely determined by the two parameters, P and T. An approximation to the optimal value of P can be made by using the EOQ formula in Equation (15.2). Since P is the time between orders, it is related to the EOQ as follows:

$$P = Q/D$$

FIGURE 15.9
A periodic review system.

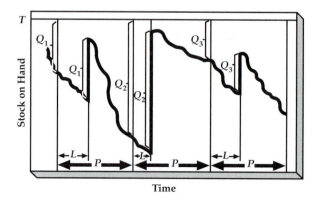

Time

Then, substituting the EOQ formula for Q, we have

$$P = \frac{Q}{D} = \frac{1}{D}\sqrt{\frac{2DS}{iC}} = \sqrt{\frac{2S}{iCD}} \qquad \textbf{(15.4)}$$

Equation (15.4) provides an approximately optimal review interval P.[6]

The target inventory level can be set by a specified service level. In this case, the target inventory is set high enough to cover demand over the lead time plus review period. This coverage time is needed because stock will not be ordered again until the next review period, and that stock will take the lead time to arrive. To achieve the specified service level, demand must be covered over the time $P + L$ at the average level plus a safety stock. Thus, we have

$$T = m' + s' \qquad \textbf{(15.5)}$$

where T = target inventory level

$\qquad m'$ = average demand over $P + L$

$\qquad s'$ = safety stock

The safety stock should be set high enough to ensure the desired service level. For safety stock, we have

$$s' = z\sigma'$$

where σ' = the standard deviation of demand over $P + L$

$\qquad z$ = safety factor

By controlling z, we can control the target inventory and the resulting service level provided.

Example

To illustrate, we will use the breakfast food example from the last section. Recall that the EOQ was 1,000 cases and the daily demand 200 cases. The optimal review interval is then

$$P = Q/D = 1{,}000/200 = 5 \text{ days}$$

The formula for target inventory is

$$T = m' + z\sigma'$$

In this case, m' is the average demand over $P + L = 5 + 4 = 9$ days. Thus, we have $m' = 9(200) = 1{,}800$. The standard deviation σ' is for the period $P + L = 9$ days. Thus, we have $\sigma' = \sqrt{9}(150) = 450$, where 150 is the daily standard deviation and 9 is the number of days.

Therefore,

$$T = 1{,}800 + z(450)$$

For a service level of 95 percent, we need $z = 1.65$. Thus,

$$T = 1{,}800 + 1.65(450) = 2{,}542$$

The P-system decision rule is to review the stock position every five days and order up to a target of 2,542 cases.

It is interesting to note, at this point, that the P system requires $1.65(450) = 742$ units of safety stock, while the same service level is provided by the Q system with only $1.65(300) = 495$ units of safety stock. The P system always requires more safety stock than a Q system for the same service level. This occurs because the P system must provide coverage over a time of $P + L$, while the Q system must protect against stockout only over the time L.

---

[6] When demand is highly uncertain, the approximation may be quite poor.

TABLE 15.3
A P-System
Example*

Day	Demand	Beginning Period on Hand	Beginning Period on Order	Beginning Period Stock Position	Amount Ordered	Amount Received
1	111	1,100	—	1,100	1,442	
2	217	989	1,442	2,431		
3	334	772	1,442	2,214		
4	124	438	1,442	1,880		
5	0	1,756	—	1,756	—	1,442
6	371	1,756	—	1,756	786	
7	135	1,385	786	2,171		
8	208	1,250	786	2,036		
9	315	1,042	786	1,828		
10	0	1,513	—	1,513	—	786
11	440	1,513	—	1,513	1,029	
12	127	1,073	1,029	2,102		
13	315	946	1,029	1,975		
14	114	631	1,029	1,660		
15	241	1,546	—	1,546	—	1,029
16	140	1,305	—	1,305	1,237	

*For this table, we have used $P = 5$ and $T = 2,542$.

This example is completed by Table 15.3, which uses the same demand figures as Table 15.2. Here, however, the review is periodic instead of continuous. A review is made in periods 1, 6, 11, and 16—that is, every five periods. The amounts ordered are 1,442, 786, 1,029, and 1,237. While the review period is fixed, the amount ordered is not.

15.7 USING P AND Q SYSTEMS IN PRACTICE

In industry, both Q and P systems, as well as modifications of them, are in wide use for independent-demand inventory management. Examples of independent demand inventories are in wholesale, retail, restaurants, hospitals, factory finished goods, and MRO inventories. The choice between Q and P systems is not a simple one and may be dictated by management practices as well as economics. There are, however, some conditions under which the P system may be preferred over the Q system:

1. The P system should be used when orders must be placed or delivered at specified intervals. An example is weekly order and delivery of canned goods to a grocery store. See the Operations Leader box for the weekly P system used by Target Stores.

2. The P system should be used when multiple items are ordered from the same supplier and delivered in the same shipment. In this case, the supplier would prefer consolidation of the items into a single order. An example is different colors of paint that might be ordered from a paint supplier. The supplier would then deliver at fixed times instead of delivering the different colors of paint at different times.

3. The P system should be used for inexpensive items that are not maintained on perpetual inventory records. An example is nuts or bolts used in a manufacturing process. In this case, the bins may be filled up daily or weekly. The bin size determines the target inventory, and the bin is filled up to target at fixed intervals. No records need be kept of each disbursement and receipt into inventory.

One of the most advanced inventory management practitioners is the highly successful Target chain.

With more than 1,300 stores carrying an average of 50,000 items each, Target, headquartered in Minneapolis, needs to make billions of decisions a year to keep shelves full enough to appear presentable while also avoiding costly overstocks.

"We couldn't do it without technology," said Richard Maguire, the chain's senior vice president for merchandise planning. Each Saturday night, Target's computerized system forecasts how much of every item in every store will be needed and then on Sunday automatically generates orders for these products to the chain's suppliers. Several of the suppliers will get an order on Monday, ship goods on Tuesday, and have them in Target stores by the end of the week.

From an average of 27 days in the late 1980s, Target has slashed its supplier-to-store period to 12 days now and plans to cut it in half again the next five years.

"That reduction in lead time means less inventory in the stores and reduces markdowns, so it enables us to have the most competitive prices," Maguire said. And, he said, merchants who had been "a little hesitant" to sign up for such swift response now embrace it, even "coming to us with ways" to move still faster. Primarily because of the improved efficiencies in the supply chain, Target stores now hold 10 percent less inventory than they did just a year ago, he said.

Source: *Star and Tribune,* December 28, 1996; and www.target.com, 2005.

STORE INVENTORY. Retail inventory replenishment utilizes a reorder point or periodic review system. © Michael Newman/PhotoEdit

In sum, the P system provides the advantage of scheduled replenishment and less record keeping. It requires, however, a somewhat larger safety stock than the Q system, as the last example illustrates. Because of this larger safety stock, the Q system is often used for expensive items where it is desirable to hold down the investment in safety stock inventory. The choice between the Q and P systems should, therefore, be made on the basis of timing of replenishment, the type of record-keeping system in use, and the cost of the item.

In practice, one also finds hybrid systems that are mixtures of P and Q inventory rules. One of these systems is characterized by min/max decision rules and periodic review. In this case, the system has both a reorder point (min) and a target (max). When the periodic review is made, no order is placed if the stock position is above the min. If the stock position is below min, an order is placed to raise the stock position to the max level.

Service Level and Inventory Level

There is an important trade-off between service level and inventory level. In the management of independent-demand inventories, one of the key considerations is customer-service levels. But customer-service levels must be balanced against investment in inventory, since higher customer-service levels require higher inventory investments. The average inventory level I is given by

$$I = Q/2 + z\sigma$$

The reasoning behind this formula is that $Q/2$ units are carried on average owing to ordering in lots of size Q, and $z\sigma$ units are carried on average owing to safety stocks. (In the case of the P system, use σ' in place of σ.) Thus, the inventory level is the sum of cycle stock ($Q/2$) and safety stock ($z\sigma$) components.

For a fixed Q and σ, the inventory level will be a function of z, which in turn also determines the service level. Thus, for given values of z, one can plot service level versus the average inventory required. Such a plot is shown in Figure 15.10.

The figure indicates that an increasing inventory level is required to achieve higher service levels. As the service level approaches 100 percent, very large inventories are required. This happens because we are assuming normally distributed demand over the lead time, and we must cover very unlikely events as the probability approaches 100 percent.

Due to the highly nonlinear relationship, it is crucial for management to compare the service-level graph with that of the inventory level before setting a service level. Selection of an arbitrary service level may be very costly since the difference of a few percentage points in service level could substantially increase the required inventory level. For instance, in Figure 15.10, an increase in service level from 95 to 99 percent (four percentage points) requires a 32 percent increase in inventory. It is, therefore, essential that management study the service level and inventory trade-offs in each situation.

The relationship between service level and inventory level helps to determine appropriate inventory turnovers. Inventory turnover can be measured by dividing the cost of goods sold by the average inventory over a specific period of time.

FIGURE 15.10
Service level versus inventory level.
($Q = 100; \sigma = 100.$)

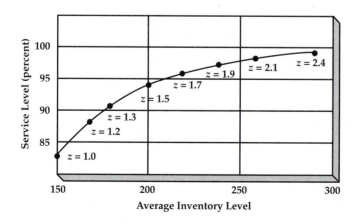

Suppose a firm is compared with its industry or with itself over time and turnover is now low. This lower turnover could be explained by either higher service levels or different ordering and holding costs. Management should look beyond turnover to the service-level policy or the cost structure inherent in the situation. On the basis of better customer service or different cost structures, management may prefer a policy that leads to turnovers that are lower than the industry norm.

Management can also choose to reduce Q and σ, thereby reducing the inventory required for a given service level. This is in line with current thinking about reduction of inventories and continuous improvement. The lot size Q can be reduced by reducing setup time (or ordering costs), as described in Chapter 17. The standard deviation of demand over the lead time can be reduced by decreasing the daily variation in demand or by decreasing the lead time. Daily variation in demand can be reduced by working with customers to smooth out demand and reduce uncertainty in their ordering patterns. Lead time can be reduced by decreasing the throughput time in the production and distribution process. How inventories have been reduced using these and other practical ideas is shown in the Operations Leader box about Subaru of New England.

15.8 ABC INVENTORY MANAGEMENT

In 1906, Vilfredo Pareto observed that a few items in any group constitute the significant proportion of the entire group.[7] At that time he was concerned that a few individuals in the economy seemed to earn most of the income. It can also be observed that a few products in a firm result in most of the sales and that, in volunteer organizations, a few people do most of the work. The law of the significant few can be applied to inventory management as well.

In inventories, a few items usually account for most of the inventory value as measured by dollar usage (demand times cost). Thus, one can manage these few items intensively and control most of the inventory value. In inventory work, the items are usually divided into three classes: A, B, and C. Class A typically contains about 20 percent of the items and 80 percent of the dollar usage. It therefore represents the most significant few. At the other extreme, class C contains 50 percent of the items and only 5 percent of the dollar usage. These items contribute very little of the dollar value of inventory. In the middle is class B, with 30 percent of the items and 15 percent of the dollar usage. The classification of inventory in this way is often called **ABC analysis** or the **80–20 rule.**

Table 15.4 is an example of an inventory with 10 items. In this case, items 3 and 6 account for a great deal of the dollar usage (73.2 percent). On the other hand, items 1, 5, 7, 8, and 10 are low in dollar usage (10.5 percent). The ABC principle, therefore, applies to this small example.

The designation of three classes is arbitrary; there could be any number of classes. Also, the exact percentage of items in each class will vary from one inventory to the next. The important factors are the two extremes: a few items that are significant and a large number of items that are relatively insignificant.

Most of the dollar usage in inventory (80 percent) can be controlled by closely monitoring the A items (20 percent). For these items, a tight control system might be used, including continuous review of stock levels, less safety stock, and close attention to record accuracy.

[7] Vilfredo Pareto, *Manual of Political Economy,* Ann A. Schwier (trans.), New York, A. M. Kelly, 1971.

OPERATIONS LEADER
Subaru Distributor Reduces Inventory by 44 Percent

A Web-based service parts logistics system reduced inventory and improved customer service for Subaru of New England, a privately owned distributorship with 60 franchised dealers that sell and service Subaru products in the New England region. To replace its legacy system, Subaru of New England needed a new inventory-planning system that would manage thousands of service parts needed to service its dealers. The new software covered every aspect of service-parts planning, including demand forecasting, optimal stock-level setting, and identification of excess inventory and critical shortages. Comprehensive "what-if" analysis enabled management to balance the trade-off between service and investment. In addition the software recommended which parts should be ordered, repaired, and replenished at any point in time.

Sean Perry, senior inventory control manager, said, "When the inventory drops to the reorder point based on lead-times, that part will show up on the Procurement screen suggesting that it be reordered. Another screen that I really find useful is the Critical Shortage screen. With this screen I can see if I'm in danger of running out of certain parts. I can then place a special air order or contact the vendor to expedite a partial delivery of the parts so that I can get a sufficient quantity in our warehouse until the complete parts order arrives. The Excess Inventory screen is also critical in my day-to-day business because it shows all the parts with quantities over a specified threshold. I can then try to get the vendor to buy back these parts or slash the prices to move the excess inventory.

"Not only have we reduced our inventory level by 44 percent, but we also increased our fill rate and dramatically simplified ordering," said Perry. "For example, we used to carry more than 100,000 oil filters in inventory, a number that has now been reduced to about 24,000 for a savings of around 76 percent. In addition, we increased our first-pass fill rate from 80 to 90 percent and decreased inventory processing time from 4–5 days to less than a day." In another three months, Subaru of New England plans to reduce inventory levels by a total of 50 percent while increasing its first pass yield to 95 percent.

Source: Abstracted from "New England Distributor Reduces Inventory Levels by 44 Percent," *APICS—The Performance Advantage*, March 2001.

TABLE 15.4
Annual Usage of Items by Dollar Value

Item	Annual Usage in Units	Unit Cost	Dollar Usage	Percentage of Total Dollar Usage
1	5,000	$ 1.50	$ 7,500	2.9%
2	1,500	8.00	12,000	4.7
3	10,000	10.50	105,000	41.2
4	6,000	2.00	12,000	4.7
5	7,500	.50	3,750	1.5
6	6,000	13.60	81,600	32.0
7	5,000	.75	3,750	1.5
8	4,500	1.25	5,625	2.2
9	7,000	2.50	17,500	6.9
10	3,000	2.00	6,000	2.4
Total			$254,725	100.0%

On the other hand, looser control might be used for C items. A periodic review system could be used to consolidate orders from the same supplier, and less record accuracy might be sufficient. Even manual systems might be used for C items. The B items require an intermediate level of attention and management control.

With computerized systems, a uniform level of control is sometimes used for all items. Nevertheless, managing inventories still requires setting priorities, and the ABC concept is often useful in doing this.

15.9   KEY POINTS

Inventory management is a key operations responsibility because it greatly affects capital requirements, costs, and customer service. This chapter provides an overview of inventory management and specific methods for the management of independent-demand inventories.

The chapter's major points include the following:

- Inventory is a stock of materials used to facilitate production or to satisfy customer demands. Inventories include raw materials, work in process, and finished goods.

- A decision rule specifies how much to order and when. In the calculation of decision rules, there are four types of inventory costs to consider: item cost, ordering (or setup) cost, carrying (or holding) cost, and stockout cost. The relevant costs to include are those that vary with the decision to be made.

- The economic order quantity assumptions include a constant demand rate, constant lead time, fixed setup time, no stockouts, lot ordering, no discounts, and a single product. Within the assumptions made, the EOQ formula minimizes the sum of holding and ordering costs.

- Any inventory problem can be solved for the optimum order quantity by using the total cost concept to minimize the appropriate sum of costs for the assumptions that apply to that particular situation.

- A continuous review system provides one way to handle random demand. When the stock position drops to the reorder point R, a fixed quantity Q is ordered. The time between orders will vary depending on actual demand. The value of Q is set equal to the EOQ. The value of R is based on the service level desired.

- A periodic review system provides another way to handle random demand. The stock position is reviewed at fixed intervals P, and an amount is ordered equal to the target inventory T minus stock position. The amount ordered at each review period will vary depending on actual demand. The value of P is set by use of the EOQ, and the value of T is based on the service level desired.

- The choice between P and Q systems should be based on the timing of replenishment, type of record keeping, and cost of the item. A periodic system should be used when inventory orders must be regularly scheduled.
- High service levels require high investment levels for a given order quantity (Q) and standard deviation (σ). Management should, therefore, study the service level and investment relationship before setting the service levels desired. Comparisons of turnover ratios do not, by themselves, provide an adequate basis for decisions on inventory level. Also, management should seek to continuously reduce Q and σ.
- The ABC inventory concept is based on the significant few and the insignificant many. The concept should be used to carefully control the significant A items and to spend less effort and cost on the B and C items.

SOLVED PROBLEMS

Problem

1. **EOQ**   In a hardware warehouse, the independent demand for a commonly used bolt is 500 units per month. The ordering cost is $30 per order placed. The carrying cost is 25 percent per year and each unit costs $.50.
   a. Based on the EOQ formula, what lot size should this product have?
   b. How often should this product be purchased?
   c. A quality team has found a way to reduce ordering costs to $5. How will that change the lot size and the frequency of purchasing for this product?

Solution

First, convert demand to the same time units as the carrying cost. In this case, the carrying cost is in years and demand is in months. The annual demand is $500 \times 12 = 6,000$ units.

a. $Q = \sqrt{\dfrac{2SD}{iC}}$

$= \sqrt{\dfrac{2 \times 30 \times 6{,}000}{.25 \times .50}}$

$= \sqrt{\dfrac{360{,}000}{.125}}$

$= 1697.06 \rightarrow 1{,}697$ units

b. The annual frequency of procurement = D/Q or $6{,}000/1{,}697 = 3.54$ times per year. To convert to months, divide 12 months per year by the annual frequency of procurement.

$\dfrac{12}{3.54} = $ every 3.39 months

$\dfrac{52}{3.54} = $ every 14.69 weeks

$\dfrac{365}{3.54} = $ every 103.11 days

c. $Q = \sqrt{\dfrac{2SD}{iC}}$

$= \sqrt{\dfrac{2 \times 5 \times 6{,}000}{25 \times .50}}$

$= \sqrt{\dfrac{60{,}000}{.125}}$

$= 692.8 \rightarrow 693$ units

The frequency of procurement = D/Q or $6{,}000/693 = 8.66$ times per year.

Problem

2. **Q System** Part number XB-2001 has an annual independent demand as spare parts of 4,000 units, a setup cost of $100, a carrying cost of 30 percent per year, and an item cost of $266.67. The production facility is open five days per week and 50 weeks per year, making a total of 250 productive days per year. The lead time for this product is nine days and the standard deviation of demand is two units per day. The company wants to have a 95 percent service level for this spare part.

a. Compute Q, using the EOQ formula.

b. Compute R.

c. If the company were using a Q system of inventory control (continuous review), interpret the results of your computations.

Solution

a. $Q = \text{EOQ}$

$= \sqrt{\dfrac{2SD}{iC}}$

$= \sqrt{\dfrac{2 \times 100 \times 4{,}000}{.3 \times 266.67}}$

$= \sqrt{10{,}000}$

$= 100$

b. Solving this part of the problem correctly requires two steps. First, the daily demand must be calculated. This is done by dividing the annual rate of demand by the number of working days per year—4,000/250 = 16 units per day. Thus, the average demand over lead time is 16 units per day over 9 days or 9 × 16 = 144 units. Second, the standard deviation of demand during lead time must be calculated. This is determined by taking the standard deviation of daily demand (two units) and multiplying by the square root of the number of days of lead time (the square root of 9).

$$R = m + z(\text{s.d. demand during lead time})$$
$$= (9 \times 16) + 1.65 \times (2 \times \sqrt{9})$$
$$= 144 + 9.9$$
$$= 153.9 \to 154 \text{ units}$$

c. Order 100 units when inventory (on hand plus on order) gets down to 154 units. On the average, 9.9 units of safety stock will be on hand when the order arrives. In 5 percent of the cases, there will be a stockout before the order arrives.

Problem

3. **P System** Consider the product described in solved problem 2 when answering the following questions:

a. How often should orders be placed for this product, if they are placed at regular intervals using a periodic review system?

b. Compute the target inventory level.

c. State the specific decision rule for this product using the information you have calculated thus far.

d. Assume it is time for a periodic review. A check of the inventory level for this product reveals that there are 60 units on hand and there are 110 units on order. What should be done?

Solution

a. $P = \dfrac{Q}{D}$ (use Q and D from the previous problem)

$$= \frac{100}{4,000}$$
$$= .025 \text{ year}$$
$$= 1.25 \text{ working weeks } (.025 \text{ year} \times 50 \text{ working weeks per year})$$
$$= 6.25 \text{ days } (0.25 \text{ year} \times 250 \text{ working days per year})$$
$$= 6 \text{ days (round off)}$$

b. $T = m' + s'$
$$= m' + z(\text{s.d. of demand during } P + L)$$
$$= (\text{average demand over } P + L) + z(\text{s.d. of demand during } P + L)$$
$$= 16 \times (6 + 9) + 1.65 \times (2 \times \sqrt{9 + 6})$$
$$= 240 + 12.8$$
$$= 252.8 \to 253$$

c. Review stock (on hand and on order) every six days and order up to a target level of 253 units.

d. Order up to the target level. The target level is 253 units. The amount of inventory on hand and on order is 60 + 110 units or 170 units total. The difference between the target level and the inventory on hand and on order is the quantity which should be ordered for delivery in nine days, 253 − (60 + 110) = 83. Order 83 units for delivery in nine days.

Discussion Questions

1. Identify the different types of inventories (raw materials, work in process, and finished goods) carried in the following organizations: gas station, hamburger stand, clothing store, and machine shop. What functions (purposes) do these inventories perform?

2. Consider the following types of items carried in a retail store: light bulbs, compact discs, and refrigerated drugs. Discuss the probable cost structure for each of these items, including item cost, carrying cost, ordering cost, and stockout cost.

3. Why is stockout cost difficult to determine? Suggest an approach that might be used to estimate it.

4. Why can the item cost be dropped from the simple EOQ formula? Are item costs important when quantity discounts are given? Why?

5. What is the difference between a requirements philosophy and a replenishment philosophy of inventory management? Why is this difference important?

6. Compare and contrast the management of finished-goods inventory in a manufacturing company with that in a retail or wholesale firm.

7. For a given service level, why will a P system require a larger inventory investment than a Q system? What factors affect the magnitude of the difference?

8. Suppose you were managing the Speedy Hardware Store. Give examples of items that might be managed by a P system and other items that might use a Q system. How do these items differ?

9. How should a manager decide on the appropriate service level for finished-goods items? Should some items have a 100 percent service level?

10. A manager was heard to complain, "I have some items that have a two-week review interval, and it takes four weeks for resupply. Every two weeks, I place orders based on the on-hand quantity in stock. Now I seem to have too much inventory." What went wrong?

11. A student was overheard saying, "The EOQ-model assumptions are so restrictive that the model would be hard to use in practice." Is it necessary to have a different model for each variation in assumptions? Why or why not?

12. What is the appropriate role of turnover criteria for managing inventory? Under what circumstances is high turnover detrimental to the firm?

13. Suppose you were managing a chain of retail department stores. The inventory in each store is computerized, but there are a large number of different items. As a top manager, how would you measure the overall inventory management performance of each store? How would you use this information in your relationship with the individual store managers?

Problems

1. The Speedy Grocery Store carries a particular brand of coffee that has the following characteristics:

   Sales = 10 cases per week
   Ordering cost = $10 per order
   Carrying charge = 30 percent per year
   Item cost = $80 per case

   a. How many cases should be ordered at a time?
   b. How often will coffee be ordered?
   c. What is the annual cost of ordering and carrying coffee?
   d. What factors might cause the company to order a larger or smaller amount than the EOQ?

2. The Grinell Machine Shop makes a line of metal tables for customers. Some of these tables are carried in finished-goods inventory. A particular table has the following characteristics:

   Sales = 200 per year
   Setup cost = $1,200 per setup (this includes machine setup for all the different parts in the table)
   Carrying cost = 20 percent per year
   Item cost = $25

   a. How many of these tables should be made in a production lot?
   b. How often will production be scheduled?

c. What factors might cause the company to schedule a different lot size than you have computed?

3. The local Toyota dealer has to decide how many spare shock absorbers of a particular type to order for repairing Toyota automobiles. This shock absorber has a demand of four units per month and they cost $25 each. The carrying charge is 20 percent per year and the ordering cost is $15 per order.

a. What is the EOQ for this item?

b. How often will the dealer reorder this part?

c. What is the annual cost of ordering and carrying this part?

 4. What is the effect on EOQ and total cost of the following types of errors for the data in problem 1?

a. A 50 percent increase in demand.

b. A 50 percent increase in carrying charge.

c. Use a spreadsheet to study the relationship between lot size and carrying cost.

5. The famous Widget Company sells widgets at the rate of 100,000 units per year. Each widget sells for $100, and it costs 30 percent to carry widgets in inventory for a year. The process of widget production has been automated over the years, and it now costs $1,000 to change over the widget production line to other products which are made on the same line.

a. What is the economical lot size for production of widgets?

b. How many lots will be produced each year?

c. What is the annual cost of carrying widgets and the annual cost of changeover?

d. What factors or changes in assumptions might cause the Widget Company to produce a larger lot than the economic lot size calculated in part *a?*

6. The Harvard Co-op orders sweatshirts with the Harvard University emblem on them for sale at $50 each. During a typical month, 1,000 sweatshirts are sold (this includes all styles and sizes ordered from a particular supplier). It costs $25 to place an order (for multiple sizes and styles) and 25 percent to carry sweatshirts in inventory for a year.

a. How many sweatshirts should the Co-op order at one time?

b. The supplier would like to deliver sweatshirts once a week in larger lot sizes than the optimal order size. How much will this cost the Co-op per year? Under what conditions would you agree to the supplier's proposal?

c. Suppose that sales increase to 1,500 sweatshirts per month, but you decide to keep the lot size the same as in part *a.* How much will this decision cost the Co-op per year?

Excel Spreadsheet Tips

Four Excel spreadsheets are provided on the student CD-ROM for this chapter to assist students in solving the chapter problems. The spreadsheet for problem 8 is shown below with different data than problem 8 to illustrate its use. Standard inputs for the Q rule are shown in the input section of the spreadsheet including costs, sales, lead time, and service level. Outputs include the EOQ and reorder point.

	B	C	D	E	F	G	H	I
17	NAME:	Example				CHAPTER 15, PROBLEM 8		
18	SECT:	***************				DATE:		
19								
20								
21	INPUT SECTION:				OUTPUT SECTION:			
22	************	***************	***************		***************	***************	***************	************
23	ANNUAL SALES:		400			EOQ =	45	
24	ORDERING COST:		$50		REORDER POINT =		9.1	
25	CARRYING COST (%):		40%			z =	1.65	
26	ITEM COST:		$50		ORDER EVERY:		28.0	DAYS
27	STANDARD DEVIATION:		0.3		***************	***************	***************	************
28	WORKING DAYS/YEAR:		250					
29	LEAD TIME (DAYS):		5					
30	SERVICE LEVEL:		95%					
31	************	***************	***************					

7. The Co-op in problem 6 has discovered that it should establish a safety stock for its sweatshirts. It wants to use a reorder point system with a two-week lead time. The demand over a two-week interval can be assumed to have an average of 500 units and a standard deviation of 250 units.
   a. What reorder point should the Co-op establish to ensure a 95 percent service level for each order placed?
   b. What reorder point should be established to ensure that no more than one stockout occurs in the course of a year?
   c. How much average inventory will the Co-op carry for part *b?* Include both cycle inventory and safety stock in your answer.
   d. How often will the Co-op turn over its inventory using the results from part *c?*

8. An appliance store carries a certain brand of TV that has the following characteristics:

   Average annual sales = 200 units
   Ordering cost = $25 per order
   Carrying cost = 25 percent per year
   Item cost = $400 per unit
   Lead time = 4 days
   Standard deviation of daily demand =.1 unit
   Working days per year = 250
   a. Determine the EOQ.
   b. Calculate the reorder point for a 95 percent service level, assuming normal demand.
   c. State the Q rule for this item.
   d. Study the effect on reorder point of changes in lead time or in standard deviation.

9. For the data given in problem 8:
   a. Determine a P system of inventory control for a 95 percent service level. Compute the values of *P* and *T.*
   b. Compare the inventory investment required for the P system and the Q system from problem 8 for various values of service level.
   c. Why does the P system require a higher inventory investment?

10. The local Toyota dealer from problem 3 is considering installing either a Q or P system for inventory control. The past standard deviation of demand has been 2.5 units per month, and the replenishment lead time is two months. A 95 percent service level is desired.
   a. If a continuous review system is used, what is the value of *Q* and *R* that should be used?

   b. If a periodic review system is used, what is the value of *P* and *T* that would be applicable?
   c. What are the pros and cons of using the P system compared to using the Q system for this part?

11. The Suregrip Tire Company carries a certain type of tire with the following characteristics:

   Average annual sales = 500 tires
   Ordering cost = $40 per order
   Carrying cost = 25 percent per year
   Item cost = $40 per tire
   Lead time = 4 days
   Standard deviation of daily demand = 1 tire
   a. Calculate the EOQ.
   b. For a Q system of inventory control, calculate the safety stock required for service levels of 85, 90, 95, 97, and 99 percent.
   c. Construct a plot of inventory investment versus service level.
   d. What service level would you establish on the basis of the graph in part *c?* Discuss.

12. For the data in problem 11:
   a. Calculate the annual turnover as a function of service level.
   b. If sales were to increase by 50 percent, what would happen to the turnover at a 95 percent service level?

13. The Easyfoot Carpet Company carries three types of carpet with the following characteristics:

Type	Annual Demand (yards)	Item Cost per Yard
A	300	$10
B	200	8
C	100	6

Assume that the items are to be ordered together from the same supplier at an ordering cost of $20 per order and an annual carrying cost of 20 percent. Also assume 300 working days in a year.
   a. Using a P system, what is the optimal ordering interval in days?
   b. How much of each type of carpet would be ordered when a combined order is placed?
   c. What is the effect on ordering interval of changing the carrying cost to 25, 30, and 35 percent?
   d. Why can't these carpets be ordered by a Q system?

14. Suppose that you are the supplier of the Easyfoot Carpet Company described in problem 13. It costs $2,000 each time you change over

your carpet-producing machine from one type of carpet to another (A, B, or C). Assume that your carrying cost is 30 percent and the other data are as given in problem 13.

a. What lot sizes would the supplier of carpet prefer to make for types A, B, and C?

b. How would you reconcile the lot sizes that the supplier would like to produce and those that the Easyfoot Carpet Company would like to buy? Mention several ways that these two differing lot sizes can be reconciled.

Selected Bibliography

Arnold, J. R. Tony. *Introduction to Materials Management,* 5th ed. Upper Saddle River, NJ: Prentice Hall, 2003.

Callioni, G., X. deMontgros, R. Shagriulder, L. Van Wassenhove, and L. Wright. "Inventory Driven Costs." *Harvard Business Review,* March 2005, pp. 135–41.

Doucette, Larissa. "Making the Most of Inventory Management." *Foodservice Equipment & Supplies* 54, no. 12 (December 2001), pp. 40–44.

Freund, Brian, and June Freund. "Hands-on VMI. " *APICS—The Performance Advantage,* March 2003, pp. 34–40.

Herring, Sean. "Inventory Management into the 21st Century." *Logistics & Transport Focus* 2, no. 7 (September 2000), pp. 43–46.

Landvater, Darryl V. *World Class Production and Inventory Management,* 2nd ed. New York: Wiley, 1997.

Pareto, Vilfredo. *Manual of Political Economy,* Ann A. Schwier (trans.). New York: A. M. Kelly, 1971.

Piasecki, Dave. "Optimizing Economic Order Quantity." *IIE Solutions* 33, no. 1 (January 2001), pp. 30–35.

Schroeder, Roger G. "Managerial Inventory Formulations with Stockout Objectives and Fiscal Constraints." *Naval Research Logistics Quarterly* 21, no. 3 (September 1974), pp. 375–88.

———. "Return on Investment as a Criterion for Inventory Methods." *Decision Sciences* 7, no. 4 (October 1976), pp. 697–704.

Silver, Edward. H., David Pyke, and John Miltenburg. *Inventory Management and Production Planning and Scheduling,* 3rd ed. New York: Wiley, 1998.

Simchi-Levi, David, Philip Kaminsky, and Edith Simchi-Levi. *Designing and Managing the Supply Chain: Concepts, Strategies and Cases.* 2nd ed. New York: McGraw-Hill, 2002.

Tersine, Richard J. *Principles of Inventory and Materials Management,* 4th ed. Upper Saddle River, NJ: Prentice Hall, 1993.

Vollmann, Thomas E., William L. Berry, D. Clay Whybark, and F. Robert Jacobs. *Manufacturing Planning and Control for Supply Chain Management,* 5th ed. New York: McGraw-Hill, 2004.

Waters, Donald. *Inventory Control and Management,* 2nd ed. New York: Wiley, 2003.

Wild, Tony. *Best Practice in Inventory Management.* New York: Wiley, 1998.

Advanced Models

This supplement presents two additional models that are useful for independent inventory demands. The first model applies to outside procurement where price discounts are given; the second applies to a gradual fill of inventory when the lot arrives uniformly over time, not all at once.

PRICE BREAKS

Outside suppliers often offer price discounts for large purchases. These discounts may be given at different procurement levels, and they may apply either to the whole order or only to the increment purchased. In this supplement, we assume that the price discounts apply to the entire procurement order. For example, the procurement price may be $2 per unit for 0 to 99 units and $1.50 per unit for 100 units and up. The cost of the units thus exhibits a jump or discontinuity at 100 units. For 99 units, the cost of the procurement order is $198, and for 100 units the cost is $150.

To solve for the economic order quantity, the procedure is to first calculate the EOQ for each different procurement price. Some of these EOQs may not be feasible because the EOQ falls outside the range of the price used to compute it. The infeasible EOQs are eliminated from further consideration. The total procurement and inventory operating cost for each feasible EOQ and each price-break quantity is then computed. The feasible EOQ or price break that results in the lowest total cost is then selected as the order quantity.

Consider the following example:

$$D = 1{,}000 \text{ units per year}$$
$$i = 20 \text{ percent per year}$$
$$S = \$10 \text{ per order}$$
$$C_1 = \$5 \text{ per unit for 0 to 199 units}$$
$$C_2 = \$4.50 \text{ per unit for 200 to 499 units}$$
$$C_3 = \$4.25 \text{ per unit for 500 units or more}$$

First calculate the three EOQs corresponding to the three values of C_i. We then obtain $Q_1 = 141$, $Q_2 = 149$, and $Q_3 = 153$. In this case, Q_2 and Q_3 are infeasible, and they are eliminated from further consideration. We then compute the total cost of procurement and inventory at the remaining EOQ and at the two price breaks. These total costs are as follows:*

$$\text{TC} = S\left(\frac{D}{Q}\right) + iC\left(\frac{Q}{2}\right) + CD$$
$$\text{TC}(141) = 10(^{1{,}000}/_{141}) + .20(5)(^{141}/_2) + 5(1{,}000)$$
$$= 5{,}141$$
$$\text{TC}(200) = 10(^{1{,}000}/_{200}) + .20(4.50)(^{200}/_2)$$
$$+ 4.50(1{,}000) = 4{,}640$$
$$\text{TC}(500) = 10(^{1{,}000}/_{500}) + .20(4.25)(^{500}/_2)$$
$$+ 4.25(1{,}000) = 4{,}482$$

* Note the annual cost *CD* of buying the units has been added to the cost equation since this cost will be affected by the discount.

FIGURE S15.1
Inventory cost with
price breaks.

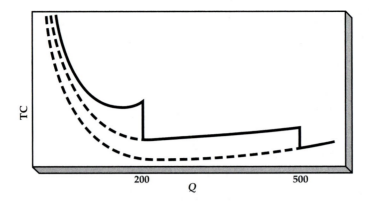

Since TC(500) is the lowest annual cost, 500 units should be ordered.

The cost behavior for the example is shown in Figure S15.1. Notice that at each price break the total cost is reduced. Therefore, the quantity at the highest price break is selected.

It is not always necessary to calculate all the EOQs and the cost at each point. A more efficient procedure follows:

1. Calculate the EOQ for the lowest cost per unit (the largest price-break quantity). If this EOQ is feasible, that is, above the price break, then the most economical quantity has been found.
2. If the EOQ is not feasible, use the next-lowest price and continue calculating EOQs until a feasible EOQ is found or until all prices have been used.
3. Next, calculate the total cost of the EOQ, if found, and the total cost at all the higher price breaks.
4. The minimum of these total costs indicates the most economic order quantity.

In the above example, this procedure would have resulted, by coincidence, in the same amount of calculation.

UNIFORM LOT DELIVERY

In some cases, the entire lot is not placed in inventory at one time but is delivered gradually. An example is a manufacturer that builds inventory at a constant production rate. Another example is a retailer that takes the lot in several shipments over a period of time.

The effect of this delivery condition on inventory is shown in Figure S15.2. The inventory level builds up gradually as both production and consumption occur. Then the inventory level is depleted as only consumption takes place.

The effect of gradual delivery is to reduce the maximum and average inventory level over that obtained in the simple EOQ case. Suppose units are produced at a rate of p units per year and consumed at a rate of D units per year (where $p > D$). Then the average inventory level will be

$$\frac{Q}{2}\left(1 - \frac{D}{p}\right)$$

This formula can be derived with the use of geometry by reference to Figure S15.2.

FIGURE S15.2
Uniform lot delivery.

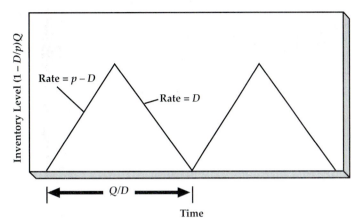

The above expression for average inventory is used in place of $Q/2$ in Equation (15.1). By minimizing the resulting expression for TC, the following EOQ formula is obtained:

$$Q = \sqrt{\frac{2SD}{iC(1 - D/p)}}$$

The EOQ in this case will always be somewhat larger than the ordinary EOQ because the factor $(1 - D/p)$ is less than 1. As p approaches D, the EOQ becomes very large, which means that production is continuous. When p is very large, the above EOQ formula approaches the ordinary EOQ. In deriving the ordinary EOQ, we assumed the entire lot arrived in inventory at once, which is equivalent to an infinite production rate p.

Supplement Problems

eXcel

1. Suppose that, for problem 1 in the chapter, the Speedy Grocery Store is offered a discount if more than 50 cases are ordered at a time. The unit item costs are $80 a case for 0 to 49 cases and $76 a case for 50 cases or more. This price of $76 applies to the entire order.

    a. Should the grocery store take the discount offer?

    b. What discount is required before the store is indifferent between taking the discount or ordering the EOQ?

2. A supplier has come to you and offered the following deal. If you buy 29 cases or less of cleaning solution, the cost will be $25 for each case. If you buy 30 or more cases, the cost will be $20 per case. Assume your cost of carrying inventory is 15 percent a year, it costs $20 for you to reorder the material, and you use 50 cases per year.

    a. How many cases should you order?

    b. Would you negotiate with this supplier for a further discount? Explain the quantities and prices

    that you would negotiate for and why these quantities and prices were selected.

3. For problem 2 in the chapter, suppose the Grinell Machine Shop produces its tables at a rate of two per day (250 working days per year).

    a. What is the optimal lot size?

    b. Draw a graph of on-hand inventory versus time.

    c. What is the maximum value of inventory?

4. A producer of electronic parts wants to take account of both production rate and demand rate in deciding on lot sizes. A particular $50 part can be produced at a rate of 1,000 units per month, and the demand rate is 200 units per month. The company uses a carrying charge of 24 percent a year, and the setup cost is $200 each time the part is produced.

    a. What lot size should be produced?

    b. If the production rate is ignored, what would the lot size be? How much does this smaller lot size cost the company on an annual basis?

    c. Draw a graph of on-hand inventory versus time.

Chapter **Sixteen**

Materials Requirements Planning

Chapter outline

Manufacturing organizations are required to deal with complexity because of numerous products, processes, parts, and uncertainties. The typical manufacturing company may have thousands of products and parts to manage, constantly shifting priorities and unpredicatable demand. However, all is not hopeless. It is possible to manage this situation through use of a computerized planning and control system called **materials requirements planning** (MRP).

Service organizations can also benefit from the use of MRP systems. Services such as restaurants, hospitals, and electric-power companies have large inventories of facilitating goods that support their service delivery systems. These inventories are difficult to manage and also require sophisticated inventory management approaches.

MRP derives its power from the very important distinction between independent-demand and dependent-demand inventories. In Chapter 15, we defined **independent-demand** inventories as those that are subject to market conditions and are thus independent of operations. Examples of independent-demand inventories are finished goods and spare parts in a manufacturing company that are used to satisfy final customer demand along with distribution inventories in retail, wholesale, and hospitals. These inventories should be managed by the order-point methods described in the last chapter.

These auto parts are subject to dependent demand. © Barry Willis/Getty Images

Dependent-demand inventories, on the other hand, are not subject to market conditions. They are dependent on demand for higher-level parts and components up to and including the master production schedule. Examples of dependent-demand inventories are raw-materials and work-in-process inventories used in manufacturing companies to support the manufacturing process itself. In a restaurant, the raw food required is dependent on the number and types of meals served. These inventories should be managed by an MRP system or by the just-in-time systems described in Chapter 17.

An MRP system is driven by the **master schedule,** which specifies the end items or output of the production function. All future demands for work in process and raw materials are dependent on the master schedule and derived by the MRP system from the master schedule. When raw-materials and work-in-process inventories are being planned, all past history of demand is irrelevant unless the future is exactly the same as the past. Since conditions are usually changing, the master schedule is a far better basis than past demand for planning raw-materials and work-in-process inventories.

The master schedule in turn is driven by the total of future expected demand including Sales and Operations Planning (S&OP), forecasts, orders from customers, or orders for finished goods inventory. The master schedule contains specific product configurations or final assembly part numbers. In contrast, the S&OP was formulated for large product families on an aggregate basis. Therefore, during master scheduling, the S&OP is broken down into actual products that will be produced.

Using MRP, the master schedule is "exploded" into purchase orders for raw materials and shop orders for scheduling the factory. For example, if the product in the master schedule is a hand-held calculator, the process of **parts explosion** will determine all the parts and components needed to make a specified number of calculator units. This process of parts explosion requires a detailed bill of materials that lists each of the parts needed to manufacture any given end item in the master schedule. The required parts may include assemblies, subassemblies, manufactured parts, and purchased parts. Parts explosion thus results in a complete list of the parts that must be ordered and the shop schedule required.

In the process of parts explosion, it is necessary to consider inventories of parts that are already on hand or on order. For example, an order for 100 end items may require a new order of only 20 pieces of a particular raw material because 50 pieces are already in stock and 30 pieces are on order.

Another adjustment made during parts explosion is for production and purchasing lead times. Starting with the master schedule, each manufactured or purchased part is offset (i.e., ordered earlier) by the amount of time it takes to get the part (the lead time). This procedure ensures that each component will be available in time to support the master schedule. If sufficient manufacturing and vendor capacity is available to meet the orders resulting from parts explosion, the MRP system will produce a valid plan for procurement and manufacturing actions. If sufficient capacity is not available, it will be necessary to replan the master schedule or to change the capacity.

MRP can be part of a larger ERP system, described in Chapter 6. The purpose of MRP is to plan and control the manufacturing function in terms of products, orders, parts, production levels, and inventories. ERP expands the information provided by MRP to planning and control of money, personnel, and all other resources. MRP is the heart of the ERP system since an inaccurate MRP system leads to inaccurate numbers in finance, marketing, accounting, and personnel.

16.1 DEFINITIONS OF MRP SYSTEMS

The typical MRP system we have been discussing can be conveniently described by Figure 16.1. At the top of the figure is the master production schedule, which is determined by customers' orders, aggregate production planning, and forecasts of future demand. The parts-explosion process, at the center of the system, is driven by three inputs: master schedule, bill of materials, and inventory records. The result of the parts-explosion process is two types of orders: purchase orders that go to vendors and shop orders that go to the factory. Before shop orders are sent to the factory, however, a check is made by materials planners on whether sufficient capacity is available to produce the parts required. If capacity is available, the shop orders are placed under control of the shop-floor control system. If capacity is not available, a change must be made by the planners in the capacity or in the master schedule through the feedback loop shown. Once the shop orders are under the shop-floor control system, the progress of these orders is managed through the shop to make sure that they are completed on time.

Figure 16.1 represents MRP as an *information system* used to plan and control inventories and capacity. Information is processed through the various parts of the system to support management decisions. If the information is accurate and timely, management can use the system to control inventories, deliver customer orders on time, and control the costs of manufacturing and services firms. In this way, the materials will be continually managed in a dynamic and changing environment.

Joseph Orlicky, in his pioneering book on MRP (1975, p. 158), has defined three principal functions of MRP as follows:

Inventory

Order the right part.

Order in the right quantity.

Order at the right time.

FIGURE 16.1 A closed-loop MRP system.

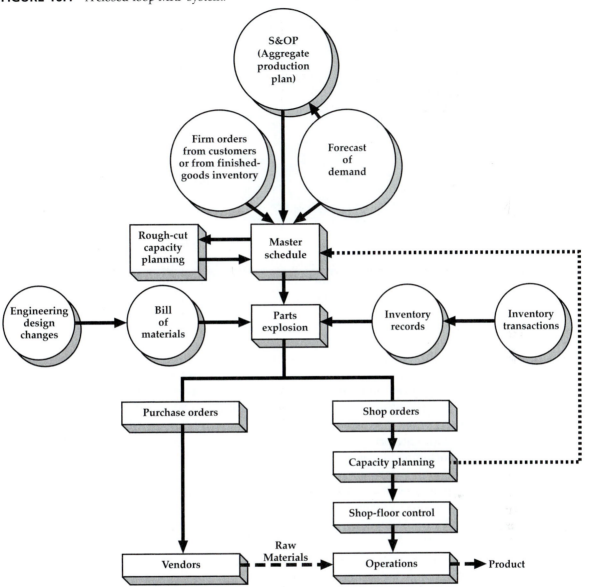

Priorities

Order with the right due date.

Keep the due date valid.

Capacity

A complete load.

An accurate (valid) load.

An adequate time span for visibility of future load.

If the MRP system in Figure 16.1 is used properly, all of Orlicky's three functions can be achieved. Although MRP is easy to understand conceptually, it can be used in a variety of different ways. This leads to two different types of MRP

PRODUCTION CONTROL. This production control employee uses a computer to track the flow of materials as part of an MRP system. © Royalty-Free/CORBIS

systems and the extension to ERP as follows:

- **Type I: An inventory control system.** The type I MRP system is a minimal inventory control system that releases manufacturing and purchase orders for the right quantities at the right time to support the master schedule. This system launches orders to control work-in-process and raw-materials inventories through proper timing of order placement. The type I system does not, however, include the capacity planning and shop-floor control modules shown in the bottom part of Figure 16.1.

- **Type II: A production and inventory control system.** The type II MRP system includes all of Figure 16.1 and is an information system used to plan and control inventories and capacities. In the type II system, the orders resulting from parts explosion are checked to see whether sufficient capacity is available. If there is not enough capacity, either the capacity or the master schedule is changed. The type II system has a feedback loop between the orders launched and the master schedule to adjust for capacity availability. As a result, this type of MRP system is called a **closed-loop system;** it controls both inventories and the capacity of resources used to support production. A type II MRP system is called a **Manufacturing Resource Planning System.**

- **An enterprise resource planning system (ERP).** An ERP system is a company-wide enterprise resource planning system used to plan and control all resources, including inventory, capacity, cash, personnel, facilities, and capital. In this case, the MRP system is integrated with all other information subsystems in the company, including accounting systems, sales and marketing systems, human resource systems, and financial systems through a common companywide database. Since everyone is working from the same information, it is possible to coordinate all company resources, not just materials and capacity.

How Detroit Diesel made the transition to an ERP system is described in the Operations Leader box. Also refer back to Chapter 6 for ERP details.

Since MRP is a simple and logical concept, one might wonder why every company does not use it. The chief reason is that the system does not fit the particular company's type of production system or the company is not aware of the potential benefits of MRP. These problems will be discussed in detail later in the chapter; also see Table 16.1 for a list of typical reasons given for not implementing MRP.

16.2 MRP VERSUS ORDER-POINT SYSTEMS

MRP calls into question many of the traditional concepts used to manage inventories. The **order-point** systems discussed in Chapter 15 do not work well for the management of inventories subject to dependent demand. Prior to the advent of MRP, however, there was no choice; the typical manufacturing and service companies managed *all* inventories with order-point systems.

OPERATIONS LEADER

Implementing ERP in a Big Way at Detroit Diesel Corp.

Managers at the Detroit Diesel Corp., a subsidiary of Penske Corp., recognized that changing business requirements were testing the limits of the firm's information systems. Outdated technology precluded further enhancement of legacy systems that had been in place for years. A new solution was in order, one that could accommodate advanced production styles, increasing numbers of new-product introductions, and, most important, ever-growing order volumes.

By the close of 1995, when the solution to Detroit Diesel's information system problems were largely in place, revenue had grown to almost $2.1 billion per year. Production lines were running on three shifts per day and into weekends, with average revenue approaching $40 million a week. Any disruption in production was out of the question. Thus, the development process and eventual cutover that led to implementation of the new system had to be virtually seamless.

Yet, the scale of enterprise precluded a clean break with the old system. A methodology sufficient to manage the transition would need to accommodate an extremely rapid cutover while maintaining links with the legacy system in some functional areas. Underlying the whole initiative, a reliable planning process that would bring a technically advanced ERP system online was required.

The end result of this activity would be a widely implemented ERP system running from "book to bill." Included in the system are order configuration and entry, work orders, inventory and shop-floor control, online engineering change orders, accounts receivable/accounts payable, advance shipping notice via electronic data interchange to and from customers, and many other functions.

Source: Goodwin, Siegert, Cardillo, and Bergmann, "Implementing ERP in a Big Way," *APICS—The Performance Advantage*, June 1996, pp. 60–64.

Some of the key distinctions between MRP and order-point systems are summarized in Table 16.2. One distinction is the **requirements philosophy** used in MRP systems versus a replenishment philosophy used in order-point systems. A **replenishment philosophy** indicates that material should be replenished when it runs low. An MRP system does not do this. More material is ordered only when a need exists as directed by the master schedule. If there are no manufacturing requirements for a particular part, it will not be replenished, even though the inventory level is low. This requirements concept is particularly important in manufacturing because demand for component parts is "lumpy." When a lot is scheduled, the component parts are needed for that lot, but demand is then zero until another lot is scheduled. If order-point systems are used for this type of lumpy demand pattern, material will be carried on hand during long periods of zero demand.

TABLE 16.1
Long-Held Attitudes in Manufacturing Companies

- "You can't forecast our business out that far."
- "We in sales are not interested in your manufacturing problems; we have enough of our own."
- "Don't ask me which customer order I want shipped first. I want them all now."
- "You can't lock up any part of this master production schedule" [sales talking].
- "You can't change any of this schedule within the first six months" [manufacturing talking].
- "That new system just can't react fast enough. We need Ed to ramrod through extra orders from time to time."
- "If I want 100 units a month out of this plant, I know from long experience I have to ask for 150."

TABLE 16.2
Comparison of
MRP and Order-
Point Systems

	MRP	Order Point
Demand	Dependent	Independent
Order philosophy	Requirements	Replenishment
Forecast	Based on master schedule	Based on past demand
Control concept	Control all items	ABC
Objectives	Meet manufacturing needs	Meet customer needs
Lot sizing	Discrete	EOQ
Demand pattern	Lumpy but predictable	Random
Types of inventory	Work in process and raw materials	Finished goods and spare parts

Another distinction between the two systems is in the use of forecasting. For order-point systems, future demand is forecast on the basis of past history of demand. These forecasts are used to replenish the stock levels. In MRP systems, past demand for component parts is irrelevant. The ordering philosophy is based on requirements generated from the master schedule. MRP is future-oriented; it derives the future demand for component parts from higher-level demand forecasts.

The ABC principle also does not work well for MRP systems. In manufacturing a product, C items are just as important as A items. For example, an automobile cannot be shipped if it lacks a fuel line or radiator cap, even though these items are relatively inexpensive C items. A meal cannot be served by a restaurant if the meat is missing. Therefore, it is necessary to control all parts, even the C items.

The time-honored EOQ is not useful in MRP systems, although modified lot-sizing formulas are available. The assumptions used to derive the traditional EOQ are badly violated by the lumpy demand patterns for component parts. Lot sizing in MRP systems should be based on discrete requirements. For example, suppose that the demand for a particular part by week is 0, 30, 10, 0, 0, and 15. Further assume that the EOQ is calculated to be 25 parts. With the EOQ or multiples of the EOQ, we could not match the requirements exactly and would, therefore, end up with remnants in inventory. These remnants from the EOQ cause unnecessary inventory-carrying costs. It would be far better to base lot sizes on the discrete demand observed. For example, with a lot-for-lot policy, we could order 30 units for the second week, 10 for the third week, and 15 for the sixth week, resulting in three orders and no carrying costs. We could also order 40 units for the second and third weeks combined, thereby saving one order but incurring a small carrying cost. With MRP systems, various discrete lot sizes need to be examined.[1]

The objective in managing independent-demand inventories with reorder-point rules is to provide a high customer service level at low inventory-operating costs. This objective is oriented toward the customer. On the other hand, the objective in managing dependent-demand inventories with MRP is to support the master production schedule. This objective is manufacturing oriented; it focuses inward rather than outward.

It should now be evident that MRP systems differ from order-point systems in almost every important dimension, and it should be clear why MRP systems are needed to control dependent-demand inventories. The next section describes the mechanics of MRP systems.

---

[1] For detailed discrete lot sizing methods see Carol Ptak, *MRP and Beyond: A Toolbox for Integrating People and Systems,* Falls Church, VA: APICS, 1996.

16.3   MRP EXAMPLE

The easiest way to understand MRP is to focus on the parts-explosion process itself. After describing this process below, by example, we will discuss the remaining elements of the MRP system.

Suppose that tables of the type shown in Figure 16.2 are being manufactured. The finished table consists of a top and a leg assembly. The leg assembly, in turn, consists of four legs, two short rails, and two long rails. In this particular example, leg assemblies are built in advance and stored in inventory. This procedure permits the table to be produced faster, as orders are received, than it could be if the table were completely assembled from individual parts. It is common practice in manufacturing companies to build assemblies for inventory in order to reduce total production lead time and to save setup costs.

The **bill of materials** (BOM) for this table is shown schematically in Figure 16.3. The finished table is at the first level of the bill. The leg assembly and tabletop are at the second level, since these parts are assembled together to produce a finished table. The pieces that go into the leg assembly are all listed at the third level. We are assuming that the parts for this table are purchased from outside; otherwise there would be a fourth level in the BOM for the wood used to make the legs, rails, and top.

Another piece of information needed prior to parts explosion is the **planned lead times** for manufactured and purchased parts, as shown in Table 16.3. For planning purposes, it takes one week to assemble the finished table from the leg assembly and top. This planned lead time includes average waiting time due to interference from other jobs, which is usually much longer than the actual working time. If the finished tables were urgently needed on a priority basis, they could be assembled in a few hours. Similarly, Table 16.3 shows that two weeks are planned for purchase of a tabletop from the time the order is placed until the tabletop is in the factory. This planned lead time could also be compressed to as little as a day or two if the tops were given high priority by the vendor.

It is now possible, using parts explosion, to construct a **materials plan** for the finished tables and all parts. The resulting materials plan is shown in Table 16.4. The master schedule in this case contains the demand for finished tables: 200 in week 4, 150 in week 5, and 100 in week 6. These quantities are listed as **gross requirements** for complete tables. As shown in the materials plan, there are 50 tables on hand at the present time (all figures in Table 16.4 are assumed to occur

FIGURE 16.2
Table example.

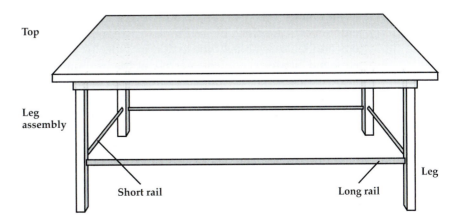

FIGURE 16.3
Bill of materials (quantity per unit shown in parentheses).

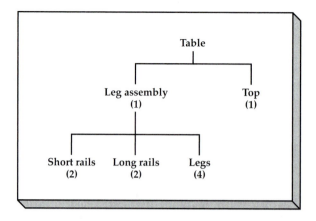

TABLE 16.3
Planned Lead Times

	Weeks
Assemble table*	1
Finished leg assembly†	1
Purchase legs	1
Purchase short rails	1
Purchase long rails	1
Purchase top	2

*Assume the tabletop and complete leg asssembly are available.
†Assume the legs, short rails, and long rails are available.

at the beginning of the week). Thus, we can subtract these available tables from the gross requirement to arrive at the **net requirement.** Then the net requirement is offset by one week, due to the planned lead time for table assembly, to arrive at planned order releases. Therefore, to meet the gross requirements of the master schedule, shop orders must be released to assemble 150 tables in week 3, 150 in week 4, and 100 in week 5.

Next, the **planned order releases** for tables are used to calculate gross requirements for tops and leg assemblies at the next level down in the BOM. The final planned order releases for tables are transferred to gross requirements for tops and leg assemblies on a one-for-one basis, since it takes one tabletop and one leg assembly to make a table. The on-hand inventory and scheduled receipts are subtracted from the gross requirements to arrive at net requirements. The net requirements are offset by lead time to arrive at planned order releases for tabletops and leg assemblies. Notice that in Table 16.4, 50 tabletops are currently on hand and 50 are scheduled to arrive at the beginning of week 2. The scheduled order for 50 tops was placed a week ago under a previous materials plan. Since there is a two-week lead time, these tops will arrive at the beginning of week 2. All materials on hand and on order must be included when doing parts explosion.

The planned order releases for leg assemblies are then used to compute gross requirements for legs, short rails, and long rails. The planned orders for leg assemblies are multiplied by 4 for legs, by 2 for short rails, and by 2 for long rails to arrive at gross requirements. A gross requirement at any level is the amount of material required to support planned orders at the next-highest level.

TABLE 16.4
Materials Plan—
Parts Explosion

	Week					
	1	2	3	4	5	6
Tables						
Gross requirements	—	—	—	200	150	100
On-hand/scheduled receipts*	50	—	—	—	—	—
Net requirements	—	—	—	150	150	100
Planned order releases	—	—	150	150	100	—
Tops						
Gross requirements	—	—	150	150	100	—
On-hand/scheduled receipts*	50	50	—	—	—	—
Net requirements	—	—	50	150	100	—
Planned order releases	50	150	100	—	—	—
Leg assembly						
Gross requirements	—	—	150	150	100	—
On-hand/scheduled receipts*	100	—	—	—	—	—
Net requirements	—	—	50	150	100	—
Planned order releases	—	50	150	100	—	—
Leg						
Gross requirements	—	200	600	400	—	—
On-hand/scheduled receipts*	150	100	—	—	—	—
Net requirements	—	—	550	400	—	—
Planned order releases	—	550	400	—	—	—
Short rail						
Gross requirements	—	100	300	200	—	—
On-hand/scheduled receipts*	50	—	—	—	—	—
Net requirements	—	50	300	200	—	—
Planned order releases	50	300	200	—	—	—
Long rail						
Gross requirements	—	100	300	200	—	—
On-hand/scheduled receipts*	—	—	—	—	—	—
Net requirements	—	100	300	200	—	—
Planned order releases	100	300	200	—	—	—

*On-hand inventory is listed in week 1. Scheduled receipts are shown in week 2 and later weeks based on orders that have already been placed and are due to arrive.

The gross-to-net calculation and the offset for lead time is then performed for each of the three remaining parts to arrive at planned order releases. This completes the parts explosion.

Table 16.4 has been constructed from the master schedule down, one level at a time, through the BOM. The materials plan for each level in the BOM was completed before moving down to the next level. For each part, the gross requirements have been reduced by on-hand and on-order inventory to arrive at net requirements. The net requirements have been offset (planned earlier) by the lead time to arrive at planned order releases. By the process of netting and offsetting, the master schedule is converted to planned order releases for each part required.

What does the materials plan in Table 16.4 tell us? First, we should immediately release purchase orders to our vendors for 50 tops, 50 short rails, and 100 long rails since these are the planned orders at the beginning of week 1. The materials plan also gives us the planned order releases for each week in the future. If the master schedule and all other conditions remain constant, these planned orders will be released when the time comes. For example, in week 2 we plan to release an order to the shop to complete 50 leg assemblies. If the materials arrive as planned, we should have on hand the legs and rails needed for this shop order: 200 legs, 100 short rails, and 100 long rails. In addition to the shop order for 50 leg assemblies, we plan to release, in week 2, purchase orders for 150 tops, 550 legs, 300 short rails, and 300 long rails. These materials will be needed to support future leg-assembly and table-assembly shop orders.

This example illustrates the construction of a **time-phased materials plan.** All **purchase orders** and **shop orders** are interrelated to provide materials when needed. If the actual lead times can be managed to meet the planned lead times, there will be no unnecessary inventory accumulations or wasted time waiting for materials in the shop, and the orders for delivery of finished tables will be shipped on time.

As a matter of fact, once any initial inventories are depleted, no finished goods inventories will be planned by the MRP system. This is because we have planned production to just equal final demand, after adjusting for available inventories. Likewise, no purchased-parts inventories are planned after initial inventories and scheduled receipts are depleted. The MRP system really cuts things close. Unless safety stocks are added for uncertainties or inventories are added to smooth out production levels, no inventory will be planned except work in process required for assembly or fabrication. The MRP logic assumes parts are available exactly when they are needed to support the production plan.

16.4   MRP ELEMENTS

Although parts explosion is the heart of MRP, it takes a good deal more to make an MRP system work. The other MRP system elements are described in this section.

Master Scheduling

The purpose of master scheduling is to specify the output of the operations function. Master scheduling drives the entire materials planning process. The master schedule has been described by Plossl (1994) as "top management's handle on the business." By controlling the master schedule, top management can control customer service, inventory levels, and manufacturing costs. Top managers cannot perform the master-scheduling task by themselves because there are too many details; therefore, they often delegate the task to a **cross-functional team.** However, top managers can review the master schedule that has been created, and they can set master-scheduling policy, thereby controlling the materials-planning function.

Top management's primary interface with manufacturing is through the aggregate production plan shown at the top of Figure 16.1. The aggregate production plan deals with families of products or product lines, not specific products, models, or options that are in the master schedule. For example, if the manufacturer makes tractors, the aggregate production plan might contain various types of tractors but not the particular size of engine, hydraulics options, or other features that the customer can select. The aggregate production planning process, described in Chapter 12, is usually part of the annual budgeting and strategic planning process and is updated on a monthly basis, for example. It seeks to make the resources (capacity), people, equipment, and facilities available for the future. As such, the master-scheduling process must work within the overall aggregate production plan, which has already been established, or seek to modify this plan if necessary.

The parts-explosion process assumes that the master schedule is feasible with respect to capacity. Using the master schedule as input, parts are exploded to produce shop orders and purchase orders. In type II systems, the shop orders are put into a capacity-planning routine and checked by materials planners to determine whether sufficient capacity is available. If sufficient capacity is not available, then either capacity or the master schedule must be changed until the master schedule is feasible.

One of the functions of master scheduling is to make sure that the final master schedule is not inflated and reflects realistic capacity constraints. All too often, the master schedule is inflated in practice on the assumption that operations will produce more output if the pressure is kept on. (This is not unlike the approach of some college professors who assign students too much homework in hopes that the students will learn more.) As a result of an inflated master schedule, the order priorities (due dates) are no longer valid. The formal MRP system then quickly breaks down, and the informal planning and control system takes over. The result is many past-due orders, expediting, and stock chasing to get the product out the door. Nothing is more insidious than an inflated master schedule that leads to invalid order due dates.

The master schedule might extend into the future for a year or more. It must extend at least beyond the longest cumulative production lead time to ensure that sufficient time is available to order all parts. Generally speaking, the master schedule should be frozen inside the production lead time to prevent unnecessary scrap and expediting due to changes during the production cycle.

Rarely is the master schedule a reflection of future demand forecasts. Rather, the master schedule is a forecast of what will be produced. It is a "build" schedule. Finished-goods inventory is a buffer between the master schedule and final customer demand, smoothing out workloads and providing fast customer service.

Bill of Materials (BOM)

The BOM is a structured list of all the materials or parts needed to produce a particular finished product, assembly, subassembly, manufactured part, or purchased part. The BOM serves the same function as a recipe used for cooking: it lists all the ingredients. It would be foolish to allow errors to creep into your favorite cooking recipes. The same is true for a BOM. If there are errors in the BOM, the proper materials will not be ordered and the product cannot be assembled and shipped. As a result, the other parts that *are* available will wait in inventory while the missing parts are expedited. Management must, therefore, insist that all BOMs are 100 percent accurate. Experience has shown that it is not too costly to have 100 percent accuracy; rather, it is too costly to tolerate imperfect BOMs.

Some companies have several BOMs for the same product. Engineering has one BOM, manufacturing has a different version, and cost accounting has still another. An MRP system requires a single BOM for the entire company. The BOM in the computer must be the correct one, and it must represent how the product is manufactured. In companies where the BOM has been used as a reference document and not a materials-planning tool, this concept of a single bill is very difficult to implement.

BOMs are constantly undergoing change as products are redesigned. Thus, an effective **engineering-change-order** (ECO) system is needed to keep the BOMs up to date. Usually an ECO coordinator must be appointed and charged with the responsibility for coordinating all engineering changes with the various departments involved.

Inventory Records

A typical computerized inventory record includes the following data segments. The item master data segment contains the part number, which is the unique item identifier, and other information such as lead time, standard cost, and so on. The inventory status segment contains a complete materials plan for each item over time. Finally, the subsidiary data segment contains information concerning outstanding orders, requested changes, detailed demand history, and the like.

In practice, constant effort is required to keep inventory records accurate. Traditionally, inventory accuracy has been ensured by the annual physical inventory count, where the plant is shut down for a day or two and everything is counted from wall to wall. It has been found that, because inexperienced people are often doing the counting, as many errors are introduced by this procedure as are corrected. After the inventory is taken, the total inventory in dollars is accurate for financial purposes because the plus and minus errors cancel out. But the counts of individual items are usually not accurate enough for MRP purposes. As a result, **cycle counting** has been developed as a substitute for the annual physical inventory.

With cycle counting, a small percentage of the items are counted each day by storeroom personnel. Errors are corrected in the records, and an attempt is made to find and correct the procedure that caused them. By developing a high regard for accuracy and adopting daily cycle counting, companies can eliminate most errors in inventory records. The result is so reliable that many auditors no longer require an annual physical inventory when an effective cycle-counting system is in place.[2]

Capacity Planning

The necessary elements for an **order-launching MRP system** (type I) have been described above. This system requires master scheduling, a BOM, inventory records, and parts explosion. The resulting order-launching system will determine correct due dates (order priorities) if sufficient capacity is available. If sufficient capacity is not available, inventories will rise, past-due orders will build up, and expediting will be used to pull orders through the factory. To correct this situation, a capacity-planning subsystem is needed.

The purpose of capacity planning is to aid management in checking on the validity of the master schedule. There are two ways this can be done: **rough-cut capacity planning** (also called resource planning) and **shop loading.** In rough-cut capacity planning, approximate labor hours and machine hours are calculated directly from the master schedule to project future capacity needs without going through the parts-explosion process. When sufficient capacity is not available, management adjusts the master schedule or changes capacity to obtain a feasible schedule. When the master schedule is feasible, then the full parts explosion is run.

When shop loading is used, a full parts explosion is run prior to capacity planning. The resulting shop orders are then loaded against work centers through the use of detailed parts-routing data. As a result, workforce and machine hours for each work center are projected into the future. If sufficient capacity is not available, management should adjust either capacity or the master schedule until it is feasible. At this point, a valid materials plan is available.

Rough-cut capacity planning requires less detailed calculation but is not as accurate as shop loading. Either of these methods or both of them can be used, depending on individual conditions and circumstances. The important point is that capacity planning should be used to close the loop in the MRP system.

[2] Accounting students should take note of this concept, since they are likely to encounter cycle counting in practice.

An alternative to capacity planning, described above, is scheduling to finite capacity. Software has been developed to implement the methods described in Chapter 13 for forward scheduling to finite capacity. These methods are being applied in situations where capacity is very expensive and scheduling is relatively simple, such as the process industries. In these cases, MRP is modified to start with a feasible finite capacity schedule, and materials are planned to arrive in time to support the feasible schedule.[3]

Purchasing

The purchasing function is greatly enhanced by the use of an MRP system. First, past-due orders are largely eliminated because MRP generates valid due dates and keeps them up to date. This permits purchasing to develop credibility with vendors since the material is really needed when purchasing says it is.

By developing and executing a valid materials plan, management can eliminate much of the order expediting that is usually done by purchasing. This allows the purchasing managers to concentrate on their prime function: qualifying vendors, looking for alternative sources of supply, and working with suppliers to ensure delivery of quality parts, on time, at low cost.

With an MRP system, it is possible to provide suppliers with reports of planned future orders. This gives vendors time to plan capacity before actual orders are placed. The practice of giving suppliers planned orders more closely interlocks them with the company's own materials plan. Many firms have gone so far as to insist that their vendors also install MRP systems so that the vendors' delivery reliability can be more readily ensured. Also, electronic data interchange (EDI) and Web-based methods are being used to transmit MRP planned orders directly from the customer's computer to the supplier's computer.

Shop-Floor Control

The purpose of the shop-floor control subsystem is to release orders to the shop floor and to manage the orders on their way through the factory to make sure that they are completed on time. The shop-floor control system helps management adjust to all the day-to-day things that go wrong in manufacturing: absenteeism among workers, machine breakdowns, loss of materials, and so on. When these unplanned complications arise, decisions must be made about what to do next. Good decisions require information on job priorities from the shop-floor control system, also called a **Manufacturing Execution System (MES).**

Job priorities are frequently calculated by dispatching rules of the type discussed in Chapter 13. When these rules are used as part of the shop-floor control system, it is possible to adjust to changing conditions and still get the work out on time. Through the use of dispatching rules, a job's production lead time can be drastically cut or increased as it goes through the shop. This is possible because a job normally spends as much as 90 percent of its time waiting in queues. If a job is behind schedule, its priority can be increased until it gets back on schedule. Similarly, a job can be slowed down if it is ahead of schedule. It is the function of the shop-floor control system to provide information to managers so they can manage production lead time dynamically.

The old notion of an accurate or good lead time must be discarded. Lead times can be managed by expanding or contracting them on the basis of priority. This concept has been popularized by the old saw, "Lead time is what you say it is." This is a very difficult concept to accept when managers are used to thinking in terms of fixed lead time or lead times as random variables.

---

[3] See Wasik and Wolfe (1990) for more details.

It is possible through a shop-floor control system to deexpedite orders—that is, to slow them down. This is not done in normal manufacturing, where orders are expedited but never deexpedited. Orders should be slowed down when the master schedule is changed or when other parts will not be available on time. This results in the minimum inventory consistent with MRP timing requirements.

To do its job properly, a shop-floor control system requires feedback reports on all jobs as they are processed. Typically, a worker notifies the system as each processing step is completed. This may be done through a computer terminal on the shop floor or by information submitted to a central office. The computer system then produces a dispatching list for each supervisor each day. The list shows the priority of each job in the work center, and if possible, the supervisor works on the highest-priority job. If materials, labor, or machines are not available for the highest-priority job, the job that is next highest in priority is done, and so on down the list.

A shop-floor control system requires valid due dates on orders. If the master schedule is inflated and the shop is overloaded, no shop-floor control system will get the work out on time. The shop-floor control system is highly dependent on proper priority and capacity planning.

When a company is using JIT for repetitive manufacturing, the shop-floor control system is replaced by a Kanban pull system, described in Chapter 17. The Kanban system relies on visual control of materials and physical signals, instead of computerized information. As a result, the shop-floor control system is greatly simplified and less costly. But JIT systems work well only for repetitive manufacturing plants; MRP shop-floor control systems are still useful for batch-oriented plants, job shops, and service operations.

16.5 OPERATING AN MRP SYSTEM

There is much more to MRP than just installing the proper computer modules. Management must operate the system in an intelligent and effective way.

One of the decisions management should make is how much **safety stock** to carry. To the surprise of many managers, little safety stock is needed if MRP is properly used. This is due to the concept of lead-time management, where both purchasing and shop lead times are effectively controlled within small variances. In purchasing, this is done by developing relationships with vendors who provide reliable deliveries. In the shop, lead times can be managed by a shop-floor control system as described above. Once the uncertainty in lead time is reduced, there is much less need for safety stock.

If safety stock were carried at the component-part level, a great deal of it would be needed to be effective. Suppose, for example, that 10 parts are required to make an assembly and each part has a 90 percent service level. The probability of having all 10 parts on hand when needed is only 35 percent.[4] It is much better, therefore, to plan and control the timing of the 10 parts than to cover all contingencies with safety stock. When safety stock is carried, it is often added at the master-schedule level. This ensures that matched sets of components, not simply an assortment of various parts, are available for final products. The purpose of safety stock at the master-schedule level is to provide flexibility to meet changing customer requirements.

[4] Probability = $(.9)^{10}$ = .35, assuming parts availabilities are independent events.

Safety lead time is a concept that should be considered for component parts. If a vendor is unreliable and the situation cannot be remedied, the planned lead time can be lengthened by adding safety lead time. This will add to inventories, however, when the vendor delivers the parts earlier than actually needed.

A third way of handling uncertainty is to plan for **safety capacity.** This approach has much merit because the spare capacity can be used to make the right parts when the need becomes known. The problem with safety stock is that it is frequently available for the wrong parts—too much of one part and too little of another. Thus, serious consideration should be given to safety capacity as an alternative to safety stock; this has not been widely done in industry. Rather, safety stock (inventory) has been considered an asset, even if it is never used, and capacity utilization of 100 percent is a desirable goal, even if excess inventories result.

Another problem in operating an MRP system is the constant danger that the **informal system** will drive out the formal system. If the formal MRP system is not used by management, the informal system will rapidly take over as material is expedited, past-due orders build up, and an atmosphere of crisis develops. The informal system is always lurking in the wings to take over. It is necessary, therefore, that management strive to maintain data accuracy, user education, and system integrity so that the formal MRP system is used to manage the company.

Coca Cola is one of the best-known brands in the world and also a noted MRP user.[5] They have kept out the informal system by meticulous attention to MRP implementation. Initial implementation began in a plant in Puerto Rico in 1987, followed by Ireland in 1988, France in 1990, and so on until all concentrate plants around the world implemented MRP. No plant was forced to use MRP and one plant at a time was converted to the MRP system. As a result significant benefits were achieved including inventory reduction of 50 to 75 percent, customer delivery performance increased to nearly 100 percent, supplier delivery performance increased from 60 percent to greater than 95 percent, and cost reduction as great as 20 percent.

If an MRP system is operating properly, it can be more than just a production and inventory control tool. The MRP system can support planning and control in all parts of the company (a type III enterprise resource planning system). For example, it can be used to drive financial planning systems—to project future total inventories, forecast purchasing budgets, and plan needs for personnel, equipment, and facilities. An MRP system used for the physical control of materials can be expanded to provide the basis for financial planning and control. MRP users are beginning to realize that detailed physical planning can be the basis for improved financial planning.

Financial planning and control are derivatives of an MRP system, being merely measured in different units—dollars instead of physical units. For too long, financial systems have been driven by transactions and assumptions different from materials control systems. The tools now exist to tie MRP and financial systems together by a simple conversion from physical units to dollars and vice versa. Physical control thus becomes the basis for financial control. It can be argued that true financial control can exist only if there is first physical control of the production process.

An MRP system can also be extended to support product costing and cost accounting. When an accurate bill of materials is in the computer, it is a relatively simple matter to calculate product costs from the labor and materials cost

[5] Chris Gray (2005).

of the component parts. As a matter of fact, a costing module is sometimes provided as part of the MRP software.

An MRP system can also be expanded into personnel planning by using a bill of labor. In this case, all the labor skills for each product are listed on the bill of labor. The labor requirements are then exploded from the master schedule in a similar way as materials requirements. This makes it possible to forecast labor requirements and to tie together labor and materials needs.

The possibilities for making MRP more than just a tool for production and inventory control are appealing. Once an MRP type II system has been implemented for materials control, the company can widen the applicability of its MRP system to the planning and control of other resources, by using an ERP system.

16.6 THE SUCCESSFUL MRP SYSTEM

It takes a great deal of effort to make MRP or ERP successful. While the points below are stated for an MRP system, they apply equally well to ERP implementation. Research indicates that five elements are required for success:

1. Implementation planning
2. Adequate computer support
3. Accurate data
4. Management support
5. User knowledge

Implementation planning should be a prerequisite to any MRP effort. Unfortunately, too many companies jump in and start implementing MRP without adequate preparation. Later, confusion and misunderstanding occur as problems arise. Advanced planning and problem-prevention efforts can help smooth out implementation efforts. Implementation planning should include education of senior management, selection of a project manager, appointment of an implementation team representing all parts of the company, preparation of objectives, identification of expected benefits and costs, and a detailed action plan. Only after this plan is prepared should selection of hardware and software, improvement of data accuracy, and other implementation activities begin. Implementation planning at Ben & Jerry's ice cream company is illustrated in the Operations Leader box.

An adequate computer system is probably one of the easiest elements of MRP to implement. Today, there are approximately 100 MRP software packages on the market. Many companies use these standard packages rather than writing their own computer programs.

An MRP system requires accurate data, which are very difficult to obtain. Many companies are accustomed to lax record keeping in manufacturing because they have always been managed by informal systems. But accurate data are required when decisions are made from information supplied by the computer.

A company that does not have an MRP system will need to create accurate BOMs as a first step. In some cases, the BOMs are in such poor condition that the company literally has to start over from the beginning. In other cases, the BOMs may be relatively accurate and require only some updating.

Once the BOMs are accurate, a system will be needed to keep them that way. This will require an engineering change coordinator who is in charge of all changes to the BOM. The coordinator should institute process controls and prevention measures to ensure quality of BOM information.

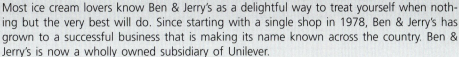

OPERATIONS LEADER

Ben & Jerry's Adds MRP to Its Recipe for Success

Most ice cream lovers know Ben & Jerry's as a delightful way to treat yourself when nothing but the very best will do. Since starting with a single shop in 1978, Ben & Jerry's has grown to a successful business that is making its name known across the country. Ben & Jerry's is now a wholly owned subsidiary of Unilever.

To gain control of this fast-growing business and to further improve profit, an MRP system has been installed. The system has three objectives. First, computerization cannot alter the freedom and flexibility of the existing work process. The reports provided by the system must be easy to customize by the users and fit the users' needs for information. Second, the system must be easy to use. This was accomplished by menu-driven methods for entering data and making system inquiries. Third, the system must be integrated. Prior to using MRP, each department had its own database and its own reports. Integration was achieved by a common companywide database.

With all these changes to its business and management process, will the firm begin to look and act differently as a business entity? "No way," says MIS director Keith Wiliams. "The only difference is that we'll be able to run our business smarter. The software assists in that process by helping us maintain control over what we have created as a business, and what we will create in the months and years ahead. I think that's going to make working here a lot more fun for our family of employees, and those that join our family of free spirits in the future."

Source: Extracted from *P&IM Review,* February 1989; and www.benandjerrys.com (2002).

Inventory records must also be accurate to support the MRP system. The initial accuracy of inventory records may be somewhat better than the BOMs, but inventory record keeping will need improvement too. The best way to improve and maintain the accuracy of inventory records is to install a system of cycle counting. Cycle counting should be used not only to correct errors but to improve the underlying record-keeping system.

All other MRP system data—such as shop routings, shop-floor status, and costs—must be initially screened for errors and then maintained in an acceptable state of accuracy. Keeping MRP data accurate for system integrity is one of the most important tasks in operating an MRP system.

The importance of **management support** to the successful MRP system can hardly be overemphasized. Many studies have shown that top-management support is the key to successful implementation of systems. But management support requires more than lip service and passive support on the manager's part. "Management participation" or "leadership" would be a better phrase. Top managers must be actively involved in installing and operating the MRP system. They must give their time, and they must change the way they operate the company. If top managers change, the climate is set for other managers also to make the changes required by the MRP system. The ultimate change required by management at all levels is to use the system and not to override it by management edicts and arbitrary decisions.

The final requirement for the successful MRP system is user knowledge at all levels of the company. An MRP system requires an entirely new approach to manufacturing. All company employees must understand how they will be affected and grasp their new roles and responsibilities. When MRP is first being

FIGURE 16.4
Types of BOM
structures.

Source: Adapted from
Elwood S. Buffa and Jeffrey
Miller, *Production Inventory
Systems Planning and Control,*
3d, ed. (Homewood, IL:
Irwin, 1979).

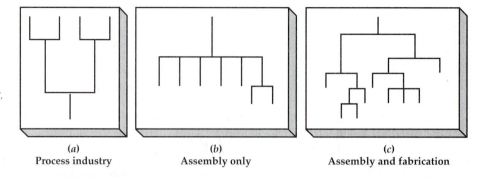

(a)
Process industry   *(b)*
Assembly only   *(c)*
Assembly and fabrication

MRP FOR SERVICES.
MRP systems can be
used for services, too.
In renovating hotel
rooms, Marriott
develops a bill of
material and a bill of
labor for each room
type and then
"explodes" the bill
throughout the
facility to summarize
its furniture and
decorating needs.
© Royalty-Free/CORBIS

installed, only a few key managers need to be educated. But as the system begins to be used, all supervisors, middle managers, and top managers need to understand MRP, including those inside and outside of manufacturing. As the MRP system is broadened in scope, the level of education within the company must be broadened too.

Users of MRP systems can be classified by the type of BOM they have. Figure 16.4*a* shows a BOM for a process company, where a given input is split into several different outputs. This occurs, for example, during the cracking and distillation of petroleum and during food processing. Figure 16.4*b* shows a BOM for a company that is in the assembly business. All parts are purchased, and the company is not vertically integrated. Finally Figure 16.4*c* is a BOM for a company that has both fabrication and assembly operations. This company—which might be a machinery or appliance manufacturer—is vertically integrated through all stages of manufacturing. Generally speaking, the most benefit from MRP is achieved by companies of the third type, which have the most complex bills of materials.

There is tremendous room for the application of MRP concepts in the service industry. If the bill of materials is replaced by a bill of labor or a bill of activities, one can explode the master schedule of output into all the activities and personnel required to deliver a particular mix of services. Some service operations will also require a bill of materials where materials are an important part of the goods-services bundle.

As an example, one electric utility has been using the MRP concept for several years in the electric hookup part of its business. When a new customer requests electrical service, a planner enters the request into a computer system for the type of service required. The computer then explodes this service request into detailed labor, material, and work activities. Each of these requirements is time-phased and accumulated over all jobs to determine whether sufficient capacity is available. When the time comes, the utility hookup crews are given work orders from the computer system, and work accomplishment is reported back to the computer. The MRP system then drives billing, labor-reporting, and other accounting systems.

The MRP concept is only beginning to be applied to service industries. There is potential in every phase of service operations, including restaurants, hotels, legal offices, health care, and many others. For an example of ERP implementation in a service industry, see the Operations Leader box about Beaumont Hospital.

16.7 KEY POINTS

Materials requirements planning is based on the concept of dependent demand. By exploding the master schedule through the BOM, it is possible to derive demand for component parts and raw materials. The MRP system can then be used to plan and control capacity, and it can be extended to business resource planning throughout a manufacturing firm.

This chapter's key points include the following:

- MRP is an information system used to plan and control manufacturing. There are three types of MRP systems: type I, an inventory control system (order launching); type II, a production and inventory control system (closed loop); and the third type, an enterprise resource planning system. Each of these systems expands the scope and use of MRP.

- The parts-explosion process has three principal inputs: master schedule, BOM, and inventory records. There are two principal outputs: purchase orders and shop orders. Parts explosion is the heart of the MRP system.

- MRP uses a requirements philosophy—parts are ordered only as required by the master schedule. Past demand for parts is irrelevant, and component inventories are *not* replenished when they reach a low level.

- Master schedules should be based on both marketing and production considerations. They should represent a realistic build plan within factory capacity. Top management should use the S&OP and master schedule to plan and control the business through a cross-functional planning team.

- The BOM contains the list of parts used to make the product. To maintain the accuracy of the bill of materials, an engineering-change-order system is needed.

- The accuracy of the inventory record system should be maintained through cycle counting. Daily cycle counting can be used in place of annual physical inventories.

- Shop-floor control (MES) is used to control the flow of materials through the factory. This is done by managing lead times dynamically as the product is manufactured. If lead times are properly managed, much safety stock can be eliminated.

- A successful MRP system requires (1) implementation planning, (2) adequate computer support, (3) accurate data, (4) management support, and (5) user knowledge. Both system and people problems must be solved to use MRP successfully. When this is done, benefits include reduced inventory, increased customer service, and improved efficiency.

- All manufacturing and service companies can benefit from MRP if it is properly installed and operated. This includes large and small companies and all industries.

STUDENT INTERNET EXERCISES

1. **INMASS MRP**
   http://www.inmass.com
   Read the software overview and describe the various MRP modules available for this software in a short report.

2. User Solutions, Inc.
   http://www.usersol.com
   Examine the reports available from the system. Describe the use of the system for MRP planning and scheduling.

3. S.F.T. Inc.
   http://www.MRP3.com
   Describe the differences among MRP, MRPII, and MRPIII.

4. SAP Inc.
   http://www.sap.com/solutions/
   Come to class prepared to discuss the SAP approach to enterprise software including the mysap supply chain management module.

SOLVED PROBLEM

Problem

1. **MRP**

   a. Using the information given below, develop a complete MRP material plan.

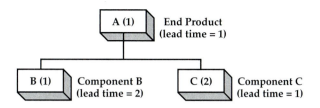

It takes one unit of B and two units of C to make one unit of A. At the beginning of time period 1, the following information is available:

Item ID	Quantity on Hand	Lead Time
A	100	1
B	150	2
C	80	1

The gross requirements of item A are 200 units for period 4 and 250 units for period 5.

b. If the lead time for item A increases by one week, and the lead time for item C also increases by one week, what will the revised materials plan look like? Are there any problems which need immediate attention?

Solution

a. The MRP materials plan is as follows:

	Period				
Item A	1	2	3	4	5
Gross requirement				200	250
On-hand/scheduled receipts	100				
Net requirement				100	250
Planned order releases			100	250	

	Period				
Item B	1	2	3	4	5
Gross requirement			100	250	
On-hand/scheduled receipts	150				
Net requirement				200	
Planned order releases		200			

	Period				
Item C	1	2	3	4	5
Gross requirement			200	500	
On-hand/scheduled receipts	80				
Net requirement			120	500	
Planned order releases		120	500		

b. The revised MRP materials plan is as follows:

	Period				
Item A	1	2	3	4	5
Gross requirement				200	250
On-hand/scheduled receipts	100				
Net requirement				100	250
Planned order releases		100	250		

Item B	Period				
	1	2	3	4	5
Gross requirement		100	250		
On-hand/scheduled receipts	150				
Net requirement			200		
Planned order releases	200				

Item C	Period				
	1	2	3	4	5
Gross requirement		200	500		
On-hand/scheduled receipts	80				
Net requirement		120	500		
Planned order releases	500				

Yes, there is a problem that needs immediate attention. Item C is behind schedule and will need to be expedited immediately to ensure that 120 units of C are available in week 2. Alternatively, the master schedule could be revised to accommodate the availability of item C. Combinations of these two alternatives could also be considered.

Discussion Questions

1. In what ways do independent-demand inventories differ from dependent-demand inventories?

2. Why is demand history irrelevant for the management of raw materials and work-in-process inventories?

3. A vendor has quoted a lead time of 10 weeks for delivery of a part. Your purchasing manager says the part can be delivered in 3 weeks if necessary. Of course, the vendor disagrees. Who is correct? Explain.

4. It has been said that MRP is an information system that does not rely on sophisticated mathematical models. Discuss the historical significance of this statement.

5. With regard to inventory management, discuss the difference between a replenishment philosophy and a requirements philosophy.

6. Can the ABC principle be applied to manufacturing component inventories? Discuss.

7. How much safety stock should be carried in an MRP system? What is the role of safety stock in MRP systems? Where should safety stock be carried?

8. What are the potential effects of an inflated master schedule?

9. Describe the advantages of cycle counting over an annual physical inventory.

10. Under what circumstances is a shop-floor control system needed?

11. Is it possible to control financial totals without physical control of materials in manufacturing?

12. A company president said his company was too small to afford an MRP system. Discuss.

13. A materials manager said that her company needed only an order-launching system. Should the loop be closed?

14. Describe how MRP concepts could be used for the following service operations:
    a. Hotel
    b. Legal office

Excel Spreadsheet Tips

Three Excel spreadsheets are provided on the student CD-ROM for this chapter to assist students in solving the chapter problems. The spreadsheet for problem 2 is shown below with different data to illustrate its use. The spreadsheet develops a material plan for the Old Hickory Furniture Company by inputting the master schedule, the on-hand inventories, and the lead times.

NAME: Old Hickory Example	SECT: *************
DATE: 14-Oct-02	CHAPTER 16, PROBLEM 2

MATERIALS PLAN
OLD HICKORY FURNITURE COMPANY

******PART******		PAST DUE ORDERS	1	2	3	4	5	6
CHAIR	GROSS REQUIREMENTS:		0	0	600	0	600	400
	ON HAND/SCHED RECEIPTS		100	0	0	0	0	0
	NET REQUIREMENTS		0	0	500	0	600	400
	PLAN. ORDER RELEASES	0	0	500	0	600	400	0
LEG	GROSS REQUIREMENTS:		0	500	0	600	400	0
ASSEMBLY	ON HAND SCHED RECEIPTS		50	0	0	0	0	0
	NET REQUIREMENTS		0	450	0	600	400	0
	PLAN. ORDER RELEASES	450	0	600	400	0	0	0
BACK	GROSS REQUIREMENTS:		0	500	0	600	400	0
ASSEMBLY	ON HAND SCHED RECEIPTS		60	0	0	0	0	0
	NET REQUIREMENTS		0	440	0	600	400	0
	PLAN. ORDER RELEASES	0	440	0	600	400	0	0
SEAT	GROSS REQUIREMENTS:		0	500	0	600	400	0
	ON HAND SCHED RECEIPTS		200	0	0	0	0	0
	NET REQUIREMENTS		0	300	0	600	400	0
	PLAN. ORDER RELEASES	300	600	400	0	0	0	0
RAILS	GROSS REQUIREMENTS:		0	2400	1600	0	0	0
	ON HAND SCHED RECEIPTS		300	0	0	0	0	0
	NET REQUIREMENTS		0	2100	1600	0	0	0
	PLAN. ORDER RELEASES	0	2100	1600	0	0	0	0
LEGS	GROSS REQUIREMENTS:		0	2400	1600	0	0	0
	ON HAND SCHED RECEIPTS		500	0	0	0	0	0
	NET REQUIREMENTS		0	1900	1600	0	0	0
	PLAN. ORDER RELEASES	0	1900	1600	0	0	0	0
TOP	GROSS REQUIREMENTS:		440	0	600	400	0	0
	ON HAND SCHED RECEIPTS		50	0	0	0	0	0
	NET REQUIREMENTS		390	0	600	400	0	0
	PLAN. ORDER RELEASES	390	600	400	0	0	0	0
SPINDLE	GROSS REQUIREMENTS:		1760	0	2400	1600	0	0
	ON HAND SCHED RECEIPTS		100	0	0	0	0	0
	NET REQUIREMENTS		1660	0	2400	1600	0	0
	PLAN. ORDER RELEASES	1660	2400	1600	0	0	0	0

CAPACITY PLAN FOR ASSEMBLY	1	2	3	4	5	6
CHAIR ASSEMBLY HOURS	0	1000	0	1200	800	0
LEG ASSEMBLY HOURS	0	600	400	0	0	0
BACK ASSEMBLY HOURS	440	0	600	400	0	0
TOTAL ASSEMBLY HOURS	440	1600	1000	1600	800	0

Problems

1. The following information is given for a particular part. Using a lead time of two weeks, complete the table.

	Week				
	1	2	3	4	5
Gross requirements			100	300	200
On-hand/scheduled receipts	80	50			
Net requirements					
Planned order releases					

eXcel 2. The Old Hickory Furniture Company manufactures chairs on the basis of the BOM shown below. At the present time, the inventories of parts and lead times are as follows:

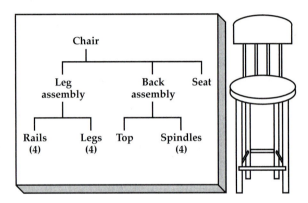

	On Hand	Weeks Lead Time
Chairs	100	1
Leg assembly	50	2
Back assembly	25	1
Seat	40	3
Rails	100	1
Legs	150	1
Top	30	2
Spindles	80	2

The company would like to produce 500 chairs in week 5 and 300 chairs in week 6.

a. Develop a materials plan for all the parts.

b. What actions should be taken now?

c. Assume it takes one hour to assemble backs, one hour to assemble legs, and two hours to finish completed chairs. Total assembly time for all three types of assembly is limited to 1,000 hours per week. Will this capacity constraint cause a bottleneck in assembly? If it does, what can be done?

d. What is the effect of changing the master schedule to 300 chairs in week 5 and 400 chairs in week 6?

3. Product A consists of subassemblies B and C. Subassembly B requires two parts of D and one part of E. Subassembly C requires one part of D and one part of F.

a. Draw a product structure tree (BOM) for this product.

b. How many parts are needed to make 200 units of finished product?

eXcel 4. The BOM for product A is given below:

Part	On Hand	Weeks Lead Time
A	75	1
B	100	2
C	50	1
D	125	2

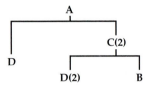

Assume the master schedule calls for 200 units of product A in week 5 and 250 units in week 6.

a. Develop a materials plan for this product.

b. What actions should be taken immediately?

c. Project the inventory ahead for each part.

d. If you were suddenly notified that part D will take three weeks to get instead of two weeks, what actions would you take?

5. The master scheduler in the ABC Widget Company is in the process of revising the master schedule. At the present time, he has scheduled 400 widgets for week 5 and is considering changing this to 500 widgets.

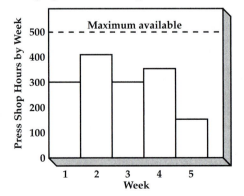

a. What information would you need to decide if you should make this change?

b. Suppose that each widget takes one hour of press time and three hours of assembly time,

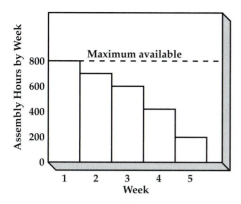

three weeks prior to delivery. Can the additional 100 widgets be made in view of the following shop loadings?

c. If the additional widgets cannot be made in part *b* above, what actions might be taken to make it possible to produce the required widgets?

6. A company makes a basic scissors consisting of three parts: the left side, the right side, and the screw that holds the sides together. At the present time, the company has the following numbers of parts on hand and on order. The lead times for reorder of each part are also shown along with a BOM and a sketch of the scissors.

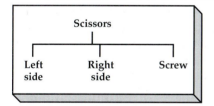

	On Hand	Weeks Lead Time	Scheduled Receipts
Scissors	100	1	
Left side	50	2	100 in week 2
Right side	75	2	200 in week 2
Screw	300	1	200 in week 1

a. Assume the master schedule calls for 300 scissors to be shipped in week 4 and 400 in week 5; work out a complete materials plan.

b. Suppose the supplier of right-hand sides calls to say that deliveries of the 200 parts on order will be one week late. What effect will this have on the materials plan?

c. If demand for scissors is uncertain and has a standard deviation of 50 units, what would you recommend the company do to maintain a 95 percent service level for scissors?

d. If the delivery of the scissors parts is unreliable and the standard deviation of delivery lead time is one week for each of the parts, what would you recommend the company do to maintain its production schedule?

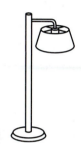

eXcel 7. A lamp consists of a frame assembly and a shade as shown below in the sketch and the bill of materials. The frame is made from a neck, a socket, and a base, which are assembled together from purchased parts. A shade is added to the frame assembly to make the finished lamp. The number of parts on hand, the parts scheduled to arrive, and the lead times to obtain more parts are shown below.

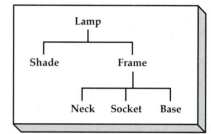

	On Hand	Weeks Lead Time	Scheduled Receipts
Lamp	200	1	—
Frame	100	2	—
Neck	0	3	—
Socket	300	2	—
Base	200	3	—
Shade	400	3	—

a. Assuming 1,000 finished lamps are required in week 7 and 1,500 in week 8, construct a complete materials plan for the lamp. What actions should be taken immediately to implement the plan?

b. If it takes 15 minutes of assembly time to assemble the parts into the frame and 5 minutes to assemble the shade and frame into a finished lamp, how much total assembly time is required in each week? What can be done if insufficient time is available in any given week?

c. If the lead time for assembly of lamps is extended from one week to two weeks, what changes will be needed in the materials plan to adjust for this change?

8. A telephone is assembled from a handset and a base. The handset in turn is assembled from a handle and a cord; and the base is assembled from a case, a circuit board, and a face plate. A BOM and a sketch of the phone, along with the numbers of parts on hand and lead times, are shown on the following page.

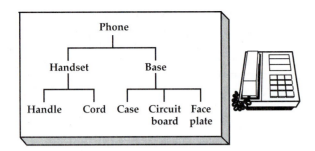

	On Hand	Weeks Lead Time
Phone	200	1
Handset	300	1
Handle	200	2
Cord	75	2
Base	250	1
Case	200	2
Circuit board	150	1
Face plate	300	2

a. Management would like to start assembling phones as soon as possible. How many phones can be made from the available parts, and when can they be delivered? Construct a materials plan to show your answer.

b. For the materials plan constructed in part *a*, develop an inventory projection of parts and finished goods on a week-by-week basis.

c. Suppose another 100 circuit boards can be obtained within one week. What effect will this have on your answer for part *a?*

9. A small toy robot is assembled from six parts: a body, a head, two arms, and two legs. The company uses a one-level bill of material to assemble

this product. The number of parts on hand and the lead times (weeks) to obtain more parts are shown below. There are no parts on order.

Toy robot

	On Hand	Lead Time
Body	25	2
Head	50	1
Arm	60	2
Leg	80	1

a. Assume that an order for 200 robots is received for the beginning of week 4 and that it takes one week to assemble the parts once they are all available. Construct a complete materials plan for the robots. What actions should be taken immediately to implement the plan?

b. The customer has called and asked if he could receive a portion of the 200 robots as soon as possible. How many robots can be assembled and delivered to him ASAP, and when would they arrive? What are the implications of this action?

c. The supplier of heads has just sent an e-mail that said it will take two weeks to deliver the heads instead of one week. What effect will this have on your material plan from part *a?*

Selected Bibliography

Anderson, John C., Roger G. Schroeder, Sharon E. Tupy, and Edna M. White. *Material Requirements Planning Systems: A Study of Implementation and Practice.* Falls Church, VA: APICS, 1981.

Bartholomew, Doug, "The ABC's of ERP." *CFO-IT*, Fall 2004, pp. 19–21.

Buffa, Elwood S., and Jeffrey Miller. *Production Inventory Systems Planning and Control,* 3rd ed. Homewood, IL: Irwin, 1979.

Burns, O. Maxie, David Turnipseed, and Water E. Riggs. "Critical Success Factors in Manufacturing Resource Planning Implementation." *International Journal of Operations Management* 11, no. 4 (1991), pp. 5–19.

Goodwin, Siegent, Cardillo, and Bergmann. "Implementing ERP in a Big Way." *APICS—The Performance Advantage,* June 1996, pp. 60–64.

Gray, Chris. "Coca Cola: Always Class A MRP II." www.partnersforexcellence.com/v2art3~htm, 2005.

Landvater, Darryl V., and Christopher D. Gray. *MRP II Standard System: A Handbook for Manufacturing Software Survival.* Falls Church, VA: APICS, 1989.

Lunn, Terry, and Susan A. Neff. *Integrating Materials Requirements Planning and Modern Business.* Falls Church, VA: APICS, 1992.

Nagendra, P. B., and S. K. Das. "Finite Capacity Scheduling Method for MRP with Lot Size Restrictions." *International Journal of Production Research* 39, no. 8 (May 2001), pp. 1603–23.

Orlicky, Joseph. *Material Requirements Planning.* New York: McGraw-Hill, 1975.

Plossl, George. *Orlicky's Material Requirement Planning,* 2nd ed. Falls Church, VA: APICS, 1994.

Ptak, Carol. *MRP and Beyond: A Toolbox for Integrating People and Systems.* Falls Church, VA: APICS, 1996.

Rondeau, Patrick J., and Lewis A. Litteral. "Manufacturing Planning and Control Systems: From Reorder Point to Enterprise Resource Planning." *Production & Inventory Management Journal* 42, no. 2 (2001), pp. 1–7.

Rudberg, Martin, and Jan Olhager. "Linking Manufacturing Strategy Decisions on Process Choice with Manufacturing Planning and Control Systems." *International Journal of Production Research* 40, no. 10 (July 2002), pp. 2335–51.

Schroeder, Roger G., John C. Anderson, Sharon E. Tupy, and Edna M. White. "A Study of MRP Benefits and Costs." *Journal of Operations Management* 2, no. 1 (October 1981), pp. 1–9.

Segerstedt, Anders. "Production and Inventory Control at ABB Motors and Volvo Wheel Loaders, Two Examples of MRP in Practical Use." *Production Planning & Control* 13, no. 3 (April 2002), pp. 317–25.

Taylor, Sam G. "Finite Capacity Scheduling Alternatives." *Production & Inventory Management Journal* 42, no. 3/4 (2001), pp. 70–74.

Toomey, John W. *MRPII: Planning for Manufacturing Excellence.* Falls Church, VA: APICS, 1996.

Vijayan, Jaikumar. "Manufacturing Execution Systems." *Computer World,* July 31, 2000.

Vollmann, Thomas E., William L. Berry, D. Clay Whybark, and F. Robert Jacobs. *Manufacturing Planning and Control for Supply Chain Management,* 5th ed. New York: McGraw-Hill, 2004.

Wasik, Arthur, and Jerry Wolfe. "Unlocking the Benefits of Finite Capacity Scheduling." *Logistics,* October 1990.

Wight, Oliver. *The Executives Guide to Successful MRP II.* New York: Wiley, 1996.

Just-in-Time Systems and Lean Thinking

Chapter outline

In this chapter, the **just-in-time** (JIT) philosophy of manufacturing will be described along with its extension to service firms and lean thinking. JIT is called a philosophy because it goes far beyond inventory control and encompasses the entire system of production. In a nutshell, JIT is an approach that seeks to eliminate all sources of waste in production activities by providing the right part at the right place at the right time.[1] Parts are therefore produced just in time to meet manufacturing requirements rather than by the traditional approach, which produces parts just in case (JIC) they are needed. The JIT system results in much less inventory, lower costs, and better quality than the JIC approach.

In this chapter, the JIT philosophy is discussed in detail and compared with MRP approaches. Even though JIT goes far beyond inventory control, it is

---

[1] Waste is defined as an activity that does not add value to the product or service.

described at this point in the book as an alternative to MRP systems for certain types of production. We also describe some concrete results that have been achieved from JIT systems, applications to services, and an implementation approach designed to gain maximum benefit from JIT. Lean thinking is discussed at the end of the chapter as an extension of JIT beyond production to design, distribution, supply chain, and services. It is important to understand JIT before discussing lean thinking.

17.1 PHILOSOPHY OF JIT

The JIT system was developed at the Toyota Motor Company in Japan.[2] Even though Schonberger (1982) indicates that JIT might be traced back to the Japanese shipbuilding industry, the modern application of JIT was popularized in the mid-1970s at Toyota by Taiichi Ohno, a Toyota vice president, and several of Ohno's colleagues. The JIT concept was then apparently first transferred to the United States about 1980 at Kawasaki's Lincoln, Nebraska, plant. Since then, many of the best corporations in the United States have implemented JIT, and it has achieved widespread use around the world.

The roots of the JIT system can probably be traced to the Japanese environment. Owing to a lack of space and lack of natural resources, the Japanese have developed an aversion to waste. They view scrap and rework as waste and thus strive for perfect quality. They also believe that inventory storage wastes space and ties up valuable materials. Anything that does not contribute value to the product is viewed as **waste.** See Table 17.1 for the seven wastes identified by

JAPANESE MANUFACTURING IN AMERICA. Japanese manufacturing methods are being widely used in America. © Rick Browne/Stock Boston

Suzaki (1987). U.S. companies, in contrast, with wide open spaces and a vast supply of raw materials, have not viewed waste in the same way. As a result, it was natural for the JIT philosophy to develop in Japan. Yet, as will be seen in this chapter, there is nothing culturally inherent in the JIT system that prevents companies anywhere in the world from using it or improving on it. Many companies now use JIT as their preferred approach.

In addition to eliminating waste, JIT has another major tenet in its philosophy—utilizing the full capability of the worker. Workers in the JIT system are charged with the responsibility for producing quality parts just in time to support the

[2] Some trace the JIT concept back to Ford Motor company because the Model T car could be produced in a few days from raw materials to the finished product.

TABLE 17.1
The Seven Wastes (none of these add value to the product or service)

- *Overproduction:* Producing more than the demand of customers resulting in unnecessary inventory, handling, paperwork, and warehouse space.
- *Waiting Time:* Operators and machines waiting for parts or work to arrive from suppliers or other operations.
- *Transportation:* Double or triple movement of materials due to poor layouts, lack of coordination, and workplace organization.
- *Processing:* Poor design or inadequate maintenance of processes requiring additional labor or machine time.
- *Inventory:* Excess inventory due to large lot sizes, obsolete items, poor forecasts, or improper production planning.
- *Motion:* Wasted movements of people or extra walking to get materials.
- *Defects:* Use of material, labor, and capacity for production of defects, sorting out bad parts, or warranty costs with customers.

Source: Adapted from Kiyoshi Suzaki, *The New Manufacturing Challenge* (New York: Free Press, 1987).

next production process. If they cannot meet this responsibility, they are required to stop the production process and call for help. In addition to greater responsibility for production, workers are also charged with improving the production process. Through quality teams, suggestion systems, and other forms of participation, workers offer improvements to the process of production. Thus, the capabilities of workers are used to a much greater extent in the JIT system than in traditional production approaches.

The objective of the JIT system is not, however, worker participation; rather, it is to improve profits and return on investment through cost reductions, inventory reductions, and quality improvements. The means for achieving these objectives are eliminating waste and involving workers in the production process. How this is done is summarized by the basic elements of JIT described in the next section.

JIT has its roots in repetitive manufacturing, which is approximately the same as mass production. **Repetitive manufacturing** is the production of standardized discrete products in high volume, for example, automobiles, electronics, and machinery. However, some of the JIT concepts are also being used for job lot or batch production, which is inherently nonrepetitive in nature, and JIT is spreading to service industries too. The use of JIT concepts at Toyota Motor Manufacturing in Georgetown, Kentucky, is described in the Operations Leader box.

17.2 ELEMENTS OF A JIT SYSTEM

Before going into detail about JIT, we will briefly summarize how the system works as a whole. This will be done by starting with the master schedule and working backward through the production process to the suppliers.

In JIT the master schedule, or final assembly schedule, is planned for a fixed period of time, say one to three months into the future, to allow work centers and suppliers to plan their respective work schedules. Within the current month, the master schedule is leveled on a daily basis. In other words, the same quantity of each product is produced each day for the entire month. Furthermore, small lots (preferably lot size equals one) are scheduled in the master schedule to provide a uniform load on the plant and suppliers during each day. The advantage of this kind of master scheduling is that it provides nearly constant

OPERATIONS LEADER
The Toyota Production System

The Toyota production system (TPS) has been transferred to the Toyota manufacturing plant in Georgetown, Kentucky, which employs 7,200 team members. The TPS includes the following elements:

- Basic Training—Training for all managers and employees in required job skills along with problem solving and continuous improvement methods.
- Jidoka—Preventing problems from occurring rather than responding to them after the fact. Workers are encouraged to stop the production line when there is a quality problem.

TOYOTA

- Standard Work—Standardization of all jobs to minimize waste and assure quality.
- A Culture of Pride—Pride is instilled by always putting people first in all decisions.
- Suggestion Program—A vigorous suggestion program is used resulting in 100,000 suggestions per year from teams or individuals.
- Supplier Relations—Suppliers deliver to the plant on a JIT basis. Supplier relations depend on mutual trust built on high performance and mutual prosperity.
- Inbound Logistics—On average only four hours of material are inside the plant. Frequent deliveries are arranged from suppliers.

This system has resulted in high quality cars being built in America with superior productivity, better than all competitors.

Source: Robert Hall, "The Americanization of the Toyota Production System," *Target* 15, no. 1 (1999).

demands on all downstream work centers and suppliers. There is nothing magic about using monthly time periods; weekly periods could be used as well if the production throughput time (cycle time) is sufficiently short.

JIT uses a simple parts withdrawal system, called "Kanban," to pull parts from one work center to the next.[3] Parts are kept in small containers, and only a specific number of these containers are provided. When all the containers are filled, the machines are shut off, and no more parts are produced until the subsequent (using) work center provides another empty container. Thus, work-in-process inventory is limited to available containers, and parts are only provided as needed. The final assembly schedule pulls parts from one work center to the next just in time to support production needs. If a process stops because of machine breakdown or quality problems, all preceding processes will automatically stop when their parts containers become full.

The objective of JIT is to produce parts in a lot size of one. In many cases, this is not economically feasible because of the cost of setup compared with inventory carrying cost. The JIT solution to this problem is to reduce the setup time as much as possible, ideally to zero. The setup time is not taken as given; rather, it is considered a cause of excess inventory. Low setup times result in small, economical lot sizes and shorter production lead times. Driving down the setup time for machines is a key to the JIT system. With shorter lead times and less material in process, the production system is also much more flexible to changes in the master schedule.

---

[3] *Kanban* means "card" or "signal" in Japanese—cards or other methods are used to signal the need for more production.

With an emphasis on **quick changeovers** and **smaller lots, multifunction workers** are required. Cross-training is needed so that workers can switch from one machine to the next and so that they can perform their own setup and maintenance. This requires a broader range of skills than traditional manufacturing. JIT requires not only broader skills but much greater teamwork and coordination since inventory is not available to cover up problems in the system. The entire production system must be more closely coordinated by the workers.

The layout of the plant is much different with JIT since inventory is held on the shop floor and not put in a storeroom between processes. Inventory is kept out in the open, so it is readily available to the next process. Since inventory is typically kept low—only a few hours or days of supply—plants can be kept much smaller because of the reduced storage space needed. One comparison showed only one-third the space was needed when compared with conventional plants.

Quality is absolutely essential with a JIT system. Not only do defects produce waste, but they can also grind the production process to a halt. Since there is no inventory to cover up mistakes, perfect or nearly perfect quality is required by a JIT system. JIT, however, facilitates improved quality since defects are quickly discovered by the next process. Quality problems rapidly gain plantwide attention as the production line stops when problems occur. A JIT system is designed to expose errors and get them corrected rather than covering them up with inventory.

Finally, supplier relations are radically changed by a JIT system. Suppliers are asked to make frequent deliveries (as many as four times per day) directly to the production line. Suppliers receive Kanban containers, just as in-plant work centers do, since suppliers are viewed as an extension of the plant. Changes in shipping procedures and close proximity of suppliers are often required to integrate suppliers effectively with JIT producers. Suppliers are also required to deliver perfect quality goods. A revolution is required in the way that we usually think of suppliers; we need to think of them as partners rather than as adversaries.

As can be seen, JIT affects practically every aspect of plant operations: lot sizing, scheduling, quality, layout, suppliers, labor relations, and so on. It will also affect every other function in the firm, particularly engineering, marketing, HR, and finance as they adjust to the new operating environment. While the effects are far-reaching, so are the potential benefits. Inventory turns of 50 to 100 times per year, superior quality, and substantial cost advantages (15 to 25 percent less) have been reported.

The objective of JIT, however, is to improve **return on investment** (ROI), as shown in Figure 17.1. ROI is increased by increases in revenues, cost reductions, and less investment. A JIT system can increase revenue by improving quality, as we have already discussed, or by giving better delivery service. Better service is provided by shorter lead times, which allow faster response to customer needs, and by better conformance to schedule commitments. Cost reductions can be obtained in materials (less scrap and rework), labor, and overhead. Finally, investment is reduced by less inventory and greater throughput of plant and equipment. When JIT is evaluated, its effect on the bottom line and on investment should be the ultimate test.

Figure 17.1 also shows how the various elements we have been describing (small lots, stable master schedule, and so on) contribute to JIT production. The most important thing to note, however, is that problem-solving activities by

FIGURE 17.1 JIT system.

Source: Adapted from Richard J. Schonberger, *Japanese Manufacturing Techniques: Nine Hidden Lessons in Simplicity* (New York: Free Press, 1982), p. 26.

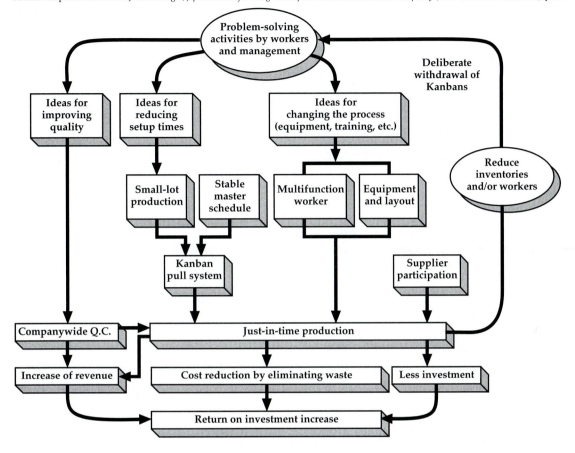

management and workers drive the whole system. These problem-solving activities are driven, in turn, by removing inventory, which is viewed as the "root of all evil." The JIT production system is, therefore, built on a philosophy of constant improvement.

An analogy for JIT is illustrated by Figure 17.2. Production is viewed as a converging system of streams, as we have previously noted in Chapter 15. The water level in the streams is viewed as inventory. At the bottom of each stream are rocks, which represent problems relating to quality, suppliers, delivery, machine breakdowns, and so forth. The traditional approach is to hold inventory high enough to cover up the rocks and thereby keep the stream flowing. The JIT approach is the opposite; the water level is lowered to expose the top of the rocks. When these rocks have been pulverized (i.e., the problems solved), the water is lowered again and more rocks are exposed. This process is repeated until all rocks are turned into pebbles and the stream flows smoothly at a low level.

This analogy is very good because it highlights the problem-solving approach that is at the heart of JIT. How this works will be described next in some detail by discussing each of the major elements of a JIT system.

FIGURE 17.2   Stream analogy.

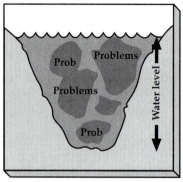
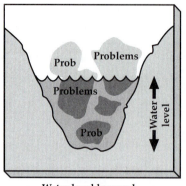
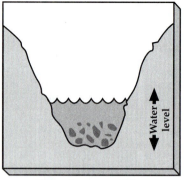

Original situation
(inventory covers problems)   **Water level lowered**
(to expose problems)   **Water flows smoothly**
(problems pulverized)

17.3   STABILIZING THE MASTER SCHEDULE

The process of production planning starts with a long-range production plan, which is then broken down into annual, monthly, and daily plans. At each point in the process, sales are considered, profit planning is done, and capacity is planned. This planning process starts with an aggregate production plan and successively refines it into specific models and products.

Master scheduling is done at the monthly (or weekly) and daily level so as to achieve a uniform load. The production horizon for specific models must be set at least one week in advance and possibly one or two months in advance, depending on lead times for production, purchasing, and capacity changes. Assume for the purpose of discussion that a one-month rolling schedule is used, where one month of production is scheduled in advance. Also assume that the schedule calls for 10,000 units of product A, 5,000 units of product B, and 5,000 units of product C. If there are 20 days of production in the month, then the daily schedule will call for 1/20 of each model produced in each day: 500A, 250B, and 250C. Furthermore, the individual units will be mixed as they go down the production line. The sequence will be |AABC|AABC|AABC|. Note how two units of A are produced for every unit of B and C. Then the sequence is continually repeated.

Production is leveled to this extent to create a **uniform load** on all work centers that support final assembly. This sequence presumes, of course, that the changeover cost between models is zero or nearly so. If this is not so, the final assembly line should be redesigned to achieve a very low setup cost. How this can be done will be described later.

In some cases, it will not be possible or economical to achieve perfectly mixed production on the final assembly line. In this case, very small lots should be scheduled, the lot size depending on the trade-off between setup and inventory carrying costs. The objective of **single-unit production,** however, should not be abandoned since it ordinarily leads to the lowest system costs.

Once the monthly master schedule has been set, this information must be transmitted to all work centers and suppliers. They will then plan their capacity in terms of numbers of workers needed, overtime, subcontracting, and possibly new equipment. Enough lead time must be given to them to obtain the resources they need to do the job.

The JIT system does not allow overproduction once the daily quota has been set. For example, if the daily quota is met in seven hours, production is stopped, and production workers do maintenance or have quality-team meetings. Similarly, if production falls behind, it is usually made up by overtime the same day. This is facilitated by shift scheduling, which allows some time between shifts. For example, a two-shift operation might be scheduled from 7 A.M. to 3 P.M. and from 5 P.M. to 1 A.M. Maintenance and overtime are then scheduled between shifts. The objective of the JIT system is to produce the right quantity each day—no more and no less.

Master scheduling, as we have described it, closely resembles customer demand on a daily basis. This minimizes finished-goods inventory since the production output is closely matched to demand. As we shall see, this type of master schedule also helps reduce work-in-process and raw-materials inventories. **Stabilizing the master schedule** is the key to stabilizing all other production processes and supplier requirements.

17.4   THE KANBAN SYSTEM

Kanban is the method of production authorization and materials movement in the JIT system. As noted earlier, Kanban, in the Japanese language, means a marker (card, sign, plaque, or other device) used to control the sequencing of jobs through a sequential process. Kanban is a subsystem of JIT; the two terms are not synonymous as some authors have indicated.

The purpose of the Kanban system is to signal the need for more parts and to ensure that those parts are produced in time to support subsequent fabrication or assembly. This is done by pulling parts through from the final assembly line. Only the final assembly line receives a schedule from the dispatching office, and this schedule is nearly the same from day to day. All other machine operators and suppliers receive production orders (Kanban cards) from the subsequent (using) work centers. If production should stop for a time in the using work centers, the supplying work centers will also soon stop since they will no longer receive Kanban orders for more material.

The Kanban system is a physical control system consisting of cards and containers. Assume for the purposes of discussion that eight containers are used between work centers A and B (A supplies B), and each container holds exactly 20 parts. The maximum inventory that can exist between these two work centers is then 160 units (8 × 20) since production at work center A will stop when all containers are filled.

In the normal course of events, the eight containers might be distributed as shown in Figure 17.3. Three containers are located at work center A in the output area filled with parts. One container is presently being filled at work center A by the machine. One full container is being moved from A to B, two full containers are sitting in the input area of work center B, and one container is being used at B. These eight containers are needed since work center A also produces parts for other work centers, machines at A may break down, and move times from A to B are not always exactly predictable.

To control movement of the containers, there are two main types of Kanban cards, **production cards** and **withdrawal** (move) **cards.** These cards are used to authorize production and to identify parts in any container. Kanban cards may be made of paper, metal, or plastic, and they generally contain the information shown in Figure 17.4. Kanban cards take the place of shop paperwork used in traditional repetitive manufacturing.

FIGURE 17.3 Kanban system.

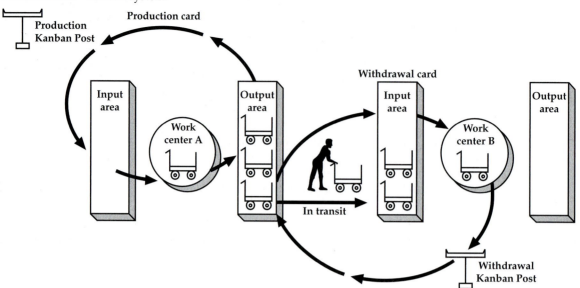

Here is how the Kanban system works, assuming containers are moved one at a time. When a container of parts is emptied at work center B, the empty container and associated withdrawal card are taken back to work center A. The production card from a full container of parts is removed from its container and replaced by the withdrawal card. The production card is then placed in the Kanban receiving post at work center A, thereby authorizing production of another container of parts. The empty container is left at work center A.

The full container of parts and its withdrawal card are moved to work center B and placed in the input area. When this container of parts is eventually used, its withdrawal card and the empty container are taken back to work center A, and the cycle is repeated.

The significant thing about the Kanban system is that it is **visual** in nature. All parts are neatly placed in containers of a fixed size. As empty containers

FIGURE 17.4 Kanban cards.

Part Number	W262		Preceding Process
Part Name	WHEEL		STAMPING A12

Box Capacity	Box Type	Issue No.	Subsequent Process
20	B	4 of 8	RUBBER TIRE B6

Withdrawal Kanban

Part Number	Y16032	Process
Part Name	WHEEL RIM	STAMPING A12
Stock Location at Which to Store:	1879-2	
Container Capacity: 20		

Production Kanban

accumulate, it is clear that the producing work center is getting behind. On the other hand, when all containers are filled, production is stopped. The production lot size is exactly equal to one container of parts.

The number of containers needed to operate a work center is a function of the demand rate, container size, and the circulating time for a container. This is illustrated by the following formula:[4]

$$n = \frac{DT}{C}$$

where n = total number of containers

D = demand rate of the using work center

C = container size in number of parts, usually less than 10 percent of daily demand

T = time for a container to complete an entire circuit: filled, wait, moved, used, and returned to be filled again (also called lead time)

Suppose that demand at the next work center is 2 parts per minute and a standard container holds 25 parts. Also assume that it takes 100 minutes for a container to make a complete circuit from work center A to work center B and back to A again, including all setup, run, move, and wait time. The number of containers needed in this case is eight.

$$n = \frac{2(100)}{25} = 8$$

The maximum inventory is equal to the container size times the number of containers = $8 \times 25 = 200$ units, since the most we can have is all containers filled.

$$\text{Maximum inventory} = nC = DT$$

Inventory can be decreased by reducing the size of the containers or the number of containers used. This is done by reducing the time required to circulate a container, including its machine setup time, run time, wait times, or move times. When any of these times has been reduced, management can remove Kanban cards from the system and a corresponding number of containers. It is the responsibility of managers and workers in a JIT system to reduce inventory by a constant cycle of improvement. **Reducing lead time** is the key.

Kanban links all work centers in a production facility and the suppliers as shown in Figure 17.5. All material is pulled through by the final assembly schedule, based on a highly visible shop-floor and supplier control system.

KANBAN SQUARE AT HONEYWELL. The Kanban square marked by the dashed rectangle signals the need for the production of a cabinet. Only one cabinet is placed on this square at a time. When the square is emptied by subsequent production, another cabinet is produced. Courtesy of Honeywell International, Inc.

[4] Safety stock can be added to the numerator of the formula to account for uncertainty in demand or the time.

FIGURE 17.5 Complete Kanban system.

Source: Robert W. Hall, *Driving the Productivity Machine: Production Planning and Control in Japan* (Falls Church, VA: American Production and Inventory Control Society, 1981).

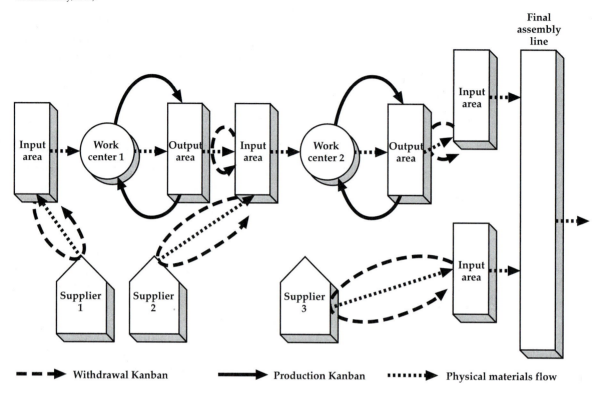

17.5 REDUCING SETUP TIME AND LOT SIZES

Reducing setup time is important since it increases available capacity, increases flexibility to meet schedule changes, and reduces inventory. As setup time approaches zero, the ideal lot size of one unit can be reached.

In conventional repetitive production, we have concentrated on reducing run times per unit and more or less ignored setup time. When long runs of thousands of units are anticipated, run times naturally are more important than setup times. A better solution is to concentrate on reducing both setup times and run times. This requires additional attention by engineers, managers, and workers to the setup process itself.

Since setup time has received so little attention, phenomenal reductions are possible. For example, at General Motors, the time required to change a die in a large punch press was reduced from 6 hours to 18 minutes. This allowed dramatic reductions in inventory from $1 million to $100,000, reductions in lead times, and greater utilization of capacity.

Single setups are being sought in many companies. Single setup refers to a setup time that has a single digit in minutes. One-touch setups are also being pursued, which refers to a setup of less than 1 minute. These low setup times can be achieved by two steps. First, external and internal setups are separated. The term "internal setup" refers to actions that require the machine to be stopped, while "external setups" can be done while the machine is operating. After separating internal and external setups, as much of the setup as possible is converted from internal to external. This is done, for example, by using two sets of dies, one inside the machine and one outside; by having quick change adjustments; and by employing cleverly designed tools and fixtures. Once the machine is stopped, it can then be quickly converted to the new product since internal setup has been minimized. Much can be done once people realize the importance of quick changeover. In some companies, the workers even practice setups in order to reduce the time. The best example of quick changeover comes from the race track. Race cars are quickly fueled, tires are changed, and the windshield washed in short pit stops by highly coordinated and trained pit crews.

Reducing setup times, lot sizes, and lead times is the engine that drives JIT. These reductions make it possible to remove Kanban cards and thus decrease inventory on a continual basis.

17.6 LAYOUT AND EQUIPMENT

Installation of a JIT system has a natural effect on **layout** and **equipment.** The plant evolves toward a more streamlined flow and automated plant because lot sizes are reduced and problems are constantly resolved making automation possible.

The effect of JIT on layout is shown in Figure 17.6. In part *a* of the figure, an initial layout is shown in which suppliers deliver to a stockroom and parts are placed in stockrooms after certain stages of production are completed. In part *b*, a JIT system has been implemented, and all stockrooms have been eliminated. In this case, all stock is kept on the shop floor as part of the JIT system. Part *c* of the figure shows that JIT has evolved to a **group technology** (GT) or cellular manufacturing layout. In this case, the work centers have been redefined so that parts can flow smoothly from one work center to the next. Most of the inventory buffers, next to each machine, have been eliminated as the parts flow from one station to the next. It is a natural consequence of JIT to evolve toward cellular manufacturing and feeder-line types of layouts. More automation is also possible as lot sizes approach one unit.

With a JIT system, superb maintenance of equipment is required. Since inventories have been cut to the bone, equipment must be kept in a good state of repair. Workers take responsibility for most of their own maintenance, which gives them more control over production. Maintenance time is also provided between shifts for routine and preventive maintenance actions.

17.7 EFFECT ON WORKERS

One of the critical things needed to make a JIT system work is **multifunction workers.** In most cases, each worker must be able to operate several machines in a group, going from one to the next to make the parts required. Since parts are not produced unless they are needed, the worker must be able to shut off the machine and move on to another job where parts are needed. The worker must also be able to set up machines, do routine maintenance, and inspect the parts. This ordinarily requires workers who are **cross-trained** in several different skills.

FIGURE 17.6 Effect of JIT on layout. JIT layout with GT.

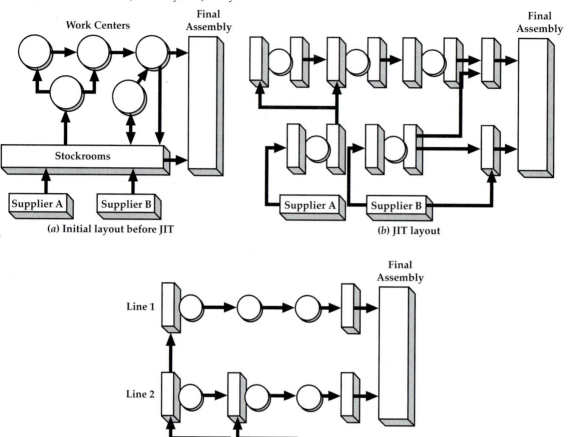

(a) Initial layout before JIT

(b) JIT layout

(c) JIT layout with GT

Moving toward a flexible workforce may require changing the way workers are paid and rewarded. Traditional pay systems are often based on seniority and job skill level. New pay systems are needed that reward workers on the basis of the number of different jobs they can perform. This will encourage workers to learn more skills and to become more flexible.

Special efforts are needed to use JIT in a union environment. Labor unions often are organized along skill or craft lines, and they do not tend to encourage flexibility in the workforce. As a result, management will need to work closely with unions to develop the kind of workforce needed for JIT.

Methods are needed to engage the workers and engineers actively in problem-solving activities. In JIT systems, quality teams and suggestion systems are used for this purpose. An environment of participation must be created in order to get all employees to contribute toward problem solving on the shop floor.

JIT cannot be implemented without full worker understanding and cooperation. Management must ensure that workers understand their new roles and accept the JIT approach to manufacturing. So many changes are required, as indicated above, that JIT cannot possibly succeed without the active and enthusiastic support of all managers, the HR function, and employees. JIT is not simply another program but a whole new approach to manufacturing.

17.8   SUPPLIERS

Just as employees are required to change, so are the company's **suppliers.** Under JIT, suppliers are treated much as internal work centers are treated. Suppliers receive Kanban cards and special containers, and they are expected to make frequent deliveries just in time for the next production stage. Suppliers are viewed as the **external factory** and as part of the production team. This is very much in line with modern supply chain thinking.

With a JIT system, several deliveries might be made each day, provided the supplier is located in the same vicinity. Suppliers located at a distance may have local warehouses where they receive bulk shipments and then break them down for frequent deliveries to the customer. This is not desirable, however, since too much inventory builds up in the pipeline and reaction time is too long. Local suppliers with short lead times are preferred.

Suppliers are given specific delivery times rather than shipment dates. For example, a supplier may be required to deliver parts at 8 A.M., 10 A.M., 12 noon, and 2 P.M. On each delivery, the supplier picks up the empty containers and associated withdrawal Kanban cards. Only that number of containers is filled for the next delivery. Deliveries are made directly to the assembly line without receiving or inspection. This requires complete confidence in the supplier's quality. It also greatly reduces paperwork, lead time, inventory, the number of receiving areas, and required storage space.

In some cases, where it is too expensive to make several deliveries each day, suppliers may get together and make round-robin deliveries. In this case, for example, one supplier may go to three other suppliers plus his own shop for the 8 A.M. delivery. Another supplier will make the 10 A.M. run, and so on. This method can save on transportation expenses for small-lot deliveries.

With the JIT system there is a tendency to use fewer suppliers. This is done to establish a long-term relationship with the supplier and to ensure the quality of parts needed. A complete reversal of thinking is needed here since we would ordinarily assume that fewer suppliers might price-gouge the customer, and more sources are needed to keep the suppliers honest. Supplier prices, however, can be kept in line with long-term contracts that include negotiated price stability. This requires a totally different type of supplier–customer relationship than we have had in the past.

Many companies have established an "integrated supplier program" to move toward a JIT system. The features of this type of program are as follows:

1. **Early supplier selection.** Suppliers are selected before the part reaches final design, so the design can be worked out completely with the suppliers.
2. **Family of parts sourcing.** A supplier takes responsibility for an entire family of parts, thereby allowing the supplier to establish group technology layouts and economic volumes.

3. **Long-term relationship.** An exclusive contract for the life of the part can be given to a supplier in exchange for a specific price schedule over the life of the part. Sometimes future price reductions or maximum increases are specified in the schedule. In other cases two or more suppliers may be used to ensure reliable supply, but nevertheless long-term relationships are established.

4. **Paperwork reduction in receiving and inspection.** This results in a direct savings to the customer and the supplier.

Changing supplier relations is one of the most important aspects of a JIT system.

17.9 IMPLEMENTATION OF JIT

The first and most successful application of JIT systems was at the Toyota Motor Company in Japan. As we have mentioned, Kawasaki U.S.A. in Nebraska started implementation of JIT in 1980. Implementation has been achieved in many other U.S. companies, including Ford, General Electric, General Motors, Eaton, Motorola, Black & Decker, Briggs and Stratton, Hewlett-Packard, IBM, John Deere, Bendix, Mercury Marine, Omark, Rockwell, Westinghouse, Tennant, 3M, and Honeywell.

Some of the effects of JIT implementation are as follows: In the auto industry, JIT has achieved inventory turns of 50 to 100, compared with 10 to 20 for traditional approaches. In motorcycle production, JIT has achieved inventory turns of about 20, compared with 3 to 5 in traditional companies. JIT has also improved quality, reduced costs, and improved flexibility in these same companies.

Implementation of JIT, however, is difficult. To facilitate implementation the following approach is suggested:

1. Obtain commitment from top management. Make sure that they know what changes will be required and that they will provide the **leadership** to adopt the JIT approach. Prepare a plan for implementation, usually with the assistance of a cross-functional team.

2. Gain the cooperation of the workforce. Strong leadership is needed on the shop floor to make JIT work. Guarantee stable employment, engage in training, and encourage participation. Small-group improvement activities such as quality teams should be used to get all employees involved in problem solving. Begin cross-training the workforce.

3. Start with the final assembly line. Level production to be almost identical every day. Reduce setup times until models can be mixed. Use standard containers for parts, and make them readily accessible to the assembly line.

4. Working backward from final assembly, reduce setup times and lot sizes in fabrication areas to match the lot sizes needed in final assembly. Remove inventory from the storerooms, and put it on the shop floor.

5. Balance fabrication rates with final assembly production rates. This may require correction of capacity shortfalls. Provide spare capacity in all areas. If any work center falls behind, it will need some spare capacity to catch up.

6. Extend JIT to the suppliers. First, stabilize their delivery schedule, and then ask for frequent deliveries. Remove the inventory needed to cover long times and variances. Help suppliers with quality assurance to meet your specifications. Negotiate long-term contracts with suppliers.

**OPERATIONS
LEADER**

*St. Lukes
Hospital and
Allegiance Inc.*

St. Lukes Episcopal Hospital in Houston used to carry a large inventory of medical supplies in its storerooms and warehouse to service its 949 beds and 38 operating rooms. Today, the storerooms have been converted into patient care areas and the inventory is gone, thanks to JIT deliveries and stockless inventory services provided by Allegiance, a medical supplies service. St. Lukes is already saving $2 million per year through these services.

JIT delivery and stockless services are provided to the hospital by Allegiance, the nation's largest medical supplies provider. Allegiance has capitalized on the strategic value of being capable of providing the right supplies to the right location, at the right time. They implemented JIT deliveries by providing frequent deliveries to hospitals. This reduced the hospital's needs for such large inventories. Then, Allegiance began an increased number of daily deliveries to the hospital, with deliveries moving directly to the department where they are needed—in a timely manner.

Allegiance and St. Lukes have teamed up in a way that is beneficial to both organizations. St. Lukes has turned an expense-generating area (the inventory storage facilities) into revenue-generating areas (additional patient services areas), and it is saving large amounts of money through eliminating wasteful inventory-carrying costs and handling costs. The benefits do not stop with reduced inventory or eliminated storerooms and warehouses. The partnership between Allegiance and St. Lukes has resulted in a new, closer working relationship between supplier and purchaser.

Source: Adapted from Milt Freudenheim, "'Partners in Inventory Control," *The New York Times,* March 3, 1991, sec. 3, p. 5; and www.allegiance.net.

JIT is the preferred method for repetitive production in industry. JIT has such a major impact that it is being compared with the Ford moving assembly line and the Taylor system as one of the great innovations in production management. The assumptions of the JIT system are certainly opposed to most of the traditional assumptions about repetitive manufacturing.

JIT is now being implemented in the service industries to limit inventories. See the Operations Leader box to learn about JIT deliveries of medical supplies to St. Lukes Hospital.

17.10 COMPARISON OF MRP AND JIT

When JIT was first introduced, much was written on MRP versus JIT because they were viewed as incompatible production control systems. More recently, we have come to recognize that MRP and JIT are compatible and can be used together in certain situations.

In discussing the relationship between MRP and JIT it is important to understand the distinction between pull and push systems of production control. A **push system,** such as MRP, pushes material into production to meet future needs. A master schedule is constructed representing future forecasts/orders, which determines what components and parts are to be ordered and pushed through production. In a **pull system,** such as JIT, material is pulled through production by the subsequent (using) work centers. Materials are provided only when there is a subsequent demand; there is no pushing of materials into production to meet future demands. Because of the lack of forward visibility, a repetitive master schedule is required for a pull system to work.

There are three situations to consider in comparing MRP and JIT: pure repetitive manufacturing, batch manufacturing, and job shop manufacturing.

1. A pure repetitive manufacturing situation is one where the master schedule is the same from day-to-day and level loaded, as we have described earlier in this chapter. In this case, a pull system, such as JIT, works very well. Since there are no changes in the end products being made from day-to-day, the component parts needed each day are the same. The only uncertainty is breakdowns in the production process. These disruptions are handled by a pull system and excellent maintenance, since production will stop when using work centers stop. There is no need for an MRP system to predict future production requirements with its more complicated, and expensive, computerized elements.

A common variation on a pure repetitive system is a system that changes from time to time but is still repetitive within a fixed planning horizon. An example is a repetitive schedule for the next five weeks, but in the sixth week the schedule will change to a different repetitive mix of products. In this case, a type I MRP system is needed for major event planning, which is a change in the future master schedule to different production rates. All work centers and suppliers must be notified in advance of the requirements for the new schedule. This can be done with a very simple MRP type I system used for planning purposes only. The JIT (pull system) is then used for execution of the plan on the shop floor. The JIT system is adjusted for major events by the MRP system.

2. A batch process might utilize a hybrid MRP-II and JIT type of system, particularly when the batches are somewhat repetitive in nature. In this case, the master schedule will not be identical from day to day but will have some repetitive elements. MRP-II is used to push material into the factory and to plan capacity, while the JIT (pull system) is used for execution on the shop floor. This makes it possible to eliminate the shop-floor control element of MRP-II with its substantial work-in-process tracking. The hybrid system works particularly well when batch production has been organized into cells so that MRP can provide shop orders to the cells rather than to each machine type. JIT is then used to pull material through each of the cells.

3. A job shop process that is batch-oriented and nonrepetitive must use MRP-II to plan and control production. An extreme example of this situation is where the factory makes products only to order and each order is different. In this case, a pull system will not work. Material must be pushed into the factory to meet future demands that are different for each order. A capacity-planning and shop-floor control system is needed to regulate the flow of materials through production. Even in this case, however, certain elements of JIT such as reduction of setup times, multifunction workers, problem solving by workers and managers, and supplier partnerships can be used. It is only the Kanban system that will not work.

As can be seen, there are various situations that are best suited to a pure JIT or a pure MRP control system. But there are many opportunities for hybrid systems too. Figure 17.7 summarizes when these various options apply.

17.11 BEYOND JIT TO LEAN THINKING

Womack, Jones, and Roos first used the term **lean production** in a popular book published in 1990 entitled *The Machine That Changed the World: The Story of Lean Production*. This book compared the efficiency of automobile assembly lines in Japan, the United States, and Europe. The conclusion was that labor productivity

FIGURE 17.7
Uses of MRP and
JIT.

Source: J. Nakane and
Robert W. Hall, "Japanese
Production Systems," in Lee
and Schwendiman (eds.),
*Management by Japanese
Systems* (New York: Praeger,
1982).

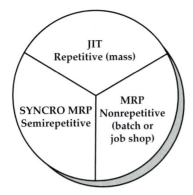

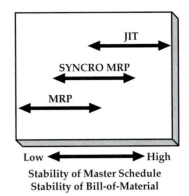

in the best plants exceeded that in the worst plants in all three countries by a factor of 2 to 1. Also, the best U.S. plants had comparable labor productivity (vehicle assembly hours) and quality to the best Japanese plants located in the United States, while the European plants lagged behind. This study demonstrated that the best plants using lean production provided a big edge in automobile assembly performance anywhere in the world. The study went on to describe lean engineering and lean distribution, thereby extending JIT concepts beyond the factory.

Womack and Jones published a subsequent book on **lean thinking** in 1996. They showed how the concepts of lean production and JIT could be extended outside production to the entire business including marketing, finance, and accounting, and these concepts could also be used in service industries. According to the authors, lean thinking consists of the following five elements:

- Specify *value* from the customer's point of view.
- Create a *value stream map* and remove waste.
- *Flow* the product or service through the system.
- *Pull* the product or service from the customer.
- Strive for *perfection*.

While JIT takes an internal view of the firm, lean thinking takes an external perspective starting with defining what the customer really values. Value can only be defined by the customer and is provided by the product or service the customer truly needs at a price the customer is willing to pay. The JIT system we have discussed in this chapter takes the product or service design as given. Lean thinking moves the analysis upstream into marketing and engineering by addressing true customer needs. Womack and Jones give the example of an airline flight. What the customer wants is to travel from point A to B safely in a short time at an affordable price. All large airlines provide acceptable safety, but often route the customer through hubs and transfer flights. What the customer wants is point-to-point service, which low-cost airlines such as Southwest, Jet Blue, and AirTran now provide. It is important, however, to carefully specify true customer value by lean thinking and not assume efficiency is only gained through economies of scale and larger aircraft using hubs, as the low-cost airlines have shown.

After specifying value, lean thinking requires describing the value stream from design and operations to suppliers and distribution. This typically involves **value stream mapping** (a variation of flowcharting from Chapter 7), as illustrated below, to identify waste in the current value stream and specification of a future value stream that eliminates waste from the customer's point of view.

The next step is to flow the product or service by reducing setup time and seeking small lots, perhaps even a lot size of one. Producing products or services in batches hides defects and leads to excessive waiting time for customers or excess inventory in the system.

Once flow is accomplished, the customer can pull the product or service through the system when requested by the customer. Customers hate to wait for a product that is being batched by the producer for the producer's convenience and is not provided when the customer wants it.

By continuous improvement, or radical change, more value can be provided seeking ultimate perfection for the customer. While everyone seeks perfection, the definition of perfection used here is an affordable product or service, delivered rapidly and on time, that meets the customers' needs.

Lean thinking is illustrated by a health care example. A large multispecialty clinic decided to apply lean thinking to its practice. A group of physicians, nurses, administrators, and technicians was assembled for two days to review the patient admission, diagnosis, and treatment process. The first task was to identify value from the patient's point of view. The group decided that patients wanted to be diagnosed and treated without errors and with a minimum of waiting. The current value stream map in Figure 17.8 was created after each team

FIGURE 17.8   Progressive health care value stream map for current state.

Adapted from Bushell, Mobley, and Shelest (2002).

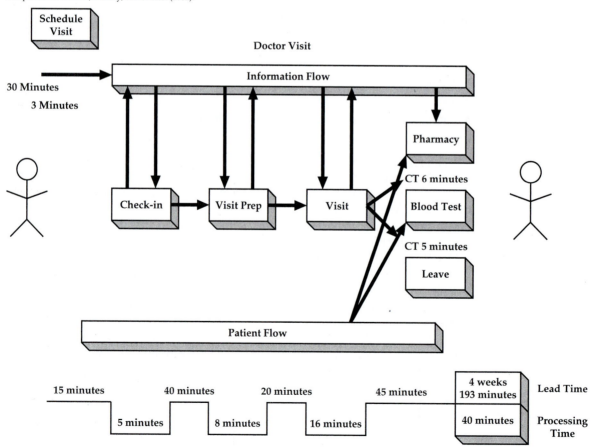

member went out to view the actual admission and examination process. They recorded patient waiting times and found waste (non-value-adding activities) such as medical errors, barriers to communication, unavailable information, wrong information, batching of customers, and correction/rework.

By brainstorming, the future value stream map was created to eliminate waste and reduce waiting times. The group realized that everything it did was for the convenience of the medical professionals, not to add value for the patient. As a result the group eliminated multiple check-in points during the same appointment, reduced waiting time during check-in (an average before the change of 40 minutes) and in the examination rooms (a previous average of 20 minutes), and reviewed possible sources of medical errors for error proofing. This process was repeated in multiple clinics as they worked toward improving patient flow, patient pull, and perfection in the system.

Lean thinking has wide applicability to any process in business including administrative, transactional, service, and manufacturing processes. It can also be used with supply chain partners to help the entire supply chain eliminate waste and create more value for the customer.

17.12 KEY POINTS

The JIT system described in this chapter is a major approach to reduce waste in manufacturing and service firms. We have seen how parts should be produced just in time rather than just in case they are needed. This is accomplished by a simple visual system of production control, constant reductions in inventories, and faster throughput.

Key points covered in the chapter are these:

- The JIT system is based on a philosophy of eliminating waste and utilizing the full capability of each worker. This system was originally developed in Japan but is now being used around the world.
- The objective of JIT is to improve return on investment. This is done by increasing revenues (through quality, delivery, and flexibility improvements), reducing costs, and reducing the investment required.
- To use JIT, the master schedule must be stabilized and leveled. This requires constant daily production, within the time frame of the master schedule, and mixed model assembly. As a result, the demand on preceding work centers is nearly constant.
- The Kanban system is used to pull parts through to meet the master assembly schedule. A fixed number of containers is provided for each part required. When these containers are full, no more parts are produced, thus limiting the inventory of each part. Constant improvement activities are encouraged by workers and management to reduce the number of containers, size of containers, and inventory.
- Reducing lot sizes, setup times, and lead times is the key to decreasing inventories in a JIT system. The objective is a lot size of one unit. This is done through small-group improvement activities and management and labor cooperative efforts.
- JIT affects plant layout by requiring much less space and encouraging movement toward group technology layouts.

1. Society of Manufacturing Engineers
   www.sme.org/leandirections
Read an article on JIT, Kaizen, or Kanban from the SME site.

2. Lean Enterprise Institute
   www.lean.org
From this site, managed by James Womack and others, read an article on lean operations and come to class prepared to discuss it.

3. Strategos
   www.strategosinc.com/kanban_game.htm
Access this site and download the Kanban game. Follow the instructions given to play the game and bring your results to class for discussion.

4. The Manager
   www.themanager.org/Knowledgebase/Operations/JIT.htm
Read an article from this site on JIT or fast-based replenishment.

- JIT requires multifunction workers who can operate several machines and perform setup, maintenance, and inspection activities. Moving toward a flexible workforce will require changing the way workers are selected, trained, evaluated, and rewarded.
- New supplier relationships must be established to make JIT work. Frequent deliveries and reliable quality are required. Often, long-term single-source contracts will be negotiated with suppliers.
- Implementation of JIT systems requires a staged progression of activities. Top management must provide leadership and support. The final assembly schedule must be leveled, followed by leveling of fabrication processes and supplier schedules. Lot sizes and lead times must be reduced for all stages of production. Intensive education of workers and management at all levels is needed.

- For production control, JIT systems are best suited to repetitive manufacturing. MRP is suited to job shop production, and mixed MRP-JIT systems are best for semirepetitive batch manufacturing.
- Lean thinking can be applied to design, manufacturing, distribution, services, and the supply chain. Lean thinking includes five elements: specify customer value, map the value stream, flow the product or service, pull from the customer, and strive for perfection.

SOLVED PROBLEMS

Problem

1. **Kanban**   A work center uses Kanban containers that hold 300 parts. To produce enough parts to fill the container, 90 minutes of setup plus run time are needed. Moving the container to the next workstation, waiting time, processing time at the next workstation, and return of empty container take 140 minutes. There is an overall demand rate of 9 units per minute.
   a. Calculate the number of containers needed for the system.
   b. What is the maximum inventory in the system?
   c. A quality team has discovered how to reduce setup time by 65 minutes. If these changes are made, can the number of containers be reduced?

Solution

a. T is the time required for a container to complete an entire circuit, in this case, 90 minutes setup and run time plus 140 minutes to move the container through the rest of the circuit.

$$n = DT/C = 9(90 + 140)/300 = 6.9 \text{ (round up to 7)}$$

b. Since production will stop when all containers are full, the maximum inventory is when all containers are full, that is, nC.

$$nC = 7(300) = 2{,}100$$

c. $n = DT/C = 9(25 + 140)/300 = 4.95$ (round up to 5)

Yes, the number of containers can be reduced from 7 to 5.

Problem

2. **Kanban**   Work center A produces parts that are then processed by work center B. Kanban containers used by the work centers hold 100 parts. The overall rate of demand is 4.5 parts per minute at work center B. The table below shows setup, run, move, and wait times for parts at each of the work centers.

	Work Center	
	A	B
Setup	4	3
Run time per unit	0.1	0.4
Move time	2	6
Wait time	10	20

a. What is the minimum number of containers needed between these two work centers?

b. Assume that two extra containers are available (at no extra cost). If these work centers were to use the two containers, what is the maximum parts per minute that could be expected to flow through these two work centers? Could the work centers handle a demand of 8.5 parts per minute?

Solution

a. T is the time required for a container to go through both work centers and back to its starting point. Therefore, $T = 4 + 3$ minutes of setup time, $100(.1 + .4)$ minutes of run time, $2 + 6$ minutes of move time, and $10 + 20$ minutes of wait time. Thus, $T = 7 + 50 + 8 + 30 = 95$ minutes.

$$n = DT/C = 4.5(95)/100 = 4.275 \text{ (round up to 5 containers)}$$

$$n = DT/C$$

$$5 + 2 = D(95)/100$$

$$D = 7 \times 100/95 = 7.37 \text{ parts per minute}$$

b. $7.37 < 8.50$, so no, the work centers cannot handle a demand rate of 8.5 units per minute if they have seven containers.

Discussion Questions

1. Visit a repetitive manufacturing facility in your area. What are the major causes of inventory? Be sure to ask about lot sizes and setup times. Would a JIT system work in this facility? Why or why not?

2. Why did the JIT approach evolve in Japan and not in the Western countries?

3. Define repetitive manufacturing and compare it with job lot or batch manufacturing.

4. Why is a stable master schedule required for JIT systems? How stable do you think the master schedule must be?

5. How can lot sizes and inventories be reduced in a JIT system? Mention specific approaches.

6. Why has repetitive manufacturing tended to use long runs and large lot sizes in the past?

7. Describe supplier relations both before and after installation of a JIT approach.

8. What are the effects of a JIT system on workers and managers?

9. Contrast and compare JIT and MRP systems.

10. What are the most critical things needed to implement JIT? Compare these things to implementation of an MRP system.

11. Will the EOQ formula work in a JIT environment? Discuss.

12. Discuss how JIT reduces costs (material, labor, overhead), not including inventory. Be specific.

13. Are there repetitive manufacturing firms that should not use JIT? Describe them.

14. What are the differences between JIT and lean thinking?

15. Find an example from the Internet of the application of lean thinking to a service operation.

16. How can lean thinking be applied to accounting, finance, or marketing processes?

Problems

1. Calculate the daily production quantities and sequences from the following monthly requirements. Assume the month has 20 production days.
   a. 5,000 A, 2,500 B, and 3,000 C
   b. 2,000 A, 3,000 B, and 6,000 C

2. Suppose a JIT work center is being operated with a container size of 25 units and a demand rate of 100 units per hour. Also assume it takes 180 minutes for a container to circulate.

   a. How many containers are required to operate this system?
   b. How much maximum inventory can accumulate?
   c. How many Kanban cards are needed?

3. Suppose a work center has a setup plus run time of 30 minutes to make 50 parts. Also assume it takes 10 minutes to move a standard container of 50 parts to the next work center, and the demand rate is one part per minute throughout the day.

a. Schedule this situation by drawing a picture of when work center A should be producing and idle and when movements of containers take place from A to B, the using work center.

b. How many standard containers are needed for this part to circulate from the picture in part *a?*

c. Use the formula $n = DT/C$ to calculate the number of containers.

4. For a particular operation, the setup time is 10 minutes at a cost of $15 in lost machine time and labor. The run time is 50 minutes to produce a standard lot of 400 parts. Assume a holding cost of $2 per part per month and a demand rate of 20,000 parts per month. It takes three hours to circulate a container of parts.

a. Calculate the EOQ for this part.

b. How many standard containers are needed?

c. If the setup time can be cut to 1 minute, recalculate the lot size and number of containers needed.

5. A company is in the business of machining parts that go through various work centers. Suppose work center A feeds work center B with parts. The following times (in minutes) are given for each work center.

	Work Center	
	A	B
Setup time	3	2
Run time (per part)	0.5	0.1
Move time	6	8

A standard Kanban container holds 50 parts that are transferred from work center A to work center B. The demand rate at work center B is four parts per minute.

a. How many Kanban containers are needed for this situation?

b. If move time is cut in half, what does this do to the number of containers needed? How much will this change reduce inventory?

6. A machine currently has a setup time of two hours and a setup cost of $10 per hour in labor and lost

machine time. It costs 25 percent to carry parts in inventory for a year, and 100 parts are produced per hour by the machine. Assume that the plant operates 2000 hours per year and that the circulation time for each Kanban container is 24 hours. Each part costs $50 to make. The demand rate for parts is 100,000 units per year.

a. What is the EOQ for this part?

b. How many Kanban containers are needed using the lot size calculated in part *a?*

c. What would be the effect of reducing the setup time in this case to 10 minutes? Recalculate the EOQ and the number of Kanban containers needed.

7. Suppose that a JIT work center is being operated with a lot size of 50 units. Assume 200 parts are being demanded per hour and it takes three hours to circulate a container, including all setup, run, move, and idle time.

a. Calculate the number of Kanban containers required.

b. What is the maximum inventory which will accumulate?

c. What can be done to reduce the inventory level? Suggest alternatives.

8. A supplier provides parts to a manufacturing company that demands JIT deliveries. At the present time it takes six hours to make a round-trip between the supplier's warehouse and the customer, including loading, travel, and unloading time. The lot size is 12 pallet loads on a truck, and the manufacturer uses 2 pallets per hour.

a. How many trucks are needed to ship the pallets to the manufacturer?

b. What is likely to happen if the truck breaks down?

c. How can the supplier ensure that the customer does not run out of parts even in the face of delivery problems or other uncertainties?

d. What will happen to the supplier if the manufacturer runs into trouble and shuts down for a period of six hours?

Selected Bibliography

Ahmad, Sohel, Roger G. Schroeder, and K. K. Sinha. "The Role of Infrastructure Practices in the Effectiveness of JIT Practices: Implications for Plant Performance." *Journal of Engineering and Technology Management* 20, no. 3 (2003), pp. 161–91.

Bushell, Sylvia, Joyce Mobley, and Becky Shelest. "Discovering Lean Thinking at Progressive Health

Care." *The Journal for Quality & Participation,* Summer 2002, pp. 20–25.

Chapman, Christopher D. "Clean House with Lean 5S." *Quality Progress,* June 2005, pp. 27–32.

Chausse, Sylvain, and Sylvain Landry. "Anatomy of Kanban: A Case Study." *Production & Inventory Management Journal* 41, no. 4 (2000), pp. 11–17.

Claunch, Jerry W. *Set-Up Time Reduction.* Falls Church, VA: APICS, 1996.

Forman, Joseph R. "Integrating JIT with MRP II." *Production and Inventory Management Review with APICS News,* March 1989, pp. 37–38.

Freudenheim, Milt. "Partners in Inventory Control." *The New York Times,* March 31, 1991, Sec. 3, p. 5.

Gupta, Surendra M., and Yousef A. Y. Al-Turki. "Flexible Kanban System." *International Journal of Operations & Production Management* 19 (1999), pp. 1065–94.

Hall, Ernest H., Jr. "Just-in-Time Management: A Critical Assessment." *Academy of Management Executive* 3, no. 4 (1989), pp. 315–18.

Hall, Robert. "The Americanization of the Toyota Production System." *Target* 15, no. 1 (1999).

Hall, Robert W. *Driving the Productivity Machine: Production Planning and Control in Japan.* Falls Church, VA: American Production and Inventory Control Society, 1981.

Inman, R. Anthony, and Satish Mehra. "JIT Applications for Service Environments." *Production and Inventory Management Journal* 32, no. 3 (1991), pp. 16–21.

Jing-Wen, Li, and Don J. Barnes. "Investigating the Factors Influencing the Shop Performance in a Job Shop Environment with Kanban-Based Production Control." *International Journal of Production Research* 38, no. 18 (2000), pp. 4683–4700.

Lovelle, Jared. "Use Value-Stream Mapping to Reveal the Benefits of Lean Manufacturing." *IIE Solutions,* February 2001.

Mason, Paul A., and Mike Parks. "The Implementation of Kanban." *Logistics Focus* 7, no. 4 (May 1999), pp. 20–25.

Monden, Yasuhiro. "Adaptive Kanban Systems Helps Toyota Maintain Just-in-Time Production." *Industrial Engineering,* May 1981, pp. 29–46.

———. *Toyota Production System: Practical Approach to Production Management.* Atlanta, GA: Industrial Engineering and Management Press, Institute of Industrial Engineering, 1983.

Nakane, J., and Robert W. Hall. "Management Specs for Stockless Production." *Harvard Business Review,* May–June 1983.

———. "Japanese Production Systems." In Lee and Schwendiman (eds.), *Management by Japanese Systems.* New York: Praeger, 1982.

Sakakibara, Sadao, Barbara Flynn, Roger Schroeder, and William Morris. "The Impact of Just-in-Time Manufacturing and Its Infrastructure on Manufacturing Performance." *Management Science* 43, no. 9 (1997), pp. 1246–57.

Schonberger, Richard J. "Kanban ('Just-in-Time') Application of Kawasaki, USA." *APICS Conference Proceedings,* 1981, pp. 188–91.

———. *Japanese Manufacturing Techniques: Nine Hidden Lessons in Simplicity.* New York: Free Press, 1982.

———. *World Class Manufacturing.* New York: Free Press, 1986.

———. *Building a Chain of Customers.* New York: Free Press, 1990.

———. *World Class Manufacturing: The Next Decade.* Falls Church, VA: APICS, 1996.

Sekine, Kenichi, and Keisuke Arai. *Kaizen and Quick Changeover: Going beyond SMED.* Falls Church, VA: APICS, 1992.

Shingo, Shigeo. *A Revolution in Manufacturing: The SMED System.* Stamford, CT: Productivity Press, 1985.

Spear, Steven, and H. Kent Bowen. "Decoding the DNA of the Toyota Production System." *Harvard Business Review,* September–October 1999, pp. 97–106.

Sugimori, Y., K. Kusunoki, F. Cho, and S. Uchikawa. "Toyota Production System and Kanban Systems Materialization of Just-in-Time and Respect for Human System." *International Journal of Production Research* 15, no. 6 (1977), pp. 553–64.

Suzaki, Kiyoshi. *The New Manufacturing Challenge.* New York: Free Press, 1987.

Tardif, Valerie. "An Adaptive Approach to Controlling Kanban Systems." *European Journal of Operational Research* 132, no. 2 (July 16, 2001), pp. 411–25.

Womack, James P., and Daniel T. Jones. *Lean Thinking: Banish Waste and Create Wealth in Your Corporation.* New York: Simon and Shuster, 1996.

Womack, James, P., Daniel T. Jones, and Daniel Roos, *The Machine That Changed the World: The Story of Lean Production.* New York: Rawson Associates, 1990.

Part **Six**

Case Studies

Introduction

Process Design

Quality

Capacity and Scheduling

Inventory

This part contains case studies designed to provide students with practice in both problem formulation and problem solution. The cases provide unstructured problems, which are more challenging than those in the text. They require integration of material from several chapters and imaginative solutions. The cases are intended to be used in an interactive classroom environment with lively discussion of the issues presented.

In April 2005, James Wallace, general manager of the Advanced Products Division at Shipper, was considering a change in manufacturing strategy. Recently, Wallace and his staff had revised the business strategy of the division. As a result, it became apparent that the marketing, engineering, and manufacturing strategies should also be revised.

The Shipper Company started in the aerospace business in the 1960s. In the early years, the company developed and produced the Echo weather satellites, which were launched into space. More recently, the Shipper Company had diversified into three divisions located in Faribault, Minnesota: the Electrical Products Division (EPD), the Materials Division (MD), and the Advanced Products Division (APD). The EPD produced a variety of circuit boards and other electrical products for mass markets. The MD produced laminated plastic materials that were sold to EPD, APD, and outside customers. The APD manufactured specialty products to customer order. The sales growth and profitability of the company have been good for the past five years, as shown in Exhibit 1. Sales and profits of the APD, however, have been somewhat erratic.

The main product of the APD is the aerostat, which is a large lighter-than-air blimp resembling the famous Goodyear blimp. These aerostats are sold to communications companies, the U.S. government, and foreign countries for communications uses. At the present time, the APD produces about 12 aerostats per year, and the aerostat accounts for about 50 percent of the APD's sales.

The APD also produces a variety of other specialty products made to customer order. These products include mine stoppers used to seal mining passages for ventilation control (see Exhibit 2) and blade liners used as inserts in helicopter blades to detect cracks. One unifying feature of these specialty products is that they are made from the laminated plastic materials supplied by the Materials Division of Shipper.

In formulating his business strategy, Wallace envisioned a gradual shift toward products that are sold to multiple customers and manufactured on a volume basis. The business strategy developed by Wallace and his staff is summarized as follows:

> APD will continue to do what it has historically done best—respond to *individual customer* design requirements and tailor new products to unique customer applications. This business is characterized by low volume but sole-source products, by customer funding for product development, and by large year-to-year variations in sales and profits.

Concurrently and increasingly, the APD will become more *market-focused* in its business and will apply resources toward market and product-development programs. Its objective shall be to reduce but not eliminate APD dependence on short-run customer-specified products or projects and to bring on stream new products with higher-volume continuous production. The APD will restrict its market development resources to certain market segments or niches of growth and to mature industries where there is a realistic opportunity and expectation of occupying a dominant or strong competitive position.

This heavy emphasis on marketing strategies will require enlargement of market research, market development, and sales distribution systems. Technologically, materials and systems engineering capabilities will have to be strengthened, as will the production engineering and production control disciplines. The company will need to concentrate heavily on planning, and it must have the patience to focus on and stick to its strategies to see them through to fruition.

EXHIBIT 1
Financial data.

	$ Thousands				
	2000	2001	2002	2003	2004
Shipper Corp.					
Sales	34,884	41,029	46,824	41,914	47,857
Profits (after tax)	1,256	1,324	1,363	1,035	1,579
APD					
Sales	5,977	6,508	4,080	7,600	5,179
Profits (after tax)	703	597	223	1,139	150

This case was prepared as a basis for class discussion, not to illustrate either effective or ineffective handling of an administrative situation.

EXHIBIT 2
Product description.

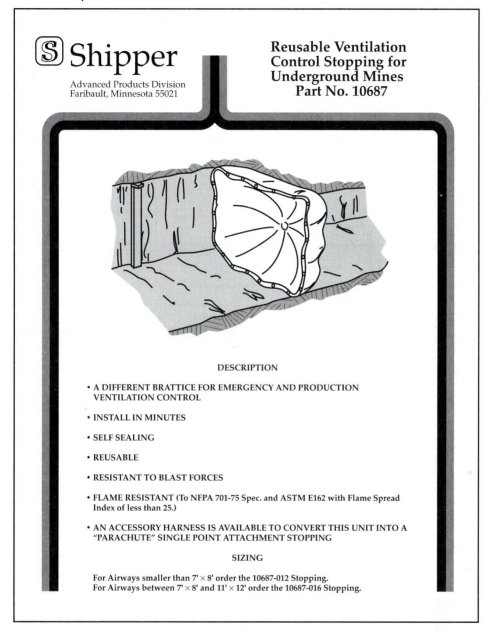

S Shipper

Advanced Products Division
Faribault, Minnesota 55021

**Reusable Ventilation
Control Stopping for
Underground Mines
Part No. 10687**

DESCRIPTION

• A DIFFERENT BRATTICE FOR EMERGENCY AND PRODUCTION
  VENTILATION CONTROL

• INSTALL IN MINUTES

• SELF SEALING

• REUSABLE

• RESISTANT TO BLAST FORCES

• FLAME RESISTANT (To NFPA 701-75 Spec. and ASTM E162 with Flame Spread
  Index of less than 25.)

• AN ACCESSORY HARNESS IS AVAILABLE TO CONVERT THIS UNIT INTO A
  "PARACHUTE" SINGLE POINT ATTACHMENT STOPPING

SIZING

For Airways smaller than 7' × 8' order the 10687-012 Stopping.
For Airways between 7' × 8' and 11' × 12' order the 10687-016 Stopping.

The business unit is growth-oriented with substantial resources directed to new-product/new-market strategies, making it a medium- to high-risk operation. Although investment in product development and capital equipment will be required, the business should retain its low-capital, high-labor-intensive character. Over the five-year planning period, sales, profits, and asset levels should produce a return on net assets (RONA) in the 30 to 40 percent range. Additionally, the business will be a net cash user.

According to Wallace, the shift in business strategy will require a corresponding change in manufacturing strategy. Manufacturing will need to develop facilities, people, and production control systems to support the gradual change from low-volume, one-of-a-kind production to higher-volume, standardized product lines. Among the results of this change in strategy could be changes in organization. The present organizational structure of the APD is shown in Exhibit 3.

EXHIBIT 3
Organization chart (detail only shown in manufacturing area).

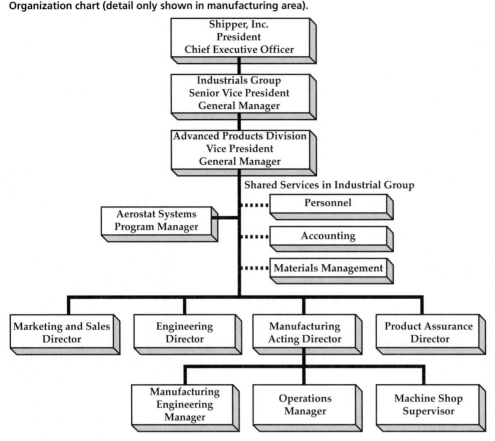

Wallace also felt that the shift in business strategy might affect the production and inventory control area. At the present time, production and inventory control is handled by two individuals who were transferred from the storeroom and the production floor. They have been trained on the job, and they have evolved a manual system of record keeping and production planning. The system appears to work quite well for the present situation, but constant expediting and stock chasing are necessary to keep production moving.

Inventory stock status is computerized by the data processing department. Receipts and disbursements are sent to data processing and then entered into the computer. Because of time lags and problems of record accuracy, the production and inventory control people also keep manual records on the most important parts.

The Shipper Company recently signed a contract with Hewlett-Packard for a new computer, which will arrive in the fall and replace the current IBM equipment. As part of the new computer conversion, the company has investigated software packages available from Hewlett-Packard. The production and inventory

control (MRP) software package appears quite good, but conversion of existing computer software will have priority over new systems. The first priority, after the new computer is installed, will be the conversion of existing accounting and financial systems.

In viewing the situation, Wallace wondered what the manufacturing strategy over the next five years should be and how the strategy should be implemented. He knew that manufacturing should support the new divisional business strategy but was unsure about exactly what direction manufacturing should take.

Discussion Questions

1. What objectives should be adopted in manufacturing with respect to cost, delivery, quality, and flexibility?

2. How should the objectives in manufacturing be achieved through process, organization, equipment, workforce, capacity, scheduling, quality management, and production and inventory control systems?

Case Study   FHE, Inc.

In March 2003, Lum Donaldson, product development engineering manager at FHE, Inc., was reviewing the process his company used to introduce new products. Donaldson was responsible for the technical direction of all new-product development and revisions of existing products. He wondered whether the procedures, organization, and project control systems used at FHE might be improved to make new-product introductions go more smoothly.

FHE is a manufacturer of pumps and related fluid-handling equipment. The company supplies products used to transfer liquids of all types, including paint, adhesives, and food products. The pumps supplied by the company are used by the automobile and appliance industries, in vehicle servicing, in home construction, and in other ways. In 2002, sales were $105,200,000 and profit after tax was $5,470,000. Over the last five years, the company has been improving both sales and profits through aggressive new-product introductions.

ORGANIZATION

The organization of the engineering, marketing, and manufacturing departments at FHE is shown in Exhibit 1. Phil Thomas, vice president of corporate development and marketing, has responsibility for both marketing and design engineering functions in the company. This arrangement is intended to facilitate cooperation between marketing and engineering, particularly on new-product introductions. Manufacturing is responsible for producing the product once it has been released to production.

On the engineering side of the organization, three technical program managers (TPMs) report to Donaldson. These program managers are generally responsible for the technical direction of the projects assigned to them. Detailed responsibilities of the TPM are shown in Exhibit 2.

On the marketing side of the organization, three product managers report to Vince Kramer, the U.S. marketing manager. These product managers are responsible for developing new-product ideas and managing the business impact of new products. Detailed responsibilities of the product manager are shown in Exhibit 3.

Manufacturing managers are responsible for designing the production process, ordering materials, scheduling production, and processing materials and components into finished products. Product specifications are given to manufacturing by engineering. Manufacturing is expected to adhere to these specifications in making the product.

A great deal of coordination is required between the product managers in marketing, the TPMs in engineering, and manufacturing to successfully introduce a new product. When problems arise, it is not always clear who has the primary responsibility for resolving them. As a result, product managers, manufacturing managers, and TPMs must work closely together during the development process.

NEW-PRODUCT DEVELOPMENT PROCESS

The new-product development process begins with a formal marketing request, which specifies in general terms the type of product needed and the market it will serve. As a result of the marketing request, a concept conference is conducted between marketing and engineering to determine whether to proceed, and if so, how. If the decision is made to proceed, a technical specification action report (TSAR) is prepared by engineering. The TSAR contains a great deal of detail on development costs, product costs, schedules, and product technical specifications. If the TSAR is approved, the project is formally authorized and engineering development begins. The project then proceeds through a series of steps, as summarized in Exhibit 4 for a typical project. These steps include actual design of the physical product, major design reviews, testing, and finally release to production if the product is successfully developed.

Although the new-product development process is well defined at FHE, Donaldson has several reservations about its operation. First, he continually encounters problems in coordinating the technical program managers and the product managers. Perhaps the division of responsibility is not as clear as it might be. Second, he is also concerned about the fluctuating workload in the engineering services department.

ENGINEERING SERVICES

The engineering services department, managed by Al Hanson, includes drafting services, the model shop, testing facilities, and technical documentation services. Because all projects use these services, the workload for engineering services is unpredictable and bottlenecks frequently occur in this department. At any one time, as many as 20 new-product development projects may be in progress, and they all seem to require the same engineering services at the same time. Hanson has continually asked the technical program managers to give him more advanced notice, but due to uncertainties in project schedules, requirements are often unknown until the last minute.

This case was prepared as a basis for class discussion, not to illustrate either effective or ineffective handling of an administrative situation.

EXHIBIT 1
Organization chart.

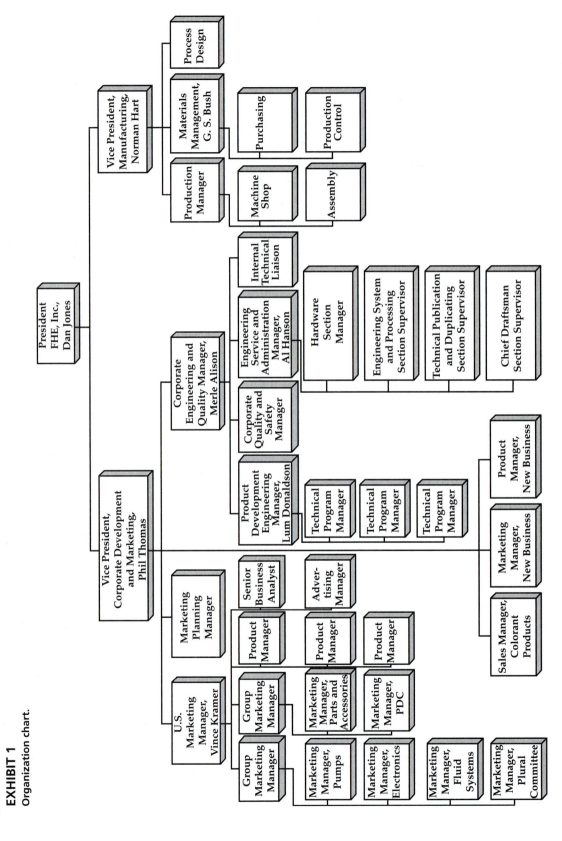

EXHIBIT 2
Position description.

TECHNICAL PROGRAM MANAGER-NEW-PRODUCT DEVELOPMENT

General Summary Statement

The technical program manager-new-product department reports to the manager of product engineering and is responsible for planning, coordinating, and directing the activities of projects in the program area(s) assigned to him or her. (A "program area" is composed of one or more projects related to a particular product application area, such as sanitary, plural components, and hydraulics.) The technical program manager-new-product department is responsible for personnel assignments and the administration and control of all design personnel reporting to him or her.

Typical Duties and Responsibilities

1. Assigns technical staff to maintain development schedules for all projects within his or her areas of program responsibility. Maintains the communication between development sections to ensure usage of critical skills and keep the state-of-the-art awareness with all personnel assigned.

2. Directs the design activities of a specific program area or areas to develop the design, select materials, prepare technical descriptions, conduct tests, meet performance, schedule, and cost objectives; is responsible for the program costs and status and presents timely reports and technical conclusions when directed; communicates with product managers, development engineers, and other design personnel; and maintains technical project files.

3. Coordinates with product management in defining technical customer specifications of currently planned product and product which is contemplated for future effort.

4. Reviews and directs the detail analysis prepared by development engineers, and is responsible for testing programs to ensure overall product design conformance to specifications. Reviews all cost inputs and directs completion of cost estimates.

5. Interfaces with all departments in the company to coordinate product design completion; negotiates work schedules with hardware and software groups, purchasing, etc.

6. Identifies technical problem areas which will result in altered time, cost, and/or performance schedules; defines alternative courses of action to meet same; and/or makes visible to management these problems so that proper corrective management action can be taken.

7. Maintains continuing contact with product management, manufacturing, fluid systems, etc., where appropriate in obtaining the best technical solutions to the problems associated with his or her program area and in ensuring that product resulting from his or her team's efforts can be economically produced.

MANUFACTURING COORDINATION

Donaldson acknowledged that once a new product is developed, it is often "thrown over the wall" to manufacturing. While manufacturing is consulted regarding technical feasibility and possible production constraints, little manufacturing input is received during product design. Donaldson commented, "Manufacturing has enough problems to worry about with today's products without bringing new products into the picture too. We try to anticipate manufacturing problems for them before release to production. Of course, there is never enough time and inevitably some problems occur after the product is released."

FHE has been considering a new CAD-CAM system as a way of coordinating marketing, engineering, and manufacturing. According to the software supplier, the new-product configuration would be entered directly into the computer and then transmitted automatically to manufacturing. This approach promised to eliminate many of the errors encountered in translation from engineering to manufacturing. After the CAD system is installed, the CAM system will be designed to interface with it. FHE felt the computer would speed up the new-product introduction cycle and eliminate many of the production problems it was currently encountering.

Discussion Questions

1. What steps should Donaldson take to improve the new-product development process at FHE?

2. What could be done to clarify the organizational relationship between product managers, technical program managers, and manufacturing managers?

3. What can be done to better manage the workload of the engineering services department?

4. Evaluate the plans and the expected results from the new CAD-CAM system.

EXHIBIT 3
Job description.

PRODUCT MANAGER RESPONSIBILITY PROFILE

A product manager's basic responsibility is to the development of new products and to ensuring that the entire product line is properly servicing the needs of the marketplace. The product manager would generally have a strong technical background and a working knowledge of marketing concepts. He or she must possess leadership qualities in that the tasks to be accomplished are through others over whom the product manager has no direct control.

MAJOR DUTIES

I. New Product
   A. Develop product strategies that are in support of corporate objectives.
   B. Coordinate project definition.
      1. Evaluate the content of new-product proposals (the product specification) and programs, responding to market opportunities identified by U.S., Eurafrica, and regional international marketing groups.
      2. Evaluate the content of the technical specification and the project schedule assuring conformity with the product specification and market timing requirements.
      3. Evaluate anticipated project costs.
      4. Analyze anticipated profitability of proposed programs (ROI).
      5. Generate the project authorization.
   C. Monitor project activity and take action where necessary to ensure integrity of project.
   D. Ensure vendor quality.
   E. Ensure the coordination of all technical resources related to new-product development and introduction; to include engineering, manufacturing, marketing, and service.
II. Existing Product
   A. Monitor product line activity and take action where required.
      1. Sales volume.
      2. Competitive postures.
      3. Relationship to changing technology.
      4. Product quality.
   B. Control product line offering (no product proliferation).
   C. Monitor engineering change order activity and take action where required.
   D. Eliminate product from the offering as appropriate.
   E. Provide technical assessment on advertising and promotional aspects of the product line (catalogs, mailers, brochures, new-product data sheets, etc.).
   F. Ensure that products comply to a variety of standards (corporate, governmental, industry, safety, etc.).
III. Competition
   A. Keep abreast of changes in product line.
   B. Maintain an in-depth knowledge of competitive product capabilities.
IV. Forecasting
   A. Unit forecast of specific product (category I).
   B. Forecast new-product quantities for Lot I build.
   C. Forecast product to meet promotional activity.
   D. Monitor all significant deviations.

EXHIBIT 4
Gantt chart.

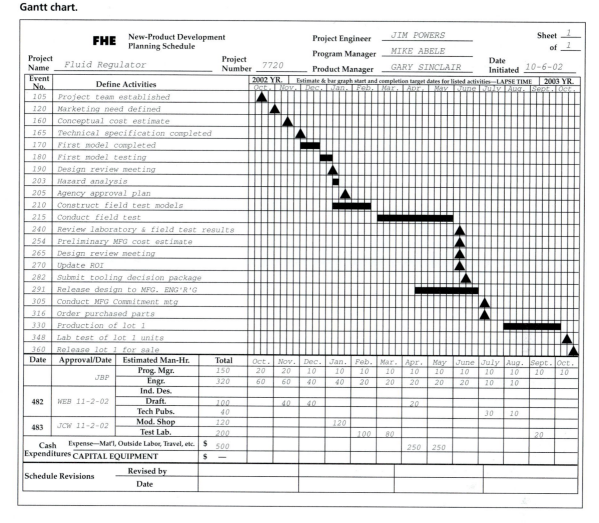

FHE New-Product Development Planning Schedule

Project Engineer _JIM POWERS_   Sheet _1_ of _1_

Program Manager _MIKE ABELE_

Project Name _Fluid Regulator_   Project Number _7720_

Product Manager _GARY SINCLAIR_   Date Initiated _10-6-02_

Event No.	Define Activities
105	Project team established
120	Marketing need defined
160	Conceptual cost estimate
165	Technical specification completed
170	First model completed
180	First model testing
190	Design review meeting
203	Hazard analysis
205	Agency approval plan
210	Construct field test models
215	Conduct field test
240	Review laboratory & field test results
254	Preliminary MFG cost estimate
265	Design review meeting
270	Update ROI
282	Submit tooling decision package
291	Release design to MFG. ENG'R'G
305	Conduct MFG Commitment mtg
316	Order purchased parts
330	Production of lot 1
348	Lab test of lot 1 units
360	Release lot 1 for sale

Date	Approval/Date	Estimated Man-Hr.	Total	Oct.	Nov.	Dec.	Jan.	Feb.	Mar.	Apr.	May	June	July	Aug.	Sept.	Oct.
	JBP	Prog. Mgr.	150	20	20	10	10	10	10	10	10	10	10	10	10	10
		Engr.	320	60	60	40	40	20	20	20	20	20	10	10		
482	WEB 11-2-02	Ind. Des.														
		Draft.	100		40	40				20						
		Tech Pubs.	40										30	10		
483	JCW 11-2-02	Mod. Shop	120				120									
		Test Lab.	200					100	80							20
Cash Expenditures	Expense—Mat'l, Outside Labor, Travel, etc.		$ 500							250	250					
	CAPITAL EQUIPMENT		$ —													

Schedule Revisions	Revised by				
	Date				

Eastern Gear, Inc., in Philadelphia, Pennsylvania, is a manufacturer of custom-made gears ranging in weight from a few ounces to over 50 pounds. The gears are made of different metals depending on the customer's requirements. Over the past year, 40 different types of steel and brass alloys have been used as raw materials. See Exhibit 1 for details.

Eastern Gear sells its products primarily to engineering research and development laboratories or very small manufacturers. As a result, the number of gears in most orders is small; rarely is exactly the same gear ordered more than once. The distribution of order sizes for March 2003 is shown in Exhibit 2.

Recently, the president of Eastern Gear decided to accept a few larger orders for 100 gears or more. Although lower prices were accepted on these orders, they helped pay the overhead. It was found that the large orders caused many of the small orders to wait for a long time before being processed. As a result, some deliveries of small orders were late.

ORDER ENTRY

When a customer wishes to order a gear, the order is taken by James Lord, sales manager and marketing vice president. The customer specifies the type of gear desired by submitting a blueprint or sketch. The quantity of gears required and the type of material are also specified by the customer. On occasion, the customer's engineer will call up after the order has been placed and request a change in the design. In these cases, it may be necessary to stop production and wait for new raw materials or for the design to be clarified. The customer's prints submitted with the order do not always contain the tolerances or finishes required during machining. As a result, the customer is contacted directly when the information is needed.

After the order is received, one copy is sent to the production supervisor, Joe Irvine, and the second copy is sent to Sam Smith, the controller. Upon receipt of the customer's order, Smith places a purchase order for the raw materials required. These materials often take from one to two weeks to arrive, depending on the supplier and the type of material ordered.

After receiving the customer order, the supervisor reviews the order and places it on file until the raw material arrives. The customer order is then routed through the shop along with the materials. In the past, the production process for most gears has taken about two weeks after receipt of raw materials. Recently this production time has increased to four weeks.

Irvine expressed concern about the bottlenecks that appear in the production process. One week the bottleneck may be in one machine center, and the next week it is in another. These bottlenecks make it difficult to get the orders out on time.

EXHIBIT 2
Sales, March 2003.

Order Size	Number of Orders	Total $ Value of Orders
1	80	$ 3,200
2	53	4,250
3	69	8,163
4	32	4,800
5	82	16,392
8	47	15,987
10	64	26,871
15	22	13,172
20	42	31,555
25	27	23,682
30	18	21,600
40	22	32,000
50	10	18,693
100	4	12,500
200	2	14,068
400	1	9,652
700	2	35,600
1,000	1	20,000
	578	$312,185

EXHIBIT 1
Raw materials.

Type of Material	2002 Usage $(000)
A	$ 36
B	10
C	15
D	43
E	110
F	18
G	32
H	75
I	40
J	60
K	30
All Others	53
Total	$522

This case was prepared as a basis for class discussion, not to illustrate either effective or ineffective handling of an administrative situation.

PHYSICAL LAYOUT AND MATERIALS FLOW

Eastern Gear utilizes a standard job-shop layout, as shown in Exhibit 3. Each work center has a common set of machines or processes. The materials flow from one work center to another, depending on the operations needed for a particular order.

A typical order will take the following path. First, the raw material, a gear blank, is sent to the milling work center. Here the teeth are cut into the edge of the gear according to the customer's specifications. Next, the gear blanks are sent to the drilling work center, where one or more holes may be drilled in the gear. The gear is then sent to a grinding center, where a finish is put on the gear teeth and the surface of the gear. Next, the gear may be sent to heat-treating if this operation is required by the customer. After the batch of gears is completed, they are inspected by the next available worker and shipped to the customer.

In Exhibit 3, note how the machines are grouped by similar type on the shop floor. For example, all

drills are located together in one work center, and all milling machines are in another work center. While this layout facilitates development of worker skills and training, it results in a jumbled flow of products through the shop.

There is constant interference of the orders being processed in the shop. The typical order spends 90 percent of its time waiting in line for a machine to become available. Only 10 percent of the time is actually spent processing the order on a machine. As a result, it takes a relatively long time (four weeks) for an order to make its way through the shop.

Large and small orders are processed together. No special work flow is utilized for different order sizes. As a matter of fact, large orders are helping to keep the shop at full capacity.

COMPANY BACKGROUND

Business has been booming at Eastern Gear. For the first two years the company lost money, but over the last several months a small profit has been made. Sales are up by 100 percent in the last quarter. See Exhibit 4 for more details.

Although sales are rapidly increasing, a recent market survey has indicated that sales can be expanded even more in the next few years. According to the market survey, sales will be $5 million in calendar year 2003 if the current delivery lead time of five to six weeks is maintained. If total delivery lead time can be reduced to the former three to four weeks, sales could be expanded to $5.5 million instead of $5 million.

Because of increased delivery lead times, the company has recently added an expediter, Matt Williams. Each morning Williams reviews the work in progress in the shop and selects those orders that

EXHIBIT 3
Layout.

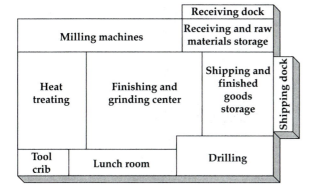

EXHIBIT 4
Financial data.

	2000	2001	2002	First Quarter, 2003
Sales	560*	1500	3100	1063
Manufacturing costs				
Materials	63	273	522	214
Labor	136	587	1,063	327
Overhead	70	216	412	140
Depreciation	172	398	422	150
Total Manufacturing Costs	441	1,474	2,419	831
Sales expenses	70	130	263	80
G & A expense	75	110	297	93
Total costs	586	1,714	2,979	1,004
Profit before tax	(26)	(214)	121	59

*All figures in thousands of dollars.

EXHIBIT 5
Organization chart.

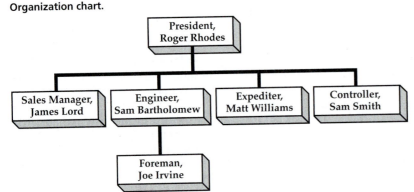

appear to be behind schedule. Each order that is behind receives a red tag, indicating that it should be treated on a rush basis. At the present time, about 20 percent of the orders have rush tags on them. Williams also spends his time looking for past-due raw materials and lost orders as well as explaining late orders to customers.

The organization chart for the company is shown in Exhibit 5. Roger Rhodes is the president and founder of Eastern Gear. He handles contacts with some of the large customers, arranges the financing needed by the company, and sits in on the weekly production meeting. During these meetings, scheduling problems, employee problems, and other production problems are discussed.

The company engineer is Sam Bartholomew. His responsibilities include design of the company's products, procurement and maintenance of equipment, and overseeing of the supervisor, Joe Irvine. Bartholomew also attends the weekly production meetings, and he spends about 10 hours a week on the factory floor talking with individual workers.

The company is currently experiencing about a 6 percent return rate on completed orders due to poor quality. In 75 percent of the cases, the returned orders have failed to undergo one or more operations or the operations have been improperly done. For example, in one returned order, all the gears were missing a hole.

Occasionally, the company will receive rush orders from its customers. In this case, the order is referred directly to Rhodes for approval. If the order is accepted, the raw materials are rush-ordered and received the next day. After receipt of the raw materials, the order is rushed through production in four days. This is accomplished by Fred Dirkson, a trusted employee, who hand-carries the rush orders through all operations. About 10 percent of the orders are handled on a rush basis.

The workforce consists of 50 employees who are highly skilled or semiskilled. The milling machine operators, for example, are highly skilled and require at least two years of vocational-technical training plus several months of on-the-job training. Within the last quarter, 10 new employees have been added to the workforce. The employees are not unionized and good labor relations exist. The workforce is managed using a family-type approach.

Discussion Questions

1. What are the major problems being faced by Eastern Gear?

2. What action should Rhodes take to solve his problems?

3. How can this case be related to operations strategy and process design concepts?

Rolf Reinschmidt, head of the Forever Sport Division of adidas-Salomon AG, was reviewing adidas' mass customization (MC) initiative: "mi adidas":

> We all talk a lot about experiences these days—experiences that consumers and retailers expect to have with brands like ours [adidas]. Well, here is an experience our brand is uniquely able to offer, differentiating us significantly from the competition and building an incredible image for the Forever Sport Division.

It was October 2001. Reinschmidt sat down in his office and reflected on his experience to date. He had been sponsoring mi adidas to create a customization experience. The journey had started many years earlier, with the company providing tailor-made shoes for top athletes. Now, customized shoes had been made available on a much broader scale. Competitors also tested the market, and a trend toward MC was visible in other industries from PCs to made-to-measure jeans. The time had come to make specific recommendations on the best course of action for mi adidas.

Reinschmidt had three alternative routes to choose from:

- *Withdraw:* Celebrate the success and PR effect accomplished to date but quietly withdraw from MC in order to focus on adidas' core business.
- *Maintain:* Maintain the developed capabilities and selectively run mi adidas fairs and planned retail tours following top events such as the Soccer World Cup and world marathon series.
- *Expand:* Expand mi adidas to multiple product categories and permanent retail installations; elevate it to brand concept status while further building volume and process expertise.

mi adidas had gained substantial momentum—it needed direction.

GLOBAL FOOTWEAR MARKET[1]
In 2000 the global footwear market was US$16.4 billion.[2] North America accounted for 48 percent, Europe 32 percent, and Asia/Pacific 12 percent of the market. The degree of concentration in the footwear segment was relatively high, with the three largest companies controlling roughly 60 percent of the market: Nike commanded 35 percent, adidas 15 percent and Reebok 10 percent market share. Nike was particularly strong in the U.S. market, with a 42 percent market share in footwear, but also led in Europe with 31 percent. Adidas was significantly stronger in the European footwear market, holding a 24 percent market share compared with its 11 percent market share in US footwear. (Refer to Exhibit 1 for regional market share information and trends for adidas, Nike and Reebok.)

ADIDAS-SALOMON AG
For over 80 years adidas had been part of the world of sports on every level, delivering state-of-the-art sports footwear, apparel, and accessories. (Refer to Exhibit 2 for a history of adidas.) In 2001 adidas-Salomon AG's total net sales reached €6.1 billion and net income amounted to €208 million. Its main brands were adidas with a 79 percent share of sales, Salomon with 12 percent, and TaylorMade-adidas Golf with 9 percent. The company employed 14,000 people and commanded an estimated 15 percent share of the world market for sporting goods. Headquartered in Herzogenaurach, Germany, it was a global leader in the sporting goods industry, offering its products in almost every country of the world: Europe accounted for 50 percent, North America for 30 percent, Asia for 17 percent, and Latin America for 3 percent of total sales.

Forever Sport Division
In 2000 adidas was reorganized into three consumer-oriented product divisions: Forever Sport, Originals and Equipment.[3] Forever Sport was the largest division with products "engineered to perform." Technological innovation and a commitment to product leadership were the cornerstones of this division. Sales fell into a few major categories: Running 32 percent, Soccer 16 percent, Basketball 11 percent, Tennis 9 percent and Others 32 percent.[4] Reinschmidt was the head of the division. He reported directly to Erich Stamminger, head of global marketing for adidas-Salomon AG.

[1] Sporting Goods Intelligence (SGI).
[2] Total market value based on wholesale prices.

[3] The reorganization officially took effect January 1, 2001. In 2002 the organization was revised again and the Forever Sport Division became the Sport Performance Division.
[4] adidas-Salomon AG, 2001 Annual Report.

EXHIBIT 1
Global footwear market: regional overview.

adidas footwear sales*		
Region	2001 Net Sales	Net Change vs. 2000
North America	€818 million	−10 %
Europe	€1,200 million	+15 %
Asia	€371 million	+39 %
Latin America	€122 million	+3 %

Note: adidas' total net sales in 2001 were €4.8 billion.

Nike footwear sales**		
Region	2001 Net Sales	Net Change vs. 2000
USA	$3,209 million	−4 %
Europe	$1,423 million	+9 %
Asia Pacific	$632 million	+14 %
Americas	$360 million	+5 %

Note: Nike's total net sales in 2001 were $9.5 billion.

Reebok footwear sales		
Region	2001 Net Sales	Net Charge vs. 2000
USA[†]	$931 million	+1 %
UK[‡]	$484 million	+1 %
Europe[‡]	$410 million	−4 %
Row[‡]	$256 million	−4 %

Note: Reebok's total net sales in 2001 were $3.0 billion.

*adidas-Salomon AG, 2001 Annual Report, year ended 12/31.
**Nike Inc., 2001 Annual Report, year ended 5/31.
[†]Reebok International, Ltd., 2001 Annual Report, Year Ended 12/31.
[‡]Footwear share of net sales estimated based on Reebok International, Ltd., 2001 Annual Report.

MI ADIDAS

"mi adidas" was envisaged as an image tool and a center of competence for the Forever Sport Division. Christoph Berger, director MC, was responsible for mi adidas and led a small but dedicated team. Berger came from an old shoemaking family and followed a traditional apprenticeship as a shoemaker himself. Having earned an Executive Master of Business Administration (EMBA), he started working for adidas in 1995. The pilot was sponsored directly by Reinschmidt and Stamminger. Without formal line authority, however, Berger had to draw implementation support from the various functions and use external contractors to complement his team. (Refer to Exhibit 3 for a project breakdown.)

mi adidas was launched in April 2000 to provide consumers with the chance to create unique athletic footwear produced to their personal specifications.

The idea was not entirely new, as adidas had provided tailor-made shoes to top athletes for many years. Now mi adidas could be experienced by many consumers at top sporting events and select retailers. The project initially offered only soccer boots but was to be expanded in 2001 to offer running shoes. For 2002 the plan was to further build volume and expand the offering into the customization of basketball and tennis footwear. (Refer to Exhibit 4 for the initial mi adidas rollout plan.)

PHASE I: THE MI ADIDAS PILOT

The first phase of the mi adidas project was a small pilot to evaluate the feasibility and prospects of mass customizing athletic shoes. The objectives were clear-cut: offer a customized product, test consumers' demands for customized products, and fulfill their expectations as far as possible. The pilot allowed

EXHIBIT 2
A short history of adidas: 1920–2001.

It all began in 1920, when Adolph "Adi" Dassler and his brother Rudolph made their first shoes in Herzogenaurach, a small village in the south of Germany. Using the few basic materials available after World War I, Rudolph began making slippers with soles made from old tires. Adi converted the slippers into gymnastics shoes and soccer shoes with nail-on studs or cleats. The idea was as simple as it was brilliant: Provide every athlete with the best possible equipment.

At the 1928 Amsterdam Olympics, German athletes showcased Dassler shoes to the world. In 1936, the brothers achieved a major breakthrough when Jesse Owens agreed to wear their shoes in the Berlin Olympics, where he won four gold medals. By 1937 the Dassler brothers were manufacturing shoes for more than 11 different sports. In 1948 the two brothers quarreled and Rudolph left to establish the Puma sports company, while Adi registered the name adidas and, the following year, adopted its now famous three diagonal stripe trademark. The first samples of adidas footwear were used at the 1952 Helsinki Olympics.

In 1954 Germany won the World Cup, wearing new screw-in studs on adidas soccer shoes. In 1963 the first adidas soccer ball was produced and clothing was added to the product range in 1967. By the Montreal Olympics in 1976, over 80 percent of medal winners were adidas-equipped athletes. Business was booming. Adidas had become a household name in the sporting arena, synonymous with sporting achievement.

In 1972 Nike entered the American market with low quality, fashionable leisurewear targeting teenagers. Reebok followed suit in 1979. Following the death of its founder in 1978 , adidas struggled through turbulent organizational and management changes and was quickly outrun by changes in the industry. Its street popularity faded as newer, more aggressive companies like Nike and Reebok stepped up the pace of competition.

In 1989 the Dassler family withdrew from the company, and the enterprise was transformed into a corporation. Bernard Tapie, a French business tycoon, took over but was soon jailed following his involvement in a soccer-fixing scandal. Subsequently, adidas was declared bankrupt and left to a number of French banks. In 1993 French-born Robert Louis-Dreyfus was appointed chairman of the executive board of adidas. Having purchased 15 percent of the company, Louis-Dreyfus was a majority shareholder and led a stunning turnaround for the company and initiated adidas' flotation on the stock market in November 1995.

In 1997 adidas acquired Salomon Group, and the company's name changed to adidas-Salomon AG. With the brands adidas (athletic footwear, apparel, and accessories), Salomon (skis, bindings, inline skates, adventure shoes and accessories), Taylor Made (golf clubs, balls, and accessories), Mavic (cycling components) and Bonfire (snowboard apparel), adidas-Salomon AG substantially broadened its portfolio of sports brands, offering products for both summer and winter sports.

In 2001 Herbert Hainer took over as chairman and CEO. adidas-Salomon AG's total net sales grew to €6.1 billion with net income of €208 million. It employed 14,000 people and commanded an estimated 15 percent world market share.

Source: http://www.adidas.com and IMD adidas case GM 743, January 26, 1999.

EXHIBIT 3
Working breakdown structure plan.

Project Management	Product Development	Product Configurator / Design tool	Marketing → Event → Communication	Information Management	Production	Logistics / Shipment	Service/ Fulfillment	Payment Tracking
• Project organization • Tracking • Budgeting / payment • Project kickoff • Project evaluation • Meetings and presentations • Handle critical situations	• Product development • Pattern engineering • Foot bed • Fit test • Sample production • Budget	• Layout • Image to transport • Configuration principle • Handling • General architecture • Potential for future • Other categories • eCommerce • Intelligence • Data flow interfaces • Budget	**Product Configuration** • Color variations • Positioning/ layout of all decorations • Clarify: stitching or printing of deco's • Cosmetics **Event** • Concept • Message we want to bring across • PR-image we want to create • Communication strategy (name of program/ product!) • Pre-event • Event organization • Postevent • Cooperation with regions • Conceptualization of product Configurator • Budget	• General IT structure • Data tracking • Handling • Storage • Research • Speed • Intelligence • Future plans • Budget	• Data reception • Creation of bills of material • Planning operation • Production on demand • QC on demand • Preparation for shipment • Packaging • Interfaces to systems and projects (e.g., scanner, payment, eCommerce, content management) • Production site selection • Budget	• Customized packaging and shipment • Define partner for shipment • Speed • Costs • Quality • Budget	• Hotline • Satisfaction panel • Returns/ replacement • Next steps • New offers • Ensure enduring customer-brand-relationship	• Clarify types of payment: → online (credit card) → credit card at event location → invoice → currencies → accounting and billing

Source: Company information.

EXHIBIT 4
Mass customization rollout plan.

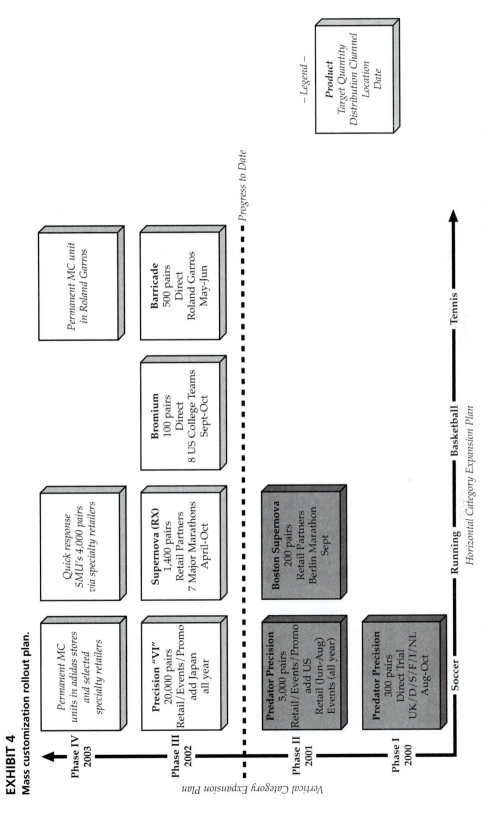

Source: Berger, C. "The Customized Revolution at adidas." *Kundenindividuelle Massenproduktion: Von Businessmodellen zu erfolgreichen Anwendungen.* Eds. M. Schenk, R. Seelmann-Eggebert, F.T. Piller. Die dritte deutsche Tagung zur Mass Customization, Frankfurt, November 8, 2001.

433

FIGURE 1
Combination logic of Predator® Precision Soccer Boot.

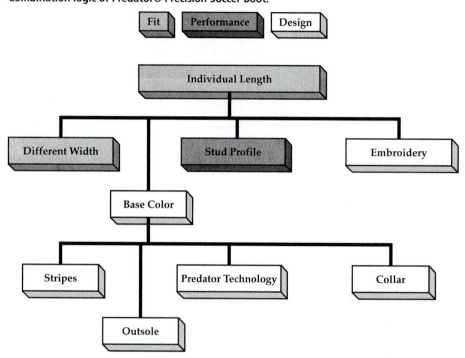

both project team and functions to gain hands-on experience in marketing, information management, production, distribution and after-service of customized shoes. It also provided a basis for a rough cost-benefit analysis and future budgeting.

Product Selection
The pilot mandate was soccer boots. A Predator® Precision boot already in production was offered for customization with regard to fit (size and width), performance (outsole types, materials, and support) and design (color combinations and embroidery).

Marketing: Event Concept and Communication
The pilot was 100 percent event based. Over a two-month period in 2000, six events were held in different European cities: Newcastle, Hamburg, Madrid, Marseille, Milan, and Amsterdam. Consumer recruitment was very selective, using local market research agencies, phone calls, written invitations and pre- and post-event questionnaires. (Refer to Exhibit 5 for details of the customer recruitment process for the pilot.) The target group was 50 participants per event and country.

The MC unit was designed in a rather neutral technology-oriented style stressing the brand's tradition as the athlete's support. A white cocoon (evoking a mysterious atmosphere with its shape and color) housed the 3-D foot scanner, the heart of the unit. A newly developed matching matrix software supported scanning and fitting. At a separate fitting terminal, a selection of sample boots was available for testing fit preferences.

In addition, a design terminal had a laptop on which the participants, assisted by adidas experts, could customize their soccer boot in terms of materials and design. The stations also displayed material and color samples to facilitate the decision-making process. (Refer to Exhibit 6 for details of the customization step and Exhibit 7 for the company press release.)

> Today, it is a brand new, revolutionary and futuristic experience. Soon it will be as normal as buying individualized glasses at an optician.

Consumer Feedback
adidas consumers greeted mi adidas with tremendous excitement.

> Consumers loved the product. 100% want a customization service available in the future.

Shortly after the introduction of mi adidas, even adidas headquarters started to receive direct inquiries

EXHIBIT 5
One-to-one communication with the event participants/recruits.

−15 days	Local market research agency contacts potential participants. Questionnaire-guided telephone interview.
−10 days	Selection of recruits based on questionnaire answers. Telephone availability-check of the recruits. Set-up of substitute list.
−7 days	Official written invitation accompanied by pre-event questionnaire.
−2 days	Ultimate check if recruits will take part in the event. Telephone invitation of substitutes as required.
Event	adidas customization experience and on-site interview
+2 weeks	Delivery of customized soccer shoes.
+6 weeks	Telephone follow-up interview.

Not only should the product and services be individualized and unique, but also the personal relationship and interaction with the consumer as being part of the customization experience. Are we prepared?

Christoph Berger, Director MC

Source: Company information.

from interested consumers who wanted to purchase a customized shoe. Franck Denglos, marketing coordinator, reflected on his experience with the mi adidas pilot:

> The concept and its execution gave consumers a strong positive impression of the brand. They left with the perception that adidas was acting as a leader. However, we have to keep in mind that their perception was highly influenced by the impressive tool, run by highly qualified adidas experts. Plus, during the pilot, the shoe was free.

COMPETITORS' FOOTWEAR CUSTOMIZATION INITIATIVES

Several competitors offered a similar service:

Nike Inc.

Nike Inc. decided to bring MC to the Web in November 1999. Nike's NIKEiD program enabled online customers to choose the color of their shoe and add a personal name of up to eight characters.[5] For this service, Nike asked the regular retail price for the shoe plus a $10 custom design fee and shipping charges. Delivery of the footwear was advertised as being within three weeks for the U.S. market. To keep fulfillment and distribution under control, however, Nike imposed an artificial ceiling

and only accepted up to 400 U.S.-based orders per day.[6]

Reebok International, Ltd

As of 2001, Reebok had not launched (or announced) its own mass customization initiative. Instead, it marketed its full foot cushion for its top of the range running shoe, the Fusion C DMX 10. Utilizing DMX®10 technology and 3-D ultralite sole material, Reebok provided 10 air pods to help distribute air for custom cushioning and to achieve the ultimate in shock absorption.[7]

New Balance Athletic Shoe, Inc.

New Balance opened its first "width center concept unit" at Harrods in London in April 2001. Coming from a long tradition of making arch supports and prescription footwear to improve shoe fit, the U.S.-based company first manufactured a performance running shoe in 1961. By 2001 New Balance featured a range of athletic shoes and outdoor footwear. Although New Balance did not offer a customization of shoes, it typically offered its products in three (at times up to five) different width sizes to optimize shoe fit.[8]

---

[5] http://nikeid.nike.com.

[6] "Nike Offers Mass Customization Online," *Computerworld,* November 23, 1999.

[7] http://www.reebok.com.

[8] http://www.newbalance.com and New Balance Athletic Shoe, Inc., press releases, April 20, 2001.

EXHIBIT 6
The customization process.

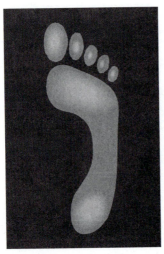

Step 1 Check in >	Step 2 Scanning >	Step 3 Fitting >	Step 4 Testing >	Step 5 Design >
Get ready for "mi adidas"! Get registered now for the chance to create your unique pair of customized shoes.	First your feet will be scanned by means of the adidas Footscan system to determine the exact length, width, and pressure distribution of each foot. This will enable you to determine which technologies your shoe will need for optimal performance.	Here you consult with an adidas fitting expert to review the results of your footscan. Then this information, combined with your personal fit preferences, is entered into a computer to determine the best-fitting shoe.	Once you have determined your personalized function and fit, you will have the opportunity to test your shoes before heading into the final design phase.	Now you can put the finishing touches on your one-of-a-kind shoes. You will be able to choose different colors, materials and even personalized embroidery— all of which can be viewed on the computer screen as you make your selections.

All that is left now is to confirm and order your customized shoe.* Within two weeks your personalized footwear will be with you ready for a new level of performance.

*Customers were not pushed to accept a customized shoe—returns upon delivery were minimal.

Source: http://www.miadidas.com.

EXHIBIT 7
Press Release: "adidas to Launch Customization Experience."

> **Custom-built footwear for consumers—Retail launch mid-2001—Pilot project unit on display at ISPO**
>
> Herzogenaurach, 02/04/2001—adidas, as the first brand in the sporting goods industry, is set to launch a pioneering "Customization Experience" project in footwear. The project starts in the Soccer category, but will be expanded into other major sports categories. With the "Customization Experience" project, adidas will give consumers the opportunity to create their own unique footwear to their exact personal specifications in terms of function, fit, and looks, thus providing services that were so far only available to soccer stars like David Beckham and Zinedine Zidane.
>
> The decision to proceed with the "Customization Experience" project was made after the successful completion and stringent evaluation of a pilot project conducted in the second half of 2000 in six European countries. During the test project some 400 pairs of the revolutionary adidas Predator® Precision soccer boots were custom built and delivered to a select group of consumers in Germany, France, England, Spain, Italy, and the Netherlands. Delivery time took two weeks on average. Consumer satisfaction was overwhelmingly positive.
>
> With the start of the "Customization Experience" project, adidas is entering the new age of the "experience economy." adidas introduces a new business model in the industry, influencing and changing the whole value chain and potentially the sporting goods marketplace, creating a new level of relationship between the consumer and the brand.
>
> The adidas "Customization Experience" unit used during the pilot project will be on display at ISPO in Munich, February 4–6, 2001. Launch in the retail marketplace is scheduled for mid 2001.

Source: adidas-Salomon AG.

Custom Foot Corp.

Custom Foot Corp. was one of the leading pioneers of mass customizing shoes in terms of fit and design. Featured in cover stories of *The New York Times, Forbes,* and *Fortune,* the company seemed to show a whole industry new ways of doing business: Custom-made Italian shoes, delivered in about three weeks, at off-the-shelf prices. But after a glorious start in 1995, Custom Foot went out of business and closed operations in summer 1998. Its concept for blending customization and mass production had failed, as the whole system could not handle the enormous complexity of the process.[9]

Creo Interactive GmbH

In 1998 Creo Interactive designed a totally new shoe based on a modular concept for the sole, the main body, and the tongue. This shoe could be produced in just 83 working steps compared with Custom Foot's 150 to 300 steps.[10] Leveraging the Internet as an interface for configuration, Creo offered pure design customization in terms of colors and patterns. By locating production in Germany, it was possible to swiftly fulfill European

market needs. However, three years into the venture, Creo Interactive closed operations in 2001.

Customatix.com of Solemates, Inc.

Based in Santa Cruz, California, Customatix.com allowed consumers to log onto its Internet site and choose from a vast array of colors, materials, graphics, and logos to create their own personalized portfolio of designs online. "150 choices you can put on the bottom of your sneakers."[11] The blueprints were then transmitted to the company's factory in China, where the shoes were manufactured and shipped to the consumer's doorstep within two weeks. The shoes retailed for $70 to $100 per pair, including import duty and delivery charges.

> The biggest problem we have is, people don't believe we can do what we do.
>
> Dave Ward, CEO of Customatix.com[12]

PHASE II: THE MI ADIDAS RETAIL TOURS

The decision to proceed with the "Customization Experience" project was made after the successful completion and stringent evaluation

[9] F. T. Piller, *Mass Customization* (Wiesbaden: Gabler Verlag, 8/2001, p. 397).
[10] F. T. Piller, "The Present and Future of Mass Customization: Do It—Now!"
[11] http://www.customatix.com.
[12] K. Smith, "Fancy Feet." *Entrepreneur's Business Start-Ups,* 7/2001.

of a pilot project conducted in the second half of 2000 in six European countries. During the test project some 400 pairs of the revolutionary adidas Predator® Precision soccer boots were custom built and delivered to a select group of consumers in Germany, France, England, Spain, Italy, and the Netherlands. Delivery time took two weeks on average. Consumer satisfaction was overwhelmingly positive.[13]

The pilot project was mainly seen as a first attempt to evaluate the requirements of "normal" consumers, as opposed to those of top athletes, with whom adidas had an ongoing relationship. Taking the successful concept of the pilot to the retail channel, however, meant facing different and new challenges. For the pilot, certain issues to do with back-end processes were adapted to current processes or not covered at all. Now, these would require more attention. In addition, a new retail unit had to be created that was smaller (10 to 20 m^2), easier to transport, more durable, and user friendly.

Retailers

Retailer interest in mi adidas was overwhelming. In Germany alone, almost 1,000 athletics specialty shops wanted to participate. However, only 50 German retail stores could be part of this second phase: the first retail tours in 2001. Soon retailer selection became a sensitive issue within adidas: Marketing preferred small athletics specialty shops for a maximal image effect and utmost retailer commitment.[14] Sales, however, favored big key accounts for reasons of relationship management. In addition, country selection was controversial: In some countries retailers were accustomed to paying a fee to a manufacturer for being able to host a promotion such as mi adidas. In other countries, retailers had never paid a fee for in-store promotions and might even demand a fee from the manufacturer instead. Depending on the final selection verdict, retailer feedback ranged from enormous enthusiasm to vast disappointment (even sporadic threats to withdraw business from adidas altogether).

Once selected, the retailers took care of consumer recruitment. To support them in marketing mi adidas, they were given a package of communication tools: CDs, posters, invitation cards, registration cards, and folders. Some retailers felt that the material was not engaging enough and demanded more support. Subsequently, the countries modified and translated the tools to fit the needs of their consumers more directly. Yet consumer turnout (and order placement) varied greatly from one retail store to another, depending on the commitment to mi adidas.

Whereas the pilot was 100 percent event based, retailers played the central role in the second phase and accounted for roughly 90 percent of the order volume. Using multiple mi adidas retail units, well over 100 retailers participated across Europe in 2001.

Customization Process

The customization process was still run by adidas experts and emphasized the "brand experience" theme. The 3-D foot scanner, however, had been replaced by a simpler Footscan™ unit, which was used in combination with a static measurement device for length and width measures. At the same time, the proprietary matching matrix software continued to evolve and directly conformed to consumer preferences in three out of four cases. The overall process had become very stable. 50 to 80 "customization experiences" could be handled per day during an event while about 15 to 20 were possible at a retail outlet.

Recent survey results seemed to confirm European consumers' interest in customized shoes. Although a focus on design customization was much simpler from a configuration perspective, consumers rated a customized design as much less important than a customized fit. In addition, individual preferences varied significantly across different European countries (and to a lesser extent also between men and women), necessitating further research for a targeted offering.[15]

Product and Pricing

The athletics footwear market was characterized by rapid product turnover. In 2001 mi adidas already featured its second product generation in soccer boots. The customized version of this soccer boot sold for a 30 percent to 50 percent price premium over the catalog price of €150.[16] In addition, the product offering was expanded into running shoes. After successful internal presentations of mi adidas for Running at the adidas global marketing meeting in

---

[13] adidas-Salomon AG, press release, April 2, 2001 (refer to **Exhibit 7** for the full press release).
[14] Some specialist stores got very excited about mi adidas and lined up local sponsors to equip entire sports teams with customized shoes while hosting the mi adidas retail unit at their outlet.

[15] S. Jäger, "Market Trends: From Mass Production to Mass Customization." EURO ShoE project, March 3, 2002, Innovation in the European Footwear Sector Conference, Milan.
[16] "Individuelle Maßanfertigung von Sportschuhen." *Schuhplus / infocomma*, October 15, 2001.

March 2001 and the Investor Day in July 2001, preparations were made to launch the project in the running market. In September 2001 mi adidas for Running was introduced to the market during the Berlin Marathon. Consumers were either recruited or invited by PR, or they were impulse buyers who passed by and became interested. Within three weeks, they received the shoes. For 2002 the plan was for mi adidas for Running to be present at all adidas-sponsored marathons (i.e., Paris, Boston, London, Madrid, Rotterdam, Prague, and Berlin) and to go on a retail tour in the relevant country after each event.

Consumers
Consumer feedback was excellent. In particular, the short delivery time and the opportunity to design their own shoes impressed the consumers. mi adidas also attracted strong interest from the press: Two television stations (Bayerischer Rundfunk and Fox TV) and many articles featured adidas' MC initiative and hailed it as a major milestone.

> Although we received this good feedback, there were several technical problems that had to be tackled. These problems caused delays and in some cases wrong production . . .

Information Management
Information management throughout the entire process was critical: Basic consumer data, product options, biometric knowledge, and product specifications had to be merged for order taking. In addition, sourcing, production, distribution, payment, and reordering required appropriate IT backing.[17]

> Information is the most important conversion factor of successful mass customization.

Many challenges in terms of the scope and integration of the required IT infrastructure remained:

a. The mi adidas kiosk system for order creation led to technical problems with synchronizing information generated offline (e.g., order numbers and customer records) with adidas backbone systems such as the sales system and customer master database.

b. The traditional sales system was not designed to process orders of individually customized shoes with detailed information on each article.

c. The IT systems for distribution needed to be extended for an organized distribution and return process.

d. Consumer data captured via mi adidas could not be transferred to the adidas CRM system.

There were ways around these problems, but they resulted in limited centralization and poor accessibility of data.

> The initial rollout was clearly under-budgeted. For example, eRoom [Exhibit 11] was chosen as the Web accessible repository for the technical documents. This decision was not entirely supported by Global IT and is seen as a short-term solution until an alternative can be found.

All development, configuration and support for mi adidas had thus far been absorbed by the business and no costs had been charged to the project budget for IT solutions, beyond the mi adidas kiosk application and scanning software. The kiosk application was developed by a contractor. However, no helpdesk was available for support and future system integration. The IT department was worried:

> The speed of implementations, the time needed to support both SAP and non-SAP countries and the limited resources Global IT presently has to support this, leads to the conclusion that we may fail to maximally deliver mi adidas globally.

mi adidas had progressed fast—calling for a completely new set of requirements.

> mi adidas, even such a small project, has forced the IT department to think about how close we are getting to our consumers and what is needed to support this development.

Production
By 1992 most sporting goods companies had outsourced the main part of their footwear production to the Far East to reduce production costs. adidas followed suit and outsourced all textile production and 96 percent of footwear production during its turnaround in the mid-1990s. The outsourced footwear production was divided between Asia (China, Indonesia, South Korea, Taiwan, Thailand, and Vietnam), Eastern Europe, and North Africa. Depending on the quality of the shoe, between 20 percent and 40 percent of production costs were related to personnel costs, which were the main driver for cost differences between regions.[18] Contract manufacturers focused on footwear assembly

[17] S. Dulio, "Technology Trends: From Rigid Mechanical Manufacturing to Mass Customization." EURO ShoE project, Innovation in the European footwear sector conference, Milan, March 3, 2002.

[18] IMD adidas case IMD-3-0743 (GM 743), January 26, 1999.

EXHIBIT 8
Traditional order and product process flow.

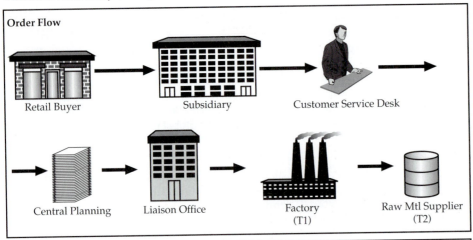

Order Flow

Retail Buyer → Subsidiary → Customer Service Desk →

→ Central Planning → Liaison Office → Factory (T1) → Raw Mtl Supplier (T2)

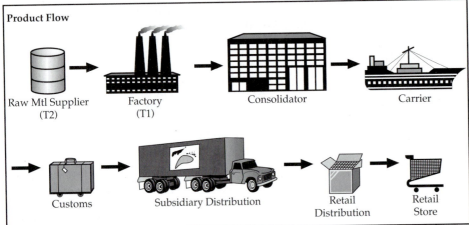

Product Flow

Raw Mtl Supplier (T2) → Factory (T1) → Consolidator → Carrier

→ Customs → Subsidiary Distribution → Retail Distribution → Retail Store

Source: Company information.

and sourced input materials from local suppliers as needed. (Refer to Exhibit 8 for a supply chain overview and Exhibit 9 for production sites.)

adidas maintained a small footwear factory in Germany, in Scheinfeld, near its headquarters. Here, models, prototypes and made-to-measure performance products could be manufactured and tested. In addition, special shoes for Olympic sports such as fencing, wrestling, weightlifting, and bobsled were made. However, Scheinfeld was not excited at the prospect of taking mi adidas production in-house. Furthermore, material provisioning for a vast set of customization options could be more costly in Scheinfeld because it was too far away from volume production sites and suppliers.

The production processes used for the mass customization shoes were the same basic processes used in mass production. For the MC events, however, a combination of development sample room and mass production facilities was used (refer to Exhibit 10 for a comparison). This combination was chosen to allow for the highest level of control and quality while providing a minimal "disruption" to the factory's daily mass production schedule.

> A program like mi adidas, without dedicated facilities, manpower and materials resources, will always be perceived as an interruption to the overall process of creating shoes.

Yet the capacity of the sample rooms was limited[19] and its operational format was not designed for

[19] For the mi adidas pilot, volume was limited and production was not a problem. In general, a development sample room, however, could not handle more than 500 to 1,000 pairs per month.

EXHIBIT 9
Three mi adidas production sites.

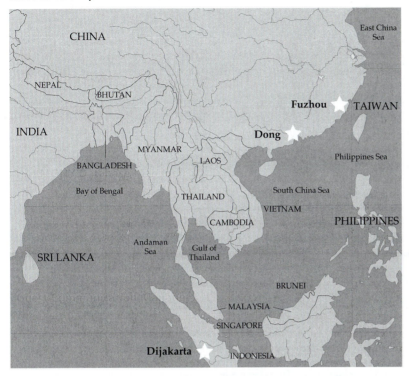

Source: www.maps.com, company information.

volume scale effects. The mass production facilities, by contrast, were not meant to handle a lot size of one[20] nor were they set up to allow for close linkage of individual product flow with corresponding customization information. Such a process was not in place and the workers lacked training and language capabilities to handle production according to detailed written product specifications.

Variability is simply not in our business model!

Although the assembly of a customized shoe was theoretically straightforward, provisioning the required material proved to be time consuming. Delays were exacerbated when material was needed that was not currently available for in-line production. In this case, special material provisioning resulted in significant inventory costs as materials for the top of the range models in question were expensive. From a production perspective, a better understanding was needed of the value–cost trade-off between the marketing perception of customer value added versus inventory and production costs

for specific customization options. For example, design customization in terms of multiple colors was not ideal from a material provisioning perspective because different shoe sizes already meant different component sizes (e.g., strip length varied with the shoe size), which would now have to be available in a range of colors. These trade-offs and the options available for new shoes should ideally play a much more prominent role right from the start—in designing products for MC. Karl-Josef Seldmeyer, vice president, head of global supply chain management, summarized his experiences:

For today's volumes, the combined complexity of fit, performance, and design is too much.

Distribution
Timely mass customization also depended on proper execution of communications and logistics to meet the seven-day lead-time from order receipt to ex-factory shipping. Starting from July 2001, the mi adidas process was changed from a pilot with deliveries direct to the final consumer to a process that involved the retailers in customization and distribution. After customization at the retailer shops, orders were no longer transferred directly to the

---

[20] Production set-ups were often made only once per day producing large batches of footwear.

EXHIBIT 10
Comparison: Classical production versus mass customization of adidas footwear.

CP (classical production)	MC (mass customization)
Production	
• Third-party production • Mass/bulk production • Weekly production planning	• Third-party production • Fast-moving lines • "On demand"
Delivery-Logistics	
• Transportation outsourced • Distribution centers (adidas owned)	• Complete outsourcing • (From factory to retailer)
Lead Time and Production Time	
70–110 days lead time Orders—delivery in dc (Distribution center) **10–12 days in production process**	**14 days lead time** Order—delivery to customer (With material in stock) = critical component **3–4 days in production process**
Delivery-Logistics	
0,70 $ seafreight (landed DC) 4,50 $ airfreight (landed DC) + customs and distribution freight	~6 $ courier service (landed retailer) per pair

Source: C. Berger, "The Customized Revolution at adidas." *Kundenindividuelle Massenproduktion: Von Businessmodellen zu erfolgreichen Anwendungen.* Eds. M. Schenk, R. Seelmann-Eggebert, F. T. Piller. Die dritte deutsche Tagung zur Mass Customization, Frankfurt, November 8, 2001.

sourcing systems. Instead, they were routed from the retailer to the respective subsidiary's sales system and from there to Logistics Ordering Systems, using the subsidiary's regular buying process. The addressee was no longer the final consumer but the individual retailer in whose shop the customization had taken place. The individual retailer was now responsible for distribution to the end consumer. (Refer to Exhibit 11 for an overview of the mi adidas order and product flow.)

Communication and Competing Initiatives
With the push into multiple product categories, communication became more difficult. In particular, the extremely technical and highly advanced customization process could not be adequately promoted as the mi adidas budget did not support targeted messaging by category. However, increasing the marketing spend was not then an option since marketing saw MC as just one of many initiatives. After all, they already supported top athletes via a special care team and tailor-made shoes made in Scheinfeld. Since it was naturally in competition for resources and management attention with other

recent initiatives, mi adidas was often seen as secondary to designated brand concepts such as "a³"[21] and "ClimaCool.™"[22] Hence a³, "Football never felt better," and Clima acted as overriding messages for the upcoming marathons, Soccer World Cup, and Roland Garros, respectively.

> Communication activity and spend needs to be regulated, ensuring that brand concepts are not undermined by ongoing mi adidas activity.

[21] a³ was a functional technology combining cushioning, stability, and light weight. It managed the foot's natural movement by dissipating harmful impact forces, stabilizing and guiding the foot through the entire footstrike, and retaining and redirecting energy from the rear foot to the front foot. adidas planned to introduce the concept for running shoes in 2002 as the most technical, functional design available.
[22] ClimaCool™ was a footwear technology concept offering 360 degrees of ventilation and moisture management. In scientific tests, it produced 20 percent dryer and 20 percent cooler feet. Targeting regular or serious athletes, adidas planned for a staggered market introduction across products in 2002.

EXHIBIT 11
mi adidas order and product process flow.

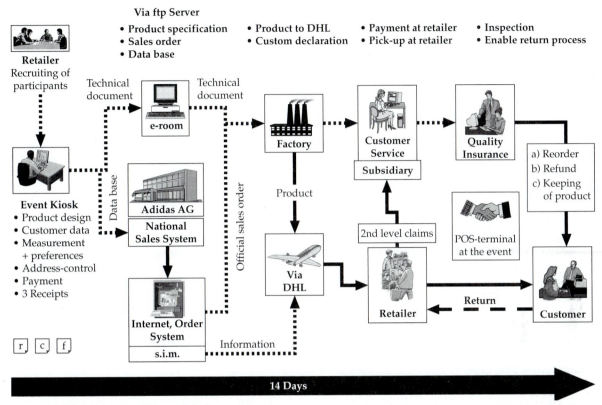

Source: C. Berger, "The Customized Revolution at adidas." *Kundenindividuelle Massenproduktion: Von Businessmodellen zu erfolgreichen Anwendungen.* Eds. M. Schenk, R. Seelmann-Eggebert, F. T. Piller. Die dritte deutsche Tagung zur Mass Customization, Frankfurt, November 8, 2001.

adidas' Own Retail Activities

To further strengthen its brand, adidas had also just stepped up its own retail activities, increasing the number of its own retail outlets from 37 in 2000 to 65 in 2001. Most notable here was the opening of two concept stores in Paris and Stockholm as well as an adidas Originals store in Berlin.[23]

Negotiating Continued Internal Support

By October 2001 mi adidas was an established initiative and the generally positive brand image effect was widely accepted within the organization. Although mi adidas had become bigger, the organizational set-up had not substantially evolved. To date, much of the support for the project from different functions of adidas was granted on a goodwill basis. As time progressed and volumes increased, it naturally became more and more difficult to persuade core business units to fully support this initiative, especially out of their own cost centers.

[23] adidas-Salomon AG, 2001 Annual Report.

The annual budget for mi adidas had basically stayed identical during its first years.

The situation was not ideal. Although the functions continued to support mi adidas and took pride in its success to date, the ultimate responsibility for mishaps, of course, rested with the project team. Should mi adidas be elevated and play a more independent role or should it be better integrated into the existing matrix to be in sync with adidas' core business, with the functions in turn assuming more accountability? A clear evaluation was made difficult by the current practice of attributing mi adidas sales to the respective countries, hindering separate accounting.

THE FUTURE OF MI ADIDAS

Reinschmidt wondered if the time was right to scale mi adidas to the next level (Phases III and IV; refer to Exhibit 4)? The pilot (Phase I) had been very successful and adidas had developed and refined important new capabilities. Consumer feedback was enthusiastic and retailers fared much better during repeat offerings of mi adidas. Yet the initial retail rollout (Phase II) had been somewhat slower than projected, falling 40 percent to 50 percent short of the targets established in the original rollout plan.

Future Alternatives

Reinschmidt had come to the conclusion that mi adidas needed clearer direction. Once again he reviewed the three generic alternatives that the company could embark on:

> mi adidas could be turned into a commercial tool over the course of the next years and now was the time to decide upon this.

Alternative I: *Withdraw*—Celebrate the success and PR effect accomplished to date but quietly withdraw from MC in order to focus on adidas' core business.

mi adidas had been launched two years earlier and now featured a soccer and running shoe. As the product life for these model cycles ended, so would mi adidas. Current commitments would be honored but any further investments in the MC initiative were to be avoided. New PR tools would soon take the place of mi adidas.

Alternative 2: *Maintain*—Maintain the developed capabilities and selectively run mi adidas fairs and planned retail tours following top events such as the Soccer World Cup and world marathon series.

mi adidas would continue in its current form and scope and be allowed limited organic growth. Investment would be minimal and MC responsibilities would be more fully integrated into the existing functions. mi adidas would be part of (and governed by) adidas' annual planning cycle. As new boots were introduced to the market, a customizable derivative of those models would be created for mi adidas; the kiosk application, promotional material and back-end processes, and the like would be adapted accordingly.

Alternative 3: *Expand*—Expand mi adidas to multiple product categories and permanent retail installations; elevate it to brand concept status while further building volume and process expertise.

mi adidas would be scaled up in terms of both volume and product categories. Increased marketing spend and revised back-end processes would support its rollout. Permanent installations at select retail stores would complement the event and retail tour concepts to foster more continuous order flow and steady volumes. Further investments would ensure a degree of independence for mi adidas and help develop MC into a potential business model in its own right for adidas.

Decision Looming

Reinschmidt had the alternatives lined up and it was up to him to come to a sensible recommendation based on the various inputs received. He had just started to summarize a set of key issues that should determine which alternative to choose, as well as his assessment of the alternatives, when he was interrupted . . .

Discussion Questions

1. Has the "mi adidas" mass customization initiative been successful to date? Why or why not?
2. What potential problems and opportunities does the current initiative present?
3. What specific manufacturing and distribution approaches would you suggest for each of the three alternatives? In other words, where should production and distribution be located and what type of process should be used for each alternative?
4. Which of the three alternatives do you recommend and why?

Lincoln Smith, manager of operations for PlasTech, stared at the income statement for fiscal year 1993. It was a disaster. Although the firm had increased revenues 20 percent, profits were down 83 percent from fiscal 1992. On many performance measures the past year had been a success: Revenues and production rates were up, and average machine setup times were down. Furthermore, these results were achieved while the firm had reformulated its marketing strategy. What had gone wrong?

PLASTECH, INC.

PlasTech was a producer of plastic pellets for use as raw material in molded plastic products. It blended raw plastic polymers with other ingredients to create new plastics with particular properties that were needed by its customers. The customers would then use these new plastics to make final products for sale to their customers. Although it manufactured tangible goods, PlasTech was primarily a service firm. PlasTech's niche was that it had the specialized equipment and expertise for blending a variety of ingredients. Many customers chose to use blenders like PlasTech because they did not want to invest in the specialized equipment or did not want to invest in developing the expertise required to properly blend the ingredients. Other customers chose to use outside blenders because the process was messy and sometimes involved hazardous chemicals. PlasTech was set up to handle hazardous wastes safely and cost-effectively.

PlasTech's production process was conceptually very simple (see Exhibit 1). Virgin plastic, in the form of small pellets, was fed, via a hopper, into a long cylindrical tube, called a "bore." While inside the bore the pellets were heated, melted, churned, and forced forward by a screw-like shaft. Chemical additives, which gave the plastic special properties (e.g., low friction, hardness, color, electrical conductivity, or oil resistance) were introduced at various points along the bore. By the time the molten mixture reached, the end of the bore, it was properly blended. The viscous plastic mixture was then extruded from the end of the bore into continuous strands of plastic. The strands were cooled in a water bath, then chopped into small pellets just like the pellets that were fed into the process.

Although the blending process appeared simple, in reality, because the blending process involved both mechanical and chemical changes and the physical state of the plastic at each point in the bore was critical, the fluid dynamics of the material as it proceeded through the bore, and hence, the design of the screw mechanism that controlled the pressure and the mixing action, was very sophisticated. Process engineers, who designed the screw, needed to understand both the physics of the production process and the polymer chemistry.

A sample screw-shaft design is shown in Exhibit 2. A typical screw was built up in a series of three- to five-inch sections, with the shape and structure of each section designed to perform a particular task. For example, a helical-screw shape was used to push plastic into the bore and increase pressure, while a spoked section was used to mix and blend. Screw configurations could be from 5 to 15 feet long depending on a particular processing requirement.

PlasTech operated six machine-paced blending lines. Each line was complete, with a feeding hopper, blending machine, water bath, and pelletizer. Two of these lines had additional specialized equipment to properly handle hazardous chemicals (e.g., water and air filtration equipment).

In this business, the virgin plastic was owned by the customer and consigned to PlasTech for processing. In order to keep their inventory costs down, customers placed orders in relatively small quantities. This practice necessitated relatively small production batch sizes and a large number of setups for PlasTech. In 1992, the average batch size was 13,000 pounds and there were 320 setups (see Exhibit 3). The average setup time was 24 hours. Setup times took so long because it took time to clean the hopper and the bore, clean and disassemble the screw shaft, and reconfigure and install the next screw. Some more time was spent (one to two hours) breaking in the new setup before product of acceptable quality was produced. Thorough and proper cleaning was critical because the smallest residual particles from a prior production run could contaminate the next batch, making it unusable.

CRISIS IN FISCAL 1992

In July 1991, PlasTech was informed that two of its customers would cease to do business with PlasTech. National Food Products had decided to purchase blending equipment of its own. Plastic Containers, Inc., was in financial trouble and going out of business. Together, these firms comprised 46 percent of the total pounds of plastic that PlasTech processed in 1992. Both companies were committed to contracts until the end of January 1992, so PlasTech had a short time to react.

This case was prepared by Assistant Professor John P. Leschke, McIntire School of Commerce, University of Virginia. Copyright © 1993 by John P. Leschke, Charlottesville, Virginia. Revision: February 26, 1996. Published with permission.

EXHIBIT 1
Schematic diagram of production process.

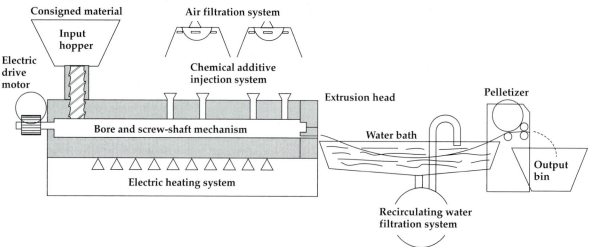

EXHIBIT 2
Schematic diagram of screw-shaft mechanism.

Drive gear   Helical-screw shapes for feeding at low pressure   Spoked sections for mixing   Helical-screw shape to stabilize and increase pressure before extrusion

In the six months before PlasTech lost nearly half of its production volume, it aggressively marketed its services to other potential customers. This effort landed two significant customers, Basic Materials Company and Plastic Components, Inc., who together replaced nearly all of the lost volume. Chastened by the experience of losing two of its largest customers, PlasTech vowed to never again be dependent on so few key contracts. PlasTech devised a new marketing strategy seeking additional work from all of its existing customers and broadening its product line. The annual production summaries in Exhibits 3 and 4 show the changes in the variety and mix of production. In making this transition, one of the directives given to the marketing area was to maintain the average price per pound while increasing the variety of products sold, without sacrificing revenues for the sake of volume. As a result of these efforts, PlasTech entered fiscal 1993 with projections of record volume and sales.

ACTIONS AND RESULTS IN FISCAL 1993
Several labor policy changes and productivity improvements were undertaken to meet the challenges that arose in 1993. A third shift was added to meet the increase in production and setup volume. Each shift was fully utilized throughout the year. Each shift was composed of six two-operator teams, one for each blending line. Wages for operator teams were reported as direct labor in financial statements. Direct labor was responsible for all production and setup. Indirect labor expenses accounted for a separate group of employees who were responsible for materials handling, machine maintenance, and other production-support activities. Concerted efforts were made to increase the production rates of the equipment so that overall capacity increased. Average throughput increased 7.4 percent, from 256.9 pounds per hour to 276.1 pounds per hour. Average setup time decreased 5 percent to 22.8 hours per setup. Exhibit 4 contains a production summary for fiscal 1993.

Despite these improvements in the operations side of the business, the financial side of the business suffered. The firm barely broke even for the year, earning less than one percent profit on sales after taxes (Exhibits 5 and 6 contain financial results for fiscal 1992 and fiscal 1993, respectively). Smith struggled with the paradox. What had gone wrong?

EXHIBIT 3
1992 production summary (fiscal year ended March 1, 1992).

Customer name	Product ID #	Production (lbs)	Production (act. hours)	Avg. Production Rate (lbs/hr)	Number of Setups	Total Actual Setup Hours	Avg. Setup Time (hrs)	Sales ($)	Avg. Sale Price ($/lb)
1 Allegheny Plastics, Inc.	PP-01-002	431,908	1,632	264.6	15	323	21.5	356,429	0.825
2	PP-12-003	503,194	2,122	237.1	64	1,613	25.2	409,893	0.815
3 National Food Products	PP-03-001	335,462	1,387	241.9	27	653	24.2	292,272	0.871
4	PP-03-002	167,731	620	270.5	12	292	24.3	146,136	0.871
5	PP-03-004	209,664	783	267.8	16	392	24.5	181,779	0.867
6	PP-06-009	419,328	1,632	256.9	32	707	22.1	359,993	0.858
7 Plastic Containers, Inc.	PP-12-001	796,723	3,084	258.3	16	384	24.0	748,500	0.939
8 Specialty Plastics	PP-08-012	209,664	832	252.0	16	392	24.5	174,650	0.833
9	PP-08-013	167,731	702	238.9	22	591	26.9	135,443	0.808
10	PP-08-014	335,462	1,469	228.4	35	845	24.1	281,579	0.839
11 Webber Packaging, Inc.	PP-12-001	29,353	114	257.5	11	238	21.6	21,386	0.729
12	PP-12-002	62,899	245	256.7	6	154	25.7	35,643	0.567
13 Ziglitz Company	PP-18-001	125,798	522	241.0	13	338	26.0	89,108	0.708
14	PE-01-001	398,363	1,176	338.7	35	758	21.7	331,479	0.832
		4,193,280	16,320	256.9	320	7,680	24.0	3,564,288	0.850

EXHIBIT 4
1993 production summary (fiscal year ended March 1, 1993).

Customer name	Product ID #	Production (lbs)	Production (act. hours)	Avg. Production Rate (lbs/hr)	Number of Setups	Total Actual Setup Hours	Avg. Setup Time (hrs)	Sales ($)	Avg. Sale Price ($/lb)
1 Allegheny Plastics, Inc.	PP-01-002	493,788	1,799	274.5	16	342	21.4	420,214	0.851
2	PP-12-003	541,256	1,946	278.1	67	1,682	25.1	449,783	0.831
3 Basic Materials Co.,	PP-01-001	75,809	257	295.0	60	1,206	20.1	65,651	0.866
4	PP-03-002	117,453	404	290.7	74	1,561	21.1	102,771	0.875
5	PP-03-004	225,911	863	261.8	30	615	20.5	203,094	0.899
6 Plastic Components, Inc.	PP-06-009	365,812	1,414	258.7	36	662	18.4	309,111	0.845
7	PP-12-001	258,914	926	279.6	36	680	18.9	218,782	0.845
8	PE-03-001	147,256	514	286.5	36	904	25.1	138,421	0.940
9	PE-03-002	604,895	2,111	286.5	36	864	24.0	530,493	0.877
10 Specialty Plastics	PP-08-012	220,469	808	272.9	18	387	21.5	184,092	0.835
11	PP-08-013	165,821	588	282.0	31	654	21.1	134,315	0.810
12	PP-08-014	400,122	1,506	265.7	43	1,097	25.5	336,102	0.840
13	PE-02-091	356,011	1,340	265.7	28	644	23.0	300,473	0.844
14	PE-04-004	105,026	367	286.2	87	2,349	27.0	89,272	0.850
15 Webber Packaging Inc.	PP-12-001	33,219	92	361.1	15	351	23.4	24,250	0.730
16	PP-12-002	65,055	184	353.6	9	194	21.6	35,845	0.551
17	PE-12-001	256,354	955	268.4	24	499	20.8	233,795	0.912
18 Ziglitz Company	PE-18-001	130,020	441	294.8	24	540	22.5	89,324	0.687
19	PE-01-001	455,933	1,616	282.1	50	1,145	22.9	375,571	0.824
20	PE-01-002	50,050	229	218.6	54	1,264	23.4	42,092	0.841
		5,069,173	18,360	276.1	774	17,640	22.8	4,283,451	0.845

EXHIBIT 5
1992 income statement (fiscal year ended March 1, 1992).

			Percent of Sales
Sales		$3,564,288	100.00%
Cost of goods sold			
Nonconsigned materials	$213,649		
Direct labor	528,000		
Indirect labor	185,000		
Utilities	633,211		
Depreciation	295,000	1,854,860	52.04%
Gross profit		$1,709,428	47.96%
Selling expenses	$819,786		
General and administrative expense	643,228	1,463,014	
Operating profit		$246,414	6.91%
Less other expenses and taxes		56,423	
Net profit after taxes		$189,991	5.33%

Fiscal Year Summary Statistics

Sales ($)	3,564,288
Production (lbs)	4,193,280
Average sale price ($/lb)	0.850
Average production cost ($/lb)	0.442
Average profit ($/lb)	0.045
Total productive time	16,320
Total setup time	7,680
Total time	24,000
Productive/total time ratio	68.0%

EXHIBIT 6
1993 income statement (fiscal year ended March 1, 1993).

			Percent of Sales
Sales		$4,283,451	100.00%
Cost of goods sold			
Nonconsigned materials	$256,757		
Direct labor	792,000		
Indirect labor	222,327		
Utilities	762,973		
Depreciation	295,000	2,329,057	54.37%
Gross profit		$1,954,394	45.63%
Selling expenses	$1,199,366		
General and administrative expense	678,459	1,877,825	
Operating profit		$76,569	1.79%
Less other expenses and taxes		45,087	
Net profit after taxes		$31,482	0.73%

Fiscal Year Summary Statistics

Sales ($)	4,283,451
Production (lbs)	5,069,173
Average sale price ($/lb)	0.845
Average production cost ($/lb)	0.459
Average profit ($/lb)	0.006
Total productive time	18,360
Total setup time	17,640
Total time	36,000
Productive/total time ratio	51.0%

Smith was not the only one concerned. The company's marketing executive, Grace Simpkins, also wanted to know what went wrong. She had worked extremely hard to successfully implement the new marketing strategy and was equally frustrated by the financial results. She had asked Smith to meet with her as soon as possible to discuss the causes and possible solutions to the firm's problems.

Lincoln Smith prepared for the meeting by going through the numbers. His first thought was to determine if the small drop in average sale price per pound accounted for the drop in earnings. He multiplied the $.005 per pound price differential by the total number of pounds produced in fiscal 1993; the result of $25,346 accounted for only a fraction of the fall in operating profit. Since nonconsigned material prices had not changed between the two years, he could not attribute the decline in profits to material cost increases. Which factors contributed to the drop in operating profits?

Smith reluctantly decided to look at direct and indirect labor productivity to see if his people were responsible for the problem. Wage rates had not changed, so it would be easy to compare labor productivity from year to year. What he found surprised him. Then he looked at the ratio of productive time to total time in the fiscal year summary statistics. What did these numbers mean?

Discussion Questions

1. Complete the income statement analysis that Lincoln Smith began by projecting the growth in each expense category and computing the variance from actual. Which factors contributed to the decline in profits?

2. What did Lincoln Smith find when he computed the direct and indirect labor productivity figures?

3. Identify and describe the root cause of the decline in operating profits. Recommend a plan of action for PlasTech.

Southwest Airlines, which began as a small Texas airline in 1971, had grown to become one of the largest airlines in the United States.[1] As of 2004, Southwest flew more than 65 million passengers a year to 59 cities in 30 states, more than 2,800 times a day.[2] While the airline industry reported greater than $5 billion in losses during 2003, that year marked Southwest Airlines' 31st consecutive year of profitability.[3]

For more than three decades, Southwest's competitive advantage stemmed from its unique business model, together with its unorthodox management style, especially that of former CEO Herb Kelleher. For example, in March 1992, Kelleher settled a dispute with Stevens Aviation over the right to use the ad slogan "Just Plane Smart," which Stevens maintained it had developed first. Kelleher and Kurt Herwald, the chairman of Stevens Aviation, had decided they would settle things the "old-fashioned way" in a best-of-three arm-wrestling match in the Dallas Sportatorium.

This unusual method of negotiation was entirely in keeping with Herb Kelleher's "disarming" style, which, for some observers, was the principal reason for Southwest's record of 31 consecutive profitable years. Many in the industry, however, pointed to a variety of other factors that ensured the Dallas-based airline would continue to maintain its top record of achievement. Others wondered how Southwest could continue its record of profitability and growth in light of the changing competitive environment in the airline industry.

HISTORY

Rollin King, a former investment counselor who had been operating a small air-taxi service in Texas, founded Southwest Airlines in 1967. The impetus behind King's organization of Southwest Airlines was his perception of a growing unmet need for improved intercity air service within Texas.

In the late 1960s, Houston, Dallas, San Antonio, and Fort Worth were among the fastest-growing cities in the United States. Although each had its own airport, a huge new airport, the Dallas–Fort Worth Regional Airport—which would serve both Dallas and Fort Worths—was then under construction. Two Texas-based carriers, Braniff International Airways and Texas International Airlines (TI), primarily served these four cities. For the most part, service to these cities by Braniff and TI consisted of "legs" of interstate flights; in other words, a Braniff flight might stop at Dallas on its way from New York to San Antonio.

In his talks with consumers before embarking on the Southwest venture, King was struck by the amount of dissatisfaction with the current service and discovered that the market was bigger than many realized. Together with his lawyer, Herb Kelleher, King was able to raise enough capital to incorporate the airline and hire Lamar Muse as president and chief executive officer. On February 20, 1968, Kelleher obtained the Certificate of Public Convenience and Necessity from the Texas Aeronautics Commission, which granted Southwest Airlines the right to provide intrastate air service between Dallas–Fort Worth, Houston, and San Antonio. Southwest's competitors reacted immediately by asking the Texas courts to enjoin issuance of the certificate, maintaining that service was already provided on the proposed routes and that the market was not large enough to support another carrier. The ensuing litigation kept the company's lawyers occupied for several years. In its first 11 months of operation, Southwest lost $3.7 million.

On June 18, 1971, amid a heavy advertising campaign to promote the new airline—as well as restraining orders issued after complaints by its competitors—Southwest launched 6 round-trip flights between Dallas's Love Field and San Antonio and 12 round-trip flights between Dallas and Houston. The takeoff proved to be less than auspicious. Some days saw the airline carrying a total of only 150 passengers on its 18 round-trip flights. Nevertheless, Muse persevered with his ideas by offering unbelievable prices, gimmicks, and creative advertising.

[1] Southwest Airlines, *Annual Report* (2003), 9.
[2] Southwest Airlines, http://www.southwest.com (accessed on 9 June 2004).
[3] Southwest Airlines, *Annual Report* (2003), 5.

EXHIBIT 1
Revenues, net income, and revenue passengers carried.

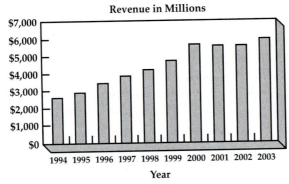

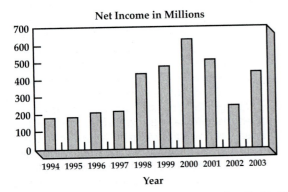

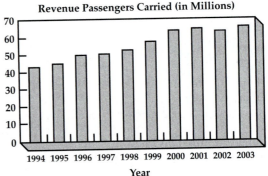

Source: Southwest Airlines, *Annual Report* (2003), 14–15.

In Texas, 1972 became the year of the fare war. To compete with Southwest, rivals slashed fares and began offering more in terms of service (e.g., free beer, hot and cold towels, one-dollar drinks on Southwest's routes, and more-frequent service). When Braniff decided to offer a half-price fare, Muse countered with a giveaway: free bottles of premium liquor to passengers who paid the full fare; passengers who did not want the liquor would pay half fare. Because corporations were accustomed to paying full fare, business travelers became the happy recipients of premium liquor. During the promotion, Southwest became not only the largest distributor in Texas of Chivas Regal, Crown Royal, and Smirnoff, but also the winner in the fare war. After 1972, Southwest consistently made a profit (see Exhibit 1 for the figures for 1994 through 2003).

HERB KELLEHER
In March 1979, Lamar Muse resigned as president and CEO of Southwest Airlines, and Herb Kelleher was named as his replacement. Kelleher, who had been a student of philosophy and literature in college and later graduated at the top of his law-school class at New York University, was wedded to the Southwest cause from the very beginning.

Early on, Kelleher established a reputation for doing the unusual. At company functions, he would appear as Elvis Presley or Roy Orbison and perform "Jailhouse Rock" or "Pretty Woman." One Halloween night, he showed up at Southwest's hangar in drag, as Corporal Klinger from the *M*A*S*H* television show, to thank the mechanics for working overtime. Although Kelleher's behavior was somewhat unconventional for a chief executive officer, his efforts paid off. His colleagues credited much of Southwest's "magic" to him.

Known for his extreme tenacity and limitless energy, Kelleher slept only four hours a night, read two or three books a week, and chain-smoked. Gary Barren, Southwest's chief operations officer, called Kelleher "the smartest, quickest lawyer—not to mention the best judge of people"—he had ever seen.[4]

[4] Charlotte Thompson and Elliott N. Weiss, "Southwest Airlines" (case study, UVA-OM-0743), University of Virginia Darden Graduate School of Business Administration, Charlottesville, 1993.

Kelleher was widely credited with much of the airline's success by promoting and maintaining both a culture that favored people and a coherent business strategy that was consistently successful yet deceptively simple. "People always want high-quality service at a lower price, provided by people who enjoy what they do," he maintained.[5] The results of Kelleher's efforts: Southwest's overall costs were the lowest of any major carrier.

OPERATIONS

Start-up
The first key decision for the airline concerned the number and type of aircraft to be used. After weeks of negotiations with representatives of several airplane manufacturers, Southwest decided to purchase three Boeing 737-200 aircraft. This decision proved to be a crucial one, as Southwest wanted to use the same type of aircraft in all its operations and also allow for future expansion. The Boeing 737-200 required fewer crew members than the aircraft used by Southwest's competitors. Maintenance costs were also lower because the airline had to maintain only one type of plane.

Scheduling
Initial decisions about scheduling were constrained by the fact that Southwest had only three airplanes. After studying flight times and on-the-ground (turnaround) times, Muse and King concluded that they could offer flights at 75-minute intervals using two planes between Dallas and Houston (the most important route) and at 150-minute intervals (2½ hours) between Dallas and San Antonio using one plane. This schedule amounted to 12 round trips a day between Dallas and Houston and 6 round trips a day between Dallas and San Antonio. Because of low weekend demand, Muse and King decided Southwest would fly less frequently on Saturdays and Sundays.

In spite of all their well-laid plans, however, scheduling soon proved to be a problem. In the first two weeks, the airline reported an average of 13.1 passengers per flight on the Dallas–Houston route and 12.9 passengers on the Dallas–San Antonio route. Owing to the lack of planes, management concluded that Southwest was unable to compete effectively, and set about to improve its schedule frequencies. Delivery of the fourth plane in late September helped immensely, but perhaps more important than the arrival of the fourth plane was the company's skill at producing a turnaround time of 10 minutes. Proving its ability to turn a constraint into a competitive advantage, Southwest was able

to initiate hourly service between Dallas and Houston and to begin flights every two hours between Dallas and San Antonio. The company did this by orchestrating maintenance and servicing to the point that no plane stayed on the ground more than 10 minutes. This development proved to be a real innovation in the industry; Southwest became known for its "quick turns."

Strategy and Service
From the beginning, Southwest's business model was to offer no-frills, low-cost flights to and from secondary airports. Management's focus was the "short-haul, point-to-point" strategy, which advocated short flights to uncrowded airports for quick turnarounds. This adherence to a short-haul strategy enabled Southwest to distinguish itself from its competitors, many of whom failed: several airlines started out in the short-haul business only to become tempted by the more glamorous routes.

Most of Southwest's competitors used a "hub-and-spoke" system in which big planes flew to major airports (hubs) and then linked up with smaller airports (spokes). Southwest developed no recognizable hub, preferring instead to maintain a "spider-web" system in which one strand at a time was spun. Kelleher's reason for implementing this strategy was that a hub-and-spoke network tied up too many valuable assets at too few pressure points, whereas a spider-web system allowed maximum flexibility to disperse assets and reduce stress in the system.

Southwest's no-frills policy included no baggage transfers, no meals, no assigned seats, and reusable boarding cards. When a passenger decided to fly Southwest, he or she would show up at the airport at the designated time, get a ticket at the counter printed out by a machine (at the time, the competition was issuing handwritten tickets), take a reusable boarding card, and board the plane to sit wherever he or she preferred. On board, the passenger could enjoy a drink or two and some peanuts, but nothing more. The reason behind the no-frills policy was that there were other things to offer customers that gave better value: frequent, reliable, on-time flights and very low prices. For Southwest, quality was not a dinner of filet mignon and a fine wine; it was on-time flights and no lost baggage.

One way the airline was able to keep its costs down was through contracting for such things as major maintenance, data processing, and legal services. Southwest also contracted for about two-thirds of its monthly jet-fuel supply and purchased the rest on the spot market.

Southwest's policy with regard to costs and services paid off: Its average number of flights per plane per day was twice the industry average; its planes

[5] Ibid.

EXHIBIT 2

Number of employees and airplanes.

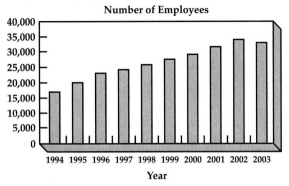

Number of Employees

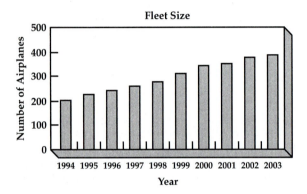

Fleet Size

were in the air 12 hours a day[6] (the industry average was 8 hours a day), which was an especially significant statistic because its flights were the shortest of any airline. Southwest's flights were also more profitable, even though short flights meant higher fuel costs and a greater number of landing fees. Southwest's secret was that it made extremely good use of its most expensive asset, planes (see Exhibit 2).

MARKETING

Positioning

Southwest decided from the beginning that it would differentiate itself from its competitors by creating a fun image. In contrast to Texas International, which was perceived as dull, and Braniff, which was seen as conservative, Southwest's personality and theme were focused on the concept of "LUV": flight attendants wore brightly colored hot pants, and in-flight drinks and peanuts were known as LUV Potions and LUV Bites.

[6] Southwest Airlines, http://www.southwest.com/about swa/press/factsheet.html (accessed on 9 March 2001).

Herb Kelleher's fun-loving personality served to reinforce Southwest's lively image among its employees and encouraged them to pass it on to passengers. Employees took to donning holiday costumes (such as rabbit garb for Easter), and every holiday became an excuse for in-flight parties with balloons and cake. Words like "young and vital," "exciting," and "dynamic" were sprinkled throughout the personality-model statement.

In 1988, under an agreement with Sea World of Texas, Southwest launched "Shamu One," its flying killer whale in the form of a 737-300 airplane. The painted plane became so popular throughout Texas that Southwest painted two others to resemble Sea World's most popular attraction.

Pricing

Pricing decisions were a particularly important part of Southwest's overall strategy. Southwest looked carefully at preoperating expenditures, operating costs, and market potential before deciding on an initial fare for routes. For its first route, the break-even capacity was 39 passengers per trip, which seemed reasonable given that the airline would have an initial price advantage over its competition. Before the break-even figure of 39 passengers per flight could be reached, however, the airline expected an initial period of deficit operations, a development it was willing to accept to get off the ground. Clearly, the marketing campaign would be crucial to the company's future decisions on pricing.

Southwest was only five months old when Muse decided to try something revolutionary for the airline industry. Because the crew had been flying an empty plane from Houston to Dallas at the end of each week for weekend servicing, Muse came up with the idea of offering a fare of $10 for this last flight of the week. Within two weeks, the plane was flying from Houston to Dallas with a full passenger load.

The success of the two-tier pricing system did not escape Muse, who soon decided to cut fares on the last flight of each day in all directions, which meant that any passenger flying Southwest after 7:00 P.M. on any day of the week would need a mere $10 to climb aboard. A few months later, Muse was able to raise both fares (regular and "night"), but he continued the two-tier pricing system because of its ability to attract passengers. Pricing was a key part of Southwest's strategy, and the company was leery of fare increases. From 1972 to 1978, Southwest did not have a single fare increase. "We base our pricing on profit rather than market share," contended Southwest's Gary C. Kelly, vice president of Finance.[7] In

[7] *AW* (March 5, 1990), 36.

2001, Southwest's average one-way airfare was about $85, and the average passenger-trip length was 652 miles.[8]

Southwest's rock-bottom prices won both admiration and scorn from competitors, many of whom immediately dropped their prices when Southwest entered their markets. A number of them were also resentful: one American Airlines executive commented, "Value isn't quality; it's getting what you pay for."[9] Some competitors accused Southwest of "airline seat dumping," although the airline made money on its routes from day one.

Promotion

Southwest defined its target market not as the passengers flying other airlines, but as the people who were using other methods of transportation. As Southwest's director of Sales and Marketing stated, "We're not competing with other carriers. We want to pull people out of backyards and automobiles and get them off the bus."[10].

Southwest's promotions were aimed primarily at regular business commuters, who constituted the majority of Southwest's traffic. Accordingly, the airline used a heavy advertising campaign and a small sales force targeted specifically at the business traveler. Initially, the company strove for name recognition, but its marketing efforts quickly expanded to create an image via mass communications. Southwest also used teaser ads announcing incredibly low fares and a follow-up phone number, as well as the Sweetheart Club, in which secretaries received one "sweetheart stamp" for each Southwest reservation they made for their bosses. For every 15 stamps, the secretary earned one free ride on Southwest.

Southwest's Expansion into New Markets

Part of Southwest's strategy was to investigate potential markets carefully. As flamboyant as Kelleher often was, he admitted to being a very cautious businessman. Cities across the United States requested that Southwest operate from their airports, but Southwest chose only the ones that fit its business model. As Gary Barron put it, "We search out markets that are overpriced and underserved."[11] Small cities and small airports meant that Southwest could get its planes in and out quickly.

Once Southwest decided to enter a market, however, it did so with full force. The airline offered so many flights that customers merely had to show up at the airport and take the next cheap flight out. This part of the strategy not only enabled the airline to spread its fixed costs over many seats, but also served a marketing function in that Southwest could really "make a statement" in a new airport. After years of patient watchfulness and careful consideration, Southwest decided to enter the California market. In 1983, it began offering flights on the San Diego–San Francisco route, but did not expand service until 1989. The California intrastate market was ideal for Southwest: it combined short-haul, high-frequency routes with good weather and a populace appreciative of Southwest's "unconventional behavior." The airline employed a relatively simple strategy of offering service in the mainly suburban areas outside Los Angeles and San Francisco at prices as low as $19 for a one-way flight. Not surprisingly, Southwest's expansion into California led to a series of fare wars as the major airlines tried to keep Southwest from stealing customers. The intensely competitive market in California saw some losers: USAir and American were forced out of the California intrastate market almost entirely. As airline analyst Harold Shenton noted, "Most of the big airlines are trying to protect long-haul revenue, so they're not dependent on local traffic, and they're weakening in the markets outside Los Angeles and San Francisco."[12]

Southwest undercut its California competitors and emerged victorious in the fare battles. The airline continued to use such tactics as offering free tickets in a "Fly One Way, Get One Way Free" campaign and a $59 unrestricted one-way fare for all intrastate California flights as part of the airline's "California State Fare" promotion. Southwest's California campaign was so successful that Southwest saved its California fliers more than $40 million in 1991.

After years of downplaying any interest in the congested airways of the East Coast, Southwest began serving Baltimore–Washington International Airport (BWI) on September 1, 1993. BWI remained Southwest's lone eastern outpost until early 1996, when Southwest added service to Tampa, Fort Lauderdale, and Orlando. In June 1996, Southwest announced its long-awaited entry into the Northeast market, with service to Providence, Rhode Island, beginning October 27, 1996.[13]

[8] Southwest Airlines, http://www.southwest.com> (accessed on 14 July 2001).
[9] *Time* (March 2, 1992), 15.
[10] Thompson and Weiss, "Southwest Airlines."
[11] *Inc.* (January 1992), 68.
[12] UPI (2 June 1991), 70.
[13] Stephen Sullivan, Richard R. Johnson, Paul W. Farris, and Marjorie Adams, "Southwest Airlines Coast-to-Coast (Condensed)" (case study, UVA-M-0464), University of Virginia Darden Graduate School of Business Administration, Charlottesville, 1995.

EXHIBIT 3

Cities served by Southwest. Southwest now flies more than 65 million passengers a year to 59 cities in 30 states, more than 2,800 times a day.

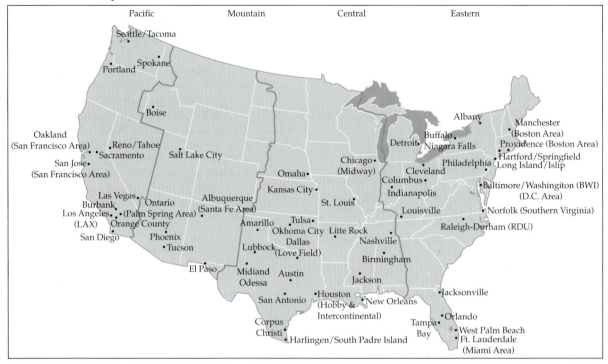

Source: Southwest Airlines, <http//:www.southwest.com> (accessed on 9 August 2004).

In April 1997, Southwest's strategy took an even larger turn with the introduction of four-hour, non-stop flights from Nashville to Los Angeles and Oakland. This move was a dramatic departure from Southwest's traditional emphasis on short-haul, point-to-point routes. In September 2002, Southwest began its first coast-to-coast route, from BWI to Los Angeles.[14]

In 2003, Southwest continued to add new city-pair routings and increase existing services in many markets, particularly in Baltimore-Washington and Chicago Midway.[15] In May 2004, Southwest announced that it would begin service to Philadelphia.[16] See Exhibit 3 for a list of the cities served by Southwest Airlines in 2004.

PERSONNEL

The company's philosophy toward recruitment remained consistent from the beginning: Southwest invested in its personnel by "spending more money to recruit and train than any of the other airlines"; its policy was to "find the right people to hire, at all levels within the organization, and spend time training them."[17]

Although Southwest's workforce was more than 82 percent unionized, the airline had not seen as much turbulence as the other carriers. The airline industry was notorious for contentious labor– management relations, but Southwest's employees enjoyed sunny relations with management. One reason for the smooth sailing was that employees had a stake in the company's success.[18] Another reason was that Southwest managed to make employees feel as if they were part of an extended family, even if it was a $5.6 billion family.

Southwest's management did not try to hide the fact that the main reason for the airline's success was the commitment of its employees. The quick turn-around time was a perfect example. As Gary Barron stated:

[14] Ibid.

[15] Southwest Airlines, *Annual Report* (2003), 9.

[16] Ibid., 8.

[17] Jody Gittell, R. John Hansman, and Anne Dunning, "Investing in Relationships—An Interview with the Southwest Airlines Management Team," *Harvard Business Review* (June 2001).

[18] Ibid.

Our employees bust their butts out there. Ground crews of 6 (12 is the industry average) perform 40 or 50 tasks during the 15 minutes that the plane is on the ground. Because of employee commitment, Southwest has consistently kept to its 15-minute "turn" (planes of major airlines spend usually an hour at the gate) and is always on time.

Another example of employee loyalty was the automatic ticket machines at Southwest counters, which took credit cards and dispensed tickets in just 20 seconds. Southwest employees built these efficient machines in their off-hours. According to Andy Donelson, station manager at Dallas's Love Field, "The machine was thought up by a bunch of guys in a bar one night in Denver."[19]

In 2003, 202,357 people applied for jobs at Southwest. Only 908 were hired.[20]

BUILDING A REPUTATION
At first, many observers believed that Southwest's fun image and no-frills flights would be the last choice for business travelers and cause the airline to take an immediate nosedive into bankruptcy, but the skeptics soon stopped laughing. Initially unprofitable, Southwest ended 1973 in the black, and celebrated its millionth passenger early in 1974. (See Exhibit 4 for a comparison of 2003 revenues, profits, and passengers for the major U.S. airlines.)

Southwest was the first U.S. domestic airline to win all three categories of the U.S. Department of Transportation's ranking report in 1992. It ranked first in on-time performance and had the smallest number of lost-baggage complaints and the lowest number of customer complaints. Southwest then proceeded to win the "Triple Crown" for the next four years, and it placed first in the Airline Quality Ratings in 1993, 1995, 1996, 1997, and 1999.

Although 2003 marked Southwest's 13th consecutive year for leading the industry with the fewest customer complaints, it had not won the Triple Crown since 1996.[21] (See Exhibit 5 for the Airline Quality Ratings for 2000 through 2003.)

CORPORATE CULTURE
Southwest was a "family-friendly place. [Management] is very flexible with scheduling, for example. There is a lot of leeway for employees to trade shifts and so on. People care about one another's families."[22]

Each year, the company hosted a banquet at which outstanding employees were recognized, much in the manner of the Emmy Awards. Kelleher could be seen at these functions mingling with employees from all levels of the company, calling them by name, laughing uproariously with them, hugging and kissing them. Even customers were brought into the family circle. Each month, Southwest invited its frequent fliers to company headquarters to interview prospective employees, the logic being that the company wanted to hire people who matched its customers in personality. Kelleher's role in the formation of Southwest's familial culture was crucial. Jim Wimberly stated that Kelleher had "a knack of really being with you, even if you're one person in a crowd of 1,000."[23] Kelleher firmly believed that employees who were committed to a mission would be more productive than uncommitted employees, and he spent a lot of his time fostering this attitude: "Southwest has its customers, the passengers; and I have my customers, the airline's employees. If the passengers aren't satisfied, they won't fly with us. If the employees aren't satisfied, they won't provide the product we need."

Once a quarter, Kelleher would join his employees to load baggage, serve drinks at 30,000 feet, or hand out boarding passes. Every Friday, he wore brightly colored shirts and shorts, regardless of the business to be conducted that day. Kelleher seemed to have found a formula that worked. In 1990, rising fuel costs made Southwest suffer a fourth-quarter loss of $4.6 million. Employees voluntarily created a "Fuel from the Heart" program in which they incurred payroll deductions to purchase fuel for the airplanes. Kelleher was so moved that he dedicated his opening letter in the company's 1990 *Annual Report* to them. "That stop-at-nothing, all-for-one, one-for-all spirit still pervades the company's corporate culture, especially among older employees."[24]

CHALLENGES FACING SOUTHWEST
Although many observers were quick to praise Southwest's unmatched record of success, some were not as enthusiastic about its future. The airline industry itself had always been a risky one. With the Iraq war, SARS concerns, a weak economy, high energy costs, and terrorism threats, the early years of the 21st century were especially difficult for the airline industry.[25] Since September 11, 2001, the major airlines continued to report billions in losses. US Airways

[19] Thompson and Weiss, "Southwest Airlines."

[20] Southwest Airlines, http://www.southwest.com (accessed on 9 June 2004).

[21] Southwest Airlines, *Annual Report* (2003), 5.

[22] Thompson and Weiss, "Southwest Airlines."

[23] *Inc.* (January 1992), 67.

[24] Pat Harris, "SJ-Southwest," http://www.simercury.com (accessed on 7 March 2001).

[25] Southwest Airlines, *Annual Report* (2003), 5.

EXHIBIT 4

Airline revenues, profits, and passengers for 2003.

ATA Member Airline Statistics—2003

	Operating Aircraft (Year-End)	Employees (Full-Time Equivalents)	Aircraft Departures	Revenue Passengers Enplaned (Thousands)	Revenue Passenger Miles[1] (Millions)	Available Seat Miles[1] (Millions)	Cargo Revenue Ton Miles (Millions)	Revenues[1] ($Millions)			Profit (Loss) ($Millions)	
								Passenger[1]	Cargo	Operating	Operating	Net
Alaska	110	10,087	180,469	15,046	14,557	20,808	73	1,788	86	2,019	(18)	(2)
Aloha	25	2,477	58,482	4,119	1,968	2,690	10	340	40	393	(8)	1
America West	140	11,107	197,484	20,031	21,266	27,843	70	2,108	35	2,223	24	45
American	743	85,555	887,114	88,151	120,004	164,780	2,012	14,236	621	17,403	(1,444)	(1,318)
ATA	66	7,328	78,402	9,386	11,840	16,373	40	1,006	21	1,398	14	13
Continental	358	34,927	371,100	38,474	56,886	74,969	865	6,556	283	7,333	30	38
Delta	523	59,525	704,759	84,076	89,154	119,912	1,349	10,272	508	14,203	(1,157)	(896)
Hawaiian	26	2,966	50,416	5,597	5,560	6,924	79	627	28	706	60	(48)
JetBlue	53	4,515	66,920	8,949	10,442	13,689	5	965	4	998	169	104
Midwest	29	2,055	37,883	2,098	1,969	2,968	7	260	4	319	(19)	(8)
Northwest	431	39,407	553,245	51,865	68,459	88,573	2,184	7,617	780	9,184	(277)	478
Southwest	387	32,972	950,572	74,719	47,940	71,789	141	5,612	97	5,937	482	442
United	528	63,612	601,361	66,018	103,857	135,867	1,888	10,619	668	13,398	(1,554)	(3,086)
US Airways	277	26,809	438,625	41,250	37,727	51,474	361	4,925	144	6,762	(421)	(465)
Subtotal	**3,696**	**383,345**	**5,176,832**	**509,779**	**591,628**	**798,659**	**9,083**	**66,931**	**3,318**	**82,277**	**(4,118)**	**(4,703)**
ABX	115	5,799	70,401	–	–	–	700	–	1,115	1,161	42	19
ASTAR[2]	41	933	20,568	–	–	–	348	–	148	153	32	18
Atlas	27	1,006	14,651	–	–	–	3,006	–	n/a	n/a	n/a	n/a
Evergreen Int'l	14	447	8,140	–	–	–	677	–	256	266	44	19
FedEx	324	114,306	359,840	–	–	–	9,487	–	8,377	16,807	474	250
Polar	15	682	5,884	–	–	–	1,115	–	n/a	n/a	n/a	n/a
UPS	246	6,098	139,958	–	–	–	4,624	–	1,215	3,046	228	40
Subtotal	**782**	**129,271**	**619,442**	**–**	**–**	**–**	**19,958**	**–**	**11,111**	**21,433**	**820**	**347**
GRAND TOTAL	**4,478**	**512,616**	**5,796,274**	**509,779**	**591,628**	**798,659**	**29,041**	**$66,931**	**$14,429**	**$103,710**	**($3,298)**	**($4,356)**

[1]Scheduled service only.

[2]Financial results reflect the period from July 14 through December 31, 2003.

n/a – Not available at time of printing.

Source: Air Transport Association, *Annual Report* (2004).

EXHIBIT 5

Performance of major U.S. air carriers: average airline quality rating (AQR) score

Airline	2003* AQR Score	Rank	2002** AQR Score	Rank	2001*** AQR Score	Rank	2000 AQR Score	Rank
Air Tran	−1.05	8	N/A	—	N/A	—	N/A	—
Alaska	−0.74	2	−0.95	2	−1.19	1	−1.54	2
America West	−0.89	4	−1.08	4	−1.75	7	−3.43	10
American	−1.24	11	−1.21	6	−1.58	6	−2.08	6
American Eagle	−2.10	13	−2.42	10	−2.14	10	N/A	—
ATA	−1.17	10	N/A	—	N/A	—	N/A	—
Atlantic Southeast	−5.76	14	N/A	—	N/A	—	N/A	—
Continental	−1.04	7	−1.10	5	−1.77	8	−2.11	7
Delta	−1.24	12	−1.26	7	−1.48	5	−1.47	1
JetBlue	−0.64	1	N/A	—	N/A	—	N/A	—
Northwest	−1.02	6	−1.39	9	−1.38	3	−1.83	5
Southwest	−0.89	3	−1.00	3	−1.42	4	−1.64	3
United	−1.11	9	−1.27	8	−1.97	9	−3.01	9
US Airways	−0.96	5	−0.85	1	−1.24	2	−1.74	4
Industry	−1.14		−1.19		−1.60		−2.05	

*Scores and rankings for 2003 reflect the addition of Air Tran, ATA, Atlantic Southeast, and JetBlue to the group of airlines tracked.
**Rankings for 2002, 2001, and 2000 reflect the removal of TWA from the group of airlines tracked.
***Scores and rankings for 2001 reflect the addition of American Eagle to the group of airlines tracked.
Note: The AQR score is a weighted average of the following: on-time, denied-boarding, mishandled baggage, and customer complaints. Average AQR scores are based on monthly AQR score calculations using AQR weighted-average method. The calendar year is used, and monthly AQR scores are totaled and divided by 12 to arrive at the AQR for the year.

Source: *Average Airline Quality Rating Report* (2004).

and United Airlines filed for bankruptcy. Other major carriers reduced capacity, eliminated jobs, and slashed costs in an effort to survive.[26]

Although Southwest managed to maintain its profitability throughout the turbulent post–September 11 period, the first few years of the 21st century posed many new challenges for Southwest. Turnover in senior management and a series of intense labor negotiations led to tension between management and union employees. Adverse labor relations were highly unusual for Southwest, an airline that had always been known for its collegial culture and approachable management. Post–September 11 security changes challenged the simplicity of Southwest's fine-tuned business model, and an influx of new, low-cost carriers that copied and improved upon Southwest's model forced the airline to rethink its no-frills offerings.

The New Generation of Low-Fare, Low-Cost Carriers

By 2004, the low-fare market that Southwest once dominated had become increasingly crowded with many low-fare, low-cost carriers that tried to emulate and, in some cases, improve upon Southwest's model. While the airlines were selling more tickets than they had the previous year, they were finding it difficult to make a profit because of a flood of cheap fares, many of them from low-cost carriers.[27] In 2004, low-fare, low-cost carriers made up 18 percent of the market; by 2010, they were expected to make up 50 percent of the market.[28]

In the 1990s, the major carriers US Airways, Continental, United, and Delta experimented with their own versions of Southwest-style no-frills, low-fare service.[29] None of them were able to emulate Southwest's model successfully. The new generation of low-cost carriers, however, did prove to be successful. JetBlue became Southwest's most formidable competitor. JetBlue was launched by David Neeleman, 39, an airline-industry veteran who served briefly as

[26] Ibid.

[27] Associated Press, "Southwest Airlines' CEO Parker Steps Down," July 16, 2004.
[28] Dan Reed, "Southwest's Challenges Grow," *USA Today*, October 16, 2002.
[29] Sullivan, Johnson, Farris, and Adams, "Southwest Airlines Coast-to-Coast (Condensed)."

an executive vice president at Southwest in 1993. Neeleman believed that most airlines treated their customers inhumanely, and believed he could improve on Southwest's model.

Like Southwest, JetBlue provided point-to-point service to large metropolitan areas with high average fares or to highly traveled markets that were underserved. It also offered low fares, reliable performance, and high-quality customer service. Unlike Southwest, JetBlue offered luxurious leather seating on brand-new planes and free, live TV at every seat. Further, JetBlue used leading-edge technology to streamline operations, offered preassigned seating (to reduce the cattle-herding ambience), and never overbooked its flights. JetBlue's model proved to be hugely successful. Since the start of JetBlue's operations, on February 11, 2000, out of New York's Kennedy Airport (JFK), the airline had put together 12 consecutive profitable quarters. JetBlue went on to boast the industry's best operating margins, top rates for on-time arrivals, and lowest costs per seat-mile. JetBlue operated 222 flights with a fleet of 53 single-class Airbus A320s serving 21 cities throughout the United States and Puerto Rico.[30]

In February 2004, United also launched a new, low-cost, low-fare carrier called Ted. Ted offered preassigned seats, music videos, and episodes of NBC sitcoms in-flight; it also offered trendy margaritas and Atkins bars for the carb-conscious.[31] In April 2003, Delta launched its own discount spin-off called Song. Song targeted affluent urban women, and featured flight attendants decked out in designer Kate Spade uniforms. Song offered apple martinis, cappuccinos with biscotti, and an in-flight exercise band, exercise ball, and how-to manual (for an $8 fee).[32] Song planned to go head-to-head with JetBlue on its lucrative New York–Fort Lauderdale route.[33] Other successful start-ups that emulated the Southwest model included AirTran Airways, Midwest Express, Frontier Airlines, American Trans Air (ATA), and, in Europe, EasyJet.[34] Virgin Atlantic's founder, Richard Branson, had also considered the launch of

an airline in the United States.[35] "It's an amenity war," said Stan Hula, ATA's vice president for planning. "Airlines used to fight with food. Turns out that wore out over time. In the end, you have to provide what the consumer wants."[36]

The New York Times reported:

> All that is forcing Southwest to rethink. It is considering moves that might have been blasphemous at the company just a few years ago: adding frills like in-flight entertainment systems and expanding its fleet beyond its trusty Boeing 737 jets. Southwest executives say no firm decisions have been made, and they give every impression that life will fundamentally be the same at the airline known for its old mustard-and-ketchup-colored planes.[37]

THE SOUTHWEST RESPONSE

Intense competition from other low-fare airlines forced Southwest to rethink its model. Kelleher had recently stated, "I recognize that we have to change our tactics frequently as competitors emerge, and as facts and circumstances change."[38] Consequently, the no-frills airline implemented aesthetic and technological improvements—initiatives that might have been considered blasphemous at the company just a few years earlier.[39]

In 2001, Southwest began renewing the interiors and exteriors of its fleet. It updated the exteriors' traditional gold, red, and orange by adding canyon blue. The airline also refurbished the interiors of new and existing planes with all-leather seats in canyon blue and saddle tan, and indicated that it would add newly designed seats for increased comfort. Southwest also worked to make its gate areas more comfortable and traveler friendly. In 2004, Southwest renovated its airport facilities at BWI, Chicago Midway, and Houston Hobby. Major expansion projects were also under way at Fort Lauderdale, Las Vegas, Long Island-Islip, Oakland, Orange County, Orlando, Phoenix, and Tampa Bay.

In June 2003, Southwest announced that its current and future fleet of Boeing 737-700s would be outfitted with blended winglets. The blended

[30] Marlene Friesen and Elliott N. Weiss, "The JetBlue Story" (case study, UVA-OM-1151), University of Virginia Darden Graduate School of Business Administration, Charlottesville, 2005.

[31] "Low-Cost Airlines-O-Matic; View from the Cheap Seats: D.C.'s Discount Airlines," *Washington Post*, 2004.

[32] Associated Press, "Airlines Hope In-Flight Exercise Will Stretch Market Share," *USA Today*, July 9, 2004.

[33] Arlyn Tobias Gajilan, "The Amazing JetBlue," *Fortune,* http://www.fortune.com/fortune/smallbusiness/articles (accessed on 3 June 2004).

[34] Sullivan, Johnson, Farris, and Adams, "Southwest Airlines Coast-to-Coast (Condensed)."

[35] Gajilan, "The Amazing JetBlue." For additional information on Virgin Atlantic's planned launch of a U.S. airline in late 2005, see http://www.virginamerica.com/Main.aspx.

[36] Ed Sperling, "Cut Costs, Not Services," *Electronic News,* http://www.reedelectronics. com/electronicnews/article/CA415986 (accessed on 7 May 2004).

[37] Micheline Maynard, "Are Peanuts No Longer Enough?" *The New York Times,* March 7, 2004.

[38] David Koenig, "Executive Sparred with Flight Attendants Union," *San Diego Union-Tribune,* August 6, 2004.

[39] Maynard, "Are Peanuts No Longer Enough?"

winglets would give the fleet a distinctive, technologically advanced look and feel, and would improve aircraft performance by extending range, saving fuel, and reducing both takeoff noise and engine-maintenance costs.

Finally, Southwest implemented several technological initiatives to streamline its operations through automation. For example, the airline began using computer-generated luggage tags at all its facilities. These tags could electronically capture luggage checked by customers. In 2004, Southwest planned to use technology that would allow customers to check their bags and obtain their transfer boarding passes by using rapid-check-in kiosks. The company also planned to offer customers the ability to check in and obtain boarding passes on southwest.com.[40]

LABOR ISSUES

Southwest maintained that its secret weapon remained its affable employees. "There hasn't been a carrier that has been able to match our people in spirit and energy and enthusiasm over the long haul," said Colleen C. Barrett, Southwest's president and chief operating officer.[41] Southwest's employees, however, were becoming tired of being in the bottom half of the industry with regard to pay, especially as they worked for one of the nation's most profitable airlines. Moreover, as Southwest's workforce grew to more than 35,000 employees, the quality of communication between management and labor deteriorated.[42] Tension between management and Southwest's unions led industry observers to question whether Southwest, the most heavily unionized U.S. carrier, could continue to maintain harmonious relations with its employees. The terms of a recent deal with flight attendants—and earlier settlements with pilots and mechanics—had raised questions about Southwest's ability to keep its costs below those of most of its competitors.[43] Southwest's total labor costs had been on the rise for several years, from just one-third of total operating costs in the mid-1990s to 41 percent of total operating costs in 2003.[44] In addition, through the first six months of 2004, Southwest's labor costs rose 6 percent over early 2003, which helped push its costs per passenger to new highs.[45]

The increased labor costs were the result of contract negotiations with Southwest's unions over the past few years, which Southwest indicated had resulted in higher compensation and enriched benefits for nine of its union groups.[46] On July 30, 2004, flight attendants at Southwest ratified a new contract, retroactive to June 2002, that gave them an average 31 percent pay raise over six years.[47] This agreement settled a two-year labor dispute with Southwest's flight attendants, and would make them the highest-paid attendants in the industry by 2007.[48] In addition, Southwest's pilots agreed to a two-year contract extension that moved them closer to what their counterparts at major airlines earned, and Southwest's mechanics also ratified a new contract—but only after rejecting a prior deal.[49] Gary Kelly, Southwest's new CEO, indicated that expensive new labor contracts were necessary to keep the airline moving forward, but warned, "We're pushing the boundary of what we can afford with our wages."[50]

MANAGEMENT TURNOVER

On July 16, 2004, James Parker, Southwest Airlines' CEO, announced that he would be stepping down, citing personal reasons for his retirement.[51] Parker, who had been appointed to his position by Kelleher three years earlier, was credited with guiding Southwest through the turbulent period after September 11, 2001. In fact, Southwest was the only major airline to post a profit in every quarter following the September 11 terrorist attacks.[52] Parker, a labor lawyer, had been Kelleher's right-hand man since 1994. He led the airline's negotiating team until April 2004, when negotiations came to a halt.[53] When the union attacked Parker personally, Kelleher stepped in to finish the negotiations. Parker announced his retirement three months later.

Southwest stated that Gary Kelly, its 49-year-old chief financial officer, would immediately replace Parker.[54] Kelly had joined Southwest as its controller in 1986, and had served as Southwest's executive vice president and chief financial officer since 2001.[55]

[40] Southwest Airlines, *Annual Report* (2003), 2–11.

[41] Maynard, "Are Peanuts No Longer Enough?"

[42] Reed, "Southwest's Challenges Grow."

[43] David Koenig, "Southwest Flight Attendants OK Contract," Associated Press, 30 July 2004.

[44] Southwest Airlines, *Annual Report* (2003).

[45] Koenig, "Southwest Flight Attendants OK Contract."

[46] "SWA Takeoff," http://www.southwest.com/swatakeoff/labor_relations.html (accessed on June 9, 2004).

[47] Koenig, "Southwest Flight Attendants OK Contract."

[48] Ibid.

[49] Reed, "Southwest's Challenges Grow."

[50] Koenig, "Southwest Flight Attendants OK Contract."

[51] Southwest Airlines, "Southwest Airlines Announces Executive Changes," news release, July 15, 2004.

[52] Southwest Airlines, *Annual Report* (2003).

[53] Reuters, "Southwest Airlines CEO Resigns," *Airwise News*, July, 15, 2004.

[54] Southwest Airlines, "Southwest Airlines Announces Executive Changes."

[55] Ibid.

For years, industry observers worried whether Southwest would continue to thrive once Herb Kelleher retired. Kelleher set the culture at Southwest, which had proved to be a source of competitive advantage. Since Kelleher's departure, in 2001, Parker had ensured that Southwest remained profitable. In 2004, however, it appeared that Southwest's collegial culture was showing signs of strain. Would Kelly be able to maintain the profitability of the airline while ensuring the continuation of Southwest's unique culture?

Discussion Questions

1. To what do you attribute the success of Southwest Airlines?

2. How significant is the 10 to 15 minutes turn-around time of Southwest's aircraft in terms of savings in investment and utilization of its aircraft compared to the competitors?

3. What challenges is Southwest facing in the future and how should they meet those challenges?

4. What should their business and operations strategy be for the future?

5. Will Gary Kelly, the new CEO, be able to maintain the profitability of Southwest Airlines while insuring the continuation of their unique culture?

Case Study   The Field Service Division of DMI

Diversified Manufacturing, Inc. (DMI), was a multibillion dollar company headquartered in Denver, Colorado, that manufactured and distributed a wide variety of electronic, photographic, and reprographic equipment used in many engineering and medical system applications. Most of the company's profits came from selling "consumables" (films and supplies) used in DMI machines. Customers bought machines on the basis of price, features, quality, and service. However, field service was becoming more important in new machine purchase decisions. According to many DMI Field Service Division managers, field service was not viewed as a critical part of DMI's corporate strategy.

DMI's Field Service Division (FSD) employed about 550 field service technicians ("techs") that covered the continental United States. (The division also provided service in Western Europe through its European subsidiary.) These techs provided important service for nearly 240,000 DMI machines in North America. Most of the technicians were concentrated in large metropolitan areas.

The Field Service Division at DMI was affected by the same trends that affected the entire field service industry:

- Although components were becoming more reliable, machines were becoming more sophisticated and more difficult to repair in the field.
- Technology change was rapid and it was a challenge to keep up.
- Product variety was increasing dramatically.
- It was becoming more and more difficult to find good technicians.

As a result of these and other challenges, the management of DMI decided to reengineer the entire field service business process.

WARRANTIES AND SERVICE CONTRACTS
Service contracts contributed significantly to the corporation's revenues and profits. Warranties or service contracts covered about 80 percent of the emergency maintenance service calls. The other 20 percent were billed to the customer based on "time and material cost" and were very profitable.[1] Service contracts

specified that "on average, our response time will be within (X) hours" where "X" was the target response time determined by a list developed several years ago that specified the standard response time by machine and by geographical zone. Zone 1 was a major metropolitan area, Zone 2 was a minor metropolitan area, and Zone 3 was a rural area. All service contracts for a particular model had the same price regardless of the target response time. The typical response time was around four hours.

NATIONAL SERVICE CENTER
DMI's National Service Center (NSC), located in a suburb of Denver, received about 3,500 calls per day. About 2,000 of these were related to emergency maintenance, either initial calls or complaints about late service. Many of the calls were from customers wanting to know when their technician would arrive. The NSC was staffed by about 40 "call-takers," who were mostly full-time employees paid a modest wage. They worked on staggered shifts to cover the entire workday for both coasts.

PROCESS FLOW
A typical incoming service call was received at the NSC and routed to one of the call-takers who entered information about the machine, caller's name, type of problem, and so forth into DMI's mainframe computer. In some cases, the call-taker attempted to help the customer fix the problem. Avoiding a single service call saved DMI about $250. However, call-takers were currently only able to avoid about 10 percent of the incoming emergency maintenance service calls. If the service call could not be avoided, the call-taker usually stated the following script: "Depending upon the availability of our technicians, you should expect to see a technician sometime between now and (now + X)." (X was the target response time based on the model number and the zone.) This information was given to the customer because many customers wanted to know when a tech would arrive on site.

Call-takers entered service call information[2] on DMI's computer system, which then sent the information electronically to the regional dispatch center assigned to that customer location. (DMI had five

[1] DMI charged "time and material" customers a minimum of $250 for a site visit. This covered the "full cost" for the visit. Profit margins on DMI parts (many of which were proprietary to DMI) were as high as 300 percent.

[2] DMI's computer system allowed for a 32-character field to describe the customer's service problem.

This case was prepared by Professor Arthur V. Hill (Curtis L. Carlson School of Management, University of Minnesota) as the basis for class discussion rather than to illustrate either effective or ineffective handling of a business situation. The case is based on a real company. All names have been disguised to protect the identity of the company. Copyright © 1996–1998 Carlson School of Management, University of Minnesota. Not to be reproduced without written permission from the Carlson School of Management (Attention: Professor Arthur Hill), University of Minnesota, Minneapolis, Minnesota 55455, USA. Published with permission.

463

regional dispatch centers with a total of about 24 dispatchers.) Service call information was printed on a small card at the dispatch center. About every hour, cards were ripped off the printer[3] and given to the dispatcher assigned to that customer location. The dispatcher placed each card on a magnetic board under the name of a tech that the dispatcher believed would be the most likely candidate for the service call—given the location of the machine, the current location of the tech, and the tech's training profile.

After completing a service call, techs were supposed to call the dispatcher in the regional dispatch center, clear the call,[4] and receive a new call assigned by the dispatcher. However, techs did not always call in right after completing a service call due to difficulty in finding a phone or to lack of incentives.[5] Techs complained that they had to wait on hold too long when they phoned the dispatcher center early in the morning, right after lunch, and late in the day. Dispatchers assigned service calls to techs based on a visual review of the magnetic dispatch board. After getting the service call from a dispatcher, a tech called the customer to give an expected time of arrival, drove to the customer site, diagnosed the problem, repaired the machine if parts were available in the van, and then phoned the dispatcher for the next call. Although some attempt was made to have the same tech always service the same customer, the dominant issue for most dispatchers was to try to get a qualified tech to the service call within the target response time. Dispatchers were instructed to never call customers.

TECHNOLOGY

Most of DMI's management were engineers and were, therefore, very open to technological solutions to management problems. Management, however, rejected a recent proposal for cellular phones because of concerns about expense and potential abuse by techs. However, serious consideration was being given to three technologies: (1) an expert system for problem diagnosis to be used by techs in the field, (2) an expert system for assigning and scheduling techs, and (3) a geographic positioning system that could be used to track tech locations at all times. DMI had already invested significantly in all three of these technologies.

SUPERVISION

Techs worked out of their homes and only went to a DMI office for training. They kept their service parts in their minivans. The area service managers tried to visit each of their approximately 20 techs about once per month. DMI's managers tended to manage "by the numbers" with emphasis on the percentage of service calls that made the response time targets. Top management was also concerned about the percentage of service calls that were short interval calls (SIC), that is, service calls that required a tech to return to a customer site within 24 hours after a repair.

PROBLEMS

No Parts Calls—Sometimes techs did not have the right parts for a repair. When this happened, the part was express mailed to the customer and the repair was done the next morning. Techs reported inventory usage when they cleared a service call. The National Service Parts Center in Denver used a "one-for-one" policy to replenish tech inventory via a two-day delivery service. DMI's management was proud of the fact that several large, well-run firms had benchmarked DMI's service parts inventory management system.

Return Logistics—Techs were instructed to return repairable boards and valuable materials[6] to Denver and to handle hazardous materials properly. DMI's management was concerned that techs were undisciplined about "return logistics" and threw away too much, including some hazardous materials.

Long Response Times—About 20 percent of all service calls did not make the target response time mentioned above. Occasionally, all of the techs in an area were busy on a service call, in training, or out sick and could not possibly make it to the service call for several days. Some customers complained that "no one ever bothered to call to let us know that you were going to be late."

Travel Times—The number of techs at DMI had declined during the last few years due to divestiture, retirements, and cost-cutting. As a result, the company was experiencing longer travel times.[7] Getting into the third-party service (servicing another company's machines) was under serious consideration.

---

[3] DMI employees were fond of calling this the "rip and strip" process.

[4] Clearing a service call involved reporting the service call number, the amount of time spent in travel, diagnosis, and repair, and then reporting the part numbers for each part used in the repair.

[5] Many techs carried an unusual set of tools in the back of their vans—long metal rods with leather grips and with metal heads at one end. These were stored in a long leather bag accompanied by a number of small white plastic spheres and small pointed wooden sticks.

[6] Some circuit boards had a book value as high as $6,000. Many boards contained valuable parts and/or metals.

[7] Travel time is a function of the number of technicians. If DMI had more technicians, it would have greater coverage of North America, and the average travel time per call would decrease.

Performance Measurement—DMI's field service management was currently using "the percent of service calls that make the target response time" as the primary measure of performance. However, some managers believed that other measures might be more useful. For example, one area manager wanted to measure techs on the number of service calls completed per day.

Utilization—The arrival rates of service calls had decreased in recent months and techs now only received about 2.1 service calls per day on average. DMI's techs could service about four service calls per day if the calls were available. Some managers, particularly some of the more financially oriented ones, wanted to see a much higher tech utilization rate.

Competition—Historically, DMI had no competition and high margins. Recently, however, Japanese competitors had entered the market with superior product technologies. In fact, some of DMI's latest machines were purchased from Hitachi. DMI's "manufacturing process" for these products was to place the DMI label on the machine and ship it to the customer.

CHALLENGES

Management put together a reengineering team that consisted of a division VP, a regional manager, a technician, a call-taker, a dispatcher, an IS person, an accounting person, and an outside consultant—all people who lived and worked in the Denver area. The reengineering team agreed that the effort should start with a process map for a service call. However, the vision for the new process was not clear. The team argued about new technologies,

better information systems,[8] a single dispatching center, a stronger service guarantee,[9] higher utilization, and a better performance measurement system. What vision was right for this business?

Discussion Questions

1. Draw the process flow chart for a service call. Where are the queues and delays in the system and what can be done to eliminate them?

2. How might the process be reengineered? Consider some technologies that might be available to help.

3. Should DMI/FSD consolidate the regional dispatch centers into one location?

4. Evaluate DMI's service guarantee. How could this be improved?

5. Why does DMI/FSD need to measure field service performance? How should performance be measured?

6. What are the strategic issues for the division and the company?

7. How could this organization become more of a learning organization?

8. Prepare an action plan to recommend to DMI/FSD management. Be prepared to present this to the rest of the class.

---

[8] The current system was a million lines of old "spaghetti code" written in COBOL and was very difficult to maintain. No one at DMI seemed to be concerned about the Y2K issue.

[9] The general manager of the division was concerned that a stronger service guarantee would cheapen the company's image and dismissed the idea with the comment, "We're not in the pizza business."

Under the leadership of its former president, Radisson Hotels Worldwide had added hotels at the rate of about one hotel every seven days. Radisson growth strategy had focused on the hotel owners and on information technology to bring guests to the hotels.

By 1997, Radisson's "growth at any cost" strategy had left Radisson with a tremendous diversity of hotel quality and an "unfocused" brand image. Alignment with hotel owners (more that hotel guests) also seemed to cause Radisson's customer service and hotel management expertise to atrophy.

In 1997 and 1998, Brian Stage, Radisson's president, and Maureen O'Hanlon, Radisson's executive vice president, took several initiatives to drive the organization towards becoming a more customer-focused brand. In their words, they "re-discovered that their primary customers should be the guests—not the owners."

Some of these initiatives included a service guarantee, a guest satisfaction measurement program, an employee satisfaction measurement program, and an information technology initiative. Stage and O'Hanlon were committed to creating the systems and programs that would bring Radisson into the 21st century as a truly "customer-driven learning organization." Their goal was to make Radisson the "most trusted and respected brand worldwide." They were hopeful that these initiatives would make a significant contribution to helping Radisson achieve these goals.

COMPANY BACKGROUND

Corporate Background
Founded in 1938 by Curtis L. Carlson, Carlson Companies, Inc., was one of America's largest privately owned corporations with total system sales of $13.4 billion in 1996 and $20 billion in 1997. Carlson Companies employed about 130,000 people world wide, including those who worked in franchised and managed operations. Headquartered in a suburb of Minneapolis, Minnesota (USA), the company was organized into four operating groups—Carlson Hospitality Worldwide, Carlson Wagonlit Travel, Carlson Marketing Group, and Carlson Leisure Group.

In 1998, Carlson Hospitality Worldwide included Radisson Hotels Worldwide, Country Inns & Suites by Carlson, TGI Friday's, Regent Hotels, Italianni's, Friday's Front Row Sports Grill, Friday's American Bar, and Radisson Seven Seas Cruises, Radisson Hotels Worldwide operated, managed, and franchised deluxe plaza hotels, all-suite hotels, inns and resorts around the world.

Radisson Hotels Worldwide
In 1962, Curt Carlson purchased the nationally known Radisson Hotel in downtown Minneapolis. The hotel was named after the French explorer, Pierre Esprit Radisson, who explored Midwestern North America in the 17th century.

By 1975, Radisson had only 10 hotels, mostly in the midwestern part of the United States. With a commitment to growth, Radisson had grown to 360 locations with over 100,000 rooms in 47 countries by 1998. As Radisson grew to become a global leader in the hospitality industry, it embraced the concept of partnering with existing hotel companies in specific geographic regions. One example of this partnership strategy was the creation of Radisson SAS Worldwide, which resulted from the partnership of Radisson with the SAS Hotel group in Europe and Radisson Moriah Hotel Group in Israel. In 1997, Radisson was pursuing similar expansion/partnership arrangements in Latin America and the Asia/pacific region. In 1997, Carlson Hospitality Worldwide announced plans to grow the number of locations from 1,100 in 1997 to over 2,000 by the year 2000.[1]

In 1997, Curt Carlson continued to retain the titles of chairman of the board and CEO, while his daughter, Marilyn Carlson Nelson, was the chief operating officer and vice chair of the Carlson Companies. Carlson's grandson, Curtis Nelson, was president/CEO of Carlson Hospitality Worldwide.

[1] Source: *Carlsonian* 8, no. 2, March/April 1997, page 4.

This case was prepared by Professor Arthur V. Hill (Curtis L. Carlson School of Management, University of Minnesota) as the basis for class discussion rather than to illustrate either effective or ineffective handling of a business situation.

The author wishes to thank Brian Stage, President, Maureen O'Hanlon, Executive VP of Marketing and Sales, Sue Geurs, Director, 100% Guest Satisfaction Program, and Scott Heintzeman, VP of Knowledge Technologies, for their invaluable assistance in writing this case.

Further information can be found at the website http://www.Radisson.com.

This case was supported by the Customer-Driven Learning Organization research project sponsored by the Quality Leadership Center at the University of Minnesota.

466

THE SERVICE CHALLENGE

Stage and O'Hanlon were very candid about the challenges facing Radisson. They felt a strong need to change from the owner-centered "growth at any cost" model, to a "champion of the guest" model. As one senior Radisson manager stated, "a brand is a promise and we broke our promise . . . the promise of delivering consistency and uniformity and quality." They felt that there was ". . . no clear-cut definition of the brand . . . no clear definition of what the Radisson brand meant." Another Radisson manager stated that:

> It was very easy to be deluded into serving the franchisee. They are the ones (customers) that we see . . . but at the end of the day only one customer is the source of cash and revenue and that is the person who stays in the room.

By early 1998, they had already "invited" 35–40 hotels to leave. However, they still needed to grow, particularly in some areas where Radisson was under-represented, but now they wanted to grow in quality as well as in number of locations.

A brochure given at the national meeting in March 1998 stated the following five strategies. (Appendix 1 is a press release that gives more details on some of these strategies.)

Strategy I. Focus on the Customer—The concept was summarized by the quote, "Quality and consistency promise guests an exceptional Radisson experience every time. Delivering at our higher service standard builds long-term guest loyalty and greater brand equity."

Strategy 2. Provide individualized marketing and services—The key idea here was that Radisson needed to use its advanced information technologies to anticipate guests' needs, recognize their preferences, and treat them individually.

Strategy 3. Develop hotels in key locations—This was a plan to establish the Radisson brand in several more key markets so that loyal Radisson guests would be able to find Radisson hotels where they needed them. The plan here was not to grow at any cost, but to find hotels and develop partnerships that met the higher Radisson standards for quality.

Strategy 4. Leverage the Carlson Companies Advantage—The idea here was to pursue synergies with the other three operating groups.

Strategy 5. Strengthen global brand presence—Stage wanted to create a cohesive message for all Radisson properties over the entire world.

Stage and O'Hanlon had initiated many programs during 1997 and 1998 to support these grand strategies. Some of the programs included:

- 100% guest satisfaction program.
- Fully integrated guest information system.
- Guest satisfaction measurement program and employee satisfaction measurement program.
- Guest recognition and rewards program.
- Genuine hospitality program.

The remainder of the case will briefly discuss some of these programs.

THE 100% GUEST SATISFACTION GUARANTEE PROGRAM

Background

Sue Geurs was appointed Director of the 100% Guest Satisfaction Guarantee Program in 1997. Geurs had been the hotel general manager in Indianapolis and knew from experience that Radisson already had an outstanding "Yes, I Can" training program that focused on service quality and service recovery. The company also had a "Second Effort Program," which attempted to recover customers who called a local number and/or an 800 number to register complaints.

Geurs began her efforts by reading everything that she could find on the subject. She conducted extensive research on other hotels including Hampton Inns and Embassy Suites. She was particularly impressed early on by a report from Hampton Inn that showed that the guests with the highest incidence of "invocations"[2] of their service guarantee also were the most loyal customers.

Financial Justification

A financial analysis of the advantages and disadvantages of the guarantee was quite a challenge. The industry-standard "allowances" (adjustments) for customer complaints was about 1 percent of sales. It was not clear if allowances would increase or decrease with the service guarantee. Professor Hill from the University of Minnesota developed a "customer defection" spreadsheet model that suggested that the cost of customer defections was quite high and that a service guarantee could be quite advantageous under a wide variety of reasonable assumptions. Exhibit 1 shows this spreadsheet analysis with values for a hypothetical hotel. The numbers in parentheses are the numbers of customers in each category.

The Design

One tough issue was the wording of the guarantee. The books and consultants often spoke highly of the

---

[2] An "invocation" was when a guest complained, "invoked" the guarantee, and received a free room night, or whatever payout the guarantee offered.

EXHIBIT 1

Hotel guest loyalty economics (with hypothetical data).

Hotel Parameters:

300	Rooms per hotel
$100	Average daily rate
75%	Occupancy rate this year
3.0	Average nights/guest stay
82,125	Room nights this year
27,375	Guest stays this year
$8,212,500	Total room sales this year

Guest Loyalty Parameters:

2	Good reports per delighted guest stay.
0	Good reports per satisfied guest stay.
10	Good reports per recovered guest stay.
10	Good reports this year needed to gain one guest stay next year.
20	Bad reports per non-recovered guest stay.
5	Bad reports per non-complaining dissatisfied guest stay.
5	Bad reports this year needed to lose one guest stay next year.

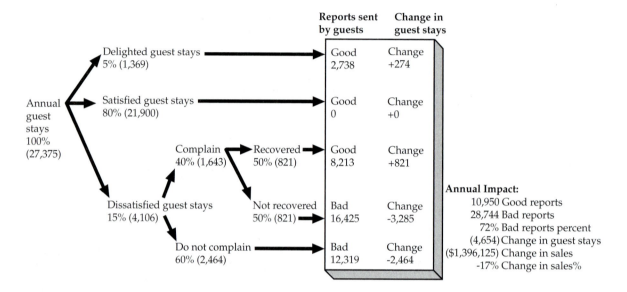

"unconditional satisfaction guarantee." However, Geurs was considering an unconditional "two-step" service guarantee that would give Radisson a chance to fix the problem before they paid for the guest's room. One proposed guarantee was written as follows:

> If you have a problem, please let us know and we'll make it right or you won't pay.

Pilot Hotel Plan

Under Geurs' leadership, Radisson's management decided to launch a pilot study to evaluate service guarantees in about 30 different pilot Radisson hotels in different market segments and locations. The plan was to evaluate the pilot by comparing the "before" and "after" measurements from Radisson's standard customer satisfaction/loyalty complaint data (from comment cards). This data measured:

- Willingness to return
- Percent advocates
- Percent defectors
- Percent complaints

Radisson's management also planned to measure the number of times that the guarantee was invoked

and how much money was spent on these "invocations." A University of Minnesota research team planned to conduct a "before" and "after" survey on "employee motivation and vision" and "organizational service learning" to discern how the service guarantee affected culture in the pilot hotels.

The service guarantee pilot test program clearly needed a strong training program to support it. The planned training program included the following initiatives:

- Enhance the "Yes, I Can" program in the general orientation to help all new employees understand the importance of the service guarantee.
- Provide information on the service guarantee for general managers and owners in a one-day format.
- Provide training to the hotel management teams on the philosophy and payback of the service guarantee.
- Teach district directors about service guarantees so that they could provide the necessary leadership to their hotels.

Geurs knew that the pilot could not test the marketing impact of the service guarantee. She also knew that it could become a "hard sell" to the hotel owners

EXHIBIT 2
Marketing with technology.

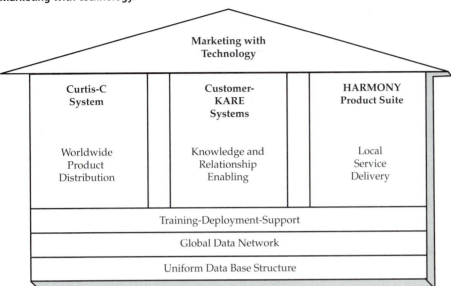

if the number of "invocations" was high and if they found that the allowances (payouts) outweighed the benefits.

As Geurs began her job as the director of this exciting (but potentially dangerous) new program, she had many challenges ahead of her. Some of these included:

1. How should Radisson word the guarantee? Should it be a "two-step" process?
2. How should hotel managers and employees be trained for the program?
3. Should the training be conducted by Radisson employees using a "train the trainer" approach or should Radisson employ a professional training firm to do the training?
4. How should they handle hotels that did not readily buy into the program?
5. Should Radisson's corporate office pay for the invocations for the test hotels?
6. What role should the guarantee play in Radisson's marketing communications?

FULLY INTEGRATED GUEST INFORMATION SYSTEM

Scott Heintzeman, VP of Knowledge Technologies for Radisson, took a number of initiatives to enhance Radisson's information technology approach to support Radisson's strategy. As suggested in Exhibit 2, the information technology approach included three "pillars"—the Curtis-C System worldwide distribution (reservation) system, the customer database (Customer-KARE Systems), and the HARMONY property management system.

Product Distribution System

This sophisticated system was the world's leading global reservations system. It helped Radisson capture business from electronic commerce and toll-free telephone services reaching into 125 countries. The worldwide computer reservations system provided instantaneous, convenient service for customers, travel agents and hotel staff. The "Curtis-C" reservation system was also accessible through airline reservations systems worldwide. Radisson's toll-free U.S. number 1-800-333-3333 was the most memorable in the hotel industry.

The CustomerKARE System

The "Customer Knowledge and Relationship Enabling" system that is on top of Radisson's information data warehouse "enables us to know and build relationships with our guests." This database had at least three uses:

- The marketing department could use this database to observe trends and manage direct marketing campaigns.
- Hotels could access customer service profiles so that they could personalize local service delivery programs (with sensitivity to guest privacy).
- Radisson Reservation Services could expedite the booking process and customize the sale to the needs and preferences of the customer.

One of the newer features of this system was the complaint management system, which could provide rich detail on (1) problem hotels, (2) problem customers, and (3) repeat common-cause problems across the organization or regions. The technology allowed the data to be "sliced and diced" any way that users wanted it.

HARMONY Property Management System

HARMONY provided "rich statistical/analytical business information" for the hotel management. This was an "executive information system" to support the general manager in evaluating staff productivity, sales patterns, employee turnover rate, etc. It also supported corporate office and hotel owners and hotel management companies. According to Heintzeman, "our next project is to create an online Information Management System for our managers that will include the very most important key performance indicators (a balanced scorecard) so that managers can look at a number of key performance indicators from their desktops." It will include an online/interactive version of their current "triage report" which provides a key set of statistics, which allow managers to assess the health of a hotel very quickly. According to Radisson's Web page,

> [HARMONY was] also a technology link between Radisson Hotels and Curtis-C, providing instantaneous guest profile information, which could be used to deliver faster, and more customized service to each guest.

The plan was to have the HARMONY property management system in place in all Radisson hotels by the end of 1998. Radisson planned on using this technology to further personalize services for guests.

PROGRAMS FOR MEASURING GUEST AND EMPLOYEE SATISFACTION

Customer Satisfaction

As mentioned above, Radisson measured customer satisfaction and loyalty primarily through hotel guest complaint cards, which measured four variables over time:

- Willingness to return
- Percent advocates
- Percent defectors
- Percent complaints

Radisson management was concerned that the number of respondents was very small and considered other means of collecting this information. In one extreme example, the Radisson Slavjanskaya hotel in Moscow received only 100 comment cards per month for 9,000 room nights. One alternative was to hire a data collection firm (such as Gallop) to randomly sample guests to collect more "transaction" detail information.

The goal of the measurement program, of course, was to measure and increase loyalty. Loyalty had several different aspects—loyalty to a particular Radisson hotel and loyalty to the brand. Radisson management was considering a program for increasing loyalty, particularly to the brand.

One of the Carlson Companies' strengths since its inception was developing "recognition" programs, such as Gold Bond Stamps that had been given away in grocery stores to promote customer loyalty, and, more recently, frequent flyer programs for many airlines. However, as of 1997, Radisson did not have its own frequent guest program. Its only guest recognition program was tied to airline frequent flyer programs.

Employee Satisfaction

Several research studies have found a strong link between employee satisfaction and customer satisfaction. Radisson management considered how they might measure and improve employee satisfaction as a part of the overall program. Some thought had been given to developing new loyalty programs for Radisson employees.

CONCLUSIONS

Radisson had initiated a program that required Radisson corporate management to call customers every Monday morning in response to complaint letters. This policy helped Radisson "make it right" for its customers and also helped Radisson management take on more of a "guest champion" role and mentality. However, O'Hanlon wondered what more Radisson could do to change the corporate structure and culture to keep close to the "guests"—and to become more of a "champion of the guests." As Radisson developed the different initiatives, Brian Stage and Maureen O'Hanlon wondered what they could do to improve their strategies and their recent quality initiatives. They also wondered if there might be other projects that they should be pursuing to accelerate their "customer-driven learning" efforts.

Discussion Questions

1. How should Radisson define and implement their service guarantee?
2. What role should information technology play in accelerating the drive to improve service quality?
3. How should Radisson measure and improve customer satisfaction and employee satisfaction?
4. How should Radisson drive commitment to service quality through their franchise organization?
5. How should Radisson align the goals of the hotel management team, hotel workers, owners, corporate management, and corporate staff with their new brand strategy?

APPENDIX 1
Radisson press release, March 23, 1998.

Radisson Hotels Worldwide Advances New Strategic Direction, Guests Are Center Stage

LAS VEGAS, Nev. (Mar. 23, 1998)—Radisson Hotels Worldwide today announced the global hotel company is on track six months after introducing the key initiatives of its new customer-focused strategic vision. This latest progress in its strategic plan aligns the global hotel company's development, marketing, technology and service strategies to higher levels of brand quality, consistency and customer satisfaction.

"Having expanded rapidly during the past decade to become a worldwide brand in the hotel industry, we are poised to take Radisson to the next level of success as a quality-driven, totally customer-focused organization," said Brian Stage, president of Radisson Hotels Worldwide. "As the Radisson brand continues to grow and mature, we are moving toward the goal of 100 percent guest satisfaction—an objective which is the foundation of our strategic agenda for the remainder of this decade and into the 21st century," he added.

There are five key strategic components to the vision for Radisson Hotels Worldwide that Stage has articulated: guest satisfaction and brand consistency; individualized marketing and guest services; strategic development of key hotels in prime locations; global brand presence; and the strengthening of the synergy among Carlson Companies.

Putting Guests First
To be the brand of choice among travelers, Radisson is focused on guest satisfaction to ensure guests receive consistent, reliable fault-free service at every Radisson hotel, every day. Radisson recently completed a pilot test of a 100 percent guest satisfaction program.

This spring, the brand will begin to implement a guest satisfaction guarantee worldwide, at every Radisson hotel. "When guests get what they expect, and more, at Radisson, they come back again and again," said Stage.

"Having a large number of hotels and being widely known are not enough," said Stage. "The Radisson brand is being defined by providing high-quality products and offering services for our guests' benefit and convenience—not ours," he added. "It is a strategy which will enable the next generation of growth and success of the Radisson brand."

Providing Individualized/Personalized Marketing and Services
Focusing on the trend of increasing customer sophistication, Radisson is moving forward to use state-of-the-art technology to custom tailor services for individual guest needs at every point of contact.

"We are developing new systems and processes that will enable Radisson to move from mass marketing to an approach that will create strong relationships with our best customers," Stage said. "Our goal is to anticipate and recognize individual customer needs, and act on those needs. The best way to win customer loyalty in the future will not be by points, premiums or miles. The next currency of customer loyalty will be convenience," explained Stage.

Radisson will soon begin to customize some of its core global marketing programs to further meet individual guests' needs. Advanced capabilities for ongoing customer data collections, enhancement, analysis and systemwide dissemination will allow the brand to deliver personalized service unlike any other hotel company.

Develop Key Hotels in Prime Locations
Over the past 15 years, Radisson's expansion strategies have rapidly grown the company from a regional hotel chain to a global brand with more than 360 hotels in 47 countries. Now that Radisson is approaching a critical mass to compete in a global marketplace, the company is directing its expansion efforts on selective, strategic developments in major markets with significant hotels. Stage said that global development will be guided by the belief that customer quality and consistency are the organization's top priority. Radisson is focused, with its franchisees as partners, to provide exceptional quality of operations and properties, and ensure a consistent, exceptional guest experience at every one of its hotels.

"Radisson is committed to continuous product improvement and has redefined specifications for the Radisson hotel product and services," he added.

Radisson is focusing on developing more hotels and resorts in major cities and leisure destinations with hotels and resorts that define the brand and meet quality standards. "Some of these developments may include equity participation and management by Radisson," Stage said.

Since Stage became president of the hotel brand in July 1997, several new Radisson hotels have been announced in key cities such as Los Angeles and Chicago, as well as new resort properties in Florida. Radisson is finalizing a partnership with the Aruban government to develop its Aruba property into a premiere Caribbean destination. Plans call for the resort to undergo a $35 million renovation before it re-opens in 1999.

APPENDIX 1
(Continued)

Strengthen Global Brand Presence

Radisson's drive to become a global brand has continued under Stage's direction. In 1998, Radisson opened its first hotels in India and Korea, and will be expanding its presence in Eastern Europe with hotels opening in Cottbus, Germany, and Vilnius, Lithuania. In the Middle East, the brand recently opened two new Jordanian Radissons in Amman and Aqaba, while Australia's newest Radisson is in Melbourne. In Canada, Sun Peaks, British Columbia, is home to a new Radisson resort. Radisson's global growth will continue with the help of strong partnerships that draw on local knowledge and resources in the theaters of the world where Radisson operates.

Leveraging Carlson Companies Synergy

Heading into the millennium, Radisson will continue to develop its global presence, while preserving the integrity of the brand. The company will seek opportunities to further capitalize on the synergy derived from Carlson Companies' four operating groups, Carlson Hospitality Worldwide, Carlson Wagonlit Travel, Carlson Leisure Group and Carlson Marketing Group. Carlson's travel agency interests include over 5,300 locations in 140 countries, providing a powerful support network for the company's hotel operations. "Making it easier for Carlson's travel businesses to book Radisson will earn us an increasing share from these giants in the global travel industry."

Carlson Marketing Group's dominance of the multi-billion dollar incentive industry offers opportunities for Radisson to attract these lucrative programs.

"This is an exciting point in Radisson's history," said Stage. "During the next five years the company will solidify its position as a leading global brand with a strong core of high-quality hotels distinguished by personalized, high-quality services to meet the needs of individual customers. We want to be sought by investors who respect the power of our brand. By taking care of guests, we'll be able to take care of our owners."

APPENDIX 2
Radisson press release, January 20, 1999.

Carlson Hospitality Worldwide Introduces New Generation Central Reservation System; "Curtis-C" Sets New Industry Standards in Technology Sophistication

OMAHA, Neb. (Jan. 20, 1999)—Continuing to set new standards and cut new ground with innovative technology, Carlson Hospitality Worldwide today introduced a new generation central reservation system, "Curtis-C" (pronounced "Courtesy"), at its worldwide reservation headquarters in Omaha, Neb. Named in honor of Curtis L. Carlson, founder and chairman of parent company Carlson Companies, Inc., Curtis-C was a three-year journey that re-invented Carlson's system into one of the most sophisticated in the hotel industry and was completed without disruption of reservation services.

Curtis-C is built upon a three-tier client server architecture, relational database and global data network utilizing the most advanced systems methodologies to harvest business and manage operations of Carlson's brands on a real time basis worldwide. The system serves Carlson's hotel and cruise ship operations including Regent International Hotels, Radisson Hotels Worldwide, Country Inns Suites By Carlson and Radisson Seven Seas Cruises.

Joining in the dedication of the new Curtis-C system were Curtis Nelson, president and CEO of Carlson Hospitality Worldwide; Eric Danziger, president of Carlson Hotels Worldwide; and Scott Heintzeman, vice president of Knowledge Technologies for Carlson Hospitality Worldwide. "The new Curtis-C system is truly a breakthrough," said Nelson. "It is a technology showcase which distinguishes us from the competition and sets new global standards for our industry. It is also a vital cornerstone in achieving the customer-focused strategic vision of Carlson Hospitality Worldwide for the next millennium," added Nelson.

"The project was completed in 'chunks' and was designed to integrate all of our worldwide systems, preparing us for massive future growth, and enables us to better focus on the individual preferences of our customers," said Heintzeman. "The capabilities of this system will allow us to not just take reservations, but to better manage our business and build fuller relationships with our customers."

In addition to taking reservations through toll-free telephone, the Global Distribution System (GDS), and the Internet, Curtis-C also interfaces with the company's more than 550 hotels worldwide via HARMONY, the company's property management system and the CustomerKARE system—or Customer Knowledge And Relationship Enabling system.

APPENDIX 2
(Continued)

In addition to HARMONY and CustomerKARE, the company systems that interface with Curtis-C include the HARMONY Database Manager which provides access to hotel inventory along with the ability to deliver reservations through several distribution systems; the Guest Communication Manager, a system which manages guest satisfaction information; and KnowledgeNet, an Intranet system that will provide hotels easy access to valuable company information. All of these components provide numerous business benefits such as creating and distributing products worldwide in seconds; making information easily accessible to customize the customer experience; allowing for synergies between applications and reducing resource requirements; and adapting to changing markets and technologies. "Curtis-C is the platform upon which we are building our customer-focused future," added Heintzeman.

Following is an overview of the core applications.

HARMONY Database Manager

The HARMONY Database Manager (HDBM) is a powerful software platform. Developed by Carlson Hospitality, the HDBM provides a hotel with PC access to electronically update rates, availability, and stay controls in the following distribution systems: Curtis-C; HARMONY; the GDS; and Internet distribution systems. "Through the HDBM, revenue management controls are literally placed in the properties' hands, thus increasing efficiency and sales effectiveness," explained Heintzeman. "Each hotel now has the ability to react immediately to a rapidly changing market. Within seconds, new rate products can be placed on the shelf, existing products modified, new selling strategies implemented and availability controls adjusted."

Guest Communication Manager

The Guest Communication Manager system supports the company's 100 percent guest satisfaction strategy. With this system, the company is able to monitor the history of service problems that occur for any individual guest and for any specific hotel. The system also allows Carlson to minimize problems by scanning for trends and patterns. "We can see if there is a common problem that continues to present itself or a specific hotel or group of hotels that need attention. The system helps us identify service problems so issues can be properly addressed," said Heintzeman.

KnowledgeNet

Because Carlson Hospitality is a global company, it is important for all hotels to have access to company information on any day, at any time. KnowledgeNet contains a wealth of information such as corporate policies; forms; reports; hotel procedures; and newsletters. In addition, KnowledgeNet eliminates the monthly printing of hotel reports and distribution to the properties. "For a company that works in a team environment, this system allows us to be more cross-functional which in turn produces a more successful bottom line," explained Heintzeman. "Managing knowledge and making that information available to the right people at the right time is the goal of every IT department, and KnowledgeNet represents the future of information management systems."

Carlson Hospitality Worldwide is a global leader in hospitality services, encompassing nearly 1,100 hotel, resort, restaurant and cruise ship operations. Specific brands include: Regent International Hotels; Radisson Hotels Worldwide; Country Inns Suites By Carlson; Carlson Lifestyle Living (Carlson Park); Carlson Vacation Ownership; Radisson Seven Seas Cruises; T.G.I. Friday's; Friday's Front Row Sports Grill; Friday's American Bar; Italianni's; AquaKnox; Star Canyon; Timpano Italian Chophouse; Samba Room and Provisions. Carlson Hospitality Worldwide is one of the major operating groups of Carlson Companies, Inc., headquartered in Minneapolis, Minn. Other Carlson Companies groups include Carlson Marketing Group, a worldwide marketing services company operating in 17 countries; Carlson Leisure Group, responsible for leisure travel ventures around the globe; and Carlson Wagonlit Travel, a world leader in business travel management.

Contact: Betsy Day, 402-498-5000, bday@carlson.com, or Kristi Arndt, 612-212-5626, karndt@carlson.com, both of Carlson Hospitality.

Source: http://www.hotel-online.com/Neo/News/PressReleases1999_1st/Jan99_CarlsonCRS.html.

The first time you tolerate anything other than a movement toward 100 percent customer satisfaction, you're on the road to mediocrity.

Frederick W. Smith,
Federal Express chairman
and chief executive officer

Federal Express Corporation (FedEx) was founded in 1973 by Frederick W. Smith. A former military pilot with a vision to create the air-express industry, Smith started his company with 14 small planes. Some 17 years later, FedEx had a fleet of 419 planes delivering packages all over the world. At the end of fiscal year (FY) 1990, the company employed 90,000 people, processed 1.5 million shipments daily, and totaled $7 billion in revenues.

Since 1973, FedEx had received 195 awards, but the most prestigious was received on December 13, 1990, when Smith accepted the Malcolm Baldrige National Quality Award (MBNQA) from the President of the United States, George Bush. Federal Express was the first company to win in the service category since the award was established in 1988. In 1990, the U.S. Department of Commerce received 160,000 requests for MBNQA applications, but only 97 companies completed the rigorous application process. (See Exhibit 1 for MBNQA application headings.)

As President Bush left the stage following the presentation of the award, Smith caught his attention and pledged his support for the potential Persian Gulf conflict with Iraq. (FedEx flew personnel and supplies into the Gulf.) The Iraq situation posed a particular challenge for FedEx, because oil prices had more than doubled between August and December 1990. Unlike the commercial airlines, FedEx did not vary its shipping rates on a regular basis. In addition, overnight-delivery growth rates were slowing, which made competitive activities from Emery, the U.S. Postal Service's express division, and Airborne more threatening than in the past. Cost was becoming a bigger factor in the overnight purchase decision as quality efforts improved service rates across the industry.

After the presentation, Smith walked offstage and joined the other 1990 MBNQA award winners (IBM Corporation, Wallace Company, and the Cadillac Division of General Motors) at a round-table discussion about the challenges facing a company that focuses on quality. The first question referred to the challenges facing FedEx. *USA Today* asked, "In tough economic times, isn't it too costly to implement quality-improvement programs that require retraining the work force?" As Smith's quotation at the beginning of this case suggests, the road to the MBNQA winner's circle has arrows pointed one way.

COMPANY PHILOSOPHY

Customer satisfaction begins with employee satisfaction. Putting people first in every action, every planning decision, every business decision requires a tremendous commitment from every manager and every employee in the company.

James L. Barksdale,
Chief Operating Officer

FedEx viewed its job as selling service; it sold the promise that a package or letter would arrive "absolutely, positively overnight." Sometimes fulfilling this promise required employees to work harder. FedEx COO Barksdale liked to use this letter from a customer to stress the idea:

The Saturday before Labor Day, I was anxiously awaiting a package being delivered to me via Federal Express. It contained materials which had to be consolidated with another package, then sent on to Europe that night. It was 4:00 P.M. when the package finally arrived; so I rushed to your local station. Unfortunately, I didn't arrive until after your closing time. I was furious. After listening to my story, Ingrid James . . . the operations manager at Emeryville . . . promised she would do whatever she could to get the package out that night. She waited 45 minutes while I compiled the materials and made sure the package made it out that night. When I arrived in my office the following Tuesday morning, I had faxes advising me that the packages were received. Having an employee like Ms. James tells me that you and your employees care about the customer's business. To me she's not just Ingrid James, she *is* Federal Express.

Barksdale agreed: "She *is* Federal Express. That says it all. Our people hold in their hands our customer's perception of quality. Clearly, the degree to which people *choose* to exert their best effort determines our success in a competitive global economy. The question is: how do we organize our companies and prepare all people to lead?" The answer,

EXHIBIT 1
Malcolm Baldrige National Quality Award application headings.

1990 Examination Categories/Items		Maximum Points
1.0	Leadership	100
	1.1 Senior executive leadership	30
	1.2 Quality values	20
	1.3 Management for quality	30
	1.4 Public responsibility	20
2.0	Information and analysis	60
	2.1 Scope and management of quality data and information	35
	2.2 Analysis of quality data and information	25
3.0	Strategic quality planning	90
	3.1 Strategic quality planning process	40
	3.2 Quality leadership indicators in planning	25
	3.3 Quality priorities	25
4.0	Human resource utilization	150
	4.1 Human resource management	30
	4.2 Employee involvement	40
	4.3 Quality education and training	40
	4.4 Employee recognition and performance measurement	20
	4.5 Employee well-being and morale	20
5.0	Quality assurance of products and services	150
	5.1 Design and introduction of quality products and services	30
	5.2 Process and quality control	25
	5.3 Continuous improvement of processes, products, and services	25
	5.4 Quality assessment	15
	5.5 Documentation	10
	5.6 Quality assurance, quality assessment, and quality improvement of support services and business processes	25
	5.7 Quality assurance, quality assessment, and quality improvement of supplier	20
6.0	Quality results	150
	6.1 Quality of products and services	50
	6.2 Comparison of quality results	35
	6.3 Business process, operational, and support service quality improvement	35
	6.4 Supplier quality improvement	30
7.0	Customer satisfaction	300
	7.1 Knowledge of customer requirements and expectations	50
	7.2 Customer relationship management	30
	7.3 Customer service standards	20
	7.4 Commitment to customers	20
	7.5 Complaint resolution for quality improvement	30
	7.6 Customer satisfaction determination	50
	7.7 Customer satisfaction results	50
	7.8 Customer satisfaction comparison	50
	Total	1000

according to the People-Service-Profit (P-S-P) philosophy, relied heavily on management's ability to create an environment that encouraged and allowed people to choose to deliver superior service. In short, Barksdale said, "Customer satisfaction begins with employee satisfaction. Our employees have been acting on their own to keep customers satisfied even before *empowerment* became a buzzword." Consequently, the P-S-P philosophy guided FedEx in all its policies and actions.

Attention to quality service emerged early in FedEx's history. For instance, FedEx advertised the company's high service levels vis-à-vis Emery in 1975 with the slogan, "Federal Express. Twice as Good as the Best in the Business." In the 1970s, service was measured by the percentage of overnight deliveries

EXHIBIT 2
Federal Express quality improvement process.

EXHIBIT 3
Federal Express problem-solving process.

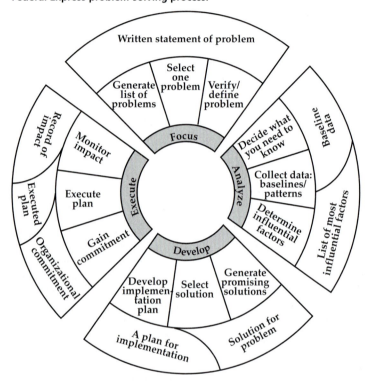

that were made on time. In the 1980s, however, FedEx managers concluded that high service percentages would not be sufficient in the future. For example, a 99 percent success rate, at FedEx's 1990 volume, translated into 2.5 million actual failures per year.

To bolster quality efforts, FedEx adopted the Quality Improvement Process (QIP). This process helped establish two important ideas to support the P-S-P philosophy. Fixrst, QIP recognized the correlation between doing things right the first time and productivity: the Q = P paradigm (quality = productivity). Second, QIP defined quality service not in statistical terms, but as performance to the standards of the customer: "100 percent" satisfaction became the uncompromising goal. Exhibit 2, which appears in the FedEx employee handbook, is a graphic representation of these philosophies.

SYSTEMS AND PROCESS

Quality Improvement
FedEx initiated a quality-education program in 1985, but the program was statistically oriented and it lost momentum. By mid-1987, the FedEx customer-service department was struggling with problems related to rapid growth in the overnight service. At this time, FedEx selected Organizational Dynamics Incorporated (ODI), an international consulting firm located in Burlington, Massachusetts, to initiate a companywide education program on quality. ODI led workshops for senior vice presidents and managing directors, and it trained managers to facilitate workshops for employees. The ODI process focused more on the thought processes in quality improvement than on statistical techniques. The goal was to get managers and employees to analyze problems in systematic and uniform ways.

The construction of the quality program rested on five modules:

1. *The Meaning of Quality* included the concepts of customer focus, total involvement, quality measurement, systems support, and continuous improvement as everyone's job.

2. *The Cost of Quality* emphasized rework and waste as the cost of not doing quality work—breaking down total costs into avoidable versus necessary costs.

3. *You and Your Customer* helped show that everyone at FedEx was both a supplier and a customer (see the section "Customer/Supplier Alignment").

4. *Continuous Improvement* developed the themes of Module 1 and showed how to meet customer needs in innovative ways.

5. *Making Quality Happen* encouraged people to take a leadership role in implementing quality programs.

Quality Action Teams
To implement the framework of ideas in the modules, FedEx instituted Quality Action Teams (QAT). The teams organized when employees saw a need to change the way they did their jobs. The QATs used a problem-solving process known as the FADE framework: *focus* on a particular problem or opportunity, *analyze* the data, *develop* solutions and action plans, and *execute* the plans for solutions (see Exhibit 3).

In addition, extensive training was given to provide the QAT members with tools to augment the FADE process—tools such as fish-bone diagrams, flow charts, action plans, and pareto analysis.

With the FADE process, FedEx elicited creative solutions through employee involvement and careful analysis. For example, one QAT in the main package-sorting hub devised mnemonic devices to help new employees remember the abbreviations for destination cities. These changes saved FedEx an estimated $3 million in training costs.

In addition to hitting improvement "home runs," the QATs focused on small, incremental changes. According to Martha Thomas, managing director of disbursements, employees were charged with the challenge of constantly changing their systems to increase their throughput. Thomas viewed the main function of the QATs as catalysts to help FedEx cultivate a culture of continuous improvement: "We are trying to encourage a culture of smaller improvements—and more of them. I think 80 percent of the problems are system problems, so you constantly have to change the system." She gave the following example:

> Our customers, in this case FedEx employees, told us that they hated to wait for expense reimbursements. We figured that, in any day, 100 percent of a day's mail is processed; it may be 10 percent of yesterday and 90 percent of the day before. Why not do 100 percent of today's mail today? Through QATs, the employees figured out how to stagger the schedule so it could be done. Now a check is written the same day we receive the expense report.

Customer Satisfaction Measurement

It should not be thought that Federal Express ignores its customers' perceptions of its performance. They have logged customer complaints since the early 80s and use the information in internal evaluations of systems. Originally, Fred Smith dubbed these customer complaints "The Hierarchy of Horrors," a listing of the eight most common customer complaints. In order they are:

> Wrong day delivery, right day late delivery, pick-up not made, lost package, customer misinformed by Federal Express, billing and paperwork mistakes, employee performance failures, and damaged package

The importance of the Hierarchy of Horrors was that it clearly indicated that there was more to measure than just on-time delivery.

EXHIBIT 4
Federal Express Service Quality Indicators (SQI).

Beginning in FY 1989, the overall quality of service was measured by the Service Quality Index (SQI). This index weighted service failures from the customers' perspective, and comprised the 12 components shown below.

Failure Type	Weighting Factor
Right day late service failures	1
Wrong day late service failures	5
Traces (not answered by COSMOS)	1
Complaints reopened by customers	5
Missing proofs of delivery (PODS)	1
Invoice adjustments requested	1
Missed pick ups	10
Lost packages	10
Damaged packages	10
Delay minutes/aircraft ("0" based)	5
Overgoods	5
Abandoned calls	1

Service Quality Indicators

In the late 1980s Federal Express decided they needed a more proactive, comprehensive, and customer-oriented measure of performance. Instead of eliminating the Hierarchy of Horrors, they borrowed from it. Breaking down the customer's concept of quality service into components, the Hierarchy of Horrors listed all the things that could go wrong with an overnight delivery. This list, combined with methods of measurement, evolved into the Service Quality Indicators (SQI, pronounced "sky") shown in Exhibit 4. SQI accounted for every package that entered the FedEx system, and each of the 12 indicators measured service quality from the customer's point of view. Each customer complaint was assigned points and given a weight. For example, a lost package had a weight of 10, and a right day/late delivery had a weight of 1. Combining the number of failures at the appropriate weights produced a record of Total Daily Failure Points. This figure was tracked, compared with projections, and communicated to every employee on a daily basis through *FXTV*, the world's largest private television station.

Anthony Byrd, a senior project analyst and author of Sections 6 and 7 of the MBNQA application, talked about the challenges of measuring quality in a service company as follows:

> The MBNQA application has manufacturing biases; it relies heavily on statistical process control (SPC). We tried to impress upon the

MBNQA examiners that quality is our basis of competition in the market place. Our strategy is to offer enhanced value through quality service, and we go beyond the quality-control measures. We go beyond sampling; we take a census of all our packages. This gives us performance figures on *every* package that goes through the system, and we communicate those figures to all the employees. This puts us in our own league.

Customer Satisfaction Surveys

Neither the Hierarchy of Horrors nor its successor, the SQI, replaced Customer Satisfaction Surveys, which act as a barometer of performance. Quarterly, a Customer Satisfaction Study was conducted by phone across Federal Express' four main market segments: base business (phone request for pick-up), U.S. export customers, manned-center customers (drop-off packages at store-front centers), and drop-box customers. On a five-point satisfaction scale, Federal Express only recognized the highest rating of completely satisfied as an acceptable level of customer satisfaction instead of combining somewhat and completely satisfied. Thus, they were only measuring improvement towards their goal of 100 percent complete customer satisfaction.

In addition to this generalized study, Federal Express also utilized Targeted Customer Satisfaction Studies (a direct-mail survey of customers who have used 1 of 10 specific FedEx processes), Federal Express Center Comment Cards, Customer Automation Studies (a survey of FedEx largest customers who use the Powership shipping and billing computer systems on-site), and the Canadian Customer Study (largest source of business outside U.S.).

Results of all the surveys were compiled to identify trends, allow for customer segmentation to a meaningful level, and provide a detailed measure of service attributes.

Customer/Supplier Alignment

The concept of an internal customer was a natural extension of the FedEx Q = P philosophy: Good relationships between customers and suppliers increase productivity. The Customer/Supplier Alignment (CSA) was a quality process for internal service. If any party requested a CSA, both parties were required to act on the request. First, one party listed and ranked the 10 most important services they provided to their internal customer. (CSA questions are listed in Exhibit 5.) Then, that same party listed how well he or she supplied the customer's needs, thereby rating his or her own performance. Next, the other party went through the same process. Jeff Campbell, a senior manager in procurement, related the following CSA experience:

EXHIBIT 5
Federal Express customer/supplier alignment.

- What do you need from me?
- What do you do with what I give you?
- Are there any gaps between what I give you and what you need?
- How well am I doing?
- What gaps can be eliminated now?
- What measures can we use to ensure requirements are being met?
- What gaps are still remaining?
- What will we do to close these remaining gaps over time?
- When can we meet again?
- What is my Service Agreement?

There is a part of Federal Express called Sort Facilities Development (SFD), which develops mini-hubs from the ground up. They are very dependent upon my department (procurement) to supply, just in time, the conveyor systems, transfer units, and controllers—anything they need—to build a sorting facility anywhere in the country. Traditionally, there had not been a good relationship between procurement and SFD, so a CSA meeting was called. When we got to the meeting, the 10 things we were *sure* that they needed from us were not even on their list! Obviously, we had some things to talk about.

Campbell added, "We also use CSA between employees and managers. If you think about it: A manager is the supplier of the resources that the employee needs to do his or her job effectively."

Guaranteed Fair Treatment Process

Employee support systems were part of the FedEx "People First" philosophy. In all departments of the company, a plaque displayed the Guaranteed Fair Treatment Procedure (GFTP). Exhibit 6 shows the steps by which an employee could appeal any eligible issue through a process of systematic reviews by progressively higher levels of management. Campbell summarized GFTP as "a three-step process that gives employees access to upper management within 21 working days." Every Tuesday, CEO Smith and COO Barksdale listened to GFTP appeals. When asked how these employees could afford the time spent on the GFTP process, Barksdale replied: "How can we afford not to? . . . Our people have helped us see that some policies

EXHIBIT 6
The FedEx guaranteed fair treatment procedure.

STEP 1: MANAGEMENT REVIEW

Complainant
- Submits written complaint to a member of management (manager, senior manager or managing director) within 7 calendar days of occurrence of the eligible issue.

Manager, Senior Manager, Managing Director
- Review all relevant information.
- Hold a telephone conference and/or meeting with complainant.
- Make decision either to uphold, modify, or overturn management's action.
- Communicate their decision in writing to complainant and Personnel matrix.

Note: When multiple levels of management exist, a consensus decision will be rendered. All of the above should occur within 10 calendar days of receipt of the complaint, unless written notice of time extension is provided to complainant and Personnel.

STEP 2: OFFICER REVIEW

Complainant
- Submits written complaint to an officer (vice president or senior vice president) of the division within 7 calendar days of Step 1 decision.

Vice President and Senior Vice President
- Review all relevant information.
- Conduct additional investigation, when necessary.
- Make decision either to uphold, modify, or overturn management's action or initiate a Board of Review.

Note: When multiple levels of management exist, a consensus decision will be rendered. All of the above should occur within 10 calendar days of receipt of the complaint, unless written notice of time extension is provided to complainant and Personnel.

STEP 3: EXECUTIVE REVIEW

Complainant
- Submits written complaint within 7 calendar days of Step 2 decision to Employee Relations Department, who investigates and prepares GFTP case file for Appeals Board review.

Appeals Board
- Reviews all relevant information.
- Makes decision to uphold, overturn, or initiate Board of Review, or take other appropriate action.
- All of the above should occur within 14 calendar days of receipt of complaint, unless written notice of time extensions are provided to complainant and Personnel.
- Responds in writing to complainant within 3 calendar days of decision with copy to Personnel matrix and the complainant's chain of command.

need revision, or perhaps need to be rethought altogether."

Survey/Feedback/Action
Exhibit 7 is a sample scoring page from the annual survey FedEx used to solicit employee feedback. This survey, Survey/Feedback/Action (SFA), supported both the People First philosophy and QIP by creating a system that charged work groups to examine management's effectiveness (see Exhibit 8). The SFA was a standard, anonymous questionnaire given each year to all employees. After six weeks, the results were returned, and the group's manager was required to have a feedback meeting to identify specific concerns or problems. The outcome of the feedback meeting was a list of clear, concise actions

EXHIBIT 7
Federal Express 1990 survey feedback action.*

Organization Name
Last Name, First Name   Management Level
Airport ID   Department
N = 8   May 1, 1990

Workgroup #1000

	Percent			
	Favorable	Sometime Fav/Unf	Unfav	# No Ans
1. Can tell my manager what I think.	86	14	0	1
2. My manager tells me what is expected.	86	0	14	1
3. Favoritism not a problem in my workgroup.	57	0	43	1
4. My manager helps us do our job better.	43	29	29	1
5. My manager listens to my concerns.	86	0	14	1
6. My manager asks for my ideas about work.	67	0	33	2
7. My manager tells me when I do a good job.	100	0	0	1
8. My manager treats me with respect.	100	0	0	1
9. My manager keeps me informed.	83	0	17	2
10. My manager does not interfere with job.	71	29	0	1
11. My manager's boss gives us support we need.	50	17	33	2
12. Upper management tells us company goals.	50	33	17	2
13. Upper management listens to ideas from my level.	0	0	100	2
14. Have confidence in the fairness of management.	17	33	50	2
15. Can be sure of a job if I do good work.	100	0	0	1
16. Proud to work for Federal Express.	100	0	0	1
17. Work leading to kind of future I want.	100	0	0	2
18. FedEx does a good job for our customers.	100	0	0	1
19. Working for Federal Express is a good deal.	100	0	0	1
20. Paid fairly for this kind of work.	57	0	43	1
21. Benefit programs meet most of my needs.	100	0	0	1
22. People cooperate within this workgroup.	100	0	0	1
23. There is cooperation between workgroups.	86	14	0	1
24. In my environment we use safe work practices.	100	0	0	2
25. Rules and procedures do not interfere.	43	14	43	1
26. Able to get supplies and resources.	86	0	14	1
27. Have enough freedom to do my job well.	100	0	0	1
28. Workgroup involved in improving service to customers.	100	0	0	3
29. 1989 SFA concerns were addressed satisfactorily.	33	17	50	2

SFA average percent favorable   76
IR index =   71
Leadership index =   78
Leadership avg =   3.8

	Favorable	Sometime Fav/Unf	Unfav	# No Ans
Local Question 1	33	17	50	2
Local Question 2	100	0	0	2
Local Question 3	0	0	100	4
Local Question 4	33	17	50	2
Local Question 5	33	33	33	2
Local Question 6	33	33	33	2
Local Question 7	60	0	40	3
Local Question 8	50	17	33	2
Local Question 9	71	0	29	1
Local Question 10	100	0	0	7

*This exhibit does not reflect actual survey results.

EXHIBIT 8
FedEx SFA and the Quality Improvement Process.

The Survey Feedback Action program shares many of the goals of the Quality Improvement Process (QIP) now used throughout Federal Express. Both programs are efforts to promote and maintain the highest quality in all operations through the involvement of all Federal Express employees. SFA is based upon some of the same "pillars of quality" used in the QIP, such as the following:

- **Total Involvement** of everyone in the organization, not just management. People execute those things to which they are committed; they become committed when they are involved.
- **Measurement** of quality. SFA provides a consistent measurement of your group's perceptions of your leadership and of the organization.
- **Continuous Improvement**—doing the right things right, better tomorrow than yesterday, and constantly looking for ways to correct or prevent problems.

SFA and QIP complement each other. Both the feedback and action steps of the SFA are opportunities for you as a manager to employ tools and processes of the QIP to ensure that your people-management skills are the most effective they can be and that the concerns of your employees are resolved.

Each phase of SFA may be viewed in terms of inputs and outputs, as follows:

	INPUT	OUTPUT
SURVEY	Your group's responses to SFA items as marked on survey forms.	Report of responses for the entire work group. Numbers are indicators (not final answers) of your group's morale.
FEEDBACK	Survey report of results. Discussion of the specific meaning of those indicators for your group.	Quality Action Plan that shows most significant problems, analysis of root causes for each problem, and at least the beginning of developed solutions.
ACTION	Your group's Quality Action Plan, executed according to the plan.	Problems corrected or improved. Improved morale according and satisfaction in the work group.

One way to view the SFA feedback meeting is as a concentrated opportunity for you to lead your group in practicing the FADE process (Focus-Analyze-Develop-Execute) on the "PEOPLE concerns" of your work group.

to be taken to address concerns and lead to improved results.

Anne Manning, a senior specialist in public relations, said of the SFA,

> Employee-satisfaction surveys exist at other companies, but the results often go into the "great black hole." At FedEx, we think *action* is the most important part—and it is monitored. If a manager is under a certain score in the Leadership index, he or she is put on a "critical" list, and a facilitator from the human resources department is assigned to that work group. The companywide Leadership index score must improve year over year; if it doesn't, *no* manager gets a bonus.

Leadership Evaluation Awareness Process
Manning continued,

> It is tough to be a manager at FedEx; you can't give orders, you have to give direction. There are lots of people who are very good at

what they do but won't make good managers, so we started the Leadership Evaluation Awareness Process (LEAP). This four-step process, which can take up to a year to complete, informs potential managers about the challenges connected with leading people:

> *Step 1* asks the candidate to consider: Is management for me? All the costs, responsibilities, and benefits are explored.

> *Step 2* is a series of written assignments on the subjects of leadership and personal development.

> *Step 3* requires peers to review the candidate, being especially candid about his or her leadership ability.

> *Step 4* has a board review the candidate's progress and conduct final interviews with the candidate.

> After successfully completing LEAP, the candidate is eligible to *apply* for a first-level management position. LEAP is difficult,

because it's important. It takes leaders to empower people; it turns people on to think they can make things happen, that they can make a difference, that they can change their jobs and make it better. But they have to have autonomy. They have to have power. For example, our customer-service reps *solve* problems: They can reimburse customers up to $250; it is their decision.

TECHNOLOGY AND INNOVATION

In leading the market of a high-value-added service, FedEx employees constantly searched for ways to serve their time-sensitive customers better. Citing the People First philosophy, Smith and Barksdale fostered a culture at FedEx that stimulated innovation. Barksdale said,

> Well-intentioned efforts are just as important as successes. And, if you hang your sales and customer-support people who try to do something that doesn't quite work—you'll get people who won't do anything. That's the reason we've tried to create a work place that encourages the motivated people who come to us to stay that way.

FedEx management operated under the assumptions that (1) a job-secure environment stimulates risk taking and innovation, and (2) a risk-taking environment leads to learning and to new solutions that will satisfy customers. To guarantee a job-secure environment, FedEx had a no layoff policy. Glen Chambers, managing director of procurement, said of this policy, "The most dramatic test of this People First commitment came when Zapmail, an electronic mail service, was discontinued in 1987. Over 1,300 people were disseminated throughout the organization; no one lost a job. That is a pretty strong commitment."

COSMOS

In applying technology to package handling, FedEx led the industry. Every package that entered the FedEx system was tracked by a central computer system, COSMOS (Customer, Operations, Service, Master On-Line System). This system was a worldwide network transmitting customer information to and receiving it in a central database in Memphis, Tennessee. The system was continuously updated with new information about package movements, customer pickups, invoices, and deliveries. In 1992, COSMOS was accessed over 250,000 times each day to determine the exact position of a package located in the FedEx system. The COSMOS system allowed customer-service representatives to handle customer inquiries with confidence.

The COSMOS system relied on a 10-digit bar code located on every overnight package. When a package was picked up, the courier passed his or her hand-held computer (Supertracker) over the bar code and entered the destination zip code and the type of service. When the courier returned to the van, the Supertracker was fitted into a port in the dispatch computer, which transmitted the information to COSMOS.

When packages arrived in the Memphis hub or one of the regional hubs, they were unloaded and sorted. Before the packages left for their destinations, they were scanned by a Supertracker to confirm their exit from the sort facility. As the package was delivered, a final scan was done by the courier to enter recipient and location information into COSMOS. The ability to give a customer accurate and timely information about a package was central to the P-S-P philosophy and FedEx's success.

Another example of FedEx's commitment to increasing productivity through technology was the Digitally Assisted Dispatch System (DADS), which communicated to approximately 30,000 couriers through interactive screens in their vans. Each courier van was equipped with the DADS, which ensured a quick response to delivery and pickup requests.

Powership

FedEx strengthened ties with its customers by providing a computerized shipping-management system (Powership). FedEx provided an electronic scale, microcomputer terminal, bar-code scanner, and printer at no charge. With the Powership system, a customer was able to print air bills for programmed addresses, download transactions to FedEx (thus eliminating clerical tasks such as reconciling invoices), manage accounts receivable, and track packages through COSMOS. By offering a complete distribution solution, FedEx had made itself indispensable to the overnight vendor.

THE FUTURE

FedEx continued to search out and develop the technologies necessary to lead the overnight industry. The company believed that such technologies as image processing of signatures and invoices, fiber-optic communications, battery technology, and expert-systems development would lead the way into the 1990s and beyond. Mike Babineaux, a senior specialist in procurement who had been hired in the 1970s when the company was a fledgling, talked as follows about the future at FedEx:

> I always say FEC doesn't just stand for "Federal Express Corporation"; it also stands for "For Ever Changing." At FedEx, change is

a matter of survival, because the business is changing so quickly. As growth slows, there seems to be more resistance to change within FedEx. It is a natural thing to do, but Federal Express will face plenty of new challenges—like the international market. We have to educate that market in the ways that overnight delivery can be a competitive weapon for any business. There will be other challenges in the future as well. I'll tell you one thing I have seen—in Fred Smith's office is a space shuttle painted FedEx colors, purple and orange! It makes me think.

BACK ON EARTH
USA Today asked, "In tough economic times, isn't it too costly to implement quality-improvement programs that require retraining the work force?" Smith replied,

Quality is the best way to reduce costs. It doesn't increase costs. We recently had the highest service level in Federal Express's history on one day, and we also calculated it was absolutely our lowest cost day. The real issue in quality is that it reduces cost by eliminating rework, repairs, and most importantly, eliminating the cost of replacing customers who have left because of the lack of quality. Anyone who's unwilling to spend on quality is really mapping a blueprint for liquidation.

Smith concluded,

One of the big things about getting employees involved in the quality process is to make them kind of have an out-of-body experience, to help them look at the world as a consumer as opposed to a producer. Employees have worked diligently over the years in a concerted effort to achieve 100 percent satisfaction, and our People First philosophy encourages that quest for quality.

Discussion Questions

1. What is the FedEx philosophy toward quality?
2. What specific elements/actions has FedEx implemented in its quality improvement history?
3. Discuss the pros and cons of each element/action from question 2.
4. What quality actions should FedEx consider for the future?

eXcel   In November 2005 John Wells, a customer service representative of Bayfield Mud Company, was summoned to the Houston, Texas, warehouse of Wet-Land Drilling, Inc., to inspect three boxcars of mud-treating agents that Bayfield Mud Company had shipped to the Houston firm. (Bayfield's corporate offices and its largest plant are located in Orange, Texas, which is just west of the Louisiana–Texas border.) Wet-Land Drilling had filed a complaint that the 50-pound bags of treating agents that it had just received from Bayfield were short-weight by approximately 5 percent.

The light-weight bags were initially detected by one of Wet-Land's receiving clerks who noticed that the railroad scale tickets indicated that the net weights were significantly less on all three of the boxcars than those of identical shipments received on October 25, 2005. Bayfield's traffic department was called to determine if lighter weight dunnage or pallets were used on the shipments. (This might explain the lighter net weights.) Bayfield indicated, however, that no changes had been made in the loading or palletizing procedures. Hence, Wet-Land randomly checked 50 of the bags and discovered that the average net weight was 47.51 pounds. They noted from past shipments that the bag net weights averaged exactly 50.0 pounds, with an acceptable standard deviation of 1.2 pounds. Consequently, they concluded that the sample indicated a significant short-weight. (The reader may wish to verify the above conclusion.) Bayfield was then contacted, and Wells was sent to investigate the complaint. Upon arrival, Wells verified the complaint and issued a 5 percent credit to Wet-Land.

Wet-Land's management, however, was not completely satisfied with only the issuance of credit for the short shipment. The charts followed by their mud engineers on the drilling platforms were based on 50-pound bags of treating agents. Lighter-weight bags might result in poor chemical control during the drilling operation and might adversely affect drilling efficiency. (Mud-treating agents are used to control the pH and other chemical properties of the cone during drilling operation.) This could cause severe economic consequences because of the extremely high cost of oil and natural gas well-drilling operations. Consequently, special use instructions had to accompany the delivery of these shipments to the drilling platforms. Moreover, the light-weight shipments had to be isolated in Wet-Land's warehouse, causing extra handling and poor space utilization. Hence, Wells was informed that Wet-Land's Drilling might seek a new supplier of mud-treating agents if, in the future, it received bags that deviated significantly from 50 pounds.

The quality control department at Bayfield suspected that the light-weight bags may have resulted from "growing pains" at the Orange plant. Because of economic conditions, oil and natural gas exploration activity had greatly increased. This increased activity, in turn, created increased demand for products produced by related industries, including drilling muds. Consequently, Bayfield had to expand from a one-shift (6:00 A.M. to 2:00 P.M.) to a two-shift (6:00 A.M. to 10:00 P.M.) operation in mid-2002 and finally to a three-shift operation (24 hours per day) in the fall of 2004.

The additional night-shift bagging crew was staffed entirely by new employees. The most experienced foremen were temporarily assigned to supervise the night-shift employees. Emphasis was placed on increasing the output of bags to meet the ever-increasing demand. It was suspected that only occasional reminders were made to double-check the bag weight-feeder. (A double-check is performed by systematically weighing a bag on a scale to determine if the proper weight is being loaded by the weight-feeder. If there is a significant deviation from 50 pounds, corrective adjustments are made to the weight-release mechanism.)

To verify this expectation, the quality control staff randomly sampled the bag output and prepared the following chart. Twenty-four bags were sampled and weighed each hour (see Exhibit 1).

Discussion Questions

1. What is your analysis of the bag-weight problem?
2. What procedures would you recommend to maintain proper quality control?

EXHIBIT 1
Sample bag weights.

Time	Avg. Weight (pounds)	Range Smallest	Range Largest	Time	Avg. Weight (pounds)	Range Smallest	Range Largest
6:00 A.M.	49.6	48.7	50.7	6:00 A.M.	46.8	41.0	51.2
7:00	50.2	49.1	51.2	7:00	50.0	46.2	51.7
8:00	50.6	49.6	51.4	8:00	47.4	44.0	48.7
9:00	50.8	50.2	51.8	9:00	47.0	44.2	48.9
10:00	49.9	49.2	52.3	10:00	47.2	46.6	50.2
11:00	50.3	48.6	51.7	11:00	48.6	47.0	50.0
12:00 noon	48.6	46.2	50.4	12:00 midnight	49.8	48.2	50.4
1:00 P.M.	49.0	46.4	50.0	1:00 A.M.	49.6	48.4	51.7
2:00	49.0	46.0	50.6	2:00	50.0	49.0	52.2
3:00	49.8	48.2	50.8	3:00	50.0	49.2	50.0
4:00	50.3	49.2	52.7	4:00	47.2	46.3	50.5
5:00	51.4	50.0	55.3	5:00	47.0	44.1	49.7
6:00	51.6	49.2	54.7	6:00	48.4	45.0	49.0
7:00	51.8	50.0	55.6	7:00	48.8	44.8	49.7
8:00	51.0	48.6	53.2	8:00	49.6	48.0	51.8
9:00	50.5	49.4	52.4	9:00	50.0	48.1	52.7
10:00	49.2	46.1	50.7	10:00	51.0	48.1	55.2
11:00	49.0	46.3	50.8	11:00	50.4	49.5	54.1
12:00 midnight	48.4	45.4	50.2	12:00 noon	50.0	48.7	50.9
1:00 A.M.	47.6	44.3	49.7	1:00 P.M.	48.9	47.6	51.2
2:00	47.4	44.1	49.6	2:00	49.8	48.4	51.0
3:00	48.2	45.2	49.0	3:00	49.8	48.8	50.8
4:00	48.0	45.5	49.1	4:00	50.0	49.1	50.6
5:00	48.4	47.1	49.6	5:00	47.8	45.2	51.2
6:00	48.6	47.4	52.0	6:00	46.4	44.0	49.7
7:00	50.0	49.2	52.2	7:00	46.4	44.4	50.0
8:00	49.8	49.0	52.4	8:00	47.2	46.6	48.9
9:00	50.3	49.4	51.7	9:00	48.4	47.2	49.5
10:00	50.2	49.6	51.8	10:00	49.2	48.1	50.7
11:00	50.0	49.0	52.3	11:00	48.4	47.0	50.8
12:00 noon	50.0	48.8	52.4	12:00 midnight	47.2	46.4	49.2
1:00 P.M.	50.1	49.4	53.6	1:00 A.M.	47.4	46.8	49.0
2:00	49.7	48.6	51.0	2:00	48.8	47.2	51.4
3:00	48.4	47.2	51.7	3:00	49.6	49.0	50.6
4:00	47.2	45.3	50.9	4:00	51.0	50.5	51.5
5:00	46.8	44.1	49.0	5:00	50.5	50.0	51.9

Case Study — Six Sigma at 3M, Inc.

On January 1, 2001, 3M announced that W. James McNerney Jr. was elected the chairman and chief executive officer of the firm (see Appendix 1 for the announcement). At the annual shareholders meeting in May 2001, McNerney announced that "At the top of my agenda is a headlong and companywide implementation of the Six Sigma approach to process and business improvement . . . I've seen firsthand how Six Sigma can energize an organization, increase sales and cash flow, satisfy customers better, and strengthen management development."

McNerney initiated a massive training program for hundreds of senior executives. Senior executives were charged with leading the training efforts for all of middle managers and coming up with a list of 100 key six sigma projects.

According to some sources, McNerney had already "sold" 3M's board of directors on the concept before he took the position.

Historically, 3M competed primarily on product leadership and quality—and almost never on price. Many 3M managers believed that the firm was already a quality company, with many high-quality products such as Post-it Products and Scotch tape commanding very high market shares in their respective markets. However, 3M's financial performance was "flat" and was not expected to improve unless some major changes were made. The decision had already been made to deploy a Six Sigma program. The question for the senior management of the firm was how to use the Six Sigma program as a key lever for transforming the firm to become more competitive.

HISTORY[1]

3M was founded in 1902 at the Lake Superior town of Two Harbors, Minnesota. Five businessmen agreed to mine a mineral deposit for grinding-wheel abrasives. But the deposits proved to be of little value, and the new Minnesota Mining and Manufacturing Company quickly moved to nearby Duluth to focus on sandpaper products.

Years of struggle ensued until the company could master quality production and a supply chain. New investors were attracted to 3M, such as Lucius Ordway, who moved the company to St. Paul in 1910. Early technical and marketing innovations began to produce successes and, in 1916, the company paid its first dividend—6 cents a share.

The world's first waterproof sandpaper, which eased the health problem of sanding dust, was developed in the early 1920s. A major milestone occurred in 1925 when Richard G. Drew, a young lab assistant, invented masking tape—an innovative step toward diversification and the first of many Scotch brand pressure-sensitive tapes.

In the following years technical progress resulted in Scotch™ Cellophane Tape for box sealing. Customers began to find many additional uses, including consumer applications. Drawing on expertise in bonding mineral grit to sandpaper, 3M brought out new adhesives to replace tacks in bonding upholstery, and sound-deadening materials for the auto industry's new metal-framed cars.

The roofing granule business (ceramic coated bits of rock) was developed in response to a need to make asphalt shingles last longer. In the early 1940s, 3M was diverted into defense materials for World War II, which was followed by new ventures, such as Scotchlite™ Reflective Sheeting for highway markings, magnetic sound recording tape, filament adhesive tape, and the start of 3M's involvement in the graphic arts with offset printing plates.

In the 1950s, 3M introduced the Thermo-Fax™ copying process, Scotchgard™ Fabric Protector, videotape, Scotch-Brite™ Cleaning Pads and several new electro-mechanical products.

In the 1960s, dry-silver microfilm, photographic products, carbonless papers, overhead projection systems, and a rapidly growing health care business of medical and dental products were introduced.

Markets were further expanded in the 1970s and 1980s into pharmaceuticals, radiology, energy control, the office market—and globally to most every country in the world.

The 1990s set new sales records of over $15 billion annually, and about 30 percent of sales coming from products created within the past four years. 3M's growth has come through a desire to participate in

[1] Source: http://www.3m.com/profile/looking/glance.jhtml May 15, 2001, and the 3M annual report for 2000.

This case was written by Professors Arthur Hill and Kevin Linderman of the Curtis L. Carlson School of Management at the University of Minnesota.

The case was prepared as the basis for class discussion rather than to illustrate either effective or ineffective handling of a business situation.

All of the content for this document was taken from public sources.

EXHIBIT 1

3M's sales history.

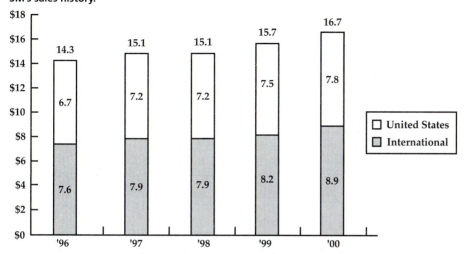

many markets where the company can make a significant contribution from core technologies, rather than be dominant in just a few markets.

In 2000, 3M was a diversified technology company with leading positions in electronics, telecommunications, industrial, consumer and office, health care, safety, and other markets. It had 2000 sales of $16.7 billion, a 6 percent increase. During 2000, 3M generated $5.6 billion (nearly 35 percent of sales) from products introduced during the previous four years, with sales over $1.5 billion from products introduced in 2000. Headquartered in St. Paul, Minnesota, the company had operations in more than 60 countries and served customers in nearly 200 countries. 3M was one of the 30 stocks that make up the Dow Jones Industrial Average and was also a component of the Standard & Poor's 500 Index.

SIX SIGMA

3M was applying many of the standard approaches to Six Sigma that had been developed by Motorola originally in 1985 and then extended to Allied Signal and GE in the mid 90s. Since then many other companies had also adopted Six Sigma as indicated in Appendix 2.

The 3M approach to Six Sigma included two different improvement models.

1. For existing processes, the five-step DMAIC model was used.

2. For new product development DFSS (Design for Six Sigma) was used.

For existing processes Six Sigma was aimed at making significant improvement in processes that were strategically selected by upper management. After selecting a process for improvement and assigning a senior executive to act as the "Champion," a Black

Belt was assigned to lead a process improvement team. The Black Belt was assigned full-time to project improvement and trained in the methods of Six Sigma and Statistics. The project team, under the Black-Belt's guidance, then worked on process improvement using the following DMAIC model.

The Six Sigma "DMAIC" Improvement Model

D	**D**efine	Requirements, goals, problems, scope
M	**M**easure	Validate problem, inputs, key steps, efficiency data
A	**A**nalyze	Develop/validate hypothesis, identify root causes, assess process design
I	**I**mprove	Remove root causes, standardize solutions, implement new process
C	**C**ontrol	Establish standard measures and reviews to maintain performance

A typical Six Sigma project lasted six months and was expected to make significant improvements both in customer satisfaction (internal or external customer) and in cost savings. The improvements were standardized and reviewed periodically to insure continuing benefit to 3M. The savings from the project were also carefully tracked by the financial organization in 3M.

The second use of Six Sigma was to design new products using the Design for Six Sigma methodology. This process started with identification of the customer's requirements and then translated those requirements eventually into product specifications. The process included not only designing the product, but reducing the inherent risk in the design processes by verifying the design with potential customers. Various tools such as Quality Function Deployment and Computer simulation of design characteristics were used during the design process.

THE SIX SIGMA PROGRAM AT 3M

3M's 2000 annual report included the following paragraphs praising the virtues of the Six Sigma program:

> *Process Improvement:* Process improvement means nothing if it doesn't lower costs, increase sales, satisfy customers, develop managers, increase cash flow and make the whole organization faster. 3M is quickly moving from multiple quality-management systems within the company to one: Six Sigma. A uniform, companywide approach shared by employees, customers and suppliers will both advance our competitiveness and improve our efficiency.

> *3M Acceleration:* This initiative targets generating even greater returns on our over $1 billion investment in R&D. The senior management team will be applying Six Sigma tools to drive time out of product development and commercialization cycles. Further, we will work as a team to sharpen our corporate focus on growth areas with the greatest returns for our investors.

3M Initiatives[2]

> Under the direction of our new Chairman, Chief Executive Officer, W. James McNerney Jr., 3M has begun the task of implementing initiatives that will lead 3M to provide a better service to its customers. Today's changing and demanding world demands the best of each element in 3M, always keeping in mind our real reason for being, Our Customers. These initiatives are focused towards long-term and short-term competitiveness because we are interested in making our clients think of us as the agile company that we are, always willing to provide the best products and services.

> *Six Sigma*—Implemented in our company, it strengthens all aspects of our business. Pursuing quality improvement under one single program, Six Sigma, 3M has been an excellent supplier to the various markets in which we participate by providing new and innovative products. Our customers demand and deserve that we do it even better and faster through 3M Acceleration.

> *E Productivity*—The future of commercial activities though electronic media is already

[2] Source: http//www.3m.com/intl/mx/englishver/mexico/quienes.htm, September 8, 2001.

present. We are changing the way we work to be more efficient, productive and to render a better service as support to our customers. To achieve this we must have the tools to be better connected, and this allows us to be ready in the rapidly growing "new" way of doing business.

> *Supply*—If we purchase in smarter and more systematic ways we will obtain cost reduction for 3M. Taking this in mind, our presence and strength in product purchasing will be translated to the generation of accessible and beneficial products for our customers.

> *Indirect Costs*—Good management of costs is critical for a sound and successful business plan, especially in critical times. At 3M, now and in the future, we seek adequate indirect cost reduction on many levels to be able to still be the preferred supplier to our customers.

JEANNE O'CONNELL'S TALK TO THE CARLSON SCHOOL OF MANAGEMENT

In a talk that Jeanne O'Connell, Director of Six Sigma Operations at 3M, gave at the Carlson School of Management in November 2001, she provided the following definition of Six Sigma at 3M:

> Six Sigma is a methodology for pursuing continuous quality improvement and reducing inherent variability. It requires a thorough process and product understanding and is clearly focused on customer-driven expectations.

She went on to share the following ideas:

Six Sigma Has a Focus on Processes

> Six Sigma is an *orderly and consistent* approach to a recurring significant business activity. Examples of a significant business activity include new product introduction, lab experiment, handling a customer call, approval of documents, manufacturing a product, filling an order, etc. All of our business activities involve a process—recognized or unrecognized, efficient or inefficient. The better our business processes, the better able we are to consistently and reliably keep our promises. Excellent business processes are essential for sustainable growth.

Ms. O'Connell described 3M's method for selecting processes for improvement as follows:

• Processes selected must be linked to the Strategic Business Plan.

EXHIBIT 2

3M's simple approach to Six Sigma.

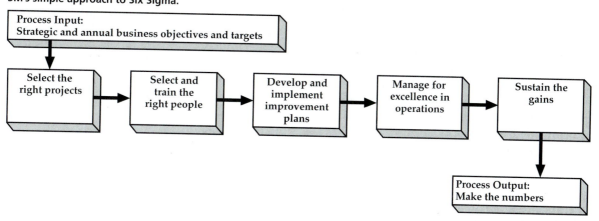

EXHIBIT 3

3M's simple approach to Six Sigma.

The Right Projects

+ The Right People

+ The Right Roadmap and Tools

+ The Right Support

= The Right Results

- Selection is prioritized based on value to the business, resources required, and timing. Factors considered in selection include growth, cost reduction and cash savings.
- All improvement processes are approved by management.
- They are formally tracked for savings and defect reduction.
- The team leader and management are held accountable

Exhibits 2 and 3 show slides that 3M uses to communicate their simple approach to Six Sigma. Exhibit 2 emphasizes that a strategic perspective drives project selection. Exhibit 3 suggests that the right results are a function of getting the previous steps right.

In answer to the question of "why Six Sigma," Jeanne O'Connell responded with the following four reasons:

- Common approach with common goals.
- Institutes a common language.
- Develops transferable skills.
- Most effective way to increase and accelerate our business performance and customer quality.

Ms O'Connell noted that 3M is moving aggressively to drive process improvement across the company. We started at the top with 3M senior leadership and are building on 3M's commitment to improvement. More than 4,000 people will have been trained by end of year 2000.

At one point in her talk, she said that "we want to change the DNA of the organization" and she even hinted that they plan to make it a requirement for all executives to be black belts.

THE SKEPTICS

Some companies have not embraced the Six Sigma approach. Skeptics in these companies point to the following issues in using Six Sigma.

- We can't afford to improve our processes to 3.4 parts per million defects as implied by Six Sigma. Also, our customers don't need this level of quality.
- Six Sigma is too complicated and involves too much statistics for our people. We need a simpler approach to process improvement.
- Six Sigma doesn't work very well for service processes or transaction-based processes that have intangible outputs and are difficult, if not impossible, to measure. Six Sigma is better suited to manufacturing.
- We can't afford the training costs and the appointment of full-time black belts for process improvement.
- Six Sigma is just the latest quality fad—it too will pass.

CHALLENGES AT 3M

As the firm went through this major transformation, many questions went through the minds of 3M managers.

1. What will the benefits of the Six Sigma program be and how will they be tracked and reported?
2. What are the costs and risks of this program?
3. What kinds of change management skills will the organization need to implement Six Sigma?
4. How should various functional areas in the organization be included in the Six Sigma initiative and what role should senior and middle management play in this change initiative?
5. What role should Six Sigma play in corporate strategy?
6. What kinds of information systems are required to support the Six Sigma initiative?
7. What are the human resource implications for deploying Six Sigma, e.g., employee selection, organizational structure (green belt, black belt, master black belt, champion)?
8. What are the most effective incentives for people involved with Six Sigma projects (black belts, team members, etc.)?

APPENDIX 1
McNerney will be 3M's new chairman and CEO.

December 5, 2000—3M announced today that W. James McNerney Jr. has been elected chairman and chief executive officer, effective Jan. 1, 2001. He succeeds L.D. DeSimone, who will remain with the company until April 1, 2001, to ensure a smooth transition. McNerney, 51, was president and CEO of GE Aircraft Engines, a world-leading supplier of jet engines with more than $10 billion in annual revenue. His GE career includes the top position at GE Lighting; president of GE Asia-Pacific; president and CEO of GE Electrical Distribution and Control; executive vice president of GE Capital, one of the world's largest financial services companies; and president of GE Information Services, a supplier of network computer services. He holds a B.A. from Yale University and an M.B.A. from Harvard University.

1997–present: President & CEO, GE Aircraft Engines, Cincinnati, OH.
1995–97: President & CEO, GE Lighting, Cleveland, OH.
1993–95: President, GE Asia-Pacific, Hong Kong.
1991–92: President and CEO, GE Electrical Distribution & Control, Plainville, CT.
1989–91: Executive Vice President, GE Financial Services and GE Capital, Stamford, CT.
1988–89: President, GE Information Services, Rockville, MD.
1982–86: GM of GE Mobile Communications.

Before joining GE in 1982, he first worked for Procter & Gamble in brand management and then as a senior manager at McKinsey & Co.

APPENDIX 2
Adopters of Six Sigma.

3M	Boeing	ComauPico	DaimlerChrysler
Allegheny Technologies	Bombardier	Commonwealth Health	Corporation
Allied Signal	Bosch	Corporation	Danaher Corporation
Amazon.com	Burlington Industries	Compaq Computer	Datacard Corporation
American Express	Canon	Corporation	Datastream Systems, Inc.
Ametek	Carlson Companies	Cooper Cameron	Dell Computer
Arcelik	Caterpiller	Corporation	Delphi Automotive
Asea Brown Boveri	Ceridian	Cooper Standard	Systems
Avery Dennison	Chromalloy	Automotive	Delta Airlines
BAE Systems	Citigroup	Cott Beverages	Digital Electronics
Baxter Healthcare	City of Fort Wayne,	Crane	Dow Chemical
BBA Nonwovens	Indiana	Cummins Engine	DuPont
Bharat Heavy Electricals	CNH Global	Company	Dura Automotive
Black & Decker	Cognis Corporation	Cytec-Fiberite Inc.	Systems

APPENDIX 2
(Continued)

Eastman Kodak	ITT Industries	Mount Carmel Health	Seagate Technology
Eaton Corporation	Jaguar	System	Sears, Roebuck &
Eli Lilly and Company	JEA	NCR Corporation	Company
Ericsson	John Deere	Nokia	Shimano
Fairchild Fasteners	Johnson & Johnson	Noranda	Siemens
First Data Corporation	Johnson Controls	Northrup	Sonoco
Flextronics International	JP Morgan Chase	Grumman Corporation	Sony
Ford Motor Company	Kaiser Aluminum	NovaStar Mortgage, Inc.	Space Systems Loral
Freudenberg	Kohler Company	Oasis Corporation	Sun Microsystems
Gateway	Landis Gardner	Owens Corning	Tata Chemicals Limited
GenCorp	Lear Corporation	PACCAR	Temasek Polytechnic
General Electric	Libby-Owens-Ford	Pilkington	Texas Instruments
Gulf States	LG Electronics	Polaroid	Textron
PaperCorporation	Lithonia Lighting	Polyclad Technologies	TIMET
Hellenic Aerospace	Lockheed Martin	PraxAir	TIMEX
Industries	Mabe	Raytheon	Toshiba
Heller Financial Inc.	Magnetek	Rexam Beverage Can	Unifi Inc.
Hitachi	Maple Leaf	Corporation	Visteon Corporation
Honda	Foods	Riverwood International	Vulcan Materials
Honeywell	Marconi	Roche Diagnostics	Company
Hoover Company	Maytag	Rohm and Haas	Vytra Health Plans
Huntsman Corporation	McKessonHBOC	Company	Walbro Engine
IBM	Mead	RR Donnelley & Sons	Management
IMI Norgren	MeridianAutomotive	Samsung	Whirlpool Corporation
IMC Global	Systems	SAMTEL	Woodward
International Paper	Motorola	Schenectady	W. C. Bradley
Invensys		International	Xerox Corporation

APPENDIX 3
3M CEO says company advancing despite tough economy; shareholders elect three directors at annual meeting.

ST. PAUL, Minnesota—May 8, 2001—W. James McNerney, Jr., 3M chairman and CEO, told more than 4,000 stockholders at the company's annual meeting that 3M achieved record sales and earnings in 2000. McNerney also said 3M is advancing despite a tough economy and described initiatives to further spur long-term growth.

In the first quarter, 3M faced the combined challenges of the sharp economic slowdown in the United States, a stronger U.S. dollar and a spike in energy costs. "We overcame these combined negative forces through continued strong international volume growth and aggressive management of costs," McNerney said.

The CEO told stockholders that 3M held sales, general and administrative costs flat compared with the first quarter last year, and that "We're committed to that same level of discipline for the rest of this year."

Future economic conditions remain very uncertain, McNerney said. "The U.S. remains weak, and while Europe and Asia Pacific were good for us in the first quarter, growth there is clearly moderating fast," he said. "Overall, there are no signs that economic conditions will improve anytime soon." Therefore, he added, 3M will maintain an intense focus on costs.

McNerney described a previously announced restructuring plan, which will result in an employment reduction of about 5,000 jobs worldwide over the next 12 months. "By selectively streamlining the organization, we make the fundamental changes necessary to sharpen 3M competitiveness, advance our market leadership across the globe, and build an even stronger 3M for the future," he said.

The CEO also described several initiatives launched recently to further accelerate 3M's growth. "At the top of my agenda is companywide implementation of the Six Sigma approach to process improvement," he said. Other initiatives

APPENDIX 3
(Continued)

include leveraging 3M's global size to drive down costs of raw materials and other supplies, reducing indirect costs, increasing returns on electronic-commerce investments and accelerating the pace of new product commercialization.

Noting that 3M will continue to invest in research and development, McNerney described the company's participation in dynamic markets, such as touch screens and light management products for electronic displays, and a new class of proprietary immune response modifier pharmaceuticals. He said international market expansion also remains a key growth driver.

McNerney thanked 3M employees for their ongoing dedication and contribution. "Around the world, our people are creating opportunities, delivering innovation, accelerating growth and working hard to fully realize this company's tremendous potential," he said.

At the meeting, 3M stockholders elected the following three directors to the company's Board of Directors, for terms ending in 2004:

- Edward A. Brennan, retired chairman of the board, president and chief executive officer, Sears, Roebuck and Co.
- W. James McNerney, Jr., chairman of the board and chief executive officer, 3M.
- Kevin W. Sharer, chairman of the board and chief executive officer, Amgen, Inc.

Shareholders also ratified the appointment of PricewaterhouseCoopers LLP as 3M's independent auditors for 2001 and rejected a stockholder proposal regarding the board member nominee process. Proponents prior to the meeting voluntarily withdrew two additional stockholder proposals regarding executive compensation.

Source: 3M Public Relations, 3M Center, Building 225-01-S-15, St. Paul, MN 55144-1000, Phone: (651) 733-8805.

APPENDIX 4
Six Sigma puts 3M on fast forward.

Process improvement isn't new to 3M. In fact, 3Mers have been good at it for a long time. Then why is Six Sigma—a process improvement methodology being implemented across the entire company—starting to make such a difference?

To learn more about this new approach, the **3M Stemwinder** editorial team met with Brad Sauer, executive director, Six Sigma. Sauer and his team are responsible for providing Six Sigma strategies, tools, training and other related support to 3M business units worldwide.

In this interview, Sauer discusses the progress that's been made since Six Sigma was introduced last February, as well as Six Sigma's long-term potential.

Q. What progress has 3M made with Six Sigma?
We've made great strides in just eight months. We're changing the way we work and are starting to see some significant results. The numbers change daily, but at this moment, about 1,700 employees have been trained in Six Sigma. We have nearly 600 projects under way and more than 3,000 people worldwide are involved in Six Sigma project teams.

A number of projects are in the control phase. That means that the new process improvement is in place and functioning. The Six Sigma team measures results over a certain time period to make sure that the gains they've achieved will be sustained. At that point, the project is closed. We'll see many projects close in the next few months and hundreds of new projects start up.

Q. Are we still planning to train all salaried employees?
Absolutely. Eventually, every salaried employee will receive at least green belt training. Green belts are trained in fundamental Six Sigma methodology.

Training is project based. That means that business units first identify the Six Sigma projects based on their business priorities, and then we train the employees who will be working on those projects. We encourage employees to look for opportunities to identify and participate in Six Sigma projects—they're in the best position to do so. And you don't have to be a green belt to participate on a team.

APPENDIX 4
(Continued)

Q. What is the focus of Six Sigma?
Business and staff units are focusing on three areas: growth, cost savings and cash generation. We're making sure we are working on those things that have the greatest impact on the company. Six Sigma isn't something separate that is being added on to what we're already doing. It's changing how we work on the most important things. For example, all of the 3M performance initiatives have Six Sigma participation.

Q. What makes Six Sigma more effective than other process improvement efforts?
In the past, 3M had a number of different systems. Six Sigma provides a single approach and a common language we all can use to improve the way we get things done. And 3M employees have really jumped right into it. That's one of the reasons we got off to such a fast start.

When we use one system, it's amazing how much information we can share and how well we can leverage what we've learned. That's been a real eye-opener. Six Sigma is helping accelerate everything we do. We're building a foundation of knowledge. So what might have taken the first team two months to do, a second team working on a similar project can do in a few weeks.

Six Sigma is a very structured approach—that is, it forces you to get data and back things up. Data is very powerful. And the ability to make data-driven decisions energizes and motivates people. It takes the subjectivity out of the work and moves teams into action very quickly.

Q. Can you give us an example?
Sure. The 3M ESPE Division is a Malcolm Baldrige award winner—world-class in terms of process improvement. They used Six Sigma to help them understand a problem they were having in a manufacturing process. They had a low yield coming out of this process and weren't sure why. Experience and intuition led them in one direction. Six Sigma data led them in a totally different direction. They believed the data, changed the process accordingly and their yield has nearly tripled. That's the power of data.

Q. Does Six Sigma apply across the company?
Everything we do is part of a process, so everyone can apply Six Sigma to their job or function, whether in manufacturing, sales, customer service, accounting, marketing—you name it. All processes have variations and can be improved. Six Sigma is a structured way to look at the problems in the process and reduce those variations.

Six Sigma can pay off in virtually any discipline. There are three keys to success. First, you need leaders who are totally committed and involved. Next, you need to make sure you're working on the most important things. And, finally, you need smart, motivated employees who can apply it. We've got all these things working for us at 3M.

Moving into New Dimensions, New Directions

Q. How will 3M customers benefit from Six Sigma?
One of the really exciting things about Six Sigma is that all of our key constituents benefit. Shareholders will see a strong, financially healthy company—a good, solid investment. Employees will be excited about their work, learning new processes, developing leadership skills. Customers will see a much more responsive 3M, a faster 3M, a 3M that can better serve them with more competitive products and services, more uniformity, and more consistent quality.

Even a project that appears to be internally focused can have a significant customer impact. For example, we have a number of projects focused on improving our receivables. When there's an error on an invoice, it doesn't get paid as promptly. Reducing the defects—the variations in that process—makes it easier for customers to do business with 3M. It's less aggravating for them and we get paid on time. It's a win for the customer and a win for us.

Q. How do you measure success?
We'll measure success in terms of the impact Six Sigma projects have on growth, cost and cash. By the end of our second year, we expect to see operating income improve by $300 million to $450 million. And we anticipate generating an additional $250 million to $400 million in cash. Right now, we're measuring data on training, such as how many people we are training versus what we think we need. We look at the effectiveness of training, the number of projects we have in progress and completed, and how they're doing.

Q. Given the continued downturn in the economy, it seems that Six Sigma is even more important now.
Absolutely. Six Sigma is even more important given the uncertainty of the external environment. Six Sigma is about controlling our destiny and doing what we can. Our commitment is unwavering, if not increasing. We'll need more Six Sigma projects. And we'll need to maintain our control plans and not lose any of the gains we've made.

APPENDIX 4
(Continued)

Q. What are Super Y's and why are they important?

In Six Sigma terms, "Y" is the output of a process. And we have a number of different areas at 3M where we have common Y's—that is, we have similar projects working to improve the same process output.

To date, we have identified three corporate-level Super Y's—DSO (Days Sales Outstanding), inventory and commercialization cycle time. For example, that means there are Six Sigma inventory projects taking place all across 3M. Work on these projects continues and produces results. But, in addition, we are bringing all of the inventory projects together, creating a larger, virtual team. This is a Super Y.

We look at common learnings, common issues and common metrics. We create a new body of knowledge that is available to all of the inventory project teams. We're leveraging what we've learned in a big way. In effect, we're making the total greater than the sum of its parts.

As we spot the need, we'll add more Super Y's. And, in addition to what we're doing at the corporate level, there are other Super Y's at the market level or in a geographical area. For example, Europe has a Super Y on pricing.

Q. Is there one Six Sigma concept that is particularly important for employees to understand?

One of the most profound aspects of Six Sigma is a concept called entitlement. In Six Sigma, entitlement represents the absolute best possible outcome that can be achieved with a given process.

Sometimes that's determined by looking at a past history and asking, "What's the best we ever did, on that golden day five years ago, when the process produced something incredible?" Other times, we might look to the outside and ask, "Who's the world's best at this particular process and what are they achieving?" You set your project goal based on that view.

Q. Is that realistic?

Yes, it is. A lot of process improvement systems seek incremental gains. Six Sigma, though the entitlement concepts, makes you look at what your true potential or opportunity is in a totally new way.

Let me explain it with some hypothetical numbers. Let's say you have a process that has an output of 20 and you want to improve on that. In incremental terms, you might seek a 10 percent improvement—and achieve an output of 22. Or let's say you even double your output—and get to 40.

You might think that's great, but is it? Even a 100 percent improvement could leave a lot of opportunity on the table unless you know what the best possible outcome could be.

In this example, the best possible outcome—your entitlement—might be 80. With that in mind, 40 looks rather puny. In reality, you should be aiming for 80—the true opportunity. Setting your goals based on entitlement is one of the most powerful elements of Six Sigma.

Source: *3M Stemwinder*, October 30–November 5, Vol. 15, No. 30, 2001.

Teri Takai, Director of Supply Chain Systems, had set aside this time on her calendar to contemplate recommendations to senior executives. The question they'd asked was widely agreed to be extremely important to Ford's future: how should the company use emerging information technologies (e.g., Internet technologies) and ideas from new high-tech industries to change the way it interacted with suppliers? Members of her team had different views on the subject.

Some argued that the new technology made it inevitable that entirely new business models would prevail, and that Ford needed to radically redesign its supply chain and other activities or risk being left behind. This group favored "virtual integration," modeling the Ford supply chain on that of companies like Dell,[1] which had aggressively used technology to reduce working capital and exposure to inventory obsolescence. Proponents of this approach argued that although the auto business was very complex, both for historical reasons and because of the inherent complexity of the automotive product, there was no reason such business models could not provide a conceptual blueprint for what Ford should attempt.

Another group was more cautious. This group believed that the differences between the auto business and relatively newer businesses like computer manufacturing were important and substantive. Some noted, for example, that relative to Dell the Ford supplier network had many more layers and many more companies, and that Ford's purchasing organization had historically played a more prominent and independent role than Dell's. These differences and others posed complications when examined closely, and it was difficult to determine the appropriate and feasible scope for redesign of the process.

As she read through the documents provided by her team, she tought about CEO Jac Nasser's recent companywide emphasis on shareholder value and customer responsiveness. It was widely acknowledged that Dell had delivered on those dimensions, but would the same methods deliver results for Ford?

[1] Information on Dell included in this case was obtained by Ford from public sources, including the 1997 Dell Annual Report, the Dell website (www.dell.com), and from "The Power of Virtual Integration: An Interview with Dell Computer's Michael Dell" by Joan Magretta, *Harvard Business Review,* March–April 1998 (reprint 98208).

COMPANY AND INDUSTRY BACKGROUND

Based in Dearborn, Michigan, the Ford Motor company was the second largest industrial corporation in the world, with revenues of more than $144 billion and about 370,000 employees. Operations spanned 200 countries. Although Ford obtained significant revenues and profits from its financial services subsidiaries, the company's core business had remained the design and manufacture of automobiles for sale on the consumer market. Since Henry Ford had incorporated in 1903, the company had produced in excess of 260 million vehicles.

The auto industry had grown much more competitive over the last two decades. Since the 1970s, the Big Three U.S. automakers—General Motors (GM), Ford, and Chrysler—had seen their home markets encroached upon by the expansion of foreign-based auto manufacturers, such as Toyota and Honda. The industry was also facing increasing over-capacity (estimated at 20 million vehicles) as developing and industrialized nations, recognizing the wealth and job-producing effects of automobile manufacturing, encouraged development and expansion of their own export-oriented auto industries.

Although manufacturers varied in their degree of market presence in different geographical regions, the battle for advantage in the industry was fast becoming global. Faced with the need to continue to improve quality and reduce cycle times while dramatically lowering the costs of developing and building cars, Ford and the other large automakers were looking for ways to take advantage of their size and global presence. One element of the effort to achieve advantage in size and scale was a movement toward industry consolidation. In the summer of 1998, Chrysler merged with Daimler-Benz to form a more global automaker. In early 1999, Ford announced that it would acquire Sweden's Volvo, and there were rumors of other deals in the works.

Previously, in 1995, Ford had embarked on an ambitious restructuring plan called Ford 2000, which included merging its North American, European, and International automotive operations into a single global organization. Ford 2000 called for dramatic cost reductions to be obtained by reengineering and globalizing corporate organizations and processes. Product development activities were consolidated into five Vehicle Centers (VCs), each responsible for development of vehicles in a particular consumer market segment (one VC was in Europe). By making processes and products globally common, Ford intended to eliminate organizational and process redundancies and realize huge economies of scale in manufacturing and purchasing. Major reengineering projects were initiated around major company processes, such as Order-To-Delivery (OTD) and Ford Production System (FPS), with goals such as reducing OTD time from more than 60 days to less than 15.

Ford's new global approach required that technology be employed to overcome the constraints usually imposed by geography on information flow. Teams on different continents needed to be able to work together as if they were in the same building. Furthermore, in virtually every reengineering project, information technology (IT) had emerged as a critical enabler. The link between reengineering success and the company's IT groups was made explicit in the Ford 2000 restructuring— IT was placed within the process reengineering organization. In the supply chain area, there was general agreement that IT could also be deployed to dramatically enhance material flows and reduce inventories—substituting information for inventory, as the expression went.

As Ford 2000 unfolded, the Internet revolution unfolded in parallel, creating new possibilities for reengineering processes within and between enterprises. Ford launched a public Internet site in mid-1995; by mid-1997 the number of visits to the site had reached more than 1 million per day. A companywide *intra*net was launched in mid-1996, and by January of 1997 Ford had in place a Business-To-Business (B2B) capability through which the intranet could be extended in a secure manner beyond company boundaries into an *extra*net, potentially connecting Ford with its suppliers. Ford teamed with Chrysler and General Motors to work on the Automotive Network Exchange (ANX), which aimed to create consistency in technology standards and processes in the supplier network, so that suppliers, already pressed to lower costs, would not have to manage different means of interaction with each automaker.

On January 1, 1999, Jac Nasser took over the CEO job from Alex Trotman. Nasser had been Trotman's second-in-command throughout the Ford 2000 rollout, and had a longstanding reputation as a tough-minded cost-cutter and a capable leader. Even before taking the helm, he had begun to focus Ford senior management on shareholder value. In the period between 1995 and 1999, Ford had seen companies with fewer physical assets and much lower revenues and profits achieve market capitalization well in excess of Ford's. Corporate staff members began to study models such as Cisco and Dell to try to understand whether Ford could produce shareholder value in the ways that these newer companies had.

As the end of 1998 approached, Ford had amassed profits of $6.9 billion, employees enjoyed record profit sharing, and return on sales (3.9 percent in 1997) was trending solidly upward. The company was the world leader in trucks. It had taken over the U.S. industry lead in profit per vehicle ($1,770) from Chrysler, and it was the most improved automaker on the 1997 J. D. Power Initial Quality Study (in fourth place overall, behind Honda, Toyota, and Nissan).

FORD'S EXISTING SUPPLY CHAIN AND CUSTOMER RESPONSIVENESS INITIATIVES

Ford had a number of initiatives under way that were aimed at positioning the company favorably for success in integrating with the extended enterprise that also included suppliers and customers. In addition, there were historical factors that would need to be taken into account in any virtual integration strategy.

Ford's Existing Supply Base

The existing supply base was, in many respects, a product of history. As the company had grown over the years so had the supply base, to the point where in the late 1980s there were several thousand suppliers of production material in a complex network of business relationships. Suppliers were picked primarily based on cost, and little regard was given to overall supply chain costs, including the complexity of dealing with such a large network of suppliers.

Beginning in the early 1990s, Ford had begun to actively try to decrease the number of suppliers the company dealt with directly. Rather than fostering strong price competition among suppliers for individual components, there was shift toward longer-term relationships with a subset of very capable suppliers who would provide entire vehicle subsystems. These "tier one" suppliers would manage relationships with a larger base of suppliers of components of subsystems—tier two and below suppliers. Ford made its expertise available to assist suppliers in improving their operations via a range of techniques, including Just-In-Time (JIT) inventory, Total Quality Management (TQM), and Statistical Process Control (SPC). In exchange for the closer relationships and long-term commitments, Ford expected yearly price reductions from suppliers. While first tier suppliers had fairly well developed IT capabilities (many interacted with Ford via Electronic Data Interchange links), they were not able to invest in new technologies at the rate Ford itself could. Also, the IT maturity (understanding and modernity of technology) decreased rapidly in lower tiers of the supply chain. As more cautious members of Takai's staff had often observed, this supply base was different in its nature and complexity from Dell's supply base.

Another major difference between Dell and Ford was organizational. At Dell, purchasing activities reported into the product development organization. At Ford, purchasing was organizationally independent of product development and had been—historically and up to the present—a powerful force within Ford. Because of the sheer volume of materials and services that Ford purchased, a very slim reduction in purchasing cost could result in very significant savings. Consequently, purchasing was involved closely in nearly every product decision. Engineers were counseled to avoid discussing prices in interactions with suppliers, as price negotiation was the sole province of purchasing agents. How this might work in a more virtually integrated system was unclear.

Ford Production System

The Ford 2000 initiative produced five major, corporationwide reengineering projects. One of these was Ford Production System (FPS). Modeled roughly on the Toyota Production System, FPS involved a multi-year project that drew on internal and external expertise worldwide. FPS was an integrated system aimed at making Ford manufacturing operations leaner, more responsive, and more efficient. It focused on key attributes of the production process, aspiring to level production and move to a more pull-based system, with synchronized production, continuous flow, and stability throughout the process. One important part of FPS was "Synchronous Material Flow" (SMF), which Ford defined as "a process or system that produces a continuous flow of material and products driven by a fixed, sequenced, and leveled vehicle schedule, utilizing flexibility and lean manufacturing concepts." One key to SMF was "In-Line Vehicle Sequencing" (ILVS), a system that used vehicle in-process storage devices (such as banks and ASRSs)[2] and computer software to assure that vehicles were assembled in order sequence. By assuring assembly in order sequence, Ford could tell

suppliers exactly when and where certain components would be needed days in advance, and buffer stocks could be dramatically reduced. If such sequenced assembly could be kept level and if it was well forecasted, the benefits would be felt throughout the supply chain. The vision was of trucks constantly in motion throughout their lives, in continuous circuits between suppliers and Ford, stopping only to refuel or change drivers, feeding a process that worked like a finely tuned and smoothly running precision instrument.

Order to Delivery

Another key process Ford reengineering initiative was Order to Delivery (OTD). The purpose of the OTD project was to reduce to 15 days the time from a customer's order to delivery of the finished product—a significant reduction versus the present performance of 45–65 days. Ford took a holistic approach to the reengineering. Pilots studies in 1997 and 1998 identified bottlenecks throughout Ford's supply chain, including its marketing, material planning, vehicle production, and transportation processes. Ford's approach to implementing an improved OTD processes relied on several elements: (1) ongoing forecasting of customer demand from dealers—before OTD Ford had never officially involved dealers in forecasting demand; (2) a minimum of 15 days of vehicles in each assembly plant's order bank to increase manufacturing stability; gaps in the order bank are filled with "suggested" dealer orders based on historical buying patterns; (3) regional "mixing centers" that optimize schedules and deliveries of finished vehicles via rail transportation; and (4) a robust order amendment process to allow vehicles to be amended for minor color and trim variations without having to submit new orders. The OTD vision was to create a lean, flexible and predictable process that harmonized the efforts of all of Ford's components to enable it to provide consumers with the right products in the right place at the right time. Ford believed that success in achieving this vision would provide better quality, higher customer satisfaction, improved customer selection, better plant productivity, stability for its supply base and lower dealer and company costs.

Ford Retail Network

On July 1, 1998, Ford launched the first of its Ford Retail Network (FRN) ventures in Tulsa, Oklahoma, under the newly formed Ford Investment Enterprises Company (FIECo). Ford Investment Enterprises was formed to take advantage of the changing face of retail vehicle distribution systems in North America. FIECo had two primary goals: (1) to be a test bed for best practices in retail distribution and drive those

---

[2] A "bank" is a storage area into which partially assembled vehicles can be directed for the purpose of removing them in a different order than the order in which they entered (i.e., resequencing). An "ASRS" or "Automated Storage and Retrieval System" is essentially a multilevel bank (vehicles are literally stored on top of each other); whereas an ordinary bank provides some resequencing flexibility, an ASRS provides the ability to access any vehicle in the bank at any time. As might be imagined, to hold a large number of vehicles and allow them to be accessed randomly, an ASRS must be very large (roughly the size of a several-story building).

practices throughout the dealer network; and (2) to create an alternate distribution channel to compete with new, publicly owned retail chains such as Auto-Nation. Ownership in the FRN varied from market to market; in some Ford would be the majority owner and in others Ford would be the minority owner. In Rochester, New York, Ford was partnering with Republic—another large, publicly owned corporation. One of the principles of the FRN was to buy all the Ford dealers in a local market so that the dealers were in competition against the "real" competition (i.e., GM, Toyota, Honda), rather than with each other. The overriding goal was for the consumer to receive the highest level of treatment and to create an experience they would want to come back to again and again. Showrooms would have a consistent look on the outside, with customized interiors for the different Ford brands—Ford, Mercury, Lincoln and Jaguar. The number of showrooms would be consolidated to focus resources on creating a superior selling experience, while the number of service outlets would increase to be closer to customer

population centers. Ford expected personnel and advertising cost savings, as well as inventory efficiencies due to economies of scale and greater use of the Internet. Ford also believed that the FRN would provide an opportunity to increase business not just in new and used vehicles, but also in parts and service, body shop operations, and Ford Credit.

DELL'S INTEGRATED SUPPLY CHAIN

See "The Power of Virtual Integration: An Interview with Dell Computer's Michael Dell," *Harvard Business Review*, March–April 1998, pages 72–84.

THE DECISION

Takai perused the neatly prepared documents that had been provided by her staff. There was a broad-based comparison between Dell and Ford on many important dimensions (Exhibit 1). Virtual integration would require changes in fundamental operations; some of the changes, framed as a shift from "push" to "pull" processes, were identified in another document (Exhibit 2). Whatever she decided, she would have to do it soon. Meetings were already scheduled

EXHIBIT 1

Dell and Ford compared.

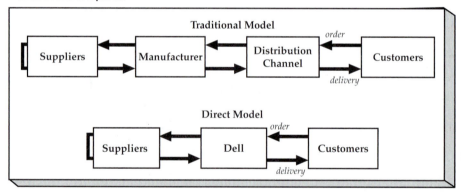

	Dell	Ford Automotive	Ford Fin. services
Employees	16,100	363,892	
Assets ($mils)	4,300	85,100	194,000
Revenue ($mils)	12,300	122,900	30,700
Net income ($mils)	944	4,700	2,200
Return on sales	7.7%	3,8%	7.2%
Cash ($mils)	320	14,500	2,200
Manufacturing facilities	3 (Texas, Ireland, Malaysia)	180 (In North and South America, Europe, Asia, Australia)	
Market capitalization ($mils)	58,469	66,886	
P/E	60	10	
5 year avg. revenue growth	55% per year	6% per year	
5 year avg. stock price growth	133% per year	33.4% per year	

EXHIBIT 1
(Continued)
Enterprise Model Comparison

A high-level comparison of the Dell and Ford Motor enterprise models is shown below.
Besides the lack of a dealer distribution channel, other key differences are Dell's ownership of
assembly plants only—all component/sub-assembly manufacturing is done by its supply
base—and the more integrated nature of Dell's Sales, R&D, and Manufacturing Operations.
All of the operating principles that underlie Dell's success have counterparts in Ford's
breakthrough objectives and key business plan initiatives.

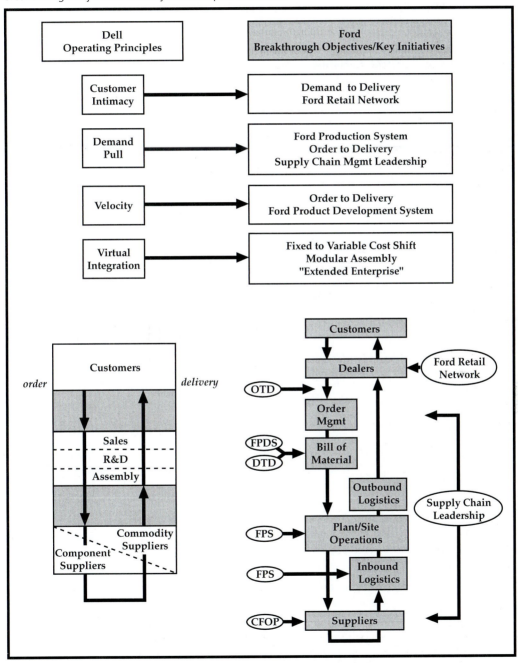

(continued)

EXHIBIT 1
(Continued)

Dell Processes	Ford
Suppliers own inventory until it is used in production	
Suppliers maintain nearby ship points, delivery time 15 minutes to 1 hour	✓
External logistics supplier used to manage inbound supply chain	✓
Customers frequently steered to PCs with high availability to balance supply and demand	✓
Demand forecasting is critical—changes are shared immediately within Dell and with supply base	
Demand pull throughout value chain "information for inventory" substitution	
Focused on strategic partnerships: suppliers down from 200 to 47	✓
Complexity is low: 50 components, 8–10 key, 100 permutations	

Sources: Dell 1998 Financial Report, Ford 1997 Annual Report, *The Wall Street Journal* Interactive.

EXHIBIT 2
Moving from push to pull.

	Process	Push	Pull
Design	Design strategy	Please everyone	Mainstream customer wants
	Vehicle combinations	More is better	Minimal
Marketing	Pricing strategy	Budget-driven	Market-driven
	Vehicle purchase incentives	Higher	Lower
Manufacturing and Supply	Capacity planning	Multiple material/capacity constraints, driven by program budget	Market-driven (no constraints, FPV/CPV +10% for vehicle, +15% for components)
	Schedule and build stability	Maximize production—make whatever you can build	Schedule from customer-driven order bank, build to schedule
Dealer Network	Dealer ordering	Orders based on allocations and capacity constraints	Orders based on customer demand
	Order to delivery times	Longer (60+ days)	Shorter (15 days or less)
	Inventory	High with low turnover	Low with rapid turnover
	Dealership model	Independent dealerships, negotiations with company	Company controlled dealerships (Ford Retail Network)

with the VP of Quality and Process Leadership, and from there the recommendations would move upward, eventually to Nasser.

Discussion Questions

1. What are the differences between the Dell and Ford supply chains?

2. Which ideas can Ford easily adopt from Dell's supply chain and which ideas would be more difficult?

3. How can Ford achieve an OTD of 15 days?

4. What changes should Teri Takai recommend in Ford's supply chain? Should she recommend radical or incremental changes?

eXcel Merriwell Bag Company is a small, family-owned corporation located in Seattle, Washington. The stock of the company is equally divided among five members of the Merriwell family (husband, wife, and three sons), but the acknowledged leader is the founder and patriarch, Ed Merriwell. Ed Merriwell formed the company 20 years ago when he resigned as a mill supervisor for a large paper manufacturer. Ironically, the same manufacturer formed a container division five years ago and is presently one of Merriwell's competitors.

COMPANY STRATEGY

The family attributes the success of Merriwell Bag Company to the fact that it has found a market niche and has no "serious" competition. Merriwell supplies stock bags to many small chain stores scattered over a wide geographical area. It ships the bags directly to small regional warehouses or drop ships directly to the individual stores. The family reasons that the large bag manufacturers cannot profitably provide service to accounts on that small a scale. In fact, Ed Merriwell formed the business with one secondhand bagging machine to provide bags for a small discount store chain and a regional chain of drug stores. These two organizations have grown tremendously over the years, and Ed Merriwell proudly points out that the bag company has grown with them. Today, these two original clients are Merriwell's largest customers.

The Merriwell family does not want its business to be too heavily reliant on any one customer. Hence, they have a policy that no single customer can account for over 15 percent of sales. In fact, Merriwell Bag Company encourages its major customers to establish alternative sources of bag supply for insurance against stockouts because of paper shortages, freight line difficulties, local trucking/warehousing strikes, and production problems that may locally affect Merriwell's ability to supply bags.

Merriwell does not aggressively pursue new bag customers, yet it has over 500 customers. The smallest customers order five bales per year (smallest order processed and shipped), and the largest order 15,000 bales per year. The number of bags per bale varies according to the weight of paper used and the size of the bag. Merriwell manufactures only pinch-bottom general merchandise bags, ranging in size from small 2" × 10" pencil bags to large 20" × 2" × 30" bags used for larger items sold in discount stores. They make no flat bottom (grocery) bags or bags that require sophisticated printing (specialty bags).

Bag labels are restricted to 20 percent face coverage and one ink color placed on one side only. Hence, Merriwell's central strategy is built around low unit cost production due to standardization, which allows a selling price that is competitive with the large bag manufacturers. At the same time, Merriwell provides the shipping and inventory services that are on too small a scale for most of the large manufacturers. The Merriwell family takes great pride in "taking care of" a customer who has an emergency need for additional bags or who would like Merriwell to warehouse a bag order for a given time because of storage problems at the customer's warehouse.

FORECASTING DEMAND

Providing this personal service requires tight inventory control and production scheduling at Merriwell's bag plant. A highly accurate demand forecast allows Merriwell to service the special customer requests by use of Merriwell's own warehouse facilities and routing schedules of the company's truck line. Heretofore, Ed Merriwell could manage the demand forecasting and production scheduling by "feel." Because of the ever-growing number of accounts and changes in personnel in customer purchasing departments, the accuracy of Merriwell's forecasting has been rapidly declining. The percentage of short-shipped accounts for particular types of bags is increasing alarmingly. Conversely, the warehouse is becoming overstocked with other types of bags. As a result, a severe demurrage penalty on three boxcars of incoming rolls of paper was recently paid because the paper warehouse was partially used to store finished bags that spilled over from the finished-bag warehouse. This caused a delay in unloading the boxcars until space could be created in the raw-material warehouse.

Demand forecasting has historically been difficult due to the seasonal nature of the product. There is always a surge in demand for bags prior to a holiday season. The exact timing of the surge in demand for particular types of bags depends upon customer stocking policies and the dates that holiday promotional activities begin.

The Merriwell family needs a forecasting method that would take this seasonal factor into consideration. Moreover, they want a method that exhibits stability because their market is relatively stable with a large number of repeat customers. Finally, they want a forecasting method that anticipates the growth patterns of their respective customers. A forecasting method with these specifications would

EXHIBIT 1
Monthly sales, 2000–2004.

	Sales (in number of bales)				
Month	**2000**	**2001**	**2002**	**2003**	**2004**
January	2,000	3,000	2,000	5,000	5,000
February	3,000	4,000	5,000	4,000	2,000
March	3,000	3,000	5,000	4,000	3,000
April	3,000	5,000	3,000	2,000	2,000
May	4,000	5,000	4,000	5,000	7,000
June	6,000	8,000	6,000	7,000	6,000
July	7,000	3,000	7,000	10,000	8,000
August	6,000	8,000	10,000	14,000	10,000
September	10,000	12,000	15,000	16,000	20,000
October	12,000	12,000	15,000	16,000	20,000
November	14,000	16,000	18,000	20,000	22,000
December	8,000	10,000	8,000	12,000	8,000
	78,000	89,000	98,000	115,000	113,000

greatly enhance the company's ability to service its market profitability. It is believed that if such a method could be applied to forecasting aggregate demand, the same method could be used to gain additional accuracy by forecasting demand of its larger customers. By having an accurate forecast of aggregate demand and demand of larger customers, the requirements of the smaller customers could be processed within the existing warehousing and shipping flexibility.

To develop such a method, the Merriwell family compiled the aggregate demand data shown in Exhibit 1. This data shows the monthly sales of bags for the past five years.

Discussion Questions

1. Develop and justify a forecasting method that fulfills the company's specifications.

2. Forecast aggregate demand by month for the year 2005.

3. In addition to forecasting demand of larger customers and aggregate demand, how might the accuracy of the forecast be improved?

4. What role should Ed Merriwell's feel of the market play in establishing new sales forecasts?

Case Study   Lawn King, Inc.

eXcel John Conner, marketing manager for Lawn King, looked over the beautiful countryside as he drove to the corporate headquarters in Moline, Illinois. John had asked his boss, Kathy Wayne, the general manager of Lawn King, to call a meeting in order to review the latest forecast figures for fiscal year 2002.[1] When he arrived at the plant, the meeting was ready to begin. Others in attendance at the meeting were James Fairday, plant manager; Joan Peterson, controller; and Harold Pinter, personnel officer.

John started the meeting by reviewing the latest situation: "I've just returned from our annual sales meeting and I think we lost more sales last year than we thought, due to back-order conditions at the factory. We have also reviewed the forecast for next year and feel that sales will be 110,000 units in fiscal year 2002. The marketing department feels this forecast is realistic and could be exceeded if all goes well."

At this point, James Fairday interrupted by saying, "John, you've got to be kidding. Just three months ago we all sat in this same room and you predicted sales of 98,000 units for fiscal '02. Now you've raised the forecast by 12 percent. How can we do a reasonable job of production planning when we have a moving target to shoot at?"

Kathy interjected, "Jim, I appreciate your concern, but we have to be responsive to changing market conditions. Here we are in September and we still haven't got a firm plan for fiscal '02, which has just started. I want to use the new forecast and develop an aggregate plan for next year as soon as possible."

John added, "We've been talking to our best customers and they're complaining about back orders during the peak selling season. A few have threatened to drop our product line if they don't get better service next year. We have to produce not only enough product but also the right models to service the customer."

MANUFACTURING PROCESS

Lawn King is a medium-sized producer of lawn mower equipment. Last year, sales were $14.5 million and pretax profits were $2 million, as shown in Exhibit 1. The company makes four lines of lawn mowers: an 18-inch push mower, a 20-inch push mower, a 20-inch self-propelled mower, and a 22-inch deluxe self-propelled mower. All these mowers are made on the same assembly line. During the year,

the line is changed over from one mower to the next to meet the actual and projected demand.

The changeover cost of the production line depends on which type of mower is being produced and the next production model planned. For example, it is relatively easy to change over from the 20-inch push mower to the 20-inch self-propelled mower, since the mower frame is the same. The self-propelled mower has a propulsion unit added and a slightly larger engine. The company estimated the changeover costs as shown in Exhibit 2.

Lawn King fabricates the metal frames and metal parts for its lawn mowers in its own machine shop. These fabricated parts are sent to the assembly line along with parts purchased directly from vendors. In the past year, approximately $8 million in parts and supplies were purchased, including engines, bolts, paint, wheels, and sheet steel. An inventory of $1 million in purchased parts is held to supply the machine shop and the assembly line. When a particular mower is running on the assembly line, only a few days of parts are kept at the plant, since supplies are constantly coming into the factory.

A total of 100 employees work at the main plant in Moline. These employees include 60 workers on the assembly line, 25 workers in the machine shop, 10 maintenance workers, and 5 office staff. A beginning assembly line worker is paid $7.15 per hour plus $2.90 an hour in benefits. Senior maintenance and machine-shop employees earn as much as $14 per hour.

It generally takes about two weeks for a new employee to reach full productivity on the assembly line. After three months, an employee can request rotation to other jobs on the line if job variety is

EXHIBIT 1

Profit and loss statement ($000).

	FY00	FY01
Sales	$11,611	$14,462
Cost of goods sold		
Materials	6,340	8,005
Direct labor	2,100	2,595
Depreciation	743	962
Overhead	256	431
Total CGS	9,439	11,993
G&A expense	270	314
Selling expense	140	197
Total expenses	9,849	12,504
Pretax profit	1,762	1,958

[1] The Lawn King 2002 fiscal year runs from September 1, 2001, to August 31, 2002.

This case was prepared as a basis for class discussion, not to illustrate either effective or ineffective handling of an administrative situation.

EXHIBIT 2

Line changeover cost matrix.

		Changed to			
		18"	20"	20" SP*	22" SP
Changed from	18"	—	$2,000	$2,000	$2,500
	20"	$2,000	—	$ 500	$1,500
	20" SP	$2,000	$ 500	—	—
	22" SP	$2,500	$1,500	$1,500	—

*SP denotes "self-propelled." Changeover cost includes the wages of the workforce used to adjust the assembly line from one model configuration to another.

EXHIBIT 3

Sales data in units.

	FY00 Forecast	FY00 Actual	FY01 Forecast	FY01 Actual	Latest FY02 Forecast
18"	30,000	25,300	23,000	22,300	24,000
20"	11,900	15,680	20,300	23,500	35,500
20" SP	15,600	14,200	20,400	21,200	31,500
22" SP	10,500	14,320	21,300	17,600	19,000
Total	68,000	69,500	85,000	84,600	110,000

desired. At least some of the workers find the work quite repetitive and boring.

The plant is unionized, but relations between the union and the company have always been good. Nevertheless, employee turnover has been high. In the past year, approximately 50 percent of the employees left the company, representing a total training cost of $42,000 for the year. There is also considerable absenteeism, especially on Mondays and Fridays, causing production disruptions. To handle this situation, six "fillers" are kept on the workforce to fill in for people who are absent on a given day. These fillers also help train the new employees when they are not needed for direct production work.

PRODUCTION PLANNING

The actual sales and forecasts are shown in Exhibit 3. Not only are the sales highly seasonal, but total sales are dependent on the weather. If the weather is good in early spring, customers will be more inclined to buy a new mower. A good grass-growing season also encourages sales during the summer.

It appears that customers are more likely to buy the high-priced self-propelled mowers in good economic times. In recessionary periods, the bottom-of-the-line 18-inch mower does better.

The production strategy in current use might be described as a one-shift level-workforce strategy with overtime used as needed. The workforce is not always exactly level due to turnover and short-run production requirements. Nevertheless, the policy is to keep the workforce as level as possible. Overtime is used when the regular workforce cannot meet production requirements.[2]

The actual monthly production output and sales for fiscal year 2001 are shown in Exhibit 4. Differences between sales and production were absorbed by the inventory. If stockouts occurred, the order was backlogged and filled from the next available production run. Lawn King utilized a 30 percent carrying cost per year for inventory.[3]

Each June, an aggregate production plan is prepared for the upcoming fiscal year. The plan shows the level of production for each model type and month of the year. The aggregate plan is used for personnel planning, inventory planning, and budget preparation. Each month during the year, the plan is revised on the basis of the latest conditions and data.

[2] Overtime work is paid at 150 percent of regular time.

[3] This cost includes capital costs (20 percent), obsolescence (5 percent), and warehouse costs (5 percent).

EXHIBIT 4
Units of production and sales, fiscal year 2001.

		18″	20″	20″ SP	22″ SP	Overtime Hours
Beginning Inventory		4,120	3,140	6,250	3,100	
Sept. 00	Production	3,000	3,100	—	—	—
	Sales	210	400	180	110	
Oct. 00	Production	—	—	3,400	3,500	—
	Sales	600	510	500	300	
Nov. 00	Production	3,000	3,800	—	—	—
	Sales	1,010	970	860	785	
Dec. 00	Production	—	—	4,400	3,750	1,000
	Sales	1,200	1,420	1,030	930	
Jan. 01	Production	4,000	4,100			1,500
	Sales	1,430	1,680	1,120	1,120	
Feb. 01	Production	—	—	4,400	3,500	1,620
	Sales	2,140	2,210	2,180	1,850	
Mar. 01	Production	3,000	3,000	2,000	—	1,240
	Sales	4,870	5,100	4,560	3,210	
Apr. 01	Production	—	—	2,000	4,500	—
	Sales	5,120	4,850	5,130	3,875	
May 01	Production	3,000	2,000	2,000	—	—
	Sales	3,210	3,310	2,980	2,650	
June 01	Production	1,000		2,000	3,000	—
	Sales	1,400	1,500	1,320	800	
July 01	Production	2,000	3,000	2,000		—
	Sales	710	950	680	1,010	
Aug. 01	Production	2,000	2,000		2,000	—
	Sales	400	600	660	960	
Total FY 01	Production	21,000	21,000	22,200	20,250	
	Sales	22,300	23,500	21,200	17,600	
End inventory (8/31/01)		2,820	640	7,250	5,750	
Nominal production rate/day (one shift)		420	400	350	300	

BACK TO THE MEETING
The meeting continued with Joan Peterson saying, "We must find a way to reduce our costs. Last year we carried too much inventory, which required a great deal of capital. At 30 percent carrying cost, we cannot afford to build up as much inventory again next year."

Harold Pinter added, "If we reduce our inventories by more nearly chasing demand, the labor force will fluctuate from month to month and our hiring and layoff costs will increase. It currently costs $800 to hire an employee, including the lower productivity on the line during the training period and the effort required to find new employees. I also believe it costs $1,500 to lay off an employee, including the severance costs and supplemental unemployment benefits that we pay."

James Fairday expressed concern that a new shift might have to be added to accommodate the higher forecast. "We are already at plant capacity, and the additional units in the new forecast can't be made with one shift. I want to be sure these sales forecasts are realistic before we go through the trouble of hiring an entire second shift."

Lunchtime had arrived and the meeting was drawing to a close. Kathy Wayne emphasized that she wanted a new production plan developed soon. "Jim, I want you to develop an aggregate production plan that considers the costs of inventory, overtime,

hiring, and layoff. If your plan results in back orders, we will have to incur greater costs later in the year to meet demand. I will not allow the same stockout situation that we experienced last year." The meeting adjourned for lunch.

Discussion Questions

1. Develop a forecast to use as a basis for aggregate production planning.
2. Develop an aggregate production plan by month for fiscal '02. Consider the use of several different production strategies. Which strategy do you recommend? Use of Excel will greatly save time in making these plans.

The World Industrial Abrasives Company produces grit used in the manufacture of sandpaper and other products. The production process starts with either aluminum oxide or silicon carbide as primary raw material, which is shipped to the company's crushing plant in railroad cars. The raw material passes through a series of crusher rollers, a furnace treatment, and screening operations to produce the finished grit in the desired sizes and shapes. The resulting grit can be glued to backing materials to form sandpaper and other abrasive products.

THE PRODUCTION PROCESS

A schematic representation of the grit production process is shown in Exhibit 1. Crude mineral is fed into a primary crush operation that produces a pea-sized grit referred to as "5 and Finer." Three pairs of secondary crushing rolls are available for processing the 5-and-Finer grit size; one pair is dedicated to aluminum oxide, another to silicon carbide, and the third pair may be used for crushing either mineral. Several different operations or machine settings can be utilized for crushing the 5-and-Finer grit size. Each secondary crushing operation normally produces three ranges of grit sizes, called splits, and a miscellaneous grit output. Because crushing operations cannot produce single grits, overproduction of some grits is often unavoidable.

Output from secondary crushing operations is normally heat-treated, giving the mineral the proper characteristics required for adherence to the backing. The capacity of this furnace treatment operation is the primary constraint on system throughput time.

Eight screening machines, each having several setups, are available for separating the furnace-treated splits into individual grits. It is the combination of secondary crushing and screening operations that determines the relative yield for each grit. A final sifting step, known as "dropping," purifies the individual grits. Approximately 10 percent of the input into the dropping operation is rejected because it is outside the quality tolerance range.

The buildup of both in-process and finished-grit inventories is an unavoidable consequence of the manufacturing process. The in-process inventory is necessary to decouple the various stages of production. The excessive finished-grit inventories are the result of the characteristics of the crushing operations, wherein single grits cannot be selectively produced. Storage of these excessive inventories represents another constraint on production. The limitations of on-site storage capacity require transportation of some mineral to a remote storage location at considerable cost.

A second unavoidable result of the production process is the recrushing of approximately 20 percent of the previously crushed mineral. Specific secondary crushing operations are dedicated to this function. The additional expense of these operations requires that original crushing and screening operations be chosen to minimize the need for recrushing.

Additionally, the difficulty of meeting the requirements exactly often results in the need to purchase finished, graded grit from outside suppliers at a premium price. This, combined with the problems of excess inventory and recrushing, requires the scheduler to make trade-off decisions. Recognition of the costs associated with each trade-off decision facilitates development of a production plan to minimize total costs.

EXHIBIT 1
Grit-crushing system-flow-process diagram.

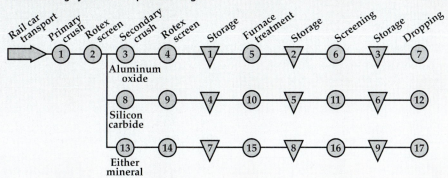

PRODUCTION SCHEDULING

Each week a printout specifying the amounts of each grit size required is given to the production scheduler. These requirements are generated by an MRP program considering final demand, inventory available, and production lead time. The scheduler's job is to determine the amount of input (silicon dioxide and aluminum oxide) and the best crushing and screening operations to be used to produce the required amounts of each grit size. In most cases, all requirements cannot be satisfied, but the scheduler attempts to come as close as possible to the required amounts of each grit size.

The development of a schedule for crushing and screening operations begins with the determination of net requirements by grit type. The scheduler analyzes the MRP requirements for an eight-week period, with primary emphasis placed on the next four weeks.

After reviewing the requirements, the scheduler selects a particular combination of crushes and screens and an input weight of silicon dioxide or aluminum oxide material. For these conditions the output of the production process is calculated. Performing the large number of calculations is a long and tedious process. The historical percentage outputs from each crushing and screening operation are obtained from a series of tables and used to predict the yields of the individual grits. Next, these yields must be compared with the requirements. If the yields do not compare favorably, the entire calculating process must be repeated using an alternative combination of crushes and screens. Because of the

time involved in performing the calculations, only a limited number of alternatives can be considered. Therefore, experienced personnel are required to select the preferred combinations in a few trials. All together, there are 19 different crushing settings, 19 different primary screening operations, and 4 secondary screening operations that might be selected by the scheduler.

THE PROBLEM

In assessing the situation, Judy Samson, a systems analyst in the manufacturing department, felt that the situation could be improved by use of an interactive computer program. The proposed system would assist the scheduler in evaluating crushing and screening options. If an optimal solution could be identified, that would be desirable, but optimality was not required by the scheduling department. The objective of the scheduling department was to meet the requirements for crushed mineral at a reasonably low cost.

Discussion Questions

1. Develop a detailed flowchart that replicates the manual method currently used by the scheduler.
2. Evaluate the advisability of using linear programming, simulation, heuristic rules, or the present scheduling method to solve this problem.
3. Develop a conceptual model to solve this problem. Specify the inputs, outputs, and computational algorithm you would use.

Joe Henry, the sole owner and president of the Consolidated Electric Company, reflected on his inventory management problems. He was a major wholesale supplier of equipment and supplies to electrical contractors, and his business hinged on the efficient management of inventories to meet his customers' needs. While Henry had built a very successful business, he was nearing retirement age and wanted to pass along a good inventory management system.

Henry's two sons-in-law were employed in the company. Carl Byerly, the older of the two, had a college degree in mathematics and was very interested in inventory formulas and computers. The other son-in-law, Edward Wright, had a degree in biology and was manager of one of the company's wholesale warehouses.

Joe Henry started the Consolidated Electric Company in the 1940s and built it into a highly profitable business. In 2004 the company had achieved $10 million dollars in sales and earned $1 million dollars in pretax profits. Consolidated Electric was currently the twelfth largest electrical wholesaler in the country.

Consolidated Electric operates through four warehouses in Iowa (Des Moines, Cedar Rapids, Sioux City, and Davenport). From these sites, contractors in Iowa, Minnesota, Nebraska, Wisconsin, Illinois, and Missouri are supplied with a wide range of electrical equipment, including wire, electrical boxes, connectors, lighting fixtures, and electrical controllers. The company stocks 20,000 separate line items in its inventory purchased from 200 different manufacturers. (A line item is defined as a particular item carried at a particular location.) These items range from less than 1 cent each to several hundred dollars for the largest electrical controllers.

Of the 20,000 line items, a great many are carried to provide a full line of service. For example, the top 2,000 items account for 50 percent of the sales and the bottom 10,000 items for only 20 percent. The remaining 8,000 items account for 30 percent of the sales.

The company has continually purged its 20,000 inventory items to carry only those that are demanded at least once a year. As Henry says, "We live and die by good customer service at a reasonable selling price. If we do not meet this objective, the customer will go to another wholesaler or buy directly from the manufacturer."

Henry explained that he currently managed inventory by using an "earn and turn" concept. According to this concept, the earnings margin multiplied by the inventory turn ratio must equal a constant value of 2.0. For example, if a particular electrical item costs $6 to purchase wholesale and is sold for $10, then the earnings margin is $4 and the earn ratio for this item is $4/$10 = .40. If this item has a turn ratio of 5 times a year (sales are 5 times the average inventory carried), then the product of earn and turn is .4(5) = 2.0. If another item earns more, it can turn slower; if it earns less, it must turn faster.

Each year, Henry sets a target earn-turn ratio for the entire business and a value for each product line. These targets are based on the estimated costs of operations and the return-on-investment goal for the company. As stated above, the current target ratio for the business is 2.0. The purchasing agents and inventory managers at each location are measured by their ability to meet the target earn-turn ratios on their product lines. The actual ratios are reported monthly.

Although earn-turn ratios work quite well in controlling profitability of the business and entire product lines, they do not work very well for individual inventory items. Some line items tend to be in excess supply, while others are often out of stock.

The inventory is currently managed by use of a Cardex system. A card for each item is kept in a large file, and a clerk posts transactions on the card as units are received or issued, thus keeping a running on-hand inventory balance. Periodically, a purchasing agent reviews the cards for a particular supplier. Then, using the order point and quantity printed on the card, the purchasing agent places an order for all items that are below their reorder point.

If the total quantities of all items required from a supplier do not meet the purchase discount minimums or a truckload lot, additional items near their reorder points are added to the order. This is not done when the total order size is too far from the minimums, since excessive inventories would build up.

The order quantity and reorder point printed on each card are based on judgment and past experience. Generally speaking, a three-month supply is ordered for low-cost items and as little as a one-month supply for expensive items. Most lines are reviewed on a weekly basis.

Over the past two years, Consolidated Electric had been converting its inventory records to the computer. At the present time, an on-hand balance is maintained on the computer, and an accurate history of all orders placed, receipts, and issues is kept. A demand history for a typical item is shown in Appendix 1.

This case was prepared as a basis for class discussion, not to illustrate either effective or ineffective handling of an administrative situation.

EXHIBIT 1

Formulas for calculating reorder points and quantities.

$$\text{Delivery delay} = \frac{\text{maximum lead time} - \text{average lead time}}{\text{average lead time}}$$

$$\text{Safety allowance} = \text{usage} \times \text{average lead time} \times .8 \times \text{delivery delay}$$

$$\text{Order point} = \text{usage} \times \text{average lead time} + \text{safety allowance}$$

$$\text{EOQ} = \sqrt{\frac{2 \times 4.36 \times \text{daily usage} \times 365}{28 \times \text{unit cost}}}$$

$$\text{Line point} = \text{daily usage} \times 7 + \text{order point}$$

Quantity to order = (order point) − (quantity on order) −(quantity on hand) + quantity allocated + EOQ

Note: The line point is used to generate orders for all items in a line which are within one week of their order points. These orders may be used to meet truckload minimums or purchase discount minimums.

Henry was anxious to automate the calculation of reorder points and order quantities, but he was unsure of the exact formulas to use. Using standard textbooks in the inventory field, Henry and Carl

Byerly developed the formulas given in Exhibit 1. The EOQ formula utilizes a carrying cost of 28 percent and an ordering cost of $4.36 per order placed. These figures were based on past cost history at the company.

The formulas were programmed into the computer and tested on a pilot basis. For some items, the formulas seemed to work quite well, but for others they resulted in drastic departures from current practice and from common sense. For example, on one electrical box, the formulas would have ordered a two-year supply. Henry wanted to get the new computerized system up as soon as possible, but he was not sure that the formulas would work properly. He wondered whether the formulas would meet the customer-service objectives of the business. Would they take advantage of truckload lots or purchase discounts whenever appropriate, and would the formulas result in reasonable inventory levels?

Discussion Questions

1. Design an inventory control system for this business.

2. Describe how the system you have designed will help the company meet customer-service and cost objectives.

APPENDIX 1
Demand history for a typical item.

PRINT1   AUDIT TRAIL

VENDOR-ABMO   CATALOG NO.-700N200A1   BRANCH-Des Moines

RECORD TYPE	CUSTOMER NUMBER	TICKET NUMBER	QUANTITY	DATE	UN	COST	SELL
SALES	12000-00	730606-0	1	8/10/04	E	16.32	21.60
SALES	19461-00	729425-0	60	8/02/04	E	16.32	18.72
SALES	22315-00	695421-0	65	7/31/04	E	16.32	18.72
SALES	34515-00	728883-0	2	7/30/04	E	16.32	21.60
SALES	02691-00	723670-0	1	7/24/04	E	16.32	21.60
SALES	02145-00	723482-0	1	7/23/04	E	16.32	21.60
SALES	81666-00	720920-0	8	7/23/04	E	16.32	18.72
SALES	02535-00	722026-0	4	7/20/04	E	16.32	21.60
SALES	81666-00	722637-0	6	7/16/04	E	16.32	18.72
SALES	01209-00	722413-0	7	7/13/04	E	16.32	18.72
SALES	81666-00	722409-0	8	7/13/04	E	16.32	18.72
SALES	23556-00	722001-0	1	7/13/04	E	16.32	18.72
SALES	51616-00	722418-0	3	7/11/04	E	16.32	21.60
SALES	81666-00	722408-0	6	7/11/04	E	16.32	18.72
SALES	26535-00	721861-0	20	7/11/04	E	16.32	18.72

PRINT1 S0015643   AUDIT TRAIL

VENDOR-ABMO   CATALOG NO.-700N200A1   BRANCH-Des Moines

RECORD TYPE	CUSTOMER NUMBER	TICKET NUMBER	QUANTITY	DATE	UN	COST	SELL
SALES	86190-00	721088-0	1	7/11/04	E	16.32	21.60
SALES	18954-00	722080-0	4	7/10/04	E	16.32	18.72
SALES	32550-00	698856-0	1	7/06/04	E	16.32	21.60
SALES	53726-00	722205-0	4	7/05/04	E	16.32	21.60
SALES	80925-02	721015-0	4	7/03/04	E	16.32	24.00
SALES	39132-00	721235-0	6	7/02/04	E	16.32	21.60
SALES	22315-00	695420-0	65	6/27/04	E	16.32	18.72
SALES	15951-00	713019-0	5	6/26/04	E	16.32	18.72
SALES	77137-00	712992-0	6	6/26/04	E	16.32	21.60
SALES	14468-00	713269-0	2	6/25/04	E	16.32	21.60
SALES	63180-00	701603-0	15	6/22/04	E	16.32	18.72
SALES	12000-00	709765-0	2	6/15/04	E	16.32	21.60
SALES	32550-00	709795-0	2	6/14/04	E	16.32	21.60
SALES	29058-00	710405-0	1	6/13/04	E	16.32	21.60
SALES	17862-00	710524-0	1	6/12/04	E	16.32	18.72

PRINT1S0015626   AUDIT TRAIL

VENDOR-ABMO   CATALOG NO.-700N200A1   BRANCH-Des Moines

RECORD TYPE	CUSTOMER NUMBER	TICKET NUMBER	QUANTITY	DATE	UN	COST	SELL
SALES	81666-00	699732-0	6	6/12/04	E	16.32	18.72
SALES	26535-00	710223-0	40	6/11/04	E	16.32	18.72
SALES	34515-00	710679-0	1	6/04/04	E	16.32	21.60
SALES	99940-00	710659-0	1	5/30/04	E	16.32	16.32
SALES	15951-00	699254-0	5	5/29/04	E	16.32	18.72
SALES	69576-00	710367-0	1	5/25/04	E	16.32	24.00
SALES	15951-00	695114-0	1	5/25/04	E	16.32	18.72
SALES	22315-00	695419-0	65	5/21/04	E	16.32	18.72
SALES	12051-00	701595-0	2	5/18/04	E	16.32	21.60
SALES	20631-00	701454-0	1	5/16/04	E	16.32	18.72
SALES	40315-00	701018-0	20	5/14/04	E	16.32	18.72
SALES	12051-00	700314-0	34	5/07/04	E	16.32	18.72
SALES	39132-00	700208-0	2	5/04/04	E	16.32	21.60
SALES	40315-00	691238-0	10	5/04/04	E	16.32	18.72
SALES	74607-02	699132-0	2	4/30/04	E	16.32	18.72

PRINT1S0015607   AUDIT TRAIL

VENDOR-ABMO   CATALOG NO.-700N200A1   BRANCH-Des Moines

RECORD TYPE	CUSTOMER NUMBER	TICKET NUMBER	QUANTITY	DATE	UN	COST	SELL
SALES	22315-00	689584-0	65	4/26/04	E	16.32	18.72
SALES	99999-00	698384-0	1	4/20/04	E	16.32	21.60
SALES	39132-00	695746-0	2	4/19/04	E	16.32	21.60
SALES	34515-00	695597-0	1	4/17/04	E	16.32	21.60
SALES	99999-00	695286-0	1	4/13/04	E	16.32	24.00
SALES	39132-00	695198-0	3	4/13/04	E	16.32	21.60

APPENDIX 1
(Continued)

PRINT1S0015607   AUDIT TRAIL

VENDOR-ABMO   CATALOG NO.-700N200A1   BRANCH-Des Moines

RECORD TYPE	CUSTOMER NUMBER	TICKET NUMBER	QUANTITY	DATE	UN	COST	SELL
SALES	12000-00	694933-0	2	4/13/04	E	16.32	21.60
SALES	36348-00	694138-0	2	4/11/04	E	16.32	18.72
SALES	99940-00	694352-0	12	4/10/04	E	16.32	16.32
SALES	40315-00	694047-0	25	4/06/04	E	15.36	17.52
SALES	19760-00	691495-0	5	4/04/04	E	15.36	20.16
SALES	17862-00	691365-0	5	4/04/04	E	15.36	17.52
SALES	17862-00	691364-0	20	4/04/04	E	15.36	17.52
SALES	34515-00	691409-0	1	4/03/04	E	15.36	20.16
SALES	83226-00	691303-0	5	4/03/04	E	15.36	20.16

PRINT1 S0015588   AUDIT TRAIL

VENDOR-ABMO   CATALOG NO.-700N200A1   BRANCH-Des Moines

RECORD TYPE	CUSTOMER NUMBER	TICKET NUMBER	QUANTITY	DATE	UN	COST	SELL
SALES	14966-00	691504-0	2	4/02/04	E	15.36	20.16
SALES	74607-02	689937-0	5	3/29/04	E	15.36	17.52
SALES	34515-00	690284-0	4	3/28/04	E	15.36	20.16
SALES	21333-00	690394-0	1	3/27/04	E	15.36	20.16
SALES	01209-00	689985-0	1	3/23/04	E	15.36	17.52
SALES	86190-00	690018-0	2	3/21/04	E	15.36	20.16
SALES	02535-00	689959-0	2	3/20/04	E	15.36	20.16
SALES	32550-00	670521-0	3	3/16/04	E	15.36	20.16
SALES	17862-00	683189-0	1	3/14/04	E	15.36	17.52
SALES	21333-00	681910-0	2	2/27/04	E	15.36	20.16
SALES	48477-00	682354-0	10	2/26/04	E	15.36	17.52
SALES	18954-00	682573-0	4	2/23/04	E	15.36	17.52
SALES	19461-00	682104-0	50	2/22/04	E	15.36	17.52
SALES	61842-00	681738-0	1	2/20/04	E	15.36	23.28
SALES	74607-02	678243-0	12	2/20/04	E	15.36	17.52

PRINT1 S0015573   AUDIT TRAIL

VENDOR-ABMO   CATALOG NO.-700N200A1   BRANCH-Des Moines

RECORD TYPE	CUSTOMER NUMBER	TICKET NUMBER	QUANTITY	DATE	UN	COST	SELL
SALES	74607-00	678239-0	7	2/20/04	E	15.36	17.52
SALES	74607-02	681673-0	5	2/19/04	E	15.36	17.52
SALES	02535-00	681458-0	2	2/13/04	E	15.36	20.16
SALES	63180-00	678329-0	12	2/12/04	E	15.36	17.52
SALES	99899-00	678188-0	1	2/07/04	E	15.36	23.28
SALES	99940-00	677897-0	1	2/02/04	E	15.36	15.36
SALES	40315-00	677869-0	8	2/02/04	E	15.36	17.52
SALES	79638-00	675976-0	4	2/01/04	E	15.36	17.52
SALES	19461-00	668836-0	10	1/30/04	E	15.36	17.52
SALES	39132-00	675497-0	1	1/26/04	E	15.36	20.16
SALES	72650-00	670481-0	25	1/24/04	E	15.36	17.52
SALES	39132-00	675474-0	10	1/23/04	E	15.36	20.16
SALES	15951-00	656858-0	2	1/15/04	E	15.36	17.52
SALES	22315-00	646309-0	100	1/15/04	E	15.36	17.52
SALES	67974-00	669143-0	2	1/12/04	E	15.36	17.52

PRINT1 S   ITEM INVENTORY FILE   Des Moines

VEND CATALOG NO.	DESCRIPTION	INV/CLS	CARRIED IN
ABMO 700N200A1	700N200A1 CONTROL RELAY	A	S

QTY. ON HAND	QTY. ON ORDER	QTY ALLOCATED	ORDER POINT	E.O.Q.		LEAD TIME
371	200	0	38	453	1	11
					2	10
					3	15
					MAX	20

QTY. SOLD BY MONTH	JUNE	MAY	APRIL	MARCH
	121	154	76	203
QTY. SOLD BY QUARTER	JAN–MAR	OCT–DEC	JUL–SEP	APR–JUN
	356	292	505	201

The following conversation was held between Joe Melaney, general manager and owner of the Toro distributorship in Galveston, Texas, and his son Joe Jr.:

Joe: I called you in this morning to discuss the future of the company. I feel that you should be involved in more of the decision making around here because you will be taking over the company soon. Roger Kirk, the district sales manager from Toro, will be contacting us next week for our spring season order. We will need to order for the entire irrigation line at that time. (See Exhibit 1.)

As you know, we have been undergoing a number of changes around the office. One of our major changes was acquiring the IBM computer system. A computer run I received this morning combined with the upcoming order date started me thinking about the figures from the new computer. I was thinking back on the circumstances that led up to the purchase of the computer a year ago in October 2001. With the way costs were skyrocketing, I had to cut down on my inventory without cutting service. The IBM representative said he could cut our inventory level by 30 percent, which sounded good enough for me. So I contracted with IBM for the new computer.

Max, our irrigation manager, swears by the numbers he gets out for order quantities.

When this package was put into our computer, they (IBM reps) said it was designed for me, but I'm not sure that I can trust it. You remember the problems IBM had getting it running. If they have problems like that, why should I trust it to tell me how to spend millions of my dollars?

Joe Jr: You mentioned that IBM designed the software for us. How did they select the decision rule used in determining the order quantities?

Joe: I can't answer that. The consultants that came in told me the best way to determine the order quantities for my company was to use an economic order quantity (EOQ) and a reorder point for every item. (See Exhibit 2.) They said this was the best because we have three set order points during the year. I'm comfortable with the order point, but I'm not sure of the EOQ. I can tell you how the EOQ was made for us. They based it on the demand quantities from the past four years. (See Exhibit 3.) IBM said that they did not see the need for any additional measures. They also said it would work very smoothly since it wasn't necessary to change the EOQ once it was in.

As I said earlier, I'm not sure of the EOQ. You know how I've depended upon my gut feel for the market in the past. I've always

EXHIBIT 1
Irrigation Products, Inc., current inventories, October 15, 2002.

Product Description	Current Inventory (units)	Current Inventory ($000)	FY 2002 Sales ($000)
Free controllers series 150—4 + 8	283	12	15
Customer controllers series 123—8 + 11	68	8	12
Monitor controllers series 176—11 + 23	51	15	26
3/4" + 1" valve globe/angle in-line	4,430	46	78
1 1/2" + 2" valve globe/angle in-line	281	6	62
Brass valves series 216	334	4	7
Pop-up bodies	50,841	20	77
570 series nozzles	90,056	14	68
Stream rotors series 300	2,043	13	144
Rain pros series 320	1,782	12	26
Gear driven rotary series 600	1,086	10	22
Gear driven rotary series 620	681	21	39
Gear driven rotary series 640	2,627	81	194
Gear driven rotary series 670	973	36	180
Totals	155,536	298	950

Prepared for use in class discussion by Roger G. Schroeder, E.R. Kunde, and Sue Flach.

EXHIBIT 2

Current computer system rules.

For order quantity size:*

$$EOQ = \sqrt{\frac{2AD}{ic}}$$

A = cost of placing an order, $

D = annual demand in units

i = "interest rate" for holding inventory for a year as a proportion of the unit cost

c = unit cost of the item, $/unit

EOQ = economic order quantity

For reorder point:

$$R = \text{average demand over the lead time} + \text{safety stock}$$

R is the reorder point where an order for more stock is placed. Currently, a 12-week lead time is used for all items in setting the reorder point.

*The current computer system uses a carrying cost i = 30% (20% cost of capital, 5% obsolescence, and 5% storage cost) and an ordering cost of $10 per order.

EXHIBIT 3

Demand for fiscal years 1999–2002.

Part #1-7287 Timing Motor with Gear Service Assembly (for Monitor Controllers)

Distributor net $12.00

Selling price $26.00

	1999	2000	2001	2002
Unit sales	30	19	22	31

Current inventory = 9 units

Reorder point = 16 units, EOQ = 12 units

Series 230, 1" Valves

Distributor net $10.35

Selling price $13.75

	1999	2000	2001	2002
Unit sales	5210	3650	4441	5673

Current inventory = 4430 units

Reorder point = 2070 units, EOQ = 173 units

Series 176, Monitor Controller

Distributor net $301.46

Selling price $400.00

	1999	2000	2001	2002
Unit sales	21	12	41	65

Current inventory = 51 units

Reorder point = 22 units, EOQ = 2 units

ordered parts based on past usage. Then I adjust the numbers according to how many golf courses I expect to be built or modified, and on the contractors'/installers' comments on how they expect the spring to go in terms of the number of installations. I also meet with friends in the building industry to see what they expect in terms of housing starts for the

EXHIBIT 4

Series 230 and 240—Automatic valves. 3/4" & 1" electric and hydraulic versions normally open, pin-type, 24 V.A.C. electric.

SERIES 230 & 240—AUTOMATIC VALVES
¾" & 1" ELECTRIC AND HYDRAULIC VERSIONS
NORMALLY OPEN, PIN-TYPE, 24 V.A.C. ELECTRIC

Application

- Underground automatic systems with G.P.M. demand of 1 G.P.M. to 50 G.P.M.
- Residential or commercial
- Electric systems
- Normally open systems—dirty or clean water
- Pin-type systems—clean water

Features

All
- Globe valve for easy installation
- Economical/competitively priced
- High flow/low pressure loss
- Manual bleed
- Smooth opening and closing
- Opens and closes at low flow and pressure
- Bleed ports protected with built-in filter

3/4"
- Corrosion resistant, glass filled nylon construction
- Small size, big performance

1"
- 230 series has manual flow control
- Corrosion resistant, Cycolac® and stainless steel construction
- Stainless steel reinforced solenoid
- Stainless steel collar over threaded 1" I.P.S. outlets

1"–230 SERIES
ELECTRIC or HYDRAULIC
with FLOW CONTROL

Specifications

3/4"
- 24 V.A.C.
  .36 amps inrush
  .18 amps holding
- Working pressure
  150 PSI maximum
  25 PSI minimum
- 3/4" I.P.S. male thread inlets
- Dimensions: 3"H, 4"W

1"
- Electric models 24 V.A.C.
  .400 amps inrush
  .200 amps holding
- Working pressure
  150 PSI maximum
  10 PSI minimum
- Dimensions: 230—6"H, 4 1/2"W
  240—4 1/2"H, 4 1/2"W

---

spring. My only other adjustments come if I think a particular product isn't moving. I feel all goods should turn over at least three times a year. There are two items I am worried about at the present time because of that exact problem. One is the timing motor with gear service assembly (Part #1-7287), a low-volume service part carried for repair of monitor controllers, and the other is the Monitor Controller (Series 176) carried as an "insurance" end product for a few specialized customers. (See Exhibits 4 and 5 for detailed descriptions of the Monitor Controller and the Series 230 valve.)

Joe Jr: I haven't heard you mention the problem of running out of products. We have been having quite a problem with running out of the Series 230 1-inch valve, a high-demand

EXHIBIT 5
Series 170—Monitor II automatic controllers: 11 & 23 station, hydraulic and electric.

SERIES 170—
MONITOR II AUTOMATIC CONTROLLERS
11 & 23 STATION, HYDRAULIC AND ELECTRIC

Application

- Heavy duty commercial
- Outdoor—wall or pedestal
- Parks—schools—cemeteries—condominiums—commercial buildings

Features

- 0–60 minute timing per station (infinite adjustment)
- 14-day programming capability—easy to set
- Automatic, semiautomatic, or manual operation
- Multicycling program—easily set
- Fused circuit protection—U.L. listed
- Dual programming on electric models (turf can be watered more frequently than shrubs)
- As many as four TORO electric valves can be operated on each station of electric models
- No time lag between stations
- Pump start circuit standard (can also be used as a master valve control circuit)
- Locks are provided for timing mechanism cover and pedestal cabinet door
- Supply line filter included on hydraulic models
- Hydraulic models resist freeze-related damage
- Controller can be operated manually even if the timing mechanism has to be removed (use Model 995-24 accessory for electric models)
- Built-in transformer on electric models
- Housing is heavy gauge steel, treated with rust inhibitor, and painted forest green
- Mounting template for easy installation in concrete included

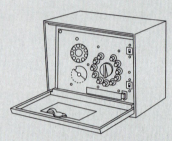

**CONTROLLER
SERIES 176**

Specifications

- 45 V.A., 24 V.A.C. transformer (built in)
- Lightning protection devices available for lightning prone areas
- Dimensions—Wall Mount 8½″ × 10¼″ × 8½″
Pedestal Mount 8¼″ × 12⅝″ × 31⅛″
- 115 V.A.C. input—24 V.A.C. output
- 2 separate ground wires required to utilize dual program
- Using normally open valves, tubing length from controller to valve should not exceed 1000 feet
- Refer to page 30 for maximum number of valves allowable per station and other technical data

part that we use all the time. How would you handle this in ordering? I know that we tend to disagree on what level of inventory should be held. I don't think you are carrying a high enough inventory level on all parts to satisfy our customers. You have always said it is criti-cal to the survival of the company that we have satisfied customers. I would tend to believe that this would require us to always have what our customers need on hand. The other problem I see resulting from stockouts is a loss of customers to our competitors. Any customer whose order

EXHIBIT 6

Irrigation division FY 2003 stocking program, terms for southern distributors.

Order Placement	Shipping Period	Dating Terms
33% 2002 Forecast Oct. 15–Oct. 30	December and January	1/2 May 15—net 1/2 June 15—net
33% 2003 Forecast Feb. 15–Feb. 30	May and June	1/2 Sept. 15—net 1/2 Oct. 15—net
33% 2003 Forecast June 15–June 30	August and September	1/2 Nov. 15—net 1/2 Dec. 15—net

EXHIBIT 7

Galveston market information.

SFDHH* $15–19M	SFDHH $20–24M	SFDHH $25–34M	SFDHH $35+	Total SFDHH	Total Population
228,545	182,607	151,110	89,375	757,000	3,640,000

Number of golf courses: 158
Number of golf course holes: 2,259
Irrigation potential market (in purchases from Toro):[†]

Small turf[‡]	$403,830	Number of cemeteries: 71
Large turf[‡]	267,048	Number of parks: 14
Parts	75,160	Number of schools: 170
Total	$846,038	

* Number of persons living in single-family dwelling households (SFDHH).
[†] This is an estimate of the market size for Toro in the area.
[‡] Small turf refers to residential installations while large turf refers to golf courses and other commercial installations.

we cannot fill will go to Rainbird, Weather Matic, or Nelson. Any of these competitors could supply the customer with comparable equipment, and once the customers have made the change, how do we get them back?

Joe: I don't have the storage capacity to carry enough inventory to protect ourselves from ever having a stockout. My philosophy has been that you can't always satisfy the customer from on-hand inventory. But you better be able to satisfy them 90 percent of the time. When you don't have it on hand, you can usually get it from another distributor. It usually is a fairly fast process because we fly the parts in. Too bad we can't place rush orders with Toro, but they hold us to their standard ordering policy (Exhibit 6).

That reminds me, we have to face a possible stockout problem this year. When I was at the country club last week, George, the general manager at the club, was talking about the number of times their sprinkler system had failed. George mentioned that he had spoken to the board about replacing the system. While the board wouldn't commit themselves until the annual meeting in December, George felt that it was going to be approved. If they installed the system, they wanted it ready to go by their annual tournament in early April. George said his first choice would be us if we could supply the system within the time specified. This contract would be a highly profitable one. As you know, the course is 390 acres, and the entire system would have to be replaced. The replacement system would rely heavily on the use of the Series 230 valves.

Because of the size of the club's system, I checked with my banker on the cost of financing. Bank notes were quoted at 18 percent. I'm not sure whether I should risk financing, so

EXHIBIT 8

Income statement (fiscal years ending June 30).

	2000	2001	2002
Net sales	$3,900,000	$3,500,000	$4,200,000
Cost of goods sold	2,800,000	2,700,000	$3,200,000
Gross profit	$1,100,000	$ 800,000	$1,000,000
Expenses			
Selling expense	$ 440,000	$ 272,000	$ 350,000
Operating expense	455,000	318,000	400,000
Fixed expense	95,000	100,000	115,000
Total expenses	$ 990,000	$ 690,000	$ 865,000
Net profit from operation	$ 110,000	$ 110,000	$ 135,000
Other expenses	$ 75,000	$ 60,000	$ 85,000
Income	15,000	10,000	25,000
Net profit before taxes	$ 50,000	$ 60,000	$ 75,000
Taxes	12,000	27,000	36,000
Net profit	$ 38,000	$ 33,000	$ 39,000

EXHIBIT 9

Balance sheet (fiscal years ending June 30).

		2000		2001		2002
Assets						
Cash		$ 10,000		$ 35,000		$ 5,000
Accts. receivable	$492,000		$ 622,000		$647,000	
Less doubtful accts.	17,000		22,000		22,000	
Net accts. receivable		475,000		600,000		625,000
Inventory		620,000		600,000		1,000,000
Total current assets		$1,105,000		$1,235,000		$1,630,000
Prepaid expenses		$ 30,000		$ 30,000		$ 20,000
Equipment (net of department)		35,000		40,000		45,000
Total fixed assets		$ 65,000		$ 70,000		$ 65,000
Total assets		$1,170,000		$1,305,000		$1,695,000
Liabilities						
Notes payable (to banks)		$ 207,000		$ 329,000		$ 700,000
Current position of long-term liabilities		20,000		20,000		20,000
Total current liabilities		$ 227,000		$ 349,000		$ 720,000
Long-term liabilities		160,000		140,000		120,000
Total liabilities		$ 387,000		$ 489,000		$ 840,000
Capital stock		$ 200,000		$ 200,000		$ 200,000
Retained earnings		583,000		616,000		655,000
Net worth		$ 783,000		$ 816,000		$ 855,000
Total liabilities and net worth		$1,170,000		$1,305,000		$1,695,000

I'm looking at cutting back in the spare parts area, where a lot of our cash is tied up. I figured that we have 25 percent of our inventory just sitting in the warehouse collecting dust. Many of these items are used by only a few of our customers. If I decide against the latter technique, we would have to rent storage space to handle the parts for the golf course installation. When I checked into this yesterday, I was quoted a price of $3.27 per square foot per year for rented warehouse storage space.

EXHIBIT 10
FY 2002 departmental analysis ($000).

	Total	Consumer Products	Commercial Products	Irrigation Products	Parts	Service
Net sales	$4200	$1800	$850	$950	$550	$50
Cost of goods sold	3200	1435	650	750	350	15
Gross profit	$1000	$365	$200	$200	$200	$35
Gross profit	23%	20%	23%	21%	36%	70%
Ending inventory	$1000	$275	$250	$295	$180	

To assist in determining the appropriate quantities and to get a little insight into the chance of the club's installing the system, I called the National Weather Service this morning. They stated they expected the driest spring in five years. I'm not sure to what extent this would affect the sales of the irrigation products. To assist in determining the effect of weather on the sales, I have gone over the demand figures and the corresponding weather for the last five years. In 2000 and 2001 I greatly overstocked. During these years, the weather was extraordinarily wet and cloudy. During 2002 the reverse conditions existed. It was an abnormally dry season, and we stocked out of most of our goods. (See Exhibit 7 for more market characteristics.)

Joe Jr: With a business that is subject to the whims of nature, why do you stay in it? Is it really worth beating your head against the wall to get the kind of return on investment that we have been getting? Even though we get a 25 percent markup on all irrigation items, the results do not always appear on the bottom line. Maybe we could manage our inventories better and really make the business worthwhile. (See Exhibits 8, 9, and 10.)

Joe: In the past I stayed in this business because I started the business. It's my baby. I felt a great deal of achievement from it. I've always planned to pass the company on to you and let you operate it. Now is the time for you to decide how you would run this company if you were in charge and if the return on investment is good enough for you to be satisfied. We also have to decide what to order from Roger Kirk when he arrives next week and what to do about using the IBM system. I have another meeting now, but I would like to get back to this discussion later.

Discussion Questions

1. What would you recommend that Joe Jr. do, assuming he takes control of Southern Toro?

2. Evaluate the importance of inventory and inventory management of the Southern Toro distributorship for both irrigation products and spare parts. Should the inventory be cut back?

3. Evaluate the current inventory management system at Southern Toro. What inventory management system would you recommend?

eXcel Dale Long, vice president of manufacturing for ToysPlus, Inc., finished reading the weekly production report for the week ended September 23, 2000. Inventories were up once again, and service levels were lower than expected. Dale wondered why these problems could not be solved once and for all. Last year he had installed a new IBM production and inventory control system on the company's mainframe computer. While the system drastically reduced inventories and improved service levels at first, things had gotten worse over the last few months.

Dale took the report and walked to Andrea Meline's office next door. Andrea had received her M.B.A. a few years ago from a prestigious business school and was now in charge of production control for the company. After exchanging the usual greetings, Dale asked Andrea why the latest figures were not better. Andrea responded, "Dale, we continue to get poor forecasts from marketing, and we have to carry more inventory than we would like in order to protect ourselves from unreliable vendor deliveries. The sales promotion that we ran last week on surplus toy trucks did not work as well as we expected." Dale interrupted, "Andrea we can no longer afford to achieve these kinds of results. You have got to find a solution. I am counting on you to come up with something to improve the situation. Otherwise we may both be out of a job."

BACKGROUND

ToysPlus is a small, privately held company in the toy industry, with sales of about $20 million a year. The company was started in 1951, manufacturing an innovative line of plastic toys and trucks that were very durable and low-priced. Over the years it has added several lines of toys and is now making 22 different toys, including games, dolls, toy vehicles, and novelty items. The company has a typical functional organization, as shown in Exhibit 1.

ToysPlus has had relatively poor financial results, as shown in Exhibit 2. Profits are only averaging 5 percent of sales, and return on assets is less than 10 percent. To improve the situation, the company has decided to make a major effort to reduce inventories and to improve customer service. In an effort to reduce costs, the company has begun to redesign the toys for manufacturability and automate its production process. The company feels that unit production costs could be reduced at least 5 percent per year by these efforts. The company also wants to achieve at least 15 inventory turns per year[1] and a service level of 95 percent. Service level is defined as the percentage of orders filled within one week of customer order. The current service level is 90 percent.

Manufacturing operations are organized around the different types of toys that are manufactured. Each type of toy has its own assembly line and its own dedicated workers. For example, three plastic toys—trucks, autos, and robots—are assembled on line 1. Only one toy can be assembled at a time on this line; then there is a changeover to the next toy. Currently, line 1 has 10 workers who engage in assembly, inspection, and packing of the toys. Some of the parts that are assembled into the finished toys are made on the company's plastic-molding machines. Other parts are purchased from outside suppliers.

[1] Inventory turns are based on the ratio of COGS to inventory.

EXHIBIT 1
Organization chart.

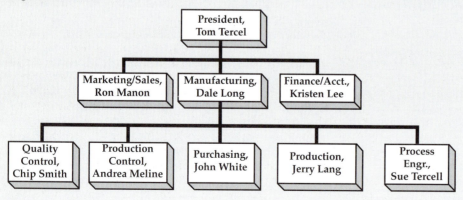

This case was prepared as a basis for class discussion, not to illustrate either effective or ineffective handling of an administrative situation.

EXHIBIT 2
Financial statements.

Profit and Loss (in $000) Year Ending June 30, 2000		Balance Sheet (in $000) As of June 30, 2000	
Net Sales	$20,100	**Assets**	
Cost of goods sold		Current assets %	
Direct labor	$2,353	Cash	$ 1,050
Materials	6,794	Accounts receivable	2,500
Overhead	2,608	Inventory	2,400
Total COGS	$11,755	Other	540
		Total curr. assets	$6,490
Gross profit	$ 8,345	Fixed assets	
		Net fixed assets	4,900
G&A expense	4,932		
Marketing costs	1,776	Total assets	$ 11,390
Profit before tax	$ 1,637	**Liabilities**	
Income tax	650	Current liabilities	
Net profit	$ 987	Notes payable	$ 3,300
		Accounts payable	3,200
		Accruals	400
		Total curr. liab.	$ 6,900
		Long-term debt	2,300
		Total liabilities	$ 9,200
		Capital stock	$ 1,500
		Retained earnings	690
		Total net worth	$ 2,190
		Total liabilities and net worth	$11, 390

Production control is based on the IBM MRP system. Every week a master schedule is prepared for the next six weeks. This master schedule specifies for assembly line 1, for example, the number of trucks, autos, and robots that will be produced in each week, as shown in Exhibit 3. Forecasts of weekly demand are received each week from marketing. Based on past experience, these forecasts are adjusted by Andrea to reflect more realistic estimates of demand. She also utilizes the lot sizes shown in the Exhibit 3 master schedule for each of the three toys. These lot sizes are based on past practice in the company. A run-out time philosophy is used to first schedule the toy that has the lowest ratio of inventory to weekly demand (the run-out time). As a result, the master schedule is prepared and entered into the computer. However, this master schedule might be infeasible when not enough parts are available in inventory or insufficient lead time remains to order more parts. As a result, the master schedule is checked for feasibility and adjusted accordingly before a final master schedule is approved.

The computer performs a parts explosion using the bill of materials and the on-hand inventories shown in Exhibit 4. Each toy requires several parts, as indicated in the bill of materials. For example, each auto requires one body, four wheels, two side windows, and one windshield. These parts are assembled, the product is inspected, and the toy is packed, which requires a total of .1 labor hour per auto. With 10 people working on the assembly line, at present, there are 350 hours of productive time available per week (35 hours each times 10). If the entire week is used to make autos, a total of 3,500 autos can be produced (350/.1). It takes .2 hour to make a truck and .15 hour to make a robot, thereby making it possible to produce a maximum of 1,750 trucks or 2,333 robots, if the entire line is devoted to either of these products. Production, however, is scheduled in lots, and the entire week is not necessarily devoted to only one toy.

In between products it takes all 10 people one hour to change the setup of the line. This changeover involves moving out the parts for the old toy, moving in the parts for the new toy, arranging the jigs and fixtures for assembly, and making trial runs to make sure that quality is right. The shop labor rate is $6 per hour for wages, fringe benefits

EXHIBIT 3

Master schedule prepared September 19, 2000.

	Week Beginning					
	Sept. 26	Oct. 3	Oct. 10	Oct. 17	Oct. 24	Oct. 31
Auto	3,500	500				3,500
Truck		1,500	1,750			
Robot				2,333	2,333	

Weekly Forecast of Demand

	Week Beginning					
	Sept. 26	Oct. 3	Oct. 10	Oct. 17	Oct. 24	Oct. 31
Auto	1,100	1,150	1,200	1,300	1,400	1,500
Truck	500	450	400	350	300	300
Robot	700	650	650	625	625	600

Products

Toy auto   Toy truck   Toy robot

EXHIBIT 4

Bill of materials.

Part Number	Description	Number Required per Unit	Cost Each	Weeks Lead Time	Current Inventory	On Order
1019	Toy auto		$3.20	1	4,000	
523	Car body	1	1.45	3	2,500	
525	Wheels	4	.30	2	9,800	
529	Side windows	2	.15	1	4,300	
531	Windshield	1	.25	2	2,620	
1021	Toy truck		$6.50		2,000	
615	Cab	1	1.70	3	1,200	800 due 10/3
617	Wheels dual	8 sets	.25	2	9,900	
619	Wheels single	2	.30	2	2,500	
621	Trailer	1	2.20	4	4,600	1,200 due 10/10
1023	Toy robot		$4.10	1	1,500	
730	Body	1	1.80	2	1,600	
732	Arms	2	.35	2	3,500	
734	Legs	2	.25	1	4,020	
736	Head	1	1.10	2	2,150	

are 33 percent additional, and there is $6 per hour charged for overhead. It costs 25 percent to carry inventory for a year. For parts and components that are ordered, it costs $25 to place each order. When the line is changed over, not only is a setup cost incurred for the labor to change the line but also an order is also triggered for each of the parts that is used to make the final product. The total setup cost of a line changeover is therefore the total of these costs.

Purchasing does not always buy the exact number of parts that are ordered by the production control department. Adjustments are made to take advantage of price breaks from suppliers or to achieve full-truckload shipments. As a result, some additional parts might be purchased in order to reduce purchasing costs. Also, suppliers do not always ship the component parts when promised. As a result, Toys-Plus carries safety stock inventory to protect the master production schedule and to keep the assembly lines running, no matter what. About one week of safety stock is carried to protect for late supplier deliveries. Management has mandated that the assembly lines will not shut down.

Dale Long has stated that the company will not lay off workers on a week-to-week basis. Thus, if demand should be less than capacity, for example by 10 percent in a week, production will be scheduled to full capacity to keep the workers busy. If this condition should continue for several weeks, workers will be laid off to adjust capacity. In a similar way, workers will be put on overtime to meet demand temporarily. But if demand exceeds normal capacity for several weeks, more workers will then be added.

A six-week rolling production schedule, based on existing capacity and lead times, is used. Each week one more week is added to keep the total master schedule horizon at six weeks. Production is adjusted each week in line with available parts, capacity, and observed demand for toys.

HAPPY HOUR

Andrea walked to General Joe's, a favorite watering hole, for happy hour with her friend from purchasing, John White. Andrea began,

> John, I don't know what I am going to do. Dale Long has laid the law down that I must reduce inventory and improve service levels. There is no alternative or excuses this time, I must do it! I'm not sure where to start. I

would like better sales forecasts, but is that realistic to expect? Can I depend on marketing? I also could reduce inventory by achieving more reliable deliveries from our suppliers. Will they cooperate? Maybe we will have to react faster in laying off and hiring workers in order to keep capacity closer to demand. What do you think of this situation? Is there a solution?

John answered,

> You must remember, Andrea, the world is filled with hustlers and liars. The salespeople lie to you about forecasts, so they can have more inventory, just in case they need it. We in purchasing lie to our suppliers about when we need the parts, so that we can be sure to get them when we really need them. You pad the production schedule a little bit, just to make sure you can meet the shipments. We all are trying to cover ourselves so that we don't run out of stock. There isn't a solution to this problem, because we are dealing with human nature. I hate to say it, but maybe top management's expectations are a bit unrealistic that inventory should be reduced and service improved. How can they expect anyone to accomplish these goals in an environment like this?

Discussion Questions

1. Calculate economic order quantities for each of the three types of toys. The EOQ formula is recommended from the supplement to Chapter 15 that considers uniform lot delivery of the toys.

2. Prepare a master production schedule for the next six weeks using the EOQs calculated in question 1 and a workforce of 10 employees. What inventory turnover ratio is achieved by this master schedule? How does this turnover compare with past levels and with management's goals?

3. Prepare a parts explosion to support the master schedule. What parts should be ordered each week?

4. What should Andrea Meline do to meet the inventory and service goals stated by management?

5. How should Andrea deal with the organization issues presented in this case?

Clem Hawkins, director of manufacturing for U.S. Stroller, leaned back in his chair as he thought about the events of the past two weeks. The president of the company, Judy Hawkins, Clem's sister, had just returned from a conference on JIT manufacturing at the University of North Carolina. After the conference, she commented to Clem,

> We have got to do something about the high inventories, poor customer service, and high costs. I think that a JIT approach would work fine for our manufacturing plant. At the conference in North Carolina we heard of many companies that have used JIT as a way to reduce cycle time, improve quality, and ultimately reduce inventory and cost. In our industry, the competition is looking for our business, and unless we do something now, we may lose our market share and margins. Clem, I want you to take a close look at the plant and get back to me on how we can go about implementing a JIT approach.

BACKGROUND

U.S. Stroller is a leader in the production and sales of baby strollers in the United States. It has historically made very high quality strollers that sell at a premium price. The company is known for its innovative designs and its good distribution system. U.S. Strollers are sold through major department stores, discount stores, and baby equipment stores. Altogether, 2,000 different sites in the United States distribute the company's products.

U.S. Stroller has been a market leader for over 50 years. At the present time it has 40 percent of the U.S. market, a competitor Graco has 20 percent of the market, and Kolcraft has 10 percent of the market. Various other companies, each with less than a 10 percent share, have the remainder of the market, including two Japanese companies that have just entered the U.S. market. The Japanese companies seem to be selling a low-price stroller that emphasizes quality and reliability of design.

U.S. Stroller started its business in 1934 with the introduction of the regular model that it still makes. While the regular model has been updated over the years for differences in fabric and style, the basic design is still the same. The regular model folds easily for storage or transportation and sells for $49 retail.

In 1955, the company introduced a deluxe model that sells for a premium price and is oriented to the upscale market. This model features a design that permits the stroller to be converted to a baby carriage as well as folding for storage or transporting. It also has an adjustable footrest, a storage basket, and locking dual front-swivel wheels. This deluxe model sells for $99 retail (see Exhibit 1 for an illustration).

In 1974, the company introduced its shopping center stroller. This model is very heavy duty, it does not fold, and it stands up well to the abuse that strollers take in shopping centers. The shopping center model sells for $149 and has been extensively marketed in the United States.

Currently, the company is selling 106,000 units per year of the three types of strollers. The amount of each type sold is shown in Exhibit 2. These amounts are divided by 52 to arrive at an average weekly usage. Sales are, of course, irregular and can vary by 25 percent from the average weekly volumes shown in Exhibit 2. Production is leveled, to the extent possible, to attain a level workforce.

The financial statements for U.S. Stroller are shown in Exhibit 3. Sales are approximately $4.5 million per year. The gross profit is 25 percent of sales, and the net profit, after tax, for the fiscal year 2005 was a disappointing 2 percent of sales. Profits have been dropping over the past two years because of price decreases and the inability to maintain margins. The balance sheet in Exhibit 3 shows that inventories are turning very slowly, at a rate of 2.4 times per year. The plant is fairly automated and includes up-to-date equipment. On an after-tax basis the company has earned 3 percent on net assets and 8 percent on owner's equity. U.S. Stroller is a privately held company.

PLANT DESCRIPTION

Strollers made by the company consist of from 20 to 30 different parts. The frame is made out of chrome-plated tubing. The tubing is bought in standard lengths and then cut to size, bent to the proper shape, and drilled with holes for assembly. Each stroller has about 10 pieces of tubing that are assembled into the final frame. Wheels for the strollers are bought from an outside vendor and attached to the tube frames. The padded seats and backs are also purchased from outside. The strollers have a plywood insert inside the seat and in the back to give added strength. These plywood pieces are cut from large 4 × 8 foot sheets by the company and then inserted into the purchased fabric pieces. U.S. Stroller also buys

This case was prepared as a basis for class discussion, not to illustrate either effective or ineffective handling of an administrative situation.

EXHIBIT 1

U.S. Stroller products.

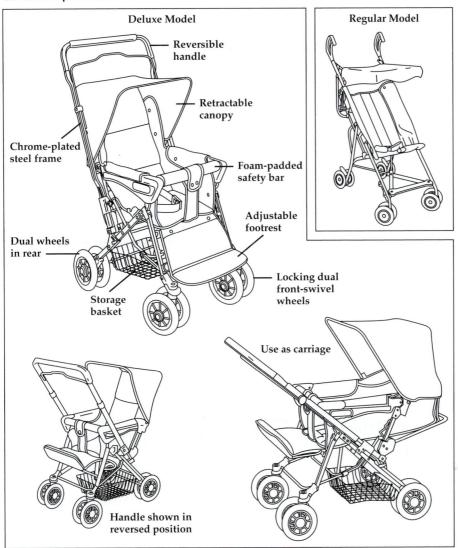

Deluxe Model

- Reversible handle
- Retractable canopy
- Chrome-plated steel frame
- Foam-padded safety bar
- Adjustable footrest
- Dual wheels in rear
- Storage basket
- Locking dual front-swivel wheels

Regular Model

Use as carriage

Handle shown in reversed position

EXHIBIT 2

Sales volumes.

	Annual Sales	Average Weekly Sales
Regular	54,000	1,040
Deluxe	24,960	480
Shopping center	27,040	520
Total	106,000	2,040

other parts needed to make a stroller, including plastic parts, bolts, fasteners, wire baskets, and so forth. Altogether, about 50 percent of the cost of a stroller consists of materials that are purchased from outside.

The plant layout has several work centers, shown in Exhibit 4. These work centers include a tube-cutting department with six nearly identical tube-cutting machines. After the tubes are cut, they are placed in tube inventory until they are needed by the tube-bending work center or the drilling work center. Tubes that require special shapes are bent by the two presses in the bending department. Bent tubes and straight tubes are taken to the drilling department and drilled with the proper holes. Jigs are used to speed up the process and to ensure that the holes are located in the right places. The drilled tubes are then put back into inventory until they are needed by final assembly. There are a total of 10 different drilling machines in the drilling work center.

EXHIBIT 3
Financial statements ($000)—fiscal year ended July 1, 2005.

Income Statement			Balance Sheet		
Sales		$4,558	Assets		
			Cash		$106
Cost of goods			Accounts rec.		480
Materials		$1,682	Inventory		1,424
Labor		894	Net plant		987
Overhead		842	Total assets		$2,997
Total		$3,418	Liabilities		
			Notes payable		$1,200
Gross profit		$1,140	Long-term debt		697
Sales expense		$ 462	Owner's equity		1,100
G&A expenses		493	Total L&OE		$2,997
Subtotal		$ 955			
Profit before tax		$ 185			
Profit after tax		91			

EXHIBIT 4
Plant layout.

EXHIBIT 5
Setup time for regular models.

Work Center	Setup Time (hours)
Tube cutting	4.2
Drilling	2.4
Tube bending	1.6
Wood saw	.5
Final assembly	2.3
Total	11.0

Final assembly consists of one assembly line used for all three types of strollers. This assembly line is changed over from one model to the next according to the final assembly schedule. The woodworking department consists of one large saw that is used to cut seat and back inserts from large plywood sheets. These seats and backs are put into inventory until they are needed by final assembly. When final assembly is begun, all parts are in inventory or are expedited in order to make the required batch of finished product. Expediting is done both inside the plant, to get the missing parts, and with outside suppliers. This expediting is started one week ahead of when the material is needed in order to get all the material in-house to support the assembly schedule for the next week.

An MRP system is used to plan and control inventories. A master production schedule is prepared on a weekly basis for eight weeks into the future. The master schedule is then frozen for four weeks to allow time to fabricate the parts required and to get the parts in from outside suppliers. Any parts that are not there when needed are expedited during the last week, as described above. New orders are only placed in week 5 or later in the master schedule.

The lot sizes for each of the strollers have been developed by use of the EOQ formula. This is done by considering the setup time of equipment and the carrying costs of inventory. The plant is scheduled on a lot-for-lot basis. For example, a lot in the master production schedule of 1,000 regular strollers is translated directly into the parts needed to produce it. This would include 1,000 stroller handles less any inventory on hand or on order. Due to lot-for-lot planning, a setup on the final assembly line also directly induces setups throughout the plant in tube cutting, drilling, bending, and seat cutting. The total

EXHIBIT 6
Economic order quantities.

Model	D Annual Sales	C Mfg. Cost	S Setup Cost	P Prod. Rate*	D Weekly Usage	1 – D/P	EOQ†
Regular	54,000	$21	$165	2,500	1,040	.584	2,400
Deluxe	24,960	$37	$185	2,000	480	.760	1,150
Shopping	27,040	$56	$170	1,800	520	.711	960

* This is the maximum weekly production rate for a single product being produced.

† $EOQ = \sqrt{\dfrac{2SD}{ic(1 - D/P)}}$

cost of a changeover at final assembly is thus the cost of changing over the final assembly line itself, plus the cost of changing over all the other production equipment affected by the lot-for-lot calculations. As shown in Exhibit 5, for the regular model, the total setup time amounts to about 11 labor hours. The shop rate is currently $15 per hour, fully loaded. Therefore, a setup for final assembly of the regular model costs $165. Similarly, the cost of changeover for the deluxe model is $185, and for the shopping center model it is $170.

Setup time includes not only changing the machine over, but also bringing in new materials and taking out the old, then making a pilot run to be sure the machine is making good parts. While there are minor setups when making different parts for the same stroller, the major setup is associated with changing over from one stroller model to another.

The EOQ calculations are shown in Exhibit 6. These calculations assume a holding charge of 25 percent per year. Note that the resulting EOQ for the regular model is 2,400 units, which is approximately one week of production, since the line can produce 2,500 regular units per week when the entire line is devoted to the regular model. Likewise, the deluxe model and the shopping center model will each require about .5 week of time to produce an EOQ.

Using the EOQs that have been calculated, a typical master production schedule is shown in Exhibit 7. This master schedule is constructed as follows. Suppose the regular model is put into production first. Then a batch of 2,400 units of regular strollers is scheduled in week 1. But 2,500 units can be produced in one week, and so with five days of production per week, the lot of 2,400 units will take 4.8 days (2,400/2,500 × 5). It will then take an average of two hours per machine to change over the line to the next stroller (time that results in lost capacity). As a result, the rest of the first week is devoted to changeover. Next, the deluxe model is scheduled in

EXHIBIT 7
Master schedule for July 2005.

		Week		
Model	1	2	3	4
Regular	2,400		2,000	400
Deluxe		1,150		1,150
Shopping		684	276	324

week 2, which requires 2.9 days of production (1,150/2,000 × 5 days) for the EOQ to be produced. Then two hours per machine are required to change over to the shopping center model. This process of scheduling is continued, resulting in the master schedule in Exhibit 7.

Inventory is maintained in finished goods ($765,000), work in process ($322,000), and raw materials ($337,000). The finished-goods inventory is distributed through three warehouses located around the country. An average of 80 days of supply is carried at each warehouse. It takes four weeks to reorder from the factory and one week for transit. Some inventory is held in safety stock. Likewise, four weeks of in-process inventory is held to provide high machine utilization and to facilitate scheduling. The company also holds 12 weeks of purchased parts in order to facilitate scheduling with vendors and to prevent line stoppages.

OPTION 1: A PULL SYSTEM
In thinking about JIT, Clem Hawkins was considering two options. Option 1 involved going to a pull system of inventory control. Under this option, three separate final assembly lines would be set up, one for each finished product. This would eliminate changeovers at final assembly. Clem was also considering mixed-model assembly, which would have a similar effect. But this could be more complicated

EXHIBIT 8
Revised schedule—pull system.

Model	Week			
	1	2	3	4
Regular	1,040	1,040	1,040	1,040
Deluxe	480	480	480	480
Shopping	520	520	520	520

and would require development of some tooling for instantaneous changeover of the line from one model to the next. Of course, setting up three assembly lines, instead of the present one line, would require additional investment (about $200,000) for jigs, fixtures, and assembly tables.

If three assembly lines were used, the master schedule would be drastically changed to the one shown in Exhibit 8. Each week the same amount is scheduled to meet the forecast, thereby putting a uniform load on the plant. This loading is, of course, required for a pull system to work. Clem thought he could also reduce the length of time that the master schedule is frozen to two weeks. This will make it possible to drastically reduce inventories at the field warehouses, to about a 15- to 30-day supply. He would like to achieve the guideline that what is ordered from the warehouses this week is scheduled to be produced next week.

Setting up permanent final assembly lines with a pull system makes it also possible to dedicate certain equipment in the plant to each of the product lines (see Exhibit 9). For example, there are six tube-cutting machines. Since about one-half of the capacity is devoted to regular strollers, three of the tube cutters could be set up permanently for regular strollers. Clem would also need 1.5 tube cutters for deluxe models and 1.5 cutters for shopping models. This presents a problem: either one machine could be dedicated to each model, or two machines could be. If one tube cutter were dedicated to each model, then one machine would be kept to change over as needed between the various models. If two machines were dedicated to each model, an additional machine would need to be purchased. Also, in this case there would be little flexibility with all dedicated machines. In a similar way, some drills and tube benders could be dedicated to each model. But the saw presents a problem since there is only one saw. Either smaller equipment must be purchased and dedicated to models, or the saw could continue to be changed over for each product.

Using the pull system, Kanban containers will be used to move inventory from one work center to the

EXHIBIT 9
Pull system layout, dedicated equipment.

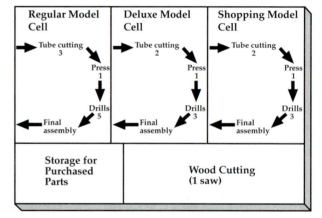

EXHIBIT 10
Cellular layout.

next. When the containers are full at a work center, all machines at the supplying work centers will be shut off, thereby limiting the maximum inventory to the number of full Kanban containers provided. The tube storage room will be eliminated, and all inventory will be held in Kanban containers on the shop floor.

A smaller storage room for purchased parts will be needed, but Clem did not think that he could supply all purchased parts directly to final assembly, at least not initially. But purchased inventories could be greatly reduced once the suppliers are also on the Kanban system. Purchased parts could be supplied on the basis of daily, or certainly weekly, deliveries for all A items and less frequently for B and C items.

OPTION 2: MANUFACTURING CELLS
In this option, a manufacturing cell would be provided for each model. The layout would look roughly like Exhibit 10. Each product would be

made in a U-shaped cell. In the regular model cell, there would be three tube-cutting machines, one bending press, five drills, and the final assembly line. This arrangement would have dedicated equipment located in close proximity to each other. Material would flow into one end of the cell and finished product out of the other end. Purchased parts would be delivered to the cell directly by the supplier or in kits from a central storage and kitting room. A kit would contain all the purchased parts needed to assemble one unit of the final product.

Two more cells would also be established: one for the deluxe model and one for the shopping center model. This would require two tube cutters, one press, and three drills in each of these cells in order to maintain the present capacity. Thus, Clem would need to purchase additional equipment (one drill, one press, and one tube cutter) at a cost of about $150,000.

There are several advantages to the use of cells. As things are moved closer together, visual control of each cell can be maintained. Any quality or maintenance problem would be readily evident. Also, the people working in the cell would gain an identity with the particular product produced. The cell takes less space and provides the advantage of fast feedback, since everything is in close proximity. Of course, a Kanban system would also be used to pull parts through each of the cells.

Many of the inventory reduction advantages described above would also be gained by the use of cells. As a matter of fact, the throughput from a cell might even be faster than the Kanban system described in option 1. As a result, less inventory would be required by a cell. On the other hand, a cell gives less flexibility to demand changes, since all equipment is dedicated to that particular product line.

SUNDAY AFTERNOON
During halftime of the Vikings and Bears football game, Clem could not help thinking about the options available for JIT manufacturing. He wondered how much each of these options would save in production costs and inventories. He also considered whether these options would have the same product quality: Would the cell produce a higher-quality product because of its close visual control? Clem decided that he would request a study of these options by his assistant, Joan Hankins. Joan had recently received her M.B.A. from UCLA and was a whiz at analyzing options such as these.

Discussion Questions

1. Evaluate the current situation facing U.S. Stroller.
2. Discuss the pros and cons of the options presented in the case.
3. What will be the impact of these options on the MRP system currently in use?
4. What option do you recommend and why?

Appendix **A**

AREAS UNDER THE STANDARD NORMAL PROBABILITY DISTRIBUTION

Values in the table represent the proportion of area under the normal curve between the mean ($\mu = 0$) and a positive value of z.

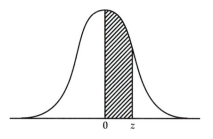

z	.00	.01	.02	.03	.04	.05	.06	.07	.08	.09
0.0	0.0000	0.0040	0.0080	0.0120	0.0160	0.0199	0.0239	0.0279	0.0319	0.0359
0.1	0.0398	0.0438	0.0478	0.0517	0.0557	0.0596	0.0636	0.0675	0.0714	0.0753
0.2	0.0793	0.0832	0.0871	0.0910	0.0948	0.0987	0.1026	0.1064	0.1103	0.1141
0.3	0.1179	0.1217	0.1255	0.1293	0.1331	0.1368	0.1406	0.1443	0.1480	0.1517
0.4	0.1554	0.1591	0.1628	0.1664	0.1700	0.1736	0.1772	0.1808	0.1844	0.1879
0.5	0.1915	0.1950	0.1985	0.2019	0.2054	0.2088	0.2123	0.2157	0.2190	0.2224
0.6	0.2257	0.2291	0.2324	0.2357	0.2389	0.2422	0.2454	0.2486	0.2517	0.2549
0.7	0.2580	0.2611	0.2642	0.2673	0.2703	0.2734	0.2764	0.2794	0.2823	0.2852
0.8	0.2881	0.2910	0.2939	0.2967	0.2995	0.3023	0.3051	0.3078	0.3106	0.3133
0.9	0.3159	0.3186	0.3212	0.3238	0.3264	0.3289	0.3315	0.3340	0.3365	0.3389
1.0	0.3413	0.3438	0.3461	0.3485	0.3508	0.3531	0.3554	0.3577	0.3599	0.3621
1.1	0.3643	0.3665	0.3686	0.3708	0.3729	0.3749	0.3770	0.3790	0.3810	0.3830
1.2	0.3849	0.3869	0.3888	0.3907	0.3925	0.3944	0.3962	0.3980	0.3997	0.4015
1.3	0.4032	0.4049	0.4066	0.4082	0.4099	0.4115	0.4131	0.4147	0.4162	0.4177
1.4	0.4192	0.4207	0.4222	0.4236	0.4251	0.4265	0.4279	0.4292	0.4306	0.4319
1.5	0.4332	0.4345	0.4357	0.4370	0.4382	0.4394	0.4406	0.4418	0.4429	0.4441
1.6	0.4452	0.4463	0.4474	0.4484	0.4495	0.4505	0.4515	0.4525	0.4535	0.4545
1.7	0.4554	0.4564	0.4573	0.4582	0.4591	0.4599	0.4608	0.4616	0.4625	0.4633
1.8	0.4641	0.4649	0.4656	0.4664	0.4671	0.4678	0.4686	0.4693	0.4699	0.4706
1.9	0.4713	0.4719	0.4726	0.4732	0.4738	0.4744	0.4750	0.4756	0.4761	0.4767
2.0	0.4772	0.4778	0.4783	0.4788	0.4793	0.4798	0.4803	0.4808	0.4812	0.4817
2.1	0.4821	0.4826	0.4830	0.4834	0.4838	0.4842	0.4846	0.4850	0.4854	0.4857
2.2	0.4861	0.4864	0.4868	0.4871	0.4875	0.4878	0.4881	0.4884	0.4887	0.4890
2.3	0.4893	0.4896	0.4898	0.4901	0.4904	0.4906	0.4909	0.4911	0.4913	0.4916
2.4	0.4918	0.4920	0.4922	0.4925	0.4927	0.4929	0.4931	0.4932	0.4934	0.4936
2.5	0.4938	0.4940	0.4941	0.4943	0.4945	0.4946	0.4948	0.4949	0.4951	0.4952
2.6	0.4953	0.4955	0.4956	0.4957	0.4959	0.4960	0.4961	0.4962	0.4963	0.4964
2.7	0.4965	0.4966	0.4967	0.4968	0.4969	0.4970	0.4971	0.4972	0.4973	0.4974
2.8	0.4974	0.4975	0.4976	0.4977	0.4977	0.4978	0.4979	0.4979	0.4980	0.4981
2.9	0.4981	0.4982	0.4982	0.4983	0.4984	0.4984	0.4985	0.4985	0.4986	0.4986
3.0	0.4987	0.4987	0.4987	0.4988	0.4988	0.4989	0.4989	0.4989	0.4990	0.4990

RANDOM NUMBER TABLE

27767	43584	85301	88977	29490	69714	94015	64874	32444	48277
13025	14338	54066	15243	47724	66733	74108	88222	88570	74015
80217	36292	98525	24335	24432	24896	62880	87873	95160	59221
10875	62004	90391	61105	57411	06368	11748	12102	80580	41867
54127	57326	26629	19087	24472	88779	17944	05600	60478	03343
60311	42824	37301	42678	45990	43242	66067	42792	95043	52680
49739	71484	92003	98086	76668	73209	54244	91030	45547	70818
78626	51594	16453	94614	39014	97066	30945	57589	31732	57260
66692	13986	99837	00582	81232	44987	69170	37403	86995	90307
44071	28091	07362	97703	76447	42537	08345	88975	35841	85771
59820	96163	78851	16499	87064	13075	73035	41207	74699	09310
25704	91035	26313	77463	55387	72681	47431	43905	31048	56699
22304	90314	78438	66276	18396	73538	43277	58874	11466	16082
17710	59621	15292	76139	59526	52113	53856	30743	08670	84741
25852	58905	55018	56374	35824	71708	30540	27886	61732	75454
46780	56487	75211	10271	36633	68424	17374	52003	70707	70214
59849	96169	87195	46092	26787	60939	59202	11973	02902	33250
47670	07654	30342	40277	11049	72049	83012	09832	25571	77628
94304	71803	73465	09819	58869	35220	09504	96412	90193	79568
08105	59987	21437	36786	49226	77837	98524	97831	65704	09514
64281	61826	18555	64937	64654	25843	41145	42820	14924	39650
66847	70495	32350	02985	01755	14750	48968	38603	70312	05682
72461	33230	21529	53424	72877	17334	39283	04149	90850	64618
21032	91050	13058	16218	06554	07850	73950	79552	24781	89683
95362	67011	06651	16136	57216	39618	49856	99326	40902	05069
49712	97380	10404	55452	09971	59481	37006	22186	72682	07385
58275	61764	97586	54716	61459	21647	87417	17198	21443	41808
89514	11788	68224	23417	46376	25366	94746	49580	01176	28838
15472	50669	48139	36732	26825	05511	12459	91314	80582	71944
12120	86124	51247	44302	87112	21476	14713	71181	13177	55292
95294	00556	70481	06905	21785	41101	49386	54480	23604	23554
66986	34099	74474	20740	47458	64809	06312	88940	15995	69321
80620	51790	11436	38072	40405	68032	60942	00307	11897	92674
55411	85667	77535	99892	71209	92061	92329	98932	78284	46347
95083	06783	28102	57816	85561	29671	77936	63574	31384	51924
90726	57166	98884	08583	95889	57067	38101	77756	11657	13897
68984	83620	89747	98882	92613	89719	39641	69457	91339	22502
36421	16489	18059	51061	67667	60631	84054	40455	99396	63680
92638	40333	67054	16067	24700	71594	47468	03577	57649	63266
21036	82808	77501	97427	76479	68562	43321	31370	28977	23896
13173	33365	41468	85149	49554	17994	91178	10174	29420	90438
86716	38746	94559	37559	49678	53119	98189	81851	29651	84215
92581	02262	41615	70360	64114	58660	96717	54244	10701	41393
12470	56500	50273	93113	41794	86861	39448	93136	25722	08564
01016	00857	41396	80504	90670	08289	58137	17820	22751	36518
34030	60726	25807	24260	71529	78920	47648	13885	70669	93406
50259	46345	06170	97965	88302	98041	11947	56203	19324	20504
73959	76145	60808	54444	74412	81105	69181	96845	38525	11600
46874	37088	80940	44893	10408	36222	14004	23153	69249	05747
60883	52109	19516	90120	46759	71643	62342	07589	08899	05985

Index